The Illinois & Michigan Canal National Heritage Corridor

The Illinois & Michigan Canal

Northern Illinois University Press
DeKalb, Illinois
1988

National Heritage Corridor

A Guide to Its History and Sources

Edited by
Michael P. Conzen
and Kay J. Carr

Foreword by
Edmund B. Thornton

Library of Congress Cataloging-in-Publication Data

The Illinois & Michigan Canal National Heritage Corridor.

Includes index.
1. Illinois and Michigan Canal National Heritage Corridor (Ill.)—History. I. Conzen, Michael P. II. Carr, Kay J. III. Title: Illinois and Michigan Canal National Heritage Corridor.
F547.I13I45 1988 977.3′5 88-5150
ISBN 0-87580-128-5

Published by the Northern Illinois University Press, DeKalb, Illinois 60115
Manufactured in the United States of America

Design by Anne Schedler

Sponsored by The Upper Illinois Valley Association

Contents

Foreword

THE HISTORY of the Illinois and Michigan Canal is also the history of the State of Illinois. From the vision of the great French explorer, Jolliet, who travelled by canoe from the waters of Lake Michigan along the channels of that shallow, meandering stream later to be known as the Chicago River, over the portage at Summit, and then down the Des Plaines River, emerged the possibility of constructing a man-made canal that would develop great commercial traffic between the Great Lakes and the Mississippi Valley.

One hundred and fifty years were to pass before serious engineering surveys were made to determine the feasibility of this ambitious project. Throughout the dozen years it took to construct the canal, the project was threatened by political and financial chaos. Construction was continually hampered by shortages of manpower and money. The commitment of the state of Illinois as well as the federal government to the project is a major chapter in the history of this state. This was, at the time, the largest single construction project ever undertaken in Illinois. Great fortunes were made and lost in the pursuit of this ambitious undertaking.

With the completion of the canal in 1848, the state had a viable water artery connecting Chicago and Lake Michigan with the navigable waters of the Illinois River at LaSalle. During the construction of the canal, Chicago grew from a village of about 4,000 people to a boom town of 40,000 people. Other towns were platted and laid out by the Canal Commission, including Ottawa. There was great speculation in land, while mass in-migration both from the East and Europe took on the proportions of a tidal wave.

Spurred by the success of the canal, the railroads followed shortly thereafter, and Illinois was crisscrossed with a myriad of new rail lines touching nearly every county in the state with the exception of some western and extreme southern counties. But it was the Illinois and Michigan Canal that was the single most important "public works project" that spurred the development of the state and the growth of the city of Chicago. Chicago and the corridor to LaSalle were developed through the sale of alternate sections of public land given to the Illinois Canal Commission by the federal government for public sale. The economic impact of the canal caused Chicago to rise literally as well as figuratively out of the mud as entire blocks were raised on jacks above the sand dunes, alluvial mud, and meander-strewn flood plain of the Chicago River.

It is interesting that now, over one hundred and fifty years since the canal was begun, a new public interest has developed in this ancient waterway. The Illinois and Michigan Canal National Heritage Corridor Commission, together with the many private organizations throughout the Corridor organized in support of this effort, have once again focused public interest on this unique waterway and its treasure of man's physical occupation spanning the period from the ancient mound-builders to twentieth century America.

It is particularly appropriate that a geographer, Professor Michael Conzen, should be the person who had the vision and professional acumen to edit this important regional source book. Much has been written over many years on the history of the Illinois and Michigan Canal and numerous related special topics. This is the first true effort to gather together references to all the key source documents and secondary writings on the subject in one bibliographic publication.

The chapters written by Professor Conzen and his associates, G. Gray Fitzsimons, Gerald W. Adelmann, and Kay J. Carr, serve as important introductions to the broader appreciation of the canal and the Heritage Corridor. The bibliography is especially useful to professional scholars, researchers, and all who would seek more detailed information on specific topics. In sum, this publication will serve as a most valuable guide in understanding the rich and complex history of the Illinois and Michigan Canal National Heritage Corridor and its role in the growth and development of the great state of Illinois.

EDMUND B. THORNTON

Preface

THE IMPETUS for this book arose from the gathering force of public interest and local organizing effort that resulted in Congressional designation of the upper Illinois Valley in August 1984, as the Illinois and Michigan Canal National Heritage Corridor. During the preceding four or five years, in which numerous initiatives aimed at awakening interest in northern Illinois in the historic, scenic, and recreational value of the corridor were undertaken, it became clear that no comprehensive guide to the documentation of the region's plethora of historical sites, structures, documentary records, and artifacts existed. It was recognized that a great deal of historical writing has been done on the region, and also that extensive collections of historical records of all kinds relating to the corridor's evolution exist in the region, the state, and elsewhere. Pulling together useful information on these resources would be no small task.

In order to gain a more coherent picture of what materials exist on the region's history, and what sources await the historian's attention, a successful proposal was made by the Upper Illinois Valley Association to the Illinois Humanities Council in 1984 to fund a program of bibliographic inventory and public presentations on the history of the corridor. A team of four bibliographers, under the senior editor's supervision, was assembled, trained, and charged with creating a comprehensive bibliographical guide to the region's rich history. The team spent three summer months in the libraries of the corridor and selected libraries elsewhere in Illinois, amassing a large collection of references to primary and secondary materials and making appropriate annotations with the ultimate goal of publishing the most useful results. The key to the plan lay in plumbing the considerable depths of the chief research libraries in the Chicago area and in Springfield, since they hold a quantitatively large proportion of all the material discovered for the guide. A sweep was then made through all the cooperating public and private libraries of the corridor to discover any additional material, particularly of a highly parochial nature, that might be unique to individual collections. Interestingly, renowned libraries such as the Chicago Historical Society and the Newberry Library prove to have material on remarkably parochial pockets of the corridor, whereas occasionally small collections offer unique items of very general interest.

A four-part public lecture series was organized as this phase of work reached conclusion, drawing on its findings and on the expertise of scholars who have studied the area's history. The symposia were held in several corridor communities (Lockport, Utica, Lemont, and Chicago) during the fall of 1984 to acquaint interested members of the public with the fruits of the bibliography project and to stimulate further curiosity about the region's historical legacy.

Several historians, geographers, and archaeologists, including members of the bibliography team, participated.

After these events, the preparation of this book began. It was decided that the bibliography would be augmented with essays offering a fresh interpretation of several key aspects of the study of the corridor's evolution. The themes adopted are highly selective and can no more than hint at the great range of subjects awaiting further and more extensive treatment. They appear, however, with the hope that they provide both a useful orientation to the nature of the corridor as a region with a rich and tangible history, and also as a context of understanding that will enhance use of the bibliography and encourage future contributions to the corridor's history.

After the bibliography team was disbanded, the onus of standardizing, checking, and collating entries in the bibliography devolved principally upon the junior editor. The wealth of material collected, over five thousand references, proved too extensive to fit within the scope of a single volume, and so a selection of about three thousand items was made for inclusion. The principal aim in selection has been to provide a balance of coverage among topics, including, for example, all serious works on topics with a small literature (such as agriculture, arts and crafts), while winnowing out repetitive and extremely minor items on well-worn topics (such as transportation history). We hope the essays and bibliography serve to further interest in the corridor's unique historical development.

M.P.C.
K.J.C.

Acknowledgments

THE RESEARCH for the major section in this book, the "Guide to Corridor Historical Sources," was supported by a grant from the Illinois Humanities Council during the summer of 1984, and the editors and bibliography team are most grateful for that support. They wish to express their particular appreciation to Gerald W. Adelmann, executive director of the Upper Illinois Valley Association, who secured the funding for and administered the grant that supported the bibliographical portion of this work; and also to Vincent L. Michael, former program coordinator of the association and current director of Chicago programs at the Landmarks Preservation Council of Illinois, who contributed so much to the project's general success; and to Vera Boozer, who coped cheerfully with many requests for assistance. We should also like to thank the Illinois and Michigan Canal National Heritage Corridor Commission for its support in preparing this volume.

A project of this scope could not have been carried through without the help of many individuals whose technical expertise smoothed what could have been an even bumpier path. In particular, the editors would like to thank Robert W. Karrow, Jr., curator of maps at the Newberry Library, who acted as the project's bibliographical consultant and trained the team for its field work. We should also like to thank the other members of the bibliography's steering committee, Kathleen N. Conzen of the University of Chicago, Michael J. Herschensohn of the Chicago Architecture Foundation, J. Carrol Moody of Northern Illinois University, Harold L. Platt of Loyola University of Chicago, Howard Rosen of the Public Works Historical Society, and Stuart Struever of Northwestern University, who gave useful advice in planning the search for bibliographical raw material. John B. Jentz, director of the Family and Community History Center at the Newberry Library, made word-processing facilities available to the bibliography project, and his assistant, Irene Hansen, spent long hours entering the bibliographic material into a computer. The Committee on Geographical Studies and the Department of History Microcomputer Laboratory at the University of Chicago also contributed word-processing facilities.

The book's completion was also dependent upon the cooperation of the many libraries, archives, and historical societies in which the research was conducted. We are particularly indebted to Virginia Sparr Brown of the Grundy County Historical Society and John Lamb of the Lewis University Illinois and Michigan Canal Archives.

We appreciate the cooperation given by the staffs of the Archives of the State of Illinois in Springfield, the Art Institute of Chicago, the Bedford Park Public Library, the Blue Island Public Library, the Bridgeview Public Library, the Center for Research Libraries, the Chicago Historical Society, the Chicago Municipal Reference Library, the Chicago Public Library, the Chicago Theological Seminary Hammond Library, the Commonwealth Edison Company Library, the Evangelical Covenant Church of America Archives, the Field Museum of Natural History Library, the Fountaindale Public Library in Romeoville, the Green Hills Public Library in Palos Hills, the Grundy County Historical Society, the Illinois Agricultural Association Library, the Illinois Historical Survey Library, the Illinois Bell Telephone Library, the Illinois and Michigan Canal Museum in Lockport, the Illinois and Michigan Canal State Trail Archives of Gebhard Woods State Park, the Illinois Department of Conservation Library, the Illinois Regional Archives Depository at Illinois State University, the Illinois Regional Archives Depository at Northern Illinois University, the Illinois State Museum, the Illinois State Historical Library, the Illinois State Geological Survey Library, the International Harvester Company Archives, the Joliet Public Library, the John Crerar Library, the Justice Public Library, the LaSalle County Historical Society Museum, the Lemont Area Historical Society's Harry J. Swanson Memorial Library, the LaSalle Public Library, the Lemont Public Library, the Lewis University Illinois and Michigan Canal Archives, the Lockport Township Public Library in Crest Hill, the Lockport Township Public Library in Lockport, the Loyola University of Chicago Archives, the Lutheran Church in America Archives, the McCormick Theological Seminary McGaw Library, the Marseilles Public Library, the Meadville Theological School of Lombard College Library, the Metropolitan Sanitary District Library, the Morris Public Library, the National Archives and Records Service's Federal Archives and Research Center in Chicago, the Newberry Library, the Norwegian-American Historical Association, the Oglesby Public Library, the Palos Heights Public Library, the Palos Park Public Library, the Peru Public Library, the Reddick Library in Ottawa, the St. Mary of the Lake Seminary's Feehan Library, the Seneca Public Library, the Summit-Argo Public Library, the Swedish-American Historical Association, the University of Chicago Joseph Regenstein Library, the University of Illinois Archives, the University of Illinois Library, the University of Illinois at Chicago Library, the Will County Historical Society Library, the Utica Public Library, and the Worth Public Library.

Illustrations

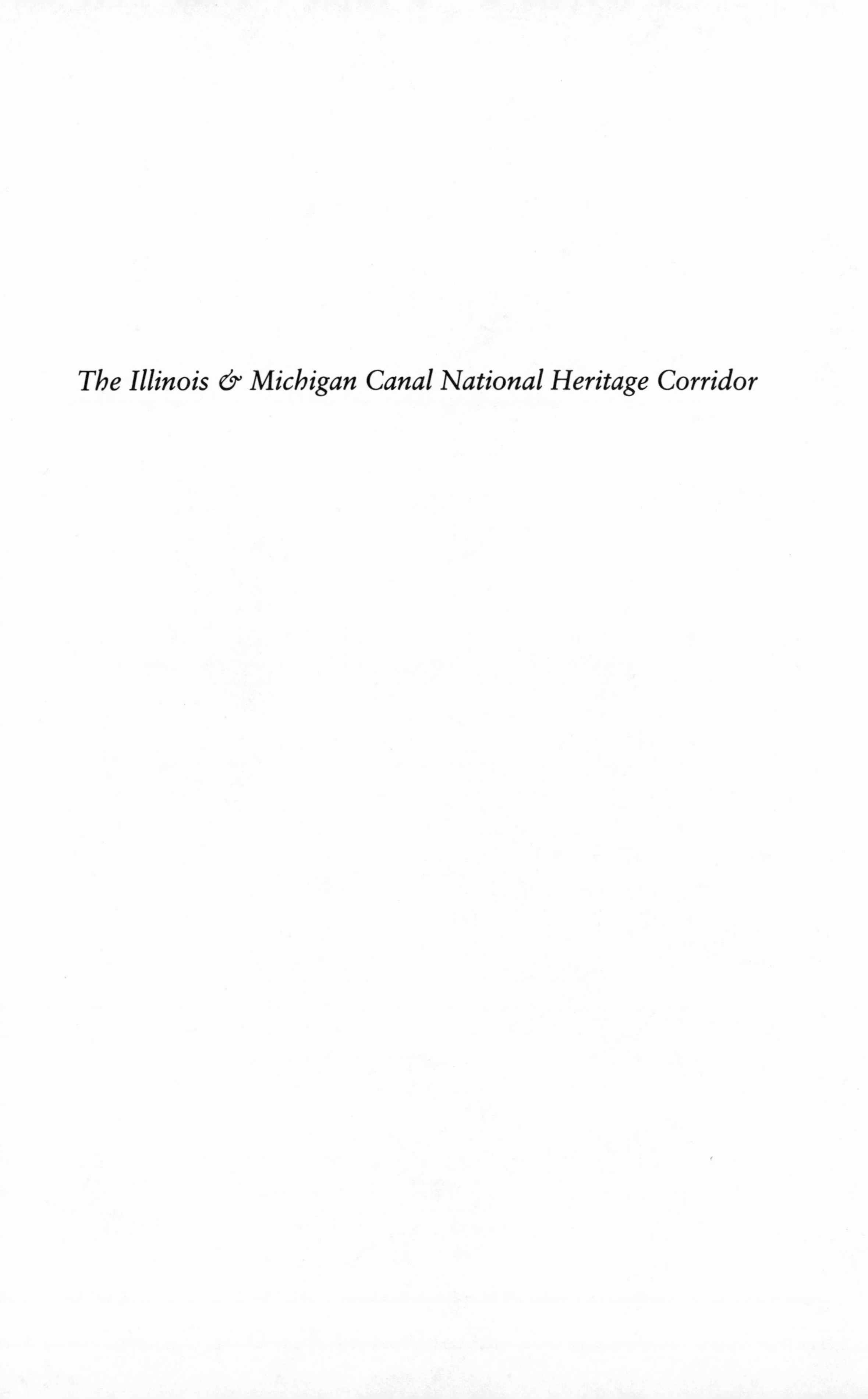

The Illinois & Michigan Canal National Heritage Corridor

One

THE HISTORICAL AND GEOGRAPHICAL DEVELOPMENT OF THE ILLINOIS AND MICHIGAN CANAL NATIONAL HERITAGE CORRIDOR

Michael P. Conzen

SINCE TIME immemorial America's heartland has played a special role in shaping the physical, social, and economic progress of what became the United States. Before European colonization the Middle West linked Amerindian settlements in northern and southern humid with western subhumid environments in a busy transition zone. Since European penetration, this connecting role has only intensified. The eastern seaboard, it is true, developed the earliest permanent European settlements and became, in its northern part at least, the urban and industrial engine of national growth. But the Middle West offered a crucial crossroads to the extraordinarily diverse agricultural and mineral resources of the continental interior and the great West. This was significant first for the French, who developed a north-south arc of occupation in an attempt to outflank the seaboard English, and then for the Americans, sprawling over the lands west of the Alleghenies, heading generally westward. In the process the Middle West became a preeminent farming and industrial region in its own right.

No single locality within the Middle West can claim to be more pivotal in these broad respects than the corridor that most directly links the Great Lakes to the Mississippi River basin. That corridor, reaching from the upper Illinois River at present-day LaSalle-Peru to the mouth of the Chicago River at Lake Michigan, invited construction of the historic Illinois and Michigan Canal and stimulated the rise of Chicago as a great commercial city at the lakeside meeting point of the Mississippi and Great Lakes waterway systems. Although the metropolis now utterly dominates the settlement pattern of northeastern Illinois, its early growth depended crucially upon the economic development of this strategic corridor. The corridor has a long and intricate history, therefore, as a small but uncommonly important region within a larger context.[1] This essay attempts to outline the most salient dimensions of that development and, in so doing, draw attention to the main features of the resulting cultural landscape that have come to express the human heritage built up in it over time.

Continental Divide: Nature Shapes the Corridor

The headwaters of the Illinois River begin extremely close to the southern margin of Lake Michigan, but in nature had no original connection with it. The principal northern branch of the Illinois is the Des Plaines River, which rises in southern Wisconsin and flows south parallel to, but five to seven miles west of, Lake Michigan's Illinois shore before turning southwest in the vicinity of the modern-day communities of Summit and Lyons. Just two or three miles east of this bend is an area of original swamp land, known as Mud Lake, which fed not only the Des Plaines River but in rainy periods also the South Branch of the Chicago River, a short stream flowing into Lake Michigan at Chicago. Between Mud Lake and the Chicago River's South Branch, then, runs a continental water divide, separating waters that flow ultimately into the Gulf of Mexico from waters that flow to the Gulf of the St. Lawrence.[2] So flat is this *interfluve* that for centuries native Indians and European adventurers, traveling through the region, could easily traverse the water gap by portaging, or carrying, their canoes across it. The increasing size of watercraft in modern times, however, meant that these headwaters could not be navigated. Commercial vessels in the nineteenth century could rarely pass farther up the Illinois at low water than present-day Peru, where the river elevation is 141 feet below the level of Lake Michigan. These striking natural circumstances have endowed the upper Illinois River and its portage connection to the Chicago River with great human interest and called forth great investments of capital and engineering skill in harnessing the corridor to serve human ends.

Geologically, the corridor passes through a zone of fairly old limestones, sandstones, and shales where older rocks of Ordovician and Silurian age to the north give way near the surface to younger coal-rich rocks of Pennsylvanian age to the south.[3] Overlying these are layers of glacially deposited drift from the numerous incursions into the area of the polar ice cap over the last million years, particularly the Lake Michigan lobe associated with the last, or Wisconsin, glaciation that left the area as recently as fifteen thousand years ago. The Illinois River valley, carved out initially before the ice age, became a major drainage channel for meltwaters from the retreating ice sheet, and it filled up with out-wash material ranging from coarse gravels to fine silts. Hence the valley floor, anywhere from a half to two miles wide, is significantly lower than the surrounding countryside. It is etched in many places by bluffs on both sides and runs southwest and westerly from the present Lake Michigan through, and roughly at right angles to, a sequence of curved topographic zones of alternating flat plains derived from former lake bottoms and gentle ridges deposited as glacial moraines. While the broad flatlands evolved a dry prairie cover, the valley itself developed wooded slopes and outer margins, with wet prairies in parts of the floodplain proper.

Nature's bequest comprised, therefore, a scenic and resourceful valley meandering through a gently undulating prairie upland rich in agriculturally valuable soils and underlain to the south by bituminous coal measures.[4] The valley itself offers a natural water "highway," together with a virtually continuous string of deposits of gravels, sands, and clays, with frequent outcroppings of building stone and occasional outcroppings of coal and cement. Only in the upper reaches of the Des Plaines River (as the northerly fork of the Illinois River above Dresden is known) is the link to Lake

Michigan obscured by a once-marshy zone that represents the continental divide. Little wonder, then, that a stage set with such inducements for travel and potential industrial development should attract a great deal of human activity from the earliest times.

Valley and Portage: Amerindian Settlements, Europeans, and the Fur Trade

Amerindian occupation of the region between the middle Mississippi valley and Lake Michigan appears to date from the earliest period following the retreat of the polar ice sheet. So far, however, archaeological evidence offers no detailed picture of the livelihood patterns or settlements of the earliest (Paleo-Indian) phase. A predominantly oak and hickory forest cover developed in the area, and the first signs of specific colonization date from the Archaic Period, prior to 1000 B.C., when deer hunting and wild plant gathering supported a dispersed population. One site in the upper Illinois valley from this era has been discovered at Starved Rock, near Ottawa.[5] More settlements are known from the subsequent Woodland Period (1000B.C.–900A.D.) when pottery made its appearance and when, later, bows and arrows and maize came into use. Indian settlements spread up the Mississippi valley as far as eastern Minnesota and around the southern half of Lake Michigan in what has been termed a *Hopewell Interaction* network that reached as far as Louisiana and Lake Ontario. In the corridor there are mounded earthworks from this period, such as the Utica Mounds on bluffs overlooking the river west of Ottawa, which were likely associated with occasional villages and seasonal camps at the base of valley bluffs. These settlements, belonging to the *Havana Hopewellian* group of the Illinois country, probably participated in interregional trade in such materials as chert (a flinty rock expecially suitable for tools and weapons), and possibly lead and copper, which would have stimulated travel through the corridor and over the shallow land portage between the headwaters of the Illinois River and Lake Michigan.[6]

The following Mississippian Period (c. 1000 A.D.–seventeenth century) saw the advent of some large, fortified towns with platform mounds, most notably Cahokia, east of St. Louis. These were centers of chiefdoms and often had satellite settlements in the vicinity. Numerous tools and extensive evidence of maize testify to the importance of agriculture in the cultures of this period. Further north in the upper Illinois valley, however, the villages, though large, lacked platform mounds, thus suggesting that they housed less stratified, more tribally organized local societies. The villages of this period were located without exception on valley bottom lands, such as the one at the Zimmerman site near Starved Rock. Tentative efforts have been made to link these settlements with the ancestors of modern aboriginal tribes—the Zimmerman dwellers with the Shawnee people, for example—but the evidence for this so far is thin.[7]

By the seventeenth century the French, far ahead of their English counterparts on the eastern seaboard, were exploring the Middle West in search of water links through the continental interior between Quebec and Louisiana. Their motives combined imperial strategy and trade with native peoples whom they sought to convert to Catholic Christianity, and this amalgam united royal and Jesuit representatives in a common enterprise. Their activities left documentary evidence for describing patterns of native Indian occupation. Although these explorers may not have mentioned every occupied site they passed, it is clear that a substantial native village known as Kaskaskia flourished at the

Zimmerman site after the middle of the seventeenth century.[8] It was visited by Louis Jolliet and Father Jacques Marquette in 1673 as they reconnoitered the Mississippi basin under commission from Count Frontenac, then governor of New France.[9] Marquette determined to return to the village to establish a mission, and he did in 1675, only to fall ill and die. He was replaced two years later by Father Claude Allouez, who maintained the mission until his death in 1689,[10] with an interruption between 1680 and 1682 following an attack on the village by the British-backed Iroquois from the east and its reestablishment by Réné-Robert Cavalier, Sieur de la Salle, and Henri de Tonty. LaSalle reputedly built Fort St. Louis on a nearby bluff to replace an earlier regional stronghold at Peoria, and this fort at Kaskaskia together with its colony of four thousand warriors controlled all the traffic on the Illinois River and the trade in furs until 1691–1692, when French operations in the valley were relocated once more at Peoria. While it lasted, the corridor saw many a *coureur du bois* (licensed fur trader) and *voyageur* (canoe man) ply his trade, principally in beaver pelts. A Jesuit mission was established at Chicago in 1696 by Father Pierre Pinet, but it failed to last more than a year.[11]

As time progressed the French centered their principal activities in the middle Mississippi valley, focusing on Fort de Chartres and its connections via the Ohio, Maumee, and Wabash rivers with Quebec, well to the south and east of the upper Illinois valley. After 1700, however, previous restrictions on who could trade with whom were removed as French influence faded in the face of belated British challenges, and the corridor saw renewed native activity. The Chicago portage became a significant channel of movement, especially for those involved in the fur trade.

Jolliet had shown extraordinary perspicacity regarding the Chicago portage in 1673, noting that "it would only be necessary to make a canal, by cutting through but half a league of prairie, to pass from the foot of the lake of the Illinois [Lake Michigan] to the river Saint Louis [Des Plaines River]" and thus sail a bark from Lake Erie to the Gulf of Mexico.[12] Although many later commentators have marvelled at Jolliet's prescience, fewer have noted LaSalle's immediate scepticism on the topic. In 1680 he wrote, "Although a canal would be possible with a great deal of expense, it would be useless because the Divine [Illinois] River is unnavigable for forty leagues, the distance to the great village of the Illinois."[13] LaSalle was technically correct, and it would be nearly a century and a half before anyone gave practical consideration to realizing Jolliet's broader vision.

The British, through their alliance with the Iroquois, gradually gained control of the fur trade throughout the region at the expense of the French, and, by 1763, wrested nominal political sovereignty from the French as well. But the upper Illinois valley remained a relative backwater until after it fell into nominal American hands in 1783. The Treaty of Greenville twelve years later transferred from Indian to United States control the strategic district around the mouth of the Chicago River, and the federal government built Fort Dearborn there, beginning in 1803. In the hinterland, or back country beyond, a westward drift of Indian tribal groups had occurred as hunting grounds to the east were threatened by white settlement, in particular bringing Potawatomis from southern Michigan to settle in the upper Illinois country.[14] This coincided with the last phase of profitable fur trading in the area, which John Jacob Astor's American Fur Company had succeeded in monopolizing by the 1820s, under the direction of John Kinzie, until the Treaty of Chicago in 1833.[15] A substantial local multiracial society in and around Chicago that had evolved under these general conditions lasted until the influx of easterners drawn to the area by the promise of a canal.[16]

Canal Politics, Surveys, and Construction

Since the birth of the new nation, American leaders had recognized the urgent need for a network of "internal improvements" to ease the problem of continental transportation. Peter B. Porter in 1810 offered to Congress the first modern proposal that included the idea of a canal across the Chicago portage, though at the time efforts on behalf of the Erie Canal in New York state were much more successful.[17] The Illinois project gained attention for strategic reasons after the War of 1812, and Indian land cessions reaching into northern Illinois in 1816 included a strip of land twenty miles wide from the upper Illinois River to the mouth of the Chicago River on Lake Michigan for this purpose. Government surveyors marked off the survey grid within this corridor in preparation for the general colonization that the canal would stimulate, while military engineers examined the corridor's topography for likely canal routes.[18] At this time Illinois entered the Union as a state, but not before its northern boundary was pushed sufficiently far north to ensure that the Chicago portage and its adjacent land corridor would be wholly within the new state's borders.

During the early 1820s the southern portions of Illinois were most settled, but pioneers were eagerly pushing up the major valleys tributary to the Mississippi River, in the Illinois River valley reaching Peoria and beyond. Northern Illinois was clearly destined to be colonized. The apparatus of statehood provided new impetus to the canal project, but it was not until 1827 that extended political maneuvering brought about a grant to the state from the federal government of the odd-numbered 640-acre sections of land within five miles of the proposed canal, the sale of which would finance the undertaking. Successive canal commissions were appointed and dissolved by the state as various financing schemes sprung up and came to nought, while successive surveys produced increasingly authoritative maps of the region. Justus Post and René Paul concluded one such survey suggesting five alternative routes a canal might take, together with comparative costs—none of which bore any practical relation to the ultimate figure. The federal land grant led to a new commission in 1829 that began the business of land sales by laying out small towns the following year at the expected termini of the canal, Ottawa and Chicago. Although new settlers were beginning to enter the district, sales were slow and revenue too slight to begin construction. The canal commission lost faith in the idea of a canal and proposed instead building a railroad. The legislature found this notion too hard to swallow, but took no alternative initiative, though it did dismiss the commission. Two years later, as settlement in the corridor picked up and land speculation boomed, yet another canal commission was created, this time with the power to borrow money. The projected canal was now to reach westward as far as the river bend near Peru. When 375 lots sold in Chicago netted $1,355,755 by June 1836, it was time to gear up.[19] Ground was broken on July 4 at Canalport (today's Bridgeport, long since annexed to Chicago) by Colonel William B. Archer, a commissioner who was also to be a major contractor. William Gooding, a professional canal engineer with experience on the Erie Canal, was hired to superintend the construction program.

At first, all went well, though labor was scarce and had to be imported from the east. The panic of 1837 was overcome, and by the following year most sections of the 100-mile canal were under contract. Problems of cash flow became acute by the early forties, however, and in 1841 work was suspended. There followed several years of political maneuvering at the end of which increased investment from European sources succeeded in refloating the enterprise and construction resumed. After much final effort the canal was opened for navigation in April 1848. The management of the canal was by that time in the hands of a three-member board of trustees, and this body managed to retire all of the outstanding debts on the $6,463,853 ultimate construction cost by 1871.[20]

The challenge of route selection and engineering design for the canal was not scientifically demanding, but it did call for organizational prowess. Essentially, the canal needed to run from the south branch of the Chicago River in a straight line over the portage zone via Mud Lake to a point where the Des Plaines branch of the Illinois River turns southwest on its ultimate course toward the Mississippi. From there it needed to parallel the river past a variety of rapids and shoals on the natural waterway to a point near Peru about a hundred miles distant from Chicago. In some stretches the canal hugs the river closely, in others it swings away to utilize the broad floodplain to maximum straight-line advantage, and in only one instance does it follow an alternate water gap not occupied by the river. The Des Plaines would supply the water, as would feeders from the Little Calumet, Kankakee, and Fox Rivers, and a 140-foot drop from the "summit" level of the junction with the Des Plaines would call for locks mainly in the central portion of the canal. Some of the more interesting structures surviving from the earliest construction period are the locks at Lockport, four miles north of Joliet, the site of the first locks west of Chicago, the canal-river crossover "at grade" at Channahon, the large aqueducts at Aux Sable and over the Fox River at Ottawa, and the steamboat turning basin at LaSalle-Peru.

The canal was built during a period and in a region that lacked a resident labor force. The promise of the canal had attracted numerous easterners to the corridor, particularly those Yankees from New England and New York, in hopes of capitalizing on its construction in one way or another. Many such individuals ended up as contractors organizing work contingents on the canal, and others as suppliers of the needed materials and provisions. In addition, widespread advertising in eastern cities brought forth a stream of poor immigrants, mostly Irish, who did the actual digging. The canal was completed just in time to hand on many of its diggers, as it were, to the goldfields of California and elsewhere, but large numbers stayed behind. Some squatted on or bought some land to try their hand at farming; others congregated in the new villages and towns to work at urban pursuits; and still others parlayed their gains into substantial rural estates and manufacturing enterprises.[21]

Town Founding and Farm Making

In the twenty-year period prior to the canal's completion, northern Illinois, in common with many areas of the upper Middle West, saw first Yankees, and then Germans and Irish begin to fill in the lands of the canal region. The mining center of Galena to the northwest was merely a town and Peoria to the southwest but a small outpost. In the canal corridor it was expectation that brought settlers in, and Chicago had swelled to twenty thousand inhabitants on this basis by the time the canal opened in 1848.

Towns, it is clear, were an integral part of canal building, and their number, timing, and location along the line of the canal were a function of institutional strategy as well as private, opportunistic initiative.[22]

The canal commissioners were put in control of alternate (odd-numbered) sections of land in a prospective canal corridor a hundred miles in length. After the legislation of 1829 the commissioners performed their first act as urban strategists by designating future town sites at Chicago and Ottawa.[23] The Chicago location, where the canal met the lake, was an obvious one, and the site and particular plat adopted showed a simple practicality. The plat was laid out on a portion of Section 9, fully controlled by the commissioners, and though it did not embrace the harbor entrance, this was well guarded by Fort Dearborn on federal land. The commissioners' plat did embrace the confluence of the North and South Branches of the Chicago River, thereby securing maximum river frontage and centrality to make the town lots appealing to purchasers.

The Ottawa location represented a more serious decision. It was not at the western extremity of the land grant, but until about 1834 opinion existed that the canal might terminate by joining the Illinois River at its confluence with the Fox River at the site of Ottawa. A county seat was needed immediately for the newly established LaSalle County, and Ottawa was centrally located for that purpose.[24] The commissioners' surveyor, James Thompson, turned luck to advantage since a portion of Section 11 in Ottawa Township suitably embraced the confluence of the Fox and Illinois rivers. In town planning terms, then, Ottawa and Chicago began life almost as carbon copies. For years the commissioners were content with two official town sites along the projected waterway, and immediate land sales not only brought in vital funds but also started Chicago and Ottawa on a path to impressive early growth. Official founding and lack of competition gave these towns a head start.

Other interests, however, developed quickly as the canal project moved forward in the early 1830s, and the canal corridor was soon colonized with additional towns. Residents of the Peru district acted on the promise that the canal would terminate there and, considering that the head of navigation on the Illinois River at low water was opposite a site on Section 16, persuaded their school officials to plat the town of Peru in 1834.[25] Simultaneously, private business interests laid out urban plats adjacent to the excellent waterpower sites located on land bought from the federal government at Joliet and Marseilles.[26]

The hundred-mile canal corridor was now beginning to fill up with town sites. Not to be outflanked, a new set of canal commissioners, with the force of updated legislation in 1836 behind them, moved to designate two more canal towns: an official western terminus town site (LaSalle) and a town to contain the canal's administrative headquarters (Lockport). The location of these new towns directly challenged the independent promoters of Peru and Joliet. LaSalle, laid out on Section 15 of Township 33, Range 1 East, directly abutted Peru to the east and vigorously engaged it in a species of twin-city rivalry that has lasted into this century.[27] The commissioners could not afford to let urban land development at the canal's western terminus be monopolized by private interests. They ensured LaSalle's competitiveness by constructing steamboat and canal boat basins within their town's plat to secure the actual transshipment trade.

Lockport's placement was more dubious but no less bold. Situated at a point where the first locks west of Chicago drop the canal from its "summit level," the site recommended itself as a suitable shipping point, waterpower site, and administrative center and was located as usual on land controlled by the canal commissioners.[28] But its position four miles north of Joliet and lacking any additional topographical openings to the surrounding countryside gave it no particular geographical "edge" over Joliet, save official prestige.

Thus, in the seven years before actual canal construction commenced, seven towns were established along its length, four through government planning and three as a result of independent business initiative. Chicago and Ottawa opened the doors to urban development in the region, although the original town site plats were so modest in size that subsequent urban success resulted in numerous additional town lot subdivisions by private interests. By 1836 the commissioners had learned to increase the scale of their townsite plats, thereby controlling more urban development at one stroke and consequently enhancing the physical unity and coherence of their town plans. Hence, LaSalle and Lockport exhibit more uniform central planning than the earlier urban foundations.

The repercussions of the 1837 depression were to strangle progress on the canal slowly, but before construction halted in 1842 one more town had been added to the corridor. The establishment of Grundy County in 1841 contained a legislative provision that the county seat, later named Morris, be located on the canal at the midpoint of its passage through the new county, and on canal land.[29] Laid out by the county commissioners in conjunction with the canal commissioners, Morris proved to be the last of the "government towns" along the canal. Its plat fronts on the canal, but besides a courthouse square reservation, its grid pattern offers nothing remarkable.

Between 1844 and 1867 four other canal towns were added to the corridor's urban system, all by private interests. Channahon and Lemont were platted in the midforties, Seneca (alias Crotty) in 1849, and Utica in 1867.[30] These were generally spontaneous towns started with a reservoir of former canal laborers turned local residents, often attracted by some local resource, such as the stone quarries in Lemont and Channahon, and built up initially by one or another local petty capitalist. Utica is the most interesting of the later foundations since it represents a relocation on the canal of a former river settlement called "Science" that had clung tenuously to existence until the canal was routed a mile to the north of it.

Ten of the twelve genuine canal towns that developed in the corridor were in place and variously thriving *before* the canal became operational in 1848. Their establishment was spread over nearly twenty years, however, and early founding gave obvious advantages to Chicago and Ottawa. Chicago's lakeshore position as a critical break-of-bulk point in the national transportation network ensured its future success on a scale the inland towns—even Peru or LaSalle, which did have modest riverboat transfer functions[31]—had no hope of matching. The half decade or so start that Ottawa had over Peru and other LaSalle County canal towns proved crucial in organizing much of the county trade north and south of the Illinois valley to become tributary to it, and its immediate selection as county seat also helped. Most canal towns grew rapidly before, during, and until shortly after the first period during which the canal had no competitor in transportation, thereafter settling into more sedate patterns of growth and maintaining their relative ranks through century's end. Late-starting places such as Channahon, Seneca, and Utica quickly found modest niches as shipping points in the valley system but stopped growing because their older, more established neighbors were too close at hand. Other than Chicago, only Joliet managed in the 1870s to separate itself from the pack and continue to grow at an impressive rate.

The I&M Canal passing through Morris. *A westward-looking view of Grundy County Courthouse and its mini-park (lower right) anchoring the old downtown. Small industrial buildings and a carpark hug the canal where warehouses and grain elevators once stood. The modern elevators now line the artificially-deepened Illinois River (left).* (Photo: Michael P. Conzen)

Towns attracted farmers to the region, and farmers' needs spurred town growth. Rural settlement developed apace when the fear of Indian attack abated after the Black Hawk War in 1832. The main problem for bona fide settlers was to secure farmland near the line of the canal without paying too much for the superior access. Government land was available after 1835 at $1.25 per acre on the even-numbered sections within the canal grant, but in numerous places it was too steep or ill-drained for good farming; that which was better often ended up in the hands of speculators.[32] Canal land generally sold for more, particularly near the canal itself, since the commissioners were out to realize the added value it represented. In both cases superior agricultural land and lots with waterpower potential sold quickly and generally to speculative interests—often local entrepreneurs who worked energetically for the profitable development of the region and themselves. In LaSalle County people such as John Crotty at Seneca; William Gentleman, William Reddick, and the Strawn family around Ottawa; and John A. Rockwell, after the breakup of his group settlement experiment in the neighborhood of LaSalle, had by the 1850s acquired acreages far beyond individual farming needs.[33]

In general settlers came not from the South, as the river connections would seem to suggest, but via the Great Lakes from the Northeast: New Yorkers and New Englanders principally, with smaller numbers from Pennsylvania and Ohio. Most families, biographies in local county histories reveal, had pioneered in previous locations that marked their westward progress. Among rural immigrants, who became pro-

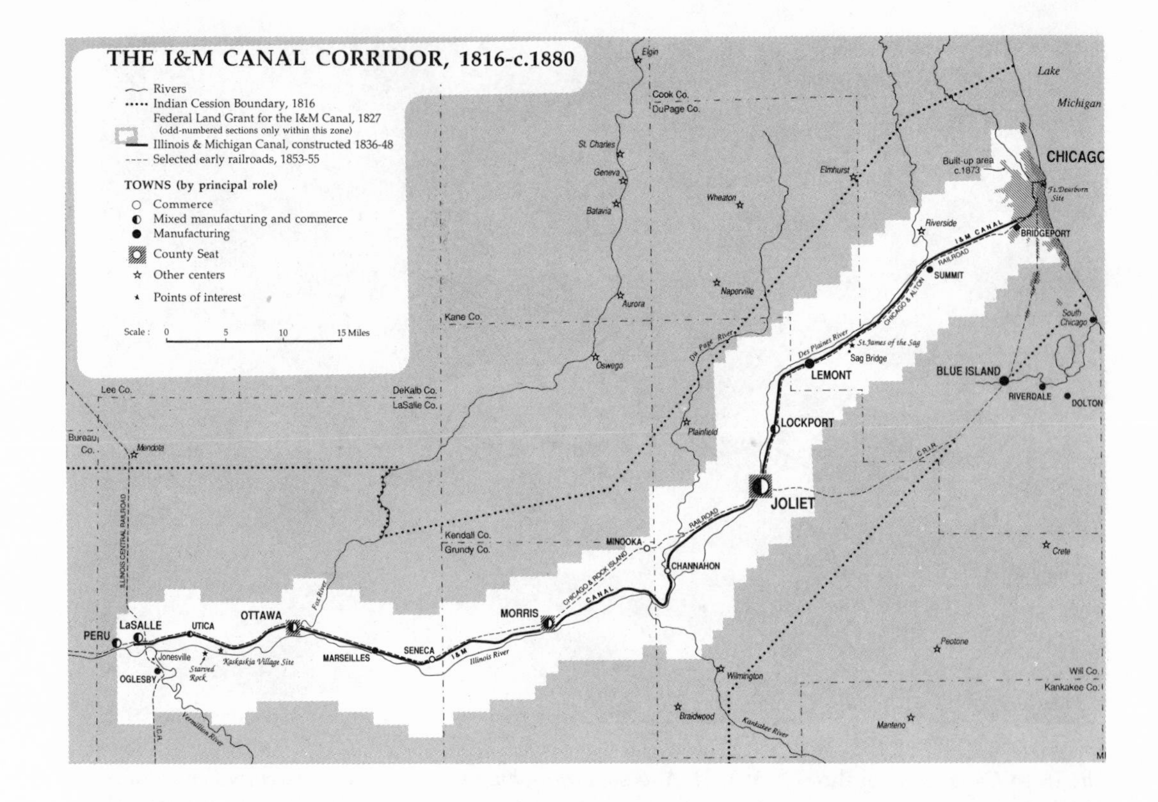

portionately more important during the 1840s, the Irish were most numerous and settled heavily along the canal, but other groups took up agricultural land in the vicinity, such as the Norwegians to the northeast of Ottawa as early as the mid-1830s.[34] Germans and Pennsylvania Dutch filled out the picture by midcentury.

Little by little, the pioneers colonized the wide open spaces between the timber stands, and by 1850 over three-quarters of LaSalle County and nearly half of Grundy County was under cultivation. Will and Cook counties saw less colonization at that date because of the higher proportions there of prairie land. Settlement along the valley bottom posed few new challenges, but the thick prairie soil was rough on traditional plows, and new machinery eventually helped to break up the knotted prairie sod better.[35] Farming soon became the foundation of the corridor's prosperity and fed the towns and the canal with the grain and other farm products that gave them a reliable economic purpose.

Canal and Railroad: Commerce and Social Life

The Illinois and Michigan Canal is significant, even among midwestern canals, for the very short period during which it served its hinterland free from the direct competition of railroads. Six years after the canal's completion the Chicago and Rock Island Railroad thundered down most of the corridor, generally parallel with and often no more than a few hundred yards away from the canal itself, connecting every town along the route, save Channahon, which consequently lapsed into economic somnolence. It would be a mistake, however, to belittle the canal's role in the region's development because of the brevity of its transport hegemony. The record of revenue from tolls and the total tonnage carried confirm the canal as a significant factor until at least

1870 in terms of valuable freight, and down to the close of the century as a medium for bulk transport.

After the canal opened, traffic built up quickly. Lumber from the Great Lakes and merchandise from the East flowed westward to the towns along its course, while farm produce from the region (principally wheat and other grains) moved east to Chicago, making the town immediately a great market for wheat, together with sugar, molasses, coffee, and other specialties from the Caribbean brought up the Mississippi.[36] Before the canal most of the trade of Illinois was tributary to St. Louis and New Orleans; afterward, it was Chicago that controlled the region's commerce. In 1845, there were about 12,000 inhabitants in the lakefront town, but within only a few short months of the canal's opening it could boast nearly 20,000, and by 1850 the total exceeded 28,000, rising to 74,500 residents four years later, the year the canal first acquired rail competition. Besides spurring Chicago's growth the canal greatly assisted Peoria through the new trade that the canal "sucked up" the Illinois River; only St. Louis lost heavily from this new geography of trade, though its wholesalers benefited from the increased volume of southern foodstuffs reaching the Great Lakes.

Passenger traffic also flourished. Packet boats left Chicago for LaSalle three times a day, traveling between four and five miles per hour and taking about twenty-five hours to cover the distance. Stagecoach travel was about twice as fast, but offered a bumpy ride. The canal boat's serene, gliding alternative, though, was not without its own discomforts: windows sealed against the threat of malaria, and a cabin fifty feet long by nine wide and seven high, in which up to ninety people sat, ate, and slept, with only a curtain at night to ensure the ladies' privacy.[37] It was freight business, however, that dominated the traffic. Most canal boats operated a crew of at least five—the captain (often the owner), a steersman, a bowsman, a driver, a cook, and one or two deck hands. The driver walked the towpath, tending the horses or, more often, the two to five mules pulling the barge. Mules had more stamina than horses for this work, and the authorities maintained state mule barns about every fifteen miles along the route. In addition, the canal scene was also peopled with lockmen, towpath walkers (checking for damage), toll collectors, and tavern keepers.[38] In villages along the way warehouses and elevators bustled with the activity of laborers loading and storing grain and other commodities; in the larger towns the public landing served as an open marketplace for businessmen, farmers, and all classes of humanity.

The canal produced steadily rising income through tolls until 1854, the year railroads connected the valley to Chicago, and then for the next decade the canal's income oscillated widely but on an upward trend until the last year of the Civil War, in which it grossed a record $300,000. The closing of the lower Mississippi River to northern trade during the Civil War was, of course, a boon to Chicago and the canal interests because trade was thereby steered directly eastward via the Great Lakes routes.

It was a period in which canal and railroad competed furiously for common cargoes, and the presence of the former substantially reduced the freight rates charged on the latter along the valley route. The railroad was initially intended to run from LaSalle to Rock Island, an extension and supplement to the canal system, not a competitor. But within a short time its promoters realized that a direct Chicago connection would be essential for the long-term future of their business, and that the canal should be challenged rather than merely supported. Railroads could operate through all seasons without interruption, handle all goods with dispatch, penetrate cities more easily, and in fact roam over land areas quite beyond the reach of canals. Consequently, the Rock Island Railroad secured a charter to build through to Chicago, connecting Joliet with Chicago by a more southerly approach away from the Des Plaines Valley. The packet-boat business soon disappeared. As a Joliet commentator noted, "Capt. Connett, the famous canal captain, had to get metamorphosed into a railroad conductor. Now we could go from Joliet in the morning, buy half the city [of Chicago]—if we had the dimes—and return at night. Lockport was left out in the cold, and she was welcome to her old canal office, over which Jolietians had growled so many years."[39]

The railroad attracted more and more of the canal's business and toll income dropped sharply between 1869 and 1878, so the canal became restricted mostly to the carriage of bulk materials for which speed was not crucial, such as lumber, grain, coal, and stone.[40] From the mid-1850s northern Illinois gained numerous railroads that tied the valley not only to Chicago, but also to the upper Mississippi, and, via the Illinois Central Railroad, which intersected with the canal at LaSalle, to the interior portions of the state north and south of the canal corridor. The general effect of this diffusion of railroad routes was to dilute the hitherto immense power of the canal to stimulate a linear corridor of economic development, and to spread the benefits of market access more widely over the state's northern section. Henceforth there would be other districts away from the major waterways capable of comparable new growth.

Heavy Industry and Waterway Improvements

The Illinois and Michigan Canal, however, had given the upper Illinois valley an enviable head start in regional development, as it had, of course, Chicago itself on the lakefront. This head start was seen not only in the shipping of locally produced farm products and long-distance commerce, but also in the energetic development of local industry, both extractive and manufacturing. Construction of the canal revealed a number of the valley's natural resources that found ready markets in Chicago and other fast-growing towns. The canal was cut through the limestone bedrock in many portions of the Des Plaines valley, and entrepreneurs quickly opened quarries in Lemont, Lockport, and Joliet. Over the years the warm-colored limestone came to epitomize the early character of these and other corridor towns, spreading wide the reputation of Lemont's "Athens Marble" and leading to Joliet's early nickname as "Stone City." Many of Chicago's early buildings were built of stone from these towns, hauled up the canal, and the industry flourished especially after Chicago's Great Fire in 1871. Quarrying continued well into the twentieth century in the Des Plaines valley, but its nature changed. Early production was of cut building stone for fine ashlar construction, but competition from superior sources—especially Indiana's Bedford Limestone—diminished this market, and the corridor's quarries turned to crushed stone aggregate for foundations and roadwork. As a consequence, new sites closer to Chicago, such as the now-huge quarries at McCook and Hodgkins, near Summit, became prominent, and the quarries further down the valley died out.

Commercial exploitation of coal began at LaSalle around 1855, using shaft mining methods, and soon the Little Vermillion River gorge across the valley from LaSalle sprouted with small company workings and miners' cottages, known today as Jonesville and Piety Hill. Here and at Morris are found the only two locations where the extensive Illinois coalfield reaches near the surface far enough north to touch the Illinois River valley. First river and canal, and then railroad, ensured profitable operations until the mining became more difficult around the First World War and other, more southerly mining sites offered cheaper, more abundant supplies.[41] The sands and clays of the region also attracted exploitation. The St. Peter sandstone that outcrops between Ottawa and Utica offers excellent, almost pure silica sand, stimulating manufacturing with this raw material immediately after the Civil War. Widespread clay deposits have also been utilized from early times, especially near Ottawa and Morris, and hydraulic cement, made at Utica from the 1840s, prospered until superior Portland cement began to be produced at what is now Oglesby, just south of LaSalle.

Given these varied and extensive raw materials, numerous waterpower sites, coal reserves, and multiplying transportation lines, manufacturing understandably gained an increasing hold over the economy of the corridor. Small water-powered mills proliferated early—particularly using the canal facilities at Lockport, Joliet, and Ottawa—processing the corn, barley, and other crops into flour, starch, and beer. The Gebhard Brewery, founded in Morris in 1866, is a representative example. In fact, a wide array of local manufacturing developed in the towns of the valley: agricultural implements, furniture and wood products, wagons, cutlery, bricks, soap, and the like. But in the 1870s a new scale of manufacturing began to emerge. In the years just after the Civil War a host of important new heavy industries made their appearance or gained prominence. A zinc-smelting and refining works was started in 1858 in LaSalle by two German mining engineers, Frederick W. Matthiessen and Edward C. Hegeler, who located there because it was the first spot on the Illinois Central Railroad where zinc ore could meet coal for smelting on its way to market.[42] This establishment prospered greatly after the war and attracted other smelters both there and to neighboring Peru, altogether employing about 850 people by 1880. In 1867, the first glass factory opened in Ottawa, based on the deep silica deposits west of town, and by 1880 it was Ottawa's most important industry. In the same year the Marseilles Manufacturing Company began production of a corn sheller, and this industry presaged the development, on the basis of excellent waterpower gained from damming the Illinois River, of a large paper and cardboard industry in that town, part of which was taken over in 1902 by the National Biscuit Company (later Nabisco) to produce cartons for its baked goods. A clock factory was started in Peru in the mid-1880s, similar to many producing intricate machinery—with low raw material inputs in relation to final value added—that sprang up in towns like those in the corridor. After two years the firm became known as the Western Clock Company (Westclox), employing about 80 workers. By 1910, when its famous "Big Ben" alarm clock was introduced, the company had nearly 900 workers and went on to become the world's largest manufacturer of alarm clocks.[43]

Perhaps most dramatic of all was the iron and steel works founded at Joliet in 1869. During the economic boom that followed the Civil War Chicago coal merchants noted the rapid expansion of the railroad network west of Lake Michigan, the proximity of the Illinois coalfield and nearby deposits of limestone, and the suitability of Chicago as a port for importing iron ore and exporting iron products and saw the opportunity to establish a local iron and steel industry somewhere in the region. At first the exact location did not seem critical, and although Joliet was not the first choice, it offered a free site and a financial subsidy and thus secured the first steel-making plant in the district, an iron rail-making mill. In 1873 two blast furnaces, a Bessemer converter (one of the earliest in the country), and a steel rail mill were added. The operation expanded rapidly, adding a wire rod mill in 1888, and two more blast furnaces by 1906, although the general growth potential was checked by the establishment of steelworks at South Chicago and later Gary, Indiana.[44] It was not long before allied manufacturing plants appeared to take advantage of the steel industry's presence. A coke plant was added in 1888 due north of the steel complex, assisting its vertical integration; American Steel & Wire Company, Phoenix Horseshoe Company, Calumet Chemical Company, General Refractories Company, Ruberoid Company, and a coal products company grew up in the vicinity. Elsewhere in Joliet, American Can Company, railroad repair shops, wallpaper mills, and other engineering firms making boilers and power machinery set up businesses. The construction of the Elgin, Joliet, and Eastern Railroad in the late 1880s, an "outer belt" railway for the Chicago region, materially helped consolidate and sustain Joliet's heavy industrial character well into the 1920s. The city symbolized a national trend toward expansion, greater productive scale, and concentration of ownership, with the attendant rise of labor unions and industrial strife it engendered.[45]

The landscape of the corridor was changing during the later nineteenth century. The growth of the surrounding farming districts slowed down and eventually reversed, as they sent their youth increasingly to the towns and factories of the valley. At the same time the corridor towns grew into an economically coherent urban subsystem within the greater Chicago hinterland. Early developments molded long-term patterns, and by about 1900 the essential economic differences among the towns had been clearly established. Each town had its own purpose to fulfill. The western third of the corridor had become studded with well-industrialized towns: Ottawa, LaSalle, and Peru (seven thousand to ten thousand population each); and there were several smaller, more specialized industrial places under twenty-five-hundred population such as Marseilles, Oglesby, and Utica. The middle third of the corridor remained more rural, with only widely spaced small towns—Seneca, Morris and tiny Channahon—to serve it. Meanwhile, the eastern third of the corridor experienced the most thorough industrial transformation, as Joliet developed into a major industrial satellite of Chicago under the powerful influence of the latter's burgeoning market and dense transportation network. As the new century dawned the territory between the two cities came under powerful new metropolitan forces that would still elude the towns further west.

These forces found expression, among other ways, in radical improvements to the waterway system. After 1870, the I&M Canal suffered not only from railroads' connecting more and more places but also from a cruel irony. Just as the canal was approaching full repayment of the debts incurred in its construction (achieved in 1871), the new state constitution of the previous year denied financial outlays for continuing canal maintenance. The two circumstances led to falling traffic and revenues, and as the canal silted up, boats moved increasingly to the Illinois River. Other pressures were building up in the region: Chicago's sewage, for one. An ingenious scheme—the Chicago Sanitary and Ship Canal—was devised to pass the metropolis's effluents down to St. Louis by reengineering the flow of the Chicago River away from Lake Michigan (the city's source of drinking water) and down a vast new "chute" handing off the waste to the Illinois River, and coincidentally providing the corridor with a widened and deepened waterway. This new canal, reaching from Chicago to Lockport, was constructed between 1890 and 1900. Also, a new branch, the Calumet Sag Channel, was built from

Sag Bridge via Blue Island to the Lake Calumet region near South Chicago, an industrial district of increasing importance. As a result of these changes, the northernmost section of the original I&M Canal, from Joliet to Chicago, was permanently closed to traffic. The new waterways functioned well, and increasing use was made of them by such industries as the Texaco oil refinery north of Lockport, built in 1911 as that company's first refinery outside its Texas-Oklahoma producing region.[46] Plans were finally laid to construct a deep shipping route between the Mississippi and Lake Michigan, which resulted in the Illinois Waterway, begun in the 1920s and completed in 1933 by the federal government. Although this and the Sanitary and Ship Canal were mammoth undertakings in terms of engineering—wider, deeper, and with huge locks, dams, and hydroelectric generating stations as integral elements—they had only a reinforcing effect on the evolving geography of the corridor and of northern Illinois. Thus, although more disruptive of their immediate environment, they could hardly be said to have been nearly as pivotal in the region's development as the original I&M Canal.

Depression, War, and Industrial Change

The upper Illinois valley enjoyed an extraordinarily long and largely uninterrupted period of bullish economic development from the close of the Civil War to the late 1920s. It had matured into a high-volume transport corridor passing through a rich corn belt countryside, punctuated at frequent intervals by industrial and commercial towns that changed their urban rankings very little. The Great Depression, however, ushered in a protracted era of general stasis that was to last into the 1970s, interrupted by the production needs of the Second World War but not otherwise marked by much change in the economic structure or social texture of the valley's communities. It was a period in which institutions of various kinds began to influence the development and mold the character of the corridor on a wholly new scale—early harbingers of the great shift toward a postindustrial service economy that the corridor, in common with other heavily industrialized districts in the nation, experienced after the middle of the century.

For one thing, metropolitan Chicago continued its territorial growth. As the central city increased in residential density, and suburbs pushed outward from the city's fringe, the surrounding countryside, besides specializing in dairy production and truck farming, offered opportunities for recreation and retreat. Rolling and wooded sites proved attractive to cemeteries and golf clubs, and a wide scatter of these appeared during the first three decades of the new century on the southern and southwestern margins of metropolitan Chicago. The Edgewood Valley Country Club, across the river from Willow Springs, founded in 1926, and Cog Hill Country Club near Lemont, established the following year, are examples.[47] Southmoor Country Club and Oak Hill Golf Club were also operating by the late 1920s, taking advantage of the attractive surroundings of the Palos Heights area. Cemeteries had similar scenic requirements, and the comparative remoteness of the area from the built-up mass of Chicago and its good drainage contributed to notable concentrations north and west of Blue Island—ten cemeteries within a two-mile radius of the town—and also between Justice and Hickory Hills.

Urban-industrial expansion affected other reaches of the corridor. The development of the silica sands west of Ottawa had earlier threatened the existence of the outstanding natural character of the Starved Rock area, leading to its designation as Illinois's first state park (1911). Interest in preserving areas of natural beauty and value was given a particular boost during the slack times of the Depression, resulting in the creation of several additional state parks in the corridor: Buffalo Rock (1929), Gebhard Woods and Illini (1934), the Illinois and Michigan Canal State Parkway (1937), and Matthiessen, next to Starved Rock (1944).[48] The Civilian Conservation Corps (CCC) made a significant impact on the corridor by developing small parks and trails along portions of the I&M Canal. In the process CCC workers stabilized and rehabilitated decaying I&M Canal structures, such as the stone locks at Channahon and Marseilles, and built numerous picnic shelters in rusticated stone, such as the one at the filled-in Hydraulic Basin in Lockport. In more recent times, state conservation and wildlife areas have followed, notably the Des Plaines Conservation Area and in the late 1970s the Goose Lake Prairie State Park.

Perhaps the most dramatic, and also most temporary, case of institutional impact on the corridor was the transformation of the small village of Seneca during World War II. In the years prior to the war a small barge-building company had taken up a riverfront site on the southeastern side of town. By early 1942 the military needed seagoing troop carriers that could unload directly on the beaches of Europe and the Pacific islands, and the Chicago Bridge and Iron Company, which owned the barge firm, won a contract to produce these landing ship tanks (LSTs). Seneca was selected for reasons of site (sandstone base at water's edge to carry the weight of numerous ships without costly piling, and deep water for boat launching) and situation (near steel supplies and on a major waterway leading to the Gulf of Mexico). For decades Seneca had been hard put to claim more than 1,000 inhabitants, but within months the Prairie Shipyard employed 8,400 workers and peaked at 10,600 workers in June 1944.[49] Emergency government housing was thrown up in "Victory Courts," trailer parks, and dormitories, which, together with private homes in the village, accommodated only about 1,500 workers. The rest were drawn from or found accommodations in other corridor towns and elsewhere, particularly Ottawa (1,900), Marseilles (700), and LaSalle (630), the vast majority commuting by automobile. Two hundred million dollars' worth of ships were built at Seneca, and by June 1945, it was all over. Much of the temporary housing was carted off or torn down, people moved away, and the town returned mostly to its former "normality," except that it now had sewers, better streets, a bank, and a new school.

The postwar period in the corridor was one of geographically varied change. In the western parts, towns pursued their traditional roles and industry lumbered on, altered in its composition by the depression and wartime, but anchored still by the larger firms that had been around at least since the late nineteenth century. Outside the towns, agriculture carried on much as usual. Around Joliet and to the east of it, however, the tempo of economic change since the 1930s was more accelerated, in terms of both shifting employment and a rising tide of suburbanization. Modern additions to the industrial character of the corridor's eastern segment have been mostly in processing along the main stem of the corridor and in fabrication along the Cal-Sag Channel and the Calumet district. More oil refineries appeared, such as the Mobil refinery south of Joliet, and the one at Lemont, now owned by Union Oil Company. Also, the spare land lying between and adjacent to the watercourses (the rerouted Des Plaines River and the Sanitary and Ship Canal) proved ideal for sewage treatment plants with their huge settling tanks and ponds. Around Blue Island and between there and South Chicago, great additions to the steel plants and heavy engineering works of the area were made during the 1940s and 1950s, the great "Indian summer" of heavy manufacturing in the Chicago region before it switched gears and succumbed to radical deindustrialization.

Large public and private institutions have continued to make a strong impact on the corridor. The triangular area between Summit, Blue Island, and Joliet, for example, developed an unlikely mixture of land uses serving the sacred, the profane, and the dead. Seminaries sprouted, prisons proliferated, and cemeteries sequestered themselves in a zone increasingly seen as a recreational haven on a grand scale. Mount Assissi Academy (1955) and Our Lady of Victory Convent (1963) joined earlier religious foundations, while the City of Chicago Correctional Farm joined the prior development in the valley of the large state correctional facility at Stateville (1925).[50] Recreation broadened in its metropolitan relevance. Country clubs and boys' camps had colonized this part of the corridor since the twenties, but after the war larger plans came to fruition. It proved more practical close to Chicago to organize county forest preserves than state parks. Although the forest preserve movement began with the Cook County District in 1916,[51] which was emulated quickly in adjoining counties, the acreages assembled were initially modest and the campaign matured only after the war. Since the 1940s large additions to these open space preserves have been made.[52] The federal government also bid for open space after the war with the relocation in the corridor of the Argonne National Laboratory from the University of Chicago campus in 1948 to conduct research into peaceful uses of the atom.

This eastern—metropolitanized—portion of the corridor, therefore, has been peppered with industrial, institutional, and recreational land uses scattered about but occupying more and more land over the last forty to fifty years. To this variegated and slowly filling mosaic have been added the bitumen, brickwork, and bric-a-brac of suburbia, filling the interstices. Historically, Chicago's suburbs pushed out along old commuter railroad lines arranged like spokes of a giant wheel, and on the city's southwestern flank the I&M corridor represented one of the nonresidential wedges between these spokes.[53] With the advance of the automobile this neat geometry broke down: it remains true that prewar suburbs due south of the city stretched thirty miles away from Chicago's Loop (and a dozen miles beyond Blue Island), whereas in the corridor's main stem Justice and Willow Springs, the last reasonably contiguous residential communities on the old Chicago and Alton line, were only fifteen miles distant. This difference is directly attributable to the physical nature of the bluff-lined valley farther south and the preemption of territory by institutional and open space preserves. In the Calumet-Sag district the nineteenth-century matrix of heavy industry and railroads continued to define the character of the area.

The advent of expressways and freeways in the southern metropolitan sector in the late 1950s began to alter spatial relations in the corridor. In eight short years (1957–1965) key freeway segments were constructed that tied the whole corridor to the heart of the metropolis in new ways. The most immediate long-distance consequences were that Ottawans and Peruvians could reach the Loop or even some of the western suburbs in two hours, drawing some types of custom away from local merchants. Also, the labor sheds of the metropolis, and those of its satellites such as Joliet, were widened, bringing to the fringes of established communities new kinds of residents with sometimes minimal attachment to their adopted domiciles. The freeways likewise improved access to the countryside for urbanites seeking weekend getaways.

When considered in terms of physical siting, freeways established a completely new pattern. They were the first transport routes not to run along the valley floor; there was by midtwentieth century precious little room left there for such space-consuming feats of engineering. Instead the freeways, Interstates 55 and 80 in particular, colonized the open farmland on the level plateau to one side of and parallel to the valley, never reaching any particular place, only passing nearby. Only where the Stevenson Expressway (I-55) needed to traverse developed districts within the city limits (between Summit and the Loop) did its designers adopt an old alignment: by constructing it on top of the abandoned I&M Canal itself. Beyond the congested areas of the 1950s, however, the purpose was both to locate the new superhighways where land was not excessively expensive to acquire and to open up new districts to development. This latter principle has transformed the geographical structure of the metropolis at the broad scale as well as at the local scale.

At the regional scale, I-55 encouraged the suburban filling in of the corridor's general farmland fringe with the development of such new residential communities as Romeoville, Bolingbrook, Brookeridge, and Darien, products of the 1960s and 1970s. At the local scale, freeway interchanges attracted new business developments and hastened many forms of urban decentralization, both close to Chicago and around the towns of the western corridor. The development of suburban shopping malls has had particularly dramatic results. In the Chicago fringe, malls have proliferated along with the "greenfield" suburbs in simple symbiosis; where malls have been added to the edges of smaller, discrete towns, their effect on the traditional downtowns of these places has often been deleterious. Joliet's central business has been especially hard hit by the competition from outlying retail centers such as the Louis Joliet Mall, and neither LaSalle's nor Peru's downtown has benefited from the establishment of the Peru Mall at the intersection of I-80 and U.S. 51. In other corridor towns without regional shopping malls on their outskirts, such as Morris and Ottawa, the traditional downtowns remain much healthier. In all cases, however, freeways have acted as magnets to pull retail and office development, even within the established parts of towns, toward them. Even in Ottawa, the central business district has developed northward along Columbus Street to include the intersection with Norris Street (Route 6), with all its fast food outlets, because that crossroads provides the key access to the freeway interchange a mile to the north, itself a focus of vigorous "commercial strip" growth.[54]

Amenities and Services: A New Era?

In the last decade or more, the corridor has witnessed a sharp swing in employment patterns away from manufacturing to service jobs. A number of long-standing industries are changing ownership, finally losing their local character, and in numerous cases being closed down. In the last decade the steelwork in Joliet was discontinued, the Westclox factory in Peru is no more, the Texaco refinery in Lockport shut down a few years ago, and Nabisco pulled out of Marseilles. There is a general shift to marketing and transportation once again, and away from the high-wage, high-skill industries that actually make things. The new oil terminals and chemical plants that line the valley between Joliet and Marseilles are highly mechanized and require relatively small work forces. So once again the

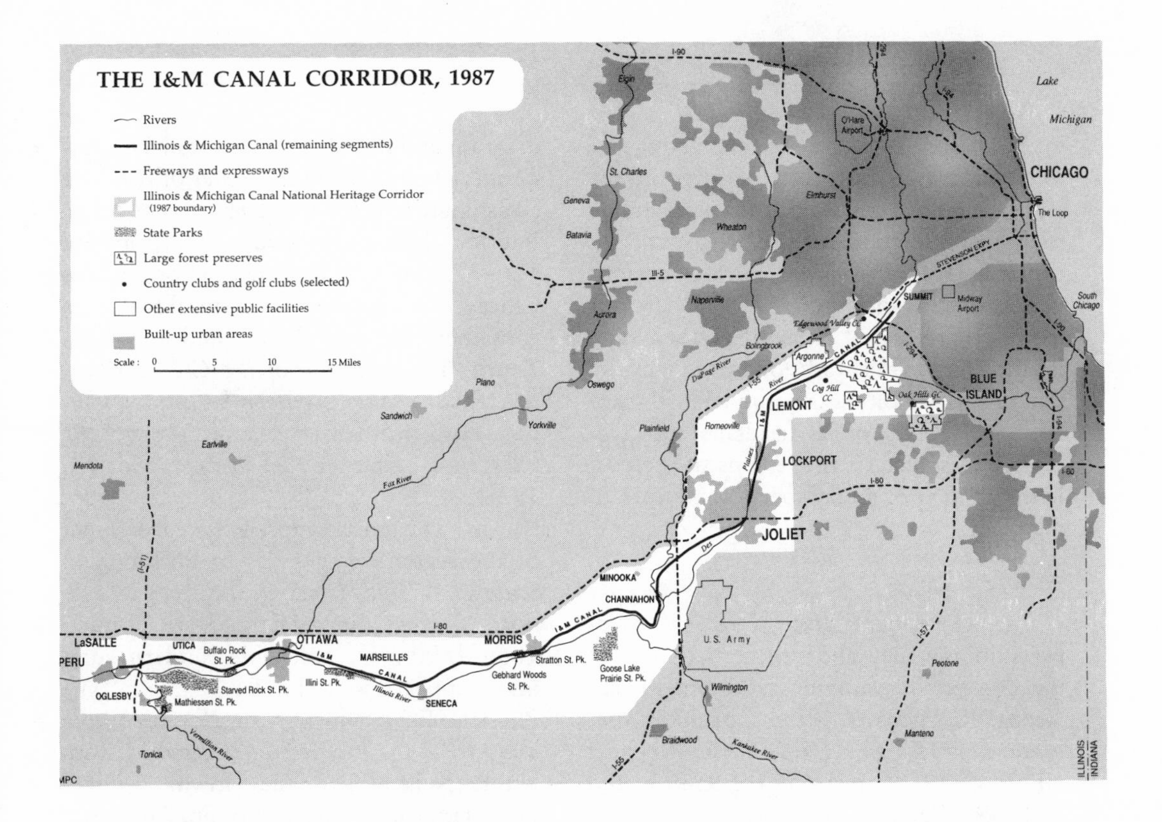

corridor's economy is defined heavily in terms of processing and transportation. The new element is the search for an alternative future, for many residents of the corridor have little desire to move away, even though their children are much more footloose and sometimes find little to keep them bound to the valley.

If manufacturing plays a diminishing role in the life of the corridor, the region's proximity to a metropolitan population of eight million is being seen increasingly as a possible source of future prosperity. The urban mass needs to breathe,and the Upper Illinois valley is rich in recreational and historical amenities that hold the potential for extensive tourist development.[55] The numerous state parks, forest preserves, wildlife conservation areas, nature trails, rivers, and waterways already provide a variety of options for such outdoors activity as hiking, boating, fishing, and swimming. The metropolitan usage of these facilities is of long standing, but bound to increase. Less recognized until recently, the historical heritage of the corridor—its transportational and industrial past and the architectural and engineering relicts in the landscape that reflect that heritage—is equally rich and potentially valuable in stimulating local and national tourism to the area. It is this historical dimension of the corridor, symbolized by its single most celebrated and unifying physical artifact, the I&M Canal, that provided a strong underpinning for the recent successful effort to gain the region designation as a "national heritage corridor."[56] Much of the valley's artifactual and documentary history remains to be fully exposed and interpreted in a coherent way. A number of museums and historical library collections exist in the corridor, but they by no means exhaust the possibilities in presenting the complex regional history of the corridor to a variety of appropriate audiences. Also, much awareness needs still to be raised among residents about the value of saving historical features in the landscape—old buildings, canal and industrial structures, and so forth—for the intrinsic interest they hold for the curious visitor and resident alike.[57] The corridor has a long record of "making history," and it can continue this tradition by recognizing that part of its future economic health may lie in the ability of its residents and promoters to articulate the lessons of the past in the context of a very specific and intriguing place.

References

1 For general discussions of the upper Illinois valley and northern Illinois in the context of national development, see George R. Taylor, *The Transportation Revolution, 1815–1860* (New York: Rinehart and Co., 1951), pp. 45–48, 95–96, and 164–69; Carter Goodrich, *Government Promotion of American Canals and Railroads, 1800–1890* (New York: Columbia University Press, 1960), pp. 138–52; and Robert D. Mitchell and Paul A. Groves, eds., *North America: The Historical Geography of a Changing Continent* (Totowa, New Jersey: Rowman and Littlefield, 1987), pp. 172–97, 321–46.

2 North America boasts three continental divides, in the form of a rough letter *H*. The two north-south divides pass along the Rocky Mountains and the Appalachian Mountains, dividing waters draining directly to the Pacific and middle Atlantic oceans from those reaching the Atlantic from the interior via the Gulfs of Mexico and St. Lawrence. These two gulfs are separated by the third, roughly east-west divide, which passes through the Chicago region. This divide lacks the physical drama of the other two, but it enabled people to traverse it and connect the adjacent regions with comparative ease. For the continental pattern of these divides, see the physiographic diagram and the water use map in *The National Atlas of the United States of America* (Washington, D.C.: U.S. Department of the Interior Geological Survey, 1970), pp. 59, 126–27. An extended discussion of the Chicago portage area as a natural feature is contained in Robert Knight and Lucius H. Zeuch, *The Location of the Chicago Portage Route of the Seventeenth Century,* Chicago Historical Society's Collection, vol. 12 (Chicago: Chicago Historical Society, 1928).

3 The most comprehensive treatment of the region's geology is to be found in State of Illinois, *Geological Survey of Illinois,* 8 vol. (Springfield: State Printer, 1866–1890). An accessible modern summary appears in Arlin D. Fentem, "The Physical Environment," in *Illinois: Land and Life in the Prairie State,* edited by Ronald E. Nelson (Dubuque, Iowa: Kendall/Hunt Publishing Co., 1978), pp. 21–107.

4 The physical geography of the corridor is discussed in detail, and with attention to examples that can be inspected in the field, in Carl O. Sauer, *Geography of the Upper Illinois Valley and History of Development,* Illinois State Geological Survey, Bulletin 27 (Urbana, Illinois: 1916), and James W. Goldthwait, *Physical Features of the Des Plaines Valley,* Illinois State Geological Survey, Bulletin 11 (Urbana, Illinois: 1909). See also F. M. Fryxell, *The Physiography of the Region of Chicago* (Chicago: University of Chicago Press, 1927).

5 For a modern overview of the prehistoric phase of native settlement of the corridor, see James A. Brown, *et al., An Inventory and Evaluation of Known Archaeological Resources in the Illinois and Michigan Canal National Heritage Corridor, Illinois,* Vol. 1 (Carbondale, Illinois: American Resources Group, 1985), pp. 45–66.

6 Michael Coe, Dean Snow, and Eliz-

abeth Benson, *Atlas of Ancient America* (New York and Oxford: Facts on File Publications, 1986), pp. 50–51.

7 Brown *et al.*, pp. 64–66.

8 Margaret K. Brown, *The First Kaskaskia: The Zimmerman Site, LaSalle, Illinois* (n.p.: LaSalle County Historical Society, 1973). This village should not be confused with a later French village established in southern Illinois on the banks of the Mississippi River.

9 Carl O. Sauer, *Seventeenth Century North America* (Berkeley, California: Turtle Island Press, 1980), pp. 137–38.

10 Joseph J. Thompson, "The Illinois Missions, I. The Jesuit Succession," *Illinois Catholic Historical Review* 1 (July 1918): 38–63.

11 Catherine Schaefer, "A Chronology of Missions and Churches in Illinois, from 1675 to 1844," *Illinois Catholic Historical Review* 1 (July 1918): 103.

12 Reuben G. Thwaites, ed., *The Jesuit Relations and Allied Documents,* Vol. 58 (Cleveland: Burrows Brothers Co., 1899), p. 105.

13 "La Salle on the Illinois Country, 1680," in Theodore C. Pease and Raymond C. Werner, eds., *Collections of the Illinois State Historical Library,* Vol. 23, French Series, Vol. 1: *The French Foundations, 1680–1693* (Springfield, Illinois: Illinois State Historical Library, 1934), p. 3.

14 Helen H. Tanner, ed., *Atlas of Great Lakes Indian History* (Norman: University of Oklahoma Press, for the Newberry Library, 1987), p. 139, and Maps 20 and 26.

15 John D. Haeger, "The American Fur Company and the Chicago of 1812–1835," *Journal of the Illinois State Historical Society* 61 (Summer 1968): 117–39.

16 Jacqueline Peterson, "'Wild' Chicago: The Formation and Destruction of a Multi-racial Community on the Midwestern Frontier, 1816–1837," in *The Ethnic Frontier: Essays in the History of Group Survival in Chicago and the Midwest,* ed. Melvin G. Holli and Peter d'A. Jones (Grand Rapids, Michigan: Wm. B. Eerdmans Publishing Co., 1977), pp. 26–71.

17 *Annals of Congress,* 11th Congress, 2nd Session, II, pp. 1388–93.

18 James W. Putnam, *The Illinois and Michigan Canal: A Study in Economic History* (Chicago: University of Chicago Press, 1918), pp. 8–9.

19 Putnam, p. 41.

20 Walter A. Howe, *Documentary History of the Illinois and Michigan Canal* (Springfield: State of Illinois Department of Public Works and Buildings, Division of Waterways, 1956).

21 Mark Wyman, *Immigrants in the Valley: Irish, Germans, and Americans in the Upper Mississippi Valley Country, 1830–1860* (Chicago: Nelson-Hall, 1984), pp. 80–84, 101.

22 The best general discussion of types of town founding in frontier America is in John W. Reps, *The Making of Urban America: A History of City Planning in the United States* (Princeton, New Jersey: Princeton University Press, 1965).

23 For a general discussion of the founding of Chicago, see Harold M. Mayer and Richard C. Wade, *Chicago: Growth of a Metropolis* (Chicago: University of Chicago Press, 1969), and Harold M. Mayer, "The Launching of Chicago: The Situation and the Site," *Chicago History* 9 (Summer 1980): 68–79.

24 C. C. Tisler, *Story of Ottawa, Illinois* (Ottawa, Illinois: Illinois Office Supply Co., 1953).

25 James Kirchherr and Russell Forster, "Peru, Illinois: Its Developmental Geography," *Bulletin of the Illinois Geographical Society* 27 (Fall 1985): 3–17.

26 William T. Chambers, "A Geographic Study of Joliet, Illinois: An Urban Center Dominated by Manufacturing."

PhD dissertation, University of Chicago, 1926; Mirah Germain, "The Historical Growth and Spatial Evolution of Marseilles, Illinois (1835 to the Present)." B.A. thesis, University of Chicago, 1985.

27 Gary L. LaGave, *LaSalle, Illinois: A Historical Sketch* (LaSalle, Illinois: Executive Committee 125th Anniversary, 1977).

28 *Lockport, Illinois: A Collective Heritage* (Lockport, Illinois: American Printers and Lithographers, for the Sesquicentennial Committee of the Bank of Lockport, 1980).

29 Virginia S. Brown, *Grundy County Illinois Landmarks Volume I* (Morris, Illinois: Grundy County Historical Society, 1981), pp. 1–7.

30 Phyllis Dillon, *History of Channahon, Homecoming of 1972* (Channahon, Illinois: By the Author, 1972); Barbara Buschman, ed., *Lemont, Illinois: Its History in Commemoration of the Centennial of its Incorporation* (Des Plaines, Illinois: King/Man Yearbook Center, 1973); *Seneca Area Centennial Celebration, The Story of 100 Years* (Seneca, Illinois: Seneca Regional Port District, 1965); Utica Junior Woman's Club, *Village of Utica, 1852–1952,* Centennial Program (n.p., 1952).

31 Still the most impressive "global" interpretation of Chicago's geographical advantages as a continental city is that in J. Paul Goode, *The Geographic Background of Chicago: A City of Destiny* (Chicago: University of Chicago Press, 1926). The somewhat boosterish overtone of the essay does not diminish the power of the fundamental regional argument made for Chicago's long-term urban success.

32 The rural settlement process of the corridor has yet to be studied in systematic detail based on the regional analysis of land records. For a useful general overview, see William V. Pooley, *The Settlement of Illinois from 1830 to 1850,* Bulletin of the University of Wisconsin, No. 220, History Series, Vol. 1, No. 4 (Madison, Wisconsin: 1908), pp. 375–95.

33 An immediate picture of the relative concentration of landownership along the margins of the upper Illinois valley can be gained from the various county landownership maps covering the area in the 1850s and 1860s. See, for example, S. B. Carter and Th. Newbarth, *Map of LaSalle County and Part of Marshall County, Illinois* (n.p., 1859).

34 Pooley, pp. 385, 388.

35 Douglas R. McManis, *The Initial Evaluation and Utilization of the Illinois Prairies, 1815–1840,* University of Chicago Department of Geography Research Paper, 94 (Chicago, 1964).

36 Putnam, p. 99.

37 Fayette B. Shaw, "Transportation in the Development of Joliet and Will County," *Journal of the Illinois State Historical Society* 30 (1937–38), p. 101.

38 Mary Y. Rathbun, *The Illinois and Michigan Canal,* second revision (Springfield, Illinois: Illinois Department of Conservation Bureau of Land and Historic Sites, 1980), pp. 38–39.

39 *History of Will County, Illinois* (Chicago: William LeBaron, Jr., and Co., 1878), p. 376.

40 Putnam, pp. 111–15.

41 Sauer, pp. 187–89.

42 Carl O. Sauer *et al., Starved Rock State Park and Its Environs,* Geographic Society of Chicago, Bulletin No. 6 (Chicago: University of Chicago Press, 1918), p. 79.

43 *Peru, Illinois, Centennial, May 25–26, 1935* (Peru, Illinois: Centennial Historical Committee, 1935), pp. 52–53.

44 Chambers, p. 19.

45 Stephen Freedman, "Organizing the Workers in a Steel Company Town: The Union Movement in Joliet, Illinois, 1870–1920," *Illinois Historical Journal* 79 (Spring 1986): 2–18.

46 James Marquis, *The Texaco*

Story: The First Fifty Years, 1902–1952 (n.p.: The Texas Company, 1953), p. 53.

47 Michael P. Conzen and David B. Hanson, "The Des Plaines Valley: Historical Landscapes of Business," *Bulletin of the Illinois Geographical Society* 23, 2 (Fall 1981): 3–17.

48 John E. Trotter, *State Park System in Illinois,* University of Chicago Department of Geography Research Paper, 74 (Chicago: 1962), p. 67.

49 Robert J. Havinghurst and H. Gerthon Morgan, *The Social History of a War-Boom Community* (New York: Longmans, Green and Company, 1951), pp. 47–50.

50 An interesting sociological history of the prison facility is found in James B. Jacobs, *Stateville: The Penitentiary in Mass Society* (Chicago: University of Chicago Press, 1977).

51 Steve Christy, "Wide-Awake Dreaming: Creation of the Cook County Forest Preserve District," *Terrain* 6 (July–August 1982): 2.

52 Alexander B. Murphy, "Issues in the Preservation and Management of Open Space for Recreational Use in Metropolitan Chicago," *Environmental Review* 10 (Spring 1986): 31–44.

53 Michael P. Conzen, "The Changing Character of Metropolitan Chicago," *Journal of Geography* 85 (September/October 1986): 224–236.

54 Brian W. Coberly, "Land Use and Residential Geography of Ottawa in 1987," Chapter 6 in *Focus on Ottawa: A Historical and Geographical Survey of Ottawa, Illinois, in the Twentieth Century,* ed. Michael P. Conzen (Chicago: University of Chicago Committee on Geographical Studies, 1987).

55 An influential series of articles by columnist John Husar entitled "Our Hidden Wilderness" appeared in the *Chicago Tribune,* September 21–25, 1980.

56 See Chapter 3 for a brief history of this extensive effort, and also Linda Legner, "A National Park Here? Why Not, Says Chicago's Super-Salesman," *Historic Preservation* (March/April 1982): 26–31.

57 Recent examples of the mounting number of feature articles on the heritage of the corridor include Deborah Slaton, "Esprit de Corridor: Illinois & Michigan Canal National Heritage Flourishes," *Inland Architect* (September/October 1986): 37–40; and Gale Kappe, "Following History's Trail: Blue herons, badgers, and Rust Belt Towns nestle on the banks of the Illinois and Michigan Canal," *Chicago* 36 (April 1987): 99–103.

Two

THE ARCHITECTURAL LEGACY AND INDUSTRIAL ARCHAEOLOGY OF THE ILLINOIS AND MICHIGAN CANAL NATIONAL HERITAGE CORRIDOR

G. Gray Fitzsimons

EXTENDING NEARLY one hundred miles from Chicago to Peru, Illinois, the Illinois and Michigan Canal National Heritage Corridor encompasses a wide range of natural and historic resources. Although its setting varies from industrialized urban centers to open prairies and thickly forested woodlands, much of the Heritage Corridor is enveloped by vast tracts of fertile farmland. Many small to medium-size towns serve this countryside, most of them situated along the Illinois and Michigan (I&M) Canal, the historic waterway that forms the central resource of the Heritage Corridor. Within these diverse landscapes is to be found a rich variety of architecture, historic engineering, and industrial sites that offer a tangible record of the region's evolution. It has been traditional in architectural accounts to emphasize high-style exemplars of residential and institutional building within particular regions, to the comparative neglect of commercial and industrial structures as well as vernacular residential structures.[1] Such a bias is not appropriate in considering the I&M Canal corridor. Since the region's preeminent significance lies in the important role it played in American commercial expansion and industrialization, particularly during the nineteenth century, a more comprehensive approach that highlights the total building history of the Heritage Corridor as a record of the special character the area acquired is needed.

The identification of historically and architecturally significant structures located along the canal began in the 1930s soon after the state had retired the I&M from commercial service. Various federal and state agencies, as well as interested individuals, conducted architectural surveys in some of the canal towns and along parts of the I&M.[2] Yet when the Heritage Corridor came into existence in 1984 the region was still in need of a comprehensive historic structures survey. Part of the legislation creating the Heritage Corridor addressed this issue and committed the National Park Service to inventory all the archaeological and historical resources within the corridor's boundaries. Consequently, the Historic American Buildings Survey/Historic American Engineering Record (HABS/HAER) Division of the National Park Service in the summer of 1985 commenced a corridorwide survey of historic architecture and engineering, and two years of survey work have so far been accomplished.[3]

In his plans for constructing the state-owned Illinois and Michigan Canal in 1836, chief engineer William Gooding divided the proposed route into three sections, the Summit, the Middle, and the Western divisions. Much of this land was wilderness with only a few primitive settlements nestled along the valley's streams and rivers. In the towns of Peru, LaSalle, Ottawa, Joliet, and Lockport there stood no more than a handful of frame and log buildings. Even the future Midwest metropolis of Chicago could boast only of Fort Dearborn and a few dozen huts, log cabins, and frame buildings. All of this would change rapidly, however, as canal construction commenced on the Summit section in the summer of 1836.

The building of the I&M did not bring about any new technological advances—indeed, Gooding relied heavily on his experience with canal construction in Ohio and Indiana—and the work was often arduously slow. Financial difficulties, harsh labor conditions, and disease hampered progress on the I&M. The collapse of canal funding in 1842 forced the state to abandon further construction work. Although the Summit and Western sections were fully excavated and even a few of the locks were partially built, little had been done on the Middle Division. The I&M remained in this unfinished condition until 1845, when the state secured additional loans to carry on the work. Finally in April 1848, the long awaited opening of the canal was realized when the first boat steamed into the Lockport section of the I&M Canal. The newly completed canal contained sixteen lift locks, about a dozen wood-frame lock-tender's houses, five aqueducts (all similarly built with stone piers supporting heavy timber trusses), five crib dams, several feeder canals, and a pumping station at Bridgeport. Packet boats traveling the ninety-six-mile length of the canal usually made the trip in one to two days. The canal commissioners chose Lockport as their headquarters, constructing for their offices a large wood-frame building with a gable roof and clapboard siding.

During its eighty-five years of operation the I&M Canal underwent a number of major alterations. Among these was the 1872 construction of the deep cut plan through Summit, thereby eliminating the Bridgeport lock and pumping station. Interestingly, Gooding, who had remained on as chief engineer, oversaw the work. The greatest change to the canal, however, came in 1900 with the completion of the Chicago Sanitary and Ship Canal. This newer, larger waterway was the preferred route for almost all of the barge traffic between Chicago and Lockport. This stretch of the I&M Canal subsequently fell into disrepair.[4]

Today the condition of the historic I&M Canal varies dramatically over its ninety-six-mile length. In the Chicago area virtually nothing remains of the canal; its prism was obliterated in the 1950s when Interstate 55 was constructed. In fact the only significant remnant of the I&M Canal within the city limits is part of the turning basin at Bridgeport. Here one may still view the eastern terminus of the I&M Canal at its junction with the South Branch of the Chicago River.

In sharp contrast to the paved-over section of the I&M Canal within the city limits of Chicago, however, the canal in Channahon where it crosses the DuPage River forms an integral part of a lovely bucolic landscape. Life-locks stand on either side of the densely forested river banks, and a dam slightly downstream creates a wide slackwater. It was here that the I&M Canal crossed the DuPage River not by means of an aqueduct but instead "at grade" by means of the slackwater dam, a tow line, and the two lift locks. Canal boats were pulled across the river behind the dam, which maintained a level of about twelve feet above the original water line. Although the locks retain much of their canal-era appearance, the former crib dam was rebuilt in concrete by the Civilian Conservation Corps in the 1930s. One other historically important structure at Channahon, the locktender's house, was built as part of the original canal operation. It is a modest two-story, wood-frame building with a slightly pitched gable roof and clapboard siding. All of the original locktender's houses were similarly built and contained a few elements borrowed from the Greek Revival style, including symmetrical fenestration and cornice returns on the gable ends. Dating from about 1848, only two other I&M Canal locktender's houses are known to survive, one in Lockport (not in its original condition) and the other at Aux Sable.[5]

Between 1848, when the I&M Canal opened, and the mid-1880s grain traffic on the canal grew steadily. Each of the canal towns had one or two grain elevators situated along the busy waterway. Even as late as the 1890s grain dealers were erecting five- and six-story elevators along the I&M Canal. They did so because shipping via the canal, though much slower than the railroads, nearly halved their costs. Nonetheless, with the decline of the I&M Canal in the early twentieth century, most of the elevators either made connections with the railroad or were torn down. Presently, there are three surviving canal-era grain elevators along the I&M Canal. The oldest one stands in Seneca, having been built in 1862 of heavy timber post and beam construction with wood siding. Similar to other grain elevators located by the canal, it was steam-powered, contained a corn sheller, and held up to 100,000 bushels of grain. The Hogan family of Seneca ran the grain elevator from the 1890s through the 1960s. It was recently purchased by the Illinois Department of Conservation, ensuring its preservation as part of the I&M Canal State Park.[6]

In addition to grain, many other locally manufactured goods were shipped via the canal. Warehouses of stone and wood construction sprang up along the I&M Canal throughout the late 1840s and 1850s. Two outstanding examples may be seen today in Lockport and in Utica. The more visually striking of the two is the Norton Building in Lockport. Built of locally quarried limestone in about 1849 by Hiram Norton, the hulking four-story building measures one hundred feet by one hundred feet. It served as a granary and general store and was operated by Norton and Company until the turn of the century. The Clark warehouse in Utica, now the LaSalle County Historical Society Museum, was erected in about 1848. James Clark probably used the two-story, sandstone building in conjunction with his cement business. In later years it housed a livery and an auto repair garage, and in the process lost its one-story wooden cupola.[7]

Although the canal played an important role in the early settlement and development of the upper Illinois valley, it was with the advent of the railroads in the 1850s that the pace of growth in the region rapidly accelerated. Three important antebellum railroads, the Chicago and Alton Railroad; the Chicago, Rock Island and Pacific Railroad; and the Illinois Central Railroad, opened up much of the remaining wilderness, permitting the cultivation of the prairie lands as well as the exploitation of the valley's rich deposits of limestone, coal, silica sand, and clay. Heavy industry soon

The I&M Canal and DuPage River at Channahon. *The lock in the foreground once raised canal boats up to the level of the river (middle ground, flowing from left to right) to cross it "at grade" before passing through another lock (far distance) on their way to Chicago. A footbridge once carried the towpath over the river at the right.* (Photo: Michael P. Conzen)

followed on the heels of railroad construction. Only a few of the early railroad stations remain. In LaSalle, where the Illinois Central crossed the Illinois River on its way to Cairo, Illinois, the original freight depot stands amidst a deserted railyard. Erected in 1857, this limestone building retains much of its early appearance. The limestone pilasters are capped with ornamental stone capitals, and the gable roof is supported by the original all-timber Queen post trusses. The freight depot was converted into an engine house around 1917 and continued in service until its abandonment in the 1970s.

The earliest surviving passenger stations in the Heritage Corridor are found in Lemont and Lockport, both products of the Chicago and Alton Railroad. They are nearly identical in appearance—gable roofs, one story in height, limestone load-bearing walls, and handsome limestone detailing around the door and window openings. Akin to the Illinois Central Railroad's LaSalle Freight Depot, the design seems to have been influenced by the Greek Revival style so popular in the early nineteenth century.[8] The famous Rock Island railroad, built parallel to the I&M Canal in 1853–1854, still has a number of its passenger stations standing along its line. The earliest of these date from the 1870s to the early 1900s. Marseilles possesses one of the later stations, built in 1917, when passenger rail traffic was still in its heyday. The design of the long, rectangular building was clearly influenced by the arts and crafts movement of the early twentieth century. It features a low-pitched intersecting gable roof covered with terra cotta tiles and wide eaves supported by ornamental wood brackets.

Traces of early industrialization in the

Elevators at Utica. *Since early days grain elevators have lined the Corridor, storing and shipping the district's farm produce. The structure on the left was built at water's edge around 1892, still tied to the canal for transport, that on the right with its back to the canal in the 1960s when only road access remained important.* (Photo: Michael P. Conzen)

upper Illinois valley may be found in the wilderness settlements of the 1830s. Pioneers built and operated sawmills, gristmills, blacksmith shops, and distilleries. Heavier industry, however, began to emerge in the 1850s and 1860s. Two in particular, stone quarrying and cement making, evolved directly from the construction of the I&M Canal. Stone quarrying was one of the major industries in Lemont, Lockport, and Joliet. Numerous quarry pits, now almost entirely abandoned, are visible in this section of the Heritage Corridor. In Lemont, the former quarry of Nathaniel J. Brown is probably the most intact nineteenth-century site. It includes the Brown residence, originally built in the 1850s and greatly modified in the 1870s; the quarry manager's residence; and the foundations of what may have been a company-owned worker's house. Unfortunately, none of the drilling machinery or masonry saws is known to survive, but the adjacent quarry and the two barns—one an impressive two-story, limestone building dating from around 1840, and the other a c. 1860 heavy timber-framed structure—form a unique pastoral industrial setting.[9]

The production of natural and hydraulic cement in Utica was first carried out in the mid-1830s. William Norton, the eldest member of an entrepreneurial family in Lockport, ran Utica's first cement works. Subsequently, James Clark purchased the property and further expanded the kilns, the grinding mill, and the quarry from which the cement produced came. A few ruins from Clark's cement works, chiefly foundations of the kilns, may be seen in Utica. By about 1870, another cement

The Illinois Central Freight Depot at LaSalle. *Built of local stone in 1857 and one of the last remaining Illinois Central Railroad structures from that era, the freight depot yet symbolizes the crossing point where for over a century and a quarter one of America's last great canals has intersected the line of the nation's first landgrant railroad.* (Photo: Michael P. Conzen)

works opened nearby at Pecamsauga Creek. Known as the Utica Cement Company, the concern manufactured Blackball Cement, operating four kilns, a steam-powered grinding and bagging mill, and a large warehouse. One of the more interesting facets of the cement works centered on the mining of limestone. The raw material came from the palisades above the kilns with mines cut into the hillside. The Blackball site, which included a small company town, ran until the First World War. The site still retains part of the brickwork of the kilns as well as the ruins of the engine house. Dozens of mine adits may be seen throughout the area.[10]

In Joliet, Ottawa, and LaSalle–Peru much of the landscape is dominated by heavy industry. Joliet's iron and steel industry achieved notoriety in the 1870s when an early Bessemer process was used in making steel rail. Located on the city's north side, the steelworks reached its peak in the 1920s and again in the 1940s when, under the ownership of U.S. Steel, it employed some seven thousand workers. Little remains of the steel-making operations; except for their foundations the open hearth furnaces, once located near the I&M Canal, have disappeared. Significantly, several mill buildings and offices, constructed of brick and limestone, are still standing, even though the sprawling steelworks has virtually closed down.[11]

In Ottawa, the silica sand industry rose to prominence in the late 1890s. Used primarily in glassmaking, silica sand was found in huge quantities west of Ottawa near the Illinois River, the site of the St. Peter's anticline that contained the fine grains of sand. These strata of sandstone contained silica sand as pure as any in the

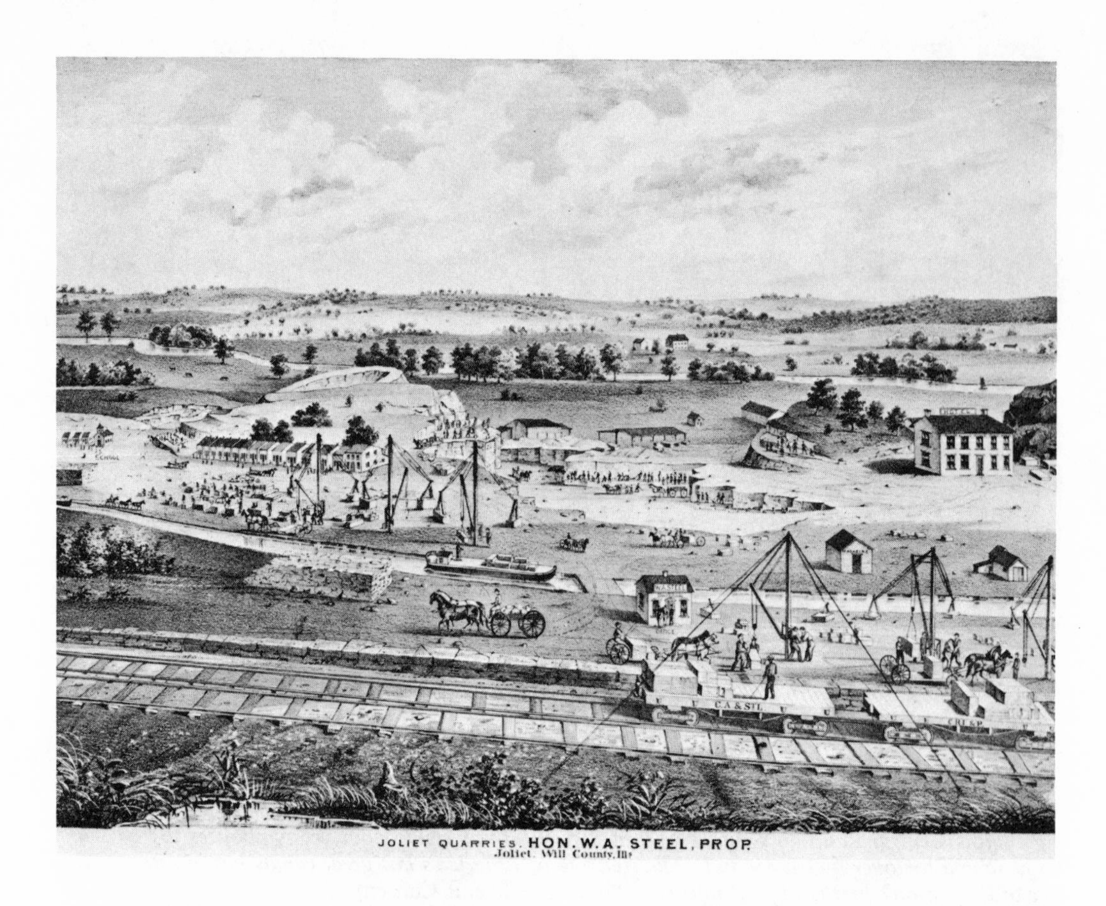

Steele's Quarry, between Lockport and Joliet. *Source for countless limestone buildings in the Corridor and especially Chicago, particularly after the 1871 fire, this quarry, pictured here in 1873, helped spread the fame of "Joliet Marble" far and wide.*

world. Ottawa Silica Company, founded in 1900 by Bedford (Indiana) native Edmund Thornton, soon became one of the largest producers of silica sand in the United States. One of the structures associated with this industry, a sand-sorting building, has become a visual landmark in Ottawa. Originally built in 1917 by U.S. Silica, chief competitor to Ottawa Silica Company, it was rebuilt with a distinctive pyramidal roof in 1929 after the latter firm acquired the site. The sorting building operated with electrically powered conveyors that transported sand to the top, where, through a gravity system, it was passed through wire screens with the fine grains settling in the bins below. The site has been idle for many years, and sadly, the sand-sorting building is slated for demolition.[12]

As with the rest of the nation, many of the upper Illinois valley manufacturers increasingly employed the technologies of mass production and hired industrial workers in far greater numbers than before. The Western Clock Company in Peru characterizes this shift in technology and factory production. Begun by a Connecticut clockmaker in 1885, the Western Clock Company was rescued from financial failure by LaSalle zinc magnate Frederick W. Matthiessen. Matthiessen saw the potential for perfecting an automatic clock-making process and financed Western Clock Company throughout the late 1890s. By 1910,

OTTAWA SILICA COMPANY
MILL 'C' COMPLEX
1917 · 1927-1929
OTTAWA, ILLINOIS

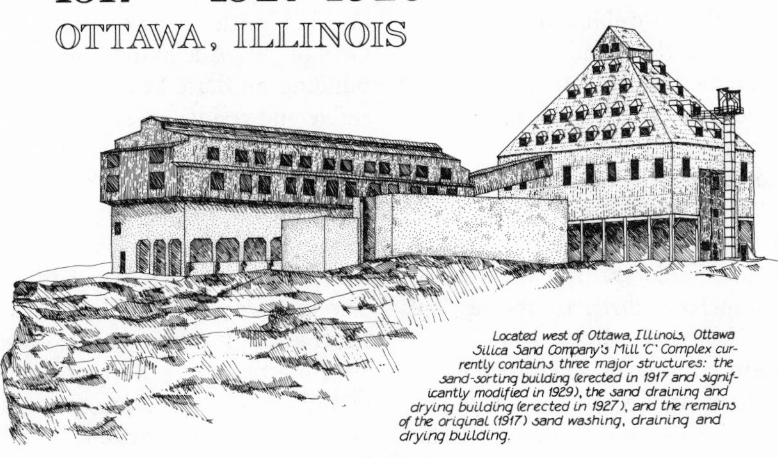

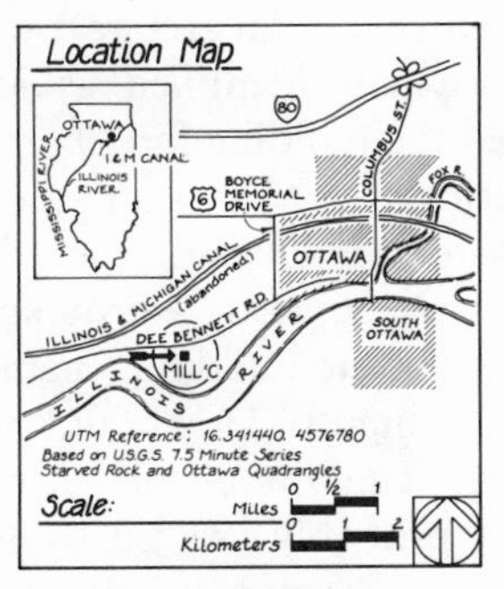

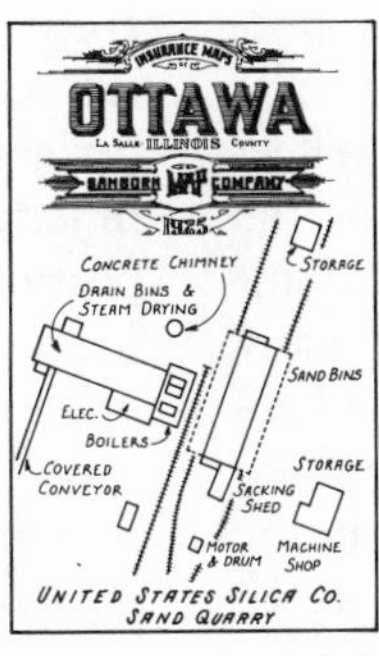

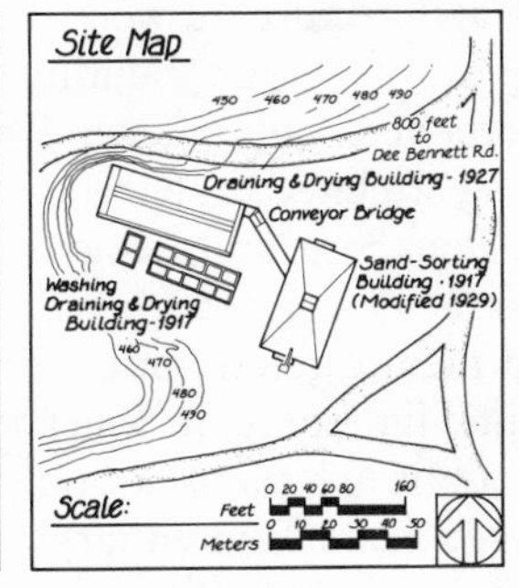

This recording project is part of the Historic American Engineering Record (HAER), a long-range program to document historically significant engineering and industrial works in the United States. The HAER program is administered by the National Park Service, a division of the U.S. Department of the Interior. Documentation of the Ottawa Silica Company Mill 'C' Complex is part of an overall historical survey of the Illinois and Michigan Canal National Heritage Corridor. Funding was provided by the National Park Service, Midwest Region.

The recording team consisted of:

Cliff Goodhart,	supervising architect;
Kelly Sarver,	architect;
Michael Drasnin,	architect;
Charles Scott,	project historian

The recording project was under the general direction of Gray Fitzsimons, I&M Canal Project Supervisor. Photographic documentation was conducted by J.T. Lowe III.

DELINEATED BY: Kelly Sarver, Cliff Goodhart, Michael Drasnin, 1986

ILLINOIS & MICHIGAN CANAL SURVEY — HISTORIC AMERICAN BUILDINGS SURVEY / HISTORIC AMERICAN ENGINEERING RECORD / NATIONAL PARK SERVICE / UNITED STATES DEPARTMENT OF THE INTERIOR | OTTAWA SILICA COMPANY MILL 'C' COMPLEX, WEST OF OTTAWA OFF DEE BENNETT ROAD | OTTAWA | LA SALLE COUNTY | ILLINOIS | SHEET 1 OF 11 | HISTORIC AMERICAN ENGINEERING RECORD IL-24

Ottawa Silica Sand-Sorting Building. *Ever since 1929 the unusual "Mill C" complex has stood as a landmark on the valley floor southwest of Ottawa, a tribute to the mining of high-grade sand in the area and to the nearby glass industry it supported.*(Photo: HABS/HAER)

Westclox, as it became known, was the largest producer of alarm clocks in the United States, employing nearly a thousand hands. Between 1910 and 1926 the factory complex more than doubled in size, employing over two thousand workers. A great deal remains from the 1920s factory expansion, including the building's starkly ornamented main entrance.[13]

The rise of agriculture and industry in the upper Illinois valley stimulated dramatic growth among the canal towns throughout the middle and late nineteenth century. Commercial districts sprang up along the tracks of the Rock Island and Chicago & Alton railroads when they were finally completed in 1854. The Heritage Corridor retains many fine examples of late nineteenth- and early-twentieth-century commercial architecture as well as important examples of public buildings. The styles, however vernacular, generally reflect the prevailing architectural trends of the time. Joliet, Lockport, and Lemont exhibit a special character derived from the many buildings in them erected with the indigenous dolomitic limestone. In Joliet spectacular stonework is exhibited not only in the well-publicized State Penitentiary (erected in 1858 with a number of later additions), but also in Frank S. Allen's Christ Episcopal Church of 1885–1887, a Gothic Revival–style building with numerous Tudor arches and a castellated tower; the Auditorium Building by G. Julian Barnes (a Joliet native), built in 1891 with elaborate granite columns and a corner turret; and Daniel H. Burnham's Public Library of 1903, an eclectic L-shaped building with a square tower in the "L" and a handsome rounded window in one gable end.[14] In Lemont one of the most outstanding examples of the use of local limestone may be found in the old Central School, originally built in 1869 and containing an 1896 addition in the Richardsonian Romanesque style by John Barnes, the brother of Julian. Lockport's downtown exhibits several vernacular commercial buildings of limestone including the Gaylord Building, erected in about 1860, and the Adelmann Block, erected in 1891 with a major addition in 1895. George W. Adelmann erected the 1891 building on State Street for use as a livery stable and residence. Similar to many livery buildings of the period, it has a parapet wall highlighted by a triangular pediment.[15]

Many other fine examples of nineteenth-century commercial buildings are seen in Morris, Ottawa, Utica, and Peru. The two-story L. W. Claypool Building in Morris stands on the corner of Liberty and Washington streets. Built of local sandstone in 1877, it features a massive metal cornice with ornamental brackets, modillions, and lozenge motifs, and a rusticated, canted corner entrance. An architect whom the local newspaper identified as Mr. Bigelow designed the building for Claypool, a longtime resident of Morris and the town's first postmaster. In Ottawa, the 200 block of Main Street contains a grouping of 1860s brick and stone buildings, namely the former Washington Hotel and the Knuessl Building. The three-story Knuessl Building was probably erected by Maximillian Knuessl, a German immigrant, and contained his pharmacy on the first floor. Up until about 1920 the Washington Hotel had a saloon on the first floor and several hotel rooms on the second and third floors. Both buildings feature ornate cast iron cornices, arched windows, and sandstone window surrounds.[16] Of the ubiquitous saloon buildings Utica has one of the more interesting, a two-story, triangular brick structure located at the intersection of Mill, Canal, and Church streets. It was erected as a saloon circa 1892 and retains much of its original appearance, including a turret with a dome. Saloons, dry goods stores, and hardware shops once lined Peru's Water Street, an area that bustled with activity throughout the lifetime of the I&M Canal.

The Rialto Theatre in Joliet. *The ornate facade of this theater, erected in 1926, more than hints at the exotic appointments inside. Complete with a Barton Grande theater pipe organ that rises through the floor of the stage, the building was exquisitely restored in 1980 to serve once more as a focus for grand entertainment.* (Photo: Michael P. Conzen)

Water Street is now only lightly traveled, yet it still retains much of its steamboat-era appearance. Two- and three-story brick commercial buildings, some with cast-iron cornices, window hoods, and sills, survive from the 1860s.[17]

As towns in the upper Illinois valley grew, additional parcels of land were surveyed and subdivided for the expanding commercial and residential districts. For example, Morris, a fairly typical canal town, was originally platted under the aegis of the canal trustees in 1842. Over the next twenty-five years additions to the original three-by-five-block plat occurred almost annually, and several additional surveys in a single year were not uncommon. The primitive log and sod houses of

The Gaylord Building in Lockport. *The original central portion of this limestone warehouse (now with arches) was constructed in 1838 at the northern edge of the town's public landing, and helped make one of the many early merchant fortunes of the Corridor. The canal banks long ago collapsed into the water.* (Photo: Michael P. Conzen)

the 1830s and 1840s gave way to frame and stone residential buildings beginning in the late 1840s and 1850s. None of the earliest settlers' houses is known to survive; however, within the Heritage Corridor a number of 1840s stone structures may be found in or near the old canal towns. One particularly interesting early residence in Peru is the Greek Revival–style Theron Brewster House, a two-and-a-half-story, L-shaped building of brick built in 1841.

Numerous examples of 1850s and 1860s residential buildings exhibiting the Greek Revival influence are seen throughout the Heritage Corridor. Many were built by Irish, Germans, and New Englanders, the predominant early immigrant groups in the Illinois Valley. The Gebhard-Weitz House in Morris, located near the I&M Canal in the 600 Block of West Washington Street, is representative of the period's wood-frame residences with Greek Revival styling. It was probably built in the 1860s and contains two stories with a gable roof and rests on a rubble limestone foundation. Coming from a German family of brewers, Louis Gebhard, following the craft of his father, opened a brewery in Morris in 1866. The brewery venture proved successful, and the Gebhard family soon became one of Morris's largest landholders. Interestingly, the later brick Gebhard residence stands nearby, as does the large four-story brewery at the western end of Main Street, the finest example of nineteenth-century brewery architecture in the Heritage Corridor.[18]

That great wealth was amassed by several of the region's nineteenth-century industrialists and landowners is evidenced in such residential buildings as the Fitzpatrick House near Lockport, the Jacob Henry

Water Street, Peru. *These largely Italianate-style wholesale businesses along the Illinois River waterfront date mostly from the 1870s when Peru competed with neighboring LaSalle for the transshipment trade at the western terminus between river and canal.* (Photo: HABS/HAER)

House in Joliet, the Reddick Mansion in Ottawa, and the Hegeler Mansion in LaSalle. The Fitzpatrick House, soon to become the headquarters of the Illinois and Michigan Canal National Heritage Corridor Commission, was built about 1860 by Patrick Fitzpatrick, an Irish immigrant. It rises two stories on a hillside overlooking the DesPlaines River and contains an intersecting gable roof, an ornamented one-story porch, and handsome limestone quoins.[19] In marked contrast to the clean lines and simple Greek Revival styling of the Fitzpatrick House, Joliet's Jacob Henry House is a heavily ornamented Second Empire–style building completed in 1876. Henry, a railroad builder, erected the three-story house with Joliet limestone, Illinois sandstone, and red brick. It features a four-story tower, a mansard roof, numerous dormers with arched windows, and a number of uniquely crafted decorative elements, of cast iron or even possibly steel, including broken scrolls, pediments, and urns.[20]

The well-known Reddick Mansion in Ottawa, a four-story brick Italianate building built in 1856–1858, anchors the city's historic Washington Square. It was designed by the Chicago firm of Olmsted and Nicholson for local politician and landowner William Reddick. Unlike most luxurious later-nineteenth-century residences, the Hegeler Mansion in LaSalle, completed in 1874 by zinc magnate Edward C. Hegeler, was situated very close to the smoke-producing smelters of the Matthiessen and

Gebhard's Brewery in Morris. *Located at the western end of Main Street on a small creek, the building was first erected in 1866 and much enlarged in 1898 with the addition of the four-story brewhouse tower. Most small towns in the Corridor supported breweries like this in the nineteenth century.* (Photo: HABS/HAER)

Hegeler zinc works. Chicago architects Allen and Irving Pond designed the four-story Second Empire–styled residence. Its original exterior was ashlar limestone but was later covered with stucco. Paul Carus, who, like Matthiessen and Hegeler, was a German chemical engineer, immigrated to America in the late nineteenth century and subsequently purchased the Hegeler Mansion. Carus eventually founded a chemical company that bore his name and now occupies the site of the old Matthiessen and Hegeler zinc works.[21]

Not surprisingly, the majority of the Heritage Corridor's historic residential buildings are more modest middle-class and working-class houses. In the larger, more heavily industrial towns the powerful industrial companies influenced the development and architecture of the nearby neighborhoods. Although there were no large tracts of company-owned workers' houses like those in Pullman (Illinois), several industrial concerns were active in real estate and invested in speculative residences. National Plate Glass Company essentially created the town of Naplate, west of Ottawa. The turn-of-the-century glassmaking company financed the construction of the town's 1910s and 1920s frame bungalows in which many of the factory workers lived. Similarly, Argo Corn Products,

The Reddick Mansion in Ottawa. *Facing historic Washington Square, site of the first Lincoln-Douglas debate, this superb Italianate residence was built in 1856 for William Reddick, prominent businessman of Ottawa. The coachhouse is to the left, and St. Columba's Catholic Church is in the background.* (Photo: Michael P. Conzen)

one of the nations's largest producers of corn starch, fashioned the town of Argo in the early 1900s and was also responsible for the construction of numerous bungalow houses. These industrial-based neighborhoods quickly assumed strong ethnic identities for the many Italians, Eastern Europeans, and black Americans who eventually settled in these communities and brought with them their own vibrant and unique cultural heritage.[22]

This essay has offered only a glimpse of the richness and variety of the Heritage Corridor's historic architecture and engineering. There is enormous scope yet for interpreting and reinterpreting the region's complex and significant evolution in the light of the buildings and other human artifacts that have been added to the area's landscape over time. It is hoped that this brief sampling of sites and structures will promote further inquiry into the history of the upper Illinois Valley.

References

1 See, for example, John Drury, *Old Illinois Houses* (Springfield: Illinois State Historical Society, 1948); and Ira J. Bach, *A Guide to Chicago's Historic Suburbs On Wheels and On Foot* (Chicago: Swallow Press, 1981). A useful local primer in reaching beyond such restricted approaches is Ruth E. Knack, ed., *Preservation Illinois: A Guide to State and Local Resources* (Springfield: Illinois Bicentennial Commission, 1977).

2 The National Park Service produced a brief historical study of the I&M Canal as early as 1937. See Charles M. Gates, "Historical Report on the Illinois

St. James of the Sag Catholic Church. *Strong symbol of the Irish contribution in building the canal and settling the region, this church dating from the 1850s occupies a magnificent site above the junction of the Calumet Sag Channel with the main canal corridor at Sag Bridge.* (Photo: Michael P. Conzen)

and Michigan Canal" (Washington, D.C.: National Park Service, 1937). This was done in conjunction with another National Park Service report, "Preliminary Draft of a Report on the Present State Park System in Illinois" (Omaha: National Park Service, 1937). More recent Park Service studies include Richard Hellinger and John Lamb, "Lockport Historic District" (Washington, D.C.: Historic American Engineering Record, National Park Service, 1979) and A. Berle Clemensen, *Illinois and Michigan Canal National Heritage Corridor, Illinois* (Denver: Denver Service Center, National Park Service, 1985).

3 By 1987, HABS/HAER had so far completed two years of survey work, covering the central business districts of Peru, LaSalle, Utica, Ottawa, Marseilles, Seneca, Morris, and Lemont. Additionally, a survey of historic industry and engineering located along both the canal and the railroads traversing the corridor was recently carried out by HABS/HAER. The work completed thus far not only has shed light on the broad patterns of settlement and development in the Upper Illinois Valley, but also has identified numerous historic canal, railroad, and industrial structures, as well as important examples of vernacular architecture.

4 A scholarly history of the Illinois and Michigan Canal is still badly needed. To date the most frequently referred to books on the I&M include James W. Putnam, *The Illinois and Michigan Canal: A Study in Economic History* (Chicago: University of Chicago Press, 1918) and Walter A. Howe, *Documentary History of the Illinois and Michigan Canal* (Springfield: State of Illinois, Department of Public Works and Buildings, Division of Waterways, 1956). For an outstanding study of early settlement in the Upper Illinois Valley, see Mark Wyman, *Immigrants in the Valley: Irish, Germans, and Americans in the Upper Mississippi Country, 1800–1860* (Chicago: Nelson, Hall Co., 1984).

5 National Park Service, Historic American Buildings Survey, "Early Canal Locks: Channahon, Illinois," two sheets of measured drawings, (1937), available at the Library of Congress, Prints and Photographs Division.

6 *History of LaSalle County, Illinois,* Vol. 2 (Chicago: Inter-State Publishing Co., 1886), 361–2; Martin J. Hogan, "The Hogan Family," in *Seneca Area Centennial Celebration: The Story of 100 Years* (n.p.: 1965).

7 Richard Hellinger and John Lamb, "Lockport Historic District" (Washington, D.C.: HAER, NPS, 1979); H. F. Kett & Co., *The Past and Present of LaSalle County, Illinois* (Chicago: H. F. Kett & Co., 1877), pp. 333–7.

8 Carlton J. Corliss, *Main Line of Mid-America: The Story of the Illinois Central Railroad* (New York: Creative Age Press, 1950); Dwight L. Agnew, "Beginning of the Rock Island Lines," *Illinois State Historical Society Journal* 46 (1953): 407–24; Historical Booklet Committee, *Marseilles Sesquicentennial, 1835–1985* (Coal City, Illinois: Bailey Printing Co., 1985), p. 16.

9 Howard L. Conrad, *Nathaniel J. Brown: Biographical Sketch and Reminiscences of a Noted Pioneer* (Chicago: n.p., 1892).

10 U. J. Hoffman, *History of LaSalle County, Illinois* (Chicago: S. J. Clarke Publishing Co., 1906), pp. 220–3; Henry C. Freeman, "The Hydraulic Cement Works of the Utica Cement Company, LaSalle, Ill.," *Transactions of the American Institute of Mining Engineers* 13 (1885): 172–180.

11 "The Illinois Steel Company's Joliet Extensions," *The Iron Age* 78 (November 15, 1906); Real Estate Research Corporation, *et al.,* "Joliet Works Reuse Strategy" for U. S. S. Realty Development

and the National Trust for Historic Preservation (1985), Chap. II.

12 *Ottawa, Old and New: A Complete History of Ottawa, Illinois, 1823–1914* (Ottawa: The Republican Times, 1912–14, 1984 reprint), pp. 114, 152; *Ottawa Daily Republican Times* (December 31, 1929).

13 Isabel Katherine Billings, "The LaSalle–Peru–Oglesby Industrial Area as a Type Unit Study in Geography," unpublished master's thesis, Illinois State Normal University, 1945.

14 Robert E. Sterling, *Joliet: A Pictorial History* (St. Louis: G. Bradley Publishing, Inc., 1986), pp. 59–60.

15 Sonia Kallick, "Transportation and Lemont," in Lemont Area Historical Society, "Lemont History and Anecdotes," (typescript, 1975, 2nd ed. 1978); U. S. Department of the Interior, Heritage Conservation and Recreation Service, *Lockport, Illinois: An HCRS Project Report* (Washington, D.C.: GPO, 1980), pp. 11–23, 46–47.

16 *Morris Herald* (April 13, 1877 and June 1, 1877); Sanborn Map Co., *Ottawa, Illinois* (New York: 1888, 1891, 1898, 1907, 1913, and 1925).

17 Sanborn Map Co., *Utica, Illinois* (New York: 1891, 1896); Louis H. Shadensack, *Peru's Water Street a Century Ago: 1860–1880* (Peru: W. H. Maze Co., 1966).

18 Lawrence and Thompson, *Classified Business Directory of the County of Grundy, Illinois* (Lawrence & Thompson's City and County Directories, 1877–1878).

19 George Woodruff, *The History of Will County, Illinois* (Chicago: Wm. LeBaron & Co., 1878), pp. 375, 423, 426.

20 Sterling, *Joliet: A Pictorial History*, p. 94.

21 Billings, "The LaSalle–Peru–Oglesby Industrial Area as a Type Unit Study in Geography."

22 *Ottawa Daily Republican Times* (December 31, 1929); Summit Bicentennial Commission Heritage Committee, *Summit Heritage* (n.p., 1977), p. 50.

Three

A PRESERVATION HISTORY OF THE ILLINOIS AND MICHIGAN CANAL CORRIDOR

Gerald W. Adelmann

PRESERVATION EFFORTS that focused on the Illinois and Michigan Canal span more than half a century and reflect to a substantial degree the evolution in aims and methods of the national conservation and historic preservation movements in the United States. With completion of the Illinois Waterway in 1933, the pioneering Illinois and Michigan Canal was permanently closed to commercial traffic. In the same year, this abandoned waterway was adopted by the Civilian Conservation Corps (CCC) in Illinois as an ambitious recreational project of the New Deal. The community-based campaign to preserve the canal as a linear park for recreational and historical purposes traces its roots to the heart of the Great Depression. This campaign culminated only recently in 1984 with the creation by Congress of the nation's first National Heritage Corridor. Over one hundred miles long and encompassing forty-two communities, the Illinois and Michigan Canal National Heritage Corridor is in the vanguard of the "urban cultural park" movement in the United States.[1]

Shifting national demographics, increasing demands on limited public open space in metropolitan regions, and high costs of urban real estate have forced the federal government to explore new approaches to national parks that address the needs of urban America.[2] For more than twenty-five years, Congress has created new park designations that respond to the opportunities for outdoor recreation near large population centers and reflect nontraditional approaches to land management and resource protection. The first federally sponsored urban parks, such as the Indiana Dunes National Lakeshore, involved large-scale purchase of land, but because of the expense of such a project, other preservation strategies for metropolitan regions became more popular. "Greenline Parks," where public and private lands coexist under various management structures, attempt to protect significant cultural and natural landscapes from overdevelopment, while allowing these areas to express their regional differences and maintain their economic vitality.[3]

Contemporary scholarly interest in historic landscapes, vernacular architecture, and commercial and industrial archeology has contributed to an understanding of the city itself as a "park" or open-air museum. Through interpretation, a city's architecture, neighborhoods, and public spaces can inform residents and visitors alike about America's ethnic, labor, and industrial heritage.[4] Lowell, Massachusetts, is probably the best example of this urban park phenomenon, where the entire city has been designated a "National Historical Park" with defined public and private responsibilities for preservation, education, and economic revitalization.[5] New York and Massachusetts have been leaders in establishing state-wide systems of urban cultural parks, which sometimes incorporate federal involvement, as at Lowell and Seneca Falls, New York. With all urban cultural parks, the management plan is complex, involving various levels of government and private interests, and invariably relying on strong local leadership. The Illinois and Michigan Canal National Heritage Corridor is no exception. For more than fifty years, the driving force behind the preservation of the canal has been persistent local citizen advocacy. The following narrative attempts to sketch the outline of this long-standing public commitment as its focus was progressively extended beyond the narrow physical limits of the canal and towpath to include the diverse resources of the surrounding landscape.

During the years preceding World War II, local CCC youth transformed the historic Illinois and Michigan Canal into a linear park of great natural beauty and unparalleled recreational opportunities in northeastern Illinois.[6] Miles of towpath were converted into hiking and bicycling trails; sections of the canal, its locks, and other canal-related structures were rehabilitated; picnic areas and shelters were constructed along the canal's banks; and state and local parks were developed on adjacent lands. Although this project was labeled the "Illinois and Michigan Canal State Park," canal lands remained under the jurisdiction of the Illinois Department of Transportation. By its constitution, the state was barred from spending any funds other than the modest rental fees for lands within the canal's ninety-foot right-of-way on maintenance or recreational development.

After the CCC was dissolved, most of the extensive improvements that this highly successful and popular project accomplished fell into disrepair. A 1956 report on the then-current use of the Illinois and Michigan Canal stated that "the major recreational facilities located along the canal are at Channahon and Gebhard Woods State Park, and at McKinley Woods Forest Preserve. Other areas were developed along the canal during the 1930s," the report continues, "but, due to a lack of maintenance, have deteriorated to such an extent as to be worthless for recreational purposes."[7]

In the general election of 1954 a referendum that amended the Illinois Constitution and allowed the state both to spend funds on canal maintenance and to sell or lease portions of the canal and its adjacent lands was passed. At the same time, the state was looking for easy access to the city of Chicago for a new major interstate expressway, which would extend south through the state to St. Louis and beyond. The easternmost section of the Illinois and Michigan Canal right-of-way, which comprised thirteen miles, was identified as an ideal economical route since the state owned the land and little community displacement would result. With the construction of the Stevenson Expressway (I-55) in the late 1950s, Bridgeport and other neighborhoods along the canal's urban eastern terminus lost the tangible link this waterway provided to their early canal heritage. The state viewed the abandoned canal primarily as surplus property and, consequently, a ready source of much-needed revenue. Plans were initiated to sell, upon market demand, certain portions of the canal to local governments and private concerns. These actions triggered an unanticipated grass-roots response that forced the state to reconsider its original intentions.

On February 8, 1971, the Illinois and Michigan Canal Task Force was appointed by the secretary of the Illinois Department of Transportation to review this complicated issue and to make recommendations for a comprehensive development and management plan for the canal. The task force immediately held public hearings to determine the concerns of local municipalities and citizens and requested Governor Richard Ogilvie to delay further sale of canal lands until a comprehensive plan could be developed.

In 1972, the services of a planning firm, Harland Bartholomew and Associates, were retained to develop a master plan for the canal that focused on historic preservation and recreational use of canal lands. As a result of this initiative, an ambitious multimillion-dollar program for canal rehabilitation was approved, and, in 1974, the entire Illinois and Michigan Canal was transferred to the jurisdiction of the Illinois Department of Conservation. Only 61.5 miles of the canal, however, was officially designated at this time as a state trail. Furthermore, the resulting comprehensive plan called for virtually no state involvement in recreational development for the reaches of the canal between Rockdale (just southwest of Joliet) and the city of Chicago. Many of these areas were already leased to industries that straddled the canal, and the plan recommended "multipurpose use" that included utility rights-of-way, industrial use, storm drainage ways, and roadways. Only certain sections of the canal were recommended for recreational purposes, and those were to be developed primarily by local jurisdictions.

A key influence during this successful crusade was a relatively new not-for-profit conservation organization, Open Lands Project, which was headquartered in Chicago and concerned with the preservation and recreational development of public open space in northeastern Illinois. Gunnar Peterson, Open Lands' executive director and a member of the state's task force, worked with such local community leaders as Tom Greenwood, John Lamb, Leonard Lock, and Harry "Scoop" Sklenar in a campaign called *Operation Greenstrip* to rally citizen support from throughout the region for official park designation of the canal by the state legislature. Some of the strongest support for park designation came from the very communities that the state excluded from its development plan. Individuals and local groups, such as "Save the Valley" in the Lemont area, continued to petition Open Lands Project for technical and political support in their drives to preserve key natural areas and valuable open space bordering on or near the historic canal along the lower Des Plaines River Valley.

Meanwhile, citizens living along the Illinois and Michigan Canal State Trail had become extremely disenchanted with the state for its failure to commit the funds necessary to implement the ambitious Harland Bartholomew plan. The limited improvements made during the 1970s in fact resulted primarily from volunteer efforts and local initiative. In 1976, for example, the LaSalle County Volunteers cleared and dredged several miles of the canal between Locks 13 and 15 in an exemplary project that allowed this section of the canal at its terminus to hold water for the first time in many years. Other important volunteer projects were undertaken in Ottawa, Marseilles, and also Lockport, where the Will County Historical Society took over the original canal office building to house its headquarters and a canal museum. In Utica, an 1848 canal warehouse was rehabilitated as the museum of the LaSalle County Historical Society. These and other projects proceeded in spite of very limited funds from the state of Illinois.

The federal government's involvement with the Illinois and Michigan Canal did not end entirely with the Civilian Conservation Corps' program of the 1930s. At that time the National Park Service had already determined that the canal was a prime cultural and recreational resource, but only in 1963 was much of the canal officially designated a national historic landmark. In 1977, the National Park Service and Bureau of Outdoor Recreation highlighted the recreational opportunities present in the lands along the Des Plaines River Valley and along undeveloped sections of the Illinois and Michigan Canal in their National Urban Recreation Study.[8] This document analyzed future open space and recreation needs for the metropolitan Chicago region.

During the summer of 1979, the Historic American Engineering Record evaluated the historical, commercial, and recreational potential of Lockport, the former canal headquarters.[9] And in the fall of the same year, at the request of Governor Thompson and the Illinois congressional delegation, the National Park Service was charged by Congress with evaluating the resources of the canal area for possible inclusion in the National Park System. The Park Service stated in the introduction to the resulting study, "Despite the volume of previous plans and studies, not one addresses the entire canal route and its larger context: the important Upper Illinois River Valley transportation system and attendant open space areas near the Chicago metropolis. Realizing that resources other than those associated with the canal might have significance, the National Park Service reconnaissance survey team decided to inspect an area larger than the canal corridor."[10] For the first time, a comprehensive approach to resource protection and land-use planning was under way along this ancient and multifaceted transportation corridor, which connects the Mississippi River and Gulf of Mexico with the Great Lakes and Atlantic Ocean.

Once more, Open Lands Project played a significant role in the preservation history of the canal. In 1978, Open Lands applied for a Historic Preservation Challenge Grant from the secretary of the interior in order to fund a survey and inventory of all significant resources, "historic, archaeological, architectural, cultural and natural," in the twenty-five-mile section of the Des Plaines River Valley from Summit to Rockdale—the official starting point of the Illinois and Michigan Canal State Trail. Although this grant was not secured, Open Lands' proposal set the stage for the comprehensive approach of the National Park Service to open space and preservation planning. After receiving initial funding from the Field Foundation of Illinois, the Illinois Humanities Council, and the Illinois Institute of Natural Resources in early 1980, Open Lands launched its Des Plaines River Valley Program, a special project that focused on the twenty-five-mile canal area excluded from the state trail designation. "The case for preservation in the lower Des Plaines is compelling," wrote Open Lands Project in its newsletter *Terrain*. "This stretch of the valley has one of the richest concentrations of Illinois' heritage, and yet it is one of the very few segments whose preservation has not been accounted for."[11] These conditions were soon to change.

The National Park Service reconnaissance survey team released its findings in June 1980 and found that "the study area

Starved Rock. *Sharp features carved by wind and water outline Devil's Nose, the most prominent facet of this massive natural formation, situated on the southern side of the Illinois River near Utica. Starved Rock State Park was created in 1911 to protect the rock, the nearby bluffs, and the dramatic ravines between them.* (Illinois Office of Tourism)

Canal Terminus at LaSalle. *Looking westward, Lock 14 (foreground), recently renovated, leads to the canalboat basin, the narrow chamber of former Lock 15 (middle ground, between stone pillars of a later railroad bridge), the steamboat basin (background), and finally the Illinois River (far distance).* (Photo: Michael P. Conzen)

appears to have substantial recreation potential based on its spaciousness, its abundant resources—especially water resources, which provide significant recreational opportunities—its convenient location and its ability to draw both regional and national visitors." [12] The team likewise concluded that the study area may also have potential for inclusion in the National Park System based on its representation of of various cultural and natural history themes. Though the Reconnaissance Survey failed to make specific recommendations for federal action, it presented a strong case for looking beyond the canal itself to the surrounding landscape. "As the study team gathered data, one recurring factor appeared," the study noted. "Although the canal has cultural integrity and historical significance in its own right, the larger context of its location adjoining the Illinois River system is equally important. This context, in turn, requires that a broader, more comprehensive area be considered in any subsequent planning." [13]

By the time the National Park Service had released its report, Open Lands Project had garnered the influential support of *Chicago Tribune* writer John Husar. His five-part, award-winning series, "Our Hidden Wilderness," which appeared in September 1980, brought to light the great preservation opportunities in the Lower Des Plaines Valley. It also inspired Senator Charles Percy; Congressman Tom Corcoran, a longtime advocate of the canal; and other members of the Illinois delegation in Congress to sponsor a bill authorizing the National Park Service to develop a conceptual plan for a hundred-mile linear park from Chicago's Navy Pier to LaSalle–Peru and to explore alternatives for implementation.

A group of more than one hundred persons was assembled into six work

A scene in the Cook County Forest Preserve. *Glacial moraines and outwash deposits of sands and clays create an undulating district of low wooded hills and ponds ideal for outdoor relaxation and pastimes.* (Photo: Peter Dring)

groups, to be concerned with (1) recreation, (2) conservation, (3) historic and cultural resources, (4) water quality, (5) land use and transportation, and (6) economic development. These groups met on three occasions and provided National Park Service staff with a tangible local consensus for the resulting conceptual plan. The group represented a broad cross section of public and private interests from throughout the study area and included representatives of the business and industrial communities. Many of these representatives expressed initial concern about the potential adverse impact of a federal "park" designation on a maturing industrial corridor, particularly one experiencing severe unemployment and a decline in traditional manufacturing.

As stated in the introduction to *Illinois and Michigan Canal Corridor: A Concept Plan,* the purpose of the National Park Service study was twofold: "The first is to provide a conceptual plan to protect and enhance the utilization of the abundant cultural and natural resources in the I&M canal corridor while at the same time providing opportunity for economic development. The second is to develop alternative implementation strategies. . . ."[14] Specific goals, objectives, and action plans for a ten-year program were agreed upon during the nine-month planning process, and a series of public meetings was held in various canal communities to present these findings to the public. Three alternatives for implementation were outlined, with only one calling for federal involvement through the creation of a federal commission to oversee development and through assistance from the National Park Service. It was this limited federal option, rather than the state and local alternatives, that the Illinois congressional delegation chose to pursue. Open Lands Project argued, "Not only does [the Illinois and Michigan Canal corridor program] seek to protect cultural and natural resources, but it actively seeks to bring about economic revitalization of the region. It regards the landscape as a whole, an environment where the development of one resource cannot take place without affecting others. In the canal corridor, where the urban and industrial are inseparable from the natural and historic, preservation must be a renewal of the whole."[15]

Although some of the more recently crafted federal designations, such as "National Historical Park," came close to reflecting the urban condition and multiple goals of the Illinois and Michigan Canal program, none was acceptable to all parties concerned. Consequently, when Senator Percy and Congressman Corcoran introduced legislation, with the cosponsorship of the entire Illinois delegation, "to retain, enhance, and interpret, for the benefit and inspiration of present and future generations, the cultural, historical, natural, recreational, and economic resources of the corridor, where feasible, consistent with industrial and economic growth,"[16] a totally new label was coined: "National Heritage Corridor."[17] This unique legislation, passed by Congress and signed into law by President Reagan on August 24, 1984, at the Conrad Hilton Hotel in Chicago, creates a federally funded commission, provides for technical assistance from the National Park Service, but does not establish any new land-use or environmental controls, nor does it call for federal ownership or management of resources. The Illinois and Michigan Canal National Heritage Corridor is seen as a partnership of federal, state, and local governments with the private sector working toward mutually agreed-upon preservation and revitalization goals.

Two new private, not-for-profit organizations were formed in 1982 during the drive for federal designation: The Friends of the I&M Canal National Heritage Corridor and the Upper Illinois Valley Association. Friends of the I&M Canal Corridor is a grass-roots support group of individuals and organizations interested in preservation and development of the corridor. The Upper Illinois Valley Association, whose board of directors is composed of leaders from business and industry, grew out of Open Lands Project, which believed that corridor industry should assume a greater role in guiding the effort. Both the association and the grass-roots group played critical roles in securing public and private support for the passage of the legislation. The Upper Illinois Valley Association continues as the only staffed private-sector organization working exclusively toward implementation of the Heritage Corridor goals.

An overview of the historic preservation movement in the United States reveals a growing shift in concern from the preservation of individual structures and sites to that of large, multiresource historic districts. Recently, this shift has become even more pronounced in the emergence of entirely new coalitions—consisting of those involved in conservation, recreation, archaeology, historic preservation, and urban planning—that were fashioned around a shared interest in growth management as a means to protect the distinctive features of our regional landscapes. Originally, preservation programs for the Illinois and Michigan Canal focused exclusively on the physical canal and its towpath; today, they have broadened to include over forty separate communities and sections of many Chicago neighborhoods, eight state parks, and numerous county and local preserves.

In microcosm, the Illinois and Michigan Canal National Heritage Corridor reflects several national trends in landscape preservation and has already served as the model for a second similar federal designation, The Blackstone River Valley National Heritage Corridor, located between Providence, Rhode Island, and Worcester, Massachusetts. The recent report of the Governor's Statewide Task Force on Recreation and Tourism recommends that a comprehensive State Heritage Corridor program be established and that technical assistance from Illinois be increased "to realize the full potential of the Illinois and Michigan Canal National Heritage Corridor, a unique State and national attraction."[18] Although the ultimate success of this most recent chapter in the preservation history of the Illinois and Michigan Canal will not become apparent for some time, innovative new projects provide hopeful signs of substantial support at the various federal, state, and local levels and of renewed public and private commitment.

References

1 The term *urban cultural park* has been applied to districts in a number of different contexts, but in general is meant to denote a large area in or adjacent to a metropolitan region symbolizing some important theme in the cultural history of the region or nation. Hence, the Lowell National Historical Park celebrates and interprets the importance of the industrial revolution in America, with special reference to the textile industry. In the case of the I&M Canal National Heritage Corridor, a new variant of the same general species, the overarching theme is the significance of transportation in national development and regional industrialization, focused on a premier transportation corridor.

2 The Conservation Foundation, *National Parks for the Future* (Washington, D.C., November 1972), pp. 67–74.

3 The Pinelands National Reserve in New Jersey is representative of a greenline park. Federal, state, and local interests have preserved more than one million acres of pine forest and wetlands in an area one-quarter the size of the state. Two-thirds of the preserve, which encompasses fifty-two

communities, remains in private ownership with certain development restrictions. For more information on greenline parks, see: Karen Schafer, "Greenlining: An Old Planting Process Saving Scenic Resources Today," *AGORA* (Landscape Architecture Foundation, Fall 1985), pp. 16–18 and Dierdre K. Hirner and James D. Mertes, "Greenlining for Landscape Preservation," *Parks & Recreation* (November 1986), pp. 30–34 and 59.

4 For a discussion of how to "read" the man-made landscape as a material record of culture, see Peirce F. Lewis, "Axioms for Reading the Landscape: Some Guides to the American Scene," in *The Interpretation of Ordinary Landscapes: Geographical Essays,* ed. D. W. Meining (Oxford University Press, New York, 1979), pp. 11–32.

5 Paul M. Bray, "The City As a Park: Weaving the Strands of Heritage in the Urban Landscape," *American Land Forum Magazine* (Winter 1985), pp. 23–27.

6 United States National Archives and Records Service, "CCC Project Reports for Illinois, SP nos. 1–5," *Records of the National Park Service,* RG 79, 1934–1936. Copies in Morris Public Library, Morris, Illinois.

7 Walter A. Howe, *Documentary History of the Illinois and Michigan Canal: Legislation, Litigation and Titles* (Springfield: Illinois Division of Waterways, 1956), p. 169.

8 United States Department of the Interior, National Park Service, Bureau of Outdoor Recreation, Lake Central Region and National Park Service, The Denver Service, "National Urban Recreation Study: Chicago/Gary" (Denver Service Center, NPS 1228, September 1977).

9 United States Department of the Interior, Heritage Conservation and Recreation Service, "Lockport, Illinois: An HCRS Project Report" (U.S. Government Printing Office, HCRS Publication Number 35, 1980).

10 United States Department of the Interior, National Park Service, *Reconnaissance Survey: Illinois and Michigan Canal, Illinois* (Washington, D.C., June, 1980), pp. 1–2.

11 Open Lands Project, *Terrain,* Vol. 4, No. 3 (July/August 1980), pp. 1–2.

12 National Park Service, *Reconnaissance Survey,* p. 6.

13 Ibid., p. 7.

14 John D. Peine and Debora A. Neurohr, *Illinois and Michigan Canal Corridor: A Concept Plan* (Ann Arbor, Michigan: National Park Service, September, 1981), p. 1.

15 *Terrain,* Vol. 5, No. 6 (December 1981), p. 1.

16 Public Law 98-398, 98th Congress (August 24, 1984), 98 Stat. 1456.

17 For a discussion of the challenges facing the National Park system in the late 20th century, *see* The Conservation Foundation, "National Parks for a New Generation: Visions, Realities, Prospects," (Washington, D.C., 1985).

18 *A Vision for Illinois' Recreation and Tourism Future: The Report of the Governor's Task Force* (Illinois Department of Conservation, 1987), p. 8.

On the one hand the steel works.
On the other hand the penitentiary.
Santa Fé trains and Alton trains
Between smokestacks on the west
And grey walls on the east.
And Lockport down the river.
Part of the valley is God's.
And part is man's.
The river course laid out
A thousand years ago.
The canals ten years back.
The sun on two canals and one river
Makes three stripes of silver
Or copper and gold
Or shattered sunflower leaves.

Talons of an iceberg
Scraped out this valley.
Claws of an avalanche loosed here

Joliet—Carl Sandburg[1]

Four

OPPORTUNITIES AND PITFALLS IN PURSUING LOCAL HISTORY IN THE CORRIDOR

Kay J. Carr

Joliet is not one of Carl Sandburg's most celebrated poems. In fact, few would argue that it compares critically with his two-volume biography of Abraham Lincoln or with some of his other poetry on midwestern cities.[2] It does, however, adequately convey the perception that Joliet's landscape is the result of both natural and manmade forces. It is not inappropriate, then, to begin an essay about local history in the Illinois and Michigan Canal National Heritage Corridor with *Joliet* since it is a source of information for researchers who are interested in the history of the area.[3] The poem is also valuable because it illustrates a point that every corridor historian ought to keep in mind, that the potential sources of local history are diverse and are often found in totally unexpected places. That is, in addition to the information one might easily expect to find in the pages of published works and in the vaults of historical societies, local history evidence can lurk in such out-of-the-way places as government pamphlets, old railroad maps, city directories, and business payrolls, as well as in local folklore, novels, and even poetry.

Sandburg's poem about Joliet also illustrates the importance of transportation facilities to the corridor and how they have affected the impressions of both residents and visitors. One may be drawn to the romance of the ancient Indian trails or the French portage routes or the canals or the railroads or the interstate highways, but the presence of a thoroughfare is and always has been at the core of the area's historic identity. A researcher, then, might do well to return often to this notion when investigating the local history of the corridor.

Before turning to the specific opportunities and pitfalls in doing corridor local history, a researcher ought to be aware of the general state of local history studies in the United States today and of the differences in intent and content between amateur and professional works in the field. Amateur local history has long been practiced by many groups of Americans who have been careful to highlight and preserve what they saw as the exciting and often unique heritage of their individual communities. In fact, amateur historians and filiopietists of the nineteenth century can be credited with having saved many community documents and artifacts that might otherwise have been neglected or destroyed with the passage of time. Recently, of course, interest in amateur local history and genealogy has enjoyed something of a renaissance. The "Roots" phenomenon of the 1970s, combined with the renewed interest in local history brought on by the activities of the nation's bicentennial celebration in 1976, spawned a tremendous amount of research into history by people who wished to learn more about their communities and their families.[4] The efforts of these lay historians over the years resulted in the collection of locally significant facts and artifacts and gave many researchers the satisfaction of knowing from where and from whom they had sprung.

At about the same time that amateur local history was making a comeback in the United States—and perhaps not entirely by coincidence—professional historians began to study local history in an entirely new way. Taking some cues from new efforts into French and English local history,[5] American professionals displayed a renewed interest in the analysis of historical topics as local phenomena in themselves rather than continuing to investigate national historical events from a local point of view. These historians were often motivated by the general atmosphere of social awareness during the 1960s and began to look for methods of analyzing historically undocumented segments of American society, or persons who previously had been accorded little distinction as actors in the tumultuous political and cultural events of the nation's past.[6] Using newly available computer and demographic techniques and previously untapped local records (which had often been lovingly preserved by the lay historians of the nineteenth century), these "new social historians" began to paint a picture of the ordinary past in distinctly local terms.[7] Most of these early social histories were on colonial New England because of the area's isolated town settlement pattern and because the early white inhabitants had been particularly careful to document their Puritan experiment in utopian communalism.[8] New Englanders were especially careful to keep meticulous vital records of local births, deaths, marriages, elections, and household inventories. And although the interest and the financial support for the same type of extensive demographic research projects have declined in recent years, social historians have since moved their subjects of local research forward in time as well as south and west across the country.[9] The more recent local works have also become more sophisticated in that they have begun to answer questions that concern the motivations of the subjects of comparable communities in addition to the study of demographic makeup and trends within each settlement.

So although lay and professional local historians might appear on the surface to be concerned with the same topics (as they often are with the same communities), their intentions and their research goals often can be entirely separate. Amateurs are usually concerned with the collection of factual material largely for its intrinsic value, whereas professionals tend to collect and use facts in order to document and analyze historical patterns of change and continuity. This is not to say, however, that lay and professional historians do not have many of the same concerns and that they cannot benefit from each other's efforts. On the contrary, amateurs often use professional works to uncover new sources of important local information and professionals are usually grateful for the facts gathered by nonprofessionals—the facts can often be woven together and used as evidence to prove their own scholarly suppositions and contentions. In either case, both amateur and professional frequently use the same sources and ought to be aware of the same opportunities and pitfalls in pursuing local history in the corridor.[10]

Of course, local history was not invented in the 1970s. Human beings have always made special efforts to record the important events in their lives, and today's interest is just the latest manifestation of a long-lived tradition. The dynamism of the nation's relatively short history, though, has made Americans simultaneously lax and meticulous in the documentation of their past, particularly on the local level. Since most of American history has been marked by an extraordinary amount of geographical mobility among the population, there has often been little time or inclination for inhabitants of frontier communities to consider the value of preserving a record of their wanderings. But once Americans began to settle, relatively speaking, into permanent communities toward the end of the nineteenth century, they began to recognize the value of preserving the memory of their pioneering experiences. In fact, Illinois—and the corridor—is well endowed with a type of systematic local history that resulted from this after-the-fact pioneer awareness: biographical collections and county histories. That is, once Americans recognized that the settlement of the frontier was drawing to a close, many were concerned that the history of the country's unprecedented expansion—and that of the participants in the process—was not being properly recorded. So entrepreneurs from various publishing establishments undertook the systematic compilation of voluminous "pioneer" biographies and county histories.[11] These "potted biographies," or "mug books," as they have affectionately come to be known, were usually sold on a subscription basis to those individuals who wished to be included as the subjects of a two- to three-hundred-word life sketch in the final work. The participants were, therefore, self-selected and were usually from the better-off segment of local society. Sometimes the sketches were even written by the subjects themselves or by their direct descendants, and they frequently boasted of entrepreneurial accomplishments and understandably excluded mention of unfavorable or unsavory episodes in the pioneers' lives.

The biographical collections and county histories of the turn-of-the-century corridor area are surely valuable to today's genealogist or local history researcher. They should, however, be used with the caveat that many facts, as well as people, were deliberately left out of the volumes. But these same volumes can be used to discern a more subtle and often overlooked change in community sensibilities to which the local researcher ought to be alert: perceptions of the "local" area to which the inhabitants refer—either indirectly in their own or their communities' written histories or directly in their jurisdictional divisions—can and did change over time. That is, although county and some city and town boundaries along the I&M Canal had become legally fixed by then, the late-nineteenth-century corridor inhabitants' perceptions regarding the borders of their "communities" and "neighborhoods" did not always coincide with present-day understandings of such divisions. Nor, for that matter, did late-nineteenth-century perceptions necessarily mirror those of early or mid-nineteenth-century inhabitants. In other words, local history, or rather the localities of history, can and did change over time, and today's researcher ought to keep this point in mind when digging into a community's past. Relevant

SCHEDULE I.—Free Inhabitants in Canal Boats in the County of Cook State of Illinois enumerated by me, on the 20 day of Nov 1850. [illegible] Ass't Marshal.

450

Dwelling-houses numbered in the order of visitation.	Families numbered in the order of visitation.	The Name of every Person whose usual place of abode on the first day of June, 1850, was in this family.	Description: Age.	Sex.	Color, White, black, or mulatto.	Profession, Occupation, or Trade of each Male Person over 15 years of age.	Value of Real Estate owned.	Place of Birth. Naming the State, Territory, or Country.	Married within the year.	Attended School within the year.	Persons over 20 y'rs of age who cannot read & write.	Whether deaf and dumb, blind, insane, idiotic, pauper, or convict.
1	2	3	4	5	6	7	8	9	10	11	12	13
5743	5209	Martin Hagan	26	m	w	Boatman		Ireland				
		Richard Skinner	28	m		"		England				
		Robert Chilvers	24	m		"		"				[illegible]
		Dennis Kain	14	m		Cook		Ireland				[illegible]
		John Stacks	25	"		Boatman		England				
5744	5210	Alfred J Horton	27	"		Canal Capt	$500	NY				
		Joseph Gardner	23	"		Boatman		Canada				
		Charles Tanner	32	"		"		NY				
		Henry Pateh	24	f		Cook		"				
		A Washburn	29	m		Canal Capt	$200	"				
		John Meadiker	40	m		Boatman	"	"				
5745	5211	Charles Mann	20	"		"		Canada				
		Margaret Manning	20	f		Cook		"				
		D Johnson	37	m		Canal Capt	$1000	Conn.				
		Alex Banger	30	"		Boatman		Unk				
		Bill	15	"		"		"				
5746	5212	W H Chase	38	"		Canal Capt	$800	Vir.				
		Cecelia Riggs	18	f		Cook		Penn				
		Nelson Almstead	22	m		Boatman		In.				
		I D Lotis	35	"		"		NY				
		John C Fish	30	"		Canal Capt		"				
		Frank Bickford	30	"		Boatman		Unk				
		William L Fish	21	"		"		NY				

The federal manuscript census. *This example evidences the meanderings of the census-taker among the canal boatmen of Bridgeport in 1850, probably hopping from boat to boat. The schedule tells of individual ages, occupations, property owned, and birthplaces, among other things.*

information about a locality may be included in less-than-obvious sources since legal boundaries and local identities may have changed any number of times over the years. For example, in the middle of the nineteenth century a German-American's ethnic origins may have meant more to him in the determination of his identification with a particular "community" than the fact that he resided in the city of LaSalle. However, another German-American in early-twentieth-century LaSalle may have identified his "community" as the north side of the city. Such changes in definitions may be highly significant and are worth looking for and taking into account. For example, a researcher might look into the degree to which local loyalties or even political and governmental institutions were shaped by the transportation priorities of the communities. Or a researcher might want to look into the effects of social and political sensibilities on the urban hierarchy of the corridor.

Local history, then, should include not only the study of changing social relationships within a particular society over time, but should also take into account the changes that have occurred in the relationships among various "communities." The researcher who plans to document the history of the Illinois and Michigan Canal

North between sect 21 & 22
C L T 34 N of R 9 E

40-00 raised a mound in
which set a post for
1/4 sect corner

70-00 timber bears N E & S W

76-25 intersected the S E boundary of the Illinois
River set a post cor.
nr of fract sect 21 & 22
from which a W Oak
14 In D bears S 78 W 58 lk
[illegible] 16 In D bears N
19 E

Land gently rolling
good soil timber Oak

The U. S. land surveyor's notebooks. *This page describes the surveyor's progress in 1821 and comments on the natural topography and vegetation cover of a section of land where Interstate 55 now crosses the Illinois River in Channahon Township, Will County.*

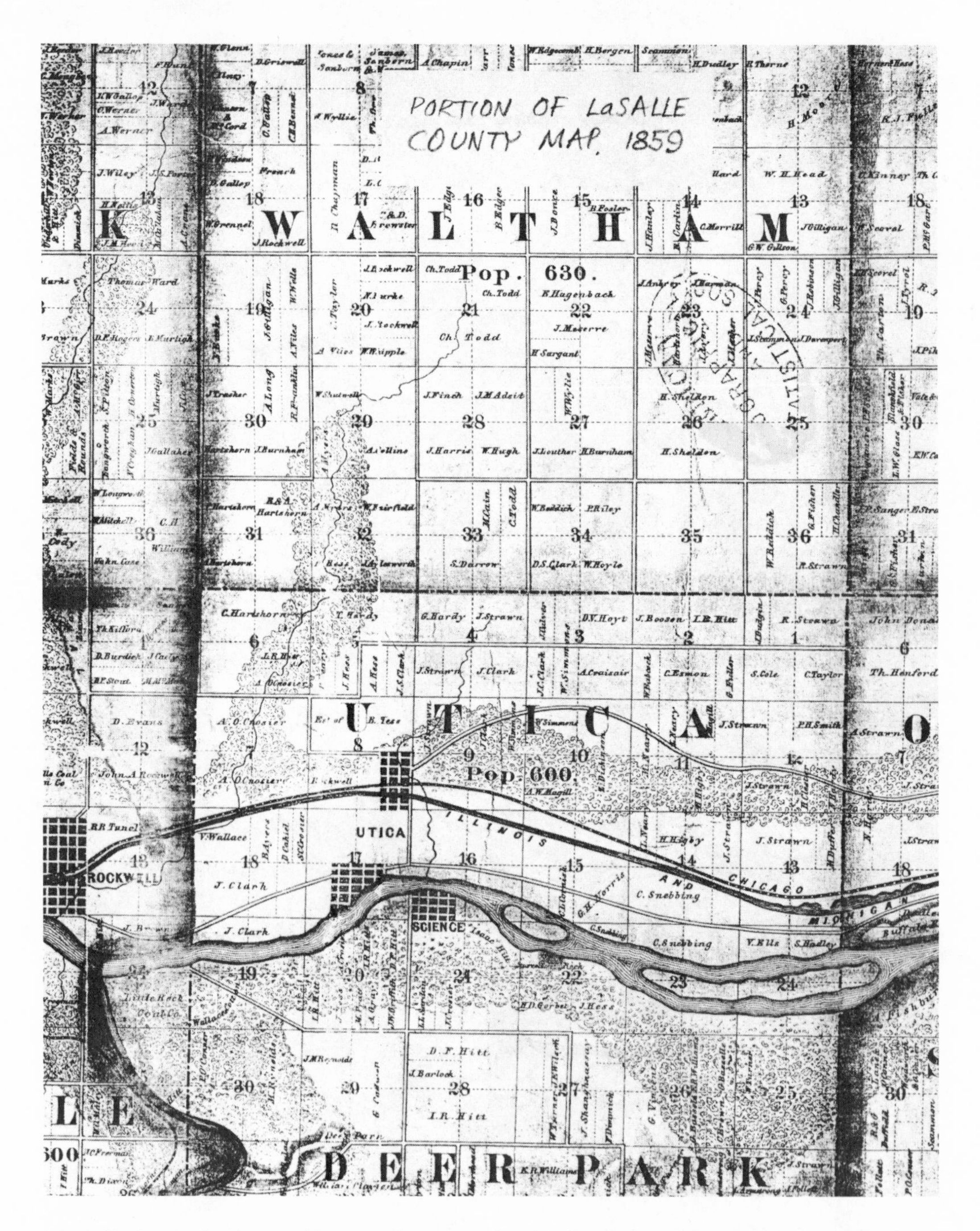

A LaSalle County landownership map of 1859. *A decade after the canal was completed, lands to the north and south were well settled, farms in proud individual ownership, and towns actively growing. Marseilles' prosperity depended on harnessing the excellent waterpower of the Illinois River for manufacturing.*

in Chicago; and Jay Pomeroy, who conducts the home farm. Mr. Harford has never been very active in politics and the only office he ever accepted was that of town clerk, in which he served for three years. He is well known in Masonic circles and belongs to Verona Lodge A. F. & A. M. at Verona, the Chapter and Commandery at Morris, and Medinah Temple, Chicago.

HARKES, William, whose abilities and achievements as a mining expert have caused his services to be eagerly sought by companies all over Grundy County, is now acting in the capacity of general superintendent of the Northern Central Coal Company of Missouri, and of the Big Four Wilmington Coal Company, at Coal City, Ill., being president of both companies. He is a native of England, and was born in 1861, a son of William and Barbara (Softleigh) Harkes, the former of whom was a captain in the Indian Army and spent the latter years of his life as a farmer in England. He passed away in his native land in 1911, when eighty-three years of age, his wife having died there in 1884. They were the parents of two children: Jane, who is the wife of John Alderton, living in England; and William.

After attending the public schools of his native county, William Harkes became a student in the English School of Mining Engineers, and upon graduating from that institution served an apprenticeship of seven years in mining engineering. Thus thoroughly prepared to follow his chosen vocation, he worked for various English firms for five years, and in 1887 came to the United States, first locating in Chicago as a mining expert. He came to Coal City in 1891 as general superintendent for the Big Four Wilmington Coal Company and the Northern Central Coal Company, of Missouri, and was made the first president of the adjoining village of Eileen. He is also president of the Harkes Coal Company of Jerome, Iowa, and is part owner of the Wilmington Foundry & Machine Co. He has been county surveyor of Grundy County. Aside from his offices he carries on a business as a general mining engineer. Mr. Harkes has shown an active and public-spirited interest in all that has affected his adopted community, and is known as one of the substantial, reliable men of Coal City. He is a friend of progress and development along all lines and can be depended upon to favor all movements making for the welfare of Coal City or its people. Fraternally, he is connected with the Modern Woodmen of America, in which he has numerous warm friends. He is a Republican in his political views, and in his religious faith is Anglican Episcopalian.

On July 1, 1892, Mr. Harkes was married in Chicago, to Miss Isabelle Gladders, born February 23, 1867, a native of England, and they have had four children: Marie Ruth, Barbara Tesla, William, and Harry C., of whom William died in infancy.

HART, Phillip, formerly a grocer of Morris, was born in Hesse-Darmstadt, Germany, December 17, 1827, but located at Morris in 1854, becoming the proprietor of what was then known as the American House. Later he opened a grocery store in Hart's block, on Liberty Street, and developed into one of the sound business men of Morris. He married in May, 1848, Elizabeth Goering, and they had the following children: Catherine, Lena, Mary, Eliza, Frederick H., George and William.

HASKINS, William G., for a number of years one of the agriculturalists of Good Farm Township, was born in Delaware County, Ohio, April 26, 1818, and came to Grundy County in 1865, first living near Gardner. In 1879 he bought eighty acres of land in Good Farm Township, and greatly improved it. On December 3, 1840, he married Martha W. Eaton and they had the following children: Jeremiah and Eliza Jane. Mr. Haskins was a Republican and served as Assessor of Good Farm Township and also as a School Director.

HENNEBERRY, David A., cashier of the Farmers First National Bank of Minooka, is a man whose career presents results of earnest endeavor which resolve themselves into a successful progress and a development towards honorable citizenship which is the goal in life to which all should work. He was born May 12, 1873, at Lorenzo, in Wilmington Township, Will County, Ill., a son of John and Catherine (O'Brien) Henneberry, the former born in County Limerick, Ireland, and the latter at Boston, Mass. After finishing his course in the local schools David A. Henneberry took a course at Bryant & Stratton's Commercial College of Chicago, and when only eighteen years old began teaching school in his native township. Until the spring of 1896, he alternated teaching school during the winter, with working on farms in the summer, but at that time bought 120 acres of land in Goose Lake Township, then known as the old Phelan farm. Within three years, he rented his property, and went to Chicago to learn the details of the grocery business. In the following spring he went to Minooka, and interested himself in a grain elevator at that point, conducting the business until June, 1903, when he lost his property by fire. He then went to work for A. K. Knapp in the grain business, and August 1, 1908, he with H. P. Dwyer organized the Farmers First National Bank of Minooka, with a capital stock of $25,000. The officers were: J. P. Clennon, president; H. P. Dwyer, vice-president; and D. A. Henneberry, cashier. This has developed into one of the leading financial institutions of the county, and its conservative policies have gained it a reasonable amount of business. It is now the only bank in the village, it having absorbed the Exchange Bank of Minooka on November 1, 1912.

On April 4, 1904, Mr. Henneberry married Margaret Brannick, who was born at Minooka in the spring of 1873, a daughter of Michael and Mary

Potted biographies in a Grundy County history. *For half a cent a word Everyman could purchase the immortality of a published summary of his lifetime exploits. Heroic or mundane, these biographies speak volumes about the origins, migrations, marriages, occupations, career experiences, and community involvements of numerous more-or-less ordinary people.*

Corridor ought to be prepared to deal with both types of social change. But one should also be prepared to contend with another often neglected change within the local history of the corridor: the changes to the physical landscape itself. That is, the stage upon which local history occurred in the area has also evolved, and these changes should be taken into account if one is to gain a fuller understanding of a community's development.

Of course, the landscapes of the corridor and its constituent communities have not always appeared as they do today. We know that, in historical times, marshes have been drained and filled, woods have been cleared and planted, and streams have been diverted and eliminated. But these are only the physical changes that have been caused by man and that have taken place over the last 150 years. If one is interested in recreating the corridor's landscape over thousands or even millions of years, one would have to consult the many geological sources that are available. In fact, since the corridor has seen many transportation and engineering improvements over the past century and a half, its geology has been, by necessity, extremely well documented by various state and federal agencies.[12] At the same time, the study of man's very earliest occupation and exploitation of the area has been both hampered and helped by the same engineering projects. Uninformed digging and dredging early in the nineteenth century sometimes caused the destruction of potential archaeological sites. For example, "Mount Joliet" near the present city of the same name exists today only in photographs and in historical documents; its mineral resources were carted off long ago.[13] However, more recent projects that have altered the landscape of the corridor—particularly the construction of the highways—have actually contributed to the study of the archaeology of the area since state and federal legislation require that all large-scale disturbances in the earth be proceeded by archaeological surveys.[14]

The very earliest information about the I&M Canal corridor's continuous use as a transportation corridor can be found in anthropological studies and in diaries and journals kept by early European explorers. The colonial French explorers, traders, and missionaries in the Great Lakes region achieved an amazing expertise in the location and exploitation of various water and animal resources. Their maps and journals can be used by the corridor researcher who wants to gain a fuller understanding of the seventeenth- and eighteenth-century regional landscape and of the native inhabitants of the area.[15] In addition, recent anthropologists have compiled a great deal of information on the lives of the Indians of the region by using both archaeological and historical sources.[16] Taken as a whole, these pre–United States sources on the corridor can be used by a local history researcher to achieve an impressionistic understanding of the precanal landscape that might be compared with the later changes that have since taken place in the physical environment.

The first systematic record of the way the corridor's landscape looked came from the American occupation and settlement of the Old Northwest. The corridor and all of northern Illinois were settled fairly late by Americans. Even though the southern part of the state had been inhabited by either Frenchmen, Englishmen, or Americans throughout the eighteenth century, the north was practically closed to American settlement until after the Black Hawk War. In the Chicago area the native Indians had to be "convinced" to leave what everybody considered a very valuable piece of real estate before American farmers and land agents were allowed to purchase that part of the public domain. Most of the I&M Canal corridor was surveyed by officials of the United States Land Office in the 1820s, earlier than the immediately surrounding lands since it was evident from the outset that the Chicago–DesPlaines rivers portage country (including the site of Chicago) was going to be a most important transportation corridor and thus was among the first land purchased from the Indian inhabitants in northern Illinois. Surveyors carefully marked a series of mile-square sections of land—in tiers of thirty-six square mile townships—all along the rivers. Their field notes are valuable to today's researcher because they describe the premodern landscape in great detail. That is, in addition to the assignment of exact cadastral positions for future real estate boundaries, the surveyors recorded their impressions of the land's potential for farming by noting the predominant land features (marshes, dry prairies, bluffs, and so on) and the presence of particular types of trees.[17] These early official impressions of the landscape can be supplemented and compared with the accounts of early travelers to the area and with the writings of the very earliest American settlers.[18] The information contained in the surveyors' notes was the raw material of the official maps of the U.S. land office. The maps were, in turn, used as the bases for advertising and recording public and private land sales.[19]

In addition to facilitating the sale of public land, the surveys were used to affix official highways and boundaries; the borders of sections and townships were often used as convenient routes for intracorridor roads and town main streets. Hence the survey accounts for the rectangular pattern of fields and roads that is so familiar to those who travel by air over northeastern Illinois. The original survey lines were also eventually used to determine county boundaries in the corridor. Officials would simply assign entire townships to particular counties whenever it became necessary to adjust the borders. The researcher who anticipates doing local history on the county level should, therefore, be aware that county boundaries regularly shifted before settling into their current configuration in the middle of the nineteenth century. The entire area of Illinois, for example, was once claimed as a county of Virginia until just after the American Revolution. Later, Illinois was a part of the Northwest and the Indiana territories. Even after becoming its own territory and later a state, Illinois county boundaries were changed whenever the increasing numbers of American settlers made it necessary. Parts of present-day Grundy County, for example, were, at various times prior to 1841, included in the Northwest Territory county of Knox; the Indiana Territory county of St. Clair; the Illinois Territory counties of St. Clair, Madison, Edwards, and Crawford; and the Illinois state counties of Crawford, Clark, Pike, Fayette, Edgar, Fulton, Putnam, Vermillion, Tazewell, LaSalle, and Grundy.[20]

Once American settlement took off in the corridor—as it did in the 1830s after the Black Hawk War—the landscape began to change much more rapidly than it had under Indian, French, or English jurisdiction. The Illinois and Michigan Canal, agricultural settlement, and road and railroad construction altered the physical appearance of the land to such an extent by the middle of the nineteenth century that the earlier inhabitants might have had trouble recognizing it. As one might expect, the documents that record these fast-paced physical alterations multiplied along with the changes themselves and are available as sources for the local researcher. The construction of the canal, for example, necessitated intense scrutiny of the area's topographical and hydraulic properties, and the number of available government water survey reports fully document the interest.[21] The printed maps from the canal-building era—showing canal rates, railroad routes, highways, and so forth—became more numerous and detailed during the middle of the last century and might be valuable to the local researcher as sources of information on transportation and settlement patterns.[22] In fact, the number of environmental local history sources increased so rapidly from the 1830s onward that a researcher who wishes to trace changes in geographical relationships over time may have to limit the scope of topical generalization or concentrate the effort on a physically smaller local place.

Unlike those in the landscape and the environment, the changes that have taken place in the cultural and social histories of the I&M Canal corridor have left very little in the way of concrete evidence. There are, of course, vestiges of past people's values and tastes in the area's architecture and in the other artifacts that have survived to the present—either through the careful vigilance of concerned citizens or through blind chance.[23] But a local researcher who is interested in documenting the often subtle variations in people's habits, mores, and life-styles must be prepared to look beyond the obvious physical evidence to less obvious sources—that may or may not have been originally created to document cultural and social achievements. The most common of these sources are those that were left behind by persons or groups of people who were indeed eager to highlight and pass on a record of their accomplishments. For example, the previously mentioned "mug books" and mass-produced county histories or the plethora of material written and left behind by social, ethnic, and religious groups at the celebration of their fifty- or one-hundred-year anniversaries were deliberate attempts to catch the attention of contemporary and future inhabitants.[24] But the careful local researcher will take advantage of these "secondary" sources by gleaning more information from them then their authors necessarily intended. That is, a researcher should be aware of the motivations behind the writing of such self-congratulatory tracts and use them as evidence for documenting changes in cultural and social assumptions. For example, it might be more fruitful to look beyond that which has been included in these histories to that which has apparently been omitted; sometimes we can learn more about the cultural and social expectations of a past people from the missing information than we can from what they decided to highlight and save.

Of course, there are other sources of social and cultural change in the corridor that are plentiful but that were not created or intended for historical use. Public and private agencies made, collected, and saved vast amounts of information for their own immediate use that the local researcher might use today to trace the paths of individuals or to recreate the atmosphere of entire communities. Probably the most popular of these sources for the recent researcher have been the federal census records from the nineteenth and early-twentieth centuries. In 1790, the United States government began to record a decennial census in order to determine the proper apportionment of representatives for each state in the new federal Congress. Before the invention of computers and earlier counting machines, the U.S. Census Bureau recorded the census by assigning a census-taker or *enumerator* to visit every residence in a given *enumeration district*. The *enumerator* would write the name of the head of each household and, depending on the idiosyncrasies of the particular census, various pieces of vital information on every member of the household onto a *census schedule*.[25] The resulting manuscript schedules of the census have proved indispensable to genealogists who have successfully traced the paths of their ancestors. But the censuses can also be used by local historians to discern social patterns within and between communities. For example, a researcher can begin to understand the significance of social relationships within a town by noting where people and their neighbors were born—that is, in which state or in which foreign country, recorded for each individual beginning in 1850—and then collating that information with other data on property ownership or population density. In addition to the federal schedules, enumerators collected census data during the early-nineteenth century for a separate Illinois census. The state census began in 1820 and was repeated every five years until 1845, when it was switched to every ten years (the last was in 1865). The data collected for the Illinois census were similar to the federal, so that the state enumeration can be used as a convenient five-year supplement.[26]

But the material contained in the county histories and in various censuses are only the most obvious sources of information on the social history of the corridor. The local researcher ought also to be aware of the many other potential sources of individual and community information. Among the most fruitful are certainly the county and city directories published for the area. Directories were the most common method by which people kept track of one another before the invention of the telephone and the diffusion of telephone books. The earliest directories covering the corridor were early state gazetteers. As time went by and as northern Illinois became more populated, however, the geographical coverage of the directories was localized more and, eventually, in addition to compendia covering the whole state, was directed toward counties and particular towns. In addition to the information contained about individuals—name, residential address, perhaps business address—directories also provide excellent sources of lists of government officials, ministers, and churches, and leaders of voluntary organizations. But the city directories were, above all, money-making ventures—sold by subscription—for their publishers. The local researcher, therefore, ought to be aware that the poorer and less-influential residents in a community were the most likely to be "missed" by directory compilers.[27]

The same sort of raw data contained in censuses and directories about individuals can also be found in land records, though with a peculiar twist. Whereas censuses and directories can be used to trace the movement of the same person over places and through time, land records hold a place (or a plot of land) constant and allow one to document its ownership by different persons through time. If a local researcher is interested in a community's economic history or the history of a particular piece of real estate, or needs to check on the whereabouts of a person at a particular point in time, the land records will probably prove a valuable, though sometimes frustrating, source. The earliest land records are those kept by the federal land office but can be supplemented, particularly if the piece of land in question is located close to the I&M Canal, with the records of the canal commissioners and subsequently, of course, the county registries of deeds.[28]

Local newspapers are similar to city directories in that, even though they were intended for immediate consumption by their readers, they can be a valuable source for today's local researcher.[29] Besides the information contained in most newspapers about the births, marriages, and deaths of community members,[30] newspapers can also be used to discern otherwise hidden trends in a community's social and political relationships. Many of the early newspapers, for example, were openly political and often reflected the social and cultural biases of certain segments of the community. Again, however, the local researcher ought to keep in mind that the information that appears to be missing from a newspaper's coverage of community affairs can be as important a source of evidence for documenting social relationships as that which is included.

In addition to governmental bodies, directory companies, and newspaper publishers, less public individuals and agencies in the past also collected data that may be of some use to the local researcher. The corridor is rich in the number of documents created by various boards and commissions that were responsible for the investigations of the effects of the area's engineering projects.[31] Early on, private companies were also alert to the corridor's industrial and settlement potential, and they have also left records that can often inform one on the social relationships within communities.[32]

Finally, it is ironic that some of the least used sources of local history in the Illinois and Michigan Canal National Heritage Corridor are also some of the most familiar pieces of information about the area to the present inhabitants. Every community, no matter how widely or narrowly defined, has its own local myths and folklore that occasionally have their bases in historical truths.[33] The problem with using local legends as a source for local history is that their bases are very often shrouded in the mists of time and are, therefore, unrecoverable. There are, however, at least two paths that a local researcher might take in order to use the myths and folklore of the corridor—which is particularly rich in local stories, some of which date to the Indians. First, listen to and read transcripts of oral histories; sometimes the information received from an individual just one generation earlier can shed more light on a dim subject.[34] And second, read the prose and poetry from and about the local place under scrutiny; sometimes a short but heart-felt past impression about a community can tell us more than a whole stack of history books.[35]

Detailed community histories of the towns in the Illinois and Michigan Canal National Heritage Corridor have to be written before we can expect to have a fuller understanding of the significance of the area to American history in general. The interest shown by historians in local history continues to provide a positive environment in which to conduct research. The sources of historical information about the corridor are certainly diverse and voluminous, but it is to be hoped that this essay and the accompanying bibliography demonstrate that they are also generally decipherable and available to those interested. The only potentially missing ingredients in the recipe for the research and writing of local corridor history are the writers, either lay or professional, who appreciate the value of documenting and interpreting the past for themselves and others and for the future. Corridor historical source materials are so rich that we must sincerely hope the writers exploiting them will proliferate. The opportunities are extensive and enticing.

References

1 Carl Sandburg, "Joliet," *Poems of the Midwest* (Cleveland and New York: The World Publishing Company, [1946]), p. 220.

2 For a sample of Sandburg's work, see *Abraham Lincoln: The Prairie Years* (New York: Harcourt, Brace, and Company, [1926]); *Abraham Lincoln: The War Years* (New York: Harcourt, Brace and Company, [1939]); *Chicago Poems* (New York: H. Holt and Company, 1916); and other works in *Poems of the Midwest.* For his autobiography, see *Always the Young Strangers* (New York: Harcourt, Brace, and Company, [1953]).

3 Beware poetic license: at the risk of appearing scientifically churlish it must be noted that Lockport is, of course, *up* the river from Joliet.

4 The publication of Alex Haley's *Roots* (Garden City, New York: Doubleday

& Company, 1976) and its later adaptation for television created an unprecedented interest in genealogical methods and sources; for examples, see "Climbing All Over the Family Trees," *Time* 109 (March 28, 1977): 54; "Everybody's Search for Roots," *Newsweek* 90 (July 4, 1977): 26–27; and "Tracing Your Own Roots—Advice from an Expert," *U.S. News and World Report* 82 (March 14, 1977): 57. For one historian's views on the Bicentennial, see Bruce Catton, "The Way I See It," *American Heritage* 28 (February 1977): 79.

5 For a review of the French and English schools of local history, see Pierre Goubert, "Local History," and Lawrence Stone, "English and United States Local History," in *Historical Studies Today,* ed. Felix Gilbert and Stephen R. Graubard (New York: W. W. Norton & Company, 1972), pp. 300–314 and 315–319.

6 This old approach to local history could be called the "George Washington slept here" school.

7 A complete review of the connections between local and social history can be found in Kathleen N. Conzen, "Community Studies, Urban History, and American Local History," in *The Past Before Us; Contemporary Historical Writing in the United States,* ed. Michael Kammen (Ithaca and London: Cornell University Press, 1980), pp. 270–291.

8 Some of the most readable treatments of early New England communities are John Demos, *A Little Commonwealth: Family Life in Plymouth Colony* (London: Oxford University Press, 1970); Kenneth A. Lockridge, *A New England Town: The First Hundred Years* (New York: W. W. Norton & Company, 1970), which is about Dedham, Massachusetts in the seventeenth and early-eighteenth centuries; Paul Boyer and Stephen Nissenbaum, *Salem Possessed: The Social Origins of Witchcraft* (Cambridge, Massachusetts: Harvard University Press, 1974); and Robert A. Gross, *The Minutemen and Their World* (New York: Hill and Wang, 1976), which deals with revolutionary Concord, Massachusetts.

9 For examples, see Peter H. Wood, *Black Majority: Negroes in Colonial South Carolina from 1670 through the Stono Rebellion* (New York: W. W. Norton & Company, 1974); Rhys Isaac, *The Transformation of Virginia: 1740–1790* (Chapel Hill: University of North Carolina Press, 1982); Paul E. Johnson, *A Shopkeeper's Millenium: Society and Revivals in Rochester, New York, 1815–1837* (New York: Hill and Wang, 1978); Don Doyle, *The Social Order of a Frontier Community: Jacksonville, Illinois, 1825–1870* (Urbana: University of Illinois Press, 1978); Roger William Lotchin, *San Francisco, 1846–1856: From Hamlet to City* (New York: Oxford University Press, 1974); Ralph Mann, *After the Gold Rush: Society in Grass Valley and Nevada City, California, 1849–1870* (Stanford, California: Stanford University Press, 1982); and Norman H. Clark, *Mill Town: A Social History of Everett, Washington, from Its Earliest Beginnings on the Shores of Puget Sound to the Tragic and Infamous Event Known as the Everett Massacre* (Seattle and London: University of Washington Press, 1970).

10 The American Association for State and Local History has published a variety of guides for local historians over the past few years. Researchers may want to consult Carol Kammen, *On Doing Local History: Reflections on What Local Historians Do, Why, and What it Means* (Nashville, Tennessee: American Assoc. for State and Local History, 1986); Houston Gwynne Jones, *Local Government Records: An Introduction to Their Management, Preservation, and Use* (Nashville, Tennessee: American Assoc. for State and Local History, 1980); Barbara Allen and Lynwood Montell, *From Memory to History: Using Oral History Sources in Local Historical Research* (Nashville, Tennessee:

American Assoc. for State and Local History, 1981); Thomas E. Felt, *Researching, Writing, and Publishing Local History* (Nashville, Tennessee: American Assoc. for State and Local History, 1976); Arthur P. Ziegler, Jr., and Walter C. Kidney, *Historical Preservation in Small Towns* (Nashville, Tennessee: American Assoc. for State and Local History, 1980); and David E. Kyvig and Myron A. Marty, *Nearby History: Exploring the Past Around You* (Nashville, Tennessee: American Assoc. for State and Local History, 1982).

11 See the Genealogy and Biography—Biographical and Genealogical Collections subsection of the Bibliography for the "mug books" and the Local History section for the county histories of the corridor. Two accounts of such publishers in Illinois can be found in Raymond and Betty Spahn, "Wesley R. Brink, History Huckster," *Journal of the Illinois State Historical Society* 58 (1965), pp. 117–38, and Michael P. Conzen, "Maps for the Masses: Alfred T. Andreas and the Midwestern County Atlas Trade," in *Chicago Mapmakers: Essays on the Rise of the City's Map Trade,* ed. Michael P. Conzen (Chicago: Chicago Historical Society, 1984), pp. 46–63. Andreas switched from county atlases to county histories in 1876 and published some early ones of northern Illinois counties (for example, LaSalle County in 1877, under the name of H. F. Kett and Company), setting a pattern followed by others (Oliver Baskin, for example, a former employee who published a Grundy County history in 1882) and culminating in his celebrated *History of Cook County* in 1884.

12 Citations of the geological surveys can be found in the The Physical Environment—Geology, The Physical Environment—Soil, the Physical Environment—Water, The Physical Environment—Climate, and the Maps and Atlases—Government Surveys subsections of the Bibliography.

13 Information on Mount Joliet can be found in Robert Knight and Lucius Zeuch, "Mount Joliet: Its Place in Illinois History and Its Location," *Journal of the Illinois State Historical Society* 23 (April 1930): 84–91.

14 The effects of the new salvage laws are outlined in American Resources Group, Ltd., *An Inventory and Evaluation of Known Archaeological Resources in the Illinois and Michigan Canal National Heritage Corridor, Illinois* (Carbondale, Illinois: 1985), pp. 108–115.

15 See the Description and Travel and Maps and Atlases sections of the Bibliography for examples of pre–United States impressions and exploration of the Corridor.

16 See the Indians, Politics, and Government—Military Affairs—Indian Wars, and the Local History—General—Old Northwest subsections of the Bibliography. In particular, see American Resources Group, Ltd., *An Inventory and Evaluation,* pp. 47–75.

17 Descriptions of the federal field notes for Illinois can be found in the Local History—Archive Sources subsection of the Bibliography.

18 See the Description and Travel section of the Bibliography.

19 For the General Land Office records in the Archives of the State of Illinois, see the Local History—Archive Sources subsection of the Bibliography.

20 For details, see Illinois, Secretary of State, *Counties of Illinois: Their Origin and Evolution, with Twenty-Three Maps Showing the Original and Present Boundary Lines of Each County of the State,* Compiled and Published by Louis L. Emmerson, Secretary of State (Springfield: Illinois State Journal Company, State Printers, 1919).

21 Sources on the federal, state, and local hydraulic surveys, are listed in The Physical Environment—Water subsection

of the Bibliography. For early canal, railroad, and highway maps, see the appropriate subsections in the Maps and Atlases section.

22 See the canal and waterway and railroads subsections of the Maps and Atlases section of the Bibliography.

23 Information on the architecture of the corridor can be found in G. Gray Fitzsimons's essay in this volume and in the Cultural Life—Architecture subsection of the Bibliography. Details about artifacts are in the Artifact Collections section of the Bibliography.

24 A number of these anniversary pamphlets can be found in the Social Environment and Cultural Life sections of the Bibliography.

25 Information on federal census manuscripts can be found in the Agriculture (agricultural schedules), Commerce and Industry (industrical schedules), Social Environment (social statistic schedules), and Genealogy and Biography (population schedules) sections of the Bibliography. Each of the entries outlines the specific information entered during each census.

26 State census citations are included in the Genealogy and Biography—Archive Sources subsection of the Bibliography.

27 Early gazetteers are listed in the Description and Travel—Gazetteers and Place Name Studies subsection and directories are listed in the Directories section of the Bibliography.

28 The early federal land records are listed in the Local History—Archive Sources subsection of the Bibliography, and the canal land records can be found in the Transportation and Communication—Archive Sources subsection. Researchers should consult the Agriculture, the Transportation and Communication, the Commerce and Industry, and the Labor sections of the guide for entries on the economic history of the corridor. The only work of economic history that deals specifically with the corridor is James William Putnam, *The Illinois and Michigan Canal: A Study in Economic History* (Chicago: University of Chicago Press, 1918).

29 Each newspaper that is known to have been published in the corridor is listed in the Newspapers section of the Bibliography, even if there are no known copies of a particular journal.

30 Some libraries and historical societies have collected vital information from past issues of their newspapers. These are listed in the Genealogy and Biography—Archive Sources subsection of the Bibliography.

31 Many of these special investigation sources can be found throughout the Transportation and Communication section of the Bibliography.

32 See the Commerce and Industry and Labor sections of the Bibliography for sources of company records.

33 See the Indians—Folklore and the Cultural Life—Folklore and Folk Art subsections of the Bibliography for sources on folklore.

34 Oral history collections are listed in the Oral History section of the Bibliography.

35 The literature of the corridor is cited in the Cultural Life—Fiction and Poetry subsection of the Bibliography.

Five

GUIDE TO CORRIDOR HISTORICAL SOURCES: AN ANNOTATED BIBLIOGRAPHY

Kay J. Carr, Chris E. Copenhaver, Stephen Freedman, and Jean M. O'Brien

MOST OF the entries in this Bibliography were gathered in the summer of 1984, just before the Upper Illinois Valley was officially designated the Illinois and Michigan Canal National Heritage Corridor. Once the bibliographic team began to look for appropriate entries in Chicago's major research libraries, it became obvious that there was a wealth of sources on the history of the corridor that might be included in a final Bibliography. Since many bibliographies and finding aids covering general Illinois materials already exist, an early decision was made to pay special attention to very local and unique materials concerning the corridor, even if this meant giving somewhat cursory treatment to more general and widely available sources. It was also decided to close the historical coverage of the Bibliography at 1940, since the postwar information boom and the proliferation of government and private documentation of the corridor would have swelled the volume to unmanageable proportions. Time constraints also made it necessary to place the geographical emphasis of the Bibliography on those areas outside the city of Chicago and along the I&M Canal. Those neighborhoods that are officially within the corridor and also within the city, therefore, are not covered to the same depth as are those communities outside the city. Researchers seeking access to sources specifically on Chicago neighborhoods are referred to the excellent and extensive treatment given them in *Annotated Bibliography of Chicago History* by Frank Jewell. Owing to similar constraints, the communities along the Calumet Sag Channel portion of the corridor are also not covered in quite the detail given the I&M Canal towns, and, again, Jewell's bibliography covers these places most helpfully.

In the interest of conserving space for unique material, each entry has been placed under only one major category in the guide. The inclusion of particular entries under major headings, however, was often a matter of judgment of the bibliography editor, since many could conceivably belong in several categories. Therefore, users should rely on their own good sense while searching for information on topics of interest by looking under various subject headings in the Bibliography. Researchers are also warned that the guide is not intended to be an exhaustive bibliography on the historical sources of the corridor. Only about three-fifths of the entries originally collected could be included in the final volume. And since historians have continued to work in the corridor, the guide does not contain references past mid-1984—although some have come to the attention of the editors and have been included.

Each entry contains at least one library code between bibliographic information and annotation. The codes are listed with their full library designations in the *Library Abbreviations* that immediately precede the bibliography. The codes are not all-inclusive (that is, they do not necessarily indicate all places that may have a particular item), but are meant simply as an indication of where the specific material in the entry has been located during the "sweep" for this compilation. An effort was made, however, to include a listing for at least one public-access library for each entry, whenever possible. Codes do not imply, therefore, that the material is available *only* at those locations. The project simply did not have resources sufficient to make this Bibliography a union list.

Contents of Guide

Library Abbreviations

CU	University of California Library, Berkeley, California
CLO	Occidental College Library, Los Angeles, California
CSmH	Henry E. Huntington Library, San Marino, California
CtY	Yale University Library, New Haven, Connecticut
DCU	Catholic University of America Library, Washington, D.C.
DLC	U.S. Library of Congress, Washington, D.C.
DNA	U.S. National Archives Library, Washington, D.C.
DHEW	U.S. Department of Health and Human Services Library, Washington, D.C.
DNLM	U.S. National Library of Medicine, Bethesda, Maryland
DSI	Smithsonian Institution Library, Washington, D.C.
FTaSU	Florida State University Library, Tallahassee, Florida
GeP—FARC	U.S. General Services Administration—Federal Archives and Records Center, East Point, Georgia
I	Illinois State Library, Springfield, Illinois
I—Ar	Illinois State Library—Archives Division, Springfield, Illinois
I—SM	Illinois State Museum, Springfield, Illinois
IAl	Hayner Public Library, Alton, Illinois
IAr	Argonne National Laboratory, Argonne, Illinois
IBlo—Ag	Illinois Agricultural Association Library, Bloomington, Illinois
IBloWM	Illinois Wesleyan University, Methodist Archives, Bloomington, Illinois
IBP	Bedford Park Public Library, Bedford Park, Illinois
IBI	Blue Island Public Library, Blue Island, Illinois
IBr	Bridgeview Public Library, Bridgeview, Illinois
ICarbS	Southern Illinois University Library, Carbondale, Illinois
IC	Chicago Public Library, Chicago, Illinois
IC—ACE	U.S. Army Corps of Engineers, North Central Division Library, Chicago, Illinois
IC—COC	Commonwealth Edison Company Library, Chicago, Illinois
IC—FARC	U.S. General Services Administration—Federal Archives and Records Center, Chicago, Illinois

IC—IHC	International Harvester Company Archives, Chicago, Illinois
ICA	Art Institute of Chicago, Chicago, Illinois
ICBT	Illinois Bell Telephone Information Center, Chicago, Illinois
ICC	Columbia College Library, Chicago, Illinois
ICCA	Evangelical Covenant Church of America Archives, Chicago, Illinois
ICD	DePaul University Library, Chicago, Illinois
ICE	Economist Newspapers, Chicago, Illinois
ICF	Field Museum of Natural History, Chicago, Illinois
ICHi	Chicago Historical Society, Chicago, Illinois
ICJ	John Crerar Library, University of Chicago, Chicago, Illinois
ICL	Loyola University Library, Chicago, Illinois
ICLT	Lutheran School of Theology, Chicago, Illinois
ICMcC	McCormick Theological Seminary, Chicago, Illinois
ICN	Newberry Library, Chicago, Illinois
ICRL	Center for Research Libraries, Chicago, Illinois
ICSD	Metropolitan Sanitary District of Greater Chicago, Chicago, Illinois
ICT	Chicago Theological Seminary, Chicago, Illinois
ICU	University of Chicago Library, Chicago, Illinois
ICUI	University of Illinois at Chicago Library, Chicago, Illinois
ICrH	Lockport Township Public Library, Crest Hill, Illinois
IDeKN	Northern Illinois University Library, DeKalb, Illinois
IDeKN—IRAD	Illinois Regional Archives Depository—Northern Illinois University, DeKalb, Illinois
	Garrett Seabury Theological Seminary, Evanston, Illinois
IEN	Northwestern University Library, Evanston, Illinois
IG	Galesburg Public Library, Galesburg, Illinois
IGK	Knox College Library, Galesburg, Illinois
IHi	Illinois State Historical Library, Springfield, Illinois
IJo	Joliet Public Library, Joliet, Illinois
IJoJ	Joliet Junior College Learning Resource Center, Joliet, Illinois
IJu	Justice Public Library, Justice, Illinois
ILa	LaSalle Public Library, LaSalle, Illinois
ILe	Lemont Public Library, Lemont, Illinois
ILeHi	Lemont Area Historical Society, Harry J. Swanson Memorial Library, Lemont, Illinois
ILo	Lockport Township Public Library, Lockport, Illinois
ILoHi	Will County Historical Society, Lockport, Illinois
ILoL	Lewis University I&M Canal Archives, Lockport, Illinois
ILomGe	DuPage County Genealogical Society, Lombard, Illinois
IMa	Marseilles Public Library, Marseilles, Illinois
IMo	Morris Public Library, Morris, Illinois

IMoGW Illinois and Michigan Canal Trail Archives, Gebhard Woods State Park, Morris, Illinois

IMoHi Grundy County Historical Society, Morris, Illinois

IMunS St. Mary of the Lake Seminary, Mundelein, Illinois

INS Illinois State University Library, Normal, Illinois

INS—IRAD Illinois Regional Archives Depository—Illinois State University, Normal, Illinois

IO Reddick Public Library, Ottawa, Illinois

IOS Starved Rock Library System, Ottawa, Illinois

IOg Oglesby Public Library, Oglesby, Illinois

IPe Peru Public Library, Peru, Illinois

IPHe Palos Heights Public Library, Palos Heights, Illinois

IPHil Green Hills Public Library, Palos Hills, Illinois

IPP Palos Park Public Library, Palos Park, Illinois

IR—ACE U.S. Army Corps of Engineers, Technical Library, Rock Island District, Rock Island, Illinois

IRo Fountaindale Public Library, Romeoville, Illinois

ISA Summit-Argo Public Library, Summit, Illinois

ISB Illinois Baptist Historical Library, Springfield, Illinois

ISCon Illinois Department of Conservation, Springfield, Illinois

ISTr Illinois Department of Transportation, Springfield, Illinois

ISe Seneca Public Library, Seneca, Illinois

IU University of Illinois Library, Urbana, Illinois

IU—Ar University of Illinois Archives, Urbana, Illinois

IU—HS Illinois Historical Survey, University of Illinois, Urbana, Illinois

IUtHi LaSalle County Historical Museum, Utica, Illinois

IWo Worth Public Library, Worth, Illinois

IaAS State University of Iowa Library, Ames, Iowa

IaCrM Iowa Masonic Library, Cedar Rapids, Iowa

IaU University of Iowa Library, Iowa City, Iowa

InG Gary Public Library, Gary, Indiana

InU Indiana University at Bloomington Library, Bloomington, Indiana

InHi Indiana Historical Society, Indianapolis, Indiana

InNd University of Notre Dame Library, Notre Dame, Indiana

LNHT Tulane University Library, New Orleans, Louisiana

MB Boston Public Library, Boston, Massachusetts

MH—BA Harvard University Graduate School of Business Administration, Baker Library, Cambridge, Massachusetts

MeB Bowdoin College Library, Brunswick, Maine

Mi Michigan State University Library, East Lansing, Michigan

MiU University of Michigan Library, Ann Arbor, Michigan

MnNSN Norwegian-American Historical Association, St. Olaf College, Northfield, Minnesota

MnU University of Minnesota Library, Minneapolis, Minnesota

MnU—I	Immigration History Research Center, University of Minnesota, Minneapolis, Minnesota
MoSU	St. Louis University Library, St. Louis, Missouri
MoU	University of Missouri Library, Columbia, Missouri
MWA	American Antiquarian Society, Worcester, Massachusetts
NjP	Princeton University Library, Princeton, New Jersey
N	New York State Library, Albany, New York
NBuC	State University of New York—College at Buffalo Library, Buffalo, New York
NIC	Cornell University Library, Ithaca, New York
NN	New York Public Library, New York, New York
NNC	Columbia University Library, New York, New York
NSyU	Syracuse University Library, Syracuse, New York
NbU	University of Nebraska Library, Lincoln, Nebraska
NcAN	National Climatic Center, Asheville, North Carolina
OCU	University of Cincinnati, Cincinnati, Ohio
OkU	University of Oklahoma Library, Norman, Oklahoma
PBL	LeHigh University Library, Bethlehem, Pennsylvania
PLatS	St. Vincent College and Archabbey Library, Latrobe, Pennsylvania
PPPrHi	Presbyterian Historical Society, Philadelphia, Pennsylvania
WHi	Wisconsin State Historical Society, Madison, Wisconsin
WMM	Marquette University Library, Milwaukee, Wisconsin
WU	University of Wisconsin Library, Madison, Wisconsin
***	No extant copies known

PART 1 General

Much of the history of the Illinois and Michigan Canal Corridor can be found in general Illinois historical sources. This section contains some of the most useful journals, bibliographies, guides, and indexes that contain information about the state. Even though many articles dealing with the corridor sites in these general sources can also be found throughout the guide, researchers might find further useful information on the area's relationship to state and national history by checking some of the following general sources.

General—*Journals and Series*

Chicago Magazine. Vol. 1–. Chicago: Contemporary Publications, 1954–.
ICU

Collections of the Illinois State Historical Library. Vols. 1–32. Springfield: Illinois State Historical Library, 1903–1945. 32 v., fronts., plates, ports., maps, plans, facsims.
DLC, ICF, ICN, ICU, IEN

Fergus Historical Series. Nos. 1–35. Chicago: Fergus Printing Co., 1876–1914. 35 v., illus., plates, ports., plan, facsims., diagr.
DLC, I, IC, ICN, ICU

Historical Research Series. No. 1–. Springfield: Illinois State Historical Library, 1964–. illus.
DLC, ICU

Illinois Libraries. Vol. 1–. Springfield: Illinois State Library, 1919–.
DLC, I, IC, ICJ, ICN, ICU, IU

Often surveys holdings of local libraries. Can be a valuable source in finding and sorting local history material.

Illinois Monthly Magazine. Vol. 1–2. Vandalia, Illinois, and Cincinnati, Ohio, 1830–1832.
DLC, ICN, ICU, IGK, IU

Superseded by *Western Monthly Magazine.*

Journal of the Illinois State Historical Society. Vol. 1–. Springfield: Illinois State Historical Society, 1908–. plates, ports., maps, facsims.
DLC, I, IC, ICHi, ICN, ICU, IEN, IU

Index to Vols. 1–25. Name changed to *Illinois Historical Journal,* 1985.

Papers in Illinois History and Transactions. Vols. 1–43. Springfield: Illinois State Historical Library, 1899–1942. 43 v., illus., ports., maps.
DLC, IC, ICN, ICU, IU

Volumes for 1937–1942 issued without series number, but constitute Nos. 44–49. Title varies from 1900 to 1936. Transactions indexed.

Publications of the Illinois State Historical Society. No. 1–. Springfield: Illinois State Historical Society, 1899–. illus., ports., maps.
DLC, IC, ICN, ICU, IU

Nos. 44–49 issued without general title and numbering. Title varies. Nos. 1–43 issued by Illinois State Historical Library. Indexed.

Studies in Illinois History. No. 1–. Macomb, Illinois: Western Illinois University, 1966–.
DLC, ICU

Each number also has a distinctive title.

General—*Bibliographies*

Bridges, Roger D., comp. "A Bibliography of Dissertations Related to Illinois History, 1884–1976." *Journal of the Illinois State Historical Society* 70 (August 1977): 208–248.
DLC, I, IC, ICHi, ICN, ICU, IEN, IU

Bridges, Roger D. comp. "Illinois Manuscripts and Archival Collections: A Checklist of Published Guides." *Journal of the Illinois State Historical Society* 66 (Winter 1973): 412–427.
DLC, I, IC, ICHi, ICN, ICU, IEN, IU

Byrd, Cecil K. *A Bibliography of Illinois Imprints, 1814–58.* Chicago: The University of Chicago Press, 1966.
ICU, WU

Indexed.

Chicago and Cook County: A Union List of Their Official Publications, Including the Semi-Official Institutions. Chicago: The University of Chicago Libraries Document Section, 1934. 230 p.
ICU

Publications of the County Board, Chicago City Council, departments of the city government, Chicago Park District, Chicago Sanitary District, Chicago Regional Port Commission, Chicago Academy of Sciences, Chicago Zoological Society, and Field Museum of Natural History.

Joliet Public Library. *Finding List of the Joliet Public Library.* Joliet: Republican Printing Company, 1901. 84 p.
DLC
Includes fictional works, bibliographies, and catalogs.

Smith, Bernice, ed. *Bibliography of Illinois Materials in the Member Libraries of the DuPage Library System.* Wheaton, Illinois: DuPage Library System, 1968.
IHi

Whitney, Ellen M. and Dunn, William R. "Illinois Sesquicentennial Publications; A Preliminary Descriptive Checklist." *Journal of the Illinois State Historical Society* 63 (Winter 1970): 422–438.
DLC, I, IC, ICHi, ICN, ICU, IEN, IU
County histories and general Illinois history.

Works Progress Administration. Federal Writers' Project, Illinois. *Selected Bibliography, Illinois: Chicago and Its Environs.* American Guide Series. Chicago: Works Progress Administration, 1937. 58 p.
ICU
Contains entries for fifty-five subject categories. Includes material on Will and southwest Cook counties.

General—*Archive Guides*

Alvord, Clarence Walworth, "... Archives of the State of Illinois." *American Historical Association, Annual Reports ... for the Year 1909* (1911): 379–463.
I, IC, ICJ, ICN, ICU

"Archival Issue. Part 1. Archives in Illinois: Archival Repositories Outside the Chicago Metropolitan Area." *Illinois Libraries* 63 (March 1981): 266–281.
DLC, I, IC, ICJ, ICN, ICU, IU

"Archival Issue. Part 2. Archival Repositories in the Chicago Metropolitan Area." *Illinois Libraries* 63 (April 1981): 283–351.
DLC, I, IC, ICJ, ICN, ICU, IU

Downs, Robert B. *Guide to Illinois Library Resources.* Chicago: Published in Cooperation with the Illinois State Library Association by the American Library Association, 1974. 565 p.
DLC, ICU
Guide to collections of manuscripts and published materials.

Harding, Bruce C. "Regional Archives Branch—Chicago." *Illinois Libraries* 57 (March 1975): 186–193.
DLC, I, IC, ICJ, ICN, ICU, IU
Describes Record Groups at Archives, including U.S. District Court, 1808–1952; Bureau of Indian Affairs, 1870–1952; Indian Census Rolls, 1880–1940; Internal Revenue Assessment Lists for Illinois, 1862–1866; Census Rolls.

Illinois State Library. "Manuscript Issue: Local History and Manuscript Collections in Illinois." *Illinois Libraries* 40 (April 1958): 277–400.
DLC, I, IC, ICJ, ICN, ICU, IU
Augustana College Archives, Chicago Historical Society, Illinois Historical Survey, Illinois State Archives, Newberry Library, Northwestern University Library, Southern Illinois University Library, University of Chicago Library, University of Illinois Library.

Illinois. State Museum, Springfield. *Handbook of Collections.* No. 1–. Springfield: Illinois State Museum, 1963–.
IU
Irregularly issued. Collected works.

Irons, Victoria and Brennan, Patricia C. *Descriptive Inventory of the Archives of the State of Illinois.* Springfield: Illinois State Archives, Office of the Secretary of State, 1978.
I—Ar, ICU
Guide to 107 record groups of territorial, state, and federal boards and offices. Includes governor, secretary of state, treasurer, auditor, superintendent of public instruction, and attorney general records. Separate index.

Nakata, Yuri. "Local Documents in Illinois Libraries: Results of Questionnaire." *Illinois Libraries* 57 (April 1975): 256–260.
DLC, I, IC, ICJ, ICN, ICU, IU
Includes responses from Alsip, Calumet City, Chicago, Romeoville, Seneca, Summit-Argo, Worth.

Norton, Margaret C., ed. "Illinois Archival Information." *Illinois Libraries* 32 (February, May, August 1950): 136–141, 214–219, 252–257, 350–359, 592–600.
DLC, I, IC, ICJ, ICN, ICU, IU
Photoreproduction and description of documents on, among other topics, the internal improvement system of 1837 and the I&M Canal.

Pease, Theodore Calvin. *The County Archives of the State of Illinois.* Collections of the Illinois State Historical Library, Vol. 12. Springfield: The Trustees of the Illinois State Historical Library, 1915. 730 p.
ICF, ICN, ICU, IEN
Bibliographical series, Vol. 3.

Pratt, Harry E. *Descriptive Lists of Various Manuscript Collections in the Illinois State Historical Library.* Springfield, 1951. 81 p.
IU

Sager, Juliet G. comp. *General Index to Collections, Journals, Publications, 1899–1928. Illinois State Historical Library.* Quincy, Illinois: The Royal Printing Co., Inc., 1930. 95 p.
DLC, ICN, ICU

Turnbaugh, Roy C., Jr. *A Guide to the County Records in the Illinois Regional Archives.* Springfield: The Illinois State Archives, Jim Edgar, secretary of state and state archivist, 1983. 376 p.
ICU
Lists county records stored at six Illinois Regional Archive Depository sites in Illinois. Site number 1, Northern Illinois University (DeKalb) contains LaSalle, Will, and DuPage county records.

Site number 3, Illinois State University (Normal) contains Grundy County records.

LaSalle County: Collector's Books, 1933–1936, 1948–1956; Chancery Records, 1854–1858, 1871–1873; Case Files, 1839–1862; County Court Records, 1872–1927, 1928–1963; Superintendent's Annual Reports, 1879–1939; School Trustee's and Treasurer's Annual Reports, 1937–1951.

Will County: Collector's Books, 1914–1965; School Superintendent's Annual Reports, 1848, 1850, 1852, 1859–1864, 1866–1877, 1882–1883; School Superintendent's Annual Reports, 1871–1884.

Grundy County: State's Attorney Fee, Fine and Forfeiture Reports, 1873–1874, 1876, 1879, 1880–1902; Grand Jury Jail Reports, 1889–1892, 1895, 1898.

General—*Miscellaneous*

Hasse, Adelaide R. *Index of Economic Material in Documents of the United States. Illinois 1809–1904.* Carnegie Institution of Washington. Publication, No. 85. Baltimore: The Lord Baltimore Press, 1909. 393 p.
DLC, ICJ
The index covers public health, education, labor, and recreation, as well as agriculture, commerce, finance, manufacturing, and transportation. The materials for the *Index* are published reports and bulletins, issued by government agencies and private associations.

Illinois. General Assembly. *Reports to the General Assembly of Illinois . . . 1838–1897.* Springfield: Illinois General Assembly, 1839–1897. 89 vols. Springfield: Illinois General Assembly, 1839–1897.
ICU, ICJ
Until 1838, the reports were published with the Journals of the Senate and House. Contains reports of superintendents of public instruction, wardens of the Illinois State Penitentiary, reports of the commissioners of the Illinois and Michigan Canal.

Illinois. Secretary of State. *Report.* Springfield: Secretary of State, 1869/1870–.
DLC, ICJ, IU
Biennial.

Lester, Daniel W., Faull, Sandra D., and Lester, Lorraine E., comps. *Cumulative Title Index to United States Public Documents, 1789–1976.* 16 v. Arlington, Virginia: United States Historical Documents Institute, 1980.
ICU
Arranged alphabetically. Researchers should look under the name of the corridor city they are studying.

Nakata, Yuri, and Strange, Michele. *Classification Scheme for Illinois State Publications: As Applied to the Documents Collection at the Library, University of Illinois at Chicago Circle, Chicago, Illinois.* Champaign: University of

Illinois Graduate School of Library Science, 1974. 39 p.
DLC, ICU, IU
Includes index.

U.S. Library of Congress. Census Library Project. *Catalog of United States Census Publications, 1790–1945.* Prepared by Henry J. Dubester. Washington, D.C.: Government Printing Office, 1950. 320 p.
DLC, ICJ, ICU
With annotations.

General—*Archive Sources*

Chicago, Illinois. Columbia College. Unpublished Manuscript. Miriam Rabban and Project Staff, comp. "Southeast Chicago Historical Project Bibliography."
ICC
A major bibliographic collection of published and unpublished materials.

Springfield, Illinois. Illinois State Historical Library. Federal Writers' Project. Illinois. Approximately 200 boxes.
IHi
Boxes 1–53: "Cities, Towns and Villages." Brief histories and descriptions of Alsip, Argo, Blue Island, Braidwood, Burnham, Calumet City, Channahon, Joliet, Justice, LaSalle, Lemont, Lockport, Marseilles, Morris, Ottawa, Palos Park, Peru, Robbins, Rockdale, Romeoville, Seneca, Utica, Worth.
Boxes 54–87: "Chicago." Material on geography, topography, climate, geology, history, transportation, bridges, streetcars, stockyards, steel, meat packers, South Lawndale, Armour Square, South Chicago, Pullman, South Deering, East Side, West Pullman, Archer Heights, McKinley Park, Clearing, Bridgeport.
Box 113: "Cook County."
Box 118: "LaSalle County."
Box 121: "Will County."
Box 136: "Will County Guide."
Boxes 150–151: "Illinois Rivers, Lakes, Parks, etc." Information on canals, Buffalo Rock, Starved Rock, sanitary districts, Chicago River, Illinois River, Fox River, DesPlaines River.
Boxes 154–180: "Annals of Agriculture." Covers 1673–1939. Contains collection of typewritten indexes to major nineteenth-century agricultural journals. Information on animal husbandry, horticulture, agricultural machinery, agronomy, agricultural institutions.
Boxes 181–192: "Religion." Information about various denominations in McKinley Park, Brighton Park, West Pullman, East Side, Bridgeport, South Chicago, Lawndale, West Side, Loop, Joliet, Lemont, Ottawa.
Boxes 193–196: "Racial Groups." Folders on various ethnic groups in Pilsen, South Chicago, Hegewisch, Pullman, Joliet, Blue Island, Calumet, Argo, Lemont, Peru, LaSalle, Braidwood, West Pullman.

PART 2 The Physical Environment

This section of the Bibliography provides a solid and thorough collection of background materials that are essential to the understanding of the physical environment of the corridor and of the environment's components. The sections on geology and water have received special attention because the area's geological, geomorphological, and hydraulic characteristics are critical to comprehending the commercial, industrial, and transportational aspects of the corridor's historical development.

For example, the various sandstone and coal deposits in the area and their extraction and usage comprise key factors in the region's economic and social history. Likewise, a researcher would find useful the sources that have been cited on the Illinois River system and the ecological impact that the region's development has had on that river system. The major debate in the construction of the Sanitary and Ship Canal by the city of Chicago revolved less around the need for a deep waterway to the Mississippi River than it did around the accompanying pollution problems caused by the canal.

Having an understanding of climate is also important since periodic severe flooding along the Illinois River system has affected the habitability and economics of the small towns and nearby farms. For those interested in conservation and park environments, there is also a section on the flora and fauna of the corridor—past and present.

The Physical Environment—*General*

Huett, J. W. *Natural History of LaSalle County, Illinois.* 2 v. Ottawa, Illinois: Fair Dealer Printing, 1897.
IU

Vol. 1 covers botany, and Vol. 2 covers zoology. A good source for information on plant life and mineral resources along the waterway.

Illinois State Laboratory of Natural History, Urbana. *Bulletin of the Illinois State Laboratory of Natural History....* Vols. 1–12. Bloomington, Illinois: Illinois State Laboratory of Natural History, 1876–1918. illus., plates, maps, tables, diagrs.
DLC, ICJ, ICN, IHi

Twelve volumes covering all aspects of Illinois natural history. Includes bibliographies.

Ladner, Elizabeth, and Trabert, Angela L. *Catalog of Environmental Literature, State of Illinois: Including Collections of Environmental Information Center, Illinois State Library and, Environmental Protection Agency.* Chicago: State of Illinois, Institute of Environmental Quality, 1974. 144 p.
IU

The Physical Environment—*Geography*

Ashton, Bessie L. *The Geonomic Aspects of the Illinois Waterway.* University of Illinois Studies in the Social Sciences, No. 14. Urbana, Illinois: University of Illinois, 1926. 177 p., illus., maps, tables, diagrs.
DLC, ICU, IU

Bibliography, pp. 158–173.

Barrows, Harlan H. *Geography of the Middle Illinois Valley.* Illinois State Geological Survey, Bulletin, No. 15. Urbana, Illinois: Phillips Bros. Printers, 1910.
IC, ICJ, ICN, ICU, IU

Reprinted 1925.

Billings, Isabel Katherine. "The LaSalle–Peru–Oglesby Industrial Area as a Type Unit Study in Geography." M.S. thesis, Illinois State University, 1945. 76 p., maps.
ILa

Covers the major industries in the region, the minor industries in the region, and the future of the tri-cities. Includes photos, charts, maps.

Bleininger, Albert Victor, Lines, E. F., and Laymen, F. E. *Portland Cement Resources of Illinois.* Illinois State Geological Survey, Bulletin, No. 17. Urbana, Illinois: University of Illinois, 1919. 121 p., plates, diagrs.
IC, ICF, ICJ, ICU

Covers Portland cement, limestone, clay, and the mines and minerals of Illinois.

Branom, Fred K. "Some Geographic Factors in the Development of Chicago." *Journal of Geography* 20 (May 1921): 176–186.
DLC, I, IC, ICU, IU

Cady, Gilbert H., Sauer, Carl O., and Cowles, Henry C. *Starved Rock State Park and Its Environs.* Chicago: University of Chicago Press, 1918. 148 p., illus., maps.
DLC, ICU

Part 1: the geography of Starved Rock area by Carl O. Sauer. Part 2: the geology of the area. Part 3: botany in the area.

Chambers, William Trout. "A Geographic Study of Joliet, Illinois, An Urban Center Dominated by Manufacturing." Ph.D. dissertation, University of Chicago, 1926. 257 p., maps, views.
ICU

An analysis of the distribution of residential and business sections of the Joliet area plus an explanation of the competitive advantages and disadvantages that the city possesses for each of its major businesses. Contains over forty pages of photographs of factories, houses, downtown stores, and institutional buildings.

Conzen, Michael P. and Hanson, David B. "The DesPlaines Valley—Historical Landscape of Business." *Bulletin of the Illinois Geographical Society* 2 (Fall 1981): 3–17.
ICU, ICUI

Concerns the evolution of the cultural landscape of the DesPlaines Valley. Identifies forces that created the landscape and argues that its heritage can be used by local communities as sources for their own histories.

Goldthwait, Walter James. *Physical Features of the Des Plaines Valley.* Illinois State Geological Survey, Bulletin, No. 11. Urbana, Illinois: University of Illinois, 1909. 103 p., illus., maps.
DLC, IC, ICF, ICJ, ICU

Goode, John Paul. *The Geographic Background of Chicago.* Chicago: University of Chicago Press, 1926. 70 p., illus., maps, diagrs.
ICU

Martin, Laura Hatch. "The Geography of DuPage County, Illinois." M.S. thesis, University of Chicago, 1911.
ICU

Mayer, Harold M. "The Launching of Chicago: The Situations and the Site." *Chicago History* 9 (Summer 1980): 68–79.
DLC, IC, ICF, ICHi, ICN, ICU, IU

"Notes on Illinois: Surface of the Country." *Illinois Monthly Magazine.* 1 (November 1830): 55–70.
DLC, ICN, ICU, IU

Generalized geographical description of Illinois. Includes commentary on the Illinois River valley and the benefits to be gained through construction of the canal.

Sauer, Carl O. *Geography of the Upper Illinois Valley and History of Its Development.* Illinois State Geological Survey, Bulletin, No. 27. Urbana, Illinois: University of Illinois, 1916. 208 p., front., illus., map, diagrs.
DLC, IC, ICF, ICJ, ICU

Tompkins, Bruce C. "The Port of Joliet and Its Relationship to the Illinois Waterway." M.S. thesis, Northern Illinois University, 1963.
IDeKN

Wittrup, Robert C. "The Functional Patterns of Ottawa, Illinois, and Environs." M.S. thesis, Illinois State University, 1951.
INS

The Physical Environment—*Geology*

Bolyard, Garrett L. "Pleistocene Features of the Palos Park Region." M.S. thesis, University of Chicago, 1923. 51 p., photos., maps, diagrs.
ICU

Bibliography, pp. 3–6.

Breta, J. H. *Geology of the Chicago Region.* 2 v. Illinois State Geological Survey, Bulletin, No. 64. Urbana, Illinois: University of Illinois, 1939. illus., maps.
DLC, IC, ICF, ICJ, ICU

Cady, Gilbert H. *Geology and Mineral Resources of the Hennepin and LaSalle Quadrangles.* Illinois State Geological Survey, Bulletin, No. 37. Urbana, Illinois: University of Illinois, 1919. 136 p., illus., maps, diagrs.
DLC, IC, ICF, ICJ, ICU

Cady, Gilbert H. *The Structure of the LaSalle Anticline.* Illinois State Geological Survey, Bulletin, No. 36. Urbana, Illinois: University of Illinois, 1920. 179 p., illus., maps, diagrs.
DLC, IC, ICF, ICJ, ICU
Bibliography, pp. 94–96.

Culver, H. E. *Geology and Mineral Resources of the Morris Quadrangle.* Illinois State Geological Survey, Bulletin, No. 43. Urbana, Illinois: University of Illinois, 1923.
DLC, IC, ICF, ICJ, ICU
Originally the author's Ph.D. dissertation, The University of Chicago, 1923.

Curner, Louis W. "Geology of the LaSalle and Streator Quadrangles." M.A. thesis, Syracuse University, 1930.
NSyU

Ekblaw, George E., and Lamar, J. E. *Sand and Gravel, Resources of Northeastern Illinois.* Illinois State Geological Survey, Circular, No. 359. Urbana, Illinois: State Geological Survey, 1964.
IC, ICJ, ICU, IU

Frye, John C. *Guide Leaflet, Geological Science Field Trip; Marseilles-Ottawa Area.* Urbana, Illinois: Illinois Dept. of Registration and Education, State Geological Survey Division, 1956. 34 p., maps.
IU
A self-study guide to the geology and physiography of the Marseilles and Ottawa quadrangles.

Frye, John C. *Guide Leaflet, Geological Science Field Trip; Morris Area.* Urbana, Illinois: Illinois Dept. of Registration and Education, State Geological Survey Division, 1961. 28 p., maps.
IMo
A guide to the geology and physiography of the Morris and Wilmington quadrangles.

Frye, John C. *Guide Leaflet, Geological Science Field Trip; Starved Rock Area.* Urbana, Illinois: Illinois Dept. of Registration and Education, State Geological Survey Division, 1962. 56 p., maps.
IO
A self-study guide to the geology and physiography of the LaSalle, Ottawa, Streator, and Wenona quadrangles.

Fryxell, Fritiof Melvin. *The Physiography of the Region of Chicago.* Chicago: University of Chicago Press, 1927. 55 p., illus., maps, diagrs.
ICF, ICU
Selected bibliography, pp. 51–52.

Fuller, J. Jay. *The Silica Sands of Ottawa.* Ottawa, Illinois: The Ottawa Silica Company, 1926.
IO
Short, concise geology and description of the silica sands of Ottawa.

Gardner, Carl L. and Associates, Inc. *Natural Resource Study. Grundy County, Illinois, 1973.* Chicago: Carl L. Gardner & Associates, 1973. 69 p., maps.
IMo
Includes climate, geology, physiography (minerals) suitability study, agricultural suitability, mineral extraction suitability, open space suitability, and pollution control programs. Includes bibliography.

"The Geological Survey." *Journal of the Illinois State Historical Society* 3 (January 1911): 116–118.
DLC, I, IC, ICHi, ICN, ICU, IEN, IU
Update on work of Illinois Geological Survey. Bulletin, No. 15, "Geography of the Middle Illinois Valley."

Gifford, John D. "The Sag—10,000 Years Ago," *Where the Trails Cross* (Spring 1977): 101–102. illus.
ICN
Geology of the Sag Bridge–Lemont area.

Griffin, Judson Roy. "The Fauna of the LaSalle Limestone." Ph.D. dissertation, University of Illinois, 1931. 1,321 p., plates.
IU

Guthrie, Ossian. *Relics Turned Up in the Drainage Canal.* Chicago: Donohue & Henneberry, Printers, [1896]. 17 p., illus.
DLC, ICU
Reprinted from the *Journal of the Western Society of Engineers.* Covers the Glacial Epoch in Northeastern Illinois.

Hathaway, John Cummins. "Roundness and Sphericity of the St. Peter Sandstone from

Ottawa, Illinois." M.S. thesis, University of Illinois, 1952.
IU

Hoover, L. R. and Schicht, R. J. *Development in Deep Sandstone Aquifer along the Illinois River in LaSalle County.* Illinois Dept. of Registration and Education, Report of Investigation, No. 59. Urbana, Illinois: State Water Survey, 1967. 23 p., maps, charts, tables.
IO

Hughes, Delores M. "Petrography of the LaSalle Limestone [Pennsylvanian], LaSalle County, Illinois." M.S. thesis. Northern Illinois University, 1972. 83 p., illus., map, diagrs.
IDeKN

Fisher, Daniel J. "Geology of the Joliet, Illinois Quadrangle." Ph.D. dissertation, University of Chicago, 1923. 160 p., illus., maps, diagr.
DLC, ICU

Also in Bulletin, No. 51, Illinois State Geological Survey. Bibliography, p. 153.

Illinois. State Geological Survey. *List of Publications of the Illinois State Geological Survey.* Urbana, Illinois: State Geological Survey, 1974. 102 p.
ICU, IU

Bibliography includes geology of Illinois, mines and minerals of Illinois, and the state's Geological Survey Bibliography.

Illinois. State Geological Survey. *List of Publications on Illinois Geology, Mineral Resources, and Mineral Industries.* Vol. 1–. Urbana, Illinois: State of Illinois, 1931–. illus., maps.
DLC, IU

Title varies, but includes periodical bibliography of Illinois geology, mines and mineral resources, and mineral industries.

Illinois. State Geological Survey. *List of Publications on Illinois Geology, Mineral Resources, and Mineral Industries. List of Published Maps and Index to List of Publications.* Vol. 1–. Urbana, Illinois: Illinois State Geological Survey, 1933–. illus., maps.
DLC

Illinois. State Geologist. *Geological Survey of Illinois.* 8 v. Springfield: State Journal Steam Press, 1866–1890. fronts., illus., plates, maps.
DLC, ICJ

A complete geological survey of Illinois by topic and county, ranging from coal to gas to limestone deposits to paleontology to fossils.

Lamar, John Everts and Willman, Harold Bowen. *High-Calcium Limestone Near Morris, Illinois.* Illinois State Geological Survey, Report of Investigations, No. 23. Urbana, Illinois: Jefferson Printing & Stationery Co., 1931. 26 p., illus., maps, tables.
IC, ICJ, ICU, IU

Langford, George. *The Wilmington Coal Fauna and Additions to the Wilmington Coal Flora from a Pennsylvanian Deposit in Will County Illinois.* [DeKalb, Illinois]: Esconi Associates, 1963. 280 p., photos., charts, map.
IJo

Includes index.

Martin, Michael David. "LaSalle Limestone [Upper Pennsylvanian] Conodonts of LaSalle County, Illinois." M.S. thesis, University of Illinois, 1974. 92 p., illus., map.
IU

Morse, Margaret L. "The Micro-Fauna from the Pennsylvania Strata Near LaSalle, Illinois." M.A. thesis, Northwestern University, 1935.
IEN

Nichols, Henry Windsor. *Early Geological History of Chicago.* Field Museum of Natural History, Geology Leaflet, No. 7. Chicago: Field Museum of Natural History, 1925. 30 p., illus., plates, maps.
ICF, ICU

Ostrum, Meredith E. *Subsurface Dolomite and Limestone Resources of Grundy and Kendall Counties.* Illinois State Geological Survey, Circular, No. 230. Urbana, Illinois: State Geological Survey, 1957.
IC, ICJ, ICU, IMo, IU

Payne, James Norman. "Subsurface Geology of the Marseilles, Ottawa, and Streator Quadrangles and Vicinity, Illinois." Ph.D. dissertation, University of Chicago, 1938. 195 p., illus., tables, plate, maps, profiles.
ICU

Same as Bulletin, No. 66, Illinois State Geological Survey. Includes bibliography.

Shepard, Charles Upham. "Geology of Upper Illinois." *The American Journal of Science and Arts* 34 (July 1838): 134–161.
IC, ICN, IU

Comments on the prairies west of Chicago, the I&M Canal route.

U.S. Dept. of Agriculture. Soil Conservation Service. *Resource Study of Northeastern Illinois. Illinois Area 2, 1967.* Lincoln, Nebraska: United States Department of Agriculture, Soil Conservation Service, 1967. 120 p., tables, maps, charts, illus.
IMo

Covers Grundy County and LaSalle County and includes soil and climate, geology and minerals, water resources, agriculture, special reports and industries, social and economic resources, and land use and people.

Willman, Harold Bowen. *Bibliography and Index of Illinois Geology through 1965; a Contribution to the Illinois Sesquicentennial Year.* Illinois State Geological Survey, Bulletin, No. 92. Urbana, Illinois: State Geological Survey, 1968. 373 p.
DLC, IC, ICF, ICJ, ICU

Willman, Harold Bowen. "General Geology and Mineral Resources of the Illinois Deep Waterway from Chicago to Peoria." Ph.D. dissertation, University of Illinois, 1931.
IU

Willman, Harold Bowen. *Geology Along the Illinois Waterway: A Basis for Environmental Planning.* Illinois State Geological Survey, Circular, No. 478. Urbana, Illinois: State Geological Survey, 1973. 48 p., maps.
IC, ICJ, ICU, IU

Bibliography, pp. 42–48.

Willman, Harold Bowen. *Summary of the Geology of the Chicago Area.* Illinois State Geological Survey, Circular, No. 460. Urbana, Illinois: State Geological Survey, 1971. 77 p., figs., map.
DLC, ICF, ICN, IJo, IU

An important source for general geology of the Chicago region.

Willman, Harold Bowen and Payne, J. Norman. *Geology and Mineral Resources of the Marseilles, Ottawa, and Streator Quadrangles.* Illinois State Geological Survey, Bulletin, No. 66. Urbana, Illinois: State Geological Survey, 1942. 388 p., illus., maps, diagrs., tables.
DLC, IC,ICF, ICJ, ICU, IU

Worthen, A. H. *Economical Geology of Illinois.* 3 v. Springfield: H. W. Rokker, State Printer and Binder, 1882. 541 p., illus.
DLC, ICJ, IU

A complete and thorough geological survey of Illinois and all of its counties by Illinois state geologist. Reprinted from the original reports of the Geological Survey with additions and amendments.

The Physical Environment—*Soil*

Alexander, J. D. and Paschke, J. E. *Soil Survey: LaSalle County, Illinois.* Agricultural Experiment Station, Soil Report, No. 91. Urbana, Illinois: University of Illinois, 1972.
IU

Hopkins, Cyril. *DuPage County Soils.* University of Illinois Agricultural Experiment Station, Soil Report No. 16. Urbana, Illinois: University of Illinois, 1917. 56 p., charts, map.
ICJ, IU

Hopkins, C. G., Mosier, J. G., Pettit, J. H., and Readhimer, H. E. *LaSalle County Soils.* University of Illinois Agricultural Experiment Station, Soil Report, No. 5. Urbana, Illinois: University of Illinois, 1913. 45 p., illus., maps.
DLC, ICJ, IDeKN—IRAD, IU

Smith, R. S., DeTurk, E. D., Bauer, F. C., and Smith, L. H. *Grundy County Soils.* Illinois Agricultural Experiment Station, Soil Report, No. 26. Urbana, Illinois: University of Illinois, 1924. 66 p., illus., maps, tables.
DLC, ICJ, IU

Smith, R. S., Ellis, O. I., DeTurk, E. D., and Smith, L. H. *Will County Soils.* Illinois Agricultural Experiment Station, Soil Report, No. 35. Urbana, Illinois: University of Illinois, 1926. 61 p., illus., maps, tables.
DLC, ICJ, IU

Thornburn, Thomas Hampton. *Surface Deposits of Illinois: A Guide for Soil Engineers.* University of Illinois Engineering Experiment Station, Circular, No. 80. Urbana, Illinois: University of Illinois, 1963. 135 p., illus., maps.
ICF

The Physical Environment—*Water*

Bartow, Edward. *Municipal Water Supplies of Illinois.* Illinois State Water Survey, Bulletin, No. 5. Urbana, Illinois: University of Illinois, 1907. 123 p., map.
DLC, IC, ICF, ICJ, ICU

Boruff, Clair S. and Buswell, A. M. *Illinois River Studies, 1925–1928.* Illinois State Water Survey, Bulletin, No. 28. Urbana, Illinois: Journal Printing Co., 1929. 127 p., maps, tables, diagrs.
DLC, IC, ICF, ICJ, ICU

Chicago. Sanitary District. Board of Trustees. *Report of George M. Wisner, Chief Engineer, Relating to Existing Lake Levels, January, 1917. Adopted by the Board of Trustees at Its Meeting Held March 1, 1917.* Chicago: Sanitary District, 1917. 7 p.
DLC, ICJ

Chicago. Sanitary District. Board of Trustees. *Report of Streams Examination, Chemic and Bacteriologic, of the Waters Between Lake Michigan and the Mississippi River at St. Louis, for the Purpose of Determining Their Condition and Quality Before and After the Opening of the Drainage Channel. Made Under the Direction of Arthur R. Reynolds, M.D., Commissioner of Health.* Chicago: The Blakeley Printing Company, 1902. 196 p., front., illus.
ICJ, ICU

Chicago. Sanitary District. Committee on Engineering. *Report on Pollution of [the] DesPlaines River and Remedies Therefore.* Chicago: Barnard and Miller, 1914. 55 p., map, tables, profiles, diagrs.
ICJ, ICU

Report made to Board of Trustees of the Sanitary District of Chicago, July, 1914.

Chicago. Sanitary District. Engineering Board of Review. *Report on the Lake Lowering Controversy and a Program of Remedial Measures. Parts 1–3.* 3 v. Chicago: Sanitary District, 1924–1927. Plates, maps, tables, diagrs.
ICU

Part 1: recommendations, including brief statement of findings and conclusions. Part 2: the technical bases for the recommendations of the board of review. Part 3: Appendix 1—Sewage Disposal, Appendix 2—Hydrology of Great Lakes.

Cooley, Lyman E. *The Illinois River: Physical Relations and the Removal of the Navigation Dams, with Supplement of the Waterway Relations of the Sanitary and Ship Canal of Chicago.* Chicago: Clohery and Co., 1914. 121 p., tables, 4 diagrs.
ICJ, ICRL

Provides a description of the physical conditions that existed in the Illinois Valley in relation to the Waterway and the Sanitary and Ship Canal of Chicago. Includes general statements about Illinois River basin, the alluvial valley, the upper and lower divisions of the Illinois River. Includes maps, surveys, reports, and flow records in relation to the Illinois River basin and the sanitary problem.

Egan, James A., Long, John H., and Zeit, F. Robert. *Report of Sanitary Investigations of the Illinois, Mississippi, and Missouri Rivers with Relation to the Effect of the Sewage of the City of Chicago and the Sanitary Conditions of the Water Supplies of the Cities of Chicago and St. Louis.* Illinois State Board of Health. Springfield: Board of Health, 1903. 23 p., diagr., maps.
DLC, ICJ

Report was compiled in 1902, but its publication was delayed until the conclusion of testimony in the suit brought by the state of Missouri in the Supreme Court of the United States against the Sanitary District of Chicago, alleging pollution of the Mississippi River.

Elmore, G. R. *Historical Water Quality Data: Chicago River, Sanitary and Ship Canal, and Calumet River Systems.* Northeastern Illinois Planning Commission, Staff Paper, No. 18. Chicago: Northeastern Illinois Planning Commission, 1977.
ICU

Includes detailed data. Identifies present problems with water quality and with past trends.

Ferguson, Harry F. *Inventory of the Pollution of DesPlaines River and Tributaries [excluding Salt Creek] from Cook–Will County Line to Wisconsin State Line and Recommendations for Abatement and Prevention of Pollution.* Springfield:

Sanitary Water Board of Cook County Forest Preserve, 1933. plates, maps, tables.
DLC, IU

Forbes, Stephen A. and Richardson, R. E. *Studies on the Biology of the Upper Illinois River.* Urbana, Illinois: State Laboratory of Natural History, 1913. 574 p.
ICU, IU

Greenfield, Robert E., Weinhold, G. A., and Buswell, A. M. *Comparison of Chemical and Bacteriological Examinations Made on Illinois River During a Season of Low and a Season of High Water: 1923–1924.* Illinois State Water Survey, Bulletin, No. 20. Urbana, Illinois: State Register, 1925. 59 p., illus., tables, diagrs.
DLC, IC, ICF, ICJ, ICU

Horner, W. W. *Water Plan for the Illinois River Basin in the States of Illinois, Wisconsin, and Indiana.* 2 v. Washington: U.S. National Resources Committee, 1936. Maps, diagrs.
ICU

Vol. 1 is a general report and Vol. 2 is a summary report.

Horton, A. H. *Water Resources of Illinois . . . With an Appendix of Water Power and Drainage Districts of Illinois.* Illinois Rivers and Lakes Commission, Bulletin, No. 14. Springfield: Illinois State Journal Company, 1914. 400 p., plates, maps, diagrs.
DLC, ICJ, ICU

Prepared in cooperation with the U.S. Geological Survey. Devotes a major section to Illinois Waterway.

Illinois. Department of Public Works and Buildings. Division of Waterways. *Floods in Illinois in 1922: Causes, Results, and Remedies.* Springfield: Illinois State Journal Co., 1922. 29 p., illus., profile, diagrs.
ICJ

Refers to flooding on Illinois River. The investigation was made by Mortimer G. Barnes, chief engineer.

Illinois. Division of Waterways. *Flood Control Report: An Engineering Study of the Flood Situation in the State of Illinois.* Chicago: State of Illinois, 1929. 402 p., maps, charts, diagrs.
ICJ, IJo

Flood control on the Illinois River, general discussion of river floods, rainfall and climate patterns, the hydraulics of the river, back water profile computations, tables, figures.

Illinois. Division of Waterways. *Preliminary Examination Report for Flood Control, Hickory Creek at Joliet, November, 1948.* n.p., 1948. 10 p., map, diagr.
DLC, IU

Illinois. Division of Waterways. *Report.* Vol. 1–. Springfield: Rivers and Lakes Commission, 1917/1918–. Illus. maps.
DLC, ICU

Annual report. Supercedes the *Report* issued by the Canal Commissioners (1836–1917).

Illinois. Division of Waterways. *Survey Report for Flood Control, Illinois and Michigan Canal and Tributaries, Joliet to Calumet–Sag Channel* Springfield: Division of Waterways, 1951. 50 p., illus., maps, diagrs., profiles, tables.
DLC, IU

Illinois. Illinois Valley Flood Control Commission. *Hearings Held by Illinois Valley Flood Control Commission on the Causes and Control of Floods in the Illinois River Valley.* [Springfield]: Illinois Valley Flood Control Commission, 1929. 261 p., maps, tables.
DLC, ICJ

Illinois. State Planning Commission. *Report on the Upper Illinois River Basin in Illinois.* Springfield: State of Illinois, Dept. of Public Works and Buildings, Division of Waterways, 1939. 62 p., maps, tables, diagrs.
DLC, ICJ, ICU

Revised edition of the report prepared for National Water Resources Survey of the National Resources Committee, 1936–1937.

Illinois. Rivers and Lakes Commission. *A Compilation of Money Spent by the Government on Various Harbors, Rivers, and Canals and the Riparian Property Holder Benefited.* Illinois Rivers and Lakes Commission, Bulletin, No. 5. Springfield: Illinois Journal Co., State Printers, 1912. 38 p.
NN

Illinois. Sanitary Water Board. *Inventory of the Pollution of Little Calumet River and Tributaries and Recommendations for the Abatement and Prevention of Pollution.* Springfield:

Sanitary Water Board, 1933. 5 p., illus., plates, maps, tables.
DLC

Illinois. State Planning Commission. *Report on the Upper Illinois River Basin in Illinois.* Revised Edition of the Report Prepared for the National Water Resources Survey of the National Resources Committee, 1936–1937. Chicago: Dept. of Public Works and Buildings, Division of Waterways, 1939. 56 p., tables, charts, maps.
ICJ, IMo, IO

Covers streams of the basin, extent and adequacy of existing water development, ground water, pollution, summary of deficiencies and future needs, and comprehensive plan of development.

Illinois. State Water Survey. *Chemical Survey of the Waters of Illinois: Report for the Years 1897–1902.* Illinois State Water Survey, Publication, No. 2. Urbana, Illinois: University of Illinois, 1903. 254 p., maps, diagrs.
DLC, ICJ

Illinois. State Water Survey. *Ground Water Supplies of the Chicago–Joliet–Chicago Heights Area.* Illinois State Water Survey, Bulletin, No. 15. Urbana, Illinois: State Water Survey Division, 1943. 285 p., maps, tables, diagrs., illus.
DLC, ICJ, ICU

Illinois. State Water Survey. *Sandstone Water Supplies of the Joliet Area.* Illinois State Water Survey, Bulletin, No. 34. Urbana, Illinois: State Water Survey Division, 1941. 128 p., illus., maps, tables.
DLC, ICJ, IU

Illinois. State Water Survey. *Some Economic Problems of the Illinois River Valley.* Illinois State Water Survey, Circular, No. 12. Urbana, Illinois: State of Illinois, 1931. 72 p., front., illus., map, diagrs.
IU

Papers presented before the economics section of the Illinois State Academy of Science, Peoria, May 8, 1931. Includes bibliography.

Ivens, J. Loreena and Motherway, Patricia A. *Annotated List of Publications, 1895–1975.* Urbana, Illinois: State Water Survey, 1975. 92 p., map.
IU

Includes index and bibliographies on Illinois water supply, climate, and water survey.

Ivens, J. Loreena and Motherway, Patricia A. *1975–1980 Supplement to Annotated List of Publications.* Urbana, Illinois: State Water Survey, Illinois Institute of Natural Resources, 1980. 36 p., map.
IU

Bibliography on Illinois water supply, climate, and water surveys.

Kofoid, Charles Atwood. *The Plankton of the Illinois River, 1894–1899, with Introductory Notes Upon the Hydrography of the Illinois River and Its Basin.* 2 v. Champaign, Illinois: State Laboratory of Natural History, 1903–1908. Plates, maps, tables, diagrs.
DLC, ICUI, IU

Bibliography, Part 1: pp. 341–354, Part 2: pp. 619–624.

Lopinot, A. C. *Channelized Streams and Ditches of Illinois.* Illinois Dept. of Conservation, Division of Fisheries, Report, No. 35. Springfield: State of Illinois, 1972. 59 p.
DLC

Rauch, John H. *Water Supplies of Illinois and the Pollution of Its Streams.* Illinois State Board of Health. Springfield: State of Illinois, 1889. 81 p., tables.
DLC, ICJ, ICU

Includes two appendices, "Chemical Investigations of the Water Supplies of Illinois," by J. J. Long, and "The Illinois River Basin in Its Relation to Sanitary Engineering," by L. E. Cooley.

Report on the Water Supply Situation in the Joliet Area. Kansas City, Missouri: Black & Veatch, 1942. 51 p.
IU

Sherman, LeRoy K. *Stream Pollution and Sewage Disposal in Illinois with Reference to Public Policy and Legislation.* Illinois Rivers and Lakes Commission, Bulletin, No. 16. Chicago: Rivers and Lakes Commission, 1915. 32 p., tables.
ICU, NN

Discusses legislation and public policy that affected the Illinois Waterway and Chicago Drainage Canal.

Smith, Walter M. *Stream Flow Data of Illinois.* Springfield: Illinois Division of Waterways, 1937. 690 p., tables.
DLC, ICU

Published in cooperation with the U.S. Geological Survey. Volume is really second edition of *Water Resources of Illinois,* published by the state of Illinois in 1914. Reprints many of the earlier data but also contains more information gathered in the interim.

"Some Reprints from Old Books and Periodicals: The Illinois River." *Journal of the Illinois State Historical Society* 2 (January 1910): 77–79.
DLC, I, IC, ICHi, ICN, ICU, IEN, IU

Extracts from Samuel R. Brown's 1817 *The Western Gazetteer.* Describes Illinois River watershed.

U.S. Army. Corps of Engineers. *Illinois River, Illinois Letter from the Secretary of War Transmitting Report from the Chief of Engineers on the Illinois River, Illinois, Covering Navigation, Flood Control, Power Development, and Irrigation. . . .* H. Doc. 182, 72nd Cong., 1st Sess., 1932. 108 p., tables, maps, profiles.
DLC, ICU

Vidal, Paul J. *DuPage County Surface Water Resources.* Springfield: Illinois Dept. of Conservation, 1969. 161 p.
ISCon

White, Max R. *Water Supply Organization in the Chicago Region.* Chicago: The University of Chicago Press, 1934. 170 p., maps, illus.
DLC, ICU

Thorough treatment and analysis of water supply system in Chicago area, pollution control therein, and comparison of Chicago with other metropolitan systems. Includes bibliography, index.

The Physical Environment—*Climate*

Changnon, Stanley A. *Illinois Weather and Climate Information: Where to Find It.* Illinois State Water Survey, Circular, No. 123. Urbana, Illinois: State Water Survey, 1975. 32 p.
DLC, ICJ, ICU

Fuller, M. L. "The Climate of Illinois: Its Permanence." *Illinois State Historical Society Transactions* 13 (1912): 54–62.
DLC, IC, ICU

Huff, Floyd A. and Vogel, John L. *Hydrometeorology of Heavy Rain Storms in Chicago and Northeastern Illinois: Phase 1, Historical Studies.* Urbana, Illinois: Illinois Dept. of Registration and Education, Illinois State Water Survey, 1976.
DLC, IU

Bibliography, pp. 62–63.

Illinois. State Water Survey. *Local Climatological Data, 1901–1962, Ottawa, Illinois.* Illinois Water Survey, Miscellaneous Publication, No. 23. Urbana, Illinois: State Water Survey, 1964. 6 p.
DLC, ICJ, ICU

Page, John Lorence. *Climate of Illinois: Summary and Analysis of Long-Time Weather Records.* Abridged ed. Illinois Agricultural Experiment Station, Bulletin, No. 532. Urbana, Illinois: University of Illinois Press, 1949.
ICU, IEN, IU

The Physical Environment—*Flora and Fauna*

Aver, Nancy A., ed. *Identification of Larval Fishes of the Great Lakes with Emphasis on the Lake Michigan Drainage.* Ann Arbor, Michigan: Great Lakes Fishery Commission, 1982. 744 p., illus.
ICF

Bibliography, pp. 677–737.

Beecher, W. J. "The Lost Illinois Prairie." *Chicago History* 2 (Spring/Summer 1973): 166–72.
DLC, IC, ICF, ICHi, ICN, ICU, IU

Bellrose, Frank Chapman, Paveglio, Fred L., Jr., and Steffeck, Donald W. *Waterfowl Populations and the Changing Environment of the Illinois River Valley.* Urbana, Illinois: Illinois Institute of Natural Resources, Natural History Survey Division, 1979. 54 p., illus.
IU

Bibliography, p. 51, includes index.

Brendel, Frederick. *Flora Peoriana: The Vegetation in the Climate of Middle Illinois.* Peoria, Illinois: J. W. Franks and Sons, Printers, 1887. 89 p.
ICF

Eifert, Virginia L. *Illinois Mammals, Today and Yesterday.* Illinois State Museum, Story of Illinois Series, No. 2. Springfield: Illinois State Museum, 1951. 38 p., illus.
DLC, ISM

Forbes, Stephen A. *Biological Investigations on the Illinois River: The Work of the Illinois Biological Station 2. The Investigation of a River System in the Interest of its Fisheries.* Urbana, Illinois: 1910. 14 p.
DLC, ICJ, ICU, IU

Ford, Edward Russell, Sanborn, Colin C., and Coursen, C. Blair. *Birds of the Chicago Region.* Illinois Audubon Society and Chicago Academy of Sciences, Bulletin, Vol. 5, Nos. 2 and 3. Chicago: Chicago Academy of Sciences, 1934. 80 p., illus.
DLC, ICF

Fraser, William E. *Native Trees, Shrubs, and Vines in LaSalle County, Illinois.* Urbana, Illinois: University of Illinois, Dept. of Landscape Architecture, n.d. 40 p.
IU

Includes bibliography. A thorough listing of flora in LaSalle County.

Glassman, Sidney F. *Grass Flora of the Chicago Region.* American Naturalist Series, Vol. 72, No. 1. Notre Dame, Indiana: University of Notre Dame Press, 1964. 49 p., map.
ICF

Bibliography, pp. 48–49.

Graber, Richard R. and Graber, Jean W. *A Comparative Study of Bird Populations in Illinois, 1906–1909 and 1956–1958.* Illinois Natural History Survey, Bulletin, Vol. 28, Art. 3. Urbana, Illinois: State Natural History Survey, 1963. 145 p., illus., map.
DLC, ICF, IU

Bibliography, pp. 516–518.

Hart, Charles A. *On the Entomology of the Illinois River and Adjacent Water, Part 1.* Illinois State Laboratory of Natural History, Bulletin, Vol. 4, Arts. 6 and 7. Springfield: H. W. Rokker, Printer and Binder, 1895. 125 p., plates.
DLC, IU

Illinois River insects.

Higley, William Kerr and Raddin, Charles S. *The Flora of Cook County, Illinois, and a Part of Lake County, Indiana.* Chicago Academy of Sciences, Bulletin, Vol. 2, No. 1. Chicago: Chicago Academy of Sciences, 1891. 168 p., front., map, illus.
ICF

Hoffmeister, Donald F. and Mohr, Carl O. *Fieldbook of Illinois Mammals.* Natural History Survey, Manual, No. 4. Urbana, Illinois: Natural History Survey, 1957. 233 p., illus., maps.
DLC, ICF, IU

Bibliography, pp. 220–222.

Hubbs, Carl L. and Lagler, Karl F. *Guide to the Fishes of the Great Lakes and Tributary Waters.* Cranbrook Institute of Science, Bulletin, No. 18. Bloomfield Hills, Michigan: The Cranbrook Institute of Science, 1941. 100 p., illus., plates.
DLC, ICF

List of references, pp. 84–91.

Illinois. Dept. of Conservation. *Illinois Game, Fish, Forests, Fur Bearing Animals.* Belleville, Illinois: Advocate Printing Co., [1931]. 75 p., illus., maps.
DLC, ICJ

Illinois. Natural History Survey. *Available Publications of the Illinois Natural History Survey and of Its Predecessors, the State Entomologist's Office and the State Laboratory of Natural History.* Vol. 1–. Urbana, Illinois: Natural History Survey Division, 1935–.
DLC, IU

Includes bibliographies.

Illinois. Natural History Survey. *Fieldbook of Illinois Wild Flowers: Six Hundred Fifty of the More Common Flowering Plants in the State.* Illinois Natural History Survey, Manual, No. 1. Urbana, Illinois: State Dept. of Registration and Education. Division of Natural History Survey, 1936. 406 p., front., illus., tables.
ICF, ICJ, IU

Illinois. Natural History Survey. *Natural History Survey of Illinois.* 4 v. Bloomington, Illinois: Reprinted by Pantagraph Printing and Stationery Co., 1913–?. illus., fronts., plates, tables, atlas of maps.
DLC, NN

Bibliographies throughout. Includes the ornithology of Illinois, fishes of Illinois, and atlas.

Illinois State Laboratory of Natural History. *Bulletin of the Illinois State Laboratory of Natural History.* Vols. 1–12. Bloomington, Illinois: State Natural History Survey, 1876/1883–1915/1917.
ICU, IU

The twelve volumes, each of which has articles on mostly statewide flora and fauna topics, deal in highly specific subject matter, mostly biological and botanical. Consult card catalogs for specific subjects. Place of publication varies.

Illinois Wildlife. Vol. 1–. Champaign, Illinois: Federation of Sportsmen's Clubs, 1945–. illus.
I, IU

Quarterly publication.

Laughlin, Kendall. *Manual of the Hawthornes of Cook and DuPage Counties of Illinois.* Standard ed. Chicago: c. 1956. 79 p., illus.
ICF

Meek, Seth Eugene and Hildebrand, S. F. *A Synoptic List of the Fishes Known to Occur Within Fifty Miles of Chicago.* Field Museum of Natural History, Publication, No. 142, Zoological Series, Vol. 7, No. 9. Chicago: Field Museum of Natural History, 1910. 115 p., illus.
DLC, ICF

Miller, Robert B. and Tehon, Lee R. *The Native and Naturalized Trees of Illinois.* Illinois Natural History Survey, Bulletin, Vol. 18. Urbana, Illinois: State Natural History Survey, 1929. 339 p.
ICF

Mills, Harlow B., Starrett, William E., and Bellrose, Frank C. *Man's Effect on the Fish and Wildlife of the Illinois River.* Illinois Natural History Survey, Biological Notes, No. 57. Urbana, Illinois: State of Illinois, 1966. 24 p.
DLC

Musselman, T. E. "A History of the Birds of Illinois." *Journal of the Illinois State Historical Society* 14 (April/July 1921): 1–73.
DLC, I, IC, ICHi, ICN, ICU, IEN, IU

Covers Illinois setting in 1818, passenger pigeons, wild fowl on Illinois River, eagles on Mississippi, demise of passenger pigeons, summer and winter birds, description of Illinois birds, and laws and clubs for protection of birds.

Parmalee, Paul W. *The Fresh-Water Mussels of Illinois.* Illinois State Museum, Popular Science Series, Vol. 8. Springfield: State of Illinois, 1967. 108 p., illus.
DLC

Bibliography, pp. 102–103.

Pearsall, Gordon S. *List of the Fauna and Flora of the Forest Preserve District of Cook County.* Chicago: The Forest Preserve District of Cook County, 1940. 35 p., illus.
DLC, ICJ

Bibliography, pp. 33–35.

Pepoon, Herman S. *An Annotated Flora of the Chicago Area, With Maps and Many Illustrations from Photographs of Topographic and Plant Features.* The Chicago Academy of Sciences Natural History Survey, Bulletin, No. 8. Chicago: R. Donnelley & Sons Company, 1927. 554 p., front., illus., maps.
DLC, ICF

Pope, Clifford H. *Amphibians and Reptiles of the Chicago Area.* Chicago: Chicago Natural History Museum, 1964. 267 p., illus., plates, maps, figures.
ICF

Covers the area west to Grundy County, Will County, and Kane and DuPage counties. Does not include LaSalle County.

Ries, Donald T., and Werner, Floyd G. "Checklist of the Birds of Starved Rock State Park and Surrounding Territory." *Illinois State Academy of Sciences Transactions* 39 (1936): 136–142.
DLC, I, ICF, ICJ

Smith, Ellen Thorne. *Chicagoland Birds: Where and When to Find Them.* Chicago: Chicago

Natural History Museum, 1958. 47 p., charts, map.
ICF

Includes bibliography.

Starrett, William Charles. *A Survey of the Mussels [Unionacea] of the Illinois River: A Polluted Stream.* Illinois Natural History, Bulletin, Vol. 30, Art. 5. Urbana, Illinois: Natural History Survey Division, 1971. 136 p., illus.
DLC, ICF

Bibliography, pp. 365–367.

Swink, Floyd A. *Plants of the Chicago Region: A Check List of the Vascular Flora of the Region; Notes on Local Distribution and Ecology.* Lisle, Illinois: Morton Arboretum, 1969. 445 p., illus.
DLC, ICF

Swink, Floyd A. and Wilhelm, Gerould. *Plants of the Chicago Region: A Check List of the Vascular Flora of the Chicago Region, with Keys, Notes on Local Distribution, Ecology, and Taxonomy, and a System for Evaluation of Plant Communities.* Lisle, Illinois: Morton Arboretum, c. 1979. 922 p., illus.
ICU

Bibliography, pp. 893–922. Highly technical. Covers all fifteen counties around Chicago, in Illinois. Excellent bibliography.

Thompson, David H. *Some Observations on the Oxygen Requirements of Fishes in the Illinois River.* Illinois Natural History Survey, Bulletin, Vol. 15, Art. 7. Urbana, Illinois: Schnepp & Barnes, Printers, 1925. 15 p., tables.
DLC, ICF, IU

Voss, John and Eifert, Virginia S. *Illinois Wild Flowers.* Illinois State Museum, Popular Science Series, Vol. 3. Springfield: State of Illinois, 2nd printing, revised, 1960. 256 p., illus.
DLC, ICU

Winterringer, Glen and Lopinot, Alvin C. *Aquatic Plants of Illinois: An Illustrated Manual Including Species Submerged, Floating, and Some of Shallow Water and Muddy Shores.* Illinois State Museum, Popular Science Series, Vol. 6. Springfield: Illinois Dept. of Registration and Education and Dept. of Conservation, Division of Fisheries, 1966. 142 p., illus.
ICU

Woodruff, Frank M. *The Birds of the Chicago Area.* Chicago Academy of Sciences Natural History Survey, Bulletin, No. 6. Chicago: Jennings & Graham, 1907. 221 p., front., plates.
DLC, ICF

Bibliography, pp. 196–205.

The Physical Environment—*Ecology*

Alvord, John W. and Burdick, Charles B. *Report of the Rivers and Lakes Commission on the Illinois River and Its Bottom Lands, with Reference to the Conservation of Agriculture and Fisheries and the Control of Floods.* Springfield: Illinois State Journal Co., 1915. 141 p., front., illus., maps, tables, diagrs.
DLC, ICJ, ICU

Forbes, Stephen A. *On the Local Distribution of Certain Illinois Fishes: An Essay in Statistical Ecology.* Illinois. State Laboratory of Natural History, Bulletin, Vol. 7, Art. 8. Urbana, Illinois: State Laboratory of Natural History, 1907. 30 p., 15 maps.
ICF, IU

"Goose Lake Prairie, Next State Conservation Loss?" *The Champaign-Urbana News-Gazette.* n.d. 1 p.
IU—HS

Shelford, Victor E. *Animal Communities in Temperate America, As Illustrated in the Chicago Region: A Study in Animal Ecology.* Geographic Society of Chicago, Bulletin, No. 5. n.p., n.d.
DLC, ICF

Bibliography, pp. 325–336.

Sinclair, Robert A., and Lubinski, Kenneth. *Long-Term Ecological Research: Illinois River and Upper Mississippi River [Large Rivers] Site Report.* Champaign, Illinois: State Water Survey, 1983. 65 p., appendices.
DLC, ICJ

Thone, Frank E. A. "Ecological Factors in [the] Region of Starved Rock, Illinois." Ph.D. dissertation, University of Chicago, 1922. 368 p., diagrs.
ICF, ICU

Reprinted in *Botanical Gazette,* Vol. 84, No. 4, Dec. 1922.

The Physical Environment—*Archive Sources*

Chicago, Illinois. Chicago Historical Society. William L. Bayley Collection.
ICHi

Copy of field notes and river survey of South Branch of the Chicago River.

Ottawa, Illinois. Reddick Library. Vertical File. Ottawa Climatological Data.
IO

Compiled locally and photocopied from Illinois publications.

Peru, Illinois. Peru Public Library. "Historical Geology of Peru, Illinois." Presented to Peru Public Library by Ernest D. Middaugh and Associates, Inc., Rockford, Illinois. Warren Grabav Geologist. 54 p., diagrs., maps, tables. (Typewritten.)
IPe

Includes paleontology.

Springfield, Illinois. Illinois State Historical Library. Henry Horner Papers. Calumet River. Pollution. Indianapolis Meeting. Chicago Sanitary District. Fox River Pollution.
IHi

Urbana, Illinois. Illinois Historical Survey Library. Water Resources Center. Papers, 1967. 85 folders.
IU—HS

Materials gathered from travel narratives and other literature concerning water resources in Illinois, 1673–1850.

New York, New York. New York Public Library. Elmer Lawrence Cothrell Papers. 16 v. and 4 boxes.
NN

Includes material on Cothrell's surveys of the Illinois River.

Asheville, North Carolina. National Climatic Center. Records of the Weather Bureau. Forty cubic feet.
NcAN

Bound volumes of Weather Maps and Bulletins and Crop Bulletins. Chicago, Illinois Station. Covers 1896–1948.

PART 3 Description and Travel

A wide variety of material relating to travel and description in the corridor is available, ranging from early exploration to the twentieth century. Narratives produced by French, English, and American explorers are available beginning in the seventeenth century and provide an important source of information on Native American populations as well. For the nineteenth century, guide books and gazetteers become available, and in the twentieth century we have a variety of place name studies. As a logical and convenient travel route, the corridor area became the subject of many diaries and travel accounts in the nineteenth and twentieth centuries. The first entries in this section list several general sources on description and travel in the corridor, including annotated bibliographies of travel accounts in the Illinois country.

Description and Travel—*General*

Angle, Paul M., ed. *Prairie State: Impressions of Illinois, 1673–1867, by Travelers and Other Observers.* Chicago: University of Chicago Press, 1968.
ICN, ICU

Buck, Solon Justice. *Travel and Description, 1765–1865, Together with a List of County Histories, Atlases, and Biographical Collections and a List of Territorial and State Laws.* Collections of the Illinois State Historical Library, No. 9. Springfield, 1917. 514 p., ports., fronts.
DLC, ICJ, ICN, ICU

Index.

Brymner, Douglas, ed. *Report on Canadian Archives 1883.* Ottawa, 1884.
DLC

Also 1885, 1886, 1887, 1888, and supplements, 1899 and 1901, by Edouard Richard.

Collection de Manuscrits Contenant Lettres, Mémoires, et Autres Documents Historiques Relatifs à la Nouvelle-France. 4 v. Quebec, 1883–1885.
DLC

Hubach, Robert R. *Early Midwestern Travel Narratives: An Annotated Bibliography, 1634–1850.* Detroit: Wayne State University Press, 1961. 149 p.
ICU, IU—HS

Matthews, William, comp. *American Diaries.* University of California Publication in English, No. 16. Berkeley and Los Angeles: University of California Press, 1945.
DLC, ICU

Annotated bibliography of diaries written before 1861.

Pierce, Bessie Louise. *As Others See Chicago: Impressions of Visitors, 1673–1933.* Chicago: University of Chicago Press, 1933. 540 p.
DLC, ICU

List of travelers' accounts, pp. 518–520.

Russell, Ruth Ida. *One Hundred Years of Travel and Trade on the Great Lakes, 1800–1900: A Selected Bibliography.* Madison, Wisconsin: Library School of the University of Wisconsin, 1939.
WU

Surrey, Nancy Maria [Miller], ed. *Calendar of Manuscripts in Paris Archives and Libraries Relating to the History of the Mississippi Valley to 1803.* Privately Printed. Washington, D.C.: Carnegie Institution of Washington, Department of Historical Research, 1926–1928.
ICN, ICU

Description and Travel—*Guide Books*

Cobb, Charles. *American Railway Guide and Pocket Companion for the United States; Containing Correct Tables for Time of Starting from All Stations, Distances, Fares, etc., on All the Railway Lines in the United States, Together with a Complete Railway Map; Also Many State Lines Running in Connection with Railroads.* New York: Dinsmore, 1850. 128 p., map.
DLC

Includes tables for packets on the I&M Canal.

Curtiss, Daniel S. *Western Portraiture and Emigrants' Guide: A Description of Wisconsin, Illinois, and Iowa; with Remarks on Minnesota,*

and Other Territories. New York: Colton, 1852. 351 p., map.
DLC, IC, ICN, IHi

Especially good accounts of Chicago and LaSalle.

Dana, Edmund. *Geographical Sketches of the Western Country: Designed for Emigrants and Settlers; Being the Result of Extensive Researches and Remarks. To Which is Added, A Summary of All the Most Interesting Matters on the Subject, Including a Particular Description of All the Unsold Public Lands, Collected from a Variety of Authentic Sources. Also, a List of the Principle Roads*. Cincinnati, Ohio: Looker, Reynolds & Company, 1819.
ICHi, ICJ, ICU

Includes commentary on the Illinois River and the proposed I&M Canal.

Darby, William. *The Emigrant's Guide to the Western and Southwestern States and Territories Comprising a Geographical and Statistical Description*. New York: Kirk & Mercein, 1818. 311 p.
DLC, IC, IHi

Includes commentary on the Illinois River and the proposal for a canal.

Ensign and Thayer's Travellers' Guide Through the States of Ohio, Michigan, Indiana, Illinois, Missouri, Iowa, and Wisconsin; with Railroad, Canal, Stage and Steamboat Routes. New York: Ensign & Thayer; Cincinnati, Ohio: R. Blanchard, 1850. 32 p., map.
DLC, ICN

Another edition, New York: Published by Horace Thayer & Company, 1852.

The Far West; a Sketch of Illinois and the Other States in the Valley of the Mississippi, Describing the Fertile Region of the Republic, the Prairies, Rivers, Minerals, Animals, Agricultural Productions, Public Lands, Plans of Internal Improvement, Manufactures, etc., with Suggestions to Emigrants, and Letters from a Rambler in the West.... Philadelphia, 1837. 46 p.
DLC

Federal Writers' Project. Illinois. *Illinois: A Descriptive and Historical Guide*. Chicago: A. C. McClurg & Co., 1939. 687 p., plates, ports., maps.
DLC, ICJ, ICU

Compiled and written by the Federal Writers' Project of the Works Project Administration. Sponsored by Henry Horner, governor. American Guide Series. Reprinted as *The WPA Guide to Illinois*. New York: Pantheon Books, 1983.

Illinois in 1837: A Sketch Descriptive of the Situation, Boundaries, Face of the Country, Prominent Districts, Prairies, Rivers, Minerals, Animals, Agricultural Productions, Public Lands, Plans of Internal Improvement, Manufactures, etc., of the State of Illinois; Also, Suggestions to Emigrants . . . Together with a Letter on the Cultivation of the Prairies, by the Hon. H. L. Ellsworth. . . . Philadelphia: S. A. Mitchell, 1837. 143 p., front., map.
DLC

Peck, John Mason. *Guide for Emigrants, Containing Sketches of Illinois, Missouri, and the Adjacent Parts*. Boston, Massachusetts: Lincoln and Edmands, 1831. 336 p., front., map.
DLC, ICU, IU

Peck covers Illinois, pp. 89–332.

Peck, John Mason. *A New Guide for Emigrants to the West, Containing Sketches of Ohio, Indiana, Illinois, Missouri, Michigan, with the Territories of Wisconsin and Arkansas, and the Adjacent Parts*. Boston, Massachusetts: Gould, Kendall & Lincoln, 1837. 381 p.
DLC, ICU, IGK, IHi, IU

Peck, John M. *The Traveller's Directory for Illinois: Containing . . . Accurate Sketches of the State, a Particular Description of Each County, and Important Business Towns, a List of the Principal Roads, State and Steamboat Routes, Land Offices, Tracts of Land Unoccupied—A Description of the Timbered and Prairie Portions of the State; the Rivers, Minerals, Animals, Internal Improvements, Climate, and Seasons—with Much Other Original and Valuable Information for the Traveller, the Emigrant, the Man of Business and the Citizen; the Whole Intended as a Companion to the New Sectional Map of Illinois*. New York: Colton, 1839. 219 p., map.
DLC, ICHi, ICN

Description and Travel—*Gazetteers and Place Name Studies*

Adams, James N. *Illinois Place Names*. Illinois. State Historical Society, Occasional Publica-

tions, No. 54. Springfield: State Historical Society, 1968. 321 p.
DLC, ICN

Reprinted from *Illinois Libraries* 50 (1968): 275–596.

Barge, William D. and Caldwell, Norman D. "Illinois Place-Names." *Journal of the Illinois State Historical Society.* 29 (April 1936/January 1937): 189–311.
DLC, I, IC, ICHi, ICN, ICU, IEN, IU

Lists sources for information on place names. Bibliography.

Beck, Lewis Caleb. *A Gazetteer of the States of Illinois and Missouri: Containing a General View of Each State, a General View of Their Counties, and a Particular Description of Their Towns, Villages, Rivers, etc., with a Map, and Other Engravings.* Albany: Printed by C. R. & Webster, 1823. 352 p., front., map.
DLC, ICF, ICN

Brookes, R[ichard]. *The General Gazetteer; or Compendious Geographical Dictionary....* London: Newbery, 1762. 756 p., maps.
DLC

Various editions, with details on Illinois increasing over time.

Brown, Samuel R. *The Western Gazetteer; or Emigrants' Directory, Containing a Geographical Description of the Western States and Territories...With an Appendix Containing a Description of the Great Northern Lakes, Indian Annuities, and Directions to Emigrants.* Auburn, New York: Southwick, Printer, 1817. 352 p.
MiU

Contains a section on Illinois that treats rivers, surfaces, products, and settlements. (Reprinted in *Illinois State Historical Society Transactions* (1908): 299–310. The reprint is not verbatim.) A section of eighteen pages on the Illinois River and tributaries is reprinted in *Journal of the Illinois State Historical Society* 2 (January 1910): 77–79.

Colby, Charles [G.] *Handbook of Illinois Accompanying Morse's New Map of the State.* New York: Blanchard, 1855. 36 p., map.
IHi

Includes sketches of the major towns along the I&M Canal.

Gerhard, Frederick. *Illinois as It Is; Its History, Geography, Statistics, Constitution, Laws, Government . . . etc. With a Prairie and Wood Map, a Geological Map, a Population Map, and Other Illustrations.* Chicago: Keen and Lee; Philadelphia: C. Desilver, 1857. 451 p., front., illus., plates, maps.
DLC

James, Uriah Pierson. *Routes of the Missouri River, Illinois River, and Northern Lakes, with Descriptions of Towns, General Features of the Country, Statistics, Tables of Distance, etc.* Cincinnati, Ohio: U. P. James, 1855. 185 p.
DLC

[Mitchell, Samuel A.] *Illinois in 1837: a Sketch Descriptive of the Situation, Boundaries, Face of the Country, Prominent Districts, Prairies, Rivers, Minerals, Animals, Agricultural Productions, Public Lands, Plans of Internal Improvement, Manufacturers, etc. of the State of Illinois; Also, Suggestions to Emigrants, Sketches of the Counties, Cities, and Principal Towns in the State; Together with a Letter on the Cultivation of the Prairies, by the Hon. H. L. Ellsworth, to Which Are Annexed the Letters from a Rambler in the West.* Philadelphia: Mitchell, 1837. 143 p., front., map.
ICHi, ICU, IHi

Peck, John Mason. *A Gazetteer of Illinois, in Three Parts: Containing a General View of the State; a General View of Each County; and a Particular Description of Each Town, Settlement, etc., Alphabetically Arranged.* Jacksonville, Illinois: R. Goudy, 1834. 376 p.
DLC, IC, ICJ, ICU, IHi

Other editions: 2nd ed., entirely rev., cor., and enl. Philadelphia: Grigg & Elliott, 1837. 328 p., and Jacksonville, Illinois: R. Goudy, 1837.

Pritchard, Edward Randolph, ed. *Illinois of To-day and its Progressive Cities . . . A Work Descriptive of the State and Its Resources: Including also Sketches of Its Important Towns, and Many of Their Prominent Citizens, Together with Cuts and Descriptions of Public Institutions, Industries, Prominent Buildings, etc.* Chicago: Illinois of To-day, 1897. illus.
DLC

Vogel, Virgil H. J. *Indian Place Names in Illinois.* Illinois State Historical Society, Pamphlet Series, No. 4. Springfield: State Historical Society, 1963. 176 p., illus., ports.
DLC, ICJ, ICN, ICU, IU

Reprinted from the *Journal of the Illinois State Historical Society* 55 (1962): 45–71, 157–189, 271–308, 385–458. Includes bibliography.

Washburne, Elihu Benjamin. *Illinois. History, Manufactures, Mining, Resources, Government, Internal Improvements, Population, Financial Condition . . . Prepared Expressly for the 9th ed. of the Encyclopedia Britannica.* Philadelphia: J. M. Stoddart, 1881. 7 p., map.
DLC

Description and Travel—*Exploration*

Alvord, Clarence W. "An Unrecognized Father Marquette Letter." *American Historical Review* 25 (1920): 676–680.
DLC, IC, ICHi, ICN, ICU, IU

Beckwith, Hiram Williams, ed. *Documents, Papers, Materials and Publications Relating to the Northwest and the State of Illinois.* Collections of the Illinois State Historical Library, No. 1. Springfield, 1903. 642 p.
DLC, ICJ, ICU

Contains documents relative to the early exploration of the corridor, including accounts of Marquette, LaSalle, Tonty, and George Rogers Clark.

Bell, John R. *The Journal of Captain John R. Bell, Official Journalist for the Stephen H. Long Expedition to the Rocky Mountains, 1820.* Edited by Harlin M. Ruller and LeRoy R. Hafen. The Far West and the Rockies Historical Series, 1820–1875, Vol. 6. Glendale, California: Arthur H. Clarke Company, 1957. 349 p., illus., port., maps.
ICN, ICU, IU

Cavelier, Jean. *The Journal of Jean Cavelier.* Chicago: Loyola University, Institute of Jesuit History, Publications, 1938. 179 p., maps.
DLC, ICL, ICU

Charlevoix, Pierre Francois Xavier de. *Histoire et Description Générale de la Nouvelle France, avec le Journal historique d'un voyage fait par ordre du Roi dans l'Amérique Septentrionnale.* 3 v. Paris: Rolin Fils, 1744. Plates, maps, plans.
ICU, InU

Charlevoix, Pierre Francois Xavier de. *History and General Description of New France.* Translated with notes, by John Gilmary Shea. New York: J. G. Shea, 1866–1872. 6 p., front., plates, port., maps, plan, facsim.
DLC, IC, ICU, IGK, IHi, InU

Another edition, New York: F. P. Harper, 1900.

Charlevoix, Pierre Francois Xavier de. *Journal of a Voyage to North America: Undertaken by Order of the French King. Containing a Geographical Description and Natural History of the Customs, Characters, Religion, Manners, and Traditions of the Original Inhabitants. In a Series of Letters to the Duchess of Lesdiquires.* 2 v. Translated from the French of P. de Charlevoix. London: Printed for R. and J. Dodsley, 1761. map.
DLC, ICU, IHi, InU

Charlevoix, Pierre Francois Xavier de. *Journal of a Voyage to North America: Translated from the French of Pierre Francois Charlevoix.* 2 v. Edited with Historical Introduction, Notes and Index, by Louise Phelps Kellogg. Chicago: The Caxton Club, 1923. front., map.
DLC, ICJ, ICU

Charlevoix, Pierre Francois Xavier de. *Letters to the Dutchess of Lesdiquieres: Giving an Account of a Voyage to Canada and Travels Through that Vast Country, and Louisiana, to the Gulf of Mexico.* London: R. Goadby, 1763.
DLC, IGK, IHi

Charlevoix, Pierre Francois Xavier de. *A Voyage to North America: Undertaken by Command of the Present King of France. Containing the Geographical Description and a Natural History of Canada and Louisiana. With the Customs, Manners, Trade and Religion of the Inhabitants . . . Also, a Description and Natural History of the Islands in the West Indies Belonging to the Different Powers of Europe.* 2 v. Dublin: Printed for J. Exshaw and J. Potts, 1766. fronts., maps.
DLC, ICU, IHi, MWA

Cox, Isaac Joslin, ed. *The Journeys of Rene Robert Cavelier, Sieur de LaSalle, as Related by his Faithful Lieutenant, Henri de Tonty; his Missionary Collegues, Fathers Zenobius Membre, Louis Hennepin, and Anastasius Donay; his Early Biographer, Father Christian LeClerq; his Trusted Subordinate, Henri Joutel; and his brother Jean Cavelier; Together with Memoirs, Commissions, etc.* 2 v. New York: Allerton Book Company, 1922. illus.
ICF
Reprinted, New York: ASM Press, 1973.

Dablon, Father Claudius. "Marquette's Journal of his First Visit to the Mississippi." *Michigan Historical Collections* 21 (1894): 467–488.
DLC, I, IC, ICN, ICU, IU, MiU

Dablon, Claudius. "Relation of the Discovery of Many Countries Situated to the South of New France, Made in 1673." *The Jesuit Relations and Allied Documents....* Vol. 58, pp. 92–109. Edited by Reuben Gold Thwaites. Cleveland, Ohio: Burrows Bros. Company, 1896–1901.
DLC, ICN, ICU
Father Dablon reports the contents of Joliet's lost journal in this account. He includes the first recommendation for a canal between Lake Michigan and the Illinois River.

Dablon, Fr. Claudius. *Relation of the Voyages, Discoveries, and Death of Father James Marquette, and the Subsequent Voyages of Father Cladius Allouez.* Prepared for publication in 1678. Collections of the Illinois State Historical Library, No. 1. Springfield, 1903.
DLC, ICU

Deliette, Sieur. *Memoir of De Gannes Concerning the Illinois Country* [1721]. Collections of the Illinois State Historical Society, No. 23, Springfield: Illinois State Historical Society, 1934. 93 p.
DLC, I, IC, ICJ, ICN, ICU
Mainly concerned with the water resources of Illinois, especially the Chicago-Illinois route.

Doty, James Duane. *Official Journal, 1820, Expedition with Cass and Schoolcraft.* Collections of the State Historical Society of Wisconsin, No. 13, Madison: Wisconsin State Historical Society, 1895. 56 p.
ICU

Garraghan, Gilbert J. "Some Hitherto Unpublished Marquettiana." *Mid-America* 18 (1936): 3–14.
DLC, IC, ICL, ICN, ICU, IU

Garraghan, Gilbert. "Some Newly Discovered Marquette and LaSalle Letters." *Archivum Historicum Societatis Jesu* 4 (1935): 268–290.
DLC, ICU, IU

Hamilton, Raphael. *Marquette's Explorations: The Narratives Reexamined.* Madison, Wisconsin: The University of Wisconsin, 1970.
DLC

Hennepin, Louis. *Description de la Louisiane, Nouvellement decouverte au sud' oüest de la Nouvelle France, par ordre du roy....* Paris: Chez la veuve Sebastien Hure, 1683.
ICN, ICRL
Various editions.

Hennepin, Louis. *A Description of Louisiana, by Father Louis Hennepin, Recollect Missionary. Translated from the Edition of 1683 and Compared with the Nouvelle Decouverte, the LaSalle Documents and Other Contemporaneous Papers.* Edited and translated by John Gilmary Shea. New York: J. G. Shea, 1880. 407 p., front., map, plates, facsim.
DLC, ICU, ICarbS, IHi
Bibliography of Hennepin, pp. 382–392.

Hennepin, Louis. *Discovery of the River Mississippi and the Adjacent Country.* American Antiquarian Society. Archaelogia Americana. Transactions and Collections, No. 1. Worcester, Massachusetts, 1820. 43 p.
DLC, ICU, MWA

Hennepin, Louis. *A New Discovery of a Vast Country in America; by Father Louis Hennepin; Reprinted from the Second London Issue of 1698, with Facsimilies of Original Title-Pages, Maps, and Illustrations, and the Addition of an Introduction, Notes, and Index by Reuben Gold Thwaites.* 2 v. Chicago: A. C. McClurg & Company, 1903. fronts., plates, maps.
DLC, IC, ICJ, ICN, ICU

Hubbard, Gurdon S. "A Voyageur of 1818." *Michigan Historical Collections* 14 (1890): 544–545.
DLC, I, IC, ICN, ICU, IU

James, Edwin, comp. *An Account of an Expedition from Pittsburgh to the Rocky Mountains, Performed in the Years 1819 and '20, by Order of the Hon. J. C. Calhoun, Secretary of War; Under the Command of Major Stephen H. Long. From the Notes of Major Long, Mr. T. Say, and Other Gentlemen of the Exploring Party.* 2 v. Philadelphia: H. C. Carey and I. Lea, 1823. Atlas, plates, maps.
ICU

Joutel, Henri. *Journal of the Last Voyage Performed by Monsr. de La Sale, to the Gulph of Mexico, to Find out the Mouth of the Mississipi River; Containing an Account of the Settlements he Endeavour'd to Make on the Coast of the Aforesaid Bay, his Unfortunate Death, and the Travels of his Companions for the Space of Eight Hundred Leages Across that Inland Country of America, Now Called Louisiana . . . till They Came into Canada, Written in French by Monsieur Joutel . . . and Translated from the Ed., just Published at Paris. With an Exact Map of that Vast Country, and a Copy of the Letters Patents Granted by the King of France to M. Crozat.* London: Printed for A. Bell, etc., 1714. 205 p., map.
DLC, ICU

Kane, Lucile, Holmquist, June D., and Gilman, Carolyn, eds. *The Northern Expeditions of Stephen H. Long: The Journals of 1817 and 1823 and Related Documents.* St. Paul, Minnesota: Minnesota Historical Society Press, 1978. 407 p., illus.
ICU

Kearny, Stephen W. *The 1820 Journal of Stephen Watts Kearny, Comprising a Narrative Account of the Council Bluff–St. Peter's Military Exploration and a Voyage Down the Mississippi River to St. Louis.* Edited by Valentine Mott Porter. St. Louis, 1908. 54 p., map.
DLC, ICHi, IHi

Describes forts, towns, and Indian villages.

Keating, William Hypolitus. *Narrative of an Expedition to the Source of the St. Peter's River, Lake Winnepeek, Lake of the Woods, etc. Performed in the Year 1823, by Order of the Hon. J. C. Calhoun, Secretary of War, Under the Command of Stephen H. Long, U.S.T.E. Compiled from the Notes of Major Long, Messrs. Say, Keating, and Calhoun, by William H. Keating.* 2 v. London: G. B. Whittaker, 1825. front., plates, map, tables.
DLC, ICU

A later edition appeared under the title *Travels in the Interior of North America.* Contains comments on Northern Illinois, Lake Michigan, and the portage.

Lahontan, Louis Armand de Lom d'Arce de. *Collection Oakes: Nouveaux Documents de Lahontan Sur le Canada et Terre-Neuve.* Edited by Gustave Lanctot. Ottawa, Canada: J. O. Patenaude, 1940.
DLC

Lahontan, Louis Armand de Lom d'Arce de. *New Voyages to North America by the Baron de Lahontan* [*1703*]. 2 v. Edited by Reuben G. Thwaites. Chicago: A. C. McClurg, 1905.
DLC, IC

Lahontan, Louis Armand de Lom d'Arce de. *Nouveaux Voyages de Mr. le baron de Lahontan dans l'Amerique Septentrionale.* 2 v. The Hague: Chez les fréres l'Honoré, 1703.
DLC, ICN, IHi

Bacqueville de la Potherie, Claude Charles Le Roy. *Voyage de l'Amérique, Contenant qui s'est passé de plus remarquable dans l'Amérique Septentrionale depuis 1534, jusqu' à present.* 4 v. Amsterdam: H. des Bordes, 1723.
ICN, IU

LaSalle, Cavelier de. "Exploration of the Mississippi." *Magazine of American History* 2 (September 1878): 551–561.
DLC, I, IC, ICHi, ICN, ICU, IU

Includes LaSalle's 1681 will, and an excerpt entitled "Arrival of LaSalle at the Illinois: Description of the Country as Far as the Junction of the Missouri with this River, Which the Discoverer Named Colbert River." Both translated and reprinted from *Découvertes et Etablissements des Français dans l'ouest et dans le sud de l'Amérique Septentrionale, Pierre Margry. Deuxième partie.* Paris: 1877.

LaSalle, Robert Cavelier de. *Relation of the Discovery and Voyages of Cavelier de LaSalle from 1679 to 1681, the Official Narrative.* Translated by Melville B. Anderson. Chicago: The Caxton Club, 1901.
DLC, ICU, IEN

LaSalle, Cavelier de. "Rivers and Peoples Discovered by LaSalle." *Magazine of American History* 2 (October 1878): 619–622.
DLC, I, IC, ICHi, ICN, ICU, IU
Taken from a detached leaf in LaSalle's handwriting. Translated and reprinted from *Découvertes et Etablissements des Français dans l'ouest et dans le sud de l'Amérique Septentrionale, etc., Pierre Margry. Deuxieme partie.* Paris, 1877.

Margry, Pierre. *Découvertes et établissements des Français dans l'ouest et dans le Sud de l'Amérique Septentrionale [1614–1754]: Mémoires et Documents Originaux.* 6 vols. Paris: Maisonneuve et Cie, 1879–1888. fronts., maps, diagrs.
ICU

Margry, Pierre. *Discoveries and Settlements of the French in Western and Southern North America [1614–1754]: Memoirs and Original Documents.* 6 v. n.p., n.d. (Microfilm).
ICU
Original is in the Burton Historical Collection, Detroit Public Library.

"Marquette's Last Journal." *Michigan Historical Collections* 21 (1894): 488–494.
DLC, I, IC, ICN, ICU, IU, MiU

Marquette, Jacques. "Of the First Voyage Made by Father Marquette Toward New Mexico." *The Jesuit Relations and Allied Documents.* Vol. 59. Edited by Reuben Gold Thwaites. pp. 86–163. Cleveland, Ohio: Burrow Bros. Company, 1896–1901.
DLC, ICN, ICU
Marquette's expedition with Joliet, 1673–1674. The return route took them through the corridor.

Memoir of the Sieur de la Salle Reporting to Monsiegneur [sic] de Seignelay the Discoveries Made by Him Under the Order of His Majesty. Collections of the Illinois State Historical Library, No. 1. Springfield, The Historical Society, 1903. 10 p.
DLC, ICU

Parkman, Francis. *LaSalle and the Discovery of the Great West.* Boston: Little, Brown, and Company, 1905.
DLC, ICJ, NN
Many earlier editions.

Quaife, Milo Milton, ed. *Pictures of Illinois One Hundred Years Ago.* Chicago: R. R. Donnelley & Sons Company, 1918. 186 p., front.
DLC, ICU
Includes Henry R. Schoolcraft's 1821 journey up the Illinois River and the 1821 Chicago Treaty.

Shea, John Gilmary. *Discovery and Exploration of the Mississippi Valley: With the Original Narratives of Marquette, Allouez, Membré, Hennepin, and Anastase Douoy.* New York: Redfield, 1852. 267 p., front., map.
DLC, ICJ, ICU, IHi

Schoolcraft, Henry R. *Travels in the Central Portions of the Mississippi Valley, Comprising Observations and Its Mineral Geography, Internal Resources, and Aboriginal Population.* New York: Collins and Hannay, 1825.
DLC, ICN

Shea, John Dawson Gilmary. *Discovery and Exploration of the Mississippi Valley: With the Original Narratives of Marquette, Allouez, Membré, Hennepin, and Anastase Douay. 2nd Ed. With a Facsimile of the Newly Discovered Map of Marquette, of Marquette's Letter, and a Steel Portrait of LaSalle.* Albany, New York: J. McDonough, 1903. 267 p., front., maps, facsim.
DLC, ICU
Reprint of 1852 edition.

Shea, John Dawson Gilmary, ed. *Early Voyages Up and Down the Mississippi by Cavelier, St. Cosme, Le Sueur, Gravier, and Guignas. With an Introduction, Notes, and an Index by John Gilmary Shea.* Albany, New York: Reprinted for J. McDonough, 1902. 191 p.
DLC, ICJ, ICU

Thwaites, Reuben Gold, ed. *Early Western Travels, 1748–1846: A Series of Annotated Reprints of the Best and Rarest Contemporary Volumes of Travel, Descriptive of the Aborigines and Social and Economic Conditions in the Middle and Far West, During the Period of Early American Settlement.* 32 v. Cleveland, Ohio: The A. H. Clark Company, 1904–1907. fronts., illus., plates, ports., maps, plan, facsims.
DLC, ICF, ICJ, ICN, ICU, IHi

Thwaites, Reuben Gold, ed. *The Jesuit Relations and Allied Documents, Travels and Explorations of the Jesuit Missionaries in New France, 1610–1791: The Original French, Latin, and Italian Texts, with English Translations and Notes; Illustrated by Portraits, Maps, and Facsimilies.* 73 v. Cleveland, Ohio: The Burrows Bros. Company, 1896–1901. front., illus., plates, maps, plans, facsim.
DLC, ICN, ICU
See especially Vols. 59, 60, 61, 64, 49, 70, 71. Index, Vols. 72,73.

Tonti, H. de. "An Account of Monsieur de la Salle's Last Expedition." *Collections of the New York Historical Society* 2 (1814): 217–341.
IC, ICN, ICU, IU

Henry de Tonty's Memoir of 1693. Collections of the Illinois State Historical Library, Vol. 1. Springfield, 1903, 36 p.
DLC, I, IC, ICJ, ICN, ICU

Tonti, Henri de. "Relation de la Louisianne; et du Mississipi, par le Chevalier de Tonti, gouverneur du Fort Saint Louis aux Illinois." In Bernard, Jean Frédéric, ed. *Recueil de Voyages au Nord.* Vol. 5, pp. 35–195. Amsterdam: 1725–1738.
DLC, ICN

Tonti, Henri de. *Relation of Henri de Tonty Concerning the Explorations of LaSalle from 1678 to 1683, 1684.* Translated by Meville B. Anderson. Chicago: The Caxton Club, 1898.
DLC, ICJ, ICN

Description and Travel—*Travel Accounts*

Benton, Colbee Chamberlain. *A Visit to Chicago in Indian Days: "Journal to the 'Far-Off West.'"* Edited by Paul M. Angle and James R. Getz. Chicago: Caxton Club, 1957. 121 p., map, notes.
ICN, ICU, IU
Diary of a journey from Windsor, Vermont, to Chicago in 1833. Contains account of Indian villages of northern Illinois on the eve of the removal of the Indians from the area.

Bryant, William C. *Letters of a Traveller, Notes of Things Seen in Europe and America.* New York: Putnam; London: Bentley, 1850. 442 p.
ICHi, ICN
Author traveled by stage to Peru.

Buckingham, J[ames] S. *The Eastern and Western States of America.* 3 v. London: Fisher, 1842.
DLC, ICHi, IHi

Buckingham, Joseph H. "Illinois as Lincoln Knew It: A Boston Reporter's Record of a Trip in 1847." Harry E. Pratt, ed. *Illinois State Historical Society Transactions, 1937* (1938): 109–187.
DLC, IC, ICU

Carpenter, Richard V. "Margaret Fuller in Northern Illinois." *Journal of the Illinois State Historical Society* 2 (January 1910): 7–22.
DLC, I, IC, ICHi, ICN, ICU, IEN, IU
Includes brief passage through DesPlaines valley.

Childs, Col. Ebenezer. "Recollections of Wisconsin Since 1820." *Wisconsin Historical Collections* 4 (1859): 153–195.
DLC, IC, ICJ, ICN, ICU
Includes account of a trip from St. Louis to Chicago via the Illinois River in 1821.

Cunynghame, Lieut. Col. Auther [A. T.] *A Glimpse at the Great Western Republic.* London: Bentley, 1851. 337 p.
DLC, IC, IHi
Author traveled from Chicago to LaSalle on the I&M Canal.

Delano, Alonzo. *Alonzo Delano's California Correspondence: Being Letters Hitherto Uncollected from the Ottawa [Illinois] "Free Trader" and the New Orleans "True Delta," 1849–1952.* Edited with an introduction and notes by Irving McKee. Sacramento Book Collectors Club. Publication, No. 5. Sacramento, California: Sacramento Book Collectors Club, 1952. 155 p., maps, view.
DLC, InU, NN
Journey from Ottawa, Illinois, overland to California and back reported in thirty-six letters.

Edwards, Governor Ninian. "Account of the Rivers, Villages and Routes from Mackinaw to St. Louis, in the Year 1812." In *Ninian W. Edwards, History of Illinois, from 1778 to 1833; and Life and Times of Ninian Edwards.* pp. 93–98. Springfield: State Journal, 1870. 549 p.
DLC

A valuable and detailed sketch based on the reports of agents.

Field, A. D. "Illinois and Its Mammoth City: Sketches of Chicago." *National Magazine* 12 (April/May 1858): 347–350, 407–411.
ICJ, ICHi, ICN
Field went to Chicago in 1835. He gives reminiscences of the city, the canal, and the surrounding country.

"Follow the Barge." *Chicago Tribune Magazine* (May 1971): 26–43. Illus.
IMa
A trip from Chicago to New Orleans in words and photographs. Historical information.

Fonda, John H. "Early Wisconsin." *Wisconsin Historical Collections* 5 (1868): 205–284.
DLC, IC, ICJ, ICN, ICU
Contains a narrative of a trip from St. Louis to Chicago by way of the Illinois River and a description of Chicago.

[**Gilman, Chandler R.**] *Life on the Lakes: Being Tales and Sketches Collected During a Trip to the Pictured Rocks of Lake Superior; by the Author of "Legends of a Log Cabin."* 2 v. New York: Dearborn, 1836.
DLC, ICHi
Author traveled from Chicago to Peoria via Ottawa on his return trip.

"The Great Lakes: Their Cities and Trade." *De Bow's Review* 15 (October 1853): 359–384.
DLC, IC, ICN, ICU, IU
Discusses Chicago and Illinois railroads and canals.

Greenough, William W. "Tour to the Western Country." *Massachusetts Historical Society Proceedings* 44 (January 1911): 339–354.
DLC, IC, ICN, IHi, ICU, IU
Author traveled through Peru and Ottawa to Chicago and provides valuable and interesting descriptions of the towns and country.

Haskins, R. S. "Valley of Lakes." *American Review, a Whig Journal* 6 (November 1847): 466–475.
DLC, I, IC, ICN, ICHi, ICU
Notes on the topography of the Northwest, the I&M Canal.

Hoffman, Charles Fenno. *A Winter in the West: By a New Yorker.* 2 v. New York: Harper & Bros., 1835.
DLC, ICU, IHi
Also published by Ann Arbor: University Microfilms (1966). March of America Facsimilies Series, No. 75. New York: Harper Bros., 1835; St. Clair Shores, Michigan: Scholarly Press, 1970; and London: R. Bentley, 1835. Includes commentary on the I&M Canal, Chicago, and Ottawa.

Jones, Abner D. *Illinois and the West, 1838: With a Township Map Containing the Latest Surveys and Improvements.* Boston: Weeks, Jordan & Company, 1838. 255 p., map.
ICF, ICU
Jones, a New Englander, made his return trip via Peru, Joliet, and Chicago.

Kelly, William. *Across the Rocky Mountains, from New York to California: With a Visit to the Celebrated Mormon Colony at the Great Salt Lake.* London: Simms & McIntyre, 1852. 240 p.
DLC, IC, ICHi, ICN
Author traveled by stage to Peru from Chicago.

Köhler, Carl. *Briefe aus Amerika: ein lehrreicher Wegweiser für deutsche Auswanderer und unterhaltendes Lesebuch für Gebildete jeden Standes; nebst einer Ubersicht der amerikanischen Munzen, des Eingangazolls der gewohnlichsten Einfahr Artikel, der Dampfschiffverbindungen Zwischen Europa und Nord-Amerika, der Eisenbahn-Kanelboot-und Dampfschiffvervindungen von New York aus nach den verschiedenen Theilen der Union, und der Entfernungen der amerikanischen Hauptstadte von einander; bearbeitet von Carl Kohler.* Darmstadt: Verlag von G. G. Lange, 1852. 234 p.
DLC, ICRL
On his return, Kohler traveled up the Illinois River and across to Chicago. Three of his letters discuss social and agricultural conditions with special reference to German emigrants.

LaTrobe, Charles J. *The Rambler in North America, 1832–1833.* 2 v. New York: Harper & Brothers, 1835.
DLC, ICU, NN

Author was in Chicago during negotiations for an Indian treaty.

Logan, James. *Notes of a Journey Through Canada, the United States of America, and the West Indies.* Edinburgh, Scotland: Fraser, 1838. 259 p., map.
DLC, ICN
Contains description of a trip by stage from Chicago to Peru.

Martineau, Harriet. *Society in America.* 3 v. London: Saunders & Otley, 1837.
DLC, ICHi
Martineau traveled as far as Joliet.

Mattson, H[ans]. *Minnen, af oferste H. Mattson.* Lund, Sweden: Gleerup, [1890]. 369 p.
DLC
Mattson's travels took him by canal boat from Chicago through LaSalle.

May, Susan Short. "Susan Short May: The Story of Her Ancestry and of Her Early Life in Illinois." *Journal of the Illinois State Historical Society* 6 (April 1913): 119–128.
DLC, I, IC, ICHi, ICN, ICU, IEN, IU
Includes account of life in a tavern on road to Ottawa.

Milburn, William H. "The Pleasures of Travel, 1846." *Journal of the Illinois State Historical Society* 35 (June 1942): 184–186.
DLC, I, IC, ICHi, ICN, ICU, IEN, IU
Travels from Peru by stage.

Paulding, James K. "Illinois and the Prairies." *Graham's American Monthly* 34 (January 1849): 16–25.
DLC, IC, ICHi, ICN
Paulding traveled up the Illinois River by steamboat and across the prairies by horseback to Chicago. He describes the towns along the way and the canal.

Raumer, Friedrich von. *Die Vereinigten Staaten von Nordamerika.* Leipzig: Brockhaus, 1845. 2 v., map.
ICHi, IU
A letter at the end of the book gives a brief account of a trip up the Illinois River to Ottawa and by stage to Chicago.

Reynolds, John. *Sketches of the Country, on the Northern Route from Belleville, Illinois, to the City of New York, and Back by the Ohio Valley: Together with a Glance at the Crystal Palace.* Belleville, Illinois: Printed by J. A. Willis and C. Johnson, 1854. 264 p.
DLC, ICN, ICU
Describes Peru, LaSalle, Ottawa, Morris, Joliet, and Chicago.

Steele, Elizabeth. *A Summer Journey in the West.* New York: S. Taylor and Company, 1841.
DLC, ICN, IGK

Storrow, Samuel A. *Narrative of a Tour in the Northwest in 1817 in a letter to Major General Jacob Brown.* n.p., [1818]. 39 p.
ICN
Contains a description of Chicago and a discussion of routes of transportation.

Sullivan, Sir Edward [R.]. *Rambles and Scrambles in North and South America.* London: Bentley, 1852. 425 p.
DLC, ICN
Author's route was through Peru.

Thomas, David. *Travels Through the Western Country in the Summer of 1816: Including Notices of the Natural History, Antiquities, Topography, Agriculture, Commerce, and Manufactures; With a Map of the Wabash Country Now Settling.* Auburn, New York: Rumsey, Printer, 1819. 320 p., map.
DLC, IC, ICJ, ICN, ICU, IHi, IU
The appendix contains a letter describing the Illinois-Michigan water route.

Williams, Mentor L. "A Tour of Illinois in 1842." *Journal of the Illinois State Historical Society* 42 (September 1949): 292–312.
DLC, I, IC, ICHi, ICN, ICU, IEN, IU
Account of an overland journey between Ottawa and Chicago. Contains descriptions of Ottawa, LaSalle, Peru, Joliet, Lockport, and the surrounding prairie.

Description and Travel—*Local Diaries and Correspondence*

Hubbard, Mrs. Mary Ann. *Family Memories.* [Chicago]: Printed for Private Circulation, 1912. 146 p., ports., front.
DLC, ICN

Sketches of Tucker and Hubbard families. Pioneer life in Illinois and Iowa.

Hubbard, Gurdon S. *Incidents and Events in the Life of Gurdon Saltonstall Hubbard: Collected from Personal Narrations and Other Sources, and Arranged by his Nephew, Henry E. Hamilton.* Chicago: Rand, etc., Printer. 1888. 189 p.
DLC, I, ICN, IU
Hubbard was an American Fur Company employee who went to Chicago in 1818 and traveled widely in Illinois, including down the Illinois River to Kaskaskia. The account runs to 1830 and includes information on the fur trade.

Description and Travel—*Portage and Trails*

The Economy Light and Power Company, Chicago, Defendants, vs. The United States of America, Complainant. In the United States District Court for the Northern District of Illinois, Eastern Division. In Chancery No. 29776. Abstract of Proofs. Chicago: The Gunthorp-Warren Printing Company, 1912.
ICN
Documentation on the Chicago portage.

[Jefferson, Thomas.] *Notes on the State of Virginia: Written in the Year 1781, Somewhat Corrected and Enlarged in the Winter of 1782, for the Use of a Foreigner of Distinction, in Answer to Certain Queries Proposed by Him . . . 1782.* Paris, Printed 1784–1785. 391 p.
ICN, ICU
Includes a description of rivers in Illinois and the Illinois-Chicago portage.

Knight, Robert. *The Location of the Chicago Portage Route of the Seventeenth Century. . . .* Chicago Historical Society Collections, Vol. 12. Chicago: Chicago Historical Society, 1928. 145 p., front., plates, maps, facsims., plans.
DLC, ICU, ICHi
Bibliography

LaSalle, Rene-Robert Cavelier, Sieur de. *LaSalle on the Illinois Country, 1680.* Collections of the Illinois State Historical Library, No. 19. Springfield, 1934. 16 p.
DLC, I, IC, ICJ, ICN, ICU
LaSalle's recommendations for linking the Illinois River with Lake Michigan.

Long, Major Stephen H. *Extract from a Report to George Graham, Esp., Acting Secretary of War, Dated Washington, March 4, 1817.* House Doc. 17, 16th Cong., 1st Sess., pp. 5–8, Serial 32. Washington: Gales & Seaton, Printers, 1819. 10 p.
ICU
Long's report describes the Illinois River, its branches, and the surrounding country and discusses the feasibility of canals via the Chicago and DesPlaines and via the St. Joseph and Kankakee rivers.

Quaife, Milo Milton. *Chicago's Highways, Old and New, from Indian Trail to Motor Road.* Chicago: D. F. Keller & Company, 1923. 278 p., front., plates, maps, plan, facsims.
DLC, ICJ, ICU
A guide to the chief points of historical interest within a day's journey of Chicago.

Rytle, John B. "The Chicago Portage." *Transactions of the Illinois State Academy of Science* 34 (1941): 63–64.
DLC, I, ICF, ICJ, ICU

Shapiro, Dena Evelyn. "Indian Tribes and Trails of the Chicago Region: A Preliminary Study of the Influence of the Indian on Early White Settlement." M.A. thesis, University of Chicago, 1929. 92 p., maps.
ICU

Description and Travel—*Archive Sources*

Chicago, Illinois. Chicago Historical Society. Benjamin F. Barker Collection. 24 items.
ICHi
Letters (1832–1840) describe conditions in Chicago and Joliet.

Chicago, Illinois. Chicago Historical Society. Judith Brown Letter File.
ICHi
Contains 1848 description of trip through Calumet swamp.

Chicago, Illinois. Chicago Historical Society. Lebbens Hascall Collections. 4 p.
ICHi
Comments about Chicago and Joliet while on a trip in 1844.

Chicago, Illinois. Chicago Historical Society. Samuel Humes Kerfoot Collection. 12 p.
ICHi

Material related to a journey down the I&M Canal in 1892.

Chicago, Illinois. Chicago Historical Society. David L. Roberts Collection. Seventeen items.
ICHi

Letters written while on trip through west, 1835. Descriptions of Chicago, Joliet, Springfield.

Chicago, Illinois. Chicago Historical Society. Albert Frederick Scharf Collections. Eighty-eight items, 1 v.
ICHi

Diary, maps, and notes on Indian villages, trails, fortifications in northern Illinois. Chicago area. Two-volume guide, 1925. Indian trails and villages of Cook, DuPage, and Will counties. Portage trails of the Old Northwest.

Chicago, Illinois. Chicago Historical Society. Henry S. Spaulding Collection. 36 p.
ICHi

Journal of steamboat trip up Mississippi and Illinois Rivers. Comments on Peoria, Joliet, and Chicago. 1848.

Chicago, Illinois. Loyola University Archives. Institute of Jesuit History Collections. Inventoried by Yolande Dembowski. 68 rolls. (Microfilm.)
ICL

Reel 3: Charlevoix, Pierre F. Histoire et description générale de la Nouvelle-France. Paris, Nyori. 1744.

Reel 4: Dumont de Montigny, F. F. Mémoires historiques sur la Louisiane. Paris, Bauche, 1753.

Reel 6: Lattontan, Baron de. Nouvaus Voyages . . . dans L'Amérique Septentrionale. LaHaye, 1703.

Reel 8: Bacqueville de la Pothene. Voyage de l'Amérique (Histoire de l'Amérique Septentrionale) Amsterdam, des Bordes, 1723.

Reel 16: Parkman's Correspondence. Copy 2. September 7, 1857–May 12, 1899.

Reel 17: Tonti, Henri de (attrib.). Dernières découvertes. Paris, 1697.

Reel 20: Marquette's trips down the Mississippi. Thevenot, Dablon, autograp., 1681.

Reel 24: Paris, Archives Nationale. Twenty-nine documents.

Reel 25: Cartes et Plans I.

Reel 26: Cartes et Plans II.

Reel 27: Mss. Français. Nouvelles Acquisitions.

Reel 28: Bib. Nat. Mss. Français, Nouvelles Acquisitions.

Reel 29: Archive Nat. Colonies.

Reel 30: Archives Nationales Colonies.

Reel 31: Arsenal Colbert Institut Marine Nazanne Moreau Museum.

Reel 32: Parkman's Papers. Regarding LaSalle.

Chicago, Illinois. Loyola University Archives. Institute of Jesuit History Collections. Uninventoried. (Microfilm.)
ICL

Reel 1: Montreal I. Correspondence de Jesuites Canadiens entre 1662 et 1741.

Reel 2: Montreal II. Journal de Bomecamts-Voyage de 1749 Catalogues Société Jésus.

Reel 4: Montreal V. Catalogues es Missen Amerique 1607 En Louisiane 1752.

Reel 38: Archives Judicieores. Touchant Adrien Jolliet et Jésuites.

Reel 46: Ottawa 3. Collection dursée en dossiers et correspondence 1675–1710.

Reel 47: Archives Judiesères-Quebec entre Armées 1651–1691.

Reel 50: Doc. in the Chicago Historical Society. Mason Collection regarding Jolliet, Biqot, Tonty.

Reel 51: Registro Mission St. Joseph, Illinois 1720–1773.

Reel 55: Maps entre 1680–1715.

Reel 58: Correspondence et lettres—Mémoires sur Missions Mississippi 1698–1706.

Reel 61: Ottawa 2. Miscellaneous Documents 1667–1705.

Reel 71: Ottawa 1. Archives Nationales 1675–1701.

Reel 98: Mémoires et Doc. d'Amérique.

Reel 116: Identification difficule, Récits de Voyages Touchant Exploration de l'embonchère du Mississippi, 1719–1722.

Reel 126: Cartes du Mississippi, Florida, Louisianne, Nouveau Mexique c. eighteenth century.

Reel 127: Documents Mission Jésuites, 1662–1699.

Chicago, Illinois. Newberry Library. Ayer Collection. Jean Cavelier. "Copre Du Journal de voyage Du Sieur Cavelier Pietre frere de Monsr. De LaSalle, Lesquels Entreprirent L an 1684." 47 p.
ICN

Photostat of original in Achivo General de Indias, Seville.

Chicago, Illinois. Newberry Library. Ayer Collection. Pierre LeMoyne Iberville. "Journal d'Iberville, Louisianne, 1699–1723." 358 p.
ICN

Collection of documents from the correspondence of Iberville and associates concerning exploration of Louisiana.

Chicago, Illinois. Newberry Library. Ayer Collection. Jacques Marquette. "Tout ce qui Regarde le Voyage du Marquette; Lettre et Journal du Frere P. Marquette, Oct. 25, 1674–Apr. 6, 1675." 70 p., map.
ICN

Photostat of original in Archives of St. Mary's College, Montreal.

Chicago, Illinois. Newberry Library. Ayer Collection. Antoine Ouilmett to James Moore, Racine, June 1, 1839. Ayer Collection. 1 p.
ICN

Reminiscences of Chicago in 1790.

Chicago, Illinois. Newberry Library. Ayer Collection. "Relation de la Découverte que Mr. de la Salle a Faite de la Liuiere de Mississipi en 1682. Et de son Retour Jusqu'è Quebec . . . La Rochelle January 17, 1683." pp. 229–264.
ICN

In "A Collection of Memoirs Concerning French Possessions, 1702–1750."

Chicago, Illinois. Newberry Library. Ayer Collection. Henry de Tonty. "Engagement Pardevant Pierre Duquet, Notaire, de deux coureurs de Bois, Jacques Nepreu et Ant. Madry, a Henry de Tonty . . . , le 27 Septembre 1684, ces deux Coureurs Devront monter au Fort Incessamment pour y faire la traite les Sauvages." 2 p.
ICN

Lockport, Illinois. Will County Historical Society. Leather-bound diary, William Trainer. 1854.
ILoHi

Springfield, Illinois. Illinois State Historical Library. Alexander Blackie diary, April 23–August 31, 1835. 22 p.
IHi

Presbyterian missionary's journey from Cincinnati, Ohio, via river to St. Louis, cross-country to Edwardsville, Springfield, Jacksonville, Quincy, Peoria, northern Illinois, and Michigan Territory. Blackie visited LaSalle and "Juliet" and includes a brief description.

Springfield, Illinois. Illinois State Historical Library. David Raynor Brees and Robert Finley Brees, Presbyterian ministers. Princeville, Illinois, dated April 22, 1835, and August 29, 1837, Ottawa, Illinois, to John Brees, Busking Ridge, New Jersey. Two items.
IHi

Letters to their father regarding living conditions in Illinois. Letter of 1837 describes a three-hundred-mile walk from Danville, Illinois, to Ottawa, Illinois.

Springfield, Illinois. Illinois State Historical Library. Brush Papers. Letters of the Brush family, Ottawa, Illinois, 1837–1909.
IHi

Civil War letters. C. H. Brush diaries, 1863, 1865, 1885/1886. Legal Papers, 1832–1867. Land entries, etc. Newspaper clippings, calling cards, etc. Daily reports of 53rd Illinois Infantry, August and September 1863, January 1864.

Springfield, Illinois. Illinois State Historical Library. Mary Ann (Posey) Craig Papers. Seventy-one items.
IHi

Covers 1830–1878. Incoming correspondence to Mary Ann (Posey) and Edward Craig. Includes letters from Chicago and Peru.

Springfield, Illinois. Illinois State Historical Library. Joseph F. Keyes Letters, 1834–1847, to Joseph F. Keyes, of Ottawa, Illinois, and Ashford, Connecticut. 17 items.
IHi

Local politics, opportunities in Illinois.

Springfield, Illinois. Illinois State Historical Library. Julia A. Moss Journals, 1838–1887. One reel of microfilm of four journals.
IHi

Trip from Mondago, New York, to Peoria County, Illinois, via Erie Canal, stage, and Illinois River; many references to Jubilee College, Bishop Chase, and successors. Also 1874 trip to Washington, New York, and Philadelphia Exposition.

Springfield, Illinois. Illinois State Historical Library. "Results of My Western Trip." Author unknown, New York, September 11, 1845. 4 p.
IHi

Opportunities for investment in Illinois real estate, specifically along the I&M Canal: Chicago, Peru, Aurora, Wilmington, Dixon. Refers to St. Louis and Peoria.

Springfield, Illinois. Illinois State Historical Library. G. N. Tatham. Journal of a Business Trip through Illinois and Michigan in 1835–1836. 40 p.
IHi

Day-by-day account of means of transportation, lodging, food, and expenses. Tatham, a surveyor, stayed at Peru. Diary contains a short note on his expenses there.

Urbana, Illinois. Illinois Historical Survey Library. Records of French Exploration in America, 1648–1762. Transcripts and photocopies of originals in Bibliotheque Nationale, Paris. 134 items.
IU—HS

Records relating to the Illinois Country, the Mississippi Valley, and Louisiana. Described in the Survey's Publication, No. 5 (1956): 95–98.

Urbana, Illinois. Illinois Historical Survey Library. France. Archives de la Marine. Records, 1684–1741. Fifty-eight items.
IU—HS

Photocopies. Described in the Survey's Publication, no. 5 (1956): 60–62.

Urbana, Illinois. Illinois Historical Survey Library. Vertical File. Michael Henry Cryder. "Some Early History of the Cryder Family Beginning From the Time They Left Ohio Until They Reach Illinois, Written in a Letter to Eugene O. Cryder, by His Father, Michael Henry Cryder in 1898." (Typewritten). 14 p.
IU—HS

The family settled in Aux Sable Township, Grundy County, in 1833. The reminiscence includes details of the family's farming operations. 1834–1855.

Utica, Illinois. LaSalle County Historical Society Museum. The Ebersoll Genealogy. One folder, 23 v.
IUtHi

Ottawa residents. Twenty-three-volume diary of Amos Ebersoll, 1840s (original and transcribed).

Utica, Illinois. LaSalle County Historical Society Museum. J. M. Woods 1874–1878 Diary. 5 v.
IUtHi

References to Ottawa.

PART 4 Indians

The user of this section of the guide should bear in mind the transitory nature of aboriginal occupance in the corridor. A migration route of great significance as well as a region of abundance and strategic importance, the region was used by a great number of Indian groups from time to time to varying degrees of intensity. *The Atlas of Great Lakes Indian History,* by Helen Hornbeck Tanner, is the definitive study of groups and locations in the area. Published material on these diverse groups is abundant and widely available. An effort was made to include resources covering the broad range of research interests. Other information is available in the documents left by French Jesuit missionaries, travelers, Indian agents, and fur traders, as well as in the special collections of the Chicago Historical Society, the Newberry Library, the Archives of the State of Illinois, and the National Archives.

Archaeological studies comprise a particularly strong component of resources available. A great many of these take the form of contract or salvage archaeology projects and reports to state agencies and private businesses. Many of these are unpublished, and only a sample have been included in this guide. For very thorough listings, the researcher should consult the archaeology bibliography produced by the Illinois State Museum or *An Inventory and Evaluation of Known Archaeological Resources in the Illinois and Michigan Canal National Heritage Corridor, Illinois,* by the American Resources Group. A variety of field notes are also available at the Illinois State Museum and the Field Museum of Natural History in Chicago.

No attempt has been made to describe pertinent resources available in Canada or abroad. Microfilms of many of these resources are available at the Loyola University archives, where Yolande Dembowski has been instrumental in collecting and describing resources and producing original research.

Indians—*General*

Bauxar, J. Joseph. "History of the Illinois Area." In *Handbook of North American Indians.* Edited by Bruce G. Trigger. Vol. 15: *Northeast,* pp. 594–601. William C. Sturtevant, general editor. Washington: Smithsonian Institution, 1978–.
ICN

Beckwith, Hiram Williams. *The Illinois and Indiana Indians.* Fergus Historical Series, No. 27. Chicago: Fergus Printing Company, 1884. 183 p.
DLC, I, IC, ICN, ICU

Callender, Charles. "Great Lakes–Riverine Sociopolitical Organization." In *Handbook of North American Indians.* Edited by Bruce G. Trigger. Vol. 15: *Northeast,* pp. 610–621. William C. Sturtevant, general editor. Washington: Smithsonian Institution, 1978–.
ICN

Callender, Charles. *Social Organization of the Central Algonkian Indians.* Milwaukee Public Museum Publications in Anthropology, No. 7. Milwaukee, Wisconsin, 1962.
NN

Fitting, James E. and Cleland, Charles. "Late Prehistorical Settlement Patterns in the Upper Great Lakes." *Ethnohistory* 16 (1969): 281–302.
ICN, IEN, IU

Foreman, Grant. "Illinois and Her Indians." *Papers in Illinois History and Transactions* (1939): 66–111.
DLC, IC, ICN, IU

Hodge, Frederick Webb, ed. *Handbook of American Indians North of Mexico.* 2 v. Bureau of American Ethnology Bulletin, No. 30. New York: Pageant Books, Inc., 1959. ports., illus.
ICN

Contains entries under individual names, tribal headings, and relevant topics.

Illinois State Archaeological Society. *Journal.* Vol. 1–7, Vol. 1–. Fairbury, Illinois, 1942–1950, 1950–. illus., ports., maps.
DLC, ICN, ICU
Quarterly.

Illinois Archaeological Survey. *Bulletin.* No. 1–. Urbana, University of Illinois, 1959–.
ICU, IU

Jablow, Joseph. *Illinois, Kickapoo, and Potawatomi Indians.* New York: Garland Publishing Company, 1974. 436 p.
DLC, ICU
A study of Indian occupancy, 1640–1832, in Royce areas 48, 96-A, 110, 177, and 98.

Lazewski, Tony. "American Indian Migration to and Within Chicago, Illinois." Ph.D. dissertation, University of Illinois, 1976.
IU

Linton, Ralph. "Indians of Illinois, Early Period." Paper prepared for the Illinois Centennial Commission, 1915. 149 p.
IU—HS
Original and two carbon copies.

Mann, Mary Estelle. "The Indians of Illinois." B.A. thesis, University of Illinois, 1893. 29 p. (Photocopy.)
IU—HS

Matson, Nehemiah. *French and Indians of Illinois River.* Princeton, Illinois: Republican Job Printing Establishment, 1874. 260 p., front., port.
DLC, ICN, ICU

Osman, Eaton G. *The Last of a Great Indian Tribe: A Chapter of Colonial History.* Chicago: A. Flanagan Company, 1923.
DLC, IO
History of Fort St. Louis. Earlier edition entitled *Starved Rock: A Chapter of Colonial History.* Chicago: A. Flanagan Company, 1895. Glossary of names. History, relics, literature of Starved Rock.

Paul, Mary Elizabeth. "The Indians of the Illinois Territory from 1815 to 1818." M.A. thesis, University of Illinois, 1932. 50 p.
IU
Chippewa, Fox, Kickapoo, Menomini, Sauk, Winnebago, Potowatomi, Ottawa.

Peterson, Jacqueline. "Ethnogenesis: Métis Development and Influence in the Great Lakes Region, 1690–1836." Ph.D. dissertation, University of Illinois at Chicago, 1977.
ICUI

Peterson, Jacqueline. "'Wild' Chicago: The Formation and Destruction of a Multiracial Community on the Midwestern Frontier, 1816–1837." In *The Ethnic Frontier: Essays in the History of Group Survival in Chicago and the Midwest.* Edited by Melvin G. Holli and Peter d'A. Jones. Grand Rapids, Michigan: William B. Eerdman's Publishing Company, 1977.
DLC, ICU

"Special Meeting of the Illinois State Historical Society, Sponsored by the Will County Historical Society." *Journal of the Illinois State Historical Society* 23 (April 1930–January 1931): 183–187.
DLC, I, IC, ICHi, ICN, ICU, IEN, IU
Program of special meeting in Joliet of the state society. Addresses over Will County prehistory, Indian wars, Chicago portage.

Strong, William Duncan. *The Indian Tribes of the Chicago Region, With Special Reference to the Illinois and the Potawatomi.* Anthropology Leaflet, No. 24. Chicago: Field Museum of Natural History, 1926. 36 p., plates.
ICF, ICN, ICU
Bibliographical references, p. 36.

Tanner, Helen Hornbeck, ed. *Atlas of Great Lakes Indian History.* Civilization of the American Indian Series, Vol. 174. Norman, Oklahoma, and Chicago: University of Oklahoma Press and The Newberry Library, 1986.
ICN

Temple, Wayne C. "Culture and Economy of the Historic Indians of Illinois." Unpublished paper, Illinois State Museum. 93 p. (Typewritten.)
ISM
In binder. Original manuscript on file in Library Manuscript Collection.

Temple, Wayne C. *Indian Villages of the Illinois Country.* Illinois State Museum, Scientific Papers, Vol. 2, Pt. 2. Springfield: Illinois State Museum, 1958. 218 p., plate, port.
ICF, ICN

Introduction by Fred Eggan. Bibliography, pp. 200–212.

Transcripts of Oral Testimony Before the Indian Claims Commission. New York: Clearwater Publishing Company, c. 1975. 1389 cards. (Microfiche.)
ICN

Tregillis, Helen Cox. *The Indians of Illinois: A History and Genealogy.* Decorah, Iowa: Amundsen Publishing Company, 1983. 134 p., illus., maps.
IO

Includes detailed name list of Indians associated with Illinois. Bibliography.

Tucker, Sara Julia [Jones], comp. *Indian Villages of the Illinois Country.* Illinois State Museum, Scientific Papers, Vol. 2. Springfield, 1942. plates., maps.
ICU, ISM

U.S. Indian Claims Commission. *Commission Findings [on Indians of Ohio, Indiana, Illinois, Southern Michigan, and Southern Wisconsin].* 3 v. New York: Garland Publishing Company, 1974.
ICN

Contains various claims findings, some of which are relevant to the corridor. Included are claims of Potawatomi, Kickapoo, Wea, Chippewa, Ottawa. Vol. 79 contains findings on Royce area 148-B, which is in the corridor. Information is included on aboriginal use and occupancy, early white settlement, dispensation of lands, Land Office, and I&M Canal statistics.

U.S. Indian Claims Commission. *The Expert Reports From the Testimony Before the Indian Claims Commission: Interim List, April 1, 1973.* New York: Clearwater Publishing Company, 1973. 32 p.
ICN

A comprehensive listing of studies conducted under the Indian Claims Commission. By docket number. Many of these studies have been published by Garland Publishing, New York. The rest are available on microfiche.

Voegelin, Erminie Wheeler. "Anthropological Report on the Ottawa, Chippewa, and Potawatomi Indians." In *Indians of Illinois and Northwestern Indiana.* New York: Garland Publishing Company, 1974. 220 p., maps.
ICN

Report presented before the Indian Claims Commission, Docket 146. Bibliography, pp. 212–217. Royce Area 117—Michigan and a portion of Indiana. Royce Areas 110, 48, 96A, 63, 117, and 98 are also treated in the volume. David B. Stout's reports on the Kickapoo, Illinois, and Potawatomi Indians cover these areas.

Voegelin, Erminie Wheeler and Blasingham, Emily J. *Anthropological Report on the Indian Occupancy of Royce Areas 77 and 78.* New York: Garland Publishing Company, 1974. 217 p., maps.
ICN

Report presented before the Indian Claims Commission, Docket 216. Royce Areas 77 and 78 encompass a large portion of the corridor. Includes statistics, detailed maps.

Villiers, M. de. "Recettes meicales employees, dans la Region des Illinois vers 1724." *Journal del la Societe des Americanistes* n.s. 18 (1926): 15–20.
DLC, ICN, ICU

Whitney, Ellen M. "Indian History and the Indians of Illinois." *Journal of the Illinois State Historical Society* 69 (May 1976): 139–146.
DLC, I, IC, ICHi, ICN, ICU, IEN, IU

Winslow, Charles S., ed. *Indians of the Chicago Region.* Chicago, 1946. 210 p., front., illus.
DLC, ICN, ICU

Indians—General Studies

Indians—*General Studies*—Illinois Confederacy

Blasingham, Emily Jane. "The Illinois Indians, 1634–1800: A Study of Depopulation." *Ethnohistory* 3 (Summer/Fall 1956): 193–224, 361–412.
ICN, IEN, IU

Blasingham, Emily Jane. *The Illinois Indians, 1634–1800: A Study in Depopulation.* Ann Arbor, Michigan: University Microfilms, 1974. (Microfilm.)
ICN

Ph.D. dissertation, Indiana University, 1956. Bibliography, pp. 143–148.

Callender, Charles. "Illinois." In *Handbook of North American Indians.* Edited by Bruce G. Trigger. Vol. 15: *Northeast,* pp. 673–680. William C. Sturtevant, general editor. Washington: Smithsonian Institution, 1978–.
ICN

Caton, J. D. *The Last of the Illinois.* Fergus Historical Series, No. 3. Chicago: Fergus Printing Company, 1876. 55 p.
DLC, ICJ

Conlin, Claire O'Connell. "A Chronological Outline of the Illinois Indians." B.S. thesis, University of Illinois, 1958. 60 p.
IU—HS

Hamy, E. T. "Note Sur d'Anciennes Peintures sur Peaux des Indiens Illinois." *Journal de la Societe des Americanistes* 2 (1897): 185–195.
DLC, ICN, ICU

Hauser, Raymond E. "An Ethnohistory of the Illinois Indian Tribe, 1673–1832." Ph.D. dissertation, Northern Illinois University, 1973. 451 p.
ICN, IDeKN

Bibliography, pp. 372–407.

Hauser, Raymond E. "The Illinois Tribe: From Autonomy and Self-Sufficiency to Dependency and Depopulation." *Journal of the Illinois State Historical Society* 69 (May 1976): 127–138.
DLC, I, IC, ICHi, ICN, ICU, IEN, IU

Hogens, Richard S. "The Early French Explorers and the Illinois Indians." *Journal of the Illinois State Archaeological Society* 2 (1952): 35–49.
DLC, ICN, ICU

Kinietz, William Vernon. "The Ethnology of the Illinois Indians." M.A. thesis, University of Chicago, 1933.
ICU

Scott, James. *The Illinois Nation: A History of the Illinois Nation of Indians from Their Discovery to the Present Day.* Streator, Illinois: Streator Historical Society, 1973. 89 p.
IO

Also bound in volume is *The Illinois Nation, Part II: A Pictoral Supplement to the History of the Illinois Nation of Indians.* 1976. 44 p., photos. Bibliography.

Wray, D. E. and Smith, H. "An Hypothesis for the Identification of the Illinois Confederacy with the Middle Mississippi Culture in Illinois." *American Antiquity* 10 (1944): 23–27.
ICN, ICU, IU

Indians—*General Studies*—Kickapoo

Callender, Charles, Pope, Richard K., and Pope, Susan M. "Kickapoo." In *Handbook of North American Indians.* Edited by Bruce G. Trigger. Vol. 15: *Northeast.* pp. 656–667. William C. Sturtevant, general editor. Washington: Smithsonian Institution, 1978–.
ICN

Indians—*General Studies*—Miami

Anson, Bert. *The Miami Indians.* Norman, Oklahoma: University of Oklahoma Press, 1970. 329 p., illus., maps, plans, ports.
ICN, ICU

The Civilization of the American Indian Series. Bibliography, pp. 304–318.

Callender, Charles. "Miami." In *Handbook of North American Indians.* Edited by Bruce G. Trigger. Vol. 15: *Northeast,* pp. 680–689. William C. Sturtevant, general editor. Washington, Smithsonian Institution, 1978–.
ICN

Indians—*General Studies*—Potawatomi

Baerreis, David S., Wheeler-Voegelin, Erminie, and Wycoco-Moore, Remedios. *Anthropological Report on the Chippewa, Ottawa, and Potawatomi Indians in Northeastern Illinois; and the Identity of the Mascoutens.* New York: Garland Publishing Company, 1974. 344 p., maps.
ICN

Report presented before the Indian Claims Commission.

Baerreis, David A. "Chieftainship Among the Potawatomi: An Exploration of Ethnohistoric Methodology." *Wisconsin Archaeologist* 54 (3): 114–134.
DLC, ICJ, ICN, ICU

Clifton, James. "Chicago Was Theirs." *Chicago History* 1 (Spring 1970): 4–17.
DLC, IC, ICF, ICHi, ICN, ICU, IU

Clifton, James A. "Potawatomi." In *Handbook of North American Indians.* Edited by Bruce G. Trigger. Vol. 15: *Northeast.* pp. 725–742. William C. Sturtevant, general editor. Washington: Smithsonian Institution, 1978–.
ICN

Clifton, James A. *The Prairie People: Continuity and Change in Potawatomi Indian Culture, 1665–1965.* Lawrence, Kansas: Regents Press of Kansas, 1977. 529 p., illus., maps.
ICF, ICU

Bibliography, pp. 485–511.

Edmunds, R. David. "A History of the Potawatomi Indians, 1615–1796." Ph.D. dissertation, University of Oklahoma, 1972.
OkU

Edmunds, Russell David. *The Potawatomis, Keepers of the Fire.* Civilization of the American Indian Series, Vol. 145. Norman, Oklahoma: University of Oklahoma Press, 1978. 367 p., illus., maps, ports.
ICF, ICN, ICU

Selected bibliography, pp. 331–346.

Schofield, William. *The Trail of the Potawatomi.* Joliet, Illinois: Will County Historical Society, 1978. 12 p.
IRo

Appended is another essay by Schofield, "Pontiac's Death and Its Consequences." 5 p.

Winger, Otho. *The Potawatomi Indians.* Elgin, Illinois: Elgin Press, 1939. 159 p., front., illus., ports.
DLC, ICN

Bibliography, p. 159. Photograph of Starved Rock. Map of Indian trails and early traces. Good, brief account of the Potawatomi in Illinois. Also treats Potawatomi in Indiana, Michigan, and Wisconsin.

Indians—*General Studies*—Sauk, Fox, Sauk and Fox

Callender, Charles. "Fox." In *Handbook of North American Indians.* Edited by Bruce G. Trigger. Vol. 15: *Northeast,* pp. 636–647. William C. Sturtevant, general editor. Washington: Smithsonian Institution, 1978–.
ICN

Callender, Charles. "Sauk." In *Handbook of North American Indians.* Edited by Bruce G. Trigger. Vol. 15: *Northeast,* pp. 648–655. William C. Sturtevant, general editor. Washington: Smithsonian Institution, 1978–.
IC

Faye, Stanley. *The Foxes' Fort—1730.* Aurora, Illinois, n.d. 40 p. (Typewritten.)
IU—HS

Paper on Starved Rock.

Faye, Stanley. "The Foxes' Fort—1730." *Journal of the Illinois State Historical Society* 28 (October 1935): 123–163.
DLC, I, IC, ICHi, ICN, ICU, IEN, IU

History of Indian reaction to French exploration. Includes map of French posts in Illinois. Footnotes.

Gussow, Zachary. *An Anthropological Report.* New York: Garland Publishing Company, 1974. 86 p., map.
ICN

Sauk and Fox Indians. Report presented before the Indian Claims Commission, Docket 135.

Gussow, Zachary. *The Historic Habitat of the Sac, Fox, and Iowa Indians.* New York: Garland Publishing Company, 1974. 62 p.
ICN

Report presented before the Indian Claims Commission, Docket 158.

Hagan, William Thomas. *The Sac and Fox Indians.* The Civilization of the American Indian Series, Vol. 48. Norman, Oklahoma: University of Oklahoma Press, 1958. 287 p., illus.
ICN, ICU

Bibliography.

Hauser, Raymond E. "An Ethnohistorical Approach to the Study of the Fox Wars, 1712–1735." M.A. thesis, Northern Illinois University, 1966. 448 p.
IDeKN

Bibliography.

Hewitt, J. N. B. "Sauk." *Bulletin of the Bureau of American Ethnology* 30 (1910): 471–480.
ICN, ICU

Manners and Customs of the Sauk Nation of Indians. New York: Garland Publishing Company, 1974. 50 p.
ICN
Presented as a report to the Indian Claims Commission, Docket 158.

Skinner, Alanson Buck. *Observations on the Ethnology of the Sauk Indians.* [Milwaukee, Wisconsin]: Public Museum of the City of Milwaukee, 1923. 180 p.
DLC, ICJ

Steward, J. F. "Further Regarding the Destruction of a Branch of the Fox Tribe of Indians." *Illinois State Historical Society Transactions* 20 (1914): 175–183.
DLC, IC, ICU
Includes Franquelin's 1684 map of Des-Plaines River Valley.

U.S. Indian Claims Commission. *Commission Findings on the Sac, Fox, and Iowa Indians.* New York: Garland Publishing Company, 1974. 385 p., maps.
ICN

Indians—*Archaeology*

Indians—*Archaeology*—General

American Resources Group, Ltd. *An Inventory and Evaluation of Known Archaeological Resources in the Illinois and Michigan Canal National Heritage Corridor, Illinois.* Vol. 1. Prepared under the Supervision of Michael J. McNerney and Vergil E. Noble, Co-Principal Investigators. Cultural Resources Management Report, No. 111. Prepared for the National Park Service, Midwest Archaeological Center. Lincoln, Nebraska, 1985. 289 p., maps, charts, tables.
ICU
Contributing authors: James A. Brown, Theodore Karamanski, Michael J. McNerney, Charles R. Moffat, and Vergil E. Noble. Compiled from 333 archaeological site survey forms used to identify 403 cultural components. Includes fifty-eight-page annotated bibliography.

Baker, Frank C., Griffin, James B., Morgan, Richard C, Neumann, George K., and Taylor, Jay L. B. *Contributions to the Archaeology of the Illinois River Valley.* Philadelphia: The American Philosophical Society, 1941. 86 p., illus., plates, charts.
ICF
Transactions of the American Philosophical Society, n.s., Vol. 32, Pt. 1.

Bauxar, J. Joseph. "Indian Villages in the Illinois Country." Unpublished paper, Illinois State Museum, 1954.
ISM

Belting, Natalia. "We Are Illinois." M.S. thesis, University of Illinois, n.d.
IU

Bluhm, Elaine A. *Chicago Area Archaeology.* Illinois Archaeological Survey Bulletin, No. 3. Springfield, 1961. 175 p., illus., plates, maps, tables.
ICF, IU
Cook County. Bibliographies.

Brown, James A., ed. *Mississippian Site Archaeology in Illinois: I. Site Reports from the St. Louis and Chicago Areas.* Illinois Archaeological Survey Bulletin, No. 8, pp. 244–246. Springfield, 1971.
IU

Brown, James A. "The Northeastern Extension of the Havana Tradition." In *Hopewellian Studies,* pp. 107–122. Edited by Joseph R. Caldwell and Robert L. Hall. Illinois State Museum Scientific Papers, No. 12. Springfield, 1964.
ISM
Cook County, Will County.

Brown, James A. "The Prairie Peninsula." Ph.D. dissertation, University of Chicago, 1965.
ICU

Buikstra, Jane E. "Mortuary Site Survey in the Lower Illinois River Region, Predictive Models Study Units I and II: Preliminary Final Report." Unpublished paper, Illinois Department of Conservation, 1978.
ISCon
Cook, Will, Grundy counties.

Griffin, James B. "Aboriginal Mortuary Customs in the Western Half of the Northeast Woodland Area." A.M. thesis, University of Chicago. 96 p., chart.
ICU

Hall, Robert L. "The Impact on Archaeology of Dredge Spoil Disposal Resulting from Nine Foot Channel Maintenance Operations in the Illinois Waterway from Beardstown to the DesPlaines–Kankakee Confluence." Paper submitted by University of Illinois at Chicago to United States Army Corps of Engineers, Chicago, 1974.
IC—ACE
Grundy County, LaSalle County.

Hall, Robert L. and Weston, Bruce R. "A Predictive Model of Archaeological Site Locations in the Upper Illinois River Valley." In *Predictive Models in Archaeological Resource Management,* pp. 21–25. Edited by Margaret Kimball Brown, Illinois Archaeological Survey, Circular, No. 3. Springfield, 1978.
ICU, IU
DuPage County, LaSalle County, Will County, Grundy County.

Keene, David, S. J. *Prehistory of the DesPlaines–Illinois River Valleys.* Chicago: Open Lands Project, 1981. 4 p. (Photocopy.)
IRo

Lawson, Publius V. "The Potawatomi." *Wisconsin Archaeologist* 19 (1920): 40–116.
ICJ, ICN, ICU

Quimby, George Irving. *Indian Culture and European Trade Goods: The Archaeology of the Historic Period in the Western Great Lakes Region.* Madison, Wisconsin: University of Wisconsin Press, 1966. 217 p., illus., map.
DLC, ICU
Bibliography, pp. 203–209.

Riffe, William Wilson. "An Analysis of the Interrelationship Among Population and Trade Structure Characteristics of Illinois Villages." Ph.D. dissertation, University of Illinois, 1967.
IU

Scharf, Albert F. *Indian Trails and Villages of Chicago and Cook, DuPage, and Will Counties, Illinois (1804) as Shown By Weapons and Implements of the Stone Age.* n.p., 1900.
IHi

Temple, Wayne C. *Indian Villages of the Illinois Country.* Scientific Papers of the Illinois State Museum, No. 2. Springfield, 1958. 218 p.
ISM

Weston, Bruce R. "Upper Illinois River Unite (II)." In *Predictive Models in Illinois Archaeology; Report Summaries,* pp. 21–32. Edited by Margaret Kimball Brown. Springfield, Illinois Department of Conservation, 1981.
ICU, ISCon
LaSalle, Grundy, Will, DuPage, Cook counties.

Weston, Bruce R. and Hall, Robert L. "A Predictive Model of Archaeological Site Locations in the Upper Illinois River Drain Basin." Paper submitted by the Department of Anthropology, University of Illinois at Chicago Circle to the Illinois Department of Conservation, 1978.
ISCon
LaSalle, Grundy, Will, DuPage, Cook counties.

Indians—*Archaeology*—LaSalle County

Allee, Mary N. "The Gentleman Farm Site and the Fisher-Heally Series in Northern Illinois." M.A. thesis, University of Chicago, 1949. 85 p.
ICU
LaSalle County.

Babson, Jane F. "The Architecture of Early Illinois Forts." *Journal of the Illinois State Historical Society* 61 (Spring 1968): 9–40.
DLC, I, IC, ICHi, ICN, ICU, IEN, IU
Compares the designs of British and French forts. Detailed description of LaSalle's Fort St. Louis at Starved Rock. Contains maps, plans, photographs.

Babson, Jane F. "Some Early Fort Types in the Northwest Territory, 1679–1832." Unpublished paper, Illinois State Historical Library, 1967.
IHi

Bauxar, J. Joseph. "Archaeological Investigations in the Starved Rock Area." Unpublished paper, Department of Anthropology, Illinois State Museum, 1953.
ISM
LaSalle County.

Blake, Leonard W. and Dean, Rosalind M. "Appendix III: Corn from Plumb Island." In *Reports on Illinois Prehistory: I,* pp. 92–93. Edited by Elaine A. Bluhm. Illinois Archaeological Survey, Bulletin, No. 4. Springfield, 1963.
IU

Bluhm, Elaine A. "Structures at Ls 13 and Ls 12." Unpublished paper, Department of Anthropology, Illinois State Museum, 1947.
ISM
LaSalle County.

Bradford, C. C. "The Starved Rock Area—Rich in Archaeology, in Indian Lore, in History." *Journal of the Illinois State Archaeological Society* (July 1943): 9–18.
DLC, ICN, ICU
LaSalle County.

Brown, James A. *The Gentleman Farm Site, LaSalle County, Illinois.* Illinois State Museum, Reports of Investigation, No. 12. Springfield, 1967.
ISM

Brown, James Allison, ed. *The Zimmerman Site; A Report on Excavations at the Grand Village of Kaskaskia, LaSalle County, Illinois, from the Reports of Kenneth G. Orr and Others.* Illinois State Museum, Report of Investigations, No. 9. Springfield, 1961. 86 p., illus.
ICU, ISM
Bibliography, pp. 84–86.

Brown, James A., William, Roger W., Barth, Mary A., and Neuman, George K. *The Gentleman Farm Site, LaSalle County, Illinois.* Illinois State Museum, Report of Investigations, No. 12. Springfield, 1967.
ISM

Brown, Margaret Kimball. "An Archaeological Survey of the Fox and DesPlaines River Valleys in Northeastern Illinois." In her "Preliminary Report of 1973 Historic Sites Survey Archaeological Reconnaissance of Selected Areas in the State of Illinois." Part I: "Summary Section A." pp. 90–95. Paper submitted by Northwestern University Archaeological Program to the United States National Park Service, Illinois Department of Conservation, and Illinois Archaeological Survey, 1974.
ISCon
LaSalle County.

Brown, Margaret Kimball. "Cultural Transformation Among the Illinois." *Michigan State University Publications of the Museum Anthropological Series* 1 (1979): 217–267.
ISM
LaSalle County.

Brown, Margaret Kimball. "Cultural Transformation Among the Illinois: The Application of a Systems Model to Archaeological and Ethnohistorical Data." Ph.D. dissertation, Michigan State University, 1973.
Mi

Brown, Margaret Kimball. *The First Kaskaskia: The Zimmerman Site, LaSalle, Illinois,* n.p., LaSalle County Historical Society, 1973. 16 p., illus.
ICF, ISM

Brown, Margaret Kimball. *The Zimmerman Site: Further Excavations at the Grand Village of Kaskaskia.* Illinois State Museum, Report of Investigations, No. 32. Springfield, 1975.
ISM
LaSalle County.

Cole, Fay-Cooper. "The Pre-History of Illinois." *Journal of the Illinois State Historical Society* 25 (January 1933): 251–260.
DLC, I, IC, ICHi, ICN, ICU, IEN, IU
References to "Great Town" of the Illinois Indians near Starved Rock. Includes bibliography.

Downer, Alan S., McCorvie, Mary R., Nickels, Martin K., and Wagner, Mark J. "Notes on a Human Burial from the Starved Rock Site, Ls-12, Starved Rock State Park, LaSalle County, Illinois." *Rediscovery* 2 (1982): 4–16.
ICarbS, IU

Fenner, Gloria J. "The Aboriginal Occupation of the Plum Island Site, LaSalle County, Illinois." M.A. thesis, University of Illinois, 1962.
IU
LaSalle County.

Fenner, Gloria J. "The Plum Island Site, LaSalle County, Illinois." In *Reports on Illinois Prehistory: I,* pp. 1–106. Edited by Elaine A. Bluhm. Illinois Archaeological Survey, Bulletin, No. 4. Springfield, 1963.
ICU, IU
LaSalle County. Maps, diagrams, charts, photographs, bibliography.

Garraghan, Gilbert. "The Great Village of the Illinois: A Topographical Problem." *Mid-America* 14 (1931): 141–151.
DLC, IC, ICL, ICN, ICU, IU
LaSalle County.

Hagen, Richard S. "The Early French Explorers and the Illinois Indians." *Journal of the Illinois State Archaeological Society* 2 (1952): 35–49.
DLC, ICN, ICU
LaSalle County.

Henriksen, Harry C. "Utica Hopewell, A Study of Early Hopewellian Occupation of the Illinois River Valley." M.A. thesis, University of Illinois, 1957.
IU
LaSalle County.

Henriksen, Harry C. "Utica Hopewell, A Study of Early Hopewellian Occupation in the Illinois River Valley." In *Middle Woodland Sites in Illinois*, pp. 1–67. Edited by Elaine Bluhm Herold. Illinois Archaeological Survey, Bulletin, No. 5. n.p., 1965.
IU
LaSalle County.

Hodges, Percy. "Preliminary Survey of the Illinois Village Site at Utica." Unpublished paper, Department of Anthropology, University of Illinois, 1929.
IU
LaSalle County.

Howard, Ruth and Gillette, Charles. "Survey of Pottery from the University of Chicago—Illinois State Museum Archaeological Expedition of the Summer 1947." Unpublished paper, Department of Anthropology, Illinois State Museum, 1947.
ISM
LaSalle County.

Jelks, Edward B. and Hawks, Preston A. "Archaeological Explorations at Starved Rock, Illinois (11-Ls-12)." Paper submitted by the Midwestern Archaeological Research Center, Illinois State University, to the Illinois Department of Conservation, 1982.
ISCon
LaSalle County.

Jelks, Edward B. and Savini, John F. "Archaeological Survey at Starved Rock and Matthiessen State Parks." Paper submitted by Archaeological Surveys, Department of Sociology, Anthropology and Social Work, Illinois State University, to the Illinois Department of Transportation, 1976.
ISTr
LaSalle County.

Keller, Gordon N. "Manifestations of the Fort Ancient Aspect in the Starved Rock Area of Northern Illinois." M.A. thesis, University of Chicago, 1949.
ICU
LaSalle County.

MacNeish, Richard S. "Archaeological Survey of the Village of Old Kaskaskia and Starved Rock." Unpublished paper, Department of Anthropology, Illinois State Museum, 1945.
ISM
LaSalle County.

Mayer-Oakes, William J. "An Early Culture at Starved Rock, Illinois." M.A. thesis, University of Chicago, 1949.
ICU
LaSalle, Illinois.

Mayer-Oakes, William J. "Starved Rock Archaic, a Pre-Pottery Horizon from Northern Illinois." *American Antiquity* 16 (1951): 313–324.
ICN, ICU, IU
LaSalle County.

McGregor, John C. "Report on Visit to Historic Site Across the River from Starved Rock and Near Ottawa." Unpublished paper, Department of Anthropology, Illinois State Museum, 1945.
ISM
LaSalle County.

Middle Woodland Sites in Illinois. Illinois Archaeological Survey Bulletin, No. 5. Urbana, Illinois: University of Illinois.
ICU, IU
Contains a study of Utica Hopewellian mound groups by Harry C. Henriksen, pp. 1–67. Includes bibliography.

Moorehead, Warren K. "Preliminary Report on Excavations at Plum Island." Unpublished paper, University of Illinois Library, n.d.
IU

Orr, Kenneth G. "Initial Report on the Zimmerman and Starved Rock Sites, LaSalle County,

Illinois." Unpublished paper, Department of Anthropology, Illinois State Museum, 1947.
ISM

Orr, Kenneth G. "Summary Statements of the Present Status of Archaeological Research in the Starved Rock Area, LaSalle County, Illinois." Unpublished paper, Department of Anthropology, Illinois State Museum, 1949.
ISM

Riley, Thomas J. "Middle Woodland Cooper from the Utica Mounds, LaSalle County, Illinois." *Wisconsin Archaeologist* 60 (1979): 26–46.
ICJ, ICN, ICU
LaSalle County.

Sauer, Carl O., Cady, Gilbert H., and Cowles, Henry C. *Starved Rock State Park and Its Environs.* Geographic Society of Chicago, Bulletin, No. 6. n.p., 1918.
DLC, I, IC, ICU, ICHi
LaSalle County.

Schnell, Gail S. *Hotel Plaza: An Early Historic Site with a Long Prehistory.* Illinois State Museum, Report of Investigations, No. 29. Springfield, 1974.
ISM, ICU
LaSalle County. Based on the author's University of Pennsylvania thesis, 1968. Bibliography. Appendix by Paul W. Parmalee.

Smith, Charles R. and Hawks, Preston A. "Phase I Archaeological Investigation of the Utica Terminal, Utica, Illinois: Interim Report." Paper submitted by the Midwestern Archaeological Research Center—Illinois State University to the United States Army Corps of Engineers—Rock Island, 1981.
IR—ACE
LaSalle County.

Tucker, Sally. "Old Kaskaskia: Preliminary Summary of Data Relating to Old Kaskaskia and the Iliniwek Indians for the Period 1670–1700." Unpublished paper, University of Chicago Library, n.d.
ICU

Westover, Allan R. and Drollinger, Harold. "Phase II Archaeological Investigation of the Utica Terminal, Utica, Illinois." Paper submitted by the Midwestern Archaeological Research Center—Illinois State University to the United States Army Corps of Engineers—Rock Island, 1982.
IR—ACE
LaSalle County.

Wiant, Michael D. and Knight, Frances R. *Archaeological Investigations at the Marseilles Training Center: The Development of a Predictive Model of Site Location.* Submitted by the Illinois State Museum Society Archaeological Research Program to the Military and Naval Department of the State of Illinois. Springfield, 1983. 38 p., maps, figures.
ISM
Bibliography.

Indians—*Archaeology*—Grundy County

Hall, Robert L. "An Archaeological Survey of the Grand Prairie in North-Central Illinois." In *Preliminary Report of 1971 Historic Sites Survey Archaeological Reconnaissance of Selected Areas in the State of Illinois.* Part I: *Summary,* pp. 72–78. Submitted by the Department of Anthropology, University of Illinois at Chicago, to the United States National Park Service, Illinois Department of Conservation, and the Illinois Archaeological Survey, 1971.
ISCon
Grundy County.

Hall, Robert L. "An Archaeological Survey of the Grand Prairie in North-Central Illinois." In *Preliminary Report of 1972 Historic Sites Survey Archaeological Reconnaissance of Selected Areas in the State of Illinois.* Part I: *Summary Section A,* pp. 70–75. Submitted by the Department of Anthropology, University of Illinois at Chicago, to United States National Park Service, Illinois Department of Conservation, and Illinois Archaeological Survey, 1972.
ISCon
Grundy County.

Koski, Ann L. "An Archaeological Survey of the Commonwealth Edison Langham (Seneca) Power Station, Grundy County, Illinois." Paper submitted by the Foundation for Illinois Archaeology to Commonwealth Edison, 1979.
IC—COC
Grundy County.

Koski, Ann L. "A Preliminary Report on the Phase II Archaeological Testing of the Dunn and Burroughs Sites, Langham Power Station, Grundy County, Illinois." Paper submitted by the Foundation for Illinois Archeology to Commonwealth Edison, 1980.
IC—COC
Grundy County.

Struever, Stuart. "Archaeological Survey of Collins Generating Station Near Morris, Grundy County, Illinois." Paper submitted by the Foundation for Illinois Archeology to Commonwealth Edison, 1972.
IC—COC
Grundy County.

Indians—*Archaeology*—Will County

Cutler, Gretchen. "Fisher Pottery Types." Unpublished paper, Department of Anthropology, University of Illinois, n.d.
IU
Will County.

Farnsworth, Kenneth B. "An Archaeological Survey of the DesPlaines Conservation Area Waterfowl Management Project, Will County, Illinois." Paper submitted by the Foundation for Illinois Archaeology to United States Army Corps of Engineers, Rock Island, 1977.
IR—ACE
Will County.

Gillette, Charles E. "The Non-Mississippi Manifestations at the Fisher Site, Will County, Illinois." M.A. thesis, University of Chicago, 1949. 84 p.
ICU
Will County.

Griffin, John W. "The Upper Mississippi Occupations of the Fisher Site, Will County, Illinois." M.A. thesis, University of Chicago, 1946. 181 p.
ICU

Klippel, Walter E. "An Archaeological Assessment and Impact Statement of the Proposed Soil Disposal Tracts for the Illinois Waterway Duplication Locks Project (Joliet-Lockport Region)." Paper submitted by the Illinois State Museum Society to the United States Army Corps of Engineers, Chicago, 1975.
IC—ACE
Will County.

Knight, Robert and Zeuch, Lucius. *Mount Joliet: Its Place in Illinois History and Its Location.* n.p., Will County Historical Society, 1980. 8 p. (Mimeographed.)
ILo
Also *Journal of the Illinois State Historical Society* 23 (April 1980): 84–91. Summarizes descriptions found in early explorers' and later cartographers' notes concerning Mount Joliet. Contains photographs of the area and two maps.

Krogman, Wilton M. "Adler Mound No. 5." Unpublished paper, The Museum, Southern Illinois University, n.d.
ICarbS

Krogman, Wilton Marion. "The Archaeology of the Chicago Area." *Illinois State Academy of Science Transactions* 23 (1931): 413–420.
DLC, I, ICJ
Will County.

Langford, George. "The Adler Mounds." Unpublished paper, The Museum, Southern Illinois University, n.d.
ICarbS

Langford, George. "The Fisher Mound and Village Site." *Illinois State Academy of Science Transactions* 22 (1929): 79–92.
DLC, I, ICJ
Will County.

Langford, George. "The Fisher Mound Group, Successive Aboriginal Occupations Near the Mouth of the Illinois River." *American Anthropologist* 29 (1927): 152–205.
IC, ICJ, ICN, ICU, IU
Will County.

Langford, George. "The Fisher Site: Exploration of the Pits." Unpublished paper, Department of Anthropology, University of Illinois, n.d.
IU
Will County.

Langford, George. "Letters to Dr. Wilton M. Krogman on 10, 13, and 19 November 1929."

Unpublished paper, The Museum, Southern Illinois University, n.d.
ICarbS

Langford, George. "Plans and Sections of Mounds 2, 3, 5, and 8." Blueprint reproductions, The Museum, Southern Illinois University, n.d.
ICarbS

Skinner, Robert R. "The Oakwood Mound, an Upper Mississippi Component." *Journal of the Illinois State Archaeological Society* 3 (1953): 2–14.
DLC, ICN, ICU
Will County.

Weedman, William and Klippel, Walter E. "An Archaeological Assessment and Impact Statement of the Proposed Soil Disposal Tracts for the Illinois Waterway Duplicate Locks Project (Joliet-Lockport Region)." Paper submitted by the Illinois State Museum Society to the United States Army Corps of Engineers, Chicago, 1975.
IC—ACE
Will County.

Indians—*Archaeology*—DuPage County

Curtis, Sue Ann, Borlin, Andrea, Bebrich, Carl A., Hendrickson, Carol, Kauffman, Barbara, Wattenmaker, Patricia, and Minc, Leah. "A Study of the Cultural Resources at the Argonne National Laboratory." Unpublished paper, Division of Environmental Impact Studies, Argonne National Laboratory, 1980.
IAr
DuPage County.

Indians—*Archaeology*—Cook County

Bennett, W. C. and Enberg, P. R. "Huber Site Near Blue Island: Report of Excavation and Survey of Collection." Unpublished paper, Department of Anthropology, Illinois State Museum, 1929.
ISM
Cook County.

Brown, James A. *Hopewell and Woodland Site Archaeology in Illinois.* Illinois Archaeological Survey Bulletin, No. 6. n.p., 1968.
IU
Cook County.

Butkus, Edmund. "Archaic Hunters of the Chicago Outlet." *Central States Archaeological Journal* 19 (1972): 114–117.
IC, ICU, IU
Cook County.

Herold, Elaine Bluhm and O'Brien, Patricia J. "The Huber Site (K-1) Cook County, Illinois." Unpublished paper, Department of Anthropology, Illinois State Museum, n.d.
ISM

Hurlbut, Henry H. *Chicago Antiquities: Comprising Original Items and Relations, Letters, Extracts, and Notes, Pertaining to Early Chicago.* Chicago, 1881.
DLC, ICHi, ICN

Koelikamp, Ted. "Paleo Points from the Chicago Area." *Central States Archaeological Journal* 20 (October 1973): 168–170.
IC, ICU, IU

Lace, Edward J. "Prehistoric Indians of the Chicago Area." *Illinois State Academy of Science Transactions* 23 (1931): 413–420.
DLC, I, ICJ

Munson, Cheryl Ann and Munson, Patrick J. "Preliminary Report on an Early Historic Site in Cook County, Illinois." *Wisconsin Archaeologist* 50 (1969): 184–188.
I, ICF, ICJ, ICN, ICU, IEN, IU

Omoto, Constance. "The Identification of a Prehistoric Indian Skeletal Series from Will County, Illinois." M.A. thesis, Indiana University, 1960.
InU
Will County.

Parmalee, Paul W. "Appendix: Vertebrate Remains from the Huber Site (K-1), Cook County, Illinois." Unpublished paper, Department of Anthropology, Illinois State Museum, n.d.
ISM

Potter, William L. *The Forts of Palos: Investigations into Two Fortified Sites Near Chicago.* n.p., By the Author, 1983. 15 p., maps. (Mimeographed.)
IPHil

Slaymaker, Charles M. III, and Slaymaker, Charles M., Jr. "Au Sagaunashke Village: The Upper Mississippian Occupation of the Knoll Spring Site, Cook County, Illinois." In *Mississip-*

pian Site Archaeology in Illinois: I. Site Reports from the St. Louis and Chicago Areas, pp. 192–244. Edited by James A. Brown. Illinois Archaeological Survey, Bulletin, No. 8. Springfield, 1921.
IU

Steward, J. F. *Lost Maramech and Earliest Chicago: A History of the Foxes and of Their Downfall Near the Great Village of Maramech; Original Investigations and Discoveries.* Chicago: F. H. Revell Company, 1903. 390 p., front., illus., facsims.
ICN, ICU

Van Stone, James W. "Canadian Trade Silver from Indian Graves in Northern Illinois." *Wisconsin Archaeologist* 51 (1970): 21–30.
I, ICF, ICJ, ICN, ICU, IEN, IU
Cook County.

Indians—*Fur Trade and Aboriginal Trade*

American Fur Company. *Calendar of the American Fur Company's Papers.* 2 v. Washington: U.S. Government Printing Office, 1945.
ICU
Annual report of the American Historical Association for the year 1944.

American Fur Company. *Guide to the Use of the Microfilm Copy of the American Fur Company Papers.* New York: New York Historical Society, 1953. 5 p. (Photocopy.)
ICU

Bridgewater, William R. "The American Fur Company." Ph.D. dissertation, Yale University, 1928.
CtY

Haeger, John D. "The American Fur Company and the Chicago of 1812–1835." *Journal of the Illinois State Historical Society* 61 (Summer 1968): 117–139. Map, photo.
DLC, I, IC, ICHi, ICN, ICU, IEN, IU
Examines fur trade in the Chicago vicinity, including the Illinois River Valley, in an effort to determine the role of the trade in urban development.

Hubbard, Gurdon Saltonstall. *The Autobiography of Gurdon Saltonstall Hubbard, Pa-pa-ma-ta-be, "The Swift Walker"; With an Introduction by Caroline M. McIlvaine.* Chicago: R. R. Donnelley, 1911. 182 p., front.
DLC, ICU

Hubbard, Gurdon Saltonstall. *Incidents and Events in the Life of Gurdon Saltonstall Hubbard, Collected from Personal Narrations and Other Sources, and Arranged by His Nephew, Henry E. Hamilton.* Chicago: Rand, McNally, Printers, 1888. 189 p., front.
DLC
Includes an account of the author's service with the American Fur Company in Michigan and Illinois, 1818–1828.

Lavender, David. *The First in the Wilderness.* Garden City, New York: Doubleday & Company, 1964.
ICN
History of the American Fur Company.

Meyor, Alfred H. *Circulation and Settlement Patterns of the Calumet Region of Northwest Indiana and Northeast Illinois (the First State of Occupance—the Pottawatomie and the Fur Trader—1830).* Albany, New York, 1954. 274 p., illus., maps.
ICN
Reprinted from the *Annals of the Association of American Geographers* 44 (September 1954).

Nute, Grace Lee. "The Papers of the American Fur Company: A Brief Estimate of Their Significance." *American Historical Review* 32 (April 1927): 519–538.
DLC, I, IC, ICN, ICU, ICHi, IU

Indians—*Ethnography*

Allouez, Jean Claude. "Narrative of a Third Voyage to the Illinois, Made by Father Claude Allouis [sic]." In *The Jesuit Relations and Allied Documents,* vol. 60, pp. 148–169. Edited by Reuben Gold Thwaites. Cleveland, Ohio, 1900.
DLC
Contains description of the Kaskaskia Village and region.

Blair, Emma H., ed. *The Indian Tribes of the Upper Mississippi Valley and Region of the Great Lakes, as Described by Nicolas Perrot, French Commandant in the Northwest; Bacqueville de la Potherie, French Royal Commissioner to Canada; Morrell Marston, American Army*

Officer; and Thomas Forsyth, United States Agent at Fort Armstrong. 2 v. Cleveland, Ohio: Arthur H. Clark, 1911–1912. fronts., plates, facsims.
DLC, ICU, InU
Bibliography, Vol. 2.

Catlin, George. *Letters and Notes on the Manners, Customs, and Condition of the North American Indians*. 2 v. Philadelphia: W. P. Hazard, 1857. front., plates.
CtY, ICarbS, ICU, NjP
Includes portraits and sketches of Illinois Indians.

Deliette, L. *Memoir Concerning the Illinois Country*. Edited by T. C. Pease and R. C. Werner. Collections of the Illinois State Historical Library, No. 23. Springfield, 1934.
DLC, ICF, ICN, ICU, IEN

Lewis, Hannah. *Narrative of Captivity and Sufferings*. New York: Garland Publishing Company, 1977. 24 p.
DLC
Covers captivities of Sauk, Fox, and other Indians of Illinois. Reprint of the 1817 edition, printed by H. Trumbell, Boston, under title *Narrative of the Captivity and Sufferings of Mrs. Hannah Lewis*.

Narrative of the Capture and Providential Escape of Misses Frances and Almira Hall, Two Respectable Young Women (Sisters) of the Ages of 16 and 18, Who Were Taken Prisoners by the Savages, at a Frontier Settlement, Near Indian Creek, in May Last, When Fifteen of the Inhabitants Fell Victims to the Bloody Tomahawk and Scalping Knife; Among Whom were the Parents of the Unfortunate Females; Likewise is Added the Interesting Narrative of the Captivity and Sufferings of Philip Brigdon, a Kentuckian, Who Fell into the Hands of the Merciless Savages in their Return to their Settlement, Three Days After the Bloody Massacre; Communicated by Persons of Respectibility Living in the Neighborhood of the Captives. n.p., 1832. 24 p.
IU, IHi, ICN
A curious account. Real names: Rachel, Sylvia.

Nichols, Frances S. *Index to Schoolcraft's Historical and Statistical Information Respecting the History, Conditions, and Prospects of the Indian Tribes of the United States*. U.S. Bureau of American Ethnology, Bulletin, No. 152. Washington: U.S. Government Printing Office, 1954. 257 p.
ICU

Scanlan, Charles M. *Indian Massacre and Captivity of the Hall Girls: Complete History of the Massacre of Sixteen Whites on Indian Creek, near Ottawa, Illinois and Sylvia Hall and Rachel Hall as Captives in Illinois and Wisconsin during the Black Hawk War, 1832*. Milwaukee, Wisconsin: Reic Publishing Company, 1915. 119 p., illus., front.
ICN
Another edition, New York: Garland Publishing Company, 1975.

Schoolcraft, Henry R. *Historical and Statistical Information Respecting the History, Conditions, and Prospects of the Indian Tribes of the United States*. 6 v. Philadelphia: Lippincott, Grambo and Company, 1852–1857.
DLC, ICRL, ICJ, ICN, ICU
Index to these volumes compiled by Frances S. Nichols, Bureau of American Ethnology, Bulletin, No. 152. Illustrated by S. Eastman.

Schoolcraft, Henry Rowe. *Personal Memoirs of a Residence of Thirty Years with the Indian Tribes on the American Frontiers; with Brief Notices of Passing Events, Facts, and Opinions, A.D. 1812 to A.D. 1842*. Philadelphia: Lippincott, Grambo and Company, 1851. 703 p., front.
DLC, ICN, ICU

Indians—*Linguistics*

Indians—*Linguistics*—General

Bloomfield, Leonard. "On the Sound System of Central Algonquian." *Language* 1 (1925): 130–156.
DLC, ICN, ICU, IU

Goddard, Ives. "Central Algonquian Languages." In *Handbook of North American Indians*. Edited by Bruce G. Trigger. Vol. 15: *Northeast*, pp. 582–587. William C. Sturtevant, general editor. Washington: Smithsonian Institution, 1978–.
ICN, ICU

Hockett, C. F. "Central Algonquian /t/ and /c/." *International Journal of American Linguistics* 22 (1957): 202–207.
DLC, ICN, ICU, IU

Hockett, C. F. "Central Algonquian Vocabulary Stems in /k/." *International Journal of American Linguistics* 23 (1957): 247–268 .
DLC, ICN, ICU, IU

Hockett, C. F. "Implications of Bloomfield's Algonquian Studies." *Language* 24 (1948): 117–135.
DLC, ICN, ICU, IU

Indians—*Linguistics*—Illinois

Neilson, J. L. Hubert [and Allouez, Claude Jean]. *Facsimile of Père Marquette's Illinois Prayer Book: Its History by the Owner, Colonel J. L. Hubert Neilson, M.D.* Quebec: Quebec Literary and Historical Society, 1908. 63 p., plates.
ICU, IO

Belting, Natalie M. "Illinois Names for Themselves and Other Groups." *Ethnohistory* 5 (1958): 285–291.
ICN, IEN, IU
Based on a manuscript Peoria dictionary and Boulanger's dictionary.

Dunn, Jacob Piatt. "Shall Indian Languages be Preserved?" *Journal of the Illinois State Historical Society* 10 (April 1918): 87–96.
DLC, I, IC, ICHi, ICN, ICU, IEN, IU
General discussion on pros and cons of preserving place names of Indian origin and pronunciation, particularly in the Illinois language.

Trowbridge, C. C. "Illinois and Miami Vocabulary and Lord's Prayer." *U.S. Catholic Historical Magazine* 3 (1891): 1–9.
DLC, IU

Indians—*Linguistics*—Miami

Volney, Constantin Francois Chasseboiuf, comte De. *A View of the Soil and Climate of the United States of America.* Philadelphia, 1804.
ICN
A vocabulary of the Miami language can be found on pp. 429–446.

Indians—*Linguistics*—Potawatomi

Hockett, C. F. "The Conjunct Modes in Ojibwa and Potawatomi." *Language* 26 (1950): 278–282.
DLC, ICN, ICU, IU

Hockett, C. F. "Potawatomi Syntax." *Language* 15 (1939): 235–248.
DLC, ICN, ICU, IU

Hockett, Charles F. "The Position of Potawatomi in Central Algonkian." *Papers of the Michigan Academy of Science, Arts and Letters* 28 (1943): 537–542.
DLC, I, ICF, ICJ, ICU, IEN, IU

Hockett, Charles F. "Potawatomi." *International Journal of American Linguistics* 14 (1948): 1–10, 63–73, 139–149, 213–225.
DLC, ICN, ICU, IU

Hockett, Charles Francis. "A Descriptive Grammar of the Potawatomi Language." Ph.D. dissertation, Yale University, 1939.
CtY
Published, "Potawatomi." *International Journal of American Linguistics* 14 (1948).

Lykins, Johnston, Jr. *The Gospel According to Matthew and Acts of the Apostles.* Louisville, Kentucky, 1844.
DLC
In Potawatomi.

Michelson, T. "The Linguistic Classification of the Potawatomi." *Proceedings of the National Academy of Sciences* 1 (1915): 450–452.
DLC, ICF, ICU, ICJ, IU

Indians—*Folklore*

Armstrong, Perry A. *The Piaza or the Devil Among the Indians.* Morris, Illinois, 1887. 48 p., illus.
DLC, ICarbS

Jones, William Anwyl. "The Tragedy of Starved Rock: The Last of the Illinois: A Legend of Starved Rock." *Illinois State Historical Society Transactions* 19 (1913): 113–114.
DLC, IC, ICU

Michelson, T. "Notes on Peoria Folk-Lore and Mythology." *Journal of American Folk-Lore* 30 (1917): 493–495.
DLC, I, IC, ICN, ICU, IU

Smith, G. H. "Three Miami Tales." *Journal of American Folk-Lore* 52 (1939): 194–208.
DLC, I, IC, ICN, ICU, IU

Trowbridge, Charles C. *Meeârmeer Traditions.* Vernon Kinietz, ed. University of Michigan Museum of Anthropology, Occasional Contributions, No. 9. Ann Arbor, Michigan, 1939.
ICF, ICJ, ICN, ICU, IEN

Indians—*Biography*

Indians—*Biography*—General

Kinzie, Juliette A. "Chicago Indian Chiefs. Biographical Information as Recorded in Letters of Juliette A. Kinzie." *Chicago Historical Society Bulletin* 1 (1935): 105–116.
IC, ICF, ICHi, ICL, ICN, ICU, IEN, IU

Indians—*Biography*—Black Hawk

Patterson, J. B., ed. *Autobiography of Ma-ka-tai-me-she-kia-kiak, or Black Hawk, Embracing the Traditions of His Nation, Various Wars in Which He Has Been Engaged, and His Account of the Cause and General History of the Black Hawk War of 1832, His Surrender and Travels through the United States, Dictated by Himself. Antoine LeClair, U.S. Interpreter .... Rock Island, Illinois, 1833. Also, Life, Death and Burial of the Old Chief, Together with a History of the Black Hawk War, ...* St. Louis, Missouri: Press of Continental Printing Company, 1882. 208 p., front., port.
ICU

Drake, Benjamin. *The Great Indian Chief of the West; or, Life and Adventures of Black Hawk.* Cincinnati, Ohio, Philadelphia: H. M. Rulison, 1856. 288 p., front., plates, ports.
ICN
First edition, Cincinnati, 1838, issued under the title *The Life and Adventures of Black Hawk: With Sketches of Keokuk, the Sac and Fox Indians, and the Late Black Hawk War.*

Jackson, Donald. "Black Hawk—the Last Campaign." *Palimpsest* 43 (February 1962): 80–94.
DLC, ICN, ICU, IU

Swisher, J. A. "Chief of the Sauks." *Palimpsest* 13 (February 1932): 41–54.
DLC, ICN, ICU, IU
Black Hawk.

Indians—*Biography*—Billy Caldwell

Clifton, James A. "Billy Caldwell's Exile in Early Chicago." *Chicago History* 6 (Winter 1977/1978): 218–228.
DLC, IC, ICF, ICN, ICU, IU

Clifton, James A. "Merchant, Soldier, Broker, Chief: A Corrected Obituary of Captain Billy Caldwell." *Journal of the Illinois State Historical Society* 71 (August 1978): 185–210.
DLC, I, IC, ICHi, ICN, ICU, IEN, IU

Clifton, James A. "Personal and Ethnic Identity on the Great Lakes Frontier: The Case of Billy Caldwell, Anglo-Canadian." *Ethnohistory* 25 (Winter 1978): 69–94.
ICN, IEN, IU

Conway, Thomas G. "An Indian Politician and Entrepreneur in the Old Northwest." *Old Northwest* 1 (March 1975): 51–62.
ICarbS, IEN, InNd
Billy Caldwell.

Indians—*Biography*—Shabbona

Dowd, James. *Built Like a Bear: Which Is a Descriptive Name for One of the Last Great Chiefs of the "Three Fires" in Illinois, Shabni (He Has Pawed Through).* Fairfield, Washington: Ye Galleon Press, 1979. 197 p., illus.
IU—HS
Bibliography, pp. 184–190.

Hatch, Luther A. *The Indian Chief Shabbona.* DeKalb, Illinois: Mrs. L. A. Hatch, 1915. 35 p.
ILa
Pamphlet.

"Historical Notes—the Life and Death of Shabbona." *Journal of the Illinois State Historical Society* 31 (September 1938): 344.
DLC, I, IC, ICHi, ICN, ICU, IEN, IU
Originally appeared in Ottawa *Free Trader* of July 23, 1859.

Matson, Nehemiah. *Memories of Shaubena with Incidents Relating to Indian Wars and the Early Settlement of the West.* Chicago: R. Grainger and Company, Printers, 1878. 269 p., illus.
ICU, IJo
Other editions.

Temple, Wayne C. *Shabbona, Friend of the Whites.* Springfield: Printed by Authority of the State of Illinois, 1957.
ISM
Reprinted from *Outdoors in Illinois* 4 (Fall/Winter 1957). 5 p. [Illinois State Museum. Report of Investigations, No. 6.]

Walters, Alta P. "Shabonee." *Journal of the Illinois State Historical Society* 17 (October 1924): 381–397.
DLC, I, IC, ICHi, ICN, ICU, IEN, IU
Compilation of a series of Old Settlers' recollections.

Indians—*Missions*

Cleary, Thomas Francis. "The History of the Catholic Church in Illinois from 1763–1844." Ph.D. dissertation, University of Illinois, 1932. 469 p.
IU
Indian missions in Illinois.

Donnelly, Joseph P. *Jacques Marquette, S. J., 1637–1675.* Chicago: Loyola University Press, 1968. 395 p., facsims., geneal. table, map.
ICU
Bibliography, pp. 341–357.

Gaston, Leroy Clifton III. "Crucifix and Calumet: French Missionary Efforts in the Great Lakes Region, 1615–1650." Ph.D. dissertation, Tulane University, 1978.
LNHT

Grover, Frank Reed. *Father Pierre Francois Pinet, S. J., and His Mission of the Guardian Angel of Chicago (l'Ange Gardien) a.d. 1696–1699: A Paper Read Before a Joint Meeting of the Chicago Historical Society and the Evanston Historical Society in the Chicago Historical Society Building, November 27, 1906.* Chicago, 1907. 28 p., front., plates, plan.
DLC, ICN, ICU

Hulst, Mrs. Cornelia (Steketee). *Indian Sketches: Pere Marquette and the Last of the Pottawatomie Chiefs.* New York: Lingmans, Green, and Company, 1912. 113 p., front., illus., maps.
ICN
Contains a chapter on Marquette's mission. The other two chapters deal mainly with the Polagon Potawatomi of Indiana.

Marquette, Jacques. "Unfinished Journal of Father Jacques Marquette, Addressed to the Reverend Father Claude Dublon, Superior of the Missions." In *The Jesuit Relations and Allied Documents,* Vol. 59, pp. 164–183. Edited by Reuben Gold Thwaites. Cleveland, Ohio, 1900.
DLC, ICU

Palm, Mary Borgias. *The Jesuit Missions of the Illinois Country, 1673–1763.* Cleveland, Ohio, 1933. 138 p., map.
DLC, ICU
Originally a Ph.D. dissertation, St. Louis University, 1931. Bibliography, pp. 124–134.

Pratt, Harry E. "Peter Cartwright and the Cause of Education." *Journal of the Illinois State Historical Society* 29 (January 1936): 271.
DLC, I, IC, ICHi, ICN, ICU, IEN, IU
Includes account of Potawatomi station school conducted by Methodists in LaSalle County.

Schaefer, Catherine. "A Chronology of Missions and Churches in Illinois from 1675 to 1844." *Illinois Catholic Historical Review* 1 (1918): 103–109.
DLC, IC, ICN, ICU

Shaw, Thomas A. *Story of the LaSalle Mission [in] Two Parts. . . .* 2 v. Chicago: M. A. Donohue & Company, [1907–1908].
ICN

Thompson, Joseph J. "Illinois Missions." *Illinois Catholic Historical Review* 1 (1918): 38–63, 185–197.
DLC, IC, ICN, ICU
Jesuit missionaries in Illinois from the 1670s to the 1840s.

Thwaites, Reuben Gold. *Father Marquette.* New York: D. Appleton and Company, 1902.
DLC, IEN

Indians—*Military Affairs, Treaties, Indian Relations*

Alvord, Clarence W. "Edward Cole, Indian Commissioner in the Illinois Country." *Journal of the Illinois State Historical Society* 3 (October 1910): 23–44.
DLC, I, IC, ICHi, ICN, ICU, IEN, IU

Armstrong, Perry A. *The Sauks and the Black Hawk War, with Biographical Sketches, etc.*

Springfield: H. W. Rokker, 1887. 726 p., illus., port.
DLC, I, IC, ICJ, ICU

Atwater, Caleb. *Remarks Made on a Tour to Prairie du Chien: Thence to Washington City, in 1829.* Columbus, Ohio: Jenkins & Glover, Printer, 1831. 296 p.
DLC, IU

Atwater was commissioned, along with two others, to treat with Indians of the Upper Mississippi Valley. Contains valuable information on Indians of Northern Illinois.

Brown, Lizzie May. "Indian Affairs in Illinois from 1815–1820." M.A. thesis, University of Minnesota, 1915. 61 p.
MnU

Chowen, Richard Henry. "The History of Treaty Making with the Potawatomi Nation of Indians." M.S. thesis, Northwestern University, 1941. 111 p.
IEN

Coulter, John Lee. *Indian Claims Commission Docket No. 15-K, Potawatomi Treaty of July 29, 1829.* n.p., n.d. illus., maps.
IU—HS

Eby, Cecil. *"That Disgraceful Affair": The Black Hawk War.* New York: W. W. Norton and Company, 1973. 354 p.
ICU

Bibliography.

Edmunds, R. David. "The Illinois River Potawatomi in the War of 1812." *Journal of the Illinois State Historical Society* 62 (Winter 1969): 341–362.
DLC, I, IC, ICHi, ICN, ICU, IEN, IU

Portraits of Tecumseh, the Prophet, Ninian Edwards. Account of Illinois Potawatomi role as British allies.

Forsyth, Thomas. "Letter-Book of Thomas Forsyth, 1814–1818." *Wisconsin State Historical Society Collections* 11 (1888): 316–355.
DLC, IC, ICJ, ICN, ICU

Consists chiefly of correspondence between Forsyth and Ninian Edwards, governor of Illinois territory, concerning their dealings with the Indian tribes as allies.

Gerwing, Anselm J. "The Chicago Indian Treaty of 1844." *Journal of the Illinois State Historical Society* 57 (Summer 1964): 117–142.
DLC, I, IC, ICHi, ICN, ICU, IEN, IU

Grad, Mary Rosina. "The Indians and French in the Illinois Region Under Three Governments." M.S. thesis, Marquette University, 1949. 144 p.
WMM

"The Illinois Indians to Captain Abner Prior, 1794." *American Historical Review* 4 (October 1898): 107–111.
DLC, IC, ICN, ICU, IU

Three letters in French, describing relations between the Illinois (Kaskaskia) and United States agents between 1791 and 1794.

Johnston, Oda B. "History of Fort Armstrong, 1816–1836." M.A. thesis, State University of Iowa, 1940. 139 p.
IaAS

The Indian neighbors and the fur trade. Kaskaskia, Peoria, Kickapoo, Sac, Fox, Winnebago, Potawatomi.

Massey, Dorothy. "The Indian Agencies at Peoria and Rock Island (A Study in the Potawatomi and Sauk and Fox Indians)." M.A. thesis, University of Wisconsin, 1923. 88 p.
WU

Miller, Otis Louis. "Indian-White Relations in the Illinois Country, 1789 to 1818." Ph.D. dissertation, Saint Louis University, 1972. 155 p.
ICN, MoU

Bibliography, pp. 140–154.

Morse, Jedidiah. *A Report to the Secretary of War of the United States, on Indian Affairs, Comprising a Narrative of a Tour Performed in the Summer of 1820, Under a Commission from the President of the United States, for the Purpose of Ascertaining for the Use of the Government, the Actual State of the Indian Tribes in Our Country.* New Haven, Connecticut: Converse, Printer, 1822. 400 p., map.
ICN, IHi, IU

Though he did not tour Illinois, Morse includes valuable information on Indians of that state. An appendix includes "Sauks, Foxes, Kickapoos, Pottawattomies, &c," by Major Morrell Marston, stationed at Fort Armstrong. Reprinted in Emma H. Blair, *Indian Tribes of the Upper Mississippi.*

Nichols, Roger L. "The Black Hawk War: Another View." *Annals of Iowa* 36 (Winter 1963): 525–533.
DLC, ICN, ICU, IU

O'Connor, Mary Helen. "Potawatomie Land Cessions in the Old Northwest." M.S. thesis, Cornell University, 1942. 106 p.
NIC

Riddell, William Renwick. "References to Illinois in French-Canadian Official Documents." *Journal of the Illinois State Historical Society* 23 (July 1930): 201–204.
DLC, I, IC, ICHi, ICN, ICU, IEN, IU

References to Indian relations, Joliet's mission.

Schoolcraft, Henry Rowe. *Travels in the Central Portions of the Mississippi Valley: Comprising Observations on Its Mineral Geography, Internal Resources, and Aboriginal Population (Performed Under the Sanction of Government, in the Year 1821)*. New York: Collins and Hannay, 1825.
DLC, ICN, ICU

Schoolcraft traveled from Peoria to Chicago on horseback as part of the Cass treaty-making expedition in 1821. Useful information on Indians is included.

Stevens, Frank E. *The Black Hawk War, Including a Review of Black Hawk's Life: Illustrated with Upward of Three Hundred Rare and Interesting Portraits and Views, by Frank E. Stevens.* Chicago: F. E. Stevens, 1903. 323 p., front., plates, ports., map, facsims.
ICN, ICU

Indians—*Archive Sources*

Chicago, Illinois. Chicago Historical Society. Albert Frederick Scharf Papers, 1859–1926.
ICHi

Diary, map, notes.

Chicago, Illinois. Chicago Historical Society. American Fur Company Records. 1,050 items and 1 v.
ICHi

Correspondence relating to fur trade and Indians in the region. Account book from Michilimackinac lists dealings with Chicago traders, 1823–1830.

Chicago, Illinois. Field Museum of Natural History. George Langford. Collected Papers on Archeology.
ICF

Includes "The Fisher Mound Group, 1927," "Stratified Indian Mounds in Will County, 1928," and "The Fisher Mound and Village Site, 1930."

Chicago, Illinois. Newberry Library. Ayer Collection. William David Barge. "Notes Collected by W. D. Barge Concerning Shabonee, the White Man's Friend." 61 p.
ICN

Chicago, Illinois. Newberry Library. Ayer Collection. Jean Baptiste Beaubien. "Two Letters to O. N. Bostwick, Chicago, Sept. 11–Oct. 24, 1923." 2 p.
ICN

Orders for goods.

Chicago, Illinois. Newberry Library. Ayer Collection. "Cass, Lewis to Alexander Wolcott, Detroit, July 3, 1828."
ICN

Treaty with the Potawatomies.

Chicago, Illinois. Newberry Library. Ayer Collection. William Clark. "Instructions to Mr. Turcotte to Deliver Messages to the Sauks and Foxes and Other Indians in Regards to the Holding of a Treaty. Signed, William Clark, Ninian Edwards and August Choteau, St. Louis, May 16, 1815.
ICN

Chicago, Illinois. Newberry Library. Ayer Collection. [De Gannes], Supposed Author. "Memorial Concerning the Illinois Country." [Montreal, 1721, Chicago, 1922]. 61 p.
ICN

Chicago, Illinois. Newberry Library. Ayer Collection. French-Illinois Dictionary. From a Manuscript of the Early Part of the Eighteenth Century. Prospectus of a Dictionary by Joseph Ignatius Boulanger.
ICN

Chicago, Illinois. Newberry Library. Ayer Collection. "Gordon, Mrs. Eleanor Lytle (Kinzie) to W. N. C. Carlton, March 6, 1912."
ICN

Potawatomi translation of the Lord's Prayer.

Chicago, Illinois. Newberry Library. Ayer Collection. "Gordon, Mrs. Eleanor Lytle (Kinzie) to Miss C. A. Smith, May 30, 1912." 3 p.
ICN

Chicago, Illinois. Newberry Library. Ayer Collection. Thomas Forsyth. "A List of Licences Granted by Thomas Forsyth, Indian Agent to Sundry Persons to Trade with the Different Indian Nations, 1822–1827." 7 p.
ICN
Photostat of Draper manuscript, Wisconsin Historical Society.

Chicago, Illinois. Newberry Library. Ayer Collection. John Kinzie. "Sketch of Hoo-wan-nee-kaw." 3 p.
ICN

Chicago. Newberry Library. Ayer Collection. John Kinzie. "Two Receipts . . . June 22, 1820, July 10, 1820."
ICN

Chicago, Illinois. Newberry Library. Ayer Collection. LeBoulanger. French-Miami-Illinois Dictionary. (Photostat.)
ICN
Original manuscript in John Carter Brown Library.

Chicago, Illinois. Newberry Library. Ayer Collection. Marquette. Facsimile of Père Marquette's Illinois Prayer Book. Quebec, 1908.
ICN

Chicago, Illinois. Newberry Library. Ayer Collection. "Farnham Russell to O. N. Bostwick, Flint Hills, Feb. 1, 1826." 2 p.
ICN

Chicago, Illinois. Newberry Library. Ayer Collection. "Instructions to Mr. Turcotte to Deliver Messages to the Sauks and Foxes . . . in Regard to Holding of a Treaty, St. Louis, May 16, 1815." 2 p.
ICN

Chicago, Illinois. Newberry Library. Ayer Collection. Michigan (Territory)-Governor, 1813–1831 (Lewis Cass). "Regulations of Indian Affairs in the Northwest Territory and Proposals for the Better Organization of the Indian Department." [Detroit, Michigan, 1815]. 37 p. (Microfilm.)
ICN

Chicago, Illinois. Newberry Library. Graff Collection. Thomas Forsyth. "Autograph Letter Signed, Adressed to William Clark." Peoria, April 9, 1824. 3 p.
ICN
About the Indians in the Peoria area.

Chicago, Illinois. Newberry Library. Graff Collection. John Latimer of Chicago. "Autograph Letter Signed, Addressed to William Clark." Chicago, October 9, 1811. 3 p.
ICN
About the situation of the Indians in the vicinity of Chicago.

Chicago, Illinois. University of Chicago. American Fur Company. Papers. 1831–1849. 37 reels microfilm.
ICU
Originals in the New York Historical Society Library.

Chicago, Illinois. University of Chicago. American Fur Company. Papers in the Public Archives of Canada. 1817–1834. 2 reels microfilm.
ICU
Original in Public Archives, Ottawa, Canada.

Chicago, Illinois. University of Chicago. American Fur Company. Papers of the Company's Agent at Mackinac. 1817–1866. 3 reels microfilm.
ICU
Original in Burton Historical Collections, Detroit Public Library.

Chicago, Illinois. University of Chicago. Department of Special Collections. Ethnohistory Collection, 16th–17th Centuries. 163 items and 140 reels microfilm.
ICU
Copies of documents relating to early settlement in the greater Mississippi Valley.

Springfield, Illinois. Archives of the State of Illinois. U.S. Surveyor General's Records for Illinois. Abstract of Conditions of Surveys of

Indian Grants and Reservations. 1850. 1 v., no index.
I—Ar
Maps showing yearly progress of Illinois surveys, 1837–1838, 1840–1843, 1848–1850, 1852.

Springfield, Illinois. Archives of the State of Illinois. U.S. Surveyor General's Records for Illinois. 10 maps, no index.
I—Ar
Maps showing yearly progress of Illinois surveys, 1837–1838, 1840–1843, 1848–1850, 1852. Abstract of conditions of surveys of Indian grants and reservations, 1850. These Indian grants border the corridor and involve Indians associated with the corridor, including Shabbona's band and Josette Beaubien.

Springfield, Illinois. Archives of the State of Illinois. U.S. Surveyor General's Records for Illinois. Terrier of Grants Made to Potawatomi Indians, May 24, 1834–November 17, 1834. index.
I—Ar
Grants are on Kankakee River just south of the corridor. Indians may be associated with Shabbona's band.

Springfield, Illinois. Illinois State Historical Library. Ninian Edwards. Ledger. Superintendent of Indian Affairs in Illinois, Aug. 1811–Dec. 1815. Includes Ledger of a Belleville, Illinois, Merchant, 1830–1831. 1 v.
IHi
Ninian Edwards's accounts with U.S. Indian Department, 1811–1815, giving agents hired, services rendered, and equipment purchased. Refers to Samuel Levering, Gen. William Clarke, John Hay, William Whiteside, Pierre Menard, etc. Entries on Illinois Indians mainly concern the capture of certain Indians "up the Illinois River" charged with murder and depredations and brief entries on Illinois River mission.

Springfield, Illinois. Illinois State Historical Library. Ninian Edwards. Letter, February 16, 1813, Elvirade, Randolph Co., Illinois Territory to Isaac Shelby, Frankfort, Kentucky. 1 p.
IHi
Report of British and Indian military affairs in Lake Michigan region. British agents at Prairie du Chien named.

Springfield, Illinois. Illinois State Historical Library. William Henry Harrison. Letter, March 5, 1809. Gov., Indiana Territory and U.S. President. Letter from Vincennes, Indiana, to Washington, D.C., giving reasons for delay in negotiating with Kickapoo and Peoria Indians for settlement of boundary south of Illinois River.
IHi

Urbana, Illinois. Illinois Historical Survey Library. U.S. Bureau of Indian Affairs Papers, 1800–1839. 51,600 p.
IU–HS
Various subjects including treaties, land titles, fur trade, Indian removals.

Urbana, Illinois. Illinois Historical Survey Library. U.S. Bureau of Indian Affairs. Letters, Letterbooks, Records, 1800–1839. 32 items, transcripts. 49 folders, photocopies. 6 reels microfilm. Inventory.
IU—HS
Copied from originals at the National Archives. Topics include treaty negotiations, fur trade, liquor traffic, Indian removals, annuities. Collection includes letters from Chicago Indian agents (1812–1820) and letters to Indian agents from Washington, D.C. (1800–1838).

Washington, D.C. National Archives. Bureau of Indian Affairs. "General Correspondence and Other Records of the Bureau 1801–1839."
DNA
Indian relations in the Chicago area.

Washington, D.C. National Archives. Bureau of Indian Affairs. "Records Relating to Indian Removal 1817–1906."
DNA
Indian relations in the Chicago area.

Washington, D.C. National Archives. Bureau of Indian Affairs. General Records of the United States Government. "Treaties with Indian Tribes and Related Papers 1778–1883."
DNA
Treaty of 1833 with the Chippewa, Ottawa, and Potawatomi.

Washington, D.C. National Archives. Records of the Bureau of Indian Affairs. Factory Records. Chicago Factory. Waste Book, 1 v., 1-inch; Ledger, 1 v., 3/4-inch; Miscellaneous Accounts, 4 inches.
DNA

Chicago "Factory" records concern Indian trade. Wastebook (1808–1810) is a day book giving a chronological record of transactions. The Ledger (1811–1812) is a record of transactions arranged by name of individual and indexed. Miscellaneous accounts (1805–1922) are arranged by year.

Washington, D.C. National Archives. Bureau of Indian Affairs. "Record of the Office of Indian Trade, 1795–1824."
DNA

Commercial and social sources.

Washington, D.C. Smithsonian Institution. National Anthropological Archives. Gravier, James. A Dictionary of the Illinois Language. 1700.
DSI

PART 5 Agriculture

The most consistent material available on agriculture in the corridor can be found in manuscript and published U.S. decennial census returns focusing on agriculture. Categories vary from census to census but generally include statistical information on farm size and value, implements, machinery, livestock, and crops produced, with more detailed information provided on some returns. Additional statistical information can be found in crop and livestock reports prepared by the Illinois Department of Agriculture and other agricultural associations. County farm bureaus and broader associations published a variety of periodicals reporting agricultural news to farmers in the area. Other archival sources include a few ledgers kept by individual farmers and documentation related to various service companies, bureaus, and associations.

Agriculture—*General*

Edwards, Everett E. *A Bibliography of the History of Agriculture in the United States.* United States Department of Agriculture, Miscellaneous Publication, No. 84. Washington, 1930.
DLC, ICU, MiU

Farmer's Reference and Account Book . . . With Catalogue for Season, 1900. LaSalle and Peru, Illinois: Castendyck Bros., [1900].
IUtHi

The Farmers' Weekly Review. . . . June 29, 1929–October 7, 1936. Joliet, Illinois.
IU

Official organ of the Will County Farm Bureau.

Grundy County, [Illinois] Farm Bureau. *Farm Bureau News. . . .* Vol. 1–. Morris, Illinois, 1920–.
IU

Hatch, Laura. "Geographical Factors in the Agriculture of DuPage County, Illinois." *Journal of Geography* 13 (March 1915): 216–223.
DLC, ICU, IU

Traces development of agriculture in the county from 1830 to 1915.

Illinois Agricultural Association and Associated Companies. *Annual Report.* Vol. 1–. n.p., Illinois Agricultural Association, 1919–.
IBlo—Ag

Provides county membership totals, rosters of officers, and county statistics for wool cooperatives, county farm supply companies, and the Country Life Insurance Company.

Illinois Agricultural Statistics. Circular. Nos. 349–445. Springfield, Illinois: U.S. Department of Agriculture and Illinois Department of Agriculture, 1924–1944.
ICU

Title varies. 1924–1944. *Illinois Crop and Live Stock Statistics.* Illinois Cooperative Crop Reporting Service and U.S. Department of Agriculture.

Illinois Farmer's Institute. *Annual Reports.* Vol. 1–[34]. Springfield: Ed. F. Hartmann, State Printer. 1896–1929.
ICRL

Contains reports of County Farm Institutes, Domestic Science Association information, occasional county by county statistics. Vol. 13 contains a short review of inland navigation, including a focus on the Illinois River System.

LaSalle County Farm Bureau News. Vol.1–47, Ottawa, Illinois. 1921–1967. illus., ports., tables. Frequency varies.
IU

Official publication of the LaSalle County Farm Bureau, and the LaSalle County Home Bureau, March 1925–October 1939.

LaSalle County Farm Directory. Cherry Valley, Illinois: G. F. Engstrom, [1942].
IO

Northwestern Prairie Farmer. Vol. 1–2. Chicago, [November,] 1858–1859.
MWA

Later the *Farmer's Advocate.*

The Orange Judd Illinois Farmer. Vol. 1–78. Chicago: The Orange Judd Farmer Publishing

Company, [1886–1930]. Semimonthly. illus, photos.
ICJ, ICRL, IU
State and local politics, crop reports, advice, occasional county-by-county statistics, market updates, home economics. Articles occasionally focus on the corridor. Service Bureau column. As of September 1, 1927, *The Illinois Farmer.*

Prairie Farmer. Vol. 1–123. Chicago, 1841–1927. illus.
DLC, I, IC, ICHi, ICJ, ICU
Frequency varies. Published 1841–April 2, 1927. Numbering irregular. Continues *Union Agriculturalist and Western Prairie Farmer.* Continued by the Illinois edition of *Prairie Farmer.* Published as *People's Illinois Weekly and Prairie Farmer,* September 2–October 5, 1882. Absorbed *Emery's Journal of Agriculture,* 1858.

Prairie Farmer's Directory of Grundy and Kendall Counties, Illinois. Chicago: Prairie Farmer Publishing Company, ca. 1917.
IMo

Prairie Farmer's Directory of Will and Southern Cook Counties, Illinois. Chicago: Prairie Farmer Publishing Company, 1918. 386 p.
ICHi, IJo
Advertisements.

Rossiter, Margaret W., comp. *A List of References for the History of Agricultural Science in America.* Davis, California, 1980. 62 p.
IDeKN—IRAD

U.S. Department of Agriculture in Cooperation with Illinois Department of Agriculture. *Illinois Crop and Livestock Statistics.* 13 v. Springfield: State Journal Company, 1924–1945.
IBlo—Ag
Title varies. Includes "Crops," 1924–1945, and "Livestock," 1925–1945.

Union Agriculturalist and Western Prairie Farmer. Vol. 1–3. Chicago: Union Agricultural Society, 1841–1843. monthly, illus.
ICRL
The organ of the Illinois Agricultural Society. Periodically includes state agricultural news, household advice, county information occasionally pertaining to the corridor, market information, politics. Officers of the Union Agricultural Society were often corridor citizens. Correspondence. After 1843, *Prairie Farmer.*

The Will County Farmer. . . . Joliet, Illinois, [1918–1927].
IU
Official publication of the Will County Farm Bureau. Monthly. Publication suspended December 1922–March 1925.

Wiser, Vivian D. *Preliminary Inventory of the Records of the Bureau of Agricultural Economics.* Washington, 1958. 212 p., diagrs.
DLC, ICU
Bibliography, pp. 208–212.

Agriculture—*Published Censuses*

U.S. Census Office. *Statistics of the United States as Collected and Returned by the Marshalls of the Several Judicial Districts, Under the Thirteenth Section of the Act for Taking the Sixth Census; Corrected at the Department of State, June 1, 1840.* Washington: Blair and Rivers, 1841. 409 p.
DLC
For county and minor civil divisions within county. Production of mines, agriculture, horticulture, capital in selected branches of business and men employed, statistics of manufacturing.

U.S. Census Office. *Agriculture of the United States in 1860.* Washington: Government Printing Office, 1864. 292 p.
DLC, ICJ, ICU
By county. Improved and unimproved acreage, cash value of farm, farm implements and machinery, total and value of livestock, crops, farms containing three acres or more by size of farm.

U.S. Census Office. *Tenth Census of the United States, 1880.* Vol. 3: *Report on the Productions of Agriculture as Returned at the Tenth Census (June 1, 1880).* Washington: Government Printing Office, 1883.
ICJ, ICU
Similar statistics to previous report. Also includes data on land tenure by county, agricultural output statistics by acreage, and volume or weight of output.

U.S. Census Office. *Eleventh Census of the United States, 1890.* Vol. 5: *Reports on the Statistics of Agriculture in the United States . . . at the Eleventh Census: 1890.* Washington: Government Printing Office, 1896. 606 p.
NN

Includes color coded national maps depicting comparative crop yields. Similar statistics to 1880 report.

U.S. Census Office. *Eleventh Census of the United States, 1890.* Vol. 12: *Report on Real Estate Mortgages in the United States at the Eleventh Census: 1890.* Washington: Government Printing Office, 1896. 943 p.
NN

Includes average mortgage per acre (1880, 1889) by county, with county map of Illinois showing average value of a farm and average value of mortgage. Number and value of mortgages for lots and farms for each year (1880–1889) by county. Total debt (1890) on acres and lots by county.

U.S. Census Office. *Eleventh Census of the United States, 1890.* Vol. 13: *Report on Farms and Homes: Proprietorship and Indebtedness in the United States at the Eleventh Census: 1890.* Washington, 1896. 646 p.
ICJ

Contains table (1880–1890) and county map (1890) of Illinois with percentages of farm and home tenancy for each county; table showing number of borrowers from local building and loan associations in Chicago, Joliet, LaSalle, and Ottawa (and borrowers as percentage of families); tables on value of rented homes and farms (1890) by county.

U.S. Census Office. *Twelfth Census of the United States, 1900.* Vol. 5: *Agriculture.* Part 1: *Farms, Live Stock, and Animal Products.* Washington: Government Printing Office, 1902. 767 p.
ICJ, ICU

Similar statistics to those found in previous reports. Also contains more detailed breakdown of land tenure (owners, part-owners, managers, owners and tenants, cash tenants, share tenants) with further breakdown by race of farmer by county, expenditures on labor and fertilizer by county. Table 41 displays number of domestic farm animals found in Chicago and Joliet.

U.S. Census Office. *Twelfth Census of the United States, 1900.* Vol. 6: *Agriculture.* Part 2: *Crops and Irrigation.* Washington: Government Printing Office, 1902.
ICJ

Acreage and output data by county. Cereal grains, hay, vegetables, fruits, nuts, flowers, nursery products, and miscellaneous crops.

U.S. Bureau of the Census. *Thirteenth Census of the United States, 1910.* Vol. 5: *Agriculture 1909 and 1910: General Report and Analysis.* Washington: Government Printing Office, 1913. 927 p.
ICU, NN

Acreage and output statistics by county.

U.S. Bureau of the Census. *Thirteenth Census of the United States, 1910.* Vol. 6: *Agriculture, 1909 and 1910. Reports by States, with Statistics for Counties: Alabama–Montana.* Washington: Government Printing Office, 1913. 977 p.
NN

Basic acreage and output statistics. Comparative statistics, 1900–1910: number of farms, total farmland, and improved farmland. Value of farm property, buildings, machinery, domestic animals. Breakdown of farm population by race and ethnicity. Statistics on land tenure and farm mortgages, including race and ethnicity of tenant farmers. Percentage of farms run by tenants by county for 1900 and 1910.

U.S. Bureau of the Census. *Fourteenth Census of the United States, 1920.* Vol. 6: *Agriculture. Reports for States with Statistics for Counties and a Summary for the United States and the North, South, and West.* Washington: Government Printing Office, 1922. 765 p.
DLC

Basic statistics on number of farms, acreage, land tenure, farm population, and farm output. Comparative county statistics for 1900, 1910, 1920.

U.S. Bureau of the Census. *Agriculture. Number of Farms, by States and Counties, 1910, 1920, 1900.* Washington: Government Printing Office, 1920. 29 p.
NN

U.S. Bureau of the Census. *United States Census of Agriculture: 1925. . . .* Part 1: *The Northern*

States. Washington: Government Printing Office, 1927. 1,318 p.
DLC, ICU

Statistics on farm size, farm tenure, farm value, mortgage debt, livestock, and farm output for 1910, 1920, and 1925 by county. Also reports value of products sold and supplies bought through farm cooperatives in 1924, by county.

U.S. Bureau of the Census. *Fifteenth Census of the United States, 1930. Agriculture, 1931–1932*. Vol. 1: *Farm Acreage and Farm Values by Townships or Other Minor Civil Divisions*. Washington: Government Printing Office, 1931. 706 p.
DLC, ICU

Number of farms, all land in farms, crop land, pasture land, woodland not used for pasture, value of farm land and buildings, all farm buildings, farmers' dwellings, and farm implements and machinery.

U.S. Bureau of the Census. *Fifteenth Census of the United States, 1930. Agriculture, 1931–1932*. Vol. 2: *Reports by States, with Statistics for Counties and a Summary for the United States*. Part 1: *The Northern States*. Washington: Government Printing Office. 1,385 p.
DLC, ICJ, ICU

Similar statistics as Vol. 1, but also includes data from 1925 and 1920 reports and a table that displays the value of cooperative marketing operations by county.

U.S. Bureau of the Census. *Fifteenth Census of the United States, 1930. Agriculture, 1931–1932*. Vol. 3: *Type of Farm. Reports by States, with Statistics for Counties and a Summary for the United States*. Part 1: *The Northern States*. Washington: Government Printing Office, 1932. 1,071 p.
ICU

Statistical breakdowns according to principal cash crop, tenure of farm operator, and total value of farm products.

U.S. Bureau of the Census. *Chickens and Chicken Eggs and Turkeys, Ducks, and Geese Raised on Farms. Chickens and Poultry Products with Selected Items by Size of Flock, for the United States, and Counties, 1930 and 1929*. Washington: Government Printing Office, 1933. 563 p.
DLC

U.S. Bureau of the Census. *United States Census of Agriculture: 1935. Reports for States with Statistics for Counties and a Summary for the United States*. Vol. 1: *Farms, Farm Acreage and Value, and Selected Livestock and Crops*. Part 1. *The Northern States*. Washington: Government Printing Office, 1936. 937 p.
DLC, ICJ

Statistics for 1930 and 1935.

U.S. Bureau of the Census. *United States Census of Agriculture: 1935 Reports for States with Statistics for Counties and a Summary for the United States*. Vol. 2: *Farms and Farm Acreage, by Size, Land of Part Owners, Farm Population, Dwellings, Labor, Years on Farm Part-Time Work, Specified Livestock and Livestock Products, Annual Legumes, Vegetables, Fruits and Miscellaneous Crops, and Irrigated Crop Land*. Part 1: *The Northern States*. Washington: Government Printing Office, 1936. 956 p.
DLC, ICJ

U.S. Bureau of the Census. *Sixteenth Census of the United States, 1940. Agriculture*. Vol. 1: *Statistics for Counties. Farms and Farm Property, with Related Information or Farms and Farm Operators, Livestock and Livestock Products, and Crops*. First and Second Series. *State Reports*. Part 1: *New England, Middle Atlantic and East North Central States*. Washington: Government Printing Office, 1942. 975 p.
DLC

Similar data as 1930 reports plus the following data by county: age of farmer, year of occupancy of farm, work of farm for pay or income, farm labor employed at specified time, inventories of automobiles, motor trucks and tractors with year of latest models, whether farm has telephone or electricity, kind of road adjoining farm.

U.S. Bureau of the Census. *Sixteenth Census of the United States, 1940. Agriculture*. Vol. 2: *Statistics for Counties. Value of Farm Products; Farms Classified by Major Source of Income; Farms Classified by Value of Products. Third Series State Reports*. Part 1: *The Northern States*.

Washington: Government Printing Office, 1942. 888 p.
DLC

Agriculture—*Bureaus, Agencies, Societies*

LaSalle County Farm Bureau News. Vol. 1–. Ottawa, Illinois, 1921–. illus., ports., tables.
IU

Official publication of LaSalle County Farm Bureau. Title varies.

Leavitt, Edward T. "Ralph Wave of Granville: Champion of Agriculture and Education." *Journal of the Illinois State Historical Society* 70 (May 1977): 161–163.
DLC, I, IC, ICHi, ICN, ICU, IEN, IU

Biographical sketch of a founder of the Buell Institute (for scientific farming) in LaSalle County.

Looking Ahead—40th Anniversary, LaSalle County Farm Bureau. [Ottawa, Illinois], 1953.
IO

Includes history of Farm Bureau.

Partners in Progress. Ottawa, Illinois: LaSalle County Farm Bureau, c. 1964. 83 p., illus., photos.
IO

Series of LaSalle County historical anecdotes.

Agriculture—*Fairs, Exhibitions*

LaSalle County Fair, Ottawa, Illinois. Ottawa, Illinois, 1912 and 1913. illus., ports.
ICHi

Premium lists, officers and directors, agricultural advertisements.

Regulations and Premiums List. LaSalle County Agricultural Board. Twenty-second Annual Fair. n.p., n.d.
IUtHi

Various publications of this sort.

Agriculture—*Archive Sources*

Chicago, Illinois. Chicago Historical Society. DuPage County, Illinois. Miscellaneous Pamphlets, and so on.
ICHi

Premium list of 1886 DuPage County Fair. Lists of officials.

DeKalb, Illinois. Northern Illinois University. Illinois Regional Archives Depository. DuPage County Farm Bureau Records. Seven boxes. 5.5 linear feet.
IDeKN—IRAD

Records include articles of incorporation, constitution and by-laws, minutes (1913–1965), financial statements and audit reports (1920–1965), printed material and publications (1911–1976), and membership cards. Inventory available at library.

DeKalb, Illinois. Northern Illinois University. Illinois Regional Archives Depository. Grundy County Farm Bureau Records. Seven boxes. Five linear feet.
IDeKN—IRAD

Contains a complete set of minutes (1914–1970), audit reports (1924–1970), attendance sheets (1931–1970). Topics covered include improved crop-raising techniques, disease control, and farm legislation. Inventory available at library.

DeKalb, Illinois. Northern Illinois University. Illinois Regional Archives Depository. Grundy Service Company Records. Fourteen boxes. Twenty-five linear feet.
IDeKN—IRAD

Records document activities of three agricultural service companies, Grundy Grain and Supply, Grundy Service, and Kendall Farmers Oil, which merged in 1971. Records cover 1928–1978 and include a company history (unpublished), minutes of Grundy Service Co. Board of Directors (1934–1961), audit reports of Grundy Service (1935–1957), minutes and audit reports of Grundy Grain and Supply (1945–1952), purchase/sales journals of Grundy Service (1929–1942). Inventory available at library.

DeKalb, Illinois. Northern Illinois University. Illinois Regional Archives Depository. Will-DuPage Service Company Records. Three boxes. Three linear feet.
IDeKN—IRAD

The company was organized by the Will County Farm Bureau in 1927. Collection includes minutes (1927–1947, 1953–1970), auditor's reports (1922–1972), supplies catalogs (1934–1938), and sixteen photographs (1935–1973). Inventory available at library.

Morris, Illinois. Morris Public Library. Joshua Collins Ledgers, 1872. 4 vols.
IMo
Farm ledgers of Morris resident.

Morris, Illinois. Morris Public Library. Grundy County. Chattel Mortgage Records, 1932–1935. 1 v. 200 p., index.
IMo
Property inventories.

Morris, Illinois. Morris Public Library. Illinois Department of Agriculture. Grundy County Centennial Farm Applications. 1973.
IHi, IMo

Morris, Illinois. Morris Public Library. Local History File. Grundy County Fair. One folder.
IMo
File includes a photocopy of the 1873 pamphlet *Premiums and Regulations of the Nineteenth Annual Fair of the Grundy County Agricultural Board to Be Held at their Grounds Adjoining the City of Morris, Illinois.* Chicago: Southard Cullaton, Book and Job Printers, 1873. 43 p. Various newspaper articles.

Morris, Illinois. Morris Public Library. Local History File. Livestock. One folder.
IMo
File includes pamphlet recounting the history of Circle A Hereford Farm, Morris, Illinois, 1933–1953. n.p., n.d. (and many catalogs more recent than 1940). "1916 Catalogue List of Polled Burham Bulls for Sale by F. A. Murray and Son." Grundy County, Illinois. n.p., [1916]. 4 p., (photocopied.), assorted newspaper clippings.

Morris, Illinois. Morris Public Library. Joshua C. Widney Ledger, 1856–1875.
IMo
Photocopy of farm ledger.

Springfield, Illinois. Archives of the State of Illinois. U.S. Department of Interior. Seventh Federal Census. Agricultural Schedules for Illinois, 1850.
I—Ar
Ninety-nine Illinois counties. 5 v. No index. Information entered for each farm includes name of owner, agent, or manager; number of acres improved and unimproved land; value of farm, implements, machinery, livestock, orchard products, market garden produce, homemade manufactures, and slaughtered animals; number of livestock; quantity of produce of all crops.

Springfield, Illinois. Archives of the State of Illinois. U.S. Department of Interior. Eighth Federal Census. Agricultural Schedules for Illinois, 1860.
I—Ar
One-hundred-two Illinois counties. 7 v. No index. Information entered for each farm includes name of owner, agent, or manager; number of acres improved and unimproved land; value of farm, implements, machinery, livestock, orchard products, market garden produce, homemade manufactures, and slaughtered animals; number of livestock; quantity of produce of all crops.

Springfield, Illinois. Archives of the State of Illinois. U.S. Department of Interior. Ninth Federal Census. Agricultural Schedules for Illinois, 1870.
I—Ar
One-hundred-two Illinois counties. 9 v. No index. Information entered for each farm includes name of owner, agent, or manager; number of acres improved and unimproved land; value of farm, implements, machinery, livestock, orchard products, forest products, market garden produce, homemade manufactures, and slaughtered animals; number of livestock; quantity of produce of all crops.

Springfield, Illinois. Archives of the State of Illinois. U.S. Department of Interior. Tenth Federal Census. Agricultural Schedules for Illinois, 1880.
I—Ar
One-hundred-two Illinois counties. 21 v. No index. Information entered for each farm includes name of individual occupying farm; tenure of individual; number of acres of improved and unimproved land; value of farm, implements, machinery, livestock, orchard produce, nursery produce, market garden produce, and forest products; estimated value of all farm productions; annual cost of building and repairing fences; amount paid for labor; numbers of live and slaughtered stock; amount of dairy products and eggs; number of acres harvested and crops yielded for cereals, sugar, broom corn,

hops, potatoes, tobacco, orchards, nurseries, and vineyards.

Springfield, Illinois. Illinois State Historical Library. Department of Agriculture. Centennial Farm Program. Project co-sponsored by the Illinois Department of Agriculture and the Illinois Production Credit Association, 1971–1972. Questionnaires, 1971–1972. 6.5 linear feet.
IHi

Folders include approved and unimproved applications for Grundy, Will, and LaSalle counties. Many applications came from corridor lands and include information on early settlers, their birthplaces, occupations, former residences, and land transactions. Some applicants trace deeds to the I&M land grant. Some farmers may have earned farms through laboring on the canal.

Springfield, Illinois. Illinois State Historical Library. Pendy Sharwood. Letter to Joseph Roby, Ottawa, Illinois. January 18, 1846. 4 p.
IHi

Rehiring of farm labor from England. Types of fencing, planting of wheat, injurious insects.

Ottawa, Illinois. Reddick Library. Vertical File. LaSalle County Farm Bureau. Charter Members. 3 p.
IO

A list compiled in 1964 includes dues-paying members, 1914. Includes location by town.

Urbana, Illinois. University of Illinois Archives. Agriculture. Dean's Office. Records. 167.3 cubic feet.
IU

Contains correspondence from LaSalle, Grundy, Will, DuPage, and Cook counties. Cook County Experiments Station, Lewis matter. Finding aid available.

Urbana, Illinois. University of Illinois Archives. Farm Account Summary Sheets, 1917–1947. 26.8 cubic feet.
IU

Farm account summary sheets on individual Illinois farms sent to the department for review, selection, tabulation, analysis, and publication in the *Farm Business Reports,* 1923–1952. Sheets show year, county, address, operator, tenancy, soil type, acreage, land value, number and value of livestock, amount and value of feed and grain, value of buildings, machinery and equipment, receipts and expenditures in each area, crop production and yields per acre, price indexes, related cost factors, and analyses of statistical data. Farms from LaSalle, Grundy, Will, DuPage, and Cook counties are included. Finding aid available.

Utica, Illinois. LaSalle County Historical Society Museum. LaSalle County Agricultural Board Minutes, 1873–1880. 1 v.
IUtHi

List of members, premiums, constitution.

PART 6 Transportation and Communication

Researchers who use this section of the Bibliography have a wide variety of places and sources at their disposal, most of which are readily accessible to the general public. These range from federal and state archives to major research libraries to local history collections—of varying quality and quantity in the towns within the corridor—to more obscure and unique civic and corporate holding centers. The Chicago Historical Society and the Illinois State Historical Library hold many original materials and manuscript collections that relate directly to the canal building projects and to the individuals who were involved in actual construction and in the legislative process.

The original records of the construction and operation of the canal are located in at least five different places. Researchers may find information at the Will County Historical Society in Lockport, the Canal Archives Center at Lewis University in Lockport, the John Crerar Library at the University of Chicago, the Gebhard Woods State Park near Morris, and the Archives of the State of Illinois in Springfield.

The researcher should be aware that the number of sources cited in this section is only a "broad sweep" of the massive amount of material available on the subject of transportation and communication in the corridor. There are literally hundreds—if not thousands—of additional sources that pertain to the subject. For example, if researchers are interested in government's role in the development and history of the corridor, they may first want to consult sources such as the *Index of Economic Material in Documents of the States of the United States. Illinois, 1809–1904,* by Adelaide R. Hasse, *CIS, U.S. Serial Guide Index,* which is a guide to congressional publications, or *U.S. Congressional Committee Hearings Index.* Also, since the U.S. Army Corps of Engineers played a major role in the construction of the various canals in the Chicago area, it would be useful to consult the several guides to Army Corps publications. For those interested in technical and engineering topics that relate to canal and sanitary history, the *Industrial Arts Index,* "Illinois and Chicago," would probably be useful. Finally, the following sources are included because they often contain useful bibliographical sections and would be helpful for further research.

Transportation and Communication—*General*

"American Waterways." *Annals of the American Academy of Political and Social Sciences* 24 (January 1908): 1–262.
DLC, I, IC, ICN, ICU, IU

Atwood, Jane Kellog. "Development of the Commerce of the Great Lakes." M.S. thesis, University of Chicago, 1915. 134 p., maps, tables.
ICU

Bibliography, pp. 129–134.

Barnes, Mortimer G. *Inland Waterways: Their Necessity, Importance, and Value in Handling the Commerce of the United States, and Reducing Transportation Costs.* Chicago: Barnard and Miller, 1920. 58 p., front., illus.
ICJ

Author was chief engineer of Illinois Division of Waterways.

Becht, J. Edwin. *Commodity Origins, Traffic, and Markets Accessible to Chicago via the Illinois Waterway.* Chicago: Illinois River Carriers' Association, 1952. 210 p., illus., maps.
DLC, IU

Also Ph.D. dissertation; University of Illinois, 1951. 238 p.

Boylan, Josephine. "Illinois Highways, 1700–1848: Roads, Rivers, Ferries, Canals." *Journal of the Illinois State Historical Society* 26 (April/July 1933): 5–59.
DLC, I, IC, ICN, ICU, IEN, IU

Bureau of Railway Economics. *An Economic Survey of Inland Waterway Transportation in the United States.* Washington: Bureau of Railway Economics, 1930. 238 p., illus., maps, tables.
ICU, MiU, MnU

Same as bureau's Special Series, No. 56. Covers inland navigation, railroads versus waterways. Includes bibliography.

Chicago Board of Trade. *The Necessity of a Ship-Canal Between the East and the West.* Chicago: Tribune Book & Job Steam Printing Office, 1863. 30 p.
ICN

Report of the proceedings of the Board of Trade, the Mercantile Association, and the businessmen of Chicago at a meeting held at Metropolitan Hall, on the evening of February 24, 1863.

Clayton, John. "How They Tinkered with a River." *Chicago History* 1 (Spring 1970): 4–17.
DLC, IC, ICF, ICHi, ICN, ICU, IU

General history of the reshaping of the river system, the construction of canals, and the development of the city's waste disposal system. With maps and photographs.

Condit, Carl W. *Chicago, 1910–1929: Building, Planning, and Urban Technology.* Chicago: University of Chicago Press, 1973. 354 p., illus., plans.
ICU

Bibliography, pp. 322–335.

Currey, Josiah Seymour. *Chicago: Its History and Its Builders . . . A Marvelous Century of Growth.* 5 v. Chicago: S. J. Clarke Publishing Co., 1912. plates, ports., maps, facsims.
DLC, ICU

Includes a brief paragraph on Oliver Newberry, who built a fleet of sail and steam vessels, including the *Illinois* and the *Michigan*. Discusses at length the formation of the Chicago River and Harbor Convention and describes the flood of the Chicago River in 1849. Index.

Dornfeld, A. A. "Chicago's Age of Sail." *Chicago History* 2 (Spring/Summer 1973): 156–165.
DLC, IC, ICF, ICHi, ICN, ICU, IU

The development of Great Lakes sailing vessels and the rise of the port of Chicago during the nineteenth century.

Dornfeld, A. A. "Steamships After 1871." *Chicago History* 6 (Spring 1977): 12–22.
DLC, IC, ICF, ICHi, ICN, ICU, IU

History of Great Lakes shipping and the development of the port of Chicago. With photographs of ships.

Drago, Harry Sinclair. *Canal Days in America: The History and Romance of Old Towpaths and Waterways.* 1st Edition. New York: C. N. Potter, Distributed by Crown Publisher, [1927]. 311 p., illus.
ICU

Bibliography, pp. 303–305. A good, general history and romance of the old towpaths and waterways. It covers the canal era from 1812 to 1862, and the construction of four thousand miles of artificial waterways. Includes over 150 photographs.

Espenshade, Esther Elizabeth. "The Economic Development and History of Chicago, 1860–1865." M.A. thesis, University of Chicago, 1931. 156 p., illus., map, chart, diagrs.
ICU

Franchere, Ruth. *Westward by Canal.* New York: Macmillan Co., 1972. 149 p., illus.
DLC

Describes the planning, building, and use of canals in nineteenth-century America and their impact on the history, economy, and westward expansion of the United States.

Goodrich, Carter, ed. *Canals and American Economic Development.* Port Washington, New York: I. J. Friedman Division, Kennikat Press, 1972. 303 p., illus.
DLC, ICU

Bibliography, pp. 256–291. A study of canal construction in America during the early nineteenth century and its relation to economic development.

Harris, Robert. *Canals and Their Architecture.* London: H. Evelyn, 1969. 233 p., illus., facsims., maps, ports.
DLC, ICU

Hartshorne, Richard. "The Lake Traffic of Chicago." Ph.D. dissertation, University of Chicago, 1924. 354 p., tables, map.
ICU

Selected bibliography, pp. 352–354.

Hatcher, Harlan Henthorne. *The Great Lakes.* New York: Oxford University Press, 1944. 384 p., front., illus. maps, plates.
DLC, ICU

Narratives on the history of the Great Lakes with some emphasis on Illinois waterways. Includes bibliography and index, pp. 371–374.

Havighurst, Walter. *Voices on the River: The Story of the Mississippi Waterways.* New York: Macmillan Co., 1964. 310 p., illus., map.
ICU

Bibliography, pp. 287–297.

Illinois. Department of Public Works and Buildings. *132 Years of Public Service: The History and Duties of the Division of Waterways.* Springfield, 1955. 24 p., illus.
DLC, ICJ, IU

Illinois. Department of Trade and Commerce. *Annual Report.* Vol. 1–. Springfield, Illinois, 1918–. tables.
DLC

Includes Illinois commerce, grain trade, and public utilities. Report year ends June 30.

MacGill, Caroline E. *History of Transportation in the United States Before 1860.* Edited by B. H. Meyer. Washington: Carnegie Institution, 1917. 678 p., maps.
ICU

Discusses I&M Canal (pp. 509–517), its role in Midwest transportation, costs, conflicts with railroads, and its crucial role in commodity transport from Chicago to St. Louis.

McKnight, Hugh. *A Source Book of Canals, Locks, and Canal Boats.* London: Ward Lock, 1974. 144 p., illus., facsims., maps, ports.
DLC

Bibliography, pp. 140–142.

Mayer, Harold M., Brockel, Harry C., and Schenker, Eric. *The Great Lakes Transportation System.* Madison, Wisconsin: University of Wisconsin Sea Grant College Program, 1976. 292 p., maps.
ICU

Discusses importance of waterway in and around Chicago and other means of transportation. Includes bibliographies.

Mayer, Harold M. *The Port of Chicago and the St. Lawrence Seaway.* University of Chicago, Dept. of Geography, Research Series, no. 49. Chicago: University of Chicago, 1957. 283 p., illus., maps.
DLC, ICU

Shipping in the Chicago area.

Merchant, Ely Othman. *A Comparison of American and European Waterways, With Special Reference to the Factors Influencing the Development of Water Transportation.* Washington: U.S. Government Printing Office, 1912. 583 p.
DLC, ICU

Originally printed as Appendix 9 to the *Final Report of the U.S. National Waterways Commission,* S. Doc. 469, 62nd Cong., 2nd Sess. Also, originally a Ph.D. dissertation, Columbia University.

Moulton, Harold G. *The American Transportation Problem.* Washington: The Brookings Institution, 1933. 915 p., illus., plates, diagrs.
DLC, ICU

Covers railroads in the United States. Transportation via canals and railroads. Selected bibliography, pp. 896–910.

Payne, Pierre Stephen Robert. *The Canal Builders: The Story of Canal Engineers Through the Ages.* New York: Macmillan, 1959. 278 p., illus.
DLC, ICU, IU

Proceedings of the National Ship Canal Convention, Held at the City of Chicago, June 2 and 3, 1863. Chicago: Tribune Co. Book & Job Printing Office, 1863. 248 p.
ILoL

Good discussion of the necessity for a ship canal to connect east with west.

Sikes, George C. *Report to the Chicago Harbor Commission on Obstacles to Chicago's Water Shipping Development. Letter of Transmittal. Chicago's Attitude Toward Water Shipping. The*

Passenger Boat Business. Bridge Hours. The Lake Freight Business. Waterways and Terminals. Suggestions for Improvement. Railroad Control Over Lake Transportation. Lack of Vessel Ownership in Chicago. Additional Inquiries Suggested. Chicago, 1908. 39 p.
ICJ

Based on interviews with shippers and vessel men, on a study and observations of local conditions, and on information gathered in visits to Milwaukee, Cleveland, Detroit, and Duluth.

Slade, W. A. *Inland Waterways: A Selected List of Recent Writings.* Washington: U.S. Library of Congress, Division of Bibliography, 1928. 19 p.
DLC, ICU

Squires, Roger. *Old Canals Revival in the United States.* Beckenham, Kent: By the Author, 1978. 48 p., illus., map.
DLC

Includes bibliographical references.

Swanson, Leslie Charles. *Canals of Mid-America.* Moline, Illinois: Swanson Publishing Co., 1964. 42 p., illus., maps.
ICU

The author devotes a chapter to the I&M Canal. Discusses five important historic landmarks and parks that remain along the canal, the history of the waterway, and its present function. Includes twenty-nine photographs.

Trout, W. E., ed. *The American Canal Guide: A Practical Guide to Historic Canals of the United States and Canada.* 2 v. Shepardstown, West Virginia: American Canal Society, c. 1975. illus., maps.
DLC

Part 3: The Mississippi and Gulf States.

U.S. Census Office. *Eleventh Census of the United States, 1890.* Vol. 14: *Report on Transportation Business in the United States at the Eleventh Census: 1890.* Pt. 2: *Transportation by Water.* Washington: Government Printing Office, 1894. 532 p.
ICU

Statistics on shipping at Chicago and Calumet ports, 1880–1889.

U.S. Congress. House. House Documents. *Examination and Survey of Chicago Harbor and Adjacent Waterways.* H. Doc., Vol. 5, 63rd Cong., 1st Sess., 1914. Thirty-two maps.
ICU

Waggoner, Madeline S. *The Long Haul West: The Great Canal Era, 1817–1850.* n.p., n.d. 320 p., illus.
DLC, ICU

Includes section on the I&M Canal as a new link in the St. Lawrence Seaway to Gulf route.

Western Society of Engineers. "Chicago Area Water Supply: A Western Society of Engineers Symposium." *Midwest Engineer* 2 (February 1950): 6–14.
DLC, I, ICJ, IU

With maps and tables. Covers the period 1888–1949.

White, Anthony G. *Architecture and Design of Ship Canals: A Selected Bibliography.* Monticello, Illinois: Vance Bibliographies, c. 1982. 7 p.
DLC

Transportation and Communication—*The Illinois and Michigan Canal*

Abbott, Carl. "Civic Pride in Chicago, 1844–1860." *Journal of the Illinois State Historical Society* 63 (Winter 1970): 399.
DLC, I, IC, ICHi, ICN, ICU, IEN, IU

Contains photographs of Michigan Avenue and I&M Canal at the LaSalle basin.

To the American and European Subscribers to the Loan for the Completion of the Illinois and Michigan Canal and to Holders of Canal Bonds Generally. Chicago, 1847. 2 p.
CSmH

Dated and signed: Chicago, Dec. 21, 1847. H. T. Dickey.

Block, Marvin W. "Henry T. Rainey of Illinois." *Journal of the Illinois State Historical Society* 65 (Summer 1972): 142–157.
DLC, I, IC, ICHi, ICN, ICU, IEN, IU

Rainey, politician and canal activist, was the only major figure whose career spanned the years of the development of the waterway.

Board of Trustees, Illinois and Michigan Canal. *Report of a Majority of the Board of Trustees of the Illinois and Michigan Canal, Made in Reply to Certain Charges Which Were Preferred by Mr.*

Chas. Oakley, Trustee on the Part of the State of Illinois, at a Meeting of Subscribers to the Loan of $1,600,000. Held in New York, on the 18th of October, 1847. Washington: J. T. Towers, 1847. 13 p.
ICJ

Board of Trustees, Illinois and Michigan Canal. *Rules, By-Laws, and Regulations, Established by the Board of Trustees . . . in Conformity with Sec. 15 of the Law of February 21, 1843; To Which Is Added the Rates of Toll for the Year 1848, and Names and Places on the Line of the Canal, with Their Distances from Each Other.* Chicago: R. L. Wilson, Daily Journal Office, 1848. 46 p.
ICHi

Board of Trustees, Illinois and Michigan Canal. *Rules, By-Laws, and Regulations, Established by the Board of Trustees . . . in Conformity with Sec. 15 of the Law of February 21, 1843; To Which Is Added the Rates of Toll for the Year 1850, and Names of the Principal Places on the Line of the Canal, with Their Distances from Each Other.* Chicago: Charles L. Wilson's Print., Journal Office, 1850. 47 p.
ICHi

Board of Trustees, Illinois and Michigan Canal. *Rules, By-Laws, and Regulations, Established by the Board of Trustees . . . in Conformity with Sec. 15 of the Law of February 21, 1843; To Which Is Added the Rates of Toll for the Year 1851.* Lockport, Illinois: Plumb & Holcomb, Printers, 1851. 28 p.
ICHi

Bruno, B. D., comp. *History of the Illinois and Michigan Canal.* LaSalle, Illinois, 1962. 11 p.
IOg

Pamphlet.

Canal Investigation. Chicago, 1847. 64 p.
ICHi

Charges, correspondence, and evidence, and the reply of Wm. Gooding, chief engineer, to the charges preferred against him by Col. Oakley, at a meeting in New York, on the 18th of October, 1847.

Chicago Democrat. Extra. Chicago: March 25, 1835. 4 p.
ICN

Contains act for the construction of Illinois and Michigan Canal.

Chicago Magazine. *The West As It Is.* Chicago, 1857. 451 p., illus., plates, ports.
IHi

Section on I&M Canal in Pt. 5.

Coles, Edward. "Communication to the Antiquarian and Historical Society of Illinois." *Illinois Monthly Magazine* 1 (October 1830): 19–29.
DLC, ICN, ICU, IU

Governor Coles's description of the routes of navigation in Illinois. Contains a call for construction of a canal connecting the Illinois River with Lake Michigan.

Cook County, Illinois. Forest Preserve District. *The Illinois and Michigan Canal.* Nature Bulletin, No. 168. Chicago, 1980. 3 p.
IPHil

A brief chronology of the I&M Canal.

Davis, George Royal. *Illinois and Michigan Canal, Remarks of the Hon. George R. Davis of Illinois in the House of Representatives, April 24, 1880.* Washington, 1880. 14 p.
ICN, IHi

Dearborn, Luther. *Illinois and Michigan Canal, Remarks of Hon. Luther Dearborn, in the Senate, Springfield, Illinois, April 1879.* n.p., n.d. 7 p.
IHi

In speeches and papers by Illinoisans collected by Dr. J. F. Snyder, Vol. A, No. 30.

Documents Relating to the Illinois and Michigan Canal. [Washington]: Thomas Allen, Printer, 1843? 21 p.
IU—HS

Garside, Charlotte. *A Short History of the Illinois and Michigan Canal.* n.p., LaSalle County Historical Society, 1971. 12 p.
ILa

Given to the society, July 24, 1965.

Gindele, Ferdinand V. *The Canal Question Discussed by Ferdinand V. Gindele, a Member of the Engineer Corps During the Deepening of the Summit Level in 1865 and 1866.* Chicago: F. Gindele, Printer, 1881. 16 p.
ICHi

Graham, R[ichard] and Philips, Joseph. [*Letter to the Secretary of War Relative to the Proposed Illinois and Michigan Canal.*] H. Doc. 17, 16th Cong., 1st Sess., c. 1820. 2 p.
ICU
Describes the various portages between Lake Michigan and the Illinois River and discusses the feasibility of the proposed canal routes.

Harlow, Alvin F. *Old Towpaths: The Story of the American Canal Era.* New York and London: D. Appleton & Co., 1926. 287 p.
DLC, IO
Includes a detailed section on the I&M Canal.

Harrison, Carter Henry *Speeches on the Illinois and Michigan Canal, and Other Subjects.* n.p., n.d. 36 p.
ICN

Hoffman, Charles F. "A Winter in the West [1835]." *Journal of the Illinois State Historical Society* 47 (Spring 1954): 98–99.
DLC, I, IC, ICHi, ICN, ICU, IEN, IU
Comments on travels in the Illinois River valley and on canal proposal.

*To the Honorable, the General Assembly of the State of Illinois, the Memorial of the Undersigned Inhabitants of Cook County Respectfully Sheweth: That the Connection of Lake Michigan with the Navigable Water of the Illinois River, is an Object of Great Commercial Importance to this State. . . .*Chicago: John Calhoun, 1834. 2 p.
I—Ar
Arguments for a canal, as opposed to a railroad.

Howard, Robert Pickrell. *The Great Canal Scrip Fraud: The Downfall of Governor Joel A. Matteson.* Selected papers in Illinois History, Vol. 1. Springfield: Illinois State Historical Society, 1980. 19 p.
IHi

The Illinois Merchants [*Table of Reference*] *And Shippers Assistant. Table of the Ready Calculation of* [*U.S.*] *Canal Tolls . . . Rates of Toll* [*I&M Canal*] *. . . Principal Merchants in Chicago . . . Galena and Chicago Rail Road . . . Map of the Illinois and Michigan Canal And the Illinois and Mississippi Rivers. . . .* New York: Mayer & Korff Lith., 1851.
ICHi

"The Illinois and Michigan Canal Centennial." *Chicago History* 1 (Spring 1948): 321–328. facsim.
DLC, IC, ICF, ICHi, ICN, ICU, IU
On the building of the canal, 1836–1848.

Illinois. Canal Commissioners. *Letter from the President of the Illinois and Michigan Canal: Concerning the Number of Engineers in the Employ of the State.* Springfield: Wm. Walters, 1846. 7 p.
ICU
Illinois General Assembly, 2nd Sess.

Illinois. Canal Commissioners. *Letter from the President of the Illinois and Michigan Canal; Giving the Number of Persons Employed at the Canal Office in Lockport.* Springfield: Wm. Walters, 1840. 1 p.
ICU
Illinois General Assembly, 2nd Sess.

Illinois. Canal Commissioners. *Reports.* Vol. 1–92. Vandalia and Springfield, Illinois: Illinois Canal Commissioners, 1825–1916.
ICJ, ICU, IHi
Reports were by the commissioners to the governors.

Illinois. Department of Conservation. *Illinois and Michigan Canal, 1848–1948.* Springfield, 1948. 35 p., illus., maps.
DLC, IU

Illinois. Department of Public Works and Buildings. Division of Waterways. *Preliminary Examination Report for Illinois and Michigan Canal Development, November, 1948.* n.p., State of Illinois, 1948. 20 p.
DLC, IU

Illinois. Department of Public Works and Buildings. Division of Waterways. *A Report of the Illinois and Michigan Canal, April 1944.* By Walter A. Rosenfield, and Thos. B. Casey. Springfield: Division of Waterways, 1944. 18 p., maps, diagr.
DLC, IHi, IU
A review of the canal's condition, the prospects for parks along its path, and the state of funding for canal-related conservation projects.

Illinois. Division of Waterways. *Preliminary Examination Report for the Illinois and Michigan Canal, November 1948.* n.p., Division of Waterways, 1948. 20 p.
IU

Illinois. Division of Waterways. *Survey Report for Flood Control, Illinois and Michigan Canal and Tributaries, Joliet to Calumet–Sag Channel.* Springfield, 1951. 50 p., illus., maps, diagrs., profiles, tables.
DLC, IU

Illinois. General Assembly. Senate. *Illinois and Michigan Canal. Mr. Forquer, from the Committee on Internal Improvements, Made the Following Report.* n.p., 1835. 16 p.
IHi

The 9th General Assembly, 1st Sess., 1834–1835, Doc. 5. Concerns the expediency of obtaining a loan on the credit of the state, for the purpose of constructing a canal.

Illinois. Governor [Thomas Carlin]. *Communication from the Governor of Illinois, Transmitting the Reports and Documents in Relation to Canal Claims.* Springfield, 1839.
IAl

Illinois. Governor. Address of Governor S. M. Cullom, at the Canal and River Convention at Ottawa, on the 17th Day of March, 1880. n.p., [1880]. 8 p.
IHi

Speech on Illinois waterways and canals.

Illinois. Historic American Buildings Survey. *Survey no: Ill-157, The Illinois and Michigan Canal.* Springfield: Department of Public Works, Division of Waterways, 1933. 2 p., blueprint, diagrs., map.
IHi

Blueprint plot showing DuPage River Dam and Locks 6 and 7. Done by WPA Preservation blueprint with map. Canal Locks 6 and 7 at Channahon, Illinois.

Illinois. Laws, Statutes, etc. *An Act for the Construction of the Illinois and Michigan Canal.* Chicago: T. O. Davis, [1836].
ICN

Done at Vandalia, the 15th day of January, 1836.

Illinois. Laws, Statutes, etc. *Acts of the Legislature of the State of Illinois, for the Construction of the Illinois and Michigan Canal, Now in Force, or Under Contracts on Said Canal have been Made.* Chicago: The Tribune Office, 1841. 35 p.
IHi, IO

With index.

Illinois. Laws, Statutes, etc. *A Law to Provide for the Completion of the Illinois and Michigan Canal and for Payment of the Canal Debt. Passed February 20, 1843.* n.p., 1845? 15 p.
IHi

A supplementary act.

Illinois. Statutes. *Bulletin, No. 27: Laws of the State of Illinois with Reference to the Powers, Duties, and Jurisdiction of the Department of Purchases and Construction, Division of Waterways; to Construct, Operate, and Maintain the Illinois Waterway; to Control and Manage the Illinois and Michigan Canal Properties; To Prevent Pollution of or Encroachment Upon all Rivers and Lakes of the State.* Chicago: Department of Purchases and Construction, Division of Waterways, 1926. 34 p.
ICU

Bulletin, No. 27. Division of Waterways.

Illinois. Rivers and Lakes Commission. *A Compilation of Money Spent by the Government of Various Harbors, Rivers, and Canals and the Riparian Property Holders Benefited.* Rivers and Lakes Commission, Bulletin, No. 5. Springfield: Illinois State Journal Co., 1912. 38 p.
ICU

Refers to harbors, rivers, and canals of Illinois.

Illinois. State Trustee of the Illinois and Michigan Canal. *Report of the State Trustee of the Illinois and Michigan Canal, Made in Relation to Certain Charges Which Were Preferred by Him Against the Chief Engineer, and Read in a Meeting . . . Held in New York on the 18th of October, 1847.* Chicago: Democrat Book & Job Office, Steam Power Press, 1848. 41 p.
ICHi

Lamb, John M. "The Great Canal Scrip Fraud." *Illinois Magazine* 16 (November 1977): 57–60. illus.
ICN

On Governor Joel Matteson's illegally redeeming I&M Canal scrip in the 1850s.

Lamb, John M. "The Illinois and Michigan Canal and Other Illinois Waterways." *Nautical Research Journal* 24 (1978): 75–80.
NN

Lee, Gary A., ed. "A Diary of the Illinois and Michigan Canal Investigation, 1843–1844, by Governor John Davis." *Papers in Illinois History and Transactions for the Year 1941* (1943): 38–72.
ICU

Putnam, James William. *The Illinois and Michigan Canal: A Study in Economic History.* Chicago: University of Chicago Press, 1918. 213 p., maps, diagrs.
ICU

Originally prepared as a doctoral dissertation at the University of Wisconsin.

Rates of Toll for the Year 1849 . . . Together with Forms of Clearances, Bills of Lading, and Names of Places Along the Line, with their Distances from Each Other. Chicago: Chas. L. Wilson, Daily Journal Office, 1849. 8 p.
ICHi

I&M Canal rates.

Rathbun, Mary Y. "Federal Maritime Grant to Help Finance Restoration of Lock # 14." *Historic Illinois* 2 (December 1979): 12–15.
ICarbS, ICU, INS

Rathbun, Mary Yeater. *The Illinois and Michigan Canal.* Printed by the Authority of the State of Illinois, Department of Conservation, Bureau of Land and Historic Sites. n.p., 1980. 50 p.
IMoGW

Detailed history of the development, construction, financing, and disuse of the canal.

Real Estate Research Corporation. *Appraisal and Study of Parts of the Illinois and Michigan Canal.* 2 v. Chicago: Real Estate Research Corp., 1966. 190 p., illus., maps, charts, diagrs., figures.
IHi, ILoL

A thorough study of the condition of the canal and what can be done for its preservation and possible uses. Prepared for State of Illinois, Division of Waterways, December 1966.

Roberts, Nathan S. *Report on the Location and Expense of a Ship Canal Around Niagara Falls. Also, from the Illinois River to Lake Michigan, With a Report of a Select Committee to the Assembly, April 14, 1834, Relating to the Connection from Oswego to the Hudson.* New York: The Railroad Journal, 1834. 16 p., map.
ICU

U.S. Army. Corps of Engineers. *Annual Report upon the Improvement of Harbors of Chicago and Calumet, Lake Michigan, and of the Illinois River. Surveys for Hennepin Canal and for the Enlargement of the Illinois and Michigan Canal, In [the] Charge of W. H. H. Benyaurd . . . Being Appendix GG of the Annual Report of the Chief of Engineers for 1883.* Washington: U.S. Government Printing Office, 1883. 53 p.
IHi

U.S. Army Corps of Engineers. . . . *Canal—Lake Michigan and Illinois River. Letter from the Secretary of War Transmitting a Report of a Survey of the Route of a Canal to Connect the Waters of Lake Michigan with Those of the Illinois River, May 25, 1832.* H. Doc. 245, 22nd Cong., 1st Sess., 1832. 7 p.
IHi

U.S. Congress. House. . . . *Canal—Lake Michigan and Illinois River. [To Accompany Bill H.R. No. 548, April 13, 1832] Mr. Mercer, from the Committee on Internal Improvements, to Which the Subject Had Been Referred, Made the Following Report.* . . . H. Rep. 445, 22nd Cong., 1st Sess., 1832.
IHi

U.S. Congress. House. *Memorial of the General Assembly of the State of Illinois, Asking for a Grant of Land to Aid Said State in Opening a Canal to Connect the Waters of Lake Michigan with the Illinois River.* H. Rep. 81, 19th Cong., 1826. 4 p.
IC

U.S. Congress. House. Committee on Interstate and Foreign Commerce. *Hearing Before Subcommittee of Committee on Interstate Commerce, House of Representatives, February 20, 1907, on the Chicago Drainage Canal and the Illinois and Michigan Canal.* Washington: U.S. Government Printing Office, 1907. 41 p.
ICJ

U.S. Congress. House. Committee on Military Affairs. . . . *Ship Canal to Connect Mississippi River and Lake Michigan [To Accompany Bill H.R. No. 288], Feb. 20, 1862. Report of the Committee on Military Affairs.* H. Rep. 37, 37th Cong., 2nd Sess., 1862. 13 p.
ICJ

U.S. Congress. House. Committee on Public Lands. *Illinois and Michigan Canal: A Report of the Committee on Public Lands to Whom was Referred "A Bill Granting Additional Quantity of Land to the State of Illinois to Aid in Completing the Illinois and Michigan Canal."* H. Rep., 28th Cong., 2nd Sess., 1845. 16 p.
ICN

U.S. Congress. House. Select Committee to Consider the Memorial of the General Assembly by the State of Illinois. . . . *Report of the Select Committee to Which Was Referred on the 3rd Ultimo, a Memorial of the General Assembly of Illinois, upon the Subject of a Canal Communication Between the Illinois River and Lake Michigan, Accompanied with a Bill to Aid the State of Illinois in the Accomplishment of the Same.* H. Rep. 53, 18th Cong., 2nd Sess., 1825. 6 p.
IHi

U.S. Congress. Senate. *Memorial of the General Assembly of the State of Illinois, On the Construction of a Canal, To Unite the Waters of Lake Michigan with the Illinois River, February 23, 1826.* S. Doc., 19th Cong., 1st Sess., 1826. 4 p.
IHi

U.S. Congress. Senate. *Message from the President of the United States, Transmitting a Communication from the Governor of the State of Illinois, with a Copy of an Act of That State, Tendering to the United States the Cession of the Illinois and Michigan Canal, upon Condition That It Shall Be Enlarged and Maintained as a Natural Waterway for Commercial Purposes.* S. Ex. Doc. 38, 48th Cong., 1st Sess., 1884. 45 p.
ICU

Walker, Charles L. *Why the United States Should Perfect the Title of the State of Illinois in the Illinois and Michigan Canal.* n.p., Illinois Canal Commissioners, 1910.
ICJ

Weik, Jesse W. "An Unpublished Chapter in the Early History of Chicago." *Journal of the Illinois State Historical Society* 7 (January 1915): 329–348.
DLC, I, IC, ICHi, ICN, ICU, IEN, IU

Biography of James M. Bucklin based on interview with him. Includes Bucklin's account of his journeys through northeastern Illinois and his work in the planning of the I&M Canal.

Westerman, George. *The Illinois and Michigan Canal: Its Past, Its Present, Plans for Its Future.* Prospect Heights, Illinois: George Westerman, 1983. 26 p., illus., maps, photos., diagrs.
IJo

A short booklet on the canal. Contains information on the canal and its importance, the need for a canal, engineering, the commercial life of the canal, people, the canal today, plans for the future, and interested organizations.

Transportation and Communication—*Sanitary and Ship Canal*

Alvord, John W. *A Review of the Chicago Sanitary and Ship Canal with Suggestions for a Harbor: An Address Before the Chicago Real Estate Board.* Chicago, 1908. 27 p.
ICJ

Anthony, Elliot. *Sanitation and Navigation.* Pt. 1: *The History of Legislation in Illinois in Regard to Canals, Including the Present Scheme for a Drainage Ship Canal.* Pt. 2: *The Story of the Erie Canal.* Chicago: The Chicago Legal News Co., 1891. 200 p., front.
ICJ

Baker, M. N. "The Chicago Drainage Canal." *Outlook* 64 (February 1900): 357–360. map.
ICU

Concise review of Chicago's drainage efforts.

Blair, F[rancis] P., Jr. *Report [of] the Committee on Military Affairs to Whom Was Referred the Resolution of the House Directing Said Committee to Inquire into the Expediency of Constructing a Ship Canal Between the Waters of Lake Michigan and the Mississippi River for the Purpose of Facilitating the Operations of the War.* H. Rep. 37, 37th Cong., 2nd Sess., 1862. 13 p.
ICJ, ICN, IHi

Description of the I&M Canal, commerce of the lakes and rivers. Discusses the desirability of constructing a deeper canal.

Bruce, William George. *The Colossal Diversion of Water into the Chicago Drainage Canal. Address by William G. Bruce . . . Delivered Before the National Rivers and Harbors Congress, Washington, D.C., December 5, 1923.* [Milwaukee, Wisconsin], 1923. 24 p.
ICJ

Contains "Where Do We Stand," about order issued by the Secretary of War in the Chicago Water Diversion Case; "What of the Future," "The Great Lakes Issue," and "The Present Status of the Chicago Water Diversion Case."

Canada. *Papers Relating to the St. Lawrence Waterway Project and the Chicago Drainage Canal.* Ottawa: F. A. Acland, Printer, 1924. 149 p.
ICU

Printed by order of the Canadian Parliament.

Canada. Commission of Conservation. *Protest Against Further Diversion of Water from Lake Michigan for the Chicago Drainage Canal.* Ottawa: R. L. Crain, Ltd., 1912. 27 p., map, diagr.
DLC, ICU

Appendix A: Application of the Sanitary District of Chicago for a permit to divert 10,000 cubic feet per second. Appendix B: Statement by Gen. Bixby, U.S. Engineers, respecting effect of lowering the level of Lake Erie. Appendix C: Memorandum by Gen. Bixby respecting the diversion of water by the Sanitary District.

Canada. Department of External Affairs. *Correspondence Relating to Diversion of the Waters of the Great Lakes by the Sanitary District of Chicago.* [*From March 27, 1912, to October 17, 1927*]. Ottawa: F. A. Acland, 1928. 70 p.
DLC, ICJ

Canada. Department of Marine and Fisheries. *Papers Relating to the Application of the Sanitary District of Chicago for Permission to Divert 10,000 Cubic Feet of Water from Lake Michigan.* Ottawa: C. H. Parmelee, 1912. 270 p., map, diagr.
DLC, ICJ, ICU

Papers relating to the pros and cons of diverting more water from Lake Michigan into the Chicago Drainage Canal.

Chicago. The Civic Federation. *A Report on the Water Supply and Sewerage Systems of the City of Chicago with a Comparative Study of Certain Other American Cities.* Chicago: The Civic Federation, 1950–1952. 117 p. illus., maps.
ICU

Report on Chicago systems of water supply, various proposals aimed at unifying the systems, and what can be learned from other cities.

Chicago. Harbor Commission. [*Final*] *Report to the Mayor and Aldermen of the City of Chicago by the Chicago Harbor Commission.* Chicago, 1909. 383 p., illus., tables, plates, maps, plan, diagr.
ICJ

Contents of the prelude, Pt. 1: "The Development of Commercial Ports," by J. P. Goode. Pt. 2: "Obstacles to Chicago's Water Shipping Development," by G. C. Sykes. Pt. 3: "The Volume and Trend of Traffic to and from the Central West," by G. G. Tunnell. Pt. 4: Special Reports.

Chicago. Sanitary District. *Building Sixty Miles of Industries: Being a Promise of the Results That Will Come from the Business-Like Development Now Under Way, of the Great Sanitary Canal District.* Chicago, 1907. 16 p., front., illus.
ICJ

Reprinted from the *Sunday Record Herald,* Chicago, April 28, 1907. A prospectus and view of industrial development that will (and has) come about as a result of the building of the Sanitary Canal.

Chicago. Sanitary District. *Facts Demonstrating the Sanitary District of Chicago's Need of and Right to the Diversion of Necessary Water to Protect the Lives and Health of its 3,500,000 Citizens and Other Millions of People Having Social and Business Relations with Them.* Chicago: Sanitary District, 1924? 82 p.
DLC

Submitted to the Committee on Rivers and Harbors, House of Representatives, 68th Cong., 1st Sess., by the Sanitary District of Chicago, a municipal corporation organized under the laws of the State of Illinois, April 1924.

Chicago. Sanitary District. *Report on the Sanitary and Ship Canal.* Chicago: Jacobs & Holmes, 1906. 34 p., illus., map.
ICJ, ICU

Chicago. Sanitary District. *The Sanitary District of Chicago, 1923.* Chicago: Webb-Linn, 1923. 32 p., maps, tables, diagr.
DLC, ICU
Covers engineering facts concerning the Sanitary District of Chicago in May of 1923.

Chicago. Sanitary District. *The Sanitary District of Chicago, 1927.* Chicago: J. T. Igoe Co., 1927. 71 p., illus., map, diagr.
ICU
Covers engineering facts concerning the Sanitary District of Chicago in June of 1927.

Chicago. Sanitary District. Board of Trustees. *Address of Hon. B. A. Eckhar, President of Board of Trustees of Sanitary District of Chicago at the Inspection of Main Drainage by the International Conference of the State Boards of Health. A Compendium of Facts and Figures Relating to the Sanitary District of Chicago—Its Formation, Progress, and Completion. June 11, 1895.* Chicago: J. F. Higgins, 1896. 22 p.
ICJ

Chicago. Sanitary District. Board of Trustees. *Comparative Tables Showing Cost of Theoretical Channels of Various Sizes in Earth and Rock, from Ashland Avenue, Chicago, to Lockport, Illinois.* Chicago: H. M. Shabad, Printer, 1893. 56 p., tables, diagrs.
ICU

Chicago. Sanitary District. Board of Trustees. *Memorandum Concerning the Drainage and Sewage Conditions in Chicago and the Diversion of 10,000 C.F.S. From Lake Michigan at Chicago.* Chicago: The Board of Trustees, 1923. 92 p., maps, illus., charts, diagrs.
ICJ, ICU, IJo
The dilution project and its objectives, water power at Lockport, sewage treatment, flood run-off from Chicago River drainage area, need of diversion, historical facts of diversion, and various other data on drainage and floods.

Chicago. Sanitary District. Board of Trustees. *Memorial Presented by the Trustees of the Sanitary District of Chicago to the Congress of the United States. Deep Waterway from Lake Michigan to the Mississippi River at St. Louis.* Chicago: J. F. Higgins, 1902. 43 p., illus., plates.
ICJ, ICU

Chicago. Sanitary District. Board of Trustees. *Memorial Presented by the Trustees of the Sanitary District of Chicago, Favoring the Widening and Deepening by the United States Government of the Chicago River from Its Mouth Through the Main and South Branch, to the Beginning of the Main Drainage Channel at Robey Street.* Chicago: F. Klein Co., 1906. 14 p., maps.
ICU

Chicago. Sanitary District. Board of Trustees. *Reports of [the] International Waterways Commission Concerning the Chicago Diversion and Terms of Treaty. O'Hanley's Report to the Canadian Government[1896]. Reprinted from "Compiled Reports of the International Waterways Commission, 1905–1913." Submitted in Accordance with the Provisions of Chapter 26, Section 27, of the Revised Statutes of Canada—Printed by Order of Parliament—Ottawa, 1913. Treaty [1910] Between the United States and Great Britain.* Chicago: The Sanitary District of Chicago, 1924. 89 p.
ICJ

Chicago. Sanitary District. Board of Trustees. *Statement by Sir Adam Beck Regarding Enormous Losses Occasioned by Diversion of Water from the Great Lakes to the Mississippi River by the Sanitary District of Chicago.* Toronto, 1923. 7 p.
ICJ

Chicago. Sanitary District. Law Department. *Laws of and in Reference to the Sanitary District of Chicago, with Annotations.* Chicago: The Chicago Sanitary District, 1916. 302 p., plans.
DLC, ICU

Chicago. Sanitary District. Law Department. *Laws of and in Reference to the Sanitary District of Chicago, with Annotations and References.* Chicago: Sanitary District, 1922. 366 p., plans.
DLC

Christensen, Daphne, ed. *Chicago Public Works: A History.* Chicago: Daphne Christensen, 1973. 238 p., illus.
ICU

Cooley, L. E. *The Lakes and Gulf Waterway. A Brief, with Illustrations and Notes, Published by the Citizens' Association. Prepared Under the Direction of [the] Committee on Main Drainage.* Chicago: Chicago Legal News Co., 1888. 85 p., maps.
IHi
Bound with Chicago drainage and waterway laws.

Illinois. General Assembly. "Amendment Authorizing Construction of Sanitary and Ship Canal." *House Journal.* 45th General Assembly. Page 1420.
ICU
Amendment authorizing construction of Sanitary and Ship Canal.

Illinois. Special Commission, Chicago Drainage Channel. *Report of the Special Commission Appointed by Hon. John R. Tanner, Governor of Illinois, under Section 27 of the "Act to Create Sanitary Districts."* Chicago: Press of Cameron Anberg & Co., 1900. 131 p., front., illus., plans, diagrs.
DLC, ICHi, ICJ
Contains the report of D. Fitzgerald, the chief engineer of the Chicago Drainage Channel, and the acts of Illinois Legislature and of Congress relating to same.

Ingersoll-Sergeant Drill Co., *The Chicago Drainage Channel.* New York, 1897? 32 p., illus.
ICJ

International Waterways Commission. U.S. and Canada. *Report Upon the Chicago Drainage Canal by the International Waterways Commission.* Washington: U.S. Government Printing Office, 1907. 54 p.
DLC, ICJ
Report of January 1887, of the commission appointed to examine the drainage and water supply of Chicago. Letter, June 29, 1906, from Lyman E. Cooley. Statement of expenditures by Sanitary District of Chicago through December 31, 1905. Permits issued by the Secretary of War to the Sanitary District of Chicago. Joint resolution of Illinois Legislature, May 27, 1889. Report of Rudolph Hering and G. W. Fuller upon methods of sewage disposal available at Chicago.

Jones, Alexander J. "The Chicago Drainage Canal and Its Forbear, The Illinois and Michigan Canal." *Illinois State Historical Society Transactions* (1907): 153–161.
DLC, IC, ICU

O'Connell, James C. *Chicago's Quest for Pure Water.* Washington: Public Works Historical Society, 1976. 19 p., illus.
ICU
A short overview of the drainage canal movement in Chicago in the late nineteenth century.

Raddin, Charles. "The Great Sanitary Waterway of Chicago." *Overland Monthly* 34 (October 1899): 301–309. illus.
I, IC, ICF, ICN, ICU, IEN, INS, IU

Randolph, Isham. *A Review . . . of John W. Alvord's "Review of the Chicago Sanitary and Ship Canal, with Suggestions for a Harbor."* Chicago, 1908. 13 p.
DLC, ICJ
Largely a cost-analysis review.

Rauch, John Henry. *A Report to the Board of Health of the City of Chicago on the Necessity of an Extension of the Sewerage of the City.* Chicago: Ottaway, Brown & Colbert, 1873. 22 p., tables.
ICU
Background of sewage problems, leading to eventual need for drainage canal.

U.S. Army. Corps of Engineers. *Diversion of Water from Lake Michigan. Report on the Sanitary District of Chicago, with Recommendations for Action on the Part of the War Department with Reference to Diversion of Water from Lake Michigan. Submitted by District Engineer, U.S. Engineer's Office, Chicago, Illinois, November 1, 1923.* Washington: U.S. Government Printing Office, 1924. 97 p., tables, diagr., profiles, charts.
DLC, ICJ, ICU
Concerning water diversion levels into Chicago Drainage Canal.

U.S. [Army] Engineering Department. Board of Engineers for Rivers and Harbors. The *Port of Chicago, Illinois . . .[Revised 1939]. Prepared by the Board of Engineers for Rivers and Harbors, War Department.* Washington: U.S. Gov-

ernment Printing Office, 1940. 194 p., tables, diagr., front., plates, maps.
DLC, ICJ

U.S. Congress. House. Committee on Public Works. *Lake Michigan Water Diversion Hearings Before the Committee of Public Works . . . to Authorize the State of Illinois and the Sanitary District of Chicago, Under the Direction of the Secretary of the Army, to Test, on a Three Year Basis, the Effect of Increasing the Diversion of Water from Lake Michigan into the Illinois Waterway, and for Other Purposes.* H. Rep. 3210, 84th Cong., 1st Sess., 1955. 125 p.
ICU

Includes memoranda submitted by the Sanitary District of Chicago, Board of Trustees, and by Great Lakes Harbors Association on the history of the Sanitary and Ship Canal and on litigation over water diversion.

U.S. Congress. House. Committee on Rivers and Harbors. *Chicago Sanitary District Canal. Hearing Before the Committee on Rivers and Harbors. . . . A Joint Resolution to Provide for the Acquisition of the Canal Now Owned by the Sanitary District of Chicago, and for Other Purposes.* H. Res. 308, 73rd Cong., 2nd Sess., 1934. 11 p.
DLC, ICU

U.S. War Department. Engineering Department. *. . . Effect of Withdrawal of Water from Lake Michigan by the Sanitary District of Chicago.* H. Doc. 6, 59th Cong., 1st Sess., Committee on Rivers and Harbors, 1906. 16 p.
ICJ

Signed: Isham Randolph, Chief Engineer.

Western Society of Engineers. *Souvenir of the Western Society of Engineers' Excursion Along the Chicago Drainage Canal on Saturday, Aug. 15, 1896.* Chicago: The Society, 1896. 32 p., illus.
ICJ

Wright, G. Frederick. "The Chicago Drainage Canal." *Nation* 60 (April 1895): 320–321.
DLC, I, ICHi, ICN, ICU, IU

Wright, John L. "The Chicago Drainage Channel." *Lippincott's Monthly Magazine* 60 (September 1897): 410–414.
DLC, IC, ICN, ICU

Transportation and Communication—*Illinois Deep Waterway*

Alvord, John W. and Burdick, Charles B. *Report Made to Former Rivers and Lakes Commission on the Illinois River and Its Bottom Lands, with Reference to the Conservation of Agriculture and Fisheries, and the Control of Floods.* Springfield: Illinois State Journal Co., 1919. 137 p., front., illus., maps, tables, diagrs.
ICJ

American Waterways. Philadelphia: American Academy of Political and Social Science, 1908. 299 p.
ICU

Contains articles on inland waterways by Theodore Roosevelt, J. E. Randsell, F. G. Newlands, W. Thayer, and R. B. Way.

Barnes, Mortimer. *The Illinois Deep Waterway: A Memorial Presented to the American Society of Civil Engineers. Presented Jan. 26, 1922.* Springfield: Illinois Legislative Joint Committee, H.J.R. 41, 1921. 21 p., map, tables.
IO

A short history and description of the commercial role of the waterway. Includes freight rates, commercial aspects, coal, why I&M Canal was important for waterway concept.

Barrett, George F. *The Waterway from the Great Lakes to the Gulf of Mexico: Facts and Records of a Century.* Chicago: The Sanitary District of Chicago, 1926, 194 p., map.
DLC, ICJ, ICU

Detailed chronology and analysis of the waterway's history and role in transportation—from early I&M Canal days to early-twentieth-century waterway concept.

Becht, J. Edwin. *Commodity Origins, Traffic, and Markets Accessible to Chicago via the Illinois Waterway.* Ann Arbor, Michigan: University Microfilms, 1951. (Microfilm.)
MiU

Bonney, Charles C. *Speech of Charles C. Bonney, of Peoria, Against an Act Entitled an "Act to Incorporate the Illinois River Improvement Company."* Peoria, Illinois: B. Foster, 1857. 16 p.
ICU

Delivered on behalf of the Common Council and citizens of Peoria, at St. Louis, June 23, 1857.

Chicago. Sanitary District. Board of Trustees. *Memorial Presented by the Trustees of the Sanitary District of Chicago to the Congress of the United States: Deep Waterway from Lake Michigan to the Mississippi River at St. Louis.* Chicago: J. F. Higgins, Printer, 1902. 43 p., illus., plates.
ICU

Chicago. Sanitary District. Engineering Board of Review. *Value of Diverted Water for Transportation, Lake Michigan to Gulf of Mexico, Being Report of Committee No. 3 of [the] Engineering Board of Review of the Sanitary District of Chicago.* Chicago: Sanitary District, 1924. 56 p.
ICJ

Citizens' Association of Chicago. *The Chicago Drainage and Waterway Laws.* Chicago: Chicago Legal News Printing, 1889. 11 p., front., maps.
IHi

Cooley, Lyman E. *The Diversion of the Waters of the Great Lakes by Way of the Sanitary and Ship Canal of Chicago: A Brief of the Facts and Issues.* Chicago: Clohesey & Co., 1913. 216 p., maps, plan, diagrs.
DLC, ICJ, ICU

Published as a rebuttal by the Sanitary District of Chicago in view of the refusal of the Secretary of War to grant a permit for increasing the diversion of water to 10,000 cubic feet per second through the Chicago Sanitary and Ship Canal. Includes statement by City of Chicago on this issue and the ruling of the Secretary of War.

Cooley, Lyman Edgar. *The Lakes and Gulf Waterway, as Related to the Chicago Sanitary Problem: The General Project of a Waterway from Lake Michigan to the Gulf of Mexico. A Preliminary Report with Appendices, Maps, and Profiles.* Chicago: Press of J. W. Weston, 1891. 92 p., front., illus., plates, maps.
DLC, ICJ, ICU

Cooley, Lyman E., ed. *The Levels of the Lakes as Affected by the Proposed Lakes and Gulf Waterway: A Discussion Before the Western Society of Engineers by George Y. Wisner [and Others].* Chicago: Citizens' Association, 1889. 36 p.
ICJ, ICU

Reprinted from the *Journal of the Association of Engineering Societies,* March 1889. Discusses how various water diversion volumes will affect the lakes.

Cooley, Lyman E. *Prospectus of a Project for a Deep Waterway and the Conservation of a Natural Resource of the State of Illinois.* Illinois Rivers and Lakes Commission, Bulletin, No. 2. Springfield: Illinois State Journal Co., 1911. 10 p.
ICU

Deneen, C. S. "Vast Wealth for the State." *Technical World Magazine* 9 (April 1908): 121–129.
DLC, IC, ICJ, ICU, IHi, IU

Article by Governor Deneen argues for development of power stations along Illinois waterway as a rationale for its construction.

East Peoria Post. *Annual Review Edition, East Peoria Post.* Vol. 21, No. 9, August 11, 1922. East Peoria, Illinois: East Peoria Post, 1922. 80 p., illus., maps, ports.
IHi

Various articles on the benefits of the waterway.

Graff, Maurice O. "The Lake Michigan Water Diversion Controversy: A Summary Statement." *Journal of the Illinois State Historical Society* 34 (December 1941): 453–471.
DLC, I, IC, ICHi, ICN, ICU, IEN, IU

The conflict between Chicago and other cities and states over the diversion of lake waters down the river system as an aid to sewage disposal.

Gross, Howard H. *A Discussion of the Proposed Deep Waterway.* Chicago? 1909. 16 p.
IHi

Guthrie, Ossian. *Lake Fluctuations.* n.p., c. 1888. 31 p.
IHi

Bound with McMath, Robert E., "The Waterway Between Lake Michigan and the Mississippi River, by Way of the Illinois River," edited by Lyman Cooley. Covers the levels of the lake as affected by the proposed lakes and gulf waterway.

Handbury, Thomas H. *Illinois River Improvement: Some Facts in Relation Thereto.* Chicago? 1888? 36 p.
IHi

Address of Maj. Thomas H. Handbury, Corps of Engineers, U.S. Army, delivered before the Illinois River Improvement Convention at Peoria, Illinois, October 11, 1887. Also press opinions and extracts from Chicago newspapers on the project.

Illinois River Improvement Convention, Peoria, 1887. *Waterway Improvement, A Matter of Great National Importance.* Peoria, Illinois: National Democrat Printing, 1887. 47 p.
DLC, IEN

Inland navigation topics. Proceedings of the Illinois River Improvement Convention, held at Peoria, Illinois, October 11 and 12, 1887.

Illinois. Board of Health. *Advance Notes of the Sanitary Investigations of the Illinois River and Its Tributaries, with Special Reference to the Effects of the Sewage of Chicago on the Des-Plaines and Illinois Rivers Prior to the Opening of the Chicago Drainage Canal.* Springfield: State Board of Health, 1900. 57 p., illus.
ICJ

Illinois. Deep Waterway Commission. *Official Report of the Deep Waterway Commission to Honorable Len Small, Governor of Illinois.* Springfield, 1922. 6 p.
DLC

Covers inland navigation.

Illinois. Department of Public Works and Buildings. Division of Waterways. *The Illinois Waterway . . . Delivered Before Illinois Society of Engineers, Jan. 26, 1922.* Springfield? Illinois Legislative Joint Committee, 1922. 21 p., illus., map.
IHi

Illinois. Division of Waterways. *Report on Drainage Districts by the Division of Waterways, 1937.* Springfield: Division of Waterways, 1937. 52 p., tables, diagr., maps.
DLC, ICU

Data on Illinois River and waterway and drainage in and around the Illinois basin, upper and lower.

Illinois. General Assembly. House. Committee on Canal River Improvements and Commerce. *Deep Waterway Debates of the 46th General Assembly of the State of Illinois.* Springfield: Illinois State Journal Co., 1910.
ICU

Illinois. General Assembly. House of Representatives. Committee on Waterways. *Waterway Proceedings. State House, Springfield, Illinois. Hall of Representatives, Wednesday, March 24, 1915. Meeting of the House Committee on Waterways. Hon. Michael L. Igoe, Chairman.* Springfield: The State of Illinois, 1915. 32 p.
IHi, INS

Concerns construction of a waterway between Lockport and Utica.

Illinois. Governor. *Special Message of Charles S. Deneen, Governor, April 25, 1911.* Springfield? 1911? 43 p.
IHi

Report by a Special Board of Engineers on Waterway, from Lockport, Illinois, to the mouth of the Illinois River.

Illinois. Internal Improvement Commission. *The Illinois Waterway Report with Plans and Estimates of Cost for [a] Waterway from Lockport, Illinois to Utica, Illinois by Way of Des-Plaines and Illinois Rivers.* Springfield: Illinois State Journal Co., 1909. 67 p., maps.
IHi

Illinois. Internal Improvement Commission. . . . *The Lakes and Gulf Waterway: A Report by the Internal Improvement Commission of Illinois to the Governor, Hon. C. S. Deneen, February, 1907.* Springfield: Phillips Bros., 1906–1907. 62 p.
DLC, ICJ, IHi

Preliminary considerations, divisions of the route, the Deep Waterway, results, and conclusions.

Illinois. Public Works and Buildings Department. Waterways Division. Internal Improvement Commission. *The Illinois Waterway Report, with Plans and Estimates of Cost for a Waterway from Lockport, Illinois to Utica, Illinois.* Internal Improvement Commission, Bulletin, No. 20. Springfield: State Journal Co., 1909.
ICU

Illinois. Rivers and Lakes Commission. *The Illinois Waterway: A Guide for Navigators from Lake Michigan to the Mississippi River via the Chicago Sanitary and Ship Canal, the Illinois and Michigan Canal, and the Illinois River.* Rivers and Lakes Commission, Bulletin, No. 10. Springfield: Illinois State Journal Co., 1914. 31 p., illus.
ICU, NN

Illinois. Rivers and Lakes Commission. *The Illinois Waterway. Report of the Board of Engineers to Governor Dunne. A Project for a Waterway of Eight Feet Minimum Depth Between Lockport and Utica and Available for Immediate Construction.* Rivers and Lakes Commission, Bulletin, No. 15. Chicago, 1914. 16 p., map.
ICU

Illinois. Rivers and Lakes Commission. *The Illinois Water-Power Waterway: An Attack by Ebin J. Ward, and Defense by Robert Isham Randolph.* Rivers and Lakes Commission, Bulletin, No. 9. Springfield: Illinois State Journal Co., 1912. 34 p.
ICU

Debate on water power on the Illinois Deep Waterway.

Illinois. Special Commission, Chicago Drainage Channel. *Report of the Special Commission Appointed by Hon. John R. Tanner, Governor of Illinois. Under Section 27 of the "Act to Create Sanitary Districts and to Remove Obstructions in the DesPlaines and Illinois Rivers and the Dams at Henry and Copperas Creek," Approved May 29, 1889.* Chicago, 1900. 131 p., illus., maps, tables.
ICJ

Illinois. University. Water Resources Center. *Future Problems and Water Resources Research Needs of the Illinois River System.* Urbana, Illinois: University of Illinois, 1977. 212 p.
IU

Special Report, No. 6. Proceedings of the annual meeting of the Water Resources Center, University of Illinois, May 1977.

Isley, Edwin K. "The Impact of Proposed Inland Waterway User Charges on Grain Transportation and Marketing: The Case of the Illinois Waterway." Ph.D. dissertation, University of Notre Dame, 1977. 138 p.
InNd

Mayer, Harold M. *The Need For Duplicate Locks on the Illinois Waterway.* Chicago? Illinois River Carrier's Association, 1960. 38 p., tables.
ICU

Includes bibliography.

Mississippi River Commission and The U.S. Army Corps of Engineers. *Report Upon Survey, with Plans and Estimates of Cost, for a Navigable Waterway 14 Feet Deep from Lockport, Illinois, by Way of DesPlaines and Illinois Rivers, to the Mouth of Said Illinois Rivers, and Thence by Way of the Mississippi River to St. Louis, Mo., and for a Navigable Waterway of 7 and 8 Feet Depth, Respectively, From the Head of Navigation of Illinois River at LaSalle, Illinois, Through Said River to Ottawa, Illinois.* Washington: Government Printing Office, 1905. 544 p., illus., maps, charts.
ILo

Post, Philip Sydney. *The Illinois Waterway. Remarks of Hon. Philip S. Post, in the House of Representatives May 23, 24 and 28, 1890.* Washington: U.S. Government Printing Office, 1890. 8 p.
IHi

Randolph, Isham. *A Counter Statement by Isham Randolph to "The Proposed Deep Waterway," A Statement by Howard H. Gross.* Springfield: Illinois State Journal Co., 1909. 6 p.
IHi

U.S. Army. Corps of Engineers. *Illinois River, Illinois. Letter from the Secretary of War Transmitting a Letter From the Chief of Engineers, United States Army, Dated December 6, 1933, Submitting a Report Together with Accompanying Papers and Illustrations, on a Survey of [the] Illinois River, Illinois, Authorized by the River and Harbor Act approved July 3, 1930. . . .*Washington: U.S. Government Printing Office, 1934. 85 p., tables, plates, map, diagrs.
DLC

U.S. Army. Corps of Engineers. *Illinois River, Illinois. Letter from the Secretary of War Transmitting a Letter from the Acting Chief of Engineers, United States Army, Dated September 30, 1941, Submitting a Report, Together with Accompanying Papers and Illustrations, on a Review of Reports on the Illinois River, Illinois, With a View to Ascertaining the Damages by Seepage and Other Factors to the Levee and Drainage Districts Bordering the River, and to Individual Landowners Within Said Districts, by the Prosecution of the Existing Navigation Project, Requested by Resolution of the Committee on Rivers and Harbors, House of Representatives, Adopted on February 10, 1937.* H. Doc. 711, 77th Cong., 2nd Sess., 1942. 77 p., tables, maps.
DLC, ICU

U.S. Army. Corps of Engineers. *Illinois Waterway Navigation Charts; Mississippi River at Gratton, Illinois, to Lake Michigan at Chicago and Calumet Harbors.* Chicago: U.S. Engineer Office, 1941. 2 p., charts.
IU

U.S. Army. Corps of Engineers. *Waterway from Lockport to the Mouth of the Illinois River. Letter from the Secretary of War, Transmitting, with a Letter from the Chief of Engineers, [a] Report by a Special Board of Engineers upon a Waterway from Lockport, Illinois, by Way of the DesPlaines and Illinois Rivers, to the Mouth of [the] Said Illinois River, and Certain Related Subjects.* H. Doc. 1374, 61st Cong, 3rd Sess., 1911. 22 p.
DLC, ICU

U.S. Congress. House. *Final Report, Waterway from Lockport, Illinois, to the Mouth of the Illinois River.* H. Doc. 762, 63rd Cong., 2nd Sess., 1923. 120 p., illus., maps, diagrs., tables.
DLC, ICU

Complete report of the Illinois Waterway regarding its construction and completion, including costs, problems, surveys.

U.S. Congress. House. Committee on Rivers and Harbors. *Illinois and Mississippi Rivers, and Diversion of Water from Lake Michigan. September 14, 1922.* Washington: U.S. Government Printing Office, 1924. 35 p.
ICU

Detailed debate and testimony of the pros and cons of Lake Michigan water diversion into the Illinois River.

U.S. Congress. House. Committee on Rivers and Harbors. *Illinois and Mississippi Rivers, and Diversion of Water from Lake Michigan. Hearings on the Subject of the Improvement of the Illinois and Mississippi Rivers, and the Diversion of Water from Lake Michigan into the Illinois River.* 2 v. 68th Cong., 1st Sess., 1924. Washington: U.S. Government Printing Office, 1924. plates, maps, tables, diagrs.
DLC, ICU

Also discusses the Chicago Sanitary District.

U.S. Congress. House. Committee on Rivers and Harbors. *Illinois Rivers, Illinois, and the Abstraction of Water from Lake Michigan.* Washington: U.S. Government Printing Office, 1926. 210 p.
ICU

U.S. Congress. House. Committee on Rivers and Harbors. *Illinois River, Illinois. Hearings Before the Committee on Rivers and Harbors, on H.R. 3029, a Bill to Authorize the Adoption of a Report Relating to Seepage and Drainage Damages on the Illinois River.* 78th Cong., 1st Sess., June 23, 1943. Washington: U.S. Government Printing Office, 1943. 13 p.
DLC, ICU

U.S. Congress. House. Committee on Rivers and Harbors. *Illinois Waterway, Illinois. Hearings Before the Committee on Rivers and Harbors, on the Subject of the Improvement of Illinois Waterway [Locks and Dams in the Illinois River].* 73rd Cong., 2nd Sess., February 8, 1934. Washington: U.S. Government Printing Office, 1934. 17 p.
DLC

U.S. Congress. House. Committee on Rivers and Harbors. *The Illinois Waterway—Diversion of Water from Lake Michigan; Hearings on H.R. Res. 148 to Permit the Diversion of Waters from Lake Michigan to Safeguard the Public Health.* 78th Cong., 1st Sess., 1943. Washington, 1943.
ICU

U.S. Congress. Senate. Committee on Public Works. *Diversion of Water from Lake Michigan. Hearings Before a Subcommittee of the Committee on Public Works, on H.R. 2 and S. 1123, Bills to Authorize the State of Illinois and the Metropolitan Sanitary District of Greater Chicago, Under the Direction of the Secretary of the Army to Test, on a Three-year Basis, the Effect of Increasing the Diversion of Water from Lake Michigan into the Illinois Waterway.* 85th Cong., 2nd Sess., July 28 to August 7, 1958. Washington: U.S. Government Printing Office, 1958. 407 p., illus., maps.
DLC, ICU

U.S. Deep Waterways Commission. *Report of the United States Deep Waterways Commission, Prepared at Detroit, Michigan, December 18–22, 1896, by the Commissioners, James B. Angell, John E. Russell, Lyman E. Cooley.* H. Doc. 192, 54th Cong., 2nd Sess., 1897. 263 p., maps, diagrs.
ICJ, ICU

Includes major section on Illinois Waterway proposals and issues, the greater issues for the Great Lakes region, and several topical reports and drawings pertaining to the Illinois Waterway and others.

U.S. War Department. Engineering Department. *Diversion of Water from Lake Michigan. Report on the Sanitary District of Chicago, with Recommendations for Action on the Part of the War Department with Reference to Diversion of Water from Lake Michigan. Submitted by District Engineer, U.S. Engineer's Office, Chicago, Illinois, Nov. 1, 1923.* Washington: U.S. Government Printing Office, 1924. 97 p., tables, diagr., profiles, charts.
DLC, ICJ

Van Meer, Gretchen L. "A Mathematical Model of Conservative Substances in the Illinois River Waterway." Ph.D. dissertation, Northwestern University, 1976. 307 p.
IEN

A civil engineering study.

Werner, Mildred Cecelia. "The History of the Deep Waterway in the State of Illinois." B.Ed. thesis, University of Illinois, 1947. illus.
IU—HS

Bibliography. Photographs in 1940s of I&M Canal locks at Lockport.

Transportation and Communication—*Calumet–Sag Channel*

Calumet and Chicago Canal and Dock Company. *Charter and By-laws.* Chicago: Republican Book & Job Printing Co., 1869. 15 p.
ICHi

Includes list of "Directors."

Calumet and Chicago Canal and Dock Company. *Charter and By-laws.* Chicago, 1871. 13 p.
ICHi

Organized April 1, 1869.

Calumet and Chicago Canal and Dock Company. *Prospectus of the Calumet and Chicago Canal and Dock Company, for the Sale and Occupation of Developed and Improved Lots, Blocks, and Acre Property at South Chicago, Illinois. . . .*[Chicago], 1874. 8 p., map.
ICN

Calumet-Sag Navigation Project; Inspection. n.p., 1955. 10 p., illus., maps, tables.
ICU

Covers the Calumet River and Sag Channel.

Chicago. Ordinances, etc. *An Ordinance Pending in the Chicago City Council Providing for the Construction of Lake Calumet Harbor Together with Certain Proposed Amendments Thereto.* Chicago: City Council, 1925. 15 p.
DLC, ICJ

Kleeman, Benton F. *Lake Calumet Harbor, Report to the Committee on Harbors, Wharves, and Bridges, City of Chicago.* Chicago: The F. J. Ringley Co., 1928. 29 p.
ICJ

A detailed plan of the proposed Lake Calumet Harbor Project. Submitted to the Mayor and City Council, by Ald. Guy Guernsey, Chairman of the Committee on Harbors, Wharves, and Bridges, October 31, 1928.

Randolph, Isham. *Argument Sustaining Prayer of the Sanitary District of Chicago for a Permit to Reverse the Flow of the Calumet River . . . to the Honorable Wm. H. Taft, Secretary of War.* Chicago: Sanitary District, 1906. 16 p.
ICJ

Van Vlissingen, Arend. *Plan and Report. Lake Calumet Harbor.* Chicago, 1920. 36 p., front., plans.
ICJ

Transportation and Communication—Railroads

Transportation and Communication—*Railroads*—Through Lines

Ackerman, William Kelly. *Early Illinois Railroads: A Paper Read Before the Chicago Historical Society Tuesday Evening, February 20, 1883.* Chicago: Fergus Printing Co., 1884. 174 p.
DLC, ICU

Covers early Illinois railroads, the Illinois Central, and various important geographical places and names.

Ackerman, William K. *Historical Sketch of the Central Railroad Together with a Brief Biographical Record of Its Incorporators and Some of Its Early Officers.* Chicago: Fergus Printing Co., 1890. 153 p.
ICJ, ICU

Ackerman, William K. *History of the Illinois Central Railroad Company and Its Representative Employees.* Chicago: Railroad Historical Co., 1900. 800 p., front., illus., ports.
ICU

Agreement Between the Pennsylvania Company, Chicago, and Alton Railroad Company, Chicago, Burlington and Quincy Railroad Company, Pennsylvania Railroad Company, Joliet and Chicago Railroad Company, and Pittsburgh, Fort Wayne and Chicago Railway Company. [Chicago, 1880.]
ICHi

Armitage, Merle. *Operations Santa Fe: Atchison, Topeka, and Santa Fe Railway System.* New York: Duell, Sloan, & Pierce, 1948. 263 p., illus., maps.
DLC, ICU

Bibliography, pp. 251–252.

Association of American Railroads. Railroad Committee for the Study of Transportation. *Railroads in This Century, A Summary of the Facts and Figures with Charts.* Washington: The Association, 1944 and 1947. 24 p.
ICRL

Association of American Railroads. Railroad Committee for the Study of Transportation. *Railway Passenger Service: A Statistical Record, by Territorial Districts, of Equipment and Operating Results of Railway Passenger Service in the United States.* Washington: The Association, 1945. 60 p., tables.
ICRL

Atchison, Topeka, and Santa Fe Railway Company. *Annual Report.* No. 1–. New York, Boston: Atchison, Topeka, and Santa Fe Railway Co., 1873–.
DLC

Title varies.

Atchison, Topeka, and Santa Fe Railway Company. *System Standards.* Dallas, Texas: Kaching Press, c. 1978. 383 p., illus.
DLC

Bradley, Glenn D. *The Story of the Santa Fe.* Boston: R. G. Badger, 1920. 288 p., front., plates, maps.
ICU

Source materials, pp. 272–279.

Brownson, Howard G. *History of the Illinois Central Railroad to 1870.* University of Illinois Studies in the Social Sciences, Vol. 1, Nos. 3 and 4. Urbana, Illinois: University of Illinois, 1915. 182 p.
DLC, ICU

Bibliography.

Bureau of Railway Economics. *Railway Economics: A Collective Catalogue of Books in Fourteen American Libraries, Prepared by the Bureau of Railway Economics.* Washington and Chicago: University of Chicago Press, 1912. 446 p.
DLC

Bureau of Railway Economics. *Railroad Consolidation, a List of References.* Washington: Bureau of Railway Economics, 1930. 83 p.
DLC, ICU

Casey, Robert J. and Douglas, W. A. S. *Pioneer Railroad: The Story of the Chicago and North*

Western System. New York: Whittlesey House, 1948. 334 p., illus., ports., maps.
IU
Bibliography.

Chicago, Aurora, and Elgin Railway Company. *Report.* No. 1–. Wheaton, Illinois: Chicago, Aurora, & Elgin Railway Co., 1925–.
DLC
Annual.

Chicago, Burlington, and Quincy Railroad. *Annual Report of the Board of Directors . . . to the Stockholders.* Nos. 15–50. Chicago: Chicago, Burlington & Quincy Railroad, 1873–1908.
DLC, ICJ, ICN, ICU
Annual.

Chicago and Northwestern Railway System. *Yesterday and Today: A History of the Chicago and Northwestern Railway System.* 3rd Ed., revised. Chicago: Winship Co., 1910.
DLC, ICJ

Chicago, Rock Island and Pacific Railway Co. *Annual Report.* No. 1–. Chicago: Chicago, Rock Island & Pacific Railway Company, 1881–.
ICU
Title varies.

Chicago, Rock Island and Pacific Railway Company. *The Chicago, Rock Island and Pacific Railway System and Representative Employees: A History of the Development of the Chicago, Rock Island and Pacific Railway, from Its Inception . . . Tracing the Progress of Steam Railroad Transportation from the Earliest Stages, in America and Abroad.* Chicago: Biographical Publishing Co., 1900. 756 p., illus., ports., maps, facsims., diagrs.
ICU

Corliss, Carlton J. *Main Line of Mid-America: The Story of the Illinois Central.* New York: Creative Age Press, 1950. 490 p., illus., map, tables.
DLC, ICJ, ICU
A comprehensive history of the Illinois Central Railroad, from its inception to its one-hundred-year anniversary. Includes index. Bibliography, pp. 405–471.

Dorin, Patrick D. *Everywhere West: The Burlington Route.* Seattle, Washington: Superior Pub. Co., c. 1976. 171 p., illus.
DLC
Includes index and bibliography, pp. 273–278. A pictorial work on the Chicago, Burlington and Quincy Railroad.

Douglas, George H. *Rail City, Chicago, U.S.A.* San Diego, California: Howell North Books, c. 1981. 338 p.
DLC, ICU
Bibliography, pp. 321–323. Includes index.

Gates, Paul W. "The Struggle for the Charter of the Illinois Central Railroad." *Illinois State Historical Society Transactions* 40 (1933): 55–66.
DLC, IC, ICU
Controversy over route of railroad. Footnotes.

Gleed, Charles S. *The Rehabilitation of the Santa Fe Railway System.* Chicago? 1912. 26 p.
ICU
Pamphlets on transportation and communication.

Gordon, Joseph Hinckley. *Illinois Railway Legislation and Commission Control Since 1870.* Urbana, Illinois: University of Illinois Press, 1904. 81 p.
DLC, IU

Gross, Joseph. *Railroads of North America: A Complete Listing of All North American Railroads, 1827–1977.* Spencerport, New Jersey: Joseph Gross, c. 1977. 174 p.
DLC

Hayes, William Edward. *Iron Road to Empire: The History of 100 Years of Progress and Achievements of the Rock Island Lines.* New York: Simmons-Boardman, 1953. 306 p., illus.
ICU
Includes bibliography.

Illinois. *An Act to Incorporate the Chicago and Milwaukee Railroad Company.* n.p., 1851.
DLC

Illinois. *An Act to Incorporate the Galena and Chicago Union Rail Road Company, Approved January 16, 1836.* n.p., n.d. 28 p.
DLC

Illinois. *An Act to Incorporate the Illinois Central Railroad Company.* St. Louis: C. Keemle, 1836. 12 p.
ICN, IHi

Illinois. Laws, Statutes, etc. *Charter of the St. Louis, Alton, and Terre Haute Railroad Company, Terre Haute and Alton Railroad Company, Belleville and Illinoistown Railway Company: With the Several Amendments Thereto: and the General Railroad Law of the State of Illinois.* St. Louis: R. P. Studley, Printers, Binders, and Lithographers, 1863. 71 p.
DLC

Illinois. Legislature. House of Representatives. Board of Commissioners of Public Works. *Message from the Governor Transmitting the Report of the Board of Public Works.* 12th Illinois Assembly, 2nd Sess., 1840. Springfield: Wm. Walter, State Printer, 1840. 8 p.
ICU

Refers to Illinois Central Railroad, Northern Cross Railroad, Alton and Mt. Carmel Railroad, Alton and Shawneetown Railroad, Peoria and Warsaw Railroad, Alton and Shelbyville Railroad, Central Branch Railroad, Maples Branch Railroad, and the Rushville and Erie Railroad.

Illinois Central Magazine. Vol. 1–42. Chicago: Illinois Central Railroad Co., 1915–1924. illus., monthly.
ICRL

Illinois Central Railroad Company. *Billigt land tilfalgs i sydlige Illinois. Illinois Central Jernbane-selskab har endnu over 150,000 acres frugtbart agerbrugsland tilfalgs for sey til ti dollars pr. acre. Baade bakkelandet og slettelandet i; sydlige Illinois afgiver avlinger af vinterhvede, mais, gron-sager, frugter, baer og tobak vaerd fra 50 dollars til flere hundrede dollars pr. acre. For faare-og Kraegavl gives der ingen bedre egn end Ozark-Bakkerne i sydlige Illinois.* Chicago: John Anderson Pub. Co., Printers, 1892. 16 p., illus., map.
IU—HS

Illinois Central Railroad Company. *Centennial Report: The Financial Story of Our First Hundred Years, 1851–1951.* Chicago: Illinois Central Railroad Co., 1951. 45 p., illus.
DLC

Illinois Central Railroad Company. *The Illinois Central Railroad Co. Offers for Sale over 2,400,000 Acres Selected Prairie, Farm and Wood Lands, in Tracts of Any Size, to Suit Purchasers, on Long Credits . . . Situated on Each Side of Their Rail-Road Extending All the Way from the Extreme North to the South of the State of Illinois.* New York: J. W. Amerman, Printer, 1855. 32 p., front., double map.
DLC, ICN

Illinois Central Railroad Company. *The Illinois Central Railroad Co. Offers for Sale over 2,000,000 Acres Selected Farming and Wood Lands, in Tracts of Forty Acres and Upwards. . . .* New York: J. W. Amerman, Printer, 1856. 64 p., maps.
DLC

Illinois Central Railroad Co. *The Illinois Central Rail-Road Co. Offers for Sale Over 2,000,000 Acres Selected Prairie, Farm and Wood Lands. . . .* New York: J. W. Amerman, Printer, 1856. 60 p., maps.
DLC

Illinois Central Railroad Co. *The Illinois Central Railroad Co. Offers for Sale Over 1,500,000 Acres Selected Farming and Wood Lands. . . .* Boston: Geo. C. Rand & Avery, Printers, 1857. 80 p., front., illus., maps.
DLC

Illinois Central Railroad Co. *A Guide to the Illinois Central Railroad Lands. The Illinois Central Railroad Co. Offers for Sale Over 1,400,000 Acres of Selected Prairie and Wood Lands, in Tracts of Forty Acres and Upwards, Suitable for Farms, on Long Credits and Low Prices, Situated on Each Side of their Railroad, Extending Through the State of Illinois.* Chicago, 1859. 60 p., front., illus., maps.
DLC

Illinois Society of Engineers. *Annual Report.* Vol. 1–43. Urbana, Illinois: Illinois Society of Engineers. 1886–1928. illus., annual.
ICRL

Johnston, Wayne Andrew. *The Illinois Central Heritage, 1851–1951; A Centenary Address.* New York: Newcomen Society in North America, 1951. 32 p., illus., ports.
DLC

Jones, Clifton Clyde. "The Agricultural Development Program of the Chicago, Burlington, and Quincy Railroad." Ph.D. dissertation, Northwestern University, 1954. 378 p.
IEN

Lewis, Bradley Glenn. "Featureless Plains Featured: The Effects of Nineteenth Century Midwestern Railroads." Ph.D. dissertation, University of Chicago, 1982. 213 p.
ICU

Bibliography, pp. 208–213.

McDonald, George B. *A Brief History of the Chicago, Rock Island and Pacific Railway.* Northwestern University Seminars in Economics, Finance and Administration, Vol. 22, No. 11. Evanston, Illinois: Northwestern University, 1908.
IEN

Marshall, James Leslie. *Sante Fe, the Railroad That Built an Empire.* New York: Random House, 1945. 465 p., illus., plates, ports., maps.
ICU

Mohr, Carolyn Curtis, comp. *Guide to the Illinois Central Archives in the Newberry Library, 1851–1906.* Chicago: Newberry Library, 1951. 210 p.
DLC, ICN, ICU

Moses, John. "Illinois in 1849 and 1852." *Magazine of Western History* 12 (July 1890): 246–251.
ICU

Discusses the Illinois Central legislation. Excerpted from Moses's *History of Illinois,* Vol. 2.

Moulton, Harold G. *Waterways Versus Railways.* Boston: Houghton Mifflin Co., 1912. 468 p., illus., diagrs.
ICU

Covers inland navigation, canal, and railways. Originally a Ph.D. dissertation, University of Chicago, 1914.

Norfolk and Western Railway Company. *Annual Report.* Vol. 1–23. Philadelphia: Norfolk and Western Railway Company, 1888–1910.
ICU

Title varies.

Overton, Richard C. *Burlington Route: A History of the Burlington Lines.* New York: Alfred A. Knopf, 1965.
ICU

Development of the CB&Q.

Overton, Richard C. *Burlington West: A Colonization History of the Burlington Railroad.* New York: Russell & Russell, 1967. 583 p., illus., facsims., maps, ports., tables, plates.
DLC

Bibliography, pp. 539–555.

Overton, Richard C. *The First Ninety Years, An Historical Sketch of the Burlington Railroad, 1850–1940.* Chicago, 1940. 39 p., illus., ports., maps, facsims.
ICU

Bibliographical note, p. 40.

Overton, Richard C. *Milepost 100: The Story of the Development of the Burlington Lines, 1849–1949.* Chicago, 1949. 62 p., illus., maps.
DLC, ICU

Bibliographical note, one page at the end.

Porter, Henry H. *H. H. Porter: A Short Autobiography Written for his Children and Grandchildren.* Chicago: By the Author, 1915. 40 p., front., plates, ports., map.
DLC, ICU

Autobiography of Chicago railroad developer. Photographs of railroad stations. Bird's eye views of city in 1853, 1913. Views of streets in 1866 and 1910.

Railway and Locomotive Historical Society. *The Chicago, Burlington and Quincy Railroad.* Railway and Locomotive Historical Society, Bulletin, No. 24. Boston: The Society, 1931. 44 p., illus., maps.
ICRL

Railway Statistics of the United States of America. Vol. 1–31. Chicago: Slason, Thompson Bureau of Railway News & Statistics. 1902–1933.
ICRL

Richardson, Helen, comp. *Chicago and Northwestern Railway Company, A Centennial Bibliography.* Washington: Bureau of Railway Economics, 1948. 168 p.
DLC

Richardson, Helen L., comp. *Illinois Central Railroad Company, A Centennial Bibliography, 1851–1951.* Washington: Bureau of Railway Economics Library, 1950. 239 p., map.
ICU

Severson, Lewis Everett. "Some Phases of the History of the Illinois Central Railroad Company Since 1870." Ph.D. dissertation, University of Chicago, 1930. 297 p., illus., maps.
ICU
Bibliography, pp. 292–297.

Sunderland, Edwin Sherwood Stonell. *Illinois Central Railroad, Main Line of Mid-America: The Simplification of its Debt Structure, 1938–1952.* New York: Pondick Press, 1952. 23 p., illus.
DLC

Sutton, Robert Mize. *The Illinois Central Railroad in Peace and War, 1858–1868.* New York: Arno Press, 1981. 240 p., plates, illus.
IU
Reprint of the 1948 edition published by the University of Illinois as a thesis. Bibliography, pp. 225–240.

Taylor, George Rogers and Neu, Irene D. *The American Railroad Network, 1861–1890.* New York: Arno Press, 1981. 113 p., maps.
DLC, ICU
Includes bibliographical references and index.

Thompson, John G. "The Early History of the Chicago, Burlington and Quincy Railroad." A.M. Thesis, University of Chicago, 1904. 23 p.
DLC, ICU

Western Railway Club, Chicago. *Official Proceedings.* Vol. 1–71. Chicago, 1888–1940.
ICRL

Wood, Struthers and Co. *Atchison, Topeka and Santa Fe Railway System: A Study of Its Progress in the Last Decade and Pertinent Comparisons with Other Trans-Continental Carriers.* New York: Wood, Struthers & Co., 1925. 80 p., illus., map.
ICU

Transportation and Communication—*Railroads*—Streetcars and Interurbans.

Chicago. Traction and Subway Commission. *Report of the Chicago Traction and Subway Commission.* Chicago: Rand McNally & Co., 1916. 113 p., illus.
ICRL

Illinois. Bureau of Labor Statistics. *The Street Railways of Chicago and Other Cities.* n.p., Campaign Committee of One Hundred Against the Humphrey Bills, 1897. 73 p.
ICJ, ICN, ICU
From the annual report of George A. Schilling, Secretary, Illinois Bureau of Labor Statistics.

Lind, Alan R. *Chicago Surface Lines: An Illustrated History.* Park Forest, Illinois: Transport History Press, 1974.
DLC

Weber, Harry P. *An Outline History of Chicago Traction.* Chicago, 1936.
ICHi
A documentary history of each line, includes those traversing southeast Chicago, Pullman, Calumet, and the neighborhoods along the canal.

Transportation and Communication—*Roads*

Illinois. Division of Highways. *General Specifications for Road Work.* Springfield, 1919. 108 p.
DLC, ICJ, IU

Illinois. Division of Highways. *The Illinois Highway Story.* Vol. 1–. Springfield, Illinois, 1953–. illus.
DLC, IU

Mann, Robert, ed. *Early Cook County Roads. Part Two—The Plank Road Era.* Nature Bulletin, No. 739. n.p., Forest Preserve District of Cook County, 1964. 1 p.
ICF

Transportation and Communication—*Bridges*

Becker, Donald N. "The Story of Chicago's Bridges." *Midwest Engineer* 5 (January 1950): 3–9.
DLC, I, ICJ, IU
Contains views and diagrams.

Illinois. Public Works and Buildings Department. Waterways Division. *Calumet Lake and the Chicago–Nickel Plate Agreement: State Supervision of Chicago Sanitary District Lands Sales. The Policy of Fixed Bridges over the Chicago River.* Bulletin, No. 26. Chicago: Blakeley Printing Co., 1926. 30 p.
ICU

Piehl, Frank J. "Shall We Gather at the River." *Chicago History* 2 (Spring/Summer 1973): 196–205.
DLC, IC, ICF, ICHi, ICN, ICU, IU

History of bridges over the Chicago River. With photographs and engravings.
ICU

Transportation and Communication—*Postal Service*

Weiser, Frederick S. *Post Offices and Postal Routes in DuPage County, Illinois in 1850.* Glen Ellyn, Illinois: DuPage Historical Review, 1950. 8 p.
ICHi

Transportation and Communication—*Telegraph and Telephone*

Dickerson, William Eugene. "Organization and Control of the Illinois Bell Telephone Company." Ph.D. dissertation, University of Chicago, 1926.
ICU

Illinois Bell Telephone Company. *Annual Report.* Vol. 1–. Chicago: Illinois Bell Telephone, 1918–.
ICBT

Transportation and Communication—*Archive Sources*

Chicago, Illinois. Chicago Historical Society. A. W. Bowen Collection. 1 v.
ICHi

Letter book kept by Bowen while postmaster at Joliet in 1845.

Chicago, Illinois. Chicago Historical Society. Calumet and Chicago Canal and Dock Company.
ICHi

Miscellaneous pamphlets on the company.

Chicago, Illinois. Chicago Historical Society. Chicago River Improvement Association, 1920. Twelve items. 29 p.
ICHi

List of owners of property on the Chicago River. List of officers and members.

Chicago, Illinois. Chicago Historical Society. Carl Culman Papers. 11 p.
ICHi

Papers related to I&M Canal, Chicago, and its bridges.

Chicago, Illinois. Chicago Historical Society. William Everett Dever Papers. Twelve thousand items.
ICHi

Includes material on Calumet Harbor project and straightening of the Chicago River.

Chicago, Illinois. Chicago Historical Society. James Herrington Collection. 1,831 letters.
ICHi

Concerning I&M Canal.

Chicago, Illinois. Chicago Historical Society. Johnson Family Papers. 20 v. Approximately fourteen hundred items.
ICHi

Letters, diaries, account books, deeds of family of Madison Yount (1817–1890) and Ann Eliza (b. 1832) Johnson. Madison Johnson was a Chicago lawyer for the Chicago, Burlington and Northern Railroad and president of the Galena and Southern Wisconsin Railroad. Unpublished guide.

Chicago, Illinois. Chicago Historical Society. John Kirk Letter Books. 8 v.
ICHi

Kirk was an itinerant salesman who traveled through the Midwest (1852–1871). Includes descriptions of Chicago's sanitary and sewage systems. Unpublished guide.

Chicago, Illinois. Chicago Historical Society. Harry Albert Musham Collection.
ICHi

Correspondence and papers including original manuscripts produced in preparation for his *Early Great Lakes Steamboats.*

Chicago, Illinois. Chicago Historical Society. George Van Zandt Collection. 41 p.
ICHi

"Recollections of my early years in Chicago," including remarks on employment with the Calumet and Chicago Canal and Dock Company. 1928.

Chicago, Illinois. Federal Archives and Records Center. Bureau of Marine Inspection and Navigation. Field Records, Chicago, Illinois. Register (Index) of Licenses Issued to Engineers. 4 v.
IC—FARC

Covers 1870–1912. Separate volumes for chief engineers (1870–1912) and assistant engineers (1873–1912). Arranged alphabetically and chronologically within each letter group by date of license issued. Information provided: date, license number, name of engineer, grade, number of renewals, name of vessel, brief description of route for which license was issued.

Chicago, Illinois. Federal Archives and Records Center. Records of the Bureau of Customs. Four cubic feet.
IC—FARC

Covers 1914–1944. Bound volumes containing data on ships using the ports on the Great Lakes. Entrance and clearance of vessels.

Chicago, Illinois. Federal Archives and Records Center. Records of the Bureau of Customs. Monthly Statistical Record of Entrances and Clearances, Various Ports. Three cubic feet.
IC—FARC

Covers the period 1908–1926. By steam and sail vessels. Separate statistics for ports of Chicago and South Chicago.

Chicago, Illinois. Federal Archives and Records Center. Records of U.S. Customs House, Chicago.
IC—FARC

Certificates of enrollment, April 17, 1865–August 23, 1888; April 10, 1903–June 30, 1913. 16 v. Includes name of vessel, owner, date and place built, home port, description, and location number.

Licenses of vessels under twenty tons, July 12, 1911–August 12, 1931. 2 v.

Consolidated certificates of enrollment and license, October 24, 1912–June 30, 1948. 6 v. Similar information as preceding.

Register (Index) of enrollments and licenses issued and surrendered, 1891–1929. 6 v.

Register of conveyances of vessels, 1883–1949. 5 v.

Records of bills of sale of enrolled vessels, March 1882–September 1888; December 1899–March 1916; May 1929–May 1952. 30 v. Includes vessel name, name and address of seller and purchaser, name of port, amount and terms of sale.

Records of mortgages of registered or enrolled vessels, 1882–1964. 13 v. Includes name and address of owner and mortgage, terms of mortgage, description of vessel.

Abstracts and certificates of records of titles issued, 1918–1941. 1 v.

Oaths for enrollment and license of merchant vessel or yacht, October 31, 1923–October 2, 1940. 6 v. Includes name and address of owner, name and citizenship of master, name and description of vessel.

Oaths on registry, license, or enrollment and license of vessel, 1922–1966. Three cartons. Similar to entry preceding but for corporate owners.

Masters oath for renewal of license of vessel, 1923–1966. 8 v. Eight cartons.

Oath or affirmation of new masters, 1930–1941, 1 v. April 29, 1919–October 26, 1966. Two cartons.

Records of endorsement of change of master, October 2, 1913–June 25, 1943. 3 v.

Chicago, Illinois. Illinois Bell Telephone Information Center. Town History Collection. Lemont. One folder.
ICBT

"Lemont Telephone Chronology," by R. L. Mahon (1882–1965). 8 p. (Typewritten.). Illinois Bell press release on history of telephone service in Lemont. Covers 1876–1965. Photograph collection. Lemont exchange building views, 1912, 1918, 1937 (new building). St. Cyril's Church and wooden residential structures (1950), barge dock (1950).

Chicago, Illinois. Illinois Bell Telephone Information Center. Town History Collection. Morris. One folder.
ICBT

"Morris Telephone Chronology," by R. L. Mahon. (1883–1967). 10 p. List of Morris subscribers, 1891 (copied from Chicago Telephone Co. Directory). Table of Exchange Statistics,

1890, 1895, 1900, 1915, 1920, 1925, 1930. Copy of *Bell Telephone News* 148 (May 1939), article on Morris, illustrated with photographs of courthouse, Liberty Street looking north from Washington, Morris Paper Mills, Morris Hospital, Lock No. 7, Morris High School, residences at Main and Calhoun. Listing of entries from engineering department file cards (1903–1957): year of project, description, cost, approval and completion dates. Photographs: two downtown scenes (1914, 1915), exterior of telephone office (1929), four snapshots of Illinois River Bridge, and four of I&M Canal locks (1935).

Chicago, Illinois. Illinois Bell Telephone Information Center. Town History Collection. LaSalle, Illinois. One folder.
ICBT

"LaSalle–Peru–Oglesby Telephone Chronology," by R. L. Mahon (1880–1965). 15 p. Reprint of 1884 LaSalle–Peru Telephone Directory. Clipping file of newspaper and magazine articles on history of LaSalle and history of telephone service in area. Floor plans of telephone exchange. Tables of statistics on telephone use in LaSalle, 1910–1925. Listing of entries from engineering department file cards (1901–1948): project description, cost, date of approval and completion. Photographs: telephone office building taken in 1926 and 1935 (located in Wilson Block, dated 1891). Interior of office (1912), exterior of office (1913), downtown views (1921, 1940s–1950s), plant department, 1912.

Chicago, Illinois. Illinois Bell Telephone Information Center. Town History Collection, Utica. One folder.
ICBT

Photographs: mostly views of downtown in 1958 during a flood, but also an undated photograph of wooden storefronts (probably 1910s). Table showing number of telephone units in Utica, 1904–1909, 1947–1969. Floor plans of Utica Telephone Exchange.

Joliet, Illinois. Joliet Public Library. Illinois Collection. I&M Canal. Two folders.
IJo

Newspaper clippings, leaflets, articles, brochures, concept plans.

Lemont, Illinois. Lemont Area Historical Society. Harry J. Swanson Memorial Library. Local History File. I&M Canal.
ILeHi

Canal newspaper clippings, brochures, I&M Canal concept plan leaflets.

Lemont, Illinois. Lemont Area Historical Society. Harry J. Swanson Memorial Library. Local History File. Railroads.
ILeHi

Chicago and Alton Schedule, 1868 (photocopy).

Lockport, Illinois. Lewis University. Canal Archives and Local History Collection. Canal History, Photographs, Articles.
ILoL

Contains files on aqueducts and culverts on canal, drawings and photographs. File on Wm. Gooding, engineer (1803–1878). City of Pekin and pictures of canal boats. Photographs of canal (approximately one hundred) by Bruce Anderson. Canal Scrip Collection and other memorabilia. Buildings associated with the canal. Maps relating to the canal. Clippings on the Irish and the canal. The "Pumping Works." State and federal laws relating to the canal. "Pictures and Plates" of locks and gates. Transcripts of oral tapes on I&M Canal. The Kankakee Canal. The Lockport Powerhouse. Numerous articles and packets on the Sanitary District of Chicago. Files on Lockport, including photographs, papers. One drawer of papers, articles, correspondence, and other material relating to "saving and preserving the Canal." Other U.S. canals.

Lockport, Illinois. Will County Historical Society. Chronology of Joliet, Rockdale, and West Joliet Telephone Service.
ILoHi

Lockport, Illinois. Will County Historical Society. Illinois and Michigan Canal Archives. More than 300,000 items.
ILoHi

Researchers should begin with the subject catalog on the I&M Canal, which provides a reference to the specific documents.

Contains estimates for work. I&M lands records, property lists. Contractors' records. Contract bids. Leases and permits. I&M Canal proceedings, annual reports (some years). Lists of land purchasers. Locks, aqueduct information. Company accounts (uses of I&M Canal). Financial accounts. Toll records. I&M Canal Commission petitions for bridges.

List of damages on the line of the I&M Canal. Petition for donation of school lots from citizens of LaSalle (1853). Petition Iroquois County feeder at Wilmington. Amendment to charter of Kankakee and Iroquois Navigation Co. Catholic congregation of Chicago. Chicago retreat for the insane (August 1954). Document dated 13 February 1836.

Lockport: 9th Street grade building of bridge abutment. Grading of 9th Street between State and Commerce. Prop. for head gates to dry dock in connection with Lock 11, Sec. 69. Field notes for filling in state property at head of basin, Sec. 67. Resolution of Board for adopting seal of office. Complete list of signed section equipment. Reports and contractor signatures as of 1839 for Sections 69–88, middle division.

Abstract of account for canal stock. Fox River feeder. Navigation and boat complaints, seizures, and files for running the locks, overload, and so forth. I&M Canal boats. Typical canal contractor's expense account. Singer Agreement. James McKay's Inn. Canal engineer appts. Archer Road orig. contract bridge on road, south branch.

Specifications for construction lock gates, 30 March 1846. Agreement to construct lock gates for Locks 2, 3, 4. Agreement for lock gates for Locks 6, 7. Accts. for parts and work done by contractors, 1848. Memo, lock gates. Est. of iron, etc. for locks, 1846. Locks information. Standard lock construction, hardware description, timber plan. Cross section of I&M Canal. Copy of survey, LaSalle County. Memo of agreement.

Misc. maps, Lockport, Joliet, LaSalle done at Joliet, May 29, 1837. 1930s resume of historical and legal matter available in vault. I&M Office. Sabbath petitions. Spec. masonry, Fox River Aque. Property for Sec. excavations. Bill for timber, Fox River feeder. Levels on masonry. Specs. on masonry-bridge-Ottawa. Specs. on lock gates. Estimate of work on Sec. 45. Fox River masonry, south branch of Chicago River, tow path bridge, inst. for foundation on Lock 1 resolutions, 1857.

Final estimate on culvert, Sec. 161–162. Estimate for crossing, Pe-Can-Sa-Ganx. Real estate reports, 1838. Petition to legislature (December 1846) by citizens of LaSalle County. Specifications for wooden culverts, iron bridges, locks, construction of sections. Teamster lists (April–November 1839). Documents on labor disputes and "Irish Trouble Makers," Petitions-Grundy Co., Ottawa (May 15, 1839). Calculation of water power, 1849. Rules for engineering department. Bills for construction and supplies.

Morris, Illinois. Gebhard Woods State Park. Illinois and Michigan Canal State Trail Archives. Canal Collection. Approximately 850 folders. **IMoGW**

Collection arranged in fifteen series. Series 1: Minutes and reports. Canal Commissioners and Board of Trustees and Reports, Division of Waterways, minutes of board (1836–1917), proceedings of commissioners (1851–1897), State Trustee's reports (1847–1868), Commission reports to governors (1865–1916), and others.

Series 2: General correspondence. Descriptions of letters (1837–1914), rates and collections (1840s), board of trustees (1850s), treasurer (1850s), and others.

Series 3: Legal Records. Land sales (1830s), debts with state (1830s), disposition of canal land, land sales (1840s–1860s), court cases (1860s), land disputes (1860s), general legal correspondence (1890s), land disputes—Lockport, Chicago, Marseilles, Blue Island and others.

Series 4: Survey Records. List of maps of I&M Canal, land sales and canal routing (1825–1829), surveys of facilities—Morris, Ottawa, Utica, and others.

Series 5: Construction Records. Construction records—Summit Bridge, locks, iron works, Marseilles, Ottawa, and others.

Series 6: Personnel Records. Personnel records (1840s, 1860s, 1880s, 1890s, 1920s), perks, duties of employees.

Series 7: Financial Records. Canal supplies (1823–1824), Payrolls (1830s, 1840s, 1850s, 1860s, 1880s, 1890s, 1910–1919, 1933–1939), expenses (1830s, 1860s), bank statements and receipts, invoices, and others.

Series 8: Lease Records. Water leases, land leases, ice cutting rights, right-of-ways, water power rights, strip leases, and others.

Series 9: Maintenance and Engineering Records. Field books, bridges (1850s, 1880s, 1910–1919, 1920s), aqueducts (1920s), towpath (1933–1934, 1950s), and others.

Series 10: Operations Records. Accidents (1840s), tolls (1840), rates (1850s, 1880s, 1890, 1900–1919), and others.

Series 11: Research Reports and Publications. Ottawa ordinances (1891), interviews, clipping, and others.

Series 12: Illinois River Improvements Records.

Series 13: Sanitary District Records and Minutes.

Series 14: Park Development Records. 1930s developments in Morris, Ottawa, Marseilles, Channahon, Willow Springs, and others.

Series 15: Photographs. Chicago Pumping Station (1913), boats (1940), aqueducts (1920s), and others.

Ottawa, Illinois. Reddick Library. Vertical File. LaSalle County History. One folder.
IO

Includes photograph of $50 share of Ottawa and Vermillion River Plank and McAdamized Road Company, 1857.

Palos Hills, Illinois. Green Hills Public Library. Vertical File. "Canal."
IPHil

Contains clippings, most on the Cal–Sag Channel. Map on I&M Canal and adjacent territory.

Romeoville, Illinois. Fountaindale Public Library. Vertical File. Transportation.
IRo

Contains assorted maps, brochures on area, and Association of American Railroads, *A Bibliography of Railroad Literature.* Washington: Association of American Railroads, Office of Information and Public Affairs, 1976. 72 p., index of authors, annotated entries.

Springfield, Illinois. Archives of the State of Illinois. Illinois and Michigan Canal Records. Approximately 1,000 v.
I—Ar

Collection arranged in 123 groups, among which are Group 5: Incoming correspondence, 1825–30.

Group 6: Reports, 1830–1831, 1833, 1836, 1838, 1845, 1847–1848, 1854, 1866–1868, 1870, 1872, 1877, 1880, 1883, 1896, 1898.

Group 7: Treasurer's Reports, 1837–1842.

Group 10: Reports of the Commissioners and Trustees to the Governor. 1845–1891, 1893, 1902, 1906, 1911, 1913–1916.

Group 11: Quarterly financial reports to the governor, 1918–1934.

Group 14: Preemption applications, 1845–1854.

Group 15: List of land patents issued by the State of Illinois, 1831–1885.

Group 16: Land patents issued by the Illinois and Michigan Canal, 1842–1878.

Group 17: Certificates for land and lots, 1848–1870.

Group 18: List of town lots sold by the Board of Canal Commissioners, 1830–1843.

Group 19: Tract books of canal land sales, 1830–1837.

Group 21: Register of lots and land sold, but not patented, 1837–1843.

Group 25: Record of forfeited and resold land, 1851–1868.

Group 28: Annual Land Sales Reports, 1848–1865.

Group 34: Journal of money received for land sales payments, 1851–1854.

Group 36: Contract bids, 1836, 1838, 1841, 1846–1848.

Group 38: Construction contracts, 1836–1847, 1891–1902.

Group 43: Rules and regulations for employees, 1845.

Group 44: Time Books, 1840–1927.

Group 45: Statistics of laborers, 1838–1840, 1845–1848.

Group 69: Register of canal expenses, 1836–1941.

Group 70: Toll rates, 1851.

Group 72: Record of tolls paid, 1849, 1852–1882, 1888, 1893–1926.

Group 75: Boat clearances, 1848–1932.

Group 76: Locktenders' reports, 1848.

Group 79: Register of Boats Locked, 1912–1925, 1936.

Group 80: Record of Articles Transported, cleared, and arrived, 1852–1907.

Group 81: Record of Boat clearances at Chicago, 1863.

Group 82: Record of boat arrivals at Chicago, 1867–1873.

Group 88: Register of boats navigating the Illinois and Michigan Canal, 1855–1932.

Group 92: Register of towpath passes, 1898–1927.

Group 105: Plats, 1830–1899.

Group 107: Grundy County field notes and surveys, 1863–1881.

Group 109: Cook, Grundy, and Will county survey, 1835–1861.

Group 121: Chicago sewerage records, 1865.

Springfield, Illinois. Illinois State Historical Library. Henry A. Gardner Letters. 2 p.
IHi

Bill for services in 1857 as Chief Engineer for Joliet & Chicago Railroad Company, 1855–1857.

Springfield, Illinois. Illinois State Historical Library. Letter of May 21, 1830, from U.S. General Land Office of List of Lands Granted by Act of Congress, March 2, 1827, to Aid in Construction of Illinois and Michigan Canal to Andrew Jackson. 5 p. (Photocopy.)
IHi

Springfield, Illinois. Illinois State Historical Library. Illinois and Michigan Canal Commissions. Papers, 1840, 1847. Six pieces.
IHi

Papers of Gov. Augustus French to Joel Manning; miscellaneous memoranda.

Springfield, Illinois. Illinois State Historical Library. Illinois and Michigan Canal. Papers. c. 1880–1900. Five items.
IHi

Concerning the canal scrip investigation of 1859.

Springfield, Illinois. Illinois State Historical Library. W. McCorristen Letter, Dec. 13, 1839, to W. McFarland, Commissioner's Office, I&M Canal, Lockport, Illinois. One piece.
IHi

Springfield, Illinois. Illinois State Historical Library. South Chicago Trades and Labor Assembly. Records. One box, 150 items.
IHi

Collection deals with Calumet-Sag harbor development project and includes correspondence, minutes, resolutions, publications, and newspaper clippings.

Summit, Illinois. Summit-Argo Public Library. Local History File. Railroads. One folder.
ISA

Contains time tables of Chicago and Joliet, and Chicago and Albany railroads, I&M Canal maps, various newspaper clippings.

Summit, Illinois. Summit-Argo Public Library. Local History File. Summit-Argo Post Office. One folder.
ISA

Contains copies of documents authorizing establishment of post office, 1914.

PART 7 Commerce and Industry

Researchers interested in documenting the commercial and industrial history of the corridor have at their disposal a wealth of materials about individual firms or entrepreneurs but few synthetic or general treatments of the subject. Financial data on individual businesses are available from incorporation records, credit ratings, tax records, and the manufacturing censuses. Researchers experienced in the use of company records for historical research may make use of one or two major archival collections and several early business ledgers that are described in the following. Those more interested in narrative accounts of company activities may consult industrial and commercial journals, booster literature, company journals and promotional materials, and general histories of the industries that were important to the development of the corridor. In addition to consulting the sources listed, researchers should examine relevant materials from the canal archives, archives from communications firms listed in the Transportation and Communication section, transcripts from lawsuits, photographic collections, and the business histories and biographical sketches of individual business leaders that are contained in the county histories.

Commerce and Industry—*General*

Annual Review of the Commerce, Manufactures, and the Public and Private Improvements of Chicago, with a Full Statement of Her System of Railroads and a General Synopsis of the Business of the City: Compiled From Several Articles Published in the Chicago Daily Press. 1852–1856/1857. 5 v. Chicago: Democratic Press. Mammoth Steam Printing Establishment, 1853–1857.
ICU

Haeger, John D. "Eastern Money and the Urban Frontier: Chicago, 1833–1842." *Journal of the Illinois State Historical Society* 64 (Autumn 1971): 267–284.
DLC, I, IC, ICHi, ICN, ICU, IEN, IU

McClear, Patrick E. "Speculation, Promotion, and the Panic of 1837 in Chicago." *Journal of the Illinois State Historical Society* 62 (Summer 1969): 135–146.
DLC, I, IC, ICHi, ICN, ICU, IEN, IU

First plat of the future city of Chicago, 1830. Role of transportation interests in the development of Chicago and the role of commerce in its survival.

McClear, Patrick E. "William Butler Ogden: A Chicago Promoter in the Speculative Era and the Panic of 1837." *Journal of the Illinois State Historical Society* 70 (November 1977): 283–291.
DLC, I, IC, ICHi, ICN, ICU, IEN, IU

Ogden had financial, real estate, manufacturing, and transportation interests in the corridor as well as in Chicago.

Taylor, Charles H. *History of the Board of Trade of the City of Chicago.* 3 v. Chicago: Robert O. Law Co., 1917. ports.
ICHi, ICJ, IU

U.S. Bureau of the Census. *Fifteenth Census of the United States, 1930. Distribution. 1933–1934.* Vol. 2: *Wholesale Distribution: State Reports with Statistics for Cities and a Summary for the United States Including County Statistics.* Washington: Government Printing Office, 1932.
DLC

Yetter, Ruby. "Some Aspects in the Commercial Growth of Chicago, 1835–1850." A.M. thesis, The University of Chicago. 1937.
ICU

Commerce and Industry—*Mining and Quarrying*

Harrington, George Bates. *Coal Mining in Illinois.* New York: Newcomen Society in North America, 1950. 24 p.
DLC, IEN

Deals partly with the Chicago, Wilmington, and Franklin Coal Company, 1866–1948.

Holmes, Leslie Arnold. "Variations in Coal Tonnage Production in Illinois, 1900–1940." Ph.D. dissertation, University of Illinois, 1942. 131 p.
DLC, ICU, IU

Illinois. Bureau of Labor Statistics. *Coal in Illinois. 1887, 1891, 1893, 1894, 1896, [6th], 10th, 12th, 13th, 15th, 16th Annual Report.* Springfield, 1887–1898.
MB

Illinois. State Geological Survey. *Cooperative Mining Series, Bulletins.* Vol. 1–33. Urbana, Illinois: State of Illinois, 1913–1930.
DLC, ICJ, IU

Illinois coal mining investigations, No. 1–15, and other topics relating to cooperative coal mining series.

Joliet Daily News, February 5, 9, 1883; *Joliet Republican,* April 1, 1889.
IHi, IJo, ILoHi

Lists area stone quarrying companies and provides information on ownership, number of employees, and wages.

LaSalle Coal Mining Company. *Charter and By-Laws.* LaSalle, Illinois: C. Boynton & Co., 1856. 20 p.
CtY, PBL

Includes report of the manager together with maps and geological sections.

Reussaw, Jerome P. "Possible Rehabilitation of the Morris Strip Mines." M.S. thesis, Northern Illinois University, 1961. 139 p., photos., maps, charts, tables, illus., bibliography.
IDeKN—IRAD

Covers physical attributes of the Morris area, cultural aspects, the coal mining era, the problem of stripped lands, local characteristics, problems and possibilities, conclusions and recommendations.

Stevens, R. P. "Contributions to the Paleontological Synchronism of the Coal Measures of Ohio and Illinois." *American Journal of Science and Arts* 76 (July 1858): 72–79.
IC, ICN, ICU, IU

Includes information on the Illinois Valley.

In the Supreme Court of Illinois, April Term, A.D. 1913: LaSalle Carbon Coal Company vs. Chicago (Sanitary District). Chicago, 1913. 1,149 p., plates, maps, tables, diagrs.
IU

Appellee (LaSalle Carbon Coal Co.) versus appellant (Sanitary District of Chicago). Judge S. C. Stough, presiding. Abstract of record.

U.S. Bureau of the Census. *Special Reports. Mines and Quarries, 1902.* Washington: Government Printing Office, 1905. 1,123 p.
DLC

Description of coal, limestone, and cement production in the corridor. County data on coal production and employment at the mines. Statewide data for limestone quarrying and cement production.

U.S. Census Office. *Tenth Census of the United States, 1880.* Vol. 15: *Report on the Mining Industries of the United States. . . .* Washington: Government Printing Office, 1886. 1,025 p.
DLC

Statistics of coal production by county and a directory of mining companies.

U.S. Census Office. *Eleventh Census of the United States, 1890.* Vol. 7: *Report on Mineral Industries in the United States at the Eleventh Census: 1890.* Washington: Government Printing Office, 1892. 858 p.
ICU

Coal production statistics by county and limestone production statistics by state. Includes data on number of employees and average wages.

Commerce and Industry—*Manufacturing*

Ahlquist, John Otto. "Illinois Manufacturing Corporations; 1821–1870." M.A. thesis, Northern Illinois University, 1966. 54 p., bibliography.
IDeKN—IRAD

Covers laws affecting many corporations in the I&M Corridor. Special laws of incorporation and development of general laws of incorporation, 1848, 1849, 1857, 1870.

American Nickeloid and Manufacturing Company. *Fiftieth Anniversary of Nickeloid Metals.* Peru, Illinois: The Company, 1848.
IPe

Appleton, John B. *The Iron and Steel Industry of the Calumet District.* University of Illinois. Studies in the Social Sciences, Vol. 13, No. 2. Urbana, Illinois: University of Illinois Press, 1925. 133 p., plates, maps.
ICU, IU

Articles of Agreement of the Ottawa Hydraulic Company. Chicago: Davis, [1836]. 12 p.
ICHi

"Edward F. Carry, 1867–1930." *Journal of the Illinois State Historical Society* 23 (July 1930): 353–357.
DLC, I, IC, ICHi, ICN, ICU, IEN, IU

Obituary of president of the Pullman Company since 1922.

Chicago Bridge and Iron Company Seneca Shipyard. *Our Prairie Shipyard: Historical Edition, 1942.* n.p., 1945. 66 p., illus.
IUtHi

Booklet on the yard constructed during World War II. Photographs cover construction and operation of the facility, including workers' homes.

Currey, Josiah. Seymour. *Manufacturing and Wholesale Industries of Chicago.* Chicago: Thomas B. Poole Co., 1918.
DLC, ICHi, ICJ

Includes information on Chicago suburbs.

Hodgdon, W. O. "A Reminiscent Story of Joliet, Illinois, with Some Up to Date References and a Few Pertinent Conclusions." *Joliet Herald,* January 1, 1911.
IJo

Assessment of Joliet industry and services. Booster piece.

Illinois Manufacturers' Association. *Directory.* First Edition, 1920. Chicago: Illinois Manufacturers' Association, 1920.
DLC, ICJ, ICRL

International Harvester Company. *1908 Works Albums.* Chicago: International Harvester, 1908. 66 p., illus.
IC—IHC

Includes descriptions of operations and photographs (interior and exterior) of company facilities including West Pullman and Wisconsin Steel Works.

Joliet Manufacturing Company. *The Eureka Direct Cylinder Force Feed Power Corn Shellers. . . .* [Joliet], 1877. 10 p., illus.
ICHi

Riley, Elmer Arthur. *The Development of Chicago and Vicinity as a Manufacturing Center Prior to 1880. . . .* Chicago: McElroy Publishing Co., 1911. 139 p., tables, maps.
ICU

Bibliography. Reprint of author's Ph.D. dissertation, University of Chicago, 1911.

Stewart, Ethelbert. "A Few Notes for an Industrial History of Illinois." *Illinois State Historical Society Transactions* 8 (1903): 118–125.
IC, ICN, ICU, IU

Brief sketch of early Illinois commerce and industry from fur trade, mining, I&M Canal, railroads.

Swanson, Leslie C. *Old Mills in the Mid-West.* Moline, Illinois: By the Author, 1963. 40 p.
DLC

Lists twenty-eight hundred mills in Iowa and Illinois used for grinding, planks, woodworking, carding.

U.S. Bureau of the Census. *Fifteenth Census of the United States, 1930: Construction Industry. Reports by States with Statistics for Counties and Cities of 100,000 Population and over, a Summary for United States, and a Study of the Location and Agencies of the Construction Industry.* Washington: Government Printing Office, 1933. 1,362 p.
DLC, ICJ, ICU, IU

Walsh, Margaret. "The Spatial Evolution of the Midwestern Pork Industry, 1835–1875." *Journal of Historical Geography* 4 (Spring 1978): 1–22.
DLC, ICU

Commerce and Industry—*Banking*

Charlton, Joseph William. "History of Banking in Illinois Since 1863." Ph.D. dissertation. University of Chicago, 1938.
ICU

Dowrie, George W. *The Development of Banking in Illinois, 1817–1863.* University of Illinois Studies in the Social Sciences, Vol. 2, No. 4.

Urbana, Illinois: University of Illinois Press, 1913. 181 p.
DLC, ICU

Hegeler, Edward C. "A Protest Against the Supreme Court of Illinois, and Also Against Its Legal and Moral Doctrine as Expressed in and Illustrated in Connection with the Case of Edward C. Hegeler vs. The First National Bank of Peru." *Illinois Reports,* Vol. 129, p. 157. Chicago: The Open Court Publishing Co., 1890.
DLC

Illinois. Auditor of Public Accounts. *Statements of Condition, Illinois State Banks, 1897–.*
DLC, ICJ, ICN
Title varies.

Morris, Henry Crittenden. *The First National Bank of Chicago, Charter Number Eight: A Brief History of Its Progress from the Day on Which It Opened for Business, July 1, 1863, to the Same Date Half a Century Later....* Chicago: M. A. Donohue & Co., 1913.
DLC

Western Underwriter. Vol. 1–. Chicago, 1897–. illus., weekly.
DLC, ICRL, IEN
Title varies.

Commerce and Industry—*Real Estate*

Abbott, Carl. "Necessary Adjuncts to Its Growth: The Railroad Suburbs of Chicago, 1854–1875." *Journal of the Illinois State Historical Society* 58 (Summer 1980): 117–131.
DLC, I, IC, ICHi, ICN, ICU, IEN, IU
Includes information on western and southwestern suburbs of Cook County.

Buettinger, Craig. "The Rise and Fall of Hiram Pearson: Mobility on the Urban Frontier." *Chicago History* 9 (Summer 1980): 112–117.
IC, ICF, ICHi, ICN, ICU, IU
Activities of a Chicago area real estate speculator during the 1830s and 1840s.

Chicago. Sanitary District. Real Estate Development Committee. *The Manufacturing Site Possibilities of the Land Along the Sanitary and Ship Canal.* Chicago: The Committee, 1916.
IU

"Edwin S. Monroe, 1859–1918." *Journal of the Illinois State Historical Society* 12 (October 1919): 485–486.
DLC, I, IC, ICHi, ICN, ICU, IEN, IU
Obituary of Joliet real estate man who was active in other civic and business ventures.

List of Canal Lots and Lands in Chicago and Vicinity, Offered for Sale by the Trustees of the Illinois and Michigan Canal, in September, 1848, and May, 1849, with the Valuations of the Several Lots and Tracts: Also, the Prices of those Sold and the Names of Purchasers. Chicago: Rees & Rucker, 1849. 31 p.
DLC, ICHi

McClear, Patrick E. "Land Speculators and Urban and Regional Development: Chicago in the 1830s." *The Old Northwest* 6 (1980): 137–151.
DLC, INS, IU
Compares activities of resident and nonresident speculators.

Zoll, Clifford Alexander. "The Methods of Real Estate Appraisal Used by Building and Loan Associations in Chicago." M.A. thesis, University of Chicago, 1929.
ICU

Commerce and Industry—*Utilities*

Ferrero, Joseph D. "Site Selection of the LaSalle County Station (electric power)." M.S. thesis, Northern Illinois University, 1975.
IDeKN

Illinois. Bureau of Labor Statistics. *History of Chicago Gas Companies: Extracts from the Forthcoming Report of the Illinois Bureau of Labor Statistics of George A. Schilling, Secretary of the Bureau of Labor.* Selected by Prof. E. W. Bemis. [Chicago: Civic Federation of Chicago, 1897]. 48 p.
ICJ, NjP

Illinois. Commerce Commission. *Opinions and Orders....* Vol. 1–12, 16–20. Springfield, 1910/1922–1940/1941.
DLC, ICJ, ICU
Continues **Illinois. Public Utilities Commission.** *Opinions and Orders.*

Illinois. Public Utilities Commission. *Opinions and Orders....* Vol. 1–8. Springfield, 1914–1921.
DLC, ICJ, ICU, IU

Illinois. Rivers and Lakes Commission. *The Conservation of Water Power in the DesPlaines and Illinois Rivers and the Improvement of These Rivers for Navigation.* Rivers and Lakes Commission, Bulletin, No. 1. Springfield: Illinois State Journal Co., 1911. 10 p.
ICU, NN

Smith, Henry Ezmard. "Organization and Administrative Procedure of the Peoples Gas, Light, and Coke Company." Ph.D. dissertation, University of Chicago, 1926.
ICU

Commerce and Industry—*Commercial Business*

Bailey, John C. W. *People's Guide to Business ... of Chicago....* Chicago: Reen and Schorer's Lithographic, 1858. 134 p.
ICHi

The Chicago Almanac and Advertiser, for the Year 1855. Chicago: Chicago Printing Co., 1855.
DLC, IC, ICHi, ICU

Chicago Association of Commerce and Industry. *Chicago, International Market: A Foreign Trade Directory of Chicago.* Chicago: 1931/1932. illus.
DLC, ICJ, ICU

Chicago Board of Trade. *A Collection of Addresses and Papers Describing the Services Rendered by the Board of Trade of the City of Chicago in the Civil War.* Chicago: The Franklin Co., 1912. 35 p.
DLC, ICHi

The Chicago Complete Business Directory for 1857 and 1858. Being Chicago: A Complete Business Directory of the City of Chicago. [Chicago], Published by Wm. F. Bartlett & Co., [1857]. 82 p.
ICHi

Chicago Business Directory. 1881/1882, 1884, 1888, 1889, 1890. 6 v. Chicago: Rand, McNally, 1881–1890. plans.
DLC, ICHi, ICJ

Chicago Central Business and Office Building Directory, 1899, 1919. 20 v. Chicago: The Winters Pub. Co., 1899–1919.
DLC, ICHi, ICJ

Chicago Office Building Directory ..., 1886–1918. 30 v. Chicago: P. H. Early, 1886–1918. illus.
DLC

The Chicago Path-Finder ... Established for the Promotion and Extension of Trade in the City of Chicago ... 1869, 1869/1870. 2 v. Chicago: Press of Church, Goodman & Donnelley, 1869. plan.
DLC, ICHi

Chicago Tribune. *Annual Review of the Trade and Commerce of the City of Chicago. 1854–1860.* Chicago: Chicago Tribune, 1855–1861.
ICRL

Chicago Tribune. *Book of Facts ... Data on Markets—Merchandising—Advertising, with Special Reference to the Chicago Territory and Chicago Newspaper Advertising.* [Chicago]: The Chicago Tribune, 1922–.
DLC, ICJ, ICU

Dunlap, Homer Herschel, Jr. "Chicago as a Competitive Market for Coal." M.A. thesis, University of Chicago, 1933.
ICU

Edwards' Chicago Business Directory ... For the Year 1866/1867.... Chicago: Edwards, Greenough & Deved, 1866. 1088 p.
DLC

Edwards' Chicago City Guide and Complete Business Directory for 1869/1870.... Chicago: R. Edwards, 1869. 477 p., illus., plan.
DLC

Frueh, Erne Rene. "Retail Merchandising in Chicago, 1833–1848." *Journal of the Illinois State Historical Society* 32 (March 1939): 149–172.
DLC, I, IC, ICHi, ICN, ICU, IEN, IU

Discusses the rise of Chicago as a merchandising center and the transportation of goods into the city as a chief factor in Chicago's rise as a retail hub.

Goss, Bert Crawford. "Factors Affecting the Origin of Livestock Receipts at the Chicago Market." M.A. thesis, University of Chicago, 1929.
ICU

The Guests' Reference Book and Directory of the First Wholesale and Retail Stores and Leading Places of Business in Chicago, 1870–1871. Chicago: P. L. Hanscom, Printers, 1870. 120 p.
DLC, ICHi

Hall, Edward Hepple. *Hall's Business Directory of Chicago: Published Annually, on the First of November. Price One Dollar.* Chicago: Hall & Company, Publishers, 1856. 94 p.
DLC, ICHi, ICN

Hurlbut, Henry Higgins, comp. . . . *Chicago Antiquities, Including Chicago Business Directory for 1839.* Chicago: Eastman & Bartlett, 1875. 21 p.
DLC, ICU

Includes 1839 pamphlet "The Laws and Ordinances of the City of Chicago."

Kwedar, Melinda F., Allen, James R., and Patterson, John A. "Illinois General Store Manuscripts, 1825–1845." *Illinois Libraries,* 62 (April 1980): 303–309.
IC, ICJ, ICN, ICU, IU

The Lakeside Business Directory and Year Book of the City of Chicago . . . 1880–1882, 1882–1883. Chicago: The Chicago Directory Co., 1880–1882.
DLC, ICHi, ICJ

A. N. Marquis and Company's Handy Business Directory of Chicago, 1886/1887, 1887/1888, 1888. 3 v. Chicago: A. N. Marquis, 1886–1888.
DLC

Merged into *Lakeside Business Directory* in 1889.

Merchants' and Manufacturers' Consolidated Business Directory of Chicago, St. Louis, Kansas City, Cincinnati, Omaha, Denver, Minneapolis, St. Paul, and Milwaukee: With a Combined List of the Representative Commercial Houses of New York, Philadelphia, Boston, Connecticut. 1889–1891. 2 v. Chicago: Commercial Publishing Co., 1889–1891.
DLC

Norris, James Wellington. *A Business Advertiser and General Directory of the City of Chicago, for the Year 1845–1846, Together with a Historical and Statistical Account: Second Year of Publication.* Chicago: J. Campbell & Co., Publishers, 1845. 156 p., front.
DLC, ICHi, ICN, ICU, IHi

Contains southwest panoramic view of Chicago in 1845.

Norris, James Wellington. *Norris' Business Directory, and Statistics of the City of Chicago for 1846.* Chicago: Eastham & Davidson, 1846. 64 p.
DLC, ICHi, ICN

Smith, A. Warren and DuMoulin, Charles A. *Chicago Business Directory and Commercial Advertiser, 1859: Containing a Classified and Alphabetical Arrangement, Representing the Mercantile, Manufacturing, Mechanical and Professional Interests of Chicago; Embracing a Complete and Reliable Co-partnership Directory; Which Exhibits, in Connection with Each Firm Name, the Full Name of the Individual Copartners.* Chicago: S. C. Griggs & Co., Publishers, [1858]. 260 p.
ICHi

Tanner, Henry, comp. *T. A. Holland & Company's Business Directory of Chicago.* . . . Chicago: T. A. Holland, 1866. 31 p.
DLC

Commerce and Industry—*Archive Sources*

Boston, Massachusetts. Harvard University. Graduate School of Business Administration. Baker Library. Illinois Land Agency. Illinois Central Railroad Company Collection, 1846–1898. 16 v. Five boxes.
MH—BA

Journals, letter books, stock books, plans, claims, and sales of titles of the Associates of the Illinois Land Agency.

Chicago, Illinois. Chicago Historical Society. Chicago Real Estate, Canal Lands. R. K. Swift. 1 v.
ICHi

Copy of register made in Land Office at Chicago for R. K. Swift, 1835–1855. Includes land in Cook and DuPage counties with date, purchaser, description.

Chicago, Illinois. Chicago Historical Society. Marseilles Water Power Company.
ICHi

Miscellaneous pamphlets on the advantages of Marseilles to manufacturers, 1880s.

Chicago, Illinois. Chicago Historical Society. Morton Family Collections. Twenty-two feet.
ICHi
Correspondence, financial records, genealogical data, and newsclippings concerning Julius Sterling Morton, his sons Joe, Paul, Mark, and Carl. Topics include family affairs, railroads, salt companies, and meat packing in Nebraska and Chicago. Argo Starch Manufacturing Co.

Chicago, Illinois. Chicago Historical Society. William Butler Ogden Business Records. 1,170 items. 3 v.
ICHi
Covers period 1835–1881. Numerous letters about canal legislation and correspondence and business records concerning Ogden's business activities and real estate holdings in Chicago and Illinois.

Chicago, Illinois. Chicago Historical Society. Ferdinand Schapper Collection.
ICHi
Collection of invoices in connection with Schapper's Drug Store in Blue Island. Chiefly from Chicago wholesale druggists but includes others from dealers in various businesses such as hardware, liquor, footwear. 1917.

Chicago, Illinois. International Harvester Company. "History of Wisconsin Steel Works." (Typewritten.)
IC—IHC

Chicago, Illinois. International Harvester Company. Payroll Book. South Chicago Furnace Company.
IC—IHC
For 1899.

Chicago, Illinois. International Harvester Company. South Chicago Furnace Company. Income Tax Return—Disposed Assets.
IC—IHC
Covers 1909–1914.

Chicago, Illinois. International Harvester Company. Wisconsin Steel Company. Articles of Association, By-Laws, Stockholders' Meetings.
IC—IHC
Covers 1906–1936. Company located in corridor.

Chicago, Illinois. International Harvester Company. Wisconsin Steel Company. By-Laws Booklet.
IC—IHC
Covers 1905–1914.

Chicago, Illinois. Loyola University. Archives. Samuel Insall Papers. 1859–1938. Eighty-five boxes.
ICL
Utility magnate. Miscellaneous documents of Public Service Co. of Northern Illinois. Photographs.

Chicago, Illinois. University of Illinois at Chicago. Philip Ream Clark Papers. Fifteen feet.
ICUI
Includes correspondence and business records in connection with Clark's tenure as president of City National Bank and Trust Company of Chicago (1932–1954). Also includes material on corporate activities of U.S. Steel (1932–1962).

Lockport, Illinois. Lewis University. Lockport Civic and Commerce Association. Correspondence.
ILoL
Covers 1932–1980.

Marseilles, Illinois. Marseilles Public Library. Local History Shelf. Miscellaneous Collection. Two bags.
IMa
Various newspaper clippings, with photograph of Crescent Paper Mill, Howe and Davidson Mill, O'Neill Implement Co., Central Roofing Co., Glen Avenue photograph from late-nineteenth century. Photograph of Spring Street Presbyterian Church. Newspaper clippings of "Ramblin' Round" by C. C. Tisler, from the *Daily Republican-Times,* Ottawa.

Morris, Illinois. Morris Public Library. Local History File. Minooka. Banks and Banking. One folder.
IMo
Contains newspaper article from 1902 on the Minooka Bank holdup. Savings passbook for First Trust and Savings Bank of Morris, 1916–1917 (Raymond Brown?). 2 v. Essay on Farmer's First National Bank, Minooka.

Springfield, Illinois. Archives of the State of Illinois. U.S. Department of Interior. Seventh Federal Census. Industrial Schedules for Illinois, 1850.
I—Ar

Ninety-nine Illinois counties. 1 v. No index. Information entered for each business includes name of corporation, company, or individual producing articles totaling $500 or more; type of business or article produced; amount of capital invested; kind, quantity, and value of raw materials used; kind of motive power used; numbers of male and female employees and average cost of wages; kind, quantity, and value of products.

Springfield, Illinois. Archives of the State of Illinois. U.S. Department of Interior. Eighth Federal Census. Industrial Schedules for Illinois, 1860.
I—Ar

One hundred-two Illinois counties. 1 v. No index. Information entered for each business includes name of corporation, company, or individual producing articles totaling $500 or more; type of business or article produced; amount of capital invested; kind, quantity, and value of raw materials used; kind of motive power used; numbers of male and female employees and average cost of wages; kind, quantity, and value of products.

Springfield, Illinois. Illinois State Historical Library. Charles S. Bond. 3 items.
IHi

Deed and bond of Charles S. Bond to Edmund L. Kimberly for land purchased in LaSalle County, 1836.

Springfield, Illinois. Illinois State Historical Library. Oscar H. Pratt and Company. Journal. November 21, 1836–May 5, 1838.
IHi

The first thirty-seven pages deal with Joliet. Then, in 1848, the records are resumed in "Auclair" [Wisconsin].

Summit, Illinois. Summit-Argo Public Library. Local History File. Corn Products Company. One folder.
ISA

Contains promotional pamphlets, *The Reflector* (company newsletter—selected issues). Photograph of surveyor's camp at Corn Products site.

Urbana, Illinois. Illinois Historical Survey Library. W. A. Shields Letters, 1935. 2 items.
IU—HS

Shields was secretary of the LaSalle Chamber of Commerce. Letters provide information on history of LaSalle and condition of the city as of 1935.

PART 8 Labor

The best documentation on the working lives of the inhabitants of the corridor can be found in citywide labor union newspapers and industrywide union journals. Reports from individual locals and letters to the editor from individual members not only describe union activities but also provide information on labor relations, social relations among ethnic groups, political activities, and cultural life. However, these sources are not indexed, so a researcher must be prepared to scan many volumes in search of information.

Corporate records, canal archives, and the censuses of manufactures (particularly the manuscript census schedules of 1850–1880) provide good sources of information on labor relations, hours, and wages. Researchers interested in documenting strike activities can consult labor journals, local newpapers, and (if the strike were serious enough) reports from the U.S. and Illinois departments of labor. Since accounts of strikes often differed according to the degree of sympathy or antipathy the writer felt toward the strikers, researchers would do best to read as many descriptions of the same event as possible (for example, in a union journal, local newspaper, business journal, and government report).

Labor—*General*

Chaney, Lucian West and Hanner, Hugh S. *The Safety Movement in the Iron and Steel Industry, 1907 to 1917.* Bulletin of the United States Bureau of Labor Statistics, No. 234. Industrial Accidents and Hygiene Series, No. 18. Washington: Government Printing Office, 1918. 299 p., tables, diagrs., plates.
DLC, MiU

Ducker, James H. *Men of the Steel Rails: Workers on the Atchison, Topeka and Santa Fe Railway, 1869–1900.* Lincoln, Nebraska: University of Nebraska Press, c. 1983. 220 p., plates.
NbU
Bibliography, pp. 205–216. Includes index.

Eaton, Charles H. "Pullman and Paternalism." *American Journal of Politics* 5 (December 1894): 571–579.
IC, ICN, ICU
Assesses the claim that Pullman was run by paternalism and concludes that it was not.

Ely, Richard T. "Pullman: A Social Study." *Harper's New Monthly Magazine* 70 (February 1885): 452–466. illus.
IC, ICHi, ICN, ICU, IU
A study of Pullman as a model company town.

"How Pullman Was Built." *Social Economist* 7 (August 1894): 85–88.
IC, ICN, ICU, IU
Describes the paternalism of Pullman.

Illinois. Bureau of Labor Statistics. *Report of the Commissioners of the State Bureaus of Labor Statistics on the Industrial, Social, and Economic Conditions of Pullman, Illinois.* Pullman, Illinois, 1884. 23 p.
MeB

Illinois. Department of Labor. *Review of Employment and Payrolls for Illinois Industries and Cities, Cost of Living, and Building Construction.* Chicago, 1940.
DLC, ICJ

Illinois. Department of Labor. Division of Statistics and Research. *Statistical Review for the Year.* Chicago, 1937. (Mimeographed.)
ICU

Lightner, David L. "Construction Labor on the Illinois Central Railroad." *Journal of the Illinois State Historical Society* 66 (Autumn 1973): 285–301.
DLC, I, IC, ICHi, ICN, ICU, IEN, IU
View of working conditions at the railroad, particularly pay rates and sickness. Also covers social problems encountered by communities near railroad construction.

Lightner, David L. *Labor on the Illinois Central Railroad, 1852–1900: The Evolution of an*

Industrial Environment. New York: The Arno Press, 1977.
DLC

Taylor, Paul Schuster. *Mexican Labor in the United States: Chicago and the Calumet Region.* University of California Publications in Economics, Vol. 7, No. 2. Berkeley: University of California Press, 1932.
ICU

Tuttle, William M., Jr. "Labor Conflict and Racial Violence: The Black Worker in Chicago, 1894–1919." *Labor History* 10 (Summer 1969): 408–432.
ICMcC, ICU, IEN, IU

Mostly a history of racial conflict in the Chicago Stockyards and the surrounding neighborhoods.

U.S. Bureau of the Census. *Thirteenth Census of the United States, 1910.* Vol. 4: *Population 1910: Occupation Statistics.* Washington: Government Printing Office, 1914. 615 p.
ICU

Detailed breakdown of occupational categories for Chicago and Joliet.

U.S. Bureau of the Census. *Fourteenth Census of the United States, 1920.* Vol. 4: *Population 1920: Occupations.* Washington: Government Printing Office, 1923. 1,309 p.
ICU

Detailed breakdown of occupations of inhabitants of Chicago and Joliet. Breakdown of population of each occupational category into age, race, and nativity for Chicago.

U.S. Bureau of the Census. *Fifteenth Census of the United States: 1930. Population.* Vol. 4: *Occupations, By States: Reports by States, Giving Statistics for Cities of 25,000 or More.* Washington: Government Printing Office, 1933. 1,796 p.
ICU

Statistics for Chicago and Joliet.

U.S. Bureau of the Census. *Sixteenth Census of the United States: 1940.* Vol. 3: *The Labor Force: Occupation, Industry, Employment and Income. Comprising the Third Series of Population Bulletins for the States.* Pt. 2: *Alabama-Indiana.* Washington: Government Printing Office, 1943. 1,052 p.
ICU

U.S. Commission on Industrial Relations. *Industrial Conditions in Chicago.* Vol. 4: *Final Report.* Washington: Government Printing Office, 1916. 284 p.
DLC, ICJ

Report of the commission.

Labor—*Unions*

Ashley, William J., ed. *The Railroad Strike of 1894.* Cambridge, England: The Church Social Union, 1895.
DLC, WHi

The statements of the Pullman Company and the report of the commission, together with an analysis of the issues.

Behen, David M. "The Chicago Labor Movement, 1874–1896: Its Philosophical Bases." Ph.D. dissertation, University of Chicago, 1954.
ICU

Bork, Hal. "The Memorial Day 'Massacre' of 1937 and Its Significance in the Unionization of the Republic Steel Corporation." M.A. thesis, University of Illinois, 1975.
IU

Evans, Chris. *History of the United Mine Workers of America.* Indianapolis: The United Mine Workers of America, 1918.
DLC, IU

Grant, Thomas Burke. "Pullman and Its Lessons." *American Journal of Politics* 5 (August 1894): 190–204.
I, IC, ICN, ICU

Assesses the extent to which George M. Pullman's policies provoked the labor disturbances of 1894. Examines in brief the European origins of Pullman's ideas.

Kinneman, Marion. "John Mitchell in Illinois." *Illinois State University Journal* 32 (September 1969): 21–35.
IU

Provides some information on the union movement among Will County miners during the late-nineteenth century.

Means, D. McG. "Principles Involved in the Recent Strike," *Forum* 17 (August 1894): 633–634.
ICN, ICU, IU

Discusses the issue of state and federal power and the role of unions in the economy, using Pullman's experience.

Scharnau, Ralph William. "Thomas J. Morgan and the United Labor Party of Chicago." *Journal of the Illinois State Historical Society* 66 (Spring 1973): 41–61.
DLC, I, IC, ICHi, ICN, ICU, IEN, IU
Discusses Morgan's role as standard-bearer of socialist thought and action in the Chicago area in the late-nineteenth and early-twentieth centuries. Covers Republican and Democratic party attempts to minimize the influence of Morgan's efforts to institutionalize the United Labor Party.

Staley, Eugene. *History of the Illinois State Federation of Labor.* Chicago: University of Chicago Press, 1930. 579 p., tables.
ICU
A general history of the labor movement in Illinois. Includes a list of all statewide officers along with their city of residence and union.

Von Holst, H. "Are We Awakened?" *Journal of Political Economy* 2 (September 1894): 485–516.
I, IC, ICJ, ICN, ICU
Comments upon the rights of labor in the wake of the Pullman Strike.

Labor—*Strikes*

Abbott, Austin. "The Legal Aspects of the Disorder at Chicago." *Outlook* 50 (July 1894): 54–55.
ICU

Brody, David. *Labor in Crisis: The Steel Strike of 1919.* Philadelphia: Lippincott, 1965.
DLC
Union organizing and strike activities in South Chicago and Joliet.

Busch, Francis X. "The Haymarket Riot and the Trial of the Anarchists." *Journal of the Illinois State Historical Society* 48 (Autumn 1955): 247–270.
DLC, I, IC, ICHi, ICN, ICU, IEN, IU
Overview of the events leading up to the riot, the riot itself, and the legal proceedings that followed.

Cleveland, Grover. "The Government in the Chicago Strike of 1894." *McClure's Magazine* 23 (July 1904): 227–240.
ICU
A discussion of the use of federal power in breaking the Pullman Strike of 1894.

Day, Stephen A. "A Celebrated Illinois Case That Made History." *Journal of the Illinois State Historical Society* 10 (July 1917): 191–206.
DLC, I, IC, ICHi, ICN, ICU, IEN, IU
General discussion of events of Pullman Strike, the role of federal intervention, particularly concerning the implications of mail disruption, and the legal battles that ensued.

Depew, Chauncey M. "Vital Points of Expert Opinion: Chauncey M. Depew on the Debs Strike." *Our Day* 13 (July/August 1894): 356–364.
ICU
Examines the origins of the Pullman–American Railway strike and the implications for state versus federal power. Taken from the *London Times* and the *New York Tribune.*

"Editorial Summary." *Public Opinion* 17 (July 1894): 305–308.
IC, ICN, ICU
A series of short commentaries including statements from Eugene Debs, President Cleveland, and excerpts from a variety of newspapers.

Eggert, Gerald G. *Railroad Labor Disputes: The Beginnings of Federal Strike Policy.* Ann Arbor: University of Michigan Press, 1967. 313 p.
IEN, InU, MiU
Begins with the 1877 railroad strikes and finishes with the aftermath of the 1894 Pullman boycott.

"The Federal Commission's Report upon the Chicago Strike," *Public Opinion* 17 (November 1894): 809–812.
IC, ICN, ICU
A summary of the commission's report, excerpts from a variety of newspapers commenting on the strike report.

Gutman, Herbert G. "The Braidwood Lockout of 1874." *Journal of the Illinois State Historical Society* 53 (Spring 1960): 5–28.
DLC, I, IC, ICHi, ICN, ICU, IEN, IU

Hall, John A. *The Great Strike on the "Q," with a History of the Organization and Growth of the Brotherhood of Locomotive Firemen, and Switchmen's Mutual Aid Association of North America.* Chicago: Elliott and Beezley, 1889.
DLC, ICJ, MiU

Harte, Walter Blackburn. "A Review of the Chicago Strike of '94." *The Arena* 10 (September 1894): 497–532.
I, IC, ICN, ICU

Preceded by a three-page commentary by Prof. Frank Parsons entitled "Chicago's Message to Uncle Sam," pp. 494–496.

Juretic, George M. "The Illinois Central Strike, 1911–1915." M.A. thesis, Northern Illinois University, 1968. 48 p., bibliography.
IDeKN—IRAD

Birth of the Illinois Central Federation, labor versus capital on the picket line, the economic effects of the strike, and craft unions and the system federation.

"The Latest Labor Crisis." *Yale Review* 3 (August 1894): 113–117.
IC, ICN, ICU

Compares the Pullman Strike to the Pittsburgh Strike of 1877 and the Southwestern Strike of 1886.

Lindsey, Almont. *The Pullman Strike: The Story of a Unique Experiment and of a Great Labor Upheaval.* Chicago: The University of Chicago Press, 1942.
DLC

McDermot, Rev. George, C.S.P. "The Pullman Strike Commission." *Catholic World* 60 (February 1895): 627–635.
DLC, I, IC, ICN, ICU, IU

Commentary on the proposals of the presidential commission appointed to investigate the causes of the Pullman Strike.

Mason, J. W. "Pullman and Its Real Lessons." *American Journal of Politics* 5 (October 1894): 392–398.
IC, ICN, ICU

Calls for an examination of methods for change apart from violence, denying that concentration on George Pullman's personality can yield fruitful conclusions.

Ogden, R. "The Report on the Chicago Strike." *Nation* 59 (November 1894): 376.
ICN, ICU, IU

Criticism of the position taken by the strike commissioners.

Pacyga, Dominic A. "Crisis and Community: The Back of the Yards 1921." *Chicago History* 6 (Fall 1977): 167–177.
DLC, IC, ICF, ICHi, ICN, ICU, IU

History of the 1921 Stockyards strike, with photographs of area residences, churches, and factories.

Perrigo, H. S. "Factional Strife in District No. 12, United Mine Workers of America, 1933." Ph.D. dissertation, University of Wisconsin, 1933.
WU

District No. 12 encompasses Illinois.

Person, Carl E. *The Lizard's Trail: A Story from the Illinois Central and Harriman Lines Strike of 1911 to 1915 Inclusive.* New York: AMS Press, 1977. 462 p.
DLC

Reprint of the 1918 edition published by Lake Pub. Co., Chicago.

Pullman, George M. "G. M. Pullman on the Strike." *Our Day* 13 (July/August 1894): 364–368.
ICU

Pullman defends his practices.

Robinson, Harry Perry. "The Humiliating Report of the Strike Commission." *Forum* 18 (January 1895): 523–553.
DLC, ICN, ICU, IU

Critique of the Pullman Strike Commission report, which examines inaccuracies within the report.

Schneirov, Richard. "Chicago's Great Upheaval of 1877." *Chicago History* 9 (Spring 1980): 2–17.
DLC, IC, ICF, ICHi, ICU, IU

The participation of immigrant unskilled laborers in the Great Railroad Strike of 1877. Much of the conflict took place near the lumber yards along the South Branch of the Chicago River.

Stead, W. T. "Incidents of Labour War in America." *Contemporary Review* 66 (July 1894): 65–76.
DLC, I, IC, ICN, ICU, IU

Contrasts British and American labor situations, using American incidents for illustration. Stresses the Illinois example.

"The Strike Commission Taking Testimony." *Public Opinion* 17 (August 1894): 514–516.
DLC, IC, ICN, ICU

Includes press commentary on the strike investigation and the actions of Governor Altgeld with regard to Pullman.

"The Strike Commission Taking Testimony at Chicago." *Public Opinion* 17 (September 1894): 542–543.
DLC, IC, ICN, ICU

Excerpts.

U.S. Congress. Senate. *Report of the Committee of Education and Labor. Violations of the Rights of Labor: The Chicago Memorial Day Incident.* S. Rep. 46, 75th Cong., 1st Sess., 1937.
ICU

Concerns the police attack on the Republic Steel Company workers during the 1937 strike.

Wish, Harvey. "The Pullman Strike: A Study in Industrial Warfare." *Journal of the Illinois State Historical Society* 32 (September 1939): 288–312.
DLC, I, IC, ICHi, ICN, ICU, IEN, IU

Discusses the strike in general terms and the similarities to other industrial environs elsewhere in the country.

Labor—*Labor Relations*

Black, Paul V. "Experiment in Bureaucratic Centralization: Employee Blacklisting on the Burlington Railroad, 1877–1892." *Business History Review* 51 (1977): 444–459.
DLC, ICJ, ICU, IU

Joliet, Illinois. Citizens Alliance. *Industrial Peace Guaranteed.* Chicago, 1904. 26 p., illus.
IU

"Lay-off Plan Upheld in Joliet Minimum Wage Case: Illinois Supreme Court Hands Down Another Decision Relating to Policemen's and Firemen's Wages." *Illinois Municipal Review* 21 (May 1942): 98–100.
ICU

Consensus suit by sixty-six Joliet city employees who in 1937 waived right to receive $175 per month minimum salary.

Montgomery, Royal E. *Industrial Relations in the Chicago Building Trades.* Chicago: University of Chicago Press, 1927.
ICU

Steel Works Club. *Classified Catalog.* Joliet, Illinois, 1911. 88 p.
IU

The Steel Works Club was a company-run recreational and educational institution that began at the Steel Works in 1889.

Labor—*Wage Studies*

Illinois. Department of Labor. Division of Statistics and Research. *Employment, Payrolls and Average Weekly Earnings in Illinois by City.* Chicago, 1933–1940.
ICJ

Labor—*Archive Sources*

Chicago, Illinois. University of Illinois at Chicago. Victor A. Olander Papers. Eight feet.
ICUI

Covers period 1884–1952. Correspondence, notes, minutes, reports, speeches, bulletins, newsletters, and clippings concerning Olander's activities as secretary of both the Illinois State Federation of Labor and the International Seaman's Union.

Urbana, Illinois. Illinois Historical Survey Library. John Hunter (1872–1955). Papers 1910–1955. Sixty-six boxes, inventory.
IU—HS

Walker served as president of the Illinois Federation of Labor (1913–1930), president of District 12 (Illinois) of the United Mine Workers of America (1906–1913, 1931–1933), and international secretary of the United Mine Workers of America Reorganized (1930–1931).

Although sociologists have written studies that deal with limited time periods in some of the corridor cities, the social history of the area has only recently been considered a legitimate scholarly subject. Researchers, therefore, need to make use of sources and documents that were not created for the task of tracing changes in the social structure. They also need to choose which categories of social interaction merit historical study; the subsections within this part of the Bibliography are an attempt to define some of those categories.

This section primarily contains listings of two types of sources. First, there are statistical compilations that can be used to discern social categories and relationships. Second, there are many works that were originally written to celebrate the accomplishments of particular ethnic, charitable, reform, and religious organizations. These contain various pieces of information that can be valuable in the study of social interaction. Researchers should also check other parts of the Bibliography (particularly those dealing with industry, labor, politics, and cultural life) for relevant information.

Social Environment—*Population (Demography)*

Bogart, Ernest L. "The Movement of the Population of Illinois, 1870–1910." *Illinois State Historical Society Transactions* (1917): 64–75.
DLC, IC, ICU

Includes a table that displays the number of foreign born and the percentage of the foreign born population in Cook, Grundy, DuPage, Will, and LaSalle counties, 1870, 1880, 1890, 1900, and 1910.

Burford, C. C. *Analysis of Population of Illinois Previous to 1840.* Urbana: University of Illinois, 1904.
ICU

Illinois. Secretary of State. *State Census, 1845. December 11, 1846: Read, Laid on the Table, and Five Hundred Copies Ordered to be Printed. . . .* n.p., 1846. 7 p., tables.
IU

"Illinois. State Census, 1835." *House Journal.* 9th General Assembly, 2nd Sess., 1835/1836. p. 372.
ICU

Totals by county of population and manufactories.

"Illinois. State Census, 1840." In *Illinois Reports,* 1840/1841. pp. 403–414. Springfield: Wm. Walters, Public Printers, 1841.
ICU

Population by counties showing totals of white males, white females, negroes and mulattoes, and manufactories.

"Illinois. State Census, 1845." In *Illinois Reports,* 1846/1847. pp. 65–71. Springfield: George R. Weber, Public Printer, 1846.
ICU

Population by counties showing totals of white males, white females, colored males and females, militias, manufactures, mills, machines, and distilleries.

U.S. Census Office. *Fifth Census: Of Enumeration of the Inhabitants of the United States, as Corrected at the Department of State, 1830.* Washington: Duff Green, 1832. 165 p.
DLC, ICU

By state, county, and minor civil division. Number of free whites, slaves, free blacks by age and sex, number of deaf and dumb and blind, number of white aliens.

U.S. Census Office. *Fifth Census: Of Enumeration of the Inhabitants of the United States, as Corrected at the Department of State, 1840.* Washington: Blain and Rives, 1841. 476 p.
ICU

Similar to 1830 census.

U.S. Census Office. *The Seventh Census of the United States, 1850. Embracing a Statistical View of Each of the States. . . .* Washington: Robert Armstrong, Public Printer, 1853. 1,022 p.
DLC, ICJ, ICU

Population by age, sex, and color for counties and minor civil divisions. Births, deaths, number of dwellings, and families by county. Statistics of colleges, academies, and schools by county. Number attending school by sex, race, and nativity by county. Adults who cannot read by sex, race, and nativity by county. Statistics of agriculture by county. Statistics of libraries by county. Statistics of church membership and church property by denomination by county.

U.S. Census Office. *Population of the United States in 1860: Compiled from the Original Returns. . . .* Washington: Government Printing Office, 1864. 694 p.
DLC, ICJ, ICU

By county. Population by age, sex, color (free and slave), and nativity. Population by color and sex for minor subdivisions.

U.S. Census Office. *Ninth Census of the United States, 1870.* Vol. 1: *Population.* Washington: Government Printing Office, 1872.
DLC, ICJ, ICU

Population by race for each county, 1790–1870. Population by race and nativity for civil divisions below county, 1850–1870. Population by nativity of persons and their parents by county. Population by state or country of birth by county. School attendance and illiteracy by race, sex, and nativity by county. Statistics of churches by denomination by county. Population by sex and age by county and minor civil division.

U.S. Census Office. *Tenth Census of the United States, 1880.* Vol. 1: *Statistics of the Population of the United States at the Tenth Census (June 1, 1880).* Washington: Government Printing Office, 1883. 961 p.
ICJ, ICU

Aggregate population by counties, 1790–1880. Population by civil division less than county. Population by race and nativity by county and for cities with over four thousand inhabitants for 1870 and 1880. State and county of birth by county. Population by age and sex by county. Persons in selected occupations for Chicago.

U.S. Census Office. *Tenth Census of the United States, 1880.* Vol. 19: *Report on the Social Statistics of Cities.* Pt. 2: *The Southern and Western States.* Washington: Government Printing Office, 1887. 843 p., maps.
ICJ, ICU

Chicago and Joliet: location, transportation facilities, climate, streets, tunnels, waterworks, gas supply, parks and amusements, drainage, pavement, cemeteries, description of government agencies and services.

U.S. Census Office. *Eleventh Census of the United States, 1890.* Vol. 1: *Report on the Population of the United States at the Eleventh Census, 1890.* Pt. 1. Washington: Government Printing Office, 1895. 968 p.
ICJ, ICU

Total population of each county, 1790–1890, and each minor civil division, 1880–1890. Breakdown of population by race and nativity (1870–1890) by county; by sex, age, race, and nativity (1890) by minor civil division. Statistics on number of families and dwellings by county and minor civil division.

U.S. Census Office. *Twelfth Census of the United States, 1900.* Vol. 2: *Population of the United States by States and Territories, Pt. 2.* Washington: Government Printing Office, 1901. 754 p.
DLC, ICJ, ICU

Similar statistics to 1890 reports plus population of Chicago and Joliet by age, sex, race, and nativity (age in five-year categories). Population of Chicago broken down by age, sex, race, nativity, and conjugal condition. School attendance data for Chicago and Joliet by sex, race, and age. Illiteracy data for Joliet and Chicago by sex, race, and age. Detailed population breakdown by occupation by sex for Chicago and Joliet. Detailed statistics on size of household for Chicago and Joliet. Statistics on farm and home ownership and rental by county. Statistics on home ownership and rental for Chicago (by ward), Joliet, LaSalle, and Ottawa.
ICU

U.S. Bureau of the Census. *Thirteenth Census of the United States, 1910.* Vol. 1: *Population, 1910: General Report and Analysis.* Washington: Government Printing Office, 1913. 1,369 p.
ICU

Population by county and minor civil division, 1890, 1900, 1910. Nativity of voting-age males, 1890, 1900, 1910, for Chicago and Joliet. School attendance and illiteracy by age group for Chicago and Joliet. Home ownership and rental by county (farm and "other") and for Chicago, Joliet, and LaSalle.

U.S. Bureau of the Census. *Thirteenth Census of the United States, 1910.* Vol. 2: *Population 1910: Reports by States, with Statistics for Counties, Cities, and Other Civil Divisions, Alabama-Montana.* Washington: Government Printing Office, 1913. 1,160 p.
ICU

Similar statistics as previous reports. New tables: age, school attendance, illiteracy, dwellings and families, sex, race, and nativity statistics placed in a single table for each county, city over twenty-five hundred, and each ward for Chicago. Tables provide country of birth for both immigrants and native born with foreign-born parents. Cities covered: Blue Island, Harvey, Marseilles, Morris, Chicago, Joliet, LaSalle.

U.S. Bureau of the Census. *Fourteenth Census of the United States, 1920.* Vol. 1: *Population, 1920: Number and Distribution of Inhabitants.* Washington: Government Printing Office, 1921. 695 p.
DLC, ICU

Number of inhabitants by county, 1850–1920, and by minor civil division, 1900–1920.

U.S. Bureau of the Census. *Fourteenth Census of the United States, 1920.* Vol. 2: *Population, 1920: General Report and Analytical Tables.* Washington: Government Printing Office, 1922. 1,410 p.
DLC, ICU

Basic demographic statistics by county and for Chicago and Joliet. Also includes tables displaying mother tongue of foreign born for Chicago and Joliet and illiteracy by age, sex, race, and nativity for Chicago and Joliet.

U.S. Bureau of the Census. *Fourteenth Census of the United States, 1920.* Vol. 3: *Population, 1920: Composition and Characteristics of the Population by States.* Washington: Government Printing Office, 1922. 1,253 p.
DLC, ICU

Similar in format to 1910 report. New tables and features: breakdown by age, race, and sex for Blue Island, Chicago, Joliet, LaSalle, and Ottawa. Ottawa included in comprehensive tables for school attendance, illiteracy, homes and dwellings, race, sex, and nativity for cities of ten thousand to twenty-five thousand population. Lockport and Peru added to similar table for places of twenty-five hundred to ten thousand.

U.S. Bureau of the Census. *Fifteenth Census of the United States, 1930. Population.* Vol. 1: *Total Population for States, Counties, and Township or Other Minor Civil Divisions; for Urban and Rural Areas; and for Cities and Other Incorporated Places.* Washington: Government Printing Office, 1931. 1,268 p.
DLC, ICU

Population of Blue Island, Calumet City, Joliet, LaSalle, and Ottawa from earliest census to 1930. Population of counties and minor civil divisions, 1910–1930. Population of incorporated places, 1920, 1930.

U.S. Bureau of the Census. *Fifteenth Census of the United States, 1930. Population.* Vol. 3: *Reports by States, Showing the Composition and Characteristics of the Population for Counties, Cities, and Townships or Other Minor Civil Divisions.* Pt. 1: *Alabama-Missouri.* Washington: Government Printing Office, 1932. 1,389 p.
DLC, ICU

New tables: breakdown of population by age, race, sex, nativity, and place of residence (urban or rural) for each township and each incorporated place with a population over one thousand (and for each community area in Chicago). Breakdown of population into occupation groups (using Dept. of Commerce industry groups) by sex and county (also for Joliet). Basic population composition statistics by county and for Blue Island, Calumet City, Joliet, LaSalle, and Ottawa.

U.S. Bureau of the Census. *Fifteenth Census of the United States, 1930. Population.* Vol. 6: *Families: Reports by States, Giving Statistics for Families and Dwellings by Counties, for Urban and Rural Areas and for Urban Places of 2,500 or More.* Washington: Government Printing Office, 1933. 1,495 p.
DLC, ICU

Classification by race, nativity, tenure, value of house, value of rent, and family size by county and for Blue Island, Calumet City, Joliet, LaSalle, Ottawa, Dolton, Lemont, Lockport, Lyons, Marseilles, Morris, Oglesby, Peru, Riverdale, and Summit.

U.S. Bureau of the Census. *Sixteenth Census of the United States, 1940. Housing.* Vol. 1: *Data for Small Areas: Selected Housing Statistics for States, Counties, and Minor Civil Divisions; for Urban and Rural Areas; for Incorporated Places; and for Metropolitan Districts: Comprising the First Series of Housing Bulletins for States.* Pt. 1: *United States Summary and Alabama-Nebraska.* Washington: Government Printing Office, 1943. 936 p.
DLC, ICU, IU

By county, township, and incorporated place of one thousand inhabitants or more (Blue Island, Riverdale, Lemont, Summit, Calumet City, Dolton, Channahon, Joliet, Rockdale, Lockport, Coal City, Morris, LaSalle, Peru, Ottawa, Crotty (Seneca), Marseilles, North Utica, and the relevant community areas in Chicago). Type of ownership, race of occupant, condition of building, persons per room. Separate tables for urban and rural dwellings. Separate table of ward statistics for cities with populations over ten thousand.

U.S. Bureau of the Census. *Sixteenth Census of the United States, 1940. Housing.* Vol. 2: *General Characteristics: Occupancy and Tenure Status, Value of Home or Monthly Rent, Size of Household, and Race of Head, Type of Structure, Housing Facilities and Equipment, and Mortgage Status. Comprising the Second Series of Housing Bulletins for the States.* Part 2: *Alabama-Indiana.* Washington: Government Printing Office, 1943. 1,019 p.
ICU

By county with separate tables for all incorporated places with populations over twenty-five hundred.

U.S. Bureau of the Census. *Sixteenth Census of the United States, 1940. Population.* Vol. 1: *Number of Inhabitants: Total Population for States, Counties, and Minor Civil Divisions; For Urban and Rural Areas; For Incorporated Places; For Metropolitan Districts; and for Census Tracts. Comprising the First Series of Population Bulletins for the States, Territories, and Possessions.* Washington: Government Printing Office, 1942. 1,236 p.
ICU

Population of the state, urban and rural, from the earliest census to 1940. Population of cities of ten thousand or more from earliest census to 1940. Area and population of counties, urban and rural, from 1920 to 1940. Population of counties by minor civil divisions from 1920 to 1940. Population of incorporated places from 1940 and 1930. Population of cities of five thousand or more by wards in 1940. Population of metropolitan districts in 1940 and 1930. Population of tracted cities by census tracts in 1940.

U.S. Bureau of the Census. *Sixteenth Census of the United States, 1940: Population.* Vol. 2: *Characteristics of the Population: Sex, Age, Race, Nativity, Citizenship, Country of Birth of Foreign-Born White, School Attendance, Education, Employment Status, Class of Worker, Major Occupation Group, and Industry Group.* Pt. 2: *Florida-Iowa.* Washington: Government Printing Office, 1943. 1,001 p.
DLC, ICU

By county (with separate tables for rural farm and rural nonfarm populations) and for Coal City, Seneca (Crotty), North Utica, Rockdale, Dolton, Lemont, Lockport, Marseilles, Morris, Peru, Riverdale, Summit, Blue Island, Calumet City, Joliet, LaSalle, Ottawa, and the relevant wards of Chicago.

U.S. Library of Congress. Census Library Project. *State Censuses.* Washington: U.S. Government Printing Offices, 1948. 73 p.
DLC, ICJ, ICU

Annotated bibliography of population censuses taken by states and territories after 1790.

Social Environment—Ethnic Groups

Social Environment—*Ethnic Groups*—General

Chicago. Department of Development and Planning. *Historic City: The Settlement of Chicago.* Chicago, 1976. 118 p., illus., maps.

ICU

Bibliography. Ethnic community maps, 1840, 1860, 1870, 1900, 1920, 1950. Illustration of construction of I&M Canal.

"Ethnic Series." *Joliet Herald News.* November 16, 20, 27; December 4, 11, 18, 21, 1980.
IJo

Articles on immigration, social life, and community institutions of Joliet ethnic groups.

Wyman, Mark. *Immigrants in the Valley; Irish, Germans, and Americans in the Upper Mississippi Country, 1830–1860.* Chicago: Nelson-Hall Inc., 1984. 258 p., illus., map.
ICU

Social history of immigrants who worked to build I&M Canal and railroads. Includes incidents and daily life in Chicago, Joliet, LaSalle, Lockport, Ottawa, Peru. Index and list of sources.

Social Environment—*Ethnic Groups*—Germans

Faust, Albert B. *The German Element in the United States with Special Reference to Its Political, Moral, Social and Educational Influence.* 2 v. New York: The Steuben Society of America, 1927.
DLC, ICJ, ICU

Definitive work on German-Americans.

Mannhardt, Emil. "Deutsche Theinehmer am Mexikanischen Kriege von LaSalle County." *Deutsch-Amerikanische Geschichtsblätter* 2 (July 1902): 48–49.
DLC, IC, ICJ, ICN, ICU, IU

In German. German-Americans from LaSalle County in the Mexican War.

Mannhardt, Emil. "Die altesten deutschen Ansiedler von Illinois: LaSalle, Bureau, Marshall and Putnam Cos." *Deutsch-Amerikanische Geschichtsblätter* 2 (April 1902): 49–62.
DLC, IC, ICJ, ICN, ICU, IU

In German. German-American settlers.

Mannhardt, Emil. "Die Deutschen in DuPage County." *Deutsch-Amerikanische Geschichtsblätter* 1 (October 1902): 33–40.
DLC, IC, ICJ, ICN, ICU, IU

In German. Germans in DuPage County.

Mannhardt, Emil. "Die Jeveraner-Kolonie in Will County, Illinois, und ihre Töchter-Kolonien." *Deutsch-Amerikanische Geschichtsblätter* 2 (January 1902): 33–39.
ICU, ICHi

In German. Will County settlement.

Pochmann, Henry A. *Bibliography of German Culture in America to 1940.* Madison, Wisconsin: University of Wisconsin Press, 1953.
DLC, ICU

Twelve thousand items. Indexed.

Tolzmann, Don Heinrich. ***German-Americana: A Bibliography.*** **Metuchen, New Jersey: Scarecrow Press, 1975.**
ICU

Lists books, pamphlets, records, photographs, dissertations, public documents, articles through 1973.

Social Environment—*Ethnic Groups*—Irish

"Irish Settlements Along the Illinois and Michigan Canal. . . ." *Chicago Times Herald.* July 24, 1898.
IHi

Review of successful Irishmen who settled in area after working on canal construction.

Onahan, William J. "Irish Settlements in Illinois." *Catholic World* 33 (May 1881): 157–162.
DLC, I, IC, ICN, ICU, IU

Focuses on the Irish settlements along the I&M Canal, describing their origins and the importance of the canal to Irish settlement in the region.

Rose, Walter R. *A Bibliography of the Irish in the United States.* New York: Tristram Shandy Publications, 1969.
IEN

Thompson, Joseph J. "The Irish in Chicago." *Illinois Catholic Historical Review* 2 (April 1920): 458–473; 3 (October 1920): 146–169.
DLC, IC, ICN, ICU

Mostly about prominent men from 1800 to 1880. Includes section in I&M Canal that demonstrates that Irish contractors received much of the construction business on the canal.

Social Environment—*Ethnic Groups*—Lithuanians

Varpas [*The Bell*]. Vol. 1–17. Lemont, Illinois: Lithuanian Alumni Association Annual. 1889–1921.
NN
Journal advocating freedom for Lithuania. In Lithuanian.

Social Environment—*Ethnic Groups*—Norwegians

Blegen, Theodore C. "Leaders in American Immigration." *Illinois State Historical Society Transactions* 38 (1931): 144–155.
DLC, IC, ICU
Includes section on Norwegian settlement in LaSalle County.

Bower, Cora Louise, ed. *From Fjord to Prairie: Norwegian-Americans in the Midwest, 1825–1975*. Chicago: Norwegian American Immigration Anniversary Commission, 1976. 166 p.
ICU
Bibliography. Includes Norwegian church history, "Fox River Settlement." Lists Sons of Norway Lodge in Ottawa.

Folkedahl, Beulah and Jacobson, Charlotte. *Guide to Manuscripts Collections of the Norwegian-American Historical Association*. Northfield, Minnesota: Norwegian-American Historical Association, 1979. 158 p., index.
ICU, MnNSN

Lipschultz, Wendy. "Norwegian Americans in LaSalle County, Illinois, 1825–1926." Thesis, Northwestern University, 1976. 43 p.
MnNSN

Lovoll, Odd S. "*The Promise of America: A History of the Norwegian-American People*. Minneapolis: University of Minnesota Press, 1984. 239 p., illus., maps.
ICU, MnNSN
Selected bibliography, pp. 223–228. Includes sections on Norwegians in LaSalle County and in Chicago.

Strand, Algot E., comp. *A History of the Norwegians of Illinois*. Chicago: J. Anderson Publishing Company, 1905.
DLC, ICJ, ICN, IEN, IU
History of Norwegians, Norwegian churches, Norwegians in Chicago. Includes biographical sketches and portraits.

Social Environment—*Ethnic Groups*—Poles

Kries, Frank. "The Racial Attitudes of the Polish Americans in Cook County." B.A. thesis, Lewis College, 1966.
ILoL

Zurawski, Joseph W. *Polish American History and Culture: A Classified Bibliography*. Chicago: Polish Museum of America, 1975. 218 p.
ICU
Over seventeen hundred entries of works in English. Indexed.

Social Environment—*Ethnic Groups*—Swedes

Olson, Ernst W. *History of the Swedes of Illinois*. 2 v. Chicago: Engberg-Holmberg Publishing Company, 1908. 918 p.
DLC, ICJ, ICU, IEG
Vol. 2 contains biographical sketches.

Social Environment—*Ethnic Groups*—Swiss

Hockings, Paul. "Albert Staub: The Story of a Wayward Immigrant." *Swiss-American Historical Society Newsletter* 14 (1978): 17–21.
DLC
Details the life of Staub, a nineteen-year-old Swiss immigrant, who committed a murder in Blue Island in 1857 and was hanged in Chicago in 1858.

Social Environment—*Ethnic Groups*—Welsh

Davies, Phillips G., ed. and trans. "Early Welsh Settlements in Illinois." *Journal of the Illinois State Historical Society* 70 (November 1977): 292–298.
DLC, I, IC, ICHi, ICN, ICU, IEN, IU
Translation of second chapter of Rev. Robert D. Thomas, *Hanes Cymry America* [*History of the Welsh in America*]. [Utica, New York, 1872]. Includes the Bridgeport Union Rolling Mill, the Welsh Union Church of Bridgeport, the Welsh Settlement at Braceville, Grundy County, and the Congregation Church of Braceville.

Social Environment—*Ethnic Groups*—Yugoslavs

Amerikanski Slovenec. Joliet, Illinois: American Slovenic Catholic Union, 1891–1941.
MnU—I
In Slovenian. Frequency varies. Moved publication to Chicago.

Ave Maria Koledar. Lemont, Illinois: Ave Maria Publishing Company, 1913–.
DLC, MnU—I
Annual publication in Slovenian. Also called *Slovenski Koledar.* Issued by Slovenski Franciskani.

Dwyer, Joseph D., ed. *Slovenes in the United States and Canada.* Minneapolis: Immigration History Research Center, University of Minnesota, 1981. 196 p.
MnU—I
Indexed by personal name. Mostly works in Slovenian.

Eterovich, Adam S. *A Guide and Bibliography to Research on Yugoslavs in the United States and Canada.* San Francisco: R & E Research Associates, 1975.
DLC

Eterovich, Adam S., ed. *Jugoslav Immigrant Bibliography.* Jugoslav-American Immigrant History Series, 1492–1900. San Francisco: 1965. 25 p.
MnU—I
Lists *Rodenje Bl. DJ. Marije* in Joliet as Croatian Catholic Church. *St. George* in Joliet as Serbian Orthodox Church.

Gobetz, Edward, ed. *Slovenian Heritage.* Willoughby Hills, Ohio: Slovenian Research Center of America, Inc., 1980. ports., photos., maps.
ILa
LaSalle, Illinois, pp. 417, 430–448.

Hail Mary. Joliet, Illinois: St. Joseph's Parish, c. 1932.
MnU—I
Monthly. Slovenian parish.

Odorizzi, Irene M. Planinsek. *Footsteps Through Time.* n.p., By the Author, 1978. 173 p., illus.
IDeKN—IRAD
References to Joliet. Photographs of "Simon Setina, Marble and Granite Monuments," Joliet, 1911. St. Joseph's School in Joliet.

Prisland, Marie. *From Slovenia—To America.* Chicago: The Slovenian Women's Union of America, 1978. 169 p., illus.
IDeKN—IRAD
Includes photographs of St. George Parish Singing Club, South Chicago, 1925, and Rev. Kazimie Zakrajsek, O.F.M., founder of Franciscan Seminary, Lemont, Illinois.

Tertiary Thoughts. Lemont, Illinois: Franciscan Fathers of the Holy Cross, c. 1946.
MnU—I
Monthly publication. Slovenian.

V Novo Bodocnost. Lemont, Illinois: St. Mary's Seminary, c. 1946.
MnU—I
In Slovenian. Frequency varies.

Zupanec, Rafko. *Spominski Album, Slovenskih Trgovcev in Obrtnikov.* Joliet, Illinois, 1913.
MnU—I
In Slovenian. Slovenian merchants in Illinois.

Social Environment—*Clubs and Social Organizations*

The Calumet Clubs. Illustrated. Chicago: Lanward Publishing Company, 1888. 73 p., plates.
ICHi
Descriptions and lists of members for Calumet, Chicago, LaSalle.

Historical Review of Activities During the First Thirty-Five Years of the District Lodge Illinois No. 8. Vasa Order of America. n.p., By the District Lodge No. 8. 336 p., photos.
ILeHi
See entry under Lodge 132 (Lemont), Lodge 147 (Lockport), and Lodge 202 (Joliet). Swedish-American organization.

Johnson, Esther L. *"Down Through the Years": the History of the Palos Park Woman's Club, 1902–1982.* Palos Park, Illinois: Palos Park Woman's Club, 1982. 51 p., illus.
IHi

LaSalle, Illinois. *Freemasons. Acacia Lodge No. 67. Rosier, June 30, 1947* [*of*] *Acacia Lodge, No. 67, A.F. & A.M., LaSalle, Illinois* [*and*]

LaSalle Chapter, No. 531, O.E.S., [LaSalle, Illinois], 1947. 23 p.
IHi

Matteson Lodge No. 175, Ancient Free and Accepted Masons, Centennial Celebration, 1855–1955. Joliet, Illinois, 1955. illus.
IJo

Joliet Masonic Lodge. Includes history of lodge.

Parsons, J. B., comp. *Patriotic Roster of LaSalle County, Illinois.* Pontiac, Illinois, 1899. 154 p., illus.
ICHi, ICN

Names and occupations of G.A.R. members.

Rules and By-laws of Mt. Joliet Lodge, No. 42, Joliet, Illinois: Constituted by Dispensation, October, 1845. By Warrant, October, 1846. Joliet, Illinois: C. & C. Zarley, Printers, 1848. 16 p.
IaCrM

Freemasons.

Rotary International, Club No. 171. *65 Years of Devotion and Accomplishment, 1915–1980: A Brief History of the Rotary Club of Morris, Illinois.* n.p., n.d., 29 p.
IMo

Includes list of charter members, 1915; list of past presidents.

Social Environment—*Charities and Social Agencies*

McCarthy, Peter H. *Twenty-two Years on Whiskey Row.* Joliet, Illinois: By the Author, 1931. 48 p., illus.
IJo

McCarthy was the superintendent of Morning Star Mission, Joliet.

U.S. Bureau of the Census. *Benevolent Institutions, 1910.* Washington: Government Printing Office, 1913. 441 p.
DLC, ICJ, ICU

Orphanages and other institutions for care of children, societies for protection of children, homes for care of adults, hospitals and sanitariums, dispensaries, and institutions for the blind and deaf listed individually and categorized by state and city. Information includes date of founding, supervising organization, population under care or supervision, receipts, and value of property.

U.S. Bureau of the Census. *Paupers in Almshouses, 1910.* Washington: Government Printing Office, 1915. 141 p.
DLC, ICU

Breakdown of population of paupers by sex, race, and nativity by county.

Social Environment—*Health and Welfare*

Connolly, Jane Francis. *The History of the Hygienic Institute for LaSalle, Peru and Oglesby, Illinois.* Thesis, St. Louis University, 1951.
MoSU

Hygienic Institute for LaSalle, Peru, and Oglesby, Illinois. *Annual Report of the Hygienic Institute Department of Health for LaSalle, Peru, and Oglesby.* Vol. 1–4. LaSalle, Illinois, 1914–1918. illus., plates.
ICJ, ICU

Report year ends April 30.

Illinois. State Board of Health. *Report of the Sanitary Investigations of the Illinois River and its Tributaries, with Special Reference to the Effect of the Sewage of Chicago on the DesPlaines and Illinois Rivers Prior to and After the Opening of the Chicago Drainage Canal.* Springfield, Illinois: Phillips Bros., State Printers, 1901. 219 p., map, diagrs.
DLC, ICJ

Contents: "Pollution of the Illinois River as Affected by the Drainage of Chicago and Other Cities," by J. A. Egan; "Chemical and Bacterial Examinations of the Waters of the Illinois River and its Principal Tributaries," by J. H. Long; "Identification of Bacteria Found in the Waters," by F. R. Zeit and G. Futerrer; "Preliminary Sanitary Survey of the Illinois River Drainage Basin," by J. A. Harman.

Kreider, George W. "William O. Ensign, M.D." *Journal of the Illinois State Historical Society* 11 (July 1918): 260.
DLC, I, IC, ICHi, ICN, ICU, IEN, IU

Obituary of William O. Ensign, M.D., first president of the LaSalle County Medical Society, 1885.

Arthritis News. Vol. 1. Ottawa, Illinois: Ottawa Arthritis Sanatorium and Diagnostic Clinic, 1942.
CLO

St. Joseph Hospital, Joliet, Illinois. *Centennial Issue. 1980–81 Annual Report*. n.p., ca. 1981.
IJo
An extensively illustrated commemorative history of the hospital and of the city.

St. Joseph's Hospital. *Annual Report*. Joliet, Illinois, n.d.
IMunS
Report year ends December 31. In charge of the Franciscan Sisters of the Sacred Heart.

Steadman, Robert F. *Public Health Organization in the Chicago Region*. Chicago: University of Chicago Press, 1930. 279 p., front., map.
DLC, ICU
Lengthy discussion of sanitary affairs, particularly drainage canals and pollution of water. Bibliography, pp. 270–272.

U.S. Census Office. *Tenth Census of the United States, 1880*. Vol. 21: *Report on the Defective, Dependent, and Delinquent Classes of the United States as Returned at the Tenth Census (June 1, 1880)*. Washington: Government Printing Office, 1888. 581 p.
ICJ, ICU
Insane, idiotic, blind, deaf, and dumb by race, sex, nativity by county. Population of Joliet Penitentiary. Police and crime statistics for Chicago, Joliet, LaSalle, and Ottawa.

U.S. Census Office. *Eleventh Census of the United States, 1890*. Vol. 2: *Report on the Insane, Feeble Minded, Deaf, Dumb, and Blind in the United States at the Eleventh Census: 1890*. Washington: Government Printing Office, 1895. 755 p.
ICU
By county with breakdown by sex, race, and nativity.

Will County Health Department. *Annual Report*. Joliet, Illinois, ca. 1943.
DNLM

Social Environment—*Reform Movements*

Armstrong, William C. *The Lundy Family and Their Descendents of Whatsoever Surname, With a Biographical Sketch of Benjamin Lundy*. New Brunswick, New Jersey: J. Heidingsfeld, 1902. 485 p., ports., index.
IBloWM
Lundy was an abolitionist in LaSalle County, Illinois.

Codding's Reply to Douglas: Substantially Codding's Speech, on Reply to Douglas, at Joliet and Geneva, in the Fall of '54. On the Kansas-Nebraska Bill, and Slavery Extension. n.p., ca. 1858. 16 p.
ICHi, IHi
Codding was a Chicago abolitionist and temperance lecturer.

Dillon, Merton L. *Benjamin Lundy and the Struggle for Negro Freedom*. Urbana: University of Illinois Press, 1966. 285 p.
DLC
Lundy was a prominent LaSalle County abolitionist editor.

Gara, Larry. "The Underground Railroad in Illinois." *Journal of the Illinois State Historical Society* 56 (Autumn 1963): 508–528.
DLC, I, IC, ICHi, ICN, ICU, IEN, IU
Fugitive slave incident in Ottawa.

"Historical Note." *Journal of the Illinois State Historical Society* 41 (March 1948): 67–74.
DLC, I, IC, ICHi, ICN, ICU, IEN, IU
Biographical sketch of Scottish-born grain dealer and abolitionist John Hossack of Ottawa, Illinois. Contains reprint of a long speech he made in his defense when on trial for violating the Fugitive Slave Law. Also contains one photograph of his house in Ottawa and another of his grain elevator on the I&M Canal.

Lawrence, George A. "Benjamin Lundy, Pioneer of Freedom." *Journal of the Illinois State Historical Society* 6 (July 1913): 174–205.
DLC, I, IC, ICHi, ICN, ICU, IEN, IU
Biographical sketch of LaSalle County abolitionist.

Lundy, Benjamin. *The Life, Travel and Opinions of Benjamin Lundy*. Philadelphia, Pennsylvania: W. D. Parrish, 1847.
DLC, IC, ICRL, IHi,

A Memorial to Benjamin Lundy, Pioneer Quaker Abolitionist, 1789–1839. Compiled by The Lundy Memorial Committee of the John Swaney School Alumni and Society of Friends

on the Occasion of the Centennial of His Death, n.p., 1939.
CSmH, NN

Short biography of LaSalle County abolitionist and publisher.

Ryan, John H. "A Chapter from the History of the Underground Railroad in Illinois." *Journal of the Illinois State Historical Society* 8 (April 1915): 23–30.
DLC, I, IC, ICHi, ICN, ICU, IEN, IU

An account of activities of Ottawa, Illinois abolitionists, and the trial of John Hossack of Ottawa for breaking the Fugitive Slave Law.

Scott, George Tressler. "Illinois' Testimonial to Mrs. Rutherford B. Hayes." *Journal of the Illinois State Historical Society* 46 (Spring 1953): 71–78.
DLC, I, IC, ICHi, ICN, ICU, IEN, IU

Six bound volumes of autographs. Mrs. Hayes was honored for banning alcohol from the White House during her husband's administration.

Strawn, Lydia, ed. "October." *The Ottawa Magazine* 1 (March 1896): 96 p., illus.
IO

Poem by Catherine C. Finch, Ottawa 1895. Article on Ottawa Women's Christian Temperance Union.

Strickland, Arvarh E. "The Illinois Background of Lincoln's Attitude Toward Slavery and the Negro." *Journal of the Illinois State Historical Society* 56 (Autumn 1963): 474–494.
DLC, I, IC, ICHi, ICN, ICU, IEN, IU

Contains a discussion of Benjamin Lundy and the Will County Anti-Slavery Society.

Will County Anti-Slavery Society. *Slave Code of the State of Illinois.* Joliet, Illinois: Will County Anti-Slavery Society, 1850. 11 p.
IHi

Abstract of laws in force in Illinois, which "affect the rights of colored people, as such, both bound and free. With notes. . . ."

Social Environment—*Sociological Studies*

Copeland, Lewis. "The Limits and Characteristics of Metropolitan Chicago." Ph.D. dissertation, University of Chicago, 1937. 275 p., maps, tables.
ICU

An assessment of the extent to which the inhabitants of the outlying counties of the Chicago metropolitan area had been brought within the economic, social, and cultural orbit of Chicago. The corridor cities of Will, Grundy, LaSalle, and southwest Cook counties are included in the analysis. Includes a chapter on the history of real estate development and evolution of land use patterns in the metropolitan area, 1830–1935.

Fleming, George Joseph. "Canal at Chicago: A Study in Political and Social History." Ph.D. dissertation, Catholic University of America, 1950.
DCU

Gillette, John Morris. *Culture Agencies of a Typical Manufacturing Group: South Chicago.* Chicago: University of Chicago Press, 1901.
ICU

An early sociological work.

Grossman, Ronald. *The Social Heritage of the DesPlaines Valley, Prepared for Open Lands Project.* Funded through Grants from Illinois Humanities Council, Field Foundation of Illinois, National Endowment for the Humanities, n.p., 1981. 6 p. (Photocopied.)
IJo

Hollinghead, August de Belmont. *Elmtown's Youth, the Impact of Social Classes on Adolescents.* New York: John Wiley & Sons, 1949. 480 p., maps, diagrs.
ICHi

Part of Committee on Human Development at University of Chicago. About Morris.

LaSalle–Peru Township High School, LaSalle, Illinois. *The Social Center, Welfare and Community Work of the Tri-Cities, LaSalle–Peru, Oglesby, Illinois. . . .* LaSalle, Illinois: LaSalle–Peru Township High School, 1915. 36 p., illus., plan.
IU, DHEW

Marrs, James Wyatt. *A High School Social Center: History and Description of the Social and Recreation Work of the LaSalle–Peru Township High School.* LaSalle, Illinois, 1921. 46 p., front., illus., ports.
IHi

Warner, William Lloyd. *Democracy in Jonesville, A Study of Quality and Inequality.* New York: Harper, 1949. 313 p., diagrs.
ICHi
About Morris, Illinois.

Social Environment—Religion

Social Environment—*Religion*—General

A Christian Brother. "The Christian Brothers at Joliet, Illinois." *Illinois Catholic Historical Review* 8 (July 1925): 82–84.
DLC, IC, ICN, ICU
On the establishment of a high school in Joliet.

Kirkham, E. Kay. *A Survey of American Church Records for the Period Before the Civil War, East of the Mississippi.* 2 v. Salt Lake City, 1958.
ICN, WHi
Vol. 1: major denominations. Vol. 2: minor denominations.

U.S. Census Office. *Eleventh Census of the United States, 1890.* Vol. 9: *Report on Statistics of Churches in the United States at the Eleventh Census: 1890.* Washington: Government Printing Office, 1894. 812 p.
ICU
Statistics by county and city for each denomination. Data include number of congregations and churches, seating capacity, value of church property, and number of communicants.

U.S. Bureau of the Census. *Religious Bodies: 1906.* Pt. 1: *Summary and General Tables.* Washington: Government Printing Office, 1910. 576 p.
DLC, ICJ, ICU, IEG
Statistics on church membership, value of church property, seating capacity of churches, debt of church organizations, and Sunday School enrollment for each denomination in Joliet. Membership statistics by denomination and by county.

U.S. Bureau of the Census. *Religious Bodies: 1916.* Pt. 1: *Summary and General Tables.* Washington: Government Printing Office, 1919. 594 p.
DLC, ICJ, ICU
Provides the same information as the 1906 report.

U.S. Bureau of the Census. *Religious Bodies: 1926.* Vol. 1: *Summary and Detailed Tables.* Washington: Government Printing Office, 1930. 769 p.
DLC, ICJ, ICU, IU
Statistics on church membership and Sunday School enrollment for each denomination in Joliet in 1920. Also, membership statistics by county and within county by denomination.

U.S. Bureau of the Census. *Religious Bodies: 1936.* Vol. 1 *Summary and Detailed Tables.* Washington: Government Printing Office, 1941. 943 p.
DLC, ICJ, ICU
Provides the same information as the 1926 report.

Social Environment—*Religion*—Missions

Schaefer, Catherine. "A Chronology of Missions and Churches in Illinois From 1675." *Illinois Catholic Historical Review* 1 (July/October 1918): 103–109, 253–256.
IC, ICN, ICU, IU
By year and location, 1675–1849.

Shaw, Thomas A. *Story of the LaSalle Mission. . . .* 2 v. Chicago: M. A. Donohue and Co., n.d.
IMunS
Catholic mission in LaSalle.

Social Environment—*Religion*—Baptists

Brown, J. Stanley. "Will County Baptist History." *Journal of the Illinois State Historical Society* 12 (October 1919): 417–421.
DLC, I, IC, ICHi, ICN, ICU, IEN, IU
Brief account of founding of Baptist churches in the county, 1834–1903.

The First Anniversary of the Ottawa Baptist Association, Held at Pawpaw Grove, Lee County, June 27 and 28, 1849. Address—. Higby, Corresponding Secretary, Ottawa, LaSalle County, Illinois. Princeton, New Jersey: Phillip Lynch, Printer, 1849. 15 p.
ISB

Association included LaSalle and Ottawa churches. Subsequent anniversary programs in 1850, 1851, 1852, 1854, 1856, 1857, 1858.

Fifth Annual Session of the Illinois River Baptist Association, Held in the Baptist Meeting House, in Lowell, LaSalle County, September 18, 19, and 20, A.D. 1840. Ottawa, Illinois: Weaver & Hise, Printers, 1840. 16 p.
ICU, IHi, ISB
Subsequent session pamphlets in 1842, 1845.

The History of the First Baptist Church of Ottawa, Illinois. Ottawa, Illinois: Republican Times Printing House, 1891. 51 p., ports.
IO
Begins in 1836.

Proceedings of the Fox River Association, at its Twentieth Annual Meeting, Held at Lockport, on the 6th and 7th of June, 1855. Oswego, Illinois: Kendall County Courier Print., 1855. 15 p., table.
ICU, IHi, ISB
Baptists.

Sechler, Earl Truman. "The Disciples of Christ in North Eastern Illinois." Masters thesis, University of Chicago, 1922.
ICU

Social Environment—*Religion*—Catholics

Achtermeier, William O. "A Calendar of the Archives of the Archdiocese of Chicago in the Feehan Memorial Library, Mundelien, Illinois: 1675–1918." 6 v. M.A. thesis, Loyola University—Chicago, 1968.
ICL

Assumption of the Blessed Virgin Mary Church. *Assumption BVM Parish (1903–1978).* South Hackensack, New Jersey: Custombook, 1977. 24 p., illus.
IMunS
West Pullman Catholic Church.

Assumption of the Blessed Virgin Mary Church (Polish). *Srebrny Jubileusz 1903–1928.* [West Pullman, Illinois, 1928.] illus., ports.
IMunS
West Pullman Catholic Church.

Burgler, J. C. *Geschichte der Kathol: Kirche Chicago's, mit besonderer Berucksichtigung des Katholischen Deutschthums.* Chicago: Wilhelm Kuhlmann, 1889. 222 p., illus.
ICHi
Woodcuts of early bishops and churches, including St. Adolphus Church in Lemont, St. Peter and Paul's Church in South Chicago, St. Benedictus Church in Blue Island, Catholic Church in Riverdale. In German.

Cathedral of St. Raymond Nonnatus. *History of the Joliet Diocese: Presented on the Occasion of the Dedication of the Cathedral of St. Raymond Nonnatus, May 26, 1955.* Joliet, Illinois, 1855. 188 p., illus. ports.
IMunS
Parish histories of St. Patrick's (Joliet), St. Dennis (Lockport), St. John's (Joliet), Immaculate Conception (Morris), St. Mary's Carmelite (Joliet), St. Joseph's (Lockport), Immaculate Conception (Braidwood), Sacred Heart (Joliet), Assumption of the Blessed Virgin Mary (Coal City), St. Joseph's (Joliet), Holy Cross (Joliet), Ss. Cyril and Methodius (Joliet), St. Anthony's (Joliet), St. Mary's Nativity (Joliet), St. Bernard's (Joliet), St. Mary's Assumption Greek Rite (Joliet), St. Raymond Nonnatus (Joliet), St. Joseph's (Rockdale), St. Thaddeus (Joliet), St. Paul the Apostle (Joliet), St. Stephen's (Joliet), St. Mary Magdalene (Joliet), St. Anne (Joliet), St. Jude (Joliet). Others: Joliet Catholic High School, Lewis College of Science and Technology, Franciscan Sisters of the Sacred Heart (Joliet), The Guardian Angel Home (Joliet), St. Francis Academy (Joliet), St. Joseph's Hospital (Joliet), Mantellate Sisters, Servants of Mary (Blue Island), College of St. Francis (Joliet).

A Cennennial Souvenior of St. Joseph's Parish, Peru, Illinois. Peru, Illinois 1954. 20 p., ports., illus.
IHi, ILa
Roster of pastors, building photographs, brief history of the parish.

Dedicated to the Sturdy Pioneers and Zealous Priests of St. John the Baptist Parish. Joliet, Illinois: Joliet Republican Printing Company, 1927. 80 p., illus., ports.
ICHi

Souvenior of diamond jubilee. Historical sketch of church, portraits of priests, advertisements.

Diamond Jubilee. Immaculate Conception B.V.M. Parish . . . 1882–1957. Chicago, 1957. 200 p., ports., plate.
ICHi
Story of the first Roman Catholic parish for the Polish people in the South Chicago area of Chicago, Illinois.

Ellis, John Tracy. *A Guide to American Catholic History.* Milwaukee, Wisconsin: Bruce Publishing Co., 1959. 147 p.
ICD, IU
Eight hundred titles.

Forty Years in the Life of the Saint Nicholas Russian Orthodox Greek Catholic Church of Joliet, Illinois. [Joliet, Illinois], 1947. 62 p., illus.
IJo
Includes history, portraits of ministers.

Fuertges, Theodore. "The History of St. Bede College and Abby, Peru, Illinois, 1889–1941." M.A. thesis, Catholic University, 1941.
DCU

Hobig, Marion A. *My God and My All.* Chicago: Franciscan Herald Press, 1977.
ICL
A history of their (Lemont) congregation.

Hoefling, Chrysantha. "No Man Can Chronicle." 1968. 8 p. (Typescript.)
ICL
Brief history of the Congregation of the Third Order of Saint Francis of Mary Immaculate (in Joliet).

Jubilate Deo, St. Francis Convent, 1865–1940. Joliet, Illinois, 1940. 23 p., illus., ports.
ICHi
Seventy-fifth anniversary booklet. History of convent with portraits. Photographs of buildings, statues.

Koenig, Rev. Msgr. Harry C. *A History of the Parishes of the Archdiocese of Chicago.* 2 v. Chicago: Archdiocese of Chicago, 1980. illus.
ICU

Koenig, Rev. Msgr. Harry C. *Caritas Christi Urget Nos: A History of the Offices, Agencies, and Institutions of the Archdiocese of Chicago.* 2 v. Chicago: Catholic Bishops of Chicago, 1981. illus.
ICU

Kuzma, George. *History of St. Joseph's Parish. Joliet, Illinois (1891–1941).* Joliet, Illinois, By the Author, 1941. 146 p., plates, ports.
IJo

O'Rourke, Alice. *The Good Work Begun: Centennial History of Peoria Diocese.* Chicago: R. R. Donnelley & Sons Company, 1970. 108 p., illus., map.
IMunS, IO
Includes LaSalle county Catholic churches: LaSalle, Marseilles, Seneca. Indexed.

"150 Years in the Kitchen": History and Cookbook of St. James at the Sag, Lemont, Illinois, Sesquicentennial Jubilee, 1833–1983. Lemont, Illinois, 1983, 283 p.
ILeHi
History and photographs interspersed with recipes.

One Hundred Twenty-fifth Anniversary of St. Patrick's Parish, LaSalle, Illinois: 1838–1963. . . . LaSalle, Illinois, 1963. 4 p., illus.
IMunS

Rodriguez, Navor. *Sintesis Historica de la Colonia Mexicana de Joliet, Illinois.* [Joliet, Illinois], n.d.
IJo
In Spanish. Indexed. Congregation formed 1914. Social and religious organizations and officers.

St. Benedict Church. Centennial: 1861–1961. Park Ridge, Illinois: Norman King Co., 1961. 131 p., illus.
IMunS
Blue Island Catholic Church.

St. Hyacinth Diamond Jubilee, 1875–1950. n.p., [1950].
ILa
Polish Catholic parish in Joliet.

St. Isidore Church. *Seventy-fifth Diamond Jubilee: 1900–1975.* [Blue Island, Illinois], 1975. illus.
IMunS
Blue Island Catholic Church.

St. John the Baptist Church, Joliet, Illinois. *100th Anniversary of the Founding of Parish of St. John's Church, 1852–1952, and the 75th Anniversary of the Arrival of Franciscans, 1877–1952.* Chicago: J. E. Marr, 1952. 110 p., illus., ports.
IMunS

"St. Mary's Croat Church, Joliet, Marks 50th Anniversary." *Zajednicar.* November 21, 1956, p. 9.
MnU—I

Saint Patrick's Parish, 1838: Dedication of the New St. Patrick's Church, May 18, 1919, Joliet, Illinois. Joliet, Illinois: Joliet Republican Printing Co., 1919. 36 p., illus.
IMunS

St. Patrick's Parish Guide . . . Christmas Day, 1912. Seneca, Illinois, 1912. 52 p., illus., ports.
ISe

St. Roch's Diamond Jubilee. LaSalle, Illinois, 1975. illus.
ILa
Slovenian parish in LaSalle, founded 1900. Founded by Franciscan Fathers of Lemont.

Saints Cyril and Methodius Church, 1844–1959. Lemont, Illinois, 1859.
ILa
Polish Catholic parish.

Schladen, Robert G. "The Beginnings of the Catholic Church in the Diocese of Peoria, Illinois." Thesis, St. Paul Seminary, St. Paul, Minnesota, n.d. 150 p. (Mimeographed.)
IMunS

Souvenir Memorial Volume of the Centennial Jubilee Observance of St. Patrick's Parish. LaSalle, Illinois: LaSalle Printing and Stationery Co., 1938. 102 p., illus., ports.
ICHi, ILa
LaSalle Mission Church in 1838 (Irish Catholics). Lists of members of 1938 societies.

Three Score Years of Church Archives: An Historical Sketch of St. Procopius Parish, Its Contributions to Chicago's Social and Religious Life. Published on the Occasion of the 60th Anniversary of Its Founding. n.p., 1935. ports., illus.
IHi
Bohemian Catholic parish in Pilsen. In Bohemian and English.

Veronica, Sister M. "A Reminiscence." *Illinois Catholic Historical Review* 11 (April 1929): 323–328.
DLC, IC, ICN, ICU
A history of St. Angelica's Academy of Morris, Illinois.

Werling, Norman G. *The First Catholic Church in Joliet, Illinois.* Chicago: The Carmelite Press, 1960. 158 p., illus., ports.
ICHi, IJo, IMunS
Contains sketch of Mount Joliet. Chapter on "Troubles on the Canal." Catholic priests arrive to help needy Irish workers on canal. Chart of Catholic church history in Will County.

Willging, Eugene P. "The Catholic Directories," *Catholic Historical Review* 20 (1934): 281–284.
DLC, IC, ICN, ICU
Lists the biographical sketches in directories, 1843–1867.

Zloty Jubileusz, Parafji, Ss. Cyryla, Metodego, 1844–1934. Lemont, Illinois, 1934.
ILeHi
In Polish. Ss. Cyril and Methodius Church in Lemont.

Župnija SV: Jozefa v Jolietu, Illinois. Njén Začétek in Naraščáj od Léta, 1891–1916. Slávnostna Izdája OB Srebŕnem Jubiléju Praznavánem, 1916. Joliet, Illinois, 1916. 135 p., illus., ports.
IJo
Index of members, 1916. In Slovenian.

Social Environment—*Religion*—Congregationalists

Brown, Anselm Byron. *Memorial Sermon, Occasioned by the Death of Rev. Joel Grant, Delivered at the Congregational Church, Lockport, Illinois, Sabbath Morning, March 8,*

*1874. . . .*Chicago: Steam Press of Cushing, Parsons & Thomas, 1874. 26 p.
ICHi

Centennial Anniversary, 1852–1952, The First Congregational Church of LaSalle, Illinois. LaSalle, Illinois, 1952. 20 p., illus.
ILa
Historical review, first members.

Directory. First Congregational Church. Peru, Illinois. n.p., 1931. 32 p.
IPe

First Congregational Church of Peru: Centennial 1837–1937. Peru, Illinois, n.d. 32 p.
IPe

History of the First Congregational Church of Peru, Illinois, 1837–1962: 125th Anniversary. n.p., 1962. 35 p., illus.
IPe

Manual of the Congregational Church and Society, Morris, Illinois. Morris, Illinois: C. E. Southard, 1867. 24 p.
ICN

Manual of the First Congregational Church in Ottawa, Illinois. Compiled January 1st, 1857. Ottawa, Illinois: Printed at the Office of the *Free Trader,* 1857. 19 p.
IO
Includes lists of pastors, deacons, and members by year of appointment, ordination, and joining.

Ninetieth Anniversary Program of the First Congregational Church of Peru, Illinois with a History From Its Beginning in 1837: Sunday, November 27 and Monday, November 28, 1927. n.p., 1927. 23 p.
IPe

Ottawa, Illinois. First Congregational Church. *Directory. . . . 1940.* [Ottawa, Illinois, 1940]. (Mimeographed.)
IHi

Sapp, Mrs. Ruth B., comp. *Commemorating the One Hundredth Anniversary of the First Congregational Church of Ottawa, Illinois.* Ottawa, Illinois: Illinois Office Supply Co., 1939. 31 p., illus., ports.
IHi, IU—HS

The Seventy-Third Annual Meeting of the Fox River Association of Congregational Churches at Marseilles, Illinois. April 8th and 9th, 1907. [Peru, Illinois], 1907.
IMa
Program.

Turner, Rev. E. B. *Forms Not Religion: A Discourse Preached on a Communion Occasion to the Congregational Church, Morris, Illinois, on the 27th of June, 1858.* Morris, Illinois: C. E. Southard, Book and Job Printer, 1858. 15 p.
ICHi, ICT, IHi
Church organized in 1848.

Social Environment—*Religion*—Episcopalians

Greggs, Clarence., comp. *Souvenir, One Hundredth Anniversary of Christ Episcopalian Church, Ottawa, Illinois . . . 1838–1938.* Ottawa, Illinois: Illinois Office Supply Co., 1938. 14 p., front., illus.
IHi
List of rectors. Records from 1852.

Parish Year Book. Christ Church (Episcopal). Joliet, Illinois: Joliet Sun Print., 1873. 23 p.
ICHi
Lists officers of parish, teachers, members. Statistics on baptisms, confirmations, marriages, burials. Minutes of meetings from 1835.

Social Environment—*Religion*—Lutherans

"Blue Island." Report and Analysis of Community Church Survey, Board of Home Missions (Augustana). Blue Island, Illinois, 1942.
ICLT
Statistics on six Lutheran churches and other denominations in Blue Island.

Centennial Book of Zion Evangelical and Reformed Church, Peru, Illinois, October 5 to 26, 1952. n.p., ca. 1952.
IPe

Deutsche Evangelische Zions Kirche . . . Andenken an die Einweihung der Vergrösserten und Verschönerten Zions Kirche der 21ten Januar, 1906. Peru, Illinois, 1906. 76 p., illus.
IHi
German Peru church. In German.

Diamond Jubilee, 1889–1964. Saint Philip's Lutheran Church. Blue Island, Illinois, 1964. 23 p., illus., ports.
ICLT
Photograph of old church, 1892–1954.

1874—One Hundred Years of Blessings—1974. St. Matthew Lutheran Church. Lemont, 1974.
ILeHi
Photographs of pastors, histories of building.

Fiftieth Anniversary, 1890–1940: St. Ausgarius Lutheran Church, Utica, Illinois, n.p., ca. 1940. 16 p., illus.
ICLT, IU—HS
History of congregation and buildings.

Fiftieth Anniversary of the Bethlehem Evangelical Lutheran Congregation . . . July 4–6, 1930. Morris, Illinois, 1930. 12 p., illus., ports.
ICHi
Scandinavian (Swedish). Statistics on baptisms, confirmations, weddings, funerals, communions, church organizations.

Fiftieth Anniversary of the Founding of Saint John's English Evangelical Lutheran Church of Joliet, Illinois. Joliet, Illinois, 1953. 20 p., ports.
ICLT
Roster of early members from 1903.

The First One Hundred Years, A Centennial History of Bethany Evangelical Lutheran Church, 1872–1972. Lemont, Illinois, 1972. 33 p., illus., ports.
ICLT
Late-nineteenth-century street scene. Photographs of the building of the present church.

Fortieth Anniversary Album, Siloa Swedish Evangelical Lutheran Church. Blue Island, Illinois, 1929. 16 p., illus.
ICLT
Advertisements. History of church buildings and church organizations. Services in English and Swedish.

To God Be the Glory: Centennial Celebration, Bethlehem Lutheran Church. A Century of Faith, 1882–1982. Joliet, Illinois, 1982. 136 p., illus.
ICCA
In Swedish. Confirmation classes from 1884.

Golden Jubilee, 1889–1939, Siloa Evangelical Lutheran Church. Blue Island, Illinois, 1939. 24 p., ports.
ICLT
Contains historical sketch. List of charter members.

Golden Jubilee Album of the Bethlehem Lutheran Church. . . . Joliet, Illinois, 1939. 160 p., illus., ports.
ICHi, ICLT, IJo
Contains history of the church, photographs and histories of societies, lists of confirmation classes from 1884. Some text in Swedish.

Golden Jubilee of the First German Evangelical Lutheran Church, 1871–1921. Joliet, Illinois, 1921. 23 p., illus.
ICLT
In English and German. Views of church. Short history.

"Hegewisch." In *Report and Analysis of Community Church Survey, Board of Home Missions.* Minneapolis, Minnesota, 1942.
ICLT
Statistical information on Lebanon and Trinity Lutheran churches by Augustana Lutheran Church. Also statistics on other church bodies in area.

The Joliet Lutheran. Vols. 1–40. Published in the Interest of the Swedish Evangelical Lutheran Bethlehem Church. Joliet, Illinois, 1919–1959.
ICLT
In Swedish and English. Monthly. Pledges of individuals to church, letters to the editor, events, church organization activities.

Jubilee Album, 1872–1947, Bethany Lutheran Church, Lemont. n.p., 1947. 28 p., illus.
ICLT
History of church and church organizations.

Kurze Geschichte der deutschen Evangelischen Zions-Gemeinde in Peru, LaSalle Co., Illinois aus vergilbten Blättern zusammengelesen und nach alten Berichten dargestellt von ihren dermaligen Pastor P. Brauns. n.p., n.d. 17 p.
ICHi

In German. Founded 1852. Names of officers. Last date mentioned, 1899.

Ninety Years of Grace, 1874–1965: St. Matthew Lutheran Church, Missouri Synod. Lemont, Illinois, 1974.
ILeHi

Siloa-Tabor Manadsblad. Luth. Siloa-Kyrkan. Blue Island, Illinois, 1919.
ICLT
In Swedish and English. Treasurer's report, donations.

Silver Jubilee, Sv. Ev. Lutheran Bethany Church. Lemont, Illinois, 1897.
ILeHi
Brief history.

65th Anniversary, 1911–1976, Our Savior's Lutheran Church, History of Our Church. Riverdale, Illinois, 1976. 6 p.
ICLT
Information on history of pastors, Sunday school, and so on.

Sustained to Serve, 1871–1971, Zion Evangelical Lutheran Church, Summit, Illinois. n.p., 1971. illus.
IBP
Photographs of church classes and groups.

Trinity Lutheran Church, 75th Anniversary, 1890–1965. [Utica, Illinois, 1965]. 9 p., illus., ports.
ICLT
Brief history. Norwegian and Swedish services.

Social Environment—*Religion*—Methodists

Dedication Souvenir Directory and Historical Sketch, The Ottawa Street Methodist Episcopal Church. [Joliet, Illinois, 1910]. 75 p., illus.
IJo
Organized 1833; advertisements.

Fiftieth Anniversary, 1924–1974, Ingalls Park Methodist Church, Joliet, Illinois. [Joliet, Illinois, 1974]. 24 p., illus.
IJo
Includes historical sketch.

The First Methodist Church, LaSalle, Illinois: Centennial Anniversary, 1950. [LaSalle, Illinois, 1950]. 16 p., illus.
IEG
History of Methodism in LaSalle; roll of ministers.

Grace United Methodist Church. Joliet, Illinois: Larkin and Avalon, c. 1970. 21 p., illus.
IJo
Formed in 1893.

Methodist Church: Seventy-fifth Anniversary Program, October 4th, 1936. Lemont, Illinois, 1936. 24 p.
IHi
Lemont Methodist church.

Richards Street United Methodist Church, Joliet, Illinois: 100 Years Serving God, 1872–1972. [Joliet, Illinois, 1972]. 12 p., illus.
IJo
Includes history.

Social Environment—*Religion*—Mormons

Kimball, Stanley B. "The Mormons in Illinois, 1838–1846: A Special Introduction." *Journal of the Illinois State Historical Society* 64 (Spring 1971): 4–21.
DLC, I, IC, ICHi, ICN, ICU, IEN, IU
Review of literature on Mormons in Illinois. LaSalle and Ottawa identified as residences for Joseph Smith relatives. Photographs. Footnotes.

Social Environment—*Religion*—Presbyterians

The First Presbyterian Church: Centennial Year, 1869–1969. (Ottawa). [Ottawa, Illinois, 1969]. illus.
IO
Church history. List of pastors from 1869.

Gage, Mrs. Lawrence F., Sr., and March, Miss Florence, comps. *A History of Brookfield Presbyterian Church.* n.p., n.d. 24 p.
IMa
Includes list of ministers, members, and friends of Marseilles church.

Gould, Nahum. "History of the Ottawa Presbytery." n.p., n.d. (Typescript.)
ICMcC

An Historical Sketch of the First Presbyterian Church of DuPage Township, Will County, Illinois: Commemorating the Celebration of the One Hundred Fifty-Fifth Anniversary of Its Organization, July 13, 1833–July 13, 1958. n.p., 1958. illus., ports.
IRo
Includes history of church. Reorganized in 1844. Photograph of old church building. List of elders and pastors from 1833.

Marshall, Albert B. *A Historical Address Delivered in the First Presbyterian Church of Morris, Illinois.* Morris, Illinois, 1876.
PPPrHi

A Memorial of Dr. James Lewis by the Central Presbyterian Church. Joliet, Illinois, 1899. 39 p., front.
ICHi, ICRL
Lewis (1836–1899) was pastor of the Central Presbyterian Church.

Social Environment—*Religion*—Universalists

Minutes of the Universalist General Convention Annual Session, 1861–1919. n.p., n.d.
ICMe
Statistics on contributions by parishes in Marseilles, Blue Island, and Joliet.

125th Anniversary Banquet Program of the Universalist Church of Joliet. Joliet, Illinois, 1961.
ICMe
Contains short history, 1844 constitution, early members.

The Universalist Companion, with an Almanac and Register. 18 v. n.p., [1836–1960].
ICMe
Title varies. Statistics of membership for Universalist church in Joliet, 1839–1960. Also information on defunct churches in Peru, Ottawa, LaSalle Prairie, Blue Island, and Marseilles.

Social Environment—*Archive Sources*

Bedford Park, Illinois. Bedford Park Public Library. Bedford Park Women's Club. Records. Seventy-five years.
IBP

Chicago, Illinois. Center for Research Libraries. American Missionary Association Manuscripts. Illinois, 1843–1878. 15 rolls microfilm.
ICRL
Correspondence from Congregational churches in Chicago, Ottawa, Joliet, Morris. Originals in Amistad Research Center, New Orleans, Louisiana.

Chicago, Illinois. Center for Research Libraries. Library of American Church Records, Nineteenth and Twentieth Centuries. Ecumenism Research Agency. (Microfilm.)
ICRL
Copies of official yearbooks, annual reports, minutes, and statistics for American Baptist Convention, 1814–1969; Assemblies of God, 1914–1965; Associated Reformed Presbyterian Church, 1803–1970; Brethren in Christ (formerly River Brethren), 1871–1970; Christian Church (Disciples), 1848–1965; Church of Christ, 1906–1963; Congregational Church, 1854–1961; Cumberland Presbyterian Church, 1810–1966; Seventh-Day Adventist Church, 1867–1970.

Chicago, Illinois. Chicago Historical Society. Zebina Eastman Collections. Seven boxes.
ICHi
Letter from Chester Hard of Ottawa to Anti-Slavery Reunion Committee giving names of other abolitionists in Ottawa area, 1874. Letter from A. M. Ebersol of LaSalle County about underground railroad in Ottawa, 1874. Letter from J. Beaumont of Joliet, planning to attend reunion, 1874. Letters from James M. Haven of San Francisco recalling abolitionist activities in Chicago and Joliet, 1875 and 1878. Letter from William Lewis of Putnam County describing burial place of Benjamin Lundy, 1864. Letter from George H. Woodruff of Will County about changes in lives of blacks, 1874.

Chicago, Illinois. Chicago Historical Society. Lemont, Illinois. Mount Assisi Convent. Miscellaneous pamphlets.
ICHi
Explanation of symbols in stained glass window.

Chicago, Illinois. Chicago Historical Society. The Ottawa Women's Club. Yearbooks. Ottawa, 1914–1915.
ICHi

Includes list of members.

Chicago, Illinois. Chicago Theological Seminary. Argo-Summit Survey. Chicago Congregational Union. Research and Survey Department, 1929–1930. One item.
ICT
Review of transportation, industry, housing, recreation, education, nationality distribution, institutions, and churches in Argo-Summit.

Chicago, Illinois. Chicago Theological Seminary. Berry, John W. Blue Island Survey. Chicago Congregational Union. Research and Survey Department, 1935. Two items.
ICT
Review of transportation, industry, housing, recreation, education, nationality distribution, institutions, and churches in Blue Island.

Chicago, Illinois. Chicago Theological Seminary. Fox River Association Minutes, 1872–1927. One folder.
ICT
Information on Congregational churches in Fox River Union (Lockport, Marseilles, Ottawa) and Chicago Association (Ottawa Free Church).

Chicago, Illinois. Chicago Theological Seminary. Materials Relative to Files.
ICT
Files of newspaper clippings on Congregational churches in Argo, Blue Island, LaSalle, Lockport, Marseilles, Morris, Ottawa, Peru.

Chicago, Illinois. Chicago Theological Seminary. South Chicago Mexican Congregational Church Records. 3 v.
ICT
Minute book, membership roll, Sunday School roll, 1932–1935. In Spanish.

Chicago, Illinois. Covenant Archives and Historical Library. Joliet Swedish Evangelical Lutheran Bethlehem Church.
ICCA
Contains fiftieth anniversary book, 1873–1923, with history of congregation (in Swedish); minutes of congregational meetings, 1885–1886, 1908–1929 (in Swedish); original constitution, n.d. (in Swedish); membership list, 1882–1937.

Chicago, Illinois. Covenant Archives and Historical Library. Lockport Swedish Evangelical Lutheran Church.
ICCA
Contains Constitution of January 19, 1873 (in Swedish); minutes of congregational meetings, 1873–1931 (in Swedish); membership list, 1892–1939; baptisms, 1917–1940; confirmation classes, 1919–1940; marriages, 1918–1940; deaths, 1917–1940; fifty-year history; centennial history.

Chicago, Illinois. Loyola University. Archives. Catholic Church Extension Society Photographs. Illinois, Joliet.
ICL
St. Francis Convent and Academy, exterior, n.d.

Chicago, Illinois. Lutheran School of Theology. Lutheran Church in America Archives. Minutes of Lutheran Conferences.
ICLT
Minutes of the biennial meetings of the General Council, 1866–1918 (German and English). Minutes of the biennial convention of the General Synod (in German and English). Yearbooks of the United Lutheran Church in America, 1917–1962. *The Lutheran,* 1919–1962. Chicago Synod Annual Convention minutes, 1896–1920. Illinois Synod I Annual Convention minutes, 1846–1867. Illinois Synod II Annual Convention minutes, 1920–1962. Wartburg Synod Annual Convention minutes, 1876–1962 (in German). Synod of the West Annual Convention minutes, 1839–1843. Northern Illinois Synod Annual Convention minutes, 1851–1919. Central Illinois Synod Annual Convention minutes, 1867–1896. Augustana Synod Annual Convention minutes, 1860–1962 (indexed). Illinois Conference minutes, 1851–1962 (includes Chicago, Fox Valley, and South Chicago Districts).

Chicago, Illinois. Meadville/Lombard Theological School. Joliet, Illinois. Universalist Church File. One folder.
ICMe
Miscellaneous correspondence, membership statistics.

DeKalb, Illinois. Northern Illinois University. Illinois Regional Archives Depository. Illinois

Nurses' Association Records. Four boxes. 2.5 feet.
IDeKN—IRAD

Grundy, Will, DeKalb, Kane, and Kendall counties. Contents include minutes, 1914–1975, unpublished histories of health facilities and nursing education programs at Joliet Junior College, Morris Hospital and Alumni Association, and St. Joseph Hospital, Joliet.

Evanston, Illinois. Garrett Seabury Theological Seminary. Illinois Local Church History Pamphlets. Vol. 4.
IEG

Contains Joliet's Ottawa Street M. E. Church. Directory, 1910.

Evanston, Illinois. Garrett Seabury Theological Seminary. Illinois Local Church History Pamphlets. Vol. 5.
IEG

Contains LaSalle's First M. E. Church, Directory, 1899; Lemont's M. E. Church, History, 1926; Marseilles's Asbury M. E. Church, Business Directory, c. 1930; Morris's First Methodist Episcopal Church, Directory and History, 1911.

Evanston, Illinois. Garrett Seabury Theological Seminary. Illinois Local Church History Pamphlets. Vol. 8.
IEG

Contains West Pullman's M. E. Church, Building Proposal, 1893.

Joliet, Illinois. Joliet Public Library. Vertical File. Joliet. Churches. One folder.
IJo

Includes various newspaper clippings on the following Joliet churches: St. Mary Magdalene, St. George Serbian Orthodox, Ss. Cyril and Methodius, Willow Avenue Presbyterian, St. John's, St. Patrick's, St. Mary's Nativity Croation, St. John Lutheran, Redeemer Lutheran, St. Stephen, Second Baptist, Central Presbyterian, Ridgewood Baptist, St. Nicholas, Ottawa Street United Methodist, Christ Episcopal.

LaSalle, Illinois LaSalle Public Library. Vertical File. LaSalle. Churches. One folder.
ILa

Contains two-page typewritten essay on Temple B'Nai Moshe in LaSalle. Synagogue in 1923.

Lemont, Illinois. Lemont Area Historical Society. Harry J. Swanson Memorial Library. Catholic Knights of Illinois, Branch No. 53, Account. Book. 1 v.
ILeHi

Dues record of Henry A. Gerbarz in St. Alphonsus Society, 1902, 1912.

Lemont, Illinois. Lemont Area Historical Society. Harry J. Swanson Memorial Library. Local History File. Lemont Knights of Pythias. One folder.
ILeHi

August 30, 1962, article, "'94 Lodge: The Knights of Pythias." Photographs of group in 1894. List of twenty-seven chapter members.

Lemont, Illinois. Lemont Area Historical Society. Harry J. Swanson Memorial Library. Local History File. Lemont United Methodist Church.
ILeHi

Miscellaneous material on church founded in 1861. Also known as "The Old Stone Church."

Lemont, Illinois. Lemont Area Historical Society. Harry J. Swanson Memorial Library. Local History File. Polish National Alliance. One folder.
ILeHi

Group 465 in Lemont formed in 1899. List of original members.

Lemont, Illinois. Lemont Area Historical Society. Harry J. Swanson Memorial Library. Local History File. St. Alphonsus Roman Catholic. One folder.
ILeHi

Souvenir of the New St. Alphonsus' Church, Lemont, 1922. Donors to Church in 1927. Photographs of pastors. Brief history, June 13, 1968. *Lemontan* article, "It's Centennial Year for St. Alphonsus." Short history, 1872.

Lemont, Illinois. Lemont Area Historical Society. Harry J. Swanson Memorial Library. Local History File. St. James Church, Sag. One folder.
ILeHi

"Ole St. James Church Has Air of Century Age." *Chicago Tribune*. February 16, 1972. Short history.

Lemont, Illinois. Lemont Area Historical Society. Harry J. Swanson Memorial Library. Local History File. St. Matthew Lutheran.
ILeHi
Contains newspaper clippings.

Lemont, Illinois. Lemont Area Historical Society. Harry J. Swanson Memorial Library. Local History File. St. Patrick's Church. One folder.
ILeHi
Includes various newspaper clippings and six-page typewritten history.

Lemont, Illinois. Lemont Area Historical Society. Harry J. Swanson Memorial Library. Local History File. Swedish Mission Church. One folder.
ILeHi
One-page summary of Mission in Lemont, torn down in 1907. Members joined Bethany Lutheran.

Lemont, Illinois. Lemont Area Historical Society. Harry J. Swanson Memorial Library. Official Record of the Proceedings of the Grand Lodge of Illinois, Knights of Pythias, Annual Conventions, 1910, 1911, 1912, 1914. 4 v.
ILeHi
Statistics and names of local lodges in LaSalle, Ottawa, Marseilles, Morris, South Chicago, Lemont, Joliet, Seneca, Blue Island, Lockport, Joliet, Peru, and South Chicago.

Lemont, Illinois. Lemont Area Historical Society. Harry J. Swanson Memorial Library. Protokalls Bok. Lodge 132, Vasa Order of America. 1 v.
ILeHi
Covers 1908–1909. Minutes of meetings and records of Lemont's Swedish Benefit Society.

Lockport, Illinois. Will County History Society. Lockport Women's Club Yearbooks.
ILoHi
For 1913/1914, 1924/1925, 1932/1933, 1934/1935, 1935/1936, 1938/1939, and 1939/1940.

Marseilles, Illinois. Marseilles Public Library. Local History Shelf. "Early Years in the History of the Brookfield Presbyterian Church, 1833–1850." By Miss Addie Marsh. 7 p.
IMa
Paper read at the Anniversary Service of Brookfield Presbyterian Church, Marseilles, Sunday, April 30, 1933.

Minneapolis, Minnesota. University of Minnesota. Immigration History Research Center. Rev. Bertrand Kotnik Papers, 1908–1965. 1.5 feet.
MnU—I
Slovenian American priest at St. Mary's Seminary, Lemont, Illinois.

Minneapolis, Minnesota. University of Minnesota. Immigration History Research Center. Kranjski-Slovenska Katoliska Jednota (Grand Carniolian Slovenian Catholic Union) Collection, 1894–1895. One inch.
MnU—I
Board of Director's Minutes, 1894–1895, of Joliet-based organization.

Morris, Illinois. Morris Public Library. Local History File. Coal City Cathedral. One folder.
IMo
Photographs and newspaper clippings. One folder.

Morris, Illinois. Morris Public Library. Morris County Medical Society. Record Book, 1901–1915, 1916–1931. 1 v.
IMo
Scrapbook of newspaper clippings.

Morris, Illinois. Morris Public Library. Morris, Illinois. Record of the Board of Health. 1 v.
IMo
Minutes of meetings, 1882–1897.

Morris, Illinois. Morris Public Library. Morris Woman's Club Yearbooks.
IMo
For 1927/1928. Includes annual calendars of the New Century Club. Some pieces date from 1896.

Northfield, Minnesota. Norwegian-American Historical Association. Johannes Johnsen Aasen Papers, 1862–1881. Eight items.
MnNSN
Daily account of a Norwegian businessman's journey in 1881 from Norway to Morris, Illinois.

Northfield, Minnesota. Norwegian-American Historical Association. Norwegians in the United States. Scrapbooks, 1923–1926. 4 v.
MnNSN
Includes history of LaSalle County congregation.

Northfield, Minnesota. Norwegian-American Historical Association. Sons of Norway Papers, 1907–1958. Four boxes.
MnNSN
Miscellaneous papers of various lodges and pamphlets containing historical sketches.

Northfield, Minnesota. Norwegian-American Historical Association. Torres Anfinsen Papers, 1819–1854. Six items.
MnNSN
Includes a letter written from Ottawa in 1851.

Ottawa, Illinois. Reddick Library. Vertical File. Ottawa. Churches. One folder.
IO
Contains material on Ottawa churches, including St. Columba Catholic, United Methodist, First Methodist, First Congregational, Seventh Day Adventist, First Baptist, First General Baptist, Southside Calvary Baptist, First Church of Christ, First Church of Christ Scientist, Church of God in Christ, First Nazarene Church, South Ottawa Church of the Nazarene, Christ Episcopal, Evangelical United Brethren, Church of Jesus Christ of Latter Day Saints, Reorganized Church of Jesus Christ of Latter Day Saints, Trinity Lutheran, Zion Lutheran, Epworth Methodist, Ottawa Bible Church, Pilgrim Holiness Church, Presbyterian Church, St. Francis Rectory, St. Mary's Catholic, St. Patrick's Rectory.

Ottawa, Illinois. Reddick Library. Young Ladies Library Association and Temperance Union. 1 v.
IO
Organized 1877. Constitution, officers, members, minutes (1877–1887).

Palos Heights, Illinois. Palos Heights Public Library. Local History Pamphlet File. Churches. One folder.
IPHe
Includes information on Sacred Heart Church, Stone Church, Reformed Church of Palos Heights, Palos United Methodist Church, Palos Park Presbyterian Church, Faith Evangelical Lutheran Church, Moraine Valley Baptist Church, Evangelical Lutheran Church of the Good Shepherd, St. Gerald's, St. Spyridon Greek Orthodox Church, St. Benedict's (Blue Island), Incarnation Parish, St. James of the Sag (Lemont), St. Alexander's.

Palos Heights, Illinois. Palos Heights Public Library. Local History Pamphlet File. Clubs and Organizations. One folder.
IPHe
Includes Palos Park Woman's Community Club.

Palos Hills, Illinois. Green Hills Public Library. Vertical File. Churches. Palos Hills. One folder.
IPHil
Contains information on St. Constantine and Helen Greek Orthodox Church, Sacred Heart Catholic.

Palos Hills, Illinois. Green Hills Public Library. Vertical File. St. James of the Sag. One folder.
IPHil
Contains "Sag Bulletin," a bimonthly newsletter of the Historical Society of St. James of the Sag, November 1971.

Palos Park, Illinois. Palos Park Public Library. Pamphlet File. Palos Park History. Churches. One folder.
IPP
File contains Winburn T. Thomas, "Church History." unpub. paper (History of the Congregational Church). "St. James Preserves Area's Irish Heritage," *Regional News,* January 14, 1982. 4 p., photos. Various news clippings, student papers, including "Religion in the Palos Area," by Greg Ozark, unpub. with information on the following churches: Reformed Church of Palos Heights, Sacred Heart Roman Catholic in Palos Hills, Palos United Methodist in Palos Heights, St. Alexander's Roman Catholic in Palos Heights.

Palos Park, Illinois. Palos Park Women's Club. Pamphlet File. Palos Park History. Palos Women's Club. One folder.
IPP

Established 1902. Includes photocopies of newspaper clippings and Esther L. Johnson, *"Down Through the Years": The History of the Palos Park Women's Club, 1902–1982*. Palos Park, Illinois: Palos Park Women's Club, 1982. 51 p., illus., ports., facsims., map.

Peru, Illinois. Peru Public Library. Churches. Scrapbook. 1 v.
IPe

Typewritten historical sketches of Peru churches, including St. Mary's Parish, St. John's Lutheran Church (German), Zion Evangelical Lutheran Church (German), St. Joseph's Catholic Church (German), First Church of Christ, St. Valentine's Parish (Polish), St. Mary's (non-German Catholic), First Congregational.

Springfield, Illinois. Archives of the State of Illinois. Inventory of Church Archives. Five cubic feet. no index.
I—Ar

Works Progress Administration 1930s notes on Illinois church archives. Uneven coverage. Files on Joliet Jewish Federation, Joliet Christ Church (Protestant Episcopal), Braidwood First Presbyterian, Coal City New Hope Presbyterian, Coal City Protestant Episcopal, St. James Mission, Marseilles St. Andrew's Mission (Protestant Episcopal), Peru St. Paul's (Protestant Episcopal), Seneca St. James Mission (Protestant Episcopal), Utica St. George's (Protestant Episcopal), Ottawa Christ Church (Protestant Episcopal), Morris St. Thomas's (Protestant Episcopal), Braidwood St. George's (Protestant Episcopal), Joliet Holy Comforter (Protestant Episcopal), Blue Island St. Aidan's Mission (Protestant Episcopal), Lockport St. John's (Protestant Episcopal), LaSalle St. Mark's (Protestant Episcopal).

Springfield, Illinois. Archives of the State of Illinois. U.S. Department of the Interior. Seventh Federal Census. Social Statistic Schedules for Illinois, 1850.
I—Ar

Ninety-one Illinois counties. 1 v. No index. Information entered for the following: Estates: value of real and personal property. Annual taxes: types, amount, method of payment. Schools: types, number, teachers, pupils, endowments. Crops: types, shortages, quantities, yields. Libraries: numbers, volumes. Newspapers: circulation, political affiliation, frequency. Churches: numbers, denominations, accommodations, value of property. Pauperism: birthplaces, costs. Crime: birthplaces. Wages: averages with and without board.

Springfield, Illinois. Archives of the State of Illinois. U.S. Department of Interior. Eighth Federal Census. Social Statistic Schedules for Illinois, 1860.
I—Ar

One hundred and two Illinois counties. 1 v. No index. Information entered for the following: Estates: value of real and personal property. Annual taxes: types, amount, method of payment. Schools: types, number, teachers, pupils, endowments. Crops: types, shortages, quantities, yields. Libraries: numbers, volumes. Newspapers: circulation, political affiliation, frequency. Churches: numbers, denominations, accomodations, value of property. Pauperism: birthplaces, costs. Crime: birthplaces. Wages: averages with and without board.

Springfield, Illinois. Archives of the State of Illinois. U.S. Department of Interior. Eighth Federal Census. Social Statistic Schedules for Illinois, 1870.
I—Ar

One hundred and two Illinois counties. 1 v. No index. Information entered for the following: Estates: value of real and personal property. Annual taxes: types, amount, method of payment. Schools: types, number, teachers, pupils, endowments. Crops: types, shortages, quantities, yields. Libraries: numbers, volumes. Newspapers: circulation, political affiliation, frequency. Churches: numbers, denominations, accomodations, value of property. Pauperism: birthplaces, costs. Crime: birthplaces. Wages: averages with and without board.

Springfield, Illinois. Illinois State Historical Library. Federal Writers' Project. Illinois. Lithuanians in Chicago and Historical Notes. One folder.
IHi

As of 1936, the largest Lithuanian community in Chicago was in Pullman, and the fifth largest was in Archer Heights. There were other settlements in West Pullman, Bridgeport, Brighton Park, and South Chicago. Folder contains about fifteen typewritten essays on immigration, church life, ethnic institutions, and Lithuanian culture.

Springfield, Illinois. Illinois State Historical Library. Federal Writers' Project. Illinois. Poles in Chicago, in Illinois, and in America. Two folders.
IHi

Folders contain about fifteen typewritten essays ranging in length from one paragraph to thirty pages. Essays provide information on settlement, churches, culture, and community institutions in Argo, Joliet, Peru, LaSalle, Lemont, and Chicago.

Springfield, Illinois. Illinois State Historical Library. Independent Order of Odd Fellows: Grand Lodge of Illinois. Records, 1851–1970. 116 feet.
IHi

Contains records of local lodges, including Blue Island Visitors Register. Lemont Financial Secretary's Ledger. Marseilles Minutes, 1874–1924, 1929–1960. Question Book, 1883–1892, 1869–1903. Membership Register, 1918–1954. Roll Book, 1930–1959. Visitors Register, 1873–1932. Receipts, 1941–1958. Cash Book, 1940–1958. Account Book, 1932–1936, 1950–1951. Minutes, 1872–1931. Question Book, 1872–1923.

Springfield, Illinois. Illinois State Historical Library. Hutchinson, Florence. "Posts of the Grand Army of the Republic, Department of Illinois." Jacksonville Area Genealogical Society, 1974. (Unpublished manuscript.)
IHi

Author copied information from the Adjutant General's Quarterly Reports of individual posts of the G.A.R. to compile genealogical information on member's name, birthplace, residence, occupation, war service, rank, company, discharge date. Information on Post 472, Lemont; Post 521, Pullman; Post 489, Riverdale; Post 109, South Chicago; Post 764, West Pullman; Post 389, Morris; Post 242, LaSalle; Post 281, Marseilles; Post 21, Ottawa; Post 14, Ottawa; Post 456, Peru; and Post 324, Seneca.

Springfield, Illinois. Illinois State Historical Library. William Royal Papers, 1823–1870. 108 items.
IHi

Royal was circuit rider, Fox River Mission. M. E. Church records, letters, documents, memoirs. Memoranda of church membership for missions: Ottawa, 1834–1855; Fox River, 1835–1836.

Springfield, Illinois. Illinois State Historical Library. Women's Christian Working Association, Presbyterian Church, Ottawa, Illinois. Autograph Album, 1880–1881. 6 v.
IHi

Presented to Mrs. Rutherford B. Hayes.

Springfield, Illinois. Illinois State Historical Library. Ottawa Driving Park Association, Ottawa. Three ledgers.
IHi

Minutes, 1905–1907, 1910–1921. Receipts and expenditures, 1905–1908, 1910–1912.

Summit, Illinois. Summit-Argo Public Library. Local History File. Churches. One folder.
ISA

Contains various pamphlets on St. Blase Church (Polish), St. Joseph Church; Shiloh Missionary Church; Record of St. Joseph School, Attendance Records, 1913–1914; Summit Congregational Church (1917); various photographs of church groups.

Summit, Illinois. Summit-Argo Public Library. Local History File. Community Organizations. One folder.
ISA

Contains pamphlets on St. Blase Mother's Club, Argo-Summit Lions, American Legion.

Summit, Illinois. Summit-Argo Public Library. Local History File. Junior Associates of the Argo-Summit Woman's Club. One folder.
ISA

Contains constitution of 1929, various correspondence, minutes of meetings, 1936–1972. Also called "The Suburbanites."

Utica, Illinois. LaSalle County Historical Society Museum. Churches Binder. 1 v.
IUtHi

Records include St. George's Episcopal in Utica (members, burials, marriages). Information and photographs on churches, including Utica Baptist, Ottawa Methodist, Ottawa Presbyterian, LaSalle Trinity United Church of Christ.

Utica, Illinois. LaSalle County Historical Society Museum. Minute Book, Post No. 135., G.A.R., 1882–97. 1 v.
IUtHi

Met at Oddfellows Hall. Includes members and dues ledger.

Military records, court records, and administrative reports of public works projects comprise the chief sources of published material in this section. However, most of the localities in the corridor have preserved government records, some of which date back to the nineteenth century. The Census Bureau also published data on taxation and expenditures of municipal and county governments. Local newspapers contain a wealth of information on local politics and government. Minutes of city council meetings were usually published in one of the daily newspapers, and political campaigns received extensive coverage.

A researcher should find out the date of municipal elections (most were held in April) and scan the newspapers for accounts of nominating sessions, editorials on particular candidates, and accounts of campaigns and elections. Since nineteenth-century newspapers were openly partisan, the researcher should, if possible, consult more than one newspaper for descriptions of particular campaigns. A similar procedure can be used for research into local participation in state and national campaigns.

Politics and Government—*Local Government*

Allen, Harry Kenneth. *Costs and Services of Local Government in Selected Illinois Counties.* Bureau of Business Research, Bulletin, No. 52. Urbana, Illinois: University of Illinois, 1936. 52 p., map, tables.
DLC, IU

Beers, Fred T. *Laws and Ordinances of the City of Peru.* Peru, Illinois: Daily News-Herald, 1890.
IPe, IUtHi

Bennett, Edward H. and Parsons, William E. *City Plan of Joliet.* Assisted by H. T. Frost. Joliet, Illinois: Joliet City Plan Commission, 1921. 44 p., front., illus., plans, diagrs.
DLC, ICJ, IU

Binmore, Henry. *Cities and Villages: A Compilation of General Laws of the State of Illinois, Governing and Regulating the Powers and Duties and the Exercise Thereof, by Cities and Villages, with Explanatory Annotations Digesting the Decisions of the Supreme and Appellate Courts to Date, and with Numerous Practical and Approved Precedents and Forms, Useful in Carrying on the Details of Executive and Legislative Business.* Chicago: E. B. Myers and Company, 1890.
DLC

Bushnell, W. and Gray, O. C. *Revised Ordinances of the City of Ottawa. . . .* Ottawa, Illinois: Ottawa Republican Book and Job Printing Office, 1855. 89 p.
IO

Seidel, John V. *Proceedings of the Council of the City of LaSalle, Illinois for the Fiscal Year Ending April 30, 1929.* LaSalle, Illinois, 1929. 123 p., tables. (Mimeographed.)
ILa

Includes financial report.

Code of Ordinances of Lockport, Illinois. Cincinnati, Ohio: Anderson Publishing Co., 1983.
ILo

Includes roster of city officials, 1904–1985.

Elazar, Daniel J. *Cities of the Prairie: The Metropolitan Frontier and American Politics.* New York: Basic Books, 1970. 514 p., maps.
ICU

Information on the demographic and political history of Joliet is included in this work on comparative urban politics.

Holbrook, James G. and McKeown, Charles J., comps. and eds. *Revised Joliet Code of 1939.* Joliet, Illinois: City Council of Joliet, 1939. 258 p., map, plan.
ICU, IU

Containing general ordinances of Joliet, as revised, cited, and amended.

Joliet, Illinois. *Annual Reports of City Officers. . . .* Various publishers, 1890/1891, 1892/1893, 1901/1902, 1903/1904, 1904/1905, 1907/1908, 1911/1912, 1914/1915, 1926/1927.
IU

Joliet City Council. *Journal of Proceeding. . . .* 41 v. Joliet, Illinois, 1890–1930.
ICU, IU, NN
Report year ends April 30.

Joliet City Council. *Track Elevation Ordinance No. 2071.* Joliet, Illinois: City Council of Joliet, 1903. 1 p.
DLC
Information on railroad crossings of Joliet.

Kelly, Robert T., arr. *The City Charter and Revised Ordinances of the City of Joliet.* Joliet, Illinois: City Council of Joliet, 1884. 374 p.
IU
Also, acts of the General Assembly of the State of Illinois, relating to the city of Joliet.

Lemont, Illinois. *Ordinances, 1882.* 6 v. Lemont, Illinois, 1882.
ICN

Madden, John F. and Stead, William H. *Revised Ordinances of the City of Ottawa.* Ottawa, Illinois: Free Trader Printing House, 1891.
IUtHi

Merriam, Charles E., Parratt, Spencer D., and Lepawsky, Albert. *The Government of the Metropolitan Region of Chicago.* Chicago: University of Chicago Press, 1933. 193 p., maps, front.
DLC, ICHi, ICJ, ICU

Miller, Glen E., comp. and ed. *Municipal Code of Lockport.* Lockport, Illinois, 1940.
DLC, ICN
General ordinances of the city of Lockport, Illinois, as revised, codified, and amended.

Morris, Illinois. City Council. *The Revised Ordinances of the City of Morris, Grundy County, Illinois.* Revised and compiled by Order of the City Council, June, 1859. n.p., [1859].
IMo

Morris, Illinois. City Council. *The Revised Ordinances of the City of Morris, Grundy County, Illinois.* Revised and Published by the Order of the City Council, April 8, A.D. 1878. Morris, Illinois: The Herald Steam Printing Rooms, 1878.
IMo

Morris, Illinois. City Council. *Revised Ordinances of the City of Morris, Illinois.* Revised and Consolidated by D. R. Anderson. Published by the Authority of City Council, D. C. Young, City Attorney. Morris: Morris Herald, 1901.
IMo

Oglesby, Illinois. *The Municipal Code of Oglesby, Illinois, 1942.* Oglesby, Illinois: City Council of Oglesby, 1943.
ICU, IU
Commission form of municipal government.

O'Neal, Frank Emerson. "County Government in Illinois: An Analysis and Proposal." A.M. thesis, University of Chicago, 1935. 102 p.
ICU

Parratt, Spencer Delbert. "The Governments of the Metropolitan Area of Chicago." Ph.D. dissertation, University of Chicago, 1932.
ICU

Ordinances of the Village of Lemont, Cook County, Illinois. Revised by J. McKenzie Cleland and Published by Authority of the President and Board of Trustees. Lemont, Illinois: Advertiser Steam Print., 1890.
ILeHi

Revised Ordinances of the City of Ottawa, LaSalle County, State of Illinois. Revised and Arranged Under the Direction of Lester H. Strawn and Herman S. Blanchard. Ottawa, Illinois: Journal Printing House, 1906. 382 p.
IO

Revised Ordinances of the Village of Blue Island, Printed and Published by Authority of the President and Board of Trustees of the Village of Blue Island. Blue Island, Illinois, 1880. 32 p.
ICHi

Schreiber, Paul H. *The Municipal Code of the City of Blue Island, Illinois.* Revised and compiled by Works Projects Administration, Illinois, 1941. Blue Island, Illinois, 1941. 384 p., tables.
DLC

Sprague, Morrill, Lagger, Louis, and Rickson, Sam C., arrs. *Charter and Revised Ordinances of the City of Joliet,* [*in*] *Will County, State of*

Illinois. Joliet, Illinois: Joliet Republican Printing Co., 1902. 583 p.
DLC

Politics and Government—*Finance and Taxation*

Cook, Walter Wellman. *The Tax Problem in Illinois*. Chicago: University of Chicago Press, 1934. 57 p., diagrs.
DLC, ICU, IU

Meyers, Herman B. *Handbook of Cook County Institutions. Review of its Business Transactions and Financial Affairs for Year 1895*. Chicago: Press of W. C. Hollister, 1896. 160 p., illus., ports.
DLC

Politics and Government—*Regional Planning*

Bach, Ira J. "A Reconsideration of the 1909 'Plan of Chicago.'" *Chicago History* 2 (Spring/Summer 1973): 132–141.
DLC, IC, ICF, ICHi, ICN, ICU, IU

Burnham, Daniel H., and Bennett, Edward H. *Plan of Chicago*. Chicago: The Commercial Club, 1909.
DLC, ICHi, ICJ

Burnham, Daniel H., Jr. and Kingery, Robert. *Planning the Region of Chicago*. Chicago: Chicago Regional Planning Association, 1956.
ICHi, ICJ

Politics and Government—*Boundaries*

Illinois. Secretary of State. *Counties of Illinois: Their Origin and Evolution, with Twenty-Three Maps Showing the Original and Present Boundary Lines of Each County of the State*. Compiled and Published by Louis L. Emmerson, Secretary of State. Springfield: Illinois State Journal Co., State Printers, 1919. 67 p., maps.
DLC, ICJ, ICU, IU

Illinois. Secretary of State. *Counties of Illinois, Their Origin and Evolution with Twenty-three Maps Showing the Original and Present Boundary Lines of Each County of the State*. Springfield: Printed by the Authority of the State of Illinois, 1934.
DLC, ICJ, IU

Rose, James A. *Counties of Illinois: Their Origin and Evolution, with Twenty-three Maps Showing the Original and the Present Boundary Lines of Each County of the State*. Springfield: Illinois State Journal Co., State Printers, 1906. 67 p., maps.
DLC, ICJ, IU

Politics and Government—*Local Political Parties and Elections*

Bennett, Fremont O. *Politics and Politicians of Chicago, Cook County, and Illinois: Memorial Volume, 1787–1888. A Complete Record of Municipal, County, State, and National Politics from the Earliest Period to the Present Time. . . .* Chicago: The Blakely Printing Co., 1886. 612 p.
DLC, ICU

Illinois Political Directory 1898–1899. 2 v. Chicago: W. L. Bodine Co., 1898.
DLC, ICJ

The Illinois Voter. Vol. 1–. Chicago: Illinois League of Women Voters, 1921–.
I, IC, ICJ, ICU
Monthly publication.

Przybylski, James Thaddeus. "Twentieth Century Elections in Illinois: Patterns of Partisan Change." Ph.D. dissertation. University of Illinois, 1972.
IU

Registered Voters in Grundy County, 1917. Compiled by the *Morris Daily Herald*. n.p., n.d. 32 p. (Typescript.)
IMo
By precinct.

Thompson, Charles M. "Elections and Election Machinery in Illinois, 1818–1848." *Journal of the Illinois State Historical Society* 7 (January 1915): 379–388.
DLC, I, IC, ICHi, ICN, ICU, IEN, IU
General description of how campaigns were run in Illinois. Contains coded map that displays vote in 1856 presidential election by county.

Townsend, Walter A. *Illinois Democracy: A History of the Party and Its Representative Members—Past and Present, George Lee Willis, Senior Author, Assisted by a Staff of*

Distinguished Party Leaders and Political Commentators. 3 v. Louisville, Kentucky: Democratic Historical Society, 1935.
DLC

Politics and Government—*State Politics*

Bean, Philip George. "Illinois Politics During the New Deal." Ph.D. dissertation, University of Illinois, 1976.
IU

Church, Charles A. *History of the Republican Party in Illinois, 1854–1912; with a Review of the Aggressions of the Slave Power, by Charles A. Church....* Rockford, Illinois: Press of Wilson Brothers Company, Printers, 1912. 248 p., port., front.
DLC, ICU

Dante, Harris L. "Reconstruction Politics in Illinois: 1860–1872." Ph.D. dissertation, University of Chicago, 1950.
ICU

Goldstein, Joel Harris. "The Effects of the Adoption of Woman Suffrage: Sex Differences in Voting Behavior—Illinois 1914–1921." Ph.D. dissertation, University of Chicago, 1973.
ICU

Illinois. Emergency Relief Commission. *Budgetary Standards and Practices in Illinois During October 1938.* n.p., 1939. 64 p.
IU

Contains tables displaying number of relief recipients and maximum monthly allotments for families on relief by county and municipality.

"Letters to Gustav Koerner, 1837–1863." *Illinois State Historical Society Transactions* 12 (1907): 222–246.
DLC, IC, ICU

Contains a letter from Joliet citizen J. McRoberts.

Lusk, David W. *Eighty Years of Illinois: Politics and Politicians, Anecdotes and Incidents. A Succinct History of the State. 1809–1889.* 3rd ed. rev. and enl. Springfield: H. W. Rokker, 1889. 126 p., front., port.
DLC, ICN, ICUB, IU

Poster, John Benjamin. "Gubernatorial Politics and State School Financing, the Case of Illinois: 1933–1940." Ph.D. dissertation, University of Chicago, 1972.
ICU

Prominent Democrats of Illinois: A Brief History of the Rise and Progress of the Democratic Party of Illinois. Biographical Sketches of Well-Known Democrats, Together with Portrait Likenesses of Many Familiar Faces.... Chicago: Democratic Publishing Co., 1899. 307 p., front., ports.
DLC, ICarbS

Raum, Green B. *History of Illinois Republicanism, Embracing a History of the Republican Party in the State to the Present Time ... With Biographies of Its Founders and Supporters ... Also a Chronological Statement of Important Political Events Since 1774.* Chicago: Rollins Pub. Co., 1900. 815 p., port., front.
DLC, ICJ, ICU

Senning, John P. "The Know-Nothing Movement in Illinois from 1854–1856." *Journal of the Illinois State Historical Society* 7 (April 1914): 7–34.
DLC, I, IC, ICHi, ICN, ICU, IEN, IU

Based partly on Will County sources. Contains maps showing percent foreign born in each county in 1850 and election returns by county for 1856.

Thompson, Charles Manfred. "The Origin and Development of the Whig Party in Illinois, 1834–1845." Ph.D. dissertation, University of Illinois, 1913.
IU

Wright, John S. "The Background and Formation of the Republican Party in Illinois, 1846–60." Ph.D. dissertation, University of Chicago, 1946.
ICU

Politics and Government—*Federal Politics*

Bowker, Mabel Edna. "The Indian Policy of the United States from 1789–1841." Ph.D. dissertation, Boston University, 1926. 345 p. illus., maps.
ICN

Bibliography, pp. 1–14. A comprehensive study that treats Indian cessions between 1789 and 1841. Illinois is included.

Carter, Clarence Edwin, ed. *The Territorial Papers of the United States.* Washington: U.S. Dept. of State, Government Printing Office, 1934.
ICN
Vol. 2 and 3: the Territory Northwest of the River Ohio, 1787–1803.
Vol. 7: the Territory of Indiana, 1800–1810.
Vol. 16 and 17: the Territory of Illinois, 1809–1818.

Hibbard, Benjamin H. *History of Public Land Policies.* New York: MacMillan Co., 1924. 591 p., illus., diagrs.
DLC, ICJ, ICU
Bibliography, pp. 573–379. Reprinted: New York: P. Smith, 1939. Madison, Wisconsin: University of Wisconsin Press, 1965. With a foreword by Paul W. Gates.

Hubbard, Paul G. "The Lincoln-McLellan Presidential Election in Illinois." Ph.D. dissertation. University of Illinois, 1949.
IU

Hunt, John Eddy. *The Acknowledgement of Deeds, Containing All the Statutes, Territorial and State, of Illinois . . . and Decisions of the Courts Construing Different Provisions of the Law.* Chicago: By the Author, 1896.
DLC

James, Harold P. "Lincoln's Own State in the Election of 1860." Ph.D. dissertation, University of Illinois, 1943.
IU

Kelly, Edith Packard, "Northern Illinois in the Great Whig Convention." *Illinois State Historical Society Trans*actions 20 (1914): 137–149.
DLC, IC, ICU
Whigs supported construction of Illinois and Michigan Canal. List of Cook County delegates.

McCarty, Dwight Gaylord. *The Territorial Governors of The Old Northwest, a Study in Territorial Administration.* Iowa City, Iowa: The State Historical Society of Iowa, 1910. 210 p.
DLC, ICU

Myer, Walter E. "The Presidential Campaign of 1860 in Illinois. . . ." A.M. thesis, University of Chicago, 1913. 63 p.
ICU

Osborn, Richards C. "Federal Indian Policy and Public Attitudes on Indian Policy in Illinois, 1818–1837." Term paper, University of Illinois, 1967. 18 p.
IU—HS

Philbrick, Francis S., ed. *The Laws of Illinois Territory, 1809–1818.* Collections of the Illinois State Historical Library, No. 25. Springfield, 1950. 386 p.
DLC, ICF, ICN, ICU, IEN

Pope, Nathaniel. *Laws of the Territory of Illinois, Revised and Digested Under the Authority of the Legislature.* 2 v. Kaskaskia, Illinois: Matthew Duncan, Printer to the Territory, 1915.
DLC

Ritze, C. C. "In Defense of Mrs. Lincoln." *Journal of the Illinois State Historical Society* 30 (April 1937): 5–69.
DLC, I, IC, ICHi, ICN, ICU, IEN, IU
Contains references to the Ottawa Lincoln-Douglas Debate.

U.S. Federal Civil Works Administration for Illinois. *Report.* n.p., 1934.
ICU, IU
The CWA was a New Deal agency that administered temporary research and public works projects during the winter of 1933/1934. The report describes each project and provides statistics by county on the number of participants in the CWA.

U.S. War Department. *Pottawatamie Indians: Letter from the Secretary of War, Transmitting the Information Required by the Resolution of the House of Representatives of the 16th District, Respecting the Treaties of the 20th, 26th, and 27th of October, 1832, with the Pottawatamie Indians. March 1, 1839. Read, and Laid upon the Table.* Washington, 1839. 13 p.
ICN
Correspondence regarding the Treaty of 1832, in which the Potawatomi ceded their lands east of the Illinois River. Correspondents include Commissioners Jonathan Jennings, John M. Davis, and Marks Crume and Secretary of War Lewis Cass.

The United States and the Indians: A Collection of Congressional Documents Relating to the

Indians. Vol. 1–. 11th Cong. Washington: Government Printing Office, 1810–. illus., maps.
ICN

Wheeler, Joanne Elizabeth. "The Origins of Populism in the Political Structure of a Midwestern State: Partisan Preference in Illinois, 1876–1892." Ph.D. dissertation, State University of New York at Buffalo, 1976.
NBuC

Politics and Government—*Crime, Justice, and Law*

Politics and Government—*Crime, Justice, and Law*—General

Anthony, Elliott. *A Digest of Cases Decided by the Supreme Court of the State of Illinois from 1819 to 1854 Including the 14th Volume of the Illinois Appellate Reports Together with Tables, Titles and References*. Philadelphia: T & E Johnson, 1855. 745 p.
ICU

Binmore, Henry. *Digest of Decisions of the Supreme Court and Appellate Courts of Illinois as Embraced in Volumes 111 to [137]: Both Inclusive Illinois Supreme Court Reports and Volumes 15 to [41]. Both Inclusive Appellate Court Reports*. 2 v. Chicago: E. B. Myers, 1890–1893.
ICU

Bowman, Ralph Waldo, comp. *A Table of Cases and Citations in the Illinois Supreme and Appellate Court Reports, with Supplement, Embracing Supreme Vols. 1–183, Appellate Vols. 1–85 Inclusive and Cases Appealed from Appellate to Supreme Court and to the U.S. Supreme Court (Vols. 168–175 Inclusive), Showing Whether Affirmed, Reversed, Etc. with All Citations of Fed., Mich., Wis., Ind., Iowa, O. and O. St., Mass., N.Y. Reps., and the L.R.A.* Chicago: The Lawyer's Cooperative Publishing Co., 1900. 298 p.
ICU

Henderson, James. Max. *Callaghan's Illinois Digest: Second Series, Covering Illinois Decisions from 300 Illinois, 367 Illinois, and from 221 Illinois Appellate Through 293 Illinois Appellate; Also Federal and United States Supreme Court Decisions Pertaining to Illinois Law from 1922 to Date; with References to Statutes, Texts, and Collateral Annotations*. Chicago: Callaghan and Co., 1938–.
ICU

Hill, Edward Judson. *Illinois State Digest: A Digest of Illinois Reports 1819 to 1887*. 6 v. Chicago: E. J. Hill, 1879–1887.
ICU

Illinois Association for Criminal Justice. *Illinois Crime Survey*. Chicago: Illinois Association for Criminal Justice in Cooperation with the Chicago Crime Commission, 1929. 1,108 p., tables, diagrs., maps.
ICU

The Illinois Citations and Table of Cases: Being a Complete Alphabetical List of Cases Under Both Parties by Title in the Illinois Supreme Court Reports, Breese to Vol. 214 Inclusive, and the Illinois Appellate Court Reports, Volumes 1 to 114 Inclusive, and Carried Through to the United States Supreme Court, Showing the Entire History of Each Case and Giving a Syllabus Index Where Every Point in the Syllabus Is Located in the Opinion . . . Arranged for the Reprint as Well as the Original Edition of the Official Volumes with Duplicate References to the National Reporter System, Followed by a Numerical Index. . . . Springfield: Fiske and Co., 1906–.
ICU

Illinois. U.S. District Court. *The Decision of How Judge Blodgett, of the United States Circuit Court, of the Northern District of Illinois Rendered May 20, 1886, in the Case of Foster vs. the City of Joliet*. Joliet, Illinois: The Press Company, Printers, 1886. 4 p.
ICHi

Longsdor, George F. *Callaghan's Illinois Digest, Complete from Breese to 300 Illinois, and from 1 to 221 Illinois Appellate, Also Including Illinois Points Found in the United States Reports and in Federal Reports to Date*. 15 v. Chicago: Callaghan and Co., 1923–1926.
ICU

U.S. Bureau of the Census. *Special Reports. Prisoners and Juvenile Delinquents in Institutions, 1904*. Washington: Government Printing Office, 1907. 295 p.
ICU

Population of the Joliet penitentiary and each county jail and workhouse broken down by sex, race, and nativity.

U.S. Census Office. *Eleventh Census of the United States, 1890.* Vol. 3: *Report on Crime, Pauperism, and Benevolence in the United States at the Eleventh Census: 1890.* Pt. 2: *General Tables.* Washington: Government Printing Office, 1895. 1,035 p.
ICU, NN

Racial and ethnic characteristics of prisoners at the Joliet penitentiary, prisoners in all county jails, paupers in each county almshouse, each hospital, and other "benevolent" institutions (by county and by institution). Also statistics on crime and local police forces for Chicago, Joliet, Ottawa, and LaSalle.

Wilken, Ralph H., comp. and ed. *Callaghan & Company's Illinois Digest: Permanent Compilation of the Cumulative Quarterly, Covering Appellate Vols. 179 to 235 Inclusive: Supreme Court Vols. 260 to 318 Inclusive.* 6 v. Chicago: Callaghan and Co., 1916–26.
ICU

Politics and Government—*Crime, Justice, and Law*—Prisons

Greene, William Robert. "Development of the Illinois State Penitentiary System." Ph.D. dissertation, Illinois State University, 1953.
INS

Greene, William Robert. "Early Development of the Illinois State Penitentiary System." *Journal of the Illinois State Historical Society* 70 (August 1977): 185–195.
DLC, I, IC, ICHi, ICN, ICU, IEN, IU

Includes a brief account of the construction of the state penitentiary outside Joliet and the controversy over the commercial use of convict labor.

Illinois. Board of Administration. *First–Seventh Annual Report, January 1, 1910 to September 30, 1916, Inclusive (Including the Biennial Reports of the State Charitable Institutions for the Above Period).* Springfield: State Printers, 1911–[1917].
ICU

Balance sheet reports for the Joliet penitentiary.

Illinois. Dept. of Public Welfare. *The Illinoisian: The Official Publication of the Illinois Prisons.* Vol. 1. Joliet, Illinois, 1940–1941.
DLC

Illinois. Dept. of Public Welfare. *Statistical Review of Prisons, Reformatories and Correctional Schools, 1939.* Springfield: Dept. of Public Welfare, 1939.
DLC

Illinois. General Assembly. House of Representatives. Special Committee to Investigate State Institutions. *Investigation of Illinois State Institutions: 45th General Assembly. 1908. Testimony, Findings, and Debates.* Chicago: Regan Printing House, 1908. 1,002 p., ports.
IHi, ICN, ICU

Includes investigation of Joliet penitentiary.

Illinois. State Penitentiary, Joliet. *Rules and Regulations . . . Approved and Adopted . . . May 6, 1899.* Joliet, Illinois, 1899. 46 p.
DLC, ICU, IU

Jacobs, James B. "Stateville: A Natural History of a Maximum Security Prison." 2 v. Ph.D. dissertation, University of Chicago, 1975.
ICU

Jacobs, James B. *Stateville: The Penitentiary in Mass Society.* Chicago: University of Chicago Press, 1977. 281 p.
ICU

The first two chapters cover the years 1925–1961.

Ragen, Joseph Edward and Finston, Charles. *Inside the World's Toughest Prison.* Springfield: C. C Thomas, 1962. 927 p., illus., 24 p.
WU

State Penitentiary Prisoners, eds. *The Joliet Prison Post.* Vol. 1–. Joliet, Illinois: Board of Commissioners and the Warden of the Illinois State Penitentiary, 1914. illus.
DLC

Monthly.

Politics and Government—*Military Affairs*

Politics and Government—*Military Affairs*—General

Collins, Holdridge Ozro. *History of the Illinois National Guard, from the Reorganization of the First Regiment in September 1874, to the*

Enactment of the Military Code, in May 1879. Chicago: Press of Black & Beach, 1884. 101 p.
DLC, ICJ, ICN, ICU

Homer's Roll of Honor: Being the Military Record of Her Sons Who Have Served the Country in the Volunteer Armies of the Republic. Lockport, Illinois, 1973. 19 p.
ILo

Revolution to Civil War. Lists rank, regiment, date of enlistment, discharge, and death of Homer Township residents. Will County.

Matheny, Willard R., comp. *Index, Soldiers of 1812, Illinois.* n.p., 1947.
ICN

Illinois. Veteran's Commission. *Honor Roll, State of Illinois, Grundy County.* n.p., 1956.
IMo

U.S. Census Office. *Sixth Census of the United States, 1840. A Census of Pensioners for Revolutionary or Military Services; with their Names, Ages, and Places of Residence . . . Under the Act for Taking the Sixth Census (1840).* Washington: Blair and Rives, 1841. 195 pp.
DLC, ICJ, ICN

Illinois, pp. 186–188.

Walker, Homer A. *Illinois Pensioners List of the Revolution, 1812, and Indian Wars.* Washington, ca. 1955. 123 p.
ICHi, ICN

Includes names of soldiers, widows, and heirs.

Politics and Government—*Military Affairs*—Indian Wars

Brown, Lizzie M. "The Pacification of the Indians After the War of 1812." *Journal of the Illinois State Historical Society* 8 (January 1916): 550–559.
DLC, I, IC, ICHi, ICN, ICU, IEN, IU

Includes description of pacification efforts in northeastern Illinois.

Clifton, James A. "Chicago, September 14, 1833: The Last Great Indian Treaty in the Old Northwest." *Chicago History* 9 (Summer 1980): 86–97.
DLC, IC, ICF, ICHi, ICN, ICU, IU

The United Band of Potawatomi, Ottawa, and Chippewa ceded five million acres in Illinois and Wisconsin.

Frazier, Arthur H. "The Military Frontier: Fort Dearborn." *Chicago History* 9 (Summer 1980): 80–85.
DLC, IC, ICF, ICHi, ICN, ICU, IU

Gerwing, Anselm J. "The Chicago Indian Treaty of 1833." *Journal of the Illinois State Historical Society* 57 (Summer 1964): 117–142. map.
DLC, I, IC, ICHi, ICN, ICU, IEN, IU

Photograph of Shabbona and white negotiators. Sketch of Chicago buildings in 1833. Map, footnotes.

Grover, Frank R. "Indian Treaties Affecting Lands in Illinois." *Journal of the Illinois State Historical Society* 8 (October 1915): 379–419.
DLC, I, IC, ICHi, ICN, ICU, IEN, IU

Treaty of Greenville (1795); Treaty of 1804 with the Sacs and Foxes; Treaty of August 24, 1816, at St. Louis; Treaty of August 29, 1821, at Chicago; Treaty of Prairie du Chien concluded August 19, 1825; Treaty of Prairie du Chien of July 29, 1829; final Treaty of Chicago, concluded September 26, 1833.

Hagan, William T. "The Sauk and Fox Treaty of 1804." *Missouri Historical Review* 51 (October 1956): 1–7.
DLC, I, IC, ICL, ICN, ICU, IU

Hauberg, John H. "The Black Hawk War, 1831–1832." *Illinois State Historical Society Transactions (1932):* 31–134.
DLC, IC, ICU

Helm, Lt. Linai T. *The Fort Dearborn Massacre: Written in 1814 by One of the Survivors.* Edited by Nelly Kinzie Gordon. Chicago: Rand, McNally & Company, 1912. 137 p., illus.
IO

Kinzie, Juliette Augusta. *Narrative of the Massacre at Chicago, August 15, 1812, and of Some Preceding Events.* Chicago: Fergus Printing Company, 1914.
ICN

Originally published in 1844.

Illinois. Military and Naval Dept. *Record of the Services of Illinois Soldiers in the Black Hawk War, 1831–32, and in the Mexican War, 1846–8, Containing a Complete Roster of Commis-*

sioned Officers and Enlisted Men of Both Wars, Taken from the Official Rolls on File in the War Department, Washington, D.C. with an Appendix, Giving a Record of the Services of the Illinois Militia, Rangers, and Riflemen, in Protecting the Frontier from the Ravages of the Indians from 1810 to 1813. Prepared and published by Authority of the Thirty-second General Assembly, by Isaac H. Elliot, Adjutant-General of the State of Illinois. Springfield: H. S. Rokker, State Printer, 1882. 343 p.
DLC, ICU
Reprinted in 1902.

Illinois. Office of the Governor. *Report of the Commissioners on Indian Disturbances, Together with a Communication from the Governor Accompanying the Same.* Vandalia, Illinois: Printed by M. Greiner, Public Printer. 6 p.
IHi

Quaife, Milo M. "The Chicago Treaty of 1833." *Wisconsin Magazine of History* 1 (March 1918): 287–303.
DLC, IC, ICN, ICU

Rouiston, Jessie Adams. "The Effect of the Black Hawk War on the Development of the Northwest." Ph.D. dissertation, University of Chicago, 1910. 47 p.
ICU

Silliman, Sue I. "The Chicago Indian Treaty of 1821." *Michigan History Magazine* 6 (1922): 194–197.
DLC, IC, ICL, ICN, ICU, IU

Treaties Between the United States of America and the Ottawa and Other Tribes of Indians, Concluded August 29, 1821, and March 28, 1836. Grand Rapids, Michigan: Enquirer Print., c. 1841. 23 p.
ICN
Caption title: "Articles of a Treaty Made and Concluded at Chicago, in the State of Illinois, Between Lewis Cass and Solomon Sibley, Commissioners of the United States, and the Ottawa, Chippewa, and Pattiwatima Nations of Indians."

Wakefield, John A. *A History of the War between the United States and the Sac and Fox Nations of Indians, and Parts of Other Disaffected Tribes of Indians, in the Years Eighteen Hundred and Twenty-Seven, Thirty-One, and Thirty-Two.* Jacksonville, Illinois: Calvin Goudy, 1834.
ICN
Reprinted as *Wakefield's History of the Black Hawk War.* Edited by Frank E. Stevens. Chicago: Caxton Club, 1908.

Wallace, Anthony F. C. *Prelude to Disaster: The Course of Indian-White Relations Which Led to the Black Hawk War of 1832.* Springfield: Illinois State Historical Library, 1970.
ICN, ICU

Webb, George W., comp. *Chronological List of Engagements Between the Regular Army of the United States and Various Tribes of Hostile Indians Which Occurred During the Years 1790–1898, Inclusive.* St. Joseph, Missouri: Wing Printing and Publishing Company, 1939. 141 p., front.
ICN, ICU

Whitney, Ellen M., comp. and ed. *The Black Hawk War, 1831–1832.* Collections of the Illinois State Historical Library, Vols. 35–38. Springfield: Illinois State Historical Library, 1970–1978.
ICN, ICU
With an introduction by Anthony F. C. Wallace. Selected from manuscripts in the Illinois State Historical Library. Bibliography, Vol. 35, pp. xix–xx.

Williams, Mentor L. "John Kinzie's Narrative of the Fort Dearborn Massacre." *Journal of the Illinois State Historical Society* 46 (Winter 1953): 343–362.
DLC, I, IC, ICHi, ICN, ICU, IEN, IU

"Young Dad Joe's Ride." *Journal of the Illinois State Historical Society* 18 (January 1926): 1001–1003.
DLC, I, IC, ICHi, ICN, ICU, IEN, IU
Explication of a poem that commemorates the activities of Young Dad Joe at Peru, during the Black Hawk War.

Young, Ella Smith. "Pioneer Life Among the Indians." *Journal of the Illinois State Historical Society* 18 (January 1926): 981–998.
DLC, I, IC, ICHi, ICN, ICU, IEN, IU
Reminiscence of her grandfather, Dad Joe Smith, and his experiences in the Black Hawk War. Peru resident.

Politics and Government—*Military Affairs*—Mexican War

Canaday, Dayton W. "Voice of the Volunteer of 1847." *Journal of the Illinois State Historical Society* 44 (Autumn 1951): 199–209.
DLC, I, IC, ICHi, ICN, ICU, IEN, IU
Concerns *On the Picket Guard,* a newspaper published in Saltillo, Mexico, by two soldiers from Ottawa, Illinois.

Illinois. Military and Naval Dept. *Official Register of the Officers of the Illinois Volunteers, for 1846.* Published by Order of the Governor of the State of Illinois. Alton, Illinois: Printed at the *Telegraph* Office, 1846. 8 p.
IHi
Issued by Adjutant General's Office.

Politics and Government—*Military Affairs*—Civil War

Burton, William L. *Descriptive Bibliography of the Civil War Manuscripts in Illinois.* Springfield: Illinois State Historical Society, 1966.
IHi, ICU
Lists papers and letters in Illinois libraries. Indexed.

Certificate of Incorporation of the Fifty-Seventh Regiment Illinois Infantry (1861–1865), Colony and Mutual Benefit Association. . . . Chicago, 1876. 24 p.
ICHi
LaSalle County men.

Civil War Roster, Will County Illinois. 2 v. Lockport, Illinois: Will County Historical Society, 1981.
ICHi, IJo
Lists name, rank, enlistment date, regiment, years of service, discharge or death date.

Cole, Arthur Charles. *The Era of the Civil War, 1848–1870.* Springfield: Illinois Centennial Commission, 1918. 499 p., front., ports., maps.
DLC, ICJ, ICU

Constitution, Proceedings and Roster of the 37th Ill. Volunteer Infantry (1861–1865) Veterans Association. Chicago: Printed by Skeen & Stuart Stationery Co., 1885. 21 p.
IHi
LaSalle County men.

Dayton, Aretas A. "Recruitment and Conscription in Illinois During the Civil War." Ph.D. dissertation, University of Illinois, 1940.
IU

Dornbusch, Charles E. *Regimental Publications and Personal Narratives of the Civil War, A Checklist, Northern States.* New York: New York Public Library: 1961.
DLC, ICU
Vol. 1, Pt. 1: Illinois. Lists locations of histories and documents of regiments and batteries. Mustering-in and -out dates of each battery.

First Reunion of the Thirty-ninth Illinois Veteran Volunteers (1861–1865), Held at Bloomington, Ill. December 18, 1866. Chicago: S. Emerson, Book and Job Printer, 1867.
ICHi
LaSalle County men.

Illinois. Adjutant General. *Grundy County Residents Who Served in the U.S. Civil War.* n.p., 1886.
IMo
Eighteen regiments.

Johnson, Kathy. *Colonel Frederick Bartleson.* Lockport, Illinois: The Will County Historical Society, 1983. 8 p. (Mimeographed.)
ILo
Bartleson was a Civil War colonel in Joliet.

Military History and Reminiscences of the Thirteenth Regiment of Illinois Volunteer Infantry (1861–1864) in the Civil War in the United States, 1861–65. Chicago: Woman's Temperance Publishing Association, 1892. 672 p., front., plates, ports., maps, facsim.
DLC
LaSalle County men.

Munden, Kenneth White. *Guide to Federal Archives Relating to the Civil War.* Washington: National Archives and Records Service, General Services Administration, 1962. 721 p., facsim.
DLC, ICU

Parsons, J. B. *Patriotic Roster [of] LaSalle County, Illinois.* Pontiac, Illinois: 1899. 154 p.
IUtHi
Names and residences of survivors.

Proceedings of the . . . 1st Reunion of the Eleventh Regiment, Illinois Volunteer Infantry

(1861–1865). . . . Ottawa, Illinois: Osman & Hapeman, Printers and Publishers, 1875.
CSmH, NjP
LaSalle County men.

Roster of the Eighth Illinois Cavalry (1861–1865). Leavenworth, Kansas: Ketcheson & Reeves, 1888. 31 p.
IHi, IU
LaSalle County men.

Schmidt, Royal Jae. *Bugles in a Dream, DuPage County in the Civil War.* Illinois Portfolio Series, No. 5. Elmhurst, Illinois: Historical Society of DuPage County, 1962. 31 p., illus.
ICN

Semi-centennial Roster, 1865–1915: Cushman's Brigade Souvenir . . . 1st Annual Reunion of 53rd Illinois Infantry (1861–1865), Ottawa, Illinois, July 22nd, 1915. Ottawa, Illinois, 1915. 26 p., illus.
IHi
Ottawa regiment.

Tusken, Roger. "In the Bastille of the Rebels." *Journal of the Illinois State Historical Society* 56 (Summer 1963): 316–339. ports.
DLC, I, IC, ICHi, ICN, ICU, IEN, IU
Excerpts from the George R. Lodge diary manuscript, made while he was a confederate prisoner. Lodge was First Lieutenant of Company G, 53rd Illinois Infantry, and a native of Ottawa.

United States. War Department. Library. *Bibliography of State Participation in the Civil War, 1861–1866.* Washington: Government Printing Office, 1913.
DLC, ICU
Lists regimental histories, government reports, and sections of county histories covering the Civil War.

Vance, J. W. *Report of the Adjutant-General of the State of Illinois . . . Containing Reports for the Years 1861–1866.* 8 v. Springfield, 1867.
DLC, ICarbS, ICJ
Vol. 1: 7th–15th regiment infantry rosters.
Vol. 2: 16th–35th regiment infantry rosters.
Vol. 3: 36th–55th regiment infantry rosters.
Vol. 4: 56th–77th regiment infantry rosters.
Vol. 5: 78th–105th regiment infantry rosters.
Vol. 6: 106th–131st regiment infantry rosters.
Vol. 7: 132nd–156th regiment infantry rosters, 1–5th regiments cavalry.
Vol. 8: 6th–17th regiment cavalry, 1st–2nd regiment artillery.

Wilson, William, comp. *History and Roster of the Surviving Members of the 4th Illinois Cavalry (1861–1864) with Their Residences.* Chicago: Straub & Hallott, Printer, 1884. 12 p., illus.
CSmH
Ottawa regiment.

Woodruff, George H. *Fifteen Years Ago: Or, the Patriotism of Will County, Designed to Preserve the Names and Memory of Will County Soldiers, Both Officers and Privates—Both Living and Dead: To Tell Something of What They Suffered, in the Great Struggle to Preserve Our Nationality.* Joliet, Illinois: J. Goodspeed, 1876. 82 p. port.
ICN

Politics and Government—*Military Affairs*—Spanish-American War

Historical Sketch, First Cavalry, Illinois National Guard: Including its Spanish War Service as the First Cavalry, Illinois Volunteers. Chicago, 1901. 84 p., illus., ports.
DLC, WHi

Illinois. Military and Naval Dept. *Adjutant General's Report, Containing the Complete Muster-out Rolls of the Illinois Volunteers who Served in the Spanish-American War, 1898 and 1899.* 5 v. n.p., 1902–1904.
ICJ, ICN, IU

Peterson, Clarence Stewart. *Known Military Dead During the Spanish-American War and the Philippine Insurrection.* Baltimore, 1958. 130 p.
DLC

Politics and Government—*Military Affairs*—World War I

Grundy County Roll of Honor: Men Who Served in World War I. Morris, Illinois: Morris Daily Herald, 1917. 14 p. (Typescript.)
IMo

Alphabetical list of names, outfits, dates of enlistment.

Service Record Book of Men and Women of Seneca, Illinois and Community, Sponsored by the American Legion Auxiliary Unit No. 457. n.p., n.d.
ISe

Vital statistics and photographs of Seneca veterans from World War I and World War II.

Politics and Government—*Archive Sources*

East Point, Georgia. Federal Archive and Records Center. *Records of the Selective Service System* [*World War I*]. (Microfilm.)
GEp—FARC

Arranged by county and then alphabetically by last name of individual. Information included is similar to the kind found in the Manuscript Census of Population, but the records only cover males aged eighteen through forty-four at the time of the draft.

Chicago, Illinois. Chicago Historical Society. Napoleon Bonaparte Bartlett Papers. Twenty-one items.
ICHi

Letters from Morris private in Company C, 76th Illinois Infantry, to members of his family. Describes life in Camp Butler and Vicksburg.

Chicago, Illinois. Chicago Historical Society. Mary Cheney Hall Papers. Fifteen items.
ICHi

Letters from Joliet resident to Mrs. Lewis Meachan of New Haven, Vermont, 1863–1865. News and activities of 100th Illinois Infantry during Civil War.

Chicago, Illinois. Chicago Historical Society. "Invitation from Jesse O. Norton to Senator James R. Doolittle." September 20, 1860.
ICHi

Norton, a Republican U.S. Representative from Joliet, invited Doolittle to address a Republican mass meeting.

Chicago, Illinois. Newberry Library. Ayer Collection. Illinois Territory-Governor, 1809–1818 (Ninian Edwards). "Six Letters to Isaac Shelby, Ill. Terr. March 7, March 14; Kaskaskia, May 18; Russelville, Logan County, Aug. 18, 1813; U.S. Saline, Illinois Terr., March 17, Elvirado, Apr. 4, 1814." 17 p.
ICN

Indians of Illinois Territory, especially the Miami; estimate of strength of other tribes.

Chicago, Illinois. Newberry Library. Ayer Collection. Indian Treaty. 1795 (Wyandots, Delawares, Shawnees, Ottawas, Chippewas, Potawatomies, Miamis, Eel River, Weas, Kickapoos, Prankashawa and Kaskaskias, U.S.). "A treaty of peace signed at Greenville, Aug. 3, 1795, between the United States of America and the above-mentioned tribes, Anthony Wayne, Commissioner; signed at Philadelphia, December 22, 1795, by George Washington, President." One leaf, parchment.
ICN

Photostat from original in Library of Congress.

Chicago, Illinois. University of Chicago Library. Illinois State Penitentiary, Joliet. Records, 1878. 1 v. 460 p.
ICU

Testimony of prisoners given to the commissioners of Illinois State Penitentiary, appointed to investigate reports of brutality. Unpublished guide.

Lockport, Illinois. Will County Historical Society. Civil War Bounty Record, 1862–1865.
ILoHi

From Will County Clerk's office.

Lockport, Illinois. Will County Historical Society. John A. Hotch Diary.
ILoHi

Hotch was a member of the 78th Illinois Infantry.

Morris, Illinois. Morris Public Library. City of Morris Bond Record. 1 v.
IMo

Covers 1930–1948. With index. Bonds were sold for local improvements.

Morris, Illinois. Morris Public Library. Local History Room. Papers on Delinquent Assessments and Tax Receipts, 1913 and 1922. One-half foot.
IMo

Morris, Illinois. Morris Public Library. George W. Smith Letters, 1862–1865. 1 v.
IMo

Compiled by Thelma R. Miller. Written during Smith's service in the Civil War. Grundy County resident. Written to wife Mary, father Thomas, children Levi, Emeline, and Albert.

Normal, Illinois. Illinois State University. Illinois Regional Archives Depository. Grundy County Records.
INS—IRAD

County Clerk records: poll books, 1842–1848; certificates of election; results of township, county, national elections, 1842–1923. Circuit Clerk/Court records: case files, 1837–1963; Grand Jury jail reports, 1879–1898; State's Attorney fee, fine, and forfeiture reports, 1873–1902.

Ottawa, Illinois. Reddick Library. Vertical File. LaSalle County. History, Military. One folder.
IO

Photographs of local Civil War recruits.

Springfield, Illinois. Archives of the State of Illinois. Historical Records Survey of the Works Progress Administration. Inventory of County Archives. 1936–1942. Twenty-four cubic feet. No index.
I—Ar

Fieldworkers' inventory work sheets on county archives include the following:

LaSalle County: Vital Statistics, County Court, County Board, Taxation, Board of Review, Drainage, Circuit Clerk, Treasurer, Recorder, Auditor, Probate Clerk, Sheriff, Coroner, Supt. of Schools, Supt. of Highways, Surveyor, County Veterinarian, Missing Records, Building Forms.

Will County: County Clerk, County Court, Vital Statistics, Taxation, County Board, Probate Clerk, Circuit Clerk, Recorder, Treasurer, County Home, Coroner, Supt. of Schools, Sheriff, Board of Review, Dept. of Public Welfare, Drainage, State's Attorney, Tuberculosis Sanitarium Hospital, Auditor, County School Nurse, Supt. of Highways, Veterinarian, Will County Courthouse—Floor Plans.

Grundy County: Vital Statistics, County Board, Board of Review, County Court, Taxation, Probate Court, Drainage, Circuit Court, Circuit Clerk, Recorder, County Treasurer, State's Attorney, Sheriff, Coroner, County Veterinarian, County Highways, Supt. of Schools, Nurse, County Farm, Old Age Assistance, Farm Bureau, Justice of Peace, Miscellaneous, Building Forms.

DuPage County: County Court, County Board, Taxation, Circuit Clerk, Probate Clerk, Treasurer, Collector, Assessor, Recorder, Auditor, Sheriff, County Coroner, Supt. of Schools, Dept. of Highways, Veterinarian, Court House, Building Forms.

Springfield, Illinois. Archives of the State of Illinois. Historical Records Survey of the Works Progress Administration. Inventory of Municipal Archives. Nine feet.
I—Ar

Blue Island: City Clerk, Accidents, Arrests, Assessments, Balances, Bids, Vital Statistics, Receipts, Police Docket, Ledgers, Letters, Licenses, Minutes of City Council, Photograph Collection, Map Collection, Real Estate, Treasurer, Ordinances, Warrants, Permits, City Surveyor.

Channahon, Office of Village Clerk: Minutes of Village Board.

Braidwood, City Clerk: Cash Book, Justice Docket, Fire Dept. Minutes, Ledgers, Police Docket, Treasurer's Journal, City Clerk Minutes, Ordinance Book, City Council Record.

Joliet Township: Expenditures for Roads and Bridges Fund, Relief Ledger, Death Certificates, Record of Expenditures, Supervisor's Record, Birth Certificates, Treasurer's Account, Auditor's Record, Highway Commissioner's Record.

Joliet Township, Police Department: Justice Docket with Index, Identification Records, Fingerprint Cards, Gun Records, Arrest Records, with index.

Joliet Township, City Clerk: City Council Proceedings with Index, Treasurer's Records, Licenses, Tax Records, Death and Birth Records, Ordinances, Fire Records.

Lockport Township, Township Clerk: Highway Commissioner's Road Records, Justice Docket, Minutes of Township Board.

Lockport Township City Clerk: Ordinances, Meeting Minutes, Deaths, Births, City Clerk Journal, Ledger, Police Docket, Treasurer.

Rockdale, City Clerk: Cash Book, Ordinances.

Summit, Village Clerk: Minutes of Village Board, Ordinances, Licenses.

Summit, Police Department: Licenses, Arrests.

Summit, Mayor's Office: Correspondence.

Summit, Collector's Office: Blueprints, Village Maps.

Summit, Treasurer: Assessment Files.

Springfield, Illinois. Archives of the State of Illinois. Illinois, Adjutant General. Military Census, 1861–1862.
I—Ar

Township lists of all Illinois men subject to military duty. 7 v. No index. Information entered for each individual: name, age, birthplace, occupation. Some lists include color of eyes, hair, and complexion, date of enlistment, and signatures of volunteers.

Springfield, Illinois. Archives of the State of Illinois. Secretary of State Record of Election Returns. 10 v. One folder. Partial index for 1818–82.
I—Ar

Covers 1818–1950 by county.

Springfield, Illinois. Illinois State Historical Library. Black Hawk War Collection. Correspondence and Muster Rolls.
IHi

Index in Curator's office for description of individual items.

Springfield, Illinois. Illinois State Historical Library. John Jay Dickey Letters.
IHi

Two letters in which Dickey writes of a stay in Ottawa to visit six recruiting officers.

Springfield, Illinois. Illinois State Historical Library. Augustus C. French Papers, 1841–1853. Approximately one thousand items.
IHi

Letters, addressed to French. Subjects include state finances, the I&M Canal, and the Illinois Central Railroad.

Springfield, Illinois. Illinois State Historical Library. Joseph Roger Papers, 1926–1971. Two thousand items.
IHi

Warden, 1933–1961, at Joliet State Penitentiary.

Springfield, Illinois. Illinois State Historical Library. Lennington Small Papers. 473 boxes.
IHi

Small was governor of Illinois, 1921–1929. Pt. 2: Correspondence, 1912, about campaign for governor, April Primary. Letters arranged by counties: Box 4: Cook through DeKalb counties. Box 5: DeWitt through Jaspar counties. Box 6: Jefferson through Macon counties. Box 9: Vermillion through LaSalle counties.

Pt. 4: Correspondence, 1924, about campaign for governor. Letters arranged by counties: Box 14: Cook County. Box 15: Crawford through Johnson counties. Box 16: Kane through Macon counties. Box 18: Richland and Will counties.

Pt. 5: Correspondence, 1928, about campaign for governor. Letters arranged by counties: Box 22: Clark through Cook (part) counties. Box 23: Cook through Edgar counties. Box 24: Edwards through Hamilton counties. Box 27: Lake through McLean counties. Box 32: Vermillion through Woodford counties.

Pt. 6: Correspondence, 1932, about campaign for governor. By county: Box 50: Gallatin through Grundy counties. Box 57: White through Will counties. Box 58: Will through Williamson counties.

Pt. 7: Correspondence, 1935–1936, about campaign for governor. By county: Boxes 66–67: Cook County. Box 69: Ford through Henry counties. Box 71: Kankakee through Lawrence counties. Box 78: Tazewell through Will counties.

Pt. 13: Correspondence, 1921–1928, regarding roads. Material arranged under Route Numbers. Boxes 171–179.

Pt. 14: Correspondence, 1921, regarding jobs and state patronage. Boxes 228–232: Cook County. Box 235: Fulton through Hamilton counties. Box 238: Kankakee through LaSalle counties. Box 251: Whiteside through Williamson counties.

Jobs and Patronage, 1925–1928: Boxes 257–262: Cook County. Box 267: Gallatin through Hamilton counties. Box 272: Kendall through LaSalle counties. Boxes 293–294: Will County.

Addresses List: Box 399. Folder 7: Cook County. Box 400, Folder 7: Grundy County. Box 401, Folder 3: LaSalle County. Box 402, Folder 27: Will County.

Springfield, Illinois. Illinois State Historical Library. Letter from James Strain to Abraham Lincoln, March 1, 1861.
IHi

Strain, lawyer in LaSalle, asked Lincoln for an appointment as a federal judge in Colorado Territory.

Springfield, Illinois. Illinois State Historical Library. War Records Section. Records and Collection, 1914–1923. 27.92 feet.
IHi

Collected materials include correspondence and reports from local American Legion posts, chambers of commerce, county food administrators, fuel administrators, liberty loan campaigns, selective service boards, war manufacturers, county Red Cross.

Summit, Illinois. Summit-Argo Public Library. Local History File. Book Box. One box.
ISA

Contains: **Jesse E. Roberts,** "The Revised Municipal Code of the Village of Summit, 1914." **Various authors,** "Summit Heritage." Summit Bicentennial Commission, 64 p., illus. ports., photos., facsims; *Roll Book of Mother's Council of Argo Community High School, 1930s.* 2 v. *Summit-Argo, Oak Lawn, Spring Forest, Justice, Clearing Business and Professional Directory and Buyer's Guide, 1928–1929.* Chicago: McDonough and Company, c. 1928. 280 p.

Utica, Illinois. LaSalle County Historical Society. Company "C," 3rd Illinois Volunteer Infantry, 1898 Scrapbook. 1 v.
IUtHi

Newspaper clippings collected by Edward Jordan.

Utica, Illinois. LaSalle County Historical Society. Soldiers Discharge Record, 1861–1865. 71 v.
IUtHi

Negative photos of discharge records. Index volume.

PART 11 Cultural Life

The cultural life of a community or of an area can be seen in both the training and the refining of its moral and intellectual faculties. This part of the Bibliography, therefore, covers the history of cultural dissemination—education, libraries, publishing—and of cultural display—literature, fine arts, architecture, and folklore.

Cultural Life—*Education*

Cultural Life—*Education*—General

U.S. Census Office. *Eleventh Census of the United States, 1890. Vol. 1: Report on Education in the United States at the Eleventh Census.* Washington: Government Printing Office, 1893. 141 p.
DLC, ICU
Statistics on teachers and school enrollment by race and sex by county.

Cultural Life—*Education*—LaSalle County

Cultural Life—*Education*—LaSalle County—*General*

Educational Counsel Bureau, LaSalle Township High School. *Report, The Bureau of Educational Counsel.* LaSalle, Illinois, 1927.
ICU, IU

First Annual Catalog of the Township High School . . . LaSalle and Peru, Illinois. July, 1899. LaSalle, Illinois: W. T. Bedford, 1899. 56 p., illus.
IPe
Includes roster of students.

LaSalle–Peru Township High School. *Ell-Ess-Pe.* 44 v. Cedar Rapids, Iowa: The Torch Press, [1897–1940].
ILa, IPe
Yearbooks of high school. Annual.

Second Annual Catalogue of the Township High School. . . . LaSalle and Peru, Illinois: 1900–1901. 56 p., illus.
ILa
Photographs of classroom scenes.

Superintendent of Schools, LaSalle County, Illinois. *Manual of the Common Schools, LaSalle County, Ill., 1927–28.* Ottawa, Illinois: Illinois Office Supply Company, 1927. 113 p.
ICU
Supplement to state course of study, by W. R. Foster.

Teachers' Manual; LaSalle County, Illinois; Supplement to the State Course of Study. 12 v. n.p., [1906–1948].
IUtHi
Manual of books, recitations, examinations, daily programs. Yearly graduates by district number. Title varies: *Manual of the Common Schools.* Also forewords to manuals [1908–1938], 17 v.

Zimmerman, Theodore Oscar. "Possibilities of Consolidation in the Schools of LaSalle County, Illinois." A.M. thesis, The University of Chicago, 1937. 92 p.
ICU

Cultural Life—*Education*—LaSalle County—*Peru*

Alumni Association Alumni Bulletin. Vol. 1–. Peru, Illinois: St. Bede College, 1909–. plates, ports.
PLatS

The Via Baeda. Peru, Illinois: St. Bede College, n.d.
DLC, ICJ
Yearbook of St. Bede Academy, Peru.

Cultural Life—*Education*—LaSalle County—*Ottawa*

Catalogue of the Officers, Teachers and Students of the Ottawa Township High School. Ottawa, Illinois, 1893–1894.
IO
Contains lithograph of building. Graduates, 1878–1894.

Catalogue of the Officers, Teachers and Students of the Ottawa Township High School. Ottawa, Illinois, 1904.
IO
Includes courses of study, requirements, graduates, 1878–1907.

Board of Education, Ottawa, Illinois. *Report, 1879/80; 1875–1890; 1895/96; 1910/11; 1913/14.* 4 v. Ottawa, Illinois, 1880–1914.
DHEW

How Firm Our Foundation, A Partial History of the Efforts of the People of the Ottawa Area to Provide Educational Opportunities for the Children of Their Communities. Ottawa, Illinois: Illinois Office Supply Co., 1959. 153 p., ports.
IO

Histories of individual schools. Photographs of buildings.

Northern Illinois Teachers' Association. *General Subject: School Management, Ottawa Ill., April 24 & 25, 1896.* Rockford, Illinois: Monitor Publishing Co., 1896. 61 p.
IMo

A school management manual. All grades.

The Ottawa Academy of Sciences: Its History, Its Failure and the Causes. An Address Before the LaSalle County Historical and Scientific Delivered at the High School Hall, Ottawa, 1901. Ottawa, Illinois [1901].
IUtHi

Typescript and original. Institution of late 1860s.

Ottawa Business University Commercial Law. Ottawa, Illinois: A Treatise on Commercial Law, with Forms of Ordinary Legal and Business Documents, and Copious Questions with References. Rochester, New York: E. R. Andrews, Printer and Bookbinder, 1890. 311 p.
IUtHi

Textbook, index.

Ottawa, Illinois. Township High School. *Dedication Week . . . October 30–November 3, 1916.* Ottawa, Illinois, 1916.
IHi

Pleasant View Luther College, Ottawa, Illinois. *The Annual Announcement.* Ottawa, Illinois: Pleasant View Luther College, n.d.
DLC

Cultural Life—*Education*—Grundy County

Cultural Life—*Education*—Grundy County—*General*

"Judge Orrin N. Carter." *Journal of the Illinois State Historical Society* 10 (October 1918): 442–445. port.
DLC, I, IC, ICHi, ICN, ICU, IEN, IU

Onetime Superintendent of Schools, Grundy County.

School Survey Committee, Grundy County, Illinois. *Final Report.* Morris, Illinois, 1948. 4 p., map.
IU

Educational surveys and education in Grundy County, Illinois.

School Survey Committee, Grundy County, Illinois. *Tentative Report.* Morris, Illinois, 1947. 38 p., maps, tables.
IU

Educational surveys and public schools in Grundy County, Illinois.

Cultural Life—*Education*—Grundy County—*Morris*

Board of Education, Morris, Illinois. *Report . . . 1872/73; 1886/87.* Morris, Illinois, 1873–1888.
DHEW

Morris Community High School. *The Illini Trail.* 16 v. n.p., [1912–1927].
IMo

Annual yearbook of high school.

Cultural Life—*Education*—Will County

Cultural Life—*Education*—Will County—*General*

Farrington, Leslie Joseph. "Development of Public School Administration in the Public Schools of Will County, Illinois, as Shown in a Comparison of Three Selected Years, 1877, 1920 and 1965." Ed.D. dissertation, Northern Illinois University, 1967.
IDeKN

School Survey Committee, Will County, Illinois. *Final Report.* n.p., 1948. 23 p. maps, tables.
IU

Educational surveys and education in Will County.

School Survey Committee, Will County, Illinois. *Tentative Report.* n.p., 1947. 20 p., maps, tables.
IU

Educational surveys and education in Will County.

Will County Community High School District 210. *A School for Tomorrow: A Plan for Building an Educational Program and the Facilities to House It.* Urbana, Illinois: Office of Field Service, College of Education, University of Illinois, 1952. 208 p., illus., maps, tables.
DLC, IU

Cultural Life—*Education*—Will County—*Joliet*

Board of School Inspectors. *Manual.* Joliet, Illinois: Board of School Inspectors, 1912. 47 p.
DHEW

Board of Education, Joliet, Illinois. *Course of Study in Social Science, Junior High School.* Joliet, Illinois, 1932. 74 p. (Mimeograph.)
IU

Board of Education, Joliet, Illinois. *Tentative Course in Elementary Science.* Joliet, Illinois, 1937. 59 p. (Mimeograph.)
IU

References at the end of each section.

Board of Education, Joliet, Illinois. *Tentative Course of Study in Art, Grades One to Six: January, 1936. Joliet Public Schools, School District No. 86, Will County, Illinois.* Joliet, Illinois, 1936. 22 p. (Mimeograph.)
IU

References, pp. 21–22.

Brown, J. Stanley. "The Joliet Township High School." *The School Review* 9 (September 1901): 417–432. illus.
ICU

Description of Joliet Township High School and its resources.

College of St. Francis. *Mary's Book.* Joliet, Illinois, n.d. front., illus.
DLC, IMunS

By the students of the College of St. Francis, under the direction of the faculty. Includes bibliography, Vol. 2, pp. 123–142.

Emerson, Lynn Arthur, comp. *Vocational Education in the Joliet Township High School.* Joliet, Illinois: Joliet Township High School Press, 1925. 148 p., front., illus., plates, diagrs.
ICRL, ICU

By the vocational staff. Compiled by L. A. Emerson, vocational director.

Fretwell, Elbert Kirtley, Jr. *Founding Public Junior Colleges: Local Initiatives in Six Communities.* Teachers College Studies in Education, Columbia University. New York: Bureau of Publication, 1954. 148 p., notes, bibliography.
ICU

Joliet Junior College and Chicago City Junior College are among the six schools studied.

Joliet Township High School. *The J, 1930.* Joliet, Illinois, 1930.
ILo

Yearbook of graduating classes of Joliet Township High School and Junior College.

Joliet Junior College. *The J.C.* 7 v. n.p., 1933–1939.
IJo

Yearbook of junior college.

Joliet Township High School. *History and Social Science Curriculum of the Joliet Township High School.* Joliet, Illinois: Press of the Joliet Township High School, [1923]. 189 p.
DHEW

By the department. Ralph H. Bush, assistant principal, head of the department. Contains bibliographies.

Joliet Township High School. *The Jollier of Joliet.* 36 v. n.p., 1906–1940.
IJo

Annual yearbook of high school.

Lane, John Joseph. "An Examination of the Process of Merger of Lewis College and the College of St. Francis, Joliet, Illinois." Ph.D. dissertation, University of Wisconsin—Madison, 1971.
WU

Rules and Regulations of the Board of School Inspectors for the Government of the Joliet Union Schools. Chicago: Rounds' Book and Decorative Printing Office, 1855/1856. 16 p., illus.
IJo

Rules and Regulations of the Board of School Inspectors, Joliet, Illinois, Revised and Adopted by the Board, February 8, 1873. Joliet, Illinois: Signal Job Printing Office, 1883. 20 p.
IJo

The Second Annual Report of the Superintendent [of] Public Schools of Joliet, Illinois to the Board of Public Instruction for the Year Ending March 31, 1871: Also a Revised Course of Study for the City Schools. Joliet, Illinois: Signal Job Printing Office, 1871. 52 p.
IJo

Shade, Chloris, ed. *Success: Vocational Information Series.* Chicago: Morgan-Dillon & Co., 1937. 55 nos. in 4 vols., diagrs.
DLC, DNLM, ICU, IaU
Directed by Chloris Shade, collaborating with teachers and associated research group, Social Science Department. For use in guidance counseling, social science, library, and general reference work. Bibliographies, Joliet Township High School.

Smolich, Robert Stephen. "An Analysis of Influences Affecting the Origin and Early Development of Three Mid-Western Public Junior Colleges—Joliet, Goshen, and Crane." Thesis, University of Texas at Austin, 1968.
ICU

Superintendent of Public Schools. *Course of Study for the Elementary Grades.* Joliet, Illinois, 1913. 104 p.
IU

Cultural Life—*Education*—Will County—*Lockport*

Lockport Township High School. *The Lock.* 12 v. n.p., 1927–1938.
ILo
Yearbook of high school.

Ott, Elmer F. *History of Lockport Schools.* n.p., 1975. 8 p. (Typescript.)
ILo

Cultural Life—*Education*—DuPage County

"The Schools of DuPage County." *Journal of the Illinois State Historical Society* 4 (October 1911): 361–362.
DLC, I, IC, ICHi, ICN, ICU, IEN, IU
From *Eclectic Journal of Education and Literary Review,* March 15, 1852.

Cultural Life—*Education*—Cook County

Cultural Life—*Education*—Cook County—*General*

Schmann, Henry Ralph. "The Organization and Administration of Schools in Cook County, Illinois, Outside of Chicago." A.M. thesis, The University of Chicago, 1936. 114 p.
ICU

Cultural Life—*Education*—Cook County—*Argo-Summit*

Argo-Summit High School. *Argolite.* n.p., 1924–.
IBP
Yearbook of high school.

Cultural Life—*Libraries and Museums*

Burgess, Jeanne Marie. "The History of the Morris Public Library." M.A. thesis, Northern Illinois University, 1969.
IMo
Bibliography.

Davison, Mabel Katherine. "The Joliet Public Library. . . ." B.L.S. thesis, University of Illinois, 1904. 39 p.
IU

Gregg, Ethel. "A Historical Sketch of the Morris Public Library." Unpublished paper, Morris Public Library, 1969. 10 p.
IMo
Includes list of 1913 Library Board Members.

Joliet, Illinois. Public Library. *Bulletin.* Joliet, Illinois, 1902–1907.
DLC, ICU
Monthly.

Joliet Public Library. *Christmas Bulletin*. Joliet, Illinois: Joliet Public Library, c. 1900. 4 p.
IU

Compiled by Mabel K. Davidson.

Joliet Public Library. *Decennial Survey*. Joliet, Illinois, 1918. 22 p.
DLC

Illustrations on front and back cover.

McIlvain, Caroline B. "Libraries as Local History Centers: The Chicago Historical Society." *Illinois State Historical Society Transactions* 11 (1906): 188–199.
DLC, IC, ICN, ICU, IU

History of CHS. Names of incorporators, officers. Manuscript collections.

"News and Comment—Activities of Local Historical Societies." *Journal of the Illinois State Historical Society* 58 (Spring 1965): 102–112.
DLC, I, IC, ICHi, ICN, ICU, IEN, IU

Includes account of LaSalle County Historical Society's efforts to convert I&M Canal warehouse in Utica into museum.

The Open Door: A Sesquicentennial Year Collection of Histories on Each of the Libraries in the Bur Oak Library System. Joliet, Illinois: Bur Oak Library System, 1968.
IJo

System libraries and founding dates: Coal City Public, 1942; Joliet Public, 1876; Lemont Public, 1944; Lockport Township, 1921; Morris Public, 1913.

A Quartet of Will County Libraries. Lockport, Illinois: Will County Historical Society, 1977.
ILoHi

Includes a history of the Lockport Township Library System (organized in 1921).

Reddick's Public Library, Ottawa, Illinois. *Finding List of the Reddick's Public Library of Ottawa, Illinois*. Ottawa: Free Trader Power Printing House, 1896. 136 p.
DLC, IU

The laws, official roster, and rules and regulations, 1896.

Waldvogel, Ruth, comp. *Lockport Township Public Library, 1921–1976*. [Lockport, Illinois, 1976]. illus.
ILo

Includes photographs of first library in 1921. History of library.

Woeckel, Allan J. "The First Sixty Years: A History of the LaSalle Public Library, 1907–1967." M.A. thesis, Northern Illinois University, 1969. 69 p. (Photocopy.)
ILa

Cultural Life—*Printing and Publishing*

Miller, Carl R. "Journalism in Illinois Before the Thirties." *Journal of the Illinois State Historical Society 11 (July 1918): 149–158.*
DLC, I, IC, ICHi, ICN, ICU, IEN, IU

Covers development of young newspapers in new river towns, their roles as molders of early public opinion, and political implications of early editors' views.

Cultural Life—*Fiction and Poetry*

Angle, Paul McClelland. . . . *Suggested Reading in Illinois History, with a Selected List of Historical Fiction*. Springfield: Illinois State Historical Society, 1935.
ICN

Balmer, Edwin and Wylie, Philip. *The Shield of Silence*. New York: Frederick A. Stokes Company, 1936. 310 p.
DLC

Novel about Lucian Myrand, who is serving a life sentence in the state penitentiary at Joliet for a murder he refuses to discuss.

Barnes, Margaret Ayer. *Edna, His Wife: An American Idyll*. Boston and New York: Houghton, Mifflin Company, 1935. 628 p.
DLC, ICU, NN

Edna, socially unsophisticated, marries a brilliant young lawyer. She does not fit into her husband's circle in the Midwest or New York. First half of book takes place from 1900 to 1914 in Blue Island and Chicago.

Bloom, Margaret. *Black Hawk's Trail*. Chicago, San Francisco, New York: Laidlaw Brothers, 1931. 233 p., illus.
NN

Allison Drake in north central Illinois in 1832. Finds safety in Ottawa before joining militia to fight Black Hawk.

Bray, Robert C. *Rediscoveries, Literature and Place in Illinois.* Urbana, Illinois: University of Illinois Press, [1982]. 167 p.
IU

Includes bibliographical references and index.

Brown, Katharine Holland. *The Hallowell Partnership.* New York: Charles Scribner's Sons, 1912. 241 p., illus.
DLC

Roderick Hallowell, Bostonian hired to help build drainage canal on the Illinois River, is joined by sister Marian. Vivid description of canal construction.

Catherwood, Mary Hartwell. *The Spirit of an Illinois Town and The Little Renault: Two Stories of Illinois at Different Periods.* Boston and New York: Houghton, Mifflin and Company, 1897. 156 p., illus.
DLC, ICU, MiU, NjP, NN

The Little Renault is story of voyageur Tonty and French child. Revealing picture of Tonty's relationship with Indians near Starved Rock.

College of St. Francis. *Burnished Gold.* Vol. 1–. Joliet, Illinois, 1936–. illus.
DLC

By the students of the College of St. Francis. Prose, poetry, and drama.

Cowdrey, Robert H. *A Tramp in Society.* Chicago: Francis J. Schulte & Company, 1891. 290 p.
DLC

Tramp Edgar Bartlett finally makes good and attempts to aid striking miners in Illinois coal fields in Coal City.

Douglas, Amanda M. *A Little Girl in Old Chicago.* New York: Dodd, Mead and Co., 1904. 324 p.
ICU, MB, NN

Social history novel of 1840s Chicago. Woven around construction of the I&M Canal.

Eggleston, George Cary. *Running the River: A Story of Adventure and Success.* New York: A. S. Barnes & Co., 1904. 295 p., illus.
DLC, ICU, MB

Commerce along the Illinois River in the 1850s.

Ellison, Jerome. *The Dam.* New York: Random House, 1941. 176 p.
DLC

Story of John Storm, 1930s engineer hired by W.P.A. to construct a dam on the Dhicato Drainage Canal.

Franchere, Ruth. *The Travels of Colin O'Dae.* New York: Thomas Y. Crowell Company, 1966. 261 p., illus.
DLC

Young Colin begins work as laborer on I&M Canal in 1836. He soon takes up with troupe of minstrels and travels on the Illinois River.

Hayes, P. C. *War Verse and Other Verse.* Joliet: By the Author, 1914. 216 p.
IJo

Poems mainly about Civil War by Will County resident.

Herrick, Frank Earl. *Poems of DuPage County.* Wheaton, Illinois: The Wheaton Daily Journal, 1937. 171 p., illus., ports.
ICHi

Holt, Alfred Hubbard. *Hubbard's Trail.* Chicago: Erle Press, 1952. 320 p.
DLC

Historical novel covering the life of Gurdon S. Hubbard, American Fur Company superintendent of Illinois River trading posts.

Kilpatrick, Thomas L. and Hoshiko, Patsy-Rose. *Illinois! Illinois! An Annotated Bibliography of Fiction.* Metuchen, New Jersey and London: The Scarecrow Press, Inc., 1979. 617 p.
ICU

Bibliography of fictional works "set entirely or in part in Illinois." Author/Title and Subject/Place Name indexes.

Masters, Edgar Lee. *Children of the Market Place.* New York: The Macmillan Company, 1922. 469 p.
DLC, ICU, MB, NjP

Story of Englishman James Miles's life in Illinois becomes entangled with building of Illinois Central Railroad and I&M Canal.

Matson, Nehemiah. *Raconteur: Four Romantic Stories Relating to Pioneer Life, Scenes in Foreign Countries, Religious Fanaticism, Love, Murder, etc.; All of Which are Founded on Fact.*

Chicago: George K. Hazlitt & Company, Printers, 1882. 219 p., illus.
DLC

"Maud Singleton" is set in the Ottawa area.

North, Jessica Nelson. *Arden Acres.* New York: Harcourt, Brace and Company, 1935. 277 p.
DLC

The Chapin family survive the Depression in a suburb near Joliet.

Parrish, Randall. *Beyond the Frontier: A Romance of Early Days in the Middle West.* Chicago: A. C. McClurg & Company, 1915.
ICN

Young Adele takes a canoe journey to the Illinois country in late-seventeenth century. Eventually finds love and peace at Fort St. Louis on Starved Rock.

Reed, Myrtle. *The Shadow of Victory: A Romance of Fort Dearborn.* New York and London: G. P. Putnam's Sons, The Knickerbocker Press, 1903. 413 p.
DLC

Excellent interpretation of Indian-White relations.

Sisson, S. Elizabeth. *Gathered Thistles: Or, A Story of Two Households.* Fremont, Nebraska: Hammand Brothers, 1897. 275 p.
CU, NNC

Two newlywed couples from New England find opposing destinies in Burton, a.k.a. Ottawa.

Tebbel, John. *Touched with Fire.* New York: E. P. Dutton & Company, Inc., 1952. 447 p.
DLC

LaSalle's last journey from Quebec to Fort St. Louis at Starved Rock.

Thorne, Jack. *Ma and Pa on the Cass Street Bus and Other Stories.* From *Joliet Herald-News.* Joliet, Illinois: Joliet Republican Printing, 1954. 96 p., illus.
IJo

Thorne, Jack. *Ma and Pa and Other Stories.* Joliet, Illinois: C. H. Peterson Company, 1939. 103 p., illus.
IJo

Daily feature, "I See by the Papers" in *Joliet Herald-News* cartoons.

Wise, Winifred E. *Swift Walker: A True Story of the American Fur Trade.* New York: Harcourt, Brace and Company, 1937. 388 p.
DLC

Fictionalized biography of Gurdon S. Hubbard, American Fur Company Superintendent of Illinois River trading posts.

Cultural Life—*Fine Arts*

"Directory of Illinois Opera Houses and Halls, 1870." *Journal of the Illinois State Historical Society* 35 (June 1942): 189–193.
DLC, I, IC, ICHi, ICN, ICU, IEN, IU

Entries for Joliet and Ottawa. Taken from O. P. Sweet, *Amusement Directory.*

Sparr, Virginia. *Prairie August.* n.p., n.d. 20 p.
IU—HS

Photocopy of a play written for the Illinois sesquicentennial competition in Morris.

Writers' Program. Illinois. *Marquette at Checagon: A Play in One Act for Ten Players, Based on Father Marquette's Enforced Stay at the Portage of Checagon during the Winter of 1674–75.* Compiled by the Workers of the Writers' Program. Chicago: Chicago Park District, 1941. 13 p. (Mimeograph.)
ICU

Cultural Life—*Architecture*

Adams, A. F. "A New Problem in Theater Design: Rialto Square Building and Theater." *Western Architect* 35 (December 1926): 155–156. plates.
DLC, IC, ICA, IU

Allen, Harold. *Photographs of Architecture in the U.S., Especially Illinois.* 5 v. Chicago, 1952–1962.
ICA

Arranged alphabetically by state and city.

Angle, Paul M. "Views of Chicago; 1866–1867." *Antiques* 63 (January 1952): 60–61.
DLC, I, IC, IU

The Art Institute of Chicago. *Chicago and New York: Architectural Interactions.* Chicago: The Art Institute of Chicago, 1984. 114 p.
ICA

Catalog of museum exhibition.

Barford, George, ed. *Architecture in Illinois.* 2nd ed. Springfield: Illinois Art Education Association, 1964. 48 p.
ICU, MoU, NIC

Brown, William T. *Architecture Evolving: An Illinois Saga.* Edited by Marilyn Hasbrouck. Collectors' 1st ed. Chicago: Teach'em Inc., 1976. 188 p., illus., plans.
DLC

Commission on Chicago Historical and Architectural Landmarks. *Chicago Landmarks, 1978: Documenting the Landmarks of Our City as Designated by the City Council of Chicago. . . .* Chicago: Commission on Chicago Historical and Architectural Landmarks, 1978.
ICU

Condit, Carl W. *The Chicago School of Architecture: A History of Commercial and Public Building in the Chicago Area, 1875–1925.* Chicago: University of Chicago Press, 1964.
CtY, MoU, WU

Coyle, J. E. "A 'Non-Collapsible School'; M. S. Cummingham School, Joliet, Illinois." *Architectural Concrete* 5 (1939): 26–28.
ICA, ICJ, IU

Cummings, Kathleen Roy. *Architectural Records in Chicago: A Guide to Architectural Research Resources in Cook County and Vicinity.* Chicago: The Art Institute of Chicago, 1981. 92 p., illus.
ICA

Detailed descriptions of holdings in Chicago-area libraries and archives including Art Institute, Chicago Historical Society, Chicago Public Library, Northwestern University, University of Chicago, and University of Illinois at Chicago.

Dibelka, James B. *Illinois Album of Public Buildings Erected During 1913–14–15–16.* Omaha, Nebraska: Polrok Publishing Company, [1917]. 94 p., illus.
DLC

"Frame Residence for William McDermitt." *Building Budget* 3 (April 1887): Three in supplement.
DLC, IC, ICA, ICN

Gayle, Margot. "A Heritage Forgotten: Chicago's First Cast Iron Buildings." *Chicago History* 7 (Summer 1978): 98–108.
DLC, IC, ICF, ICHi, ICN, ICU, IU

Chicago's Iron Front buildings, 1854–1890. Contains photographs and lithographs of buildings.

Historic American Buildings Survey. *Chicago and Nearby Illinois Areas: List of Measured Drawings, Photographs and Written Documentation in the Survey, 1966.* J. William Rudd, comp. Park Forest, Illinois: Prairie School Press, 1966. 32 p.
ICA, ICU, IU

Historic American Buildings Survey. *Illinois. Photographs of Buildings.* 3 v. n.p., n.d. 471 photographs.
ICA

Vols. 1–2: Chicago. Vol. 3: Illinois outside Chicago.

Historic American Buildings Survey. *Northern Illinois, 1716–1867, Comprising a Series of Fifty Plates of Measured Drawings of Pioneer Architecture, Selected as Characteristic of Those Made by a Group of Architects and Draftsmen in Chicago From January to May, 1934.* Sponsored by the National Park Service, U.S. Department of the Interior. Federal C.W.A. Project No. 67 and Illinois C.S.A., IERC Project No. 7523, Earl H. Reed, Jr., District Officer, Thomas E. Tallmidge, Chairman, Advisory Committee. 1934. Chicago: Lake Photoprint Company, 1934. Forty-seven plates, three plans.
ICHi, IU

Fifty plates of pioneer architecture.

Historic American Buildings Survey. *Northern Illinois, 1833–1872.* Chicago: Lake Photoprint Company, 1937. Forty-seven plates; three plans.
IU

Fifty plates of pioneer architecture.

Historic American Buildings Survey. Microfiche Edition. Cambridge, England: Chadwick-Healy, Ltd., 1980.
ICA

By state and county. Corridor structures featured in buildings survey: John Hossack house, Ottawa; Early Canal Lock, Channahon; Green House, Plainfield (1834); Pullman Company, administration buildings and shops; Babson Stable and Service Building, 283 Gatesby Lane, Riverside (1915); John Wentworth Farmhouse, Summit (1868).

Historic American Buildings Survey. *Northern Illinois, 1837–1872.* Chicago: Lake Photoprint Company, 1936. Forty-six plates; four plans.
DLC
Plates of pioneer architecture.

Hitchcock, Henry R. *American Architectural Books: A List of Books, Portfolios and Pamphlets on Architecture and Related Subjects Published in America Before 1895.* Minneapolis: University of Minnesota Press, 1962. 130 p.
MnU

Illinois. Board of Examiners of Architects. *Biennial Report.* Vol. 1–. Chicago, Springfield, 1899–.
DLC, ICJ

Illinois Historic Structures Survey. *Inventory of Architecture Before World War II in Calumet City, Chicago Heights, Country Club Hills, Flossmoor, Harvey, Homewood, Lansing, Matteson, Olympia Fields, Thornton in Cook County, Interior Report.* Chicago, 1973. 10 p., maps.
ICHi
Lists five structures (with addresses) in Calumet. Also contains map with locations of structures indicated.

Illinois Historic Structures Survey. *Inventory of Architecture Before World War II in Lemont, Cook County.* Interim Report. Chicago, 1973. 4 p., map.
ICHi

Illinois Historic Structures Survey. *Inventory of Historic Structures . . . Interim Report Prepared by the IHSS, a Division of the Illinois Historic Sites Survey, Conducted Under the Auspices of the Illinois Department of Conservation.* 5 v. Chicago, 1972–.
ICHi
Vol. 1: newsletters, counties, A–H. Vol. 2: counties, I–O. Vol. 3: counties, P–W. Vol. 4: towns except Chicago. Vol. 5: Chicago neighborhoods.

Illinois Society of Architects. Chicago Architectural Exhibition League. *Yearbook . . . and Catalogue of the 7th–41st Annual Exhibition, 1894–1928.* Chicago, 1894–1928.
DLC

Illinois Society of Architects. *Handbook For Architects and Builders.* 1st–35th ed. Chicago: Published Under the Auspices of the Illinois Society of Architects, [1898]–1939.
DLC

"Illustration." *Building Budget* 2 (December 1886): 150 and plate.
DLC, IC, ICA, ICN
Concerns Caton House (1886).

Koeper, Frederick. *Illinois Architecture from Territorial Times to the Present: A Selective Guide.* Chicago: University of Chicago Press, 1968. 304 p., illus.
ICU, IaU, MB, NjP
Historic buildings in Chicago and Ottawa.

Larson, G. E. "Bathhouse for Blue Island, Illinois." *Architectural Concrete* 6 (1940): 26–27.
ICJ, IU

Lowe, David. "Greek Revival Architecture in Chicago." *Chicago History* 4 (Fall 1975): 157–166.
DLC, IC, ICF, ICHi, ICN, ICU, IU
Covers 1830–1850. With lithographs and drawings.

Madden, Betty I. *Arts, Crafts, and Architecture in Early Illinois.* Urbana, Illinois: University of Illinois Press, 1974.
DLC, ICU

Mercantile Advancement Co. *Majestic Chicago: Its Mammoth Structures. . . .* Chicago, 1900. 176 p.
ICHi
Page 73 concerns Joliet Pioneer Stone Co.

O'Donnell, Thomas Edward. "An Outline of the History of Architecture in Illinois." *Illinois State Historical Society Transactions* 38 (1931): 124–143.
DLC, IC, ICU
Begins with mound building, through French, English, Americans. Source of materials.

O'Donnell, Thomas Edward. "Recording the Early Architecture of Illinois in the Historical American Buildings Survey." *Illinois State*

Historical Society Transactions 41 (1934): 185–213.
DLC, IC, ICU

A summary of the findings of the Historic American Buildings Survey of the 1930s.

Pointer, Norbert J. II. "Pullman: A New Town Takes Shape on the Illinois Prairie." *Historical Preservation* 22 (April/June 1970): 26–35.
ICJ, ICN, ICU

Pond, I. R. "The Life of Architecture: Residence of Herman Hegeler and Julius Hegler at LaSalle, Illinois." *Architectural Record* 18 (August 1905): 156.
DLC, I, IC, ICA, ICJ, ICN, ICU

Schlacks, Henry John. *The Work of Henry John Schlacks, Ecclesiologist. . . .* Chicago: Press of Henneberry Company, 1903. 79 p., illus.
NNC

Mostly illustrations of Chicago church architecture.

"Store and Office Building for Messrs. Abbot and Reichman." *Building Budget* 3 (April 1887): three in supplement.
DLC, IC, ICA, ICN

"Store and Tenement Building for Monroe and Seiggert." *Building Budget* 3 (April 1887): three in supplement.
ICA

Tallmadge, Thomas E. *Architecture in Old Chicago.* Chicago: University of Chicago Press, 1941. 218 p., illus., plates.
ICA

Tallmadge, Thomas Eddy. *A History of Architecture in Illinois, 1818–1918: The Thirty-First Annual Chicago Architectural Exhibition, Given Jointly by the Illinois Chapter, American Institute of Architects, the Chicago Architectural Club, The Illinois Society of Architects, with Cooperation of the Art Institute of Chicago, April 4th to May 1st, 1918.* Chicago, 1918.
ICA

Terp, George William. "A Series of Investigations in Early Architectural Construction in the State of Illinois." M.A. thesis, Armour Institute of Technology, 1934. Thirty-eight illus.; five plans.
ICA

"Two-Story Residence For Henry Biroth at Blue Island, Illinois." *Building Budget* 3 (July 1887): 97.
DLC, IC, ICA, ICN

"United States Post-Office, Joliet, Illinois." *American Architect & Building News* 70 (December 1900): 70; plate follows 104.
ICA

Webster, James Carson. *Architecture of Chicago and Vicinity.* [Media], Pennsylvania: Society of Architectural Historians, 1965. 72 p., illus., plans.
DLC

Westfall, C. William. *Concerning the Character of the Architectural Legacy of the Illinois and Michigan Canal Corridor between Summit and Joliet.* Chicago: Open Lands Project, 1981. 6 p.
ICHi

Cultural Life—*Folklore and Folk Art*

Donovan, Helen Martin. *Starved Rock Legendary.* Chicago: The O'Donnell Printing Company, 1915. 44 p.
DLC

Two stories: "Lolomi of the Illinois: A Legend of Lover's Leap," and "Dave and Mary: A Tale of Starved Rock Twenty Years Ago." Same plot, different time periods.

Harris, Jesse. "Illinois Folklore, Past and Present." *Midwest Folklore* 4 (Fall 1954): 134–138.
DLC, ICN, ICU, IHi, InU, IU

Review of previous studies. Footnotes.

Illinois Folklore. Vol. 1–2. Carbondale, Illinois: Illinois Folklore Society, 1947–1948.
IU

Janvein, Mary W. "Some Reprints from Old Books and Periodicals: The Legend of Starved Rock." *Journal of the Illinois State Historical Society* 2 (January 1910): 82–87.
DLC, I, IC, ICHi, ICN, ICU, IEN, IU

Account of Indian legend from *Peterson's Magazine,* Vol. 30, No. 6, Philadelphia, December 1856.

Writers' Program. *Stories from Illinois History.* Compiled by Workers of the Writers' Program of the WPA in the state of Illinois. Chicago, 1941.
DLC

Cultural Life—*Archive Sources*

Chicago, Illinois. Chicago Historical Society. Chicago Architectural Archive. Architectural Drawings Collection.
ICHi

Solon Spencer Beman: Pullman, Illinois—Arcade Building, Standard Knitting Mills, Pullman Market Hall (1885). Daniel Hudson Burnham: Crane Company Building (manufacturing), West 14th Place at Canal Street. Jobson and Hubbard: Pullman, Illinois—Alterations of Arcade Building (1923). Rlelamp and Whitmore: Additions to Aviation Buildings, 6048 South Cicero Avenue (1934).

Chicago, Illinois. Chicago Historical Society. William Gooding Collections. 1 p.
ICHi

Resolution of School District No. 6, Lockport, expressing satisfaction with work of Principal O. S. Westcott, 1867.

Chicago, Illinois. Chicago Historical Society. Illinois Register of Historic Places: (Application Forms). c. 1970–. maps.
ICHi

Photocopies of application forms and supporting evidence.

Chicago, Illinois. Chicago Historical Society. Illinois Society of Architects Records. Twenty-seven document cases. 3 v.
ICHi

Covers period 1901–1940.

Joliet, Illinois. Joliet Public Library. Vertical File. Joliet Public Library. History.
IJo

Newspaper clippings. Pamphlet on John Lambert, Joliet financier who built present structure and gave to library in 1903. Decennial Survey, 1908–1918. 8 p. (Typewritten.)

Lemont, Illinois. Lemont Area Historical Society. Harry J. Swanson Memorial Library. Class Autograph Book, 1928/1929. 1 v.
ILeHi

Autograph book of Catherine Gerhary, first year of Lemont High School, 1928/1929.

Lemont, Illinois. Lemont Area Historical Society. Harry J. Swanson Memorial Library. Lemont Township High School Yearbook. n.p., 1920.
ILeHi

Lemont, Illinois. Lemont Area Historical Society. Harry J. Swanson Memorial Library. Local History File. Lemont Folklore.
ILeHi

Talk given by Gene Graczyk, May 1977, at Lemont Area Historical Society.

Lemont, Illinois. Lemont Area Historical Society. Harry J. Swanson Memorial Library. Local History File. Lemont. Old Central School.
ILeHi

Detail from *Atlas of Cook County,* 1882, showing sites of school lands. School founded in 1869.

Lemont, Illinois. Lemont Area Historical Society. Harry J. Swanson Memorial Library. Local History File. Sag Bridge Ghost.
ILeHi

Account of Sag Bridge Ghost by *Chicago Tribune* writer.

Marseilles, Illinois. Marseilles Public Library. Local History Shelf. Nathan A. Fleming Collection. 1 v.
IMa

Collection of fifty-three poems written by Fleming (1891–1971), Marseilles resident. "An Ode to the Illinois and Michigan Canal," p. 41. "Cleaning Up the Illinois and Michigan Tadpole Sewer," p. 42.

Morris, Illinois. Morris Public Library. *EM–HI.* Collection. One box.
IMo

Contains school newspapers, 1926, 1931/1932, and yearbook.

Morris, Illinois. Morris Public Library. Local History File. Coal City High School.
IMo

Contains 1904 graduation program, 1936 yearbook, and alumni directory.

Morris, Illinois. Morris Public Library. Morris Board of Education. Public School Attendance Records, 1856–1864. 1 v.
IMo

Morris, Illinois. Morris Public Library. Morris Board of Education, District No. 1. Record of Proceedings of the Board of Education, 1859–1875, 1876–1899.
IMo

Morris, Illinois. Morris Public Library. Morris High School Catalogue, 1924. 1 v., illus. 100 p.
IMo

Photographs of buildings. Index. Group photographs.

Morris, Illinois. Morris Public Library. Morris Public Library Records.
IMo

Contains land deeds to Morris Public Library property. Morris Public Library Establishment Petition, 1911. Monthly Reports, 1914–1937. Registered Borrowers' Records (with index), 1911, 1926–1930, 1940–1951. Records Relating to Children's Room, Established in 1938. Photograph Scrapbook, 1920. Correspondence, 1911–1936. Board Minutes, 1911–1975.

Morris, Illinois. Morris Public Library. Physics Record. 1 v.
IMo

Botany Physics Record, laboratory notes and drawings of Mabel Aker, Morris High School, winter 1903.

Morris, Illinois. Morris Public Library. Ruth Jorstad Scrapbook.
IMo

"The Girl Graduate." Scrapbook of Morris Community High School of 1918. News clippings, programs, notes, and photographs.

Ottawa, Illinois. Reddick Library. Vertical File. Ottawa. Schools.
IO

Contains, "100 Years of Education; Ottawa Township High School." Photographs, 1978. Class pictures. "Graduates of Ottawa High School (1875–1877) and Ottawa Township High School (1878–1978)," 1978. Photographs of classes, Ottawa Hatchery. "Lincoln School Diamond Jubilee, 1897–1972," 1972.

Palos Hills, Illinois. Green Hills Public Library. Photograph File. Resurrection Mary.
IPHil

"Meet the Folks on Archer—the Dead Ones," *Chicago Tribune,* Tempo Section, October 29, 1982.

Palos Hills, Illinois. Green Hills Public Library. Vertical File. Little Red School House. Two folders.
IPHil

Newspaper clippings and pamphlets concerning an 1886 schoolhouse that now serves as a nature center for the Cook County Forest Preserve.

Palos Park, Illinois. Palos Park Public Library. Pamphlet File. Palos Park History. Library. One folder.
IPP

File contains "History of the Palos Park Library," by Palos Park Women's Club Historian, Ester L. Johnson, 3 p. (Typewritten, Photocopy.) Photocopied newspaper clippings regarding the erection of the Palos Park Public Library building in 1982.

Palos Park, Illinois. Palos Park Public Library. Pamphlet File. Palos Park History. Schools. One folder.
IPP

Includes essays on history of schools, photos of classrooms, and various newspaper clippings.

Peru, Illinois. Peru Public Library. Maud Powell Scrapbook.
IPe

Maud Powell (1868–1920) is described as the greatest woman violinist of her day. Powell was born in Peru. Her family moved away in 1870. Scrapbook includes typewritten biographical sketches, newspaper articles, programs of performances, and three letters.

Springfield, Illinois. Illinois State Historical Library. Federal Writers' Project. Illinois. Plays and Radio Scripts. Seven boxes.
IHi

Box 297: "Father of Chicago," by Onah Spencer. "The Massacre at Fort Dearborn," "All is Fair," "The Story of Pullman," "The City Called Packingtown," by David Eskind. Box 300: "The Opening Wedge (LaSalle)," "This is Our Truth" (John Hossack).

Summit, Illinois. Summit-Argo Public Library. Local History File. Argo Community High School. One folder.
ISA

Contains newspaper clippings from the *DesPlaines Valley News, Chicago Tribune, The Economist, Chicago Sun-Times, Chicago Daily News.*

Summit, Illinois. Summit-Argo Public Library. Local History File. Community Theaters. One folder.
ISA

Contains various newspaper clippings, 1920s theater programs.

Summit, Illinois. Summit-Argo Public Library. Local History File. District 104. One folder.
ISA

Summit, Illinois. Summit-Argo Public Library. Local History File. One folder.
ISA

Contains program of the Grand Mary Ball for the benefit of the Argo-Summit Library, 1934 (mostly advertising), various newspaper clippings.

Urbana, Illinois. Illinois Historical Survey Library. American Institute of Architects. Central Illinois Chapter. Records, 1917–1951. Five boxes. Inventory.
IU—HS

Utica, Illinois. LaSalle County Historical Society Museum. District 141, Ottawa, Illinois Schools. Financial Records, 1895–1942. 10 v.
IUtHi

Utica, Illinois. LaSalle County Historical Society Museum. District 141, Ottawa, Illinois Schools. Minutes, Board of Education, 1872–1947. 8 v.
IUtHi

Utica, Illinois. LaSalle County Historical Society Museum. Collection of Children's Books by Leo Edwards.
IUtHi

Leo Edwards, Utica native.

Utica, Illinois. LaSalle County Historical Society Museum. LaSalle County College and Seminary Fund Commissioners. Account Book, 1838–1855. 1 v.
IUtHi

Utica, Illinois. LaSalle County Historical Society Museum. 1918 Yearbook. LaSalle–Peru Township High School. 206 p. 1 v.
IUtHi

Classes, sports, organizations.

Utica, Illinois. LaSalle County Historical Society Museum. Official Diary, Ottawa High School, 1916–1920. 1 v.
IUtHi

Utica, Illinois. LaSalle County Historical Society Museum. Ottawa Free School Journal. 1861–1881. 2 v.
IUtHi

Utica, Illinois. LaSalle County Historical Society Museum. Picture Book. Zez Confrey Collection.
IUtHi

Pictures and illustrations of Zez Confrey (composer, born in LaSalle County), his music, newspaper articles.

Utica, Illinois. LaSalle County Historical Society Museum. Record of Loans of School Money, 1868–1884, Township 32N, Range 3E. 1 v.
IUtHi

Utica, Illinois. LaSalle County Historical Society Museum. School Commissioners Account Book, 1856–1865. 1 v.
IUtHi

LaSalle County townships.

Washington, D.C. Library of Congress. American Folklife Center. Chicago Ethnic Arts Project Collection. 335 recordings, 3,700 slides, 300 rolls film.
DLC

Center undertook field survey of Chicago ethnic arts traditions at request of Illinois Arts Council in 1977. Information for following groups: Afro-American, Austrian, Chicano, Chinese, Croation, Cuban, Czech, Danish, Finnish, German, Greek, Irish, Italian, Japanese, Jewish, Korean, Lithuanian, Macedonian, Native American, Norwegian, Polish, Puerto Rican, Serbian, Slovak, Slovenian, Swedish, Ukrainian.

PART 12 Recreation and Sports

Long recognized for its recreational value, the corridor boasts parks, outdoor recreational facilities, and overnight accommodations in abundance from Chicago to LaSalle–Peru. Descriptive articles on Shabbona Park, the Illinois and Michigan Canal State Park, and other parks and forest preserves provide information on activities and attractions of these sites. An abundance of materials is available on Starved Rock, including histories, legends, descriptions, and guides.

Recreation and Sports—*General*

Joliet Park Commissioners, Recreation Department. *Report of the Activities.* Joliet, Illinois, n.d.
IU

Illinois and Michigan Canal Task Force. *Interim Report on Comprehensive Development Planning for the Illinois and Michigan Canal.* n.p., 1973. maps.
IO

This important report presents the historical and recreational developments being proposed by the state for I&M development plans and use and/or disposal of those canal lands not usable. Filed with 78th General Assembly, State of Illinois.

Program. Ottawa Chautauqua. Ottawa, Illinois, 1902.
IO

Includes photograph of bridge at Deer Park. View of Fox River. Advertisements.

Recreation and Sports—*Parks*

Bennett, Albert. *Starved Rock Beautiful (Illinois State Park Souvenir Edition): An Authentic History of This Enchanting Resort. A Guide to the Glens and Canyons with Maps and Routes on How to Get There. Compiled in the Interest of Tourists and the Lovers of the Beautiful.* Ottawa, Illinois: Ottawa Printing Company, 1914. 46 p., photos., maps.
IO, ILa

Republished in 1941 by the Starved Rock Publishing Company.

Burnham, D. H., Jr., and Kingery, Robert. *Parks, Forests and Recreation in the Region of Chicago, Featuring the Forest Preserve District of Cook County, Illinois.* Prepared by John B. Morrill from *Planning the Region of Chicago.* Reprint ed., n.p., 1970. 23 p., photos.
IPP

Cook County, Illinois. Board of Forest Preserve Commissioners. *Forest Preserves of Cook County Owned and Controlled by the Forest Preserve District of Cook County in the State of Illinois.* Chicago: Clohesy & Company, 1918, 1921. 145 p., 223 p., illus., ports., plans, tables.
DLC, ICJ, ICU

Cook County, Illinois. Board of Forest Preserve Commissioners. *Forest Preserve Trails.* [Chicago, 1934]. maps.
ICJ

"Dedication of Shabbona Park, LaSalle County, Illinois, August 29, 1906." *Publications of the Illinois State Historical Library* 12 (1908): 332–341.
DLC, I, IC, ICF, ICJ, ICN, ICU

A memorial to the settlers slain in the Indian Creek Massacre, May 20, 1882.

Descriptive Handbook of the Summer Resort of Illinois, At Starved Rock, and the Picturesque Scenery of LaSalle County, Illinois. Chicago: Klein & Company, 1891. 40 p.
ILa

In English and German.

Ellenburg, Naomi L. *The Heritage of Starved Rock.* n.p., Naomi Ellenburg, n.d. 41 p., photos.
IO

A short history of the park and its environs.

Hammond, John D. *The Cliffs, Glens and Canyons of the Illinois Valley in LaSalle County, Illinois.* Ottawa, Illinois: Free Trader Publishing House, 1894. illus., maps.
IO

Poem "Our Valley," photographs of Starved Rock Hotel, Buffalo Rock, Deer Park, tourist car route.

Hanson Engineers Incorporated. *Restoration Study Lock 1, Illinois and Michigan Canal State Park, Lockport, Illinois.* Springfield, 1978.
IPP

Hanson, Phil. "Six Decades of Change in the Palos Woodlands." *Field Museum of Natural History Bulletin* (May 1980): 12–13. photos.
IPP

Hayes, William P. "Development of the Forest Preserve District of Cook County, Illinois." M.A. thesis, DePaul University, 1949. 38 p.
IPP

Bibliography.

"Historical News." *Journal of the Illinois State Historical Society* 25 (October 1932): 241–245.
DLC, I, IC, ICHi, ICN, ICU, IEN, IU

Includes plans of LaSalle County Historical Society to erect museum at Starved Rock State Park.

Illinois. Department of Public Works and Buildings. *What to See and How to See Starved Rock State Park, Together with a Short History of the Park, Its Various Automobile Roads Thereto, and Trails.* Springfield, 1924. 15 p., illus., map.
DLC

Various editions.

"The Illinois Park Commission: Investigations, Starved Rock." *Journal of the Illinois State Historical Society* 2 (October 1909): 101–103.
DLC, I, IC, ICHi, ICN, ICU, IEN, IU

Bill of General Assembly creating Illinois Park Commission in response to efforts of LaSalle County Historical Society to preserve Starved Rock.

Illinois Valley Railway Company. *The Illini Trail; Descriptive of the Valley of the Illinois, Points of Scenic Beauty and Historical Interest, Including the Story of Starved Rock.* n.p., 1905. 41 p., illus.
IU

Includes LaSalle County and Illinois Valley in general.

James, James Alton. "The Beginning of a State Park System for Illinois." *Illinois State Historical Society Transactions* 43 (1936): 53–62.
DLC, IC, ICU

History of Starved Rock State Park, early state park legislation.

Jessup, Theodore. "Starved Rock and Its Neighborhood." *Illinois State Historical Society Transactions* 11 (1906): 203–213.
DLC, IC, ICU

Geologic survey of area, roads, photograph of rock.

Kingery, Robert. "The State Parks and Illinois History." *Illinois State Historical Society Transactions* 43 (1936): 63–67.
DLC, IC, ICU

Information about restoration of I&M Canal from Chicago to LaSalle. Trails in Starved Rock State Park. Photographs of Starved Rock, I&M towpath near Channahon, and other state parks.

"Laws Relating to Historical Matters and Interests Passed by the Forty-Seventh General Assembly of Illinois." *Journal of the Illinois State Historical Society* 4 (July 1911): 246–249.
DLC, I, IC, ICHi, ICN, ICU, IEN, IU

Account of General Assembly's appropriation of $150,000 for the purchase of Starved Rock.

"Legislation Before the Present General Assembly Relating to Historical Matters and Affairs." *Journal of the Illinois State Historical Society* 4 (April 1911): 120–121.
DLC, I, IC, ICHi, ICN, ICU, IEN, IU

Outlines Illinois State Park Commission report that recommends the purchase of Starved Rock by the state.

Lemont, Illinois. Lemont Area Historical Society. *Save the Valley Association: Open Space for a Better Community, Box 383, Lemont, Illinois.* n.p., n.d.
ILeHi

A series of leaflets, bound together, outlining Lemont area conservation efforts.

McDonnell, John B. and Reeve, Lloyd Eric. *Starved Rock Through the Centuries: French and Indian History and Traditions. Indian Legends, Beliefs, and Customs, with a Complete Map of Rock Park.* Champaign, Illinois: The Service Press, 1924. 79 p., ports., map, illus.
IO

"Monument Unveiled: Dedication of Shabbona Park, LaSalle County, Illinois, August 29,

1906." *Illinois State Historical Society Transactions* 12 (1907): 332–341. photo., port.
DLC, IC, ICU

Taken from the *Ottawa Journal,* August 30, 1906.

Osman, Eaton Goodell. *Starved Rock: A Chapter of Colonial History. . . .* 2nd ed. Chicago: A. Flanagan Company, 1911. 210 p., front., illus., ports., maps, facsim.
DLC, ICU

Osman, Eaton G. *Starved Rock: A Historical Sketch.* Ottawa, Illinois: The Free Trader Printing House, 1895. 84 p., photos.
IO

Covers the earliest history of the park, its legends, and real events.

Paape, Charles W. *Starved Rock: History and Romance in the Heart of the West.* Elmhurst, Illinois: Charles W. Paape, 1938. 31 p., maps, photos.
ILa

Includes "How Starved Rock Got Its Name," "The Story of the Rocks," "The Indians," "The Fur Traders and Missionaries," "The Settlers," and "The Establishment of the Park."

Rhoades, H. A. "Legends of the Starved Rock Country." *Journal of the Illinois State Historical Society* 6 (January 1914): 509–516.
DLC, I, IC, ICHi, ICN, ICU, IEN, IU

Includes geological history of park and variety of Indian and French legends.

Starved Rock: A Brief History Illustrated with Engravings and Maps Showing Automobile Routes from Points in Northern Illinois. Aurora, Illinois: Amell Publishing Company, 1912. 47 p., illus., maps.
ICHi

"State of Illinois Buys Starved Rock." *Journal of the Illinois State Historical Society* 4 (January 1912): 532–533.
DLC, I, IC, ICHi, ICN, ICU, IEN, IU

Account of state purchasing site for park for $146,000.

Tisler, C. C. and Tisler, Aleita V. *Starved Rock: Birth Place of Illinois.* n.p., 1956.
IO

Concise work on the meaning, significance, and key events in the Starved Rock story.

University of Illinois. Office of Recreation and Park Resources. Department of Recreation and Park Administration. *A Comprehensive Plan: LaSalle County Conservation District, Ottawa, Illinois.* 4 v. Urbana, Illinois: University of Illinois, 1969.
IO

Vol. 1: Leisure behavior attitudes and interests of the citizens of LaSalle County. Vol. 2: Program services in conservation and outdoor recreation in LaSalle County. Vol. 3: Conservation and outdoor resources for LaSalle County. Vol. 4: Organization and administration of the LaSalle County Conservation District.

Wojtas, Ed. "Historic, Colorful I&M Canal, Now Popular Recreational Area." *Champaign-Urbana Courier,* 6 June 1958, pp. 19, 21.
IU—HS

Channahon State Park in Will County.

Recreation and Sports—*Outdoor Recreation*

Flanagan, John T. "Hunting in Early Illinois." *Journal of the Illinois State Historical Society* 72 (1979): 2–11.
DLC, I, IC, ICHi, ICN, ICU, IEN, IU

Includes accounts of hunting in northeastern Illinois and descriptions of game birds and animals.

Husar, John. "Our Hidden Wilderness." *Chicago Tribune,* 21–24 September 1980, 30 p., photos., maps, illus.
IJo

Chicago Tribune, five-part series on the canal area, from Summit to Joliet.

Illinois Paddling Council. *Three-Hundredth Anniversary: Discovery of the Illinois Country; Louis Jolliet-Jacques Marquette, 1673–1973.* Evanston, Illinois: Illinois Paddling Council, 1973. illus., map.
IMa

Standard history.

Prairie Club, Chicago. *Outdoors with the Prairie Club: Written by Members of the Club.* Comp. Emma Doeserich, Mary Sherburne, Anna B. Wey. Chicago: Paquin Publishers, 1941. 354 p., illus.
ICRL

The club was organized for the promotion of outdoor recreation in the form of walks and outings in the Chicago area, the dissemination of knowledge of the attractions of the country adjacent to the city, and the preservation of suitable area in which such recreation may be pursued. A variety of articles and topics relevant to I&M corridor and various rivers and forests.

Saturday Afternoon Walks in the Forests, Fields, Hills and Valleys About the City Under the Auspices of the Prairie Club. Chicago, n.d.
ICRL
Club organized to take excursions. Lists of officers and directors. Weekend trips to Starved Rock, Palos Park, Sag Bridge, DesPlaines Valley, Willow Springs, Lemont, Joliet. Photographs of rivers, Starved Rock.

Vierling, Philip E. *A Self-Guided Loop Hiking Trail to the Chicago Portage National Historic Site. Illinois Country Hiking Guide*. n.p., 1973. 48 p., maps.
ISA
Bibliography.

Recreation and Sports—*Archive Sources*

Lemont, Illinois. Lemont Area Historical Society. Harry J. Swanson Memorial Library. Local History File. Two Baseball Scorebooks (1906 and 1908).
ILeHi

Morris, Illinois. Morris Public Library. Local History File. Parks.
IMo
Contains newspaper clippings and brochures on local parks and various issues dealing with parks.

Morris, Illinois. Morris Public Library. Local History File. Goose Lake Prairie State Park. One folder.
IMo
Contains newspaper clippings, pamphlet with a checklist of birds in Prairie State Park, essay on the history of the prairie in Illinois, and various state pamphlets.

Ottawa, Illinois. Reddick Library. Pamphlet File. Starved Rock State Park. One folder.
IO
Assorted articles on the Park from the *Daily Republican*. Letter from James James to C. C. Tisler on the creation of the park. Guide to Ottawa, Starved Rock, including historical sketches, recreational sketches, photographs. Brochure.

Utica, Illinois. LaSalle County Historical Society Museum. Amusement Scrap Book. Amusement Book.
IUtHi
Contains sports teams' portraits, centennial memorabilia, views of bridges, advertisements, certificates of incorporation, various catalogs, county fair brochures, various pictures of LaSalle County life, and parades from the 1850s to 1950s.

Utica, Illinois. LaSalle County Historical Society Museum. Bands and Amusements. Picture Scrap Book.
IUtHi
Contains pictures, papers, and leaflets on bands, sheet music, advertisements.

PART 13 Local History

This section of the Bibliography contains those sources that emphasize the histories of particular places—regions, counties, or towns. Local histories written during various periods and for various purposes are included, along with primary sources from which a researcher might attempt his own syntheses. Before doing so, however, one should be aware of at least two caveats. First, today's local historians ought to recognize that earlier works were usually constructed in order to immortalize the accomplishments of individuals or groups of persons, and they ought to be used in light of that fact. Second, researchers ought also to rely on the other parts of the Bibliography to gain a full understanding of the cultural, social, political, and economic conditions in the corridor's locales.

Local History—*General*

Directory of Local History Collections in Northern Illinois. Chicago: [The] Genealogy and Local History Interest Group of the Illinois Regional Library Council, 1981. 39 p.
DLC

Foster, Olive S. *Illinois: A Student's Guide to Localized History.* New York: Teachers College, Columbia University, 1968. 28 p.
DLC

Annotated bibliography. Pamphlet.

Peterson, Clarence Stewart. *Consolidated Bibliography of County Histories in Fifty States in 1961.* 2nd ed. Baltimore, Maryland: Genealogical Publishing Co., 1963.
DLC

Zachert, Donald. "Research Projects in Illinois History." *Journal of the Illinois State Historical Society* 66 (Winter 1973): 404–411.
DLC, I, IC, ICHi, ICN, ICU, IEN, IU

Local History—*Illinois*

Breese, Sidney. *The Early History of Illinois, From Its Discovery by the French, in 1673, Until Its Cession to Great Britain in 1763, Including the Narrative of Marquette's Discovery of the Mississippi.* Chicago: E. B. Myers, 1884. 422 p., front., port., maps.
DLC, IC, ICU

Edited by Thomas Hoyne. Biographical memoir by Melville W. Fuller.

Brown, Henry. *The History of Illinois, From Its First Discovery and Settlement to the Present Time.* New York: J. Winchester, 1844. 492 p., map.
DLC, ICU

Buck, Solon J. *Illinois in 1818.* Springfield: The Illinois Centennial Commission, 1917. 362 p., front., illus., plates, ports., map, facsims.
ICJ, ICU

Bibliography, pp. 321–326.

Differding, Virginia M. *The Prairie Sings to Me: Explorations into Northern Illinois' Past, Adapted from a Series of Articles Developed by Northern Illinois University for Newspapers Throughout the Region.* DeKalb, Illinois: Northern Illinois University, 1977. 42 p., illus.
DLC, IDeKN—IRAD

Bibliography, p. viii. Illinois history, addresses, essays, lectures. Frontier and pioneer life.

Ford, Thomas. *A History of Illinois, from its Commencement as a State in 1818, to 1847; Containing a Full Account of the Black Hawk War, the Rise, Progress, and Fall of Mormonism, the Alton and Lovejoy Riots, and Other Important and Interesting Events.* Chicago: S. C. Griggs; New York: Ivison & Phinney, 1854. 447 p.
DLC, IC, ICHi, ICU, IHi

Howard, Robert D. *Illinois: A History of the Prairie State.* Grand Rapids, Michigan: William B. Eerdmans Publishing Company, 1972. 626 p., illus.
DLC, ICU

Illinois. Centennial Commission. *The Centennial History of Illinois.* 5 v. Springfield: Centennial Commission, 1918–1920.
ICJ, ICU, IU

Vol. 1: *The Illinois Country, 1673–1818,* by C. W. Alvord. Vol. 2: *The Frontier State, 1818–1848,* by T. C. Pease. Vol. 3: *The Era of the Civil War, 1848–1870,* by A. C. Cole. Vol. 4:

The Industrial State, 1870–1893, by E. L. Bogart. Vol. 5: *The Modern Commonwealth, 1893–1918,* by E. L. Bogart and C. M. Thompson.

Joliet Herald News. *Illinois Sesquicentennial Edition.* August 17, 1968.
IJo

Subjects covered include stone quarrying, early travel, architecture of Chicago Street, archaelology of area, Lockport fire of 1895, early settlers, LaSalle expeditions, Black Hawk War, history of industry, history of religious congregations, history of the EJ&E Railroad, history of the I&M Canal, the Great Sauk Trail, histories of Will County communities.

Jones, Abner Dumont. *Illinois and the West: With a Township Map, Containing the Latest Surveys and Improvements.* Boston, Massachusetts: Weeks, Jordan and Company; Philadelphia: W. Marshall, 1838. 255 p., front., map.
DLC, ICJ, IHi, IU

Mather, Irwin F. *The Making of Illinois: Historical Sketches. . . .* Chicago: A. Flanagan, 1900, 1911, 1913, 1916, 1917, 1922, 1926, 1931, 1935. front., illus., ports, maps.
DLC, ICarbS, ICJ, ICU

Matson, Nehemiah. *Pioneers of Illinois, Containing a Series of Sketches Relating to Events That Occurred Previous to 1813: Also Narratives of Many Thrilling Incidents Connected with the Early Settlement of the West, Drawn from History, Tradition and Personal Reminiscences.* Chicago: Knight & Leonard, Printers, 1882. 206 p., front.
DLC, ICarbS, ICN, ICU

Moses, John. *Illinois, Historical and Statistical, Comprising the Essential Facts of Its Planting and Growth as a Province, County, Territory, and State. . . .* 2 v. Chicago: Fergus Printing Company, 1889–1892. fronts., illus., plates, ports., maps, facsims.
DLC, I, ICJ, ICN, IU

Includes population and election statistics.

Quaife, Milo Milton. *Pictures of Illinois One Hundred Years Ago.* Chicago: R. R. Donnelley, 1918. 186 p., front., port.
DLC, ICJ

Reynolds, John. *The Pioneer History of Illinois, Containing the Discovery, in 1673, and the History of the Country to the Year Eighteen Hundred and Eighteen, When the State Government was Organized.* Belleville, Illinois: N. A. Randall, 1852. 348 p.
DLC, IC, ICN, ICU, IEN, IU

Also published in Chicago: Fergus Printing Company, 1887. 459 p., front., ports., plan.

Woodruff, George H. *Fifty Years Ago: Or, Gleanings Respecting the History of Northern Illinois a Few Years Previous to, and During the Black Hawk War.* Joliet, Illinois: Joliet Republic and Sun Printing, 1883. 62 p.
ICN

Writers' Program. Illinois. *Illinois Historical Anecdotes.* Compiled by the Workers of the Writers' Program of the Work Projects Administration in the State of Illinois. Official Sponsor: Division of Department Reports, State of Illinois. Cooperating Sponsor: Chicago Library Club. Chicago, 1940. 93 p.
DLC, ICU

Writers' Program. Illinois. *Pioneer Days in Illinois.* Compiled by the Workers of the Writers' Program of the Works Project Administration in the State of Illinois. Official Sponsor: Division of Department Reports, State of Illinois. Cooperating Sponsor: Chicago Library Club. Chicago, 1940. 78 p.
DLC, ICN, ICU

Local History—*Land Disposal*

Chisholm, Roger K. *The Value of Certain Tracts of Land in Illinois in the Years 1803, 1818, 1819, and 1820.* Memphis, Tennessee: Chisholm, 1975. 340 figures.
ICN

Dockets 15-D, 311, 314-A, 315, Indian Claims Commission. Analysis of early settlement in Royce areas 48, 96a, 98, 110 and a fraction of 180. The study includes statistical information as well as descriptive, and discusses in various places Grundy and LaSalle counties. Some corridor towns are described.

Complete List of the Lots and Lands Conveyed to the Trustees of the Illinois and Michigan Canal, Showing Size of Lots, Appraisal, Sales in Sept. 1848, and May, 1849, Names of Purchas-

ers, etc. Compiled by Order of the Board February, 1850. Chicago: Printed at the Democrat Office, 1850. 151 p.
ICHi

Gates, Paul Wallace. "Charts of Public Land Sales and Entries." *Journal of Economic History* 24 (1964): 22–28.
DLC, ICU, IEN, IU

Gates, Paul Wallace. "The Disposal of the Public Domain in Illinois, 1848–1856." *Journal of Economic and Business History* 3 (1931): 216–240.
DLC, IC, ICN, ICU, IU

Grover, Frank R. "Indian Treaties Affecting Lands in the Present State of Illinois." *Journal of the Illinois State Historical Society* 8 (October 1915): 379–419.
DLC, I, IC, ICHi, ICN, ICU, IEN, IU

Hammer, Raymond, ed. "Squatters in Territorial Illinois." *Illinois Libraries* 59 (May 1977): 308–382.
DLC, I, IC, ICJ, ICN, ICU, IU

Applications and permissions for settlement registered at Kaskaskia Land Office 1807 and preemption reports in Kaskaskia Land District in 1813.

List of Canal Lots and Lands in Chicago and Vicinity, Offered for Sale by the Trustees of the Illinois and Michigan Canal, in September 1848, and May 1849 with the Valuations of the Several Lots and Tracts: Also, the Prices of Those Sold and the Names of Purchasers. Chicago: Rees & Rucker, Daily Democrat Steam Press, 1849. 31 p.
ICHi

List of Lots and Lands in Chicago and Vicinity, Offered for Sale by the Trustees of the Illinois and Michigan Canal, in September, 1848, With the Valuations and Names of the Purchasers of Those Which Were Sold, and the Prices Sold for, etc. Chicago: Rees & Rucker, Daily Democrat Steam Press, 1849. 31 p.
ICHi

Smith, Clifford Neal. *Federal Land Series: A Calendar of Archival Materials on the Land Patents Issued by the United States Government, with Subject, Tract, and Name Indexes.* Vol. 3: [*1810–1814*]. Chicago: American Library Association, 1980. maps.
DLC

Two maps of Illinois, one indicating the District Land Office jurisdiction, the second adding the boundaries of the I&M Canal grant. The volume contains land transactions, but Illinois falls outside the time frame.

Local History—*Old Northwest*

Alvord, Clarence W. *The Critical Period, 1763–1765.* Edited with Introduction and Notes, by Clarence Walworth Alvord . . . and Clarence Edwin Carter. Springfield: The Trustees of the Illinois State Historical Library, 1915. 597 p., front., ports., facsims.
DLC, ICN, ICU

Alvord, Clarence Walworth. *Mississippi Valley in British Politics; A Study of the Trade, Land Speculation, and Experiments in Imperialism Culminating in the American Revolution.* 2 v. Cleveland, Ohio: The Arthur H. Clark Company, 1927. maps.
DLC, ICRL, ICU, WHi

Bibliography.

Alvord, Clarence Walworth, ed. *The New Regime, 1765–1767.* Collections of the Illinois Historical Library, No. 11. Springfield, 1916. 700 p., ports., front., map, facsim.
ICU

Introduction and notes by Clarence W. Alvord and Clarence Edwin Carter.

Attig, Chester Jacob. "The Institutional History of the Northwest Territory, 1787–1802." Ph.D. dissertation, The University of Chicago, 1921. 288 p., maps.
DLC, ICU

Bibliography.

Blanchard, Rufus. *The Discovery and Conquest of the Northwest: Including the Early History of Chicago, Detroit, Vincennes, St. Louis, Ft. Wayne, Prairie du Chien, Marietta, Cincinnati, Cleveland, etc., etc., and Incidents of Pioneer Life in the Region of the Great Lakes and the Mississippi Valley.* Chicago: Cushing, Thomas & Company, 1880. 484 p., front., plates, maps.
DLC, ICU

Kinzie, Juliette Augusta (Magill). *"Mrs. John Kinzie." Wau-bun, the "Early Day" in the North-West.* New York: Derby & Jackson; Cincinnati: H. W. Derby, 1856. 598 p., front., plates.
DLC, ICF, ICU

Narrative of travel in Wisconsin and Illinois. 2nd Edition, Chicago: D. B. Cooke, 1857. Other editions: Philadelphia: J. B. Lippincott, 1873. 309 p. Edition with notes and introduction by Eleanor Kinzie Gordon, Chicago and New York: Rand, McNally, 1901. 393 p., plates, ports., front., facsim. New edition, with an introduction and notes by R. Gold Thwaites, Chicago: The Caxton Club, 1901. 451 p., facsim., front., plates, ports., maps. Edition with notes and introduction by Louise Phelps Kellogg, Centennial edition, Menasha, Wisconsin: National Society of Colonial Dames in Wisconsin, 1948.

Kohlmeier, Albert Ludwig. *The Old Northwest as a Keystone of the Arch of American Federal Union: A Study in Commerce and Politics.* Bloomington, Indiana: The Principia Press, Inc., 1938. 257 p.
DLC, ICU, IU, WHi

Bibliographical footnotes.

Malin, James C. *Indian Policy and Westward Expansion.* University of Kansas Humanistic Studies, Bulletin, No. 2. Lawrence, Kansas: University of Kansas, 1921. 108 p., illus., maps.
DLC, ICU, WHi

Peck, John Mason. *Annals of the West: Embracing a Concise Account of Principal Events Which Have Occurred in the Western States and Territories, from the Discovery of the Mississippi Valley to the Year Eighteen Hundred and Fifty.* 2nd ed. St. Louis: J. R. Albach, 1850. 808 p.
DLC

Quaife, Milo Milton. *Chicago and the Old Northwest, 1673–1835: A Study of the Evolution of the Northwestern Frontier, Together with a History of Fort Dearborn. . . .* Chicago: The University of Chicago Press, 1913. 480 p., front., plates, ports., map, facsims.
DLC, ICU

Annotated bibliography.

Scheiber, Harry N., comp. *The Old Northwest: Studies in Regional History, 1787–1910.* Lincoln: University of Nebraska Press, 1969. 395 p., map.
DLC, ICU

Bibliographical footnotes.

Webber, Joe D., ed. "Indian Cessions Within the Northwest Territory." "Maps Showing Location of Cessions." "Index to Indian Treaties." *Illinois Libraries* 61 (June 1979): 508–564.
DLC, I, IC, ICJ, ICN, ICU, IU

Includes two maps of Illinois. Index lists year, tribe, and state along with page and volume.

Local History—*Historic Places*

Adelman, William. *Pilsen and the West Side: A Tour Guide to Ethnic Neighborhoods, Architecture, Restaurants, Wall Murals, and Labor History, with Special Emphasis on Events Connected with the Great Upheaval of 1877.* n.p., [1978]. 85 p., illus., maps.
ICHi

Tour includes Hull House; "Praha," site of O'Leary cottage; "Little Italy," site of Auditorium; Jane Addams Housing Project; Mategrano's Restaurant; Gennaro's Restaurant; Chiarugi Hardware; Holy Family Church . . . Vertical Lift Bridge . . . Blue Island intersection (poem about same).

Brown, Virginia Sparr, ed. *Grundy County, Illinois Landmarks: A Guide to Places of Historic Interest in Aux Sable, Erienna, Goose Lake, Nettle Creek, Saratoga, Wauponsee, and Morris Townships.* Morris, Illinois: Grundy County Historical Society, 1981. 93 p., maps.
ICHi, IMoHi

Bibliography. Plan of Dresden in 1835. Points of interest in county include Morris Township: courthouse square, courthouse, soldier's monument, Indian pole, Shabonna's grave, Driving Park, W. G. Stratton State Park, Shakey Bridge, Gebhard Woods, I&M aqueduct.

Erienna Township: I&M Canal towpath, Old Stag Road, Buggy Wash, Gypsy Camp, Hoge's Woods, largest tree in Illinois (120 feet high, circumference 27 feet, 4 inches), Hillcroft Farm, fords across Illinois River, Mt. Carmel Cemetery, Sugar Island, Weitz Cover, Rock Island R.R. Right-of-Way, interurban, R. W. Hoge School, Circle A. Farm, Stockdale Young School, Erienna School, Clarkson Site, Castle Denger, Wide Waters on I&M, Crist Island, Five Mile Bridge, Barry School, Horron City, Holderman Farmstead, Praire Road, Long Point School.

Gerding, Earl T. and Thorton, Edmund B. *Historical Architectural Tour of Ottawa, Illinois.* Sponsored by Fine Arts Commission of Ottawa Growth Foundation, May 28, 1961. [Ottawa, Illinois, 1961]. 8 p.
IHi

Ruth Knack, ed. *Preservation Illinois: A Guide to State and Local Resources.* Springfield: Illinois Department of Conservation, Division of Historic Sites, 1977. 288 p., illus.
DLC
Includes index, historic sites of Illinois, conservation and restoration, federal aid to historic sites, and local histories.

Jensen, George Peter. *Historic Chicago Sites.* Chicago: Creative Enterprises, 1953. 185 p., illus.
DLC, ICU

Petterchak, Janice. "Historical Markers Program." *Journal of the Illinois State Historical Society* 67 (June 1974): 324–339.
DLC, I, IC, ICHi, ICN, ICU, IEN, IU
Lists historical points of interest in Illinois by county.

Springfield, Illinois. Illinois State Historical Library. Federal Writers' Project (Illinois). *Joliet Guide.* American Guide Series. Sponsored by the City of Joliet, Illinois. n.p., 1938. 103 p. (Typewritten.)
IHi
Includes a historical chronology (1673–1936), listing of points of interest, major businesses and industries, history of the effects of the canals.

The Will County Historical Society. *Will County Tours.* Joliet, Illinois, 1968. 10 p., maps. (Typewritten).
ICHi
Includes tours of Joliet, East Joliet–Lockport, Channahon–Morris, Plainfield. Poem about Joliet by Carl Sandburg.

Local History—*Illinois Valley*

Gray, James. *The Rivers of America: The Illinois.* As Planned and Started by Constance L. Skinner. New York: Farrar and Rinehart [1940]. 335 p., illus.
DLC, ICU
An account of places and events that occurred along the Illinois River.

Conger, John Leonard and Hull, William E. *History of the Illinois River Valley.* 3 v. Chicago: S. J. Clarke Publishing Company, 1932.
DLC, IMo, InU
Vol. 1: Contains seventeen chapters on Illinois River valley's history and commercial, social, and economic development. I&M Canal, pp. 175–193. Vols. 2 and 3: Biographical collections.

"Forgotten Towns." *Chicago Tribune—Suburban Tribune,* Friday, August 3, 1984.
IPHil
Towns in the corridor that did not survive, including Beardstown (Kankakee City).

The Illinois Valley. Chicago: Windsor Publications, 1970. 48 p., photos.
IOg
Includes profiles of the Illinois valley, Illinois Valley Area Chamber of Commerce, Illinois Valley Community College, Illinois valley industry.

Lamb, John. *A Corridor in Time.* Romeoville, Illinois: Lewis University, 1987.
ILoL
Produced for the sesquicentennial of the construction of the I&M Canal in 1836. This is the most balanced pamphlet-length introduction to the corridor's historical development.

Lamb, John M. "Early Days on the Illinois and Michigan Canal." *Chicago History* 3 (Winter 1974/1975): 168–176.
DLC, IC, ICF, ICHi, ICN, ICU, IU

Smith, Hermon Dunlap. *The DesPlaines River, 1673–1940: A Brief Consideration of Its Homes and History.* Lake Forest, Illinois: By the Author, 1940. 28 p., front., map, illus.
DLC

Woodruff, George. *Fifty Years Ago: Or Gleanings Respecting the History of Northern Illinois a Few Years Previous to and During the Black Hawk War.* Joliet, Illinois: Joliet Republican and Sun Printing, 1883.
ICN, IU

Local History—LaSalle County

Local History—*LaSalle County*—County Histories

Baldwin, Elmer. *History of LaSalle County, Illinois: Its Topography, Geology, Botany, Natural History, History of the Mound Builders, Indian Tribes, French Explorations, and a Sketch of the Pioneer Settlers of Each Town to 1840, with an Appendix, Giving the Present Status of the County, its Population, Resources, Manufacturers and Instituions....* Chicago: Rand, McNally & Company, 1877. 552 p., maps, plans.
ICN, ICU, IMoHi

Barge, William D. *The Genesis of LaSalle County.* Chicago, 1919. 22 p. (Typewritten.)
ICHi

Foster, W. R. *Stories of Pioneer Days by Eighth Grade Graduates of Village and Rural Schools Class of 1931 Commemorating the Centennial Anniversary of LaSalle County, Illinois, 1831–1931.* Ottawa, Illinois: Illinois Office Supply Company, 1931. 112 p., illus., map.
ICHi, IMa, IO, IU
Sixty essays on townships, cemeteries, early settlers.

History of LaSalle County, Illinois, Together with Sketches of Its Cities, Villages and Towns, Educational, Religous, Civil, Military, and Political History, Portraits of Prominent Persons, and Biographies of Representative Citizens: Also a Condensed History of Illinois, Embodying Accounts of Prehistoric Races, Aborigines, Winnebago and Black Hawk Wars, and a Brief Review of Its Civil and Political History. 2 v. Chicago: Inter-state Publishing Company, 1886. 1,688 p., illus., ports.
ICN, ICU
Includes Old Settlers' Society reports, county press, sketches of prominent physicians, history of public buildings, county and municipal officers, church histories. Vol. 2: Township histories.

Hoffman, U. J. *History of LaSalle County, Illinois ... Together with Biographical Sketches of Many of Its Prominent and Leading Citizens and Illustrious Dead....* Chicago: Clarke, 1906. 1,177 p., illus., ports.
ICN
Includes sketches of 1824 to 1840 pioneers in county towns. Norwegian settlements. Ottawa street scenes, 1860, 1875. Ottawa public buildings, 1906.

"LaSalle County, 150 Years." *The Daily Times* (Ottawa). September 16, 1981.
IMa
Souvenir edition. Articles on Naplate (c. 1947), Utica, Mexican War, Ottawa, Reddick Mansion, Marseilles bridge. Photographs of LaSalle street scenes and I&M Canal.

LaSalle, Illinois. Centennial Committee. *LaSalle, Illinois: An Historical Sketch.* LaSalle, Illinois, 1952. 66 p., illus.
IEN, ICN, ICU, IHi
Includes bibliography.

O'Byrne, Michael Cyprian. *History of LaSalle County, Illinois.* 3 v. Chicago: Lewis Publishing Company, 1924.
ICHi, ICN

The Past and Present of LaSalle County, Illinois, Containing a History of the County: Its Cities, Towns, etc., a Biographical Directory of its Citizens, War Record of Its Volunteers in the Late Rebellion, Portraits of Early Settlers and Prominent Men, General and Local Statistics, Map of LaSalle County, History of Illinois, Constitution of the United States, Miscellaneous Matters, etc., etc. Chicago: H. F. Klett & Company, 1877. 653 p., fronts., map, ports.
ICN, ICU
Abstract of Illinois state laws, interest table, map of LaSalle County, Civil War company lists, geology, Indian inhabitants, Old Settlers' Association records, church histories, organization officers.

Pencil Sketches [of] Ottawa and Vicinity, Including the Program of the Thirtieth Reunion and Picnic of the Old Settlers of LaSalle County. 2 v. Ottawa, Illinois, 1898 and 1899. illus.
IO
Advertisements; view of Columbus Street.

Perrin, J. Nick. "The Oldest Civil Record in the West." *Illinois State Historical Society Transactions* 6 (1901): 63–65.
DLC, IC, ICU
Brief discussion of LaSalle County.

Sandham, William R. "Lewis Bayley, Early Settler of LaSalle County." *Journal of the Illinois State Historical Society* 15 (October 1922–January 1923): 670–676.
DLC, I, IC, ICHi, ICN, ICU, IEN, IU
Covers the early settlement in LaSalle County of Lewis Bai[y]ley, as first "white child" born in county, his early life, marriage, and other family members' activities.

Local History—*LaSalle County*—Peru

Beebe, Henry S. *The History of Peru.* Peru, Illinois: J. F. Linton, Printer and Publisher, 1858. 162 p.
ICHi, ICN, IGK, IHi, IU
Includes information on early elections, newspapers, churches, canal work, railroads, depressions of 1850s. Special census of city includes nativity of 3,652 inhabitants.

Peru, Illinois. Historical Committee. *Peru, Illinois Centennial, May 25–26, 1935.* [Peru, Illinois, 1935]. 63 p., illus.
ICHi, ICU
History of churches: Zion Evangelical, 1852; St. Joseph's, 1854 (Mission of LaSalle's St. Patrick), German-speaking; St. Mary's, 1867, English-speaking; St. Valentine's, 1889, Polish-speaking; St. John's English Lutheran, 1919; First Church of Christ Scientist, 1909. Clubs and lodges: Young Men's Athlethic Club, 1901; American Legion, 1919; Rotary, 1921; Masons, 1841; Knights of Pythias, 1896. Photographs of buildings (mills on river front), canal. Bird's-eye view map showing locations of churches about 1868.

Peru, Illinois 125th Birthday Celebration, July 1,2,3,4, 1960. Historical Program. Peru, Illinois: Quad-City Printing Co., [1960]. unpaged.
IPe

Shadensack, Louis H. *Peru's Water Street a Century Ago, 1860–1880.* Peru, Illinois: W. H. Maze Company, 1966. 31 p., illus., map.
IHi

Starkey, Wilbur F. *A Pictorial History of Peru, Illinois and Part of the Illinois and Michigan Canal.* n.p., 1958. 91 p., illus. (Typewritten.)
IHi, IU—HS
Discussion of settlement, town growth, and development of political and cultural institutions.

Struever, Carl C. *Our Community: Past, Present and Future.* Peru, Illinois, 1967. 24 p.
IOg
Includes short history of LaSalle and Peru, Matthieson and Hegeler Zinc Company, Westclox, Oglesby (first known as Kenosha; Oglesby incorporated 1902), Portland Cement Industry.

Local History—*LaSalle County*—LaSalle

The Articles of Association of the Rockwell Land Company, LaSalle County, Illinois. Cleveland, Ohio: F. B. Penniman, 1836. 12 p.
ICHi
Proprietors of Rockwell surveyed town south of what later became LaSalle.

"The Bell News Visits Your Hometown: LaSalle–Peru–Oglesby." *Illinois Bell Telephone News* 42 (March 1952): 6–8. illus.
ICHi

Cummings, Elizabeth. *LaSalle, Illinois, An Historical Sketch.* LaSalle, Illinois, 1952. 66 p., illus., maps.
ICHi, ICN, ILa, IMa, IPe
Photograph of downtown Morris, c. 1870s. Other railroad and street scenes from late-nineteenth century, canal, IC bridges, bibliography.

Hennessey, A. L. *LaSalle and Peru, Illinois, Illustrated.* Portland, Maine: Chisholm Bros., 1897. 12 p., plates.
IHi

LaGave, Gary Lloyd. *LaSalle, Illinois, a Historical Sketch.* Edited by Elizabeth Cummings and Patricia Connolly. LaSalle, Illinois: [Executive Committee 125th Anniversary], 1977. 26 p., illus.
IHi, IU—HS

The LaSalle Tribune. Twentieth Anniversary Souvenir Edition, 1891–1911. LaSalle, Illinois: W. T. Bedford [1911].
ILa

Various articles on LaSalle history, businesses, and town life. Includes various advertisements.

Local History—*LaSalle County*—Oglesby

Bent, J. R. "Early History of Oglesby." *Daily Post Tribune,* March 9, 1940. 14 p. (Typewritten.)
IOg

Information on Chicago, Milwaukee, and St. Paul Railroad. Lehigh Portland Cement Company, school, Marquette Portland Cement Company, history of the Oglesby Library (1902), Union Church (1867), Sacred Heart Parish (1900, Catholic, Polish-Lithuanian Catholic), St. Constantine (Catholic, Lithuanian, c. 1900), Oglesby Coal Company.

City of Oglesby, LaSalle County, Illinois, 1902–1977. Diamond Jubilee. n.p., [1977]. 56 p.
IOg

Includes photographs of Oglesby mayors; aerial view of Oglesby, Oglesby song, written in 1951 by Ray Auler, photographs of street scenes, industries, buildings, portraits, schools, churches, and residences, historical sketch by Ray Brolley.

City of Oglesby, LaSalle County, Illinois, 1902–1952. Golden Anniversary Jubilee. n.p., [1952].
IOg

Includes "Oglesby—A Progressive City," by D. L. Mattiazza, superintendent of schools, 5 p. Photographs include portraits, aerial view of Oglesby, Swing Bridge at Deer Park, statue of Richard J. Oglesby, Baptist Church, Union Church, Holy Family Church. Advertisements.

Local History—*LaSalle County*—Utica

Utica, Illinois. Father Marquette Memorial Committee. *Dedication, Father Marquette Memorial, Sunday October 14, 1951.* [Utica, Illinois], 1951. 12 p., illus., port.
IHi

Program booklet.

Johnson, Albert. *Detailed Financial Report of Village of North Utica—A Corporation.* Utica, Illinois, 1923. 48 p.
IUtHi

Reports of deaths, births, fires, and so on.

Utica Junior Woman's Club. *Village of Utica, 1852–1952 Centennial Program.* n.p., 1952.
IO

Local History—*LaSalle County*—Ottawa

"The Bell News Visits Your Home Town: Ottawa, One Hundred Years of Progress." *Illinois Bell Telephone News* 43 (May 1953): 6–9. illus.
ICHi

Carrol, Edward Vincent. "An Examination of Ottawa, Illinois, 1830–1870." B.A. thesis, University of Illinois, 1977.
IO, IU

"Celebration of the Fiftieth Anniversary of the Lincoln-Douglas Debates of 1858: The Ottawa Meeting." *Journal of the Illinois State Historical Society* 1 (July and October 1908): 3–6.
DLC, I, IC, ICHi, ICN, ICU, IEN, IU

Account of town's celebration of debate's anniversary, August 21, 1908. Artifacts, addresses, visitors.

Conzen, Michael P., ed. *Focus on Ottawa: A Historical and Geographical Survey of Ottawa, Illinois, in the Twentieth Century.* Chicago: The University of Chicago, Committee on Geographical Studies, 1987.
DLC, ICHi, ICN, ICU, IO

First National Bank, Ottawa. *Eighty-Eight Years Ago.* Ottawa, Illinois: Office Supply Company, 1953. 16 p., illus.
ICHi

Aerial views of Ottawa in 1952. Old Settlers picnic in 1871, Ottawa Turnverein in 1866, Electric Railway in 1889.

Hackensmith, C. W. *Boyhood Remembrances of Ottawa, Illinois.* Iowa Falls, Iowa: General Publishing and Binding Telephone, 1971. 56 p., illus.
IO

Family history of German-American family in Ottawa.

To the Minister of Foreign Affairs of Norway. Chicago: C. L. Ricketts, 1934. 6 p.
IHi

Photostatic reproduction of the invitation to attend the centenary celebration in and around the city of Ottawa, Illinois, in honor of the founding of the first permanent Norwegian settlement in the United States.

Nattinger, E. A., comp. *Ottawa in Nineteen Hundred: A Souvenir of the City, Industrial, Commercial, Educational, Professional, Social, Religious, and Scenic.* Ottawa, Illinois: E. A. Nattinger, June 1900. 138 p., illus., ports., maps, plans.
IHi

. . . *Ottawa; Beautiful, Resourceful Pioneer City of Illinois, Capital of the Second County in the State. . . .* Ottawa, Illinois: Republican Times, 1897. 82 p., illus., ports.
ICHi, ICN
Includes plan of Ottawa in 1838, bird's-eye view in 1895, Illinois Valley Coal Company, U.S. Silica Company.

Ottawa, Illinois. Republican Times. *53rd Year Edition.* Ottawa, Illinois: Sapp and Nattinger, 1897. 82 p., illus., ports.
IO

Raymond, W. J. and Tieste, W. F. *Ottawa, Illinois: Historical, Biographical, and Commercial.* Ottawa, Illinois: Raymond & Tieste, 1881. 20 p.
ICN
A review of its manufacturing and jobbing, wholesaling and retailing, in dry goods, groceries, boots and shoes, furnishing goods, clothing, crockery, drugs, tobacco, lumber, carpets, furniture, coal, hardware, and hotel business.

The Republican Times. *Ottawa: Old and New; A Complete History of Ottawa, Illinois, 1823–1914.* Ottawa, Illinois: The Republican Times, 1823–1914. 208 p., illus.
ICN, IU

Tisler, C. C. *Lincoln Was Here, for Another Go at Douglas.* Jackson, Tennessee: McCowat-Mercer Press, 1958. 60 p., illus.
ICHi, ICU, IO
About Ottawa. History of Lincoln and Douglas debate with letters to residents from Lincoln.

Tisler, C. C. *Story of Ottawa, Illinois.* Ottawa, Illinois: Illinois Office Supply Company, 1953. 51 p.
IO
Written for the Centennial Commission of the city of Ottawa.

Townley, Wayne C. *Two Judges of Ottawa.* Carbondale, Illinois: Egypt Book House, 1948. 43 p.
IO
Judges T. Lyle Dickey and John Dean Caton. The book is a town history of the 1830–1860 period, with several photographs and engravings of residential structures.

Local History—*LaSalle County*—Marseilles

Carney, Mary Vance. *The Story of Marseilles, 1835–1960: Dedicated to the Oldest Native-Born Residents of Marseilles in 1960.* Ottawa, Illinois: Historical Booklet Committee, 1960. 52 p., illus.
ICHi, IO
Includes chapter on influences of canal and railroad. Histories of churches, schools, Marseilles Manufacturing Company. Street scene photograph in 1900. Surveyor's plat of 1835.

Germain, Mirah. "The Historical Growth and Spatial Evolution of Marseilles, Illinois (1835 to the Present)." B.A. thesis, University of Chicago, 1985.
IMa
Divides the town's history into four distinct periods of economic growth and spatial evolution: 1835–1866, small-scale industry; 1867–1900, large-scale industry; 1901–1929, great prosperity; 1930–1985, cessation of spatial development.

Marseilles, Illinois. Greater Marseilles Club. *Marseilles.* Marseilles, Illinois, 1921. 8 p., folder, illus.
IHi

Marseilles Bicentennial Commission. *The Story of Marseilles.* [Marseilles, Illinois]: 1976. illus., 99 p.
IHi, IMa
Poem by Nathan A. Fleming, Sr., "Marseilles 1835–1935," plat of Marseilles, photographs of buildings, Marseilles blocks on I&M Canal (photographs). Church histories:

Universalist (1859), St. Andrew's Episcopal (1868), Brookfield Presbyterian (1833), Congregational (1860), St. Joseph's Catholic (1862), Church of the Nazarene (1931), Church of God (1931), Baptist (1866), Methodist (1868), Trinity Lutheran (1866), Immanuel Lutheran (1892, Norwegian), early schools, migration of Norwegians, Italians, and Kentuckians.

Marseilles Sesquicentennial, 1835–1985. "Say Mar-Sales, Where Life Begins at 150." Coal City, Illinois: Printed by Bailey Printing, 1985. 144 p., illus., maps.
IMa
Thirty-one sections on all aspects of Marseilles history, including bridges, churches, schools, I&M Canal, businesses.

Local History—*LaSalle County*—Seneca

Seneca Area Centennial Celebration, The Story of 100 Years: July 27 through August 1, 1965. Seneca, Illinois: Seneca Regional Port District, 1965. 68 p., illus.
IHi, IMa, IO
Advertising. Information on Jeremiah Crotty and other early settlers, St. Patrick's Church, Stavanger Lutheran Church, Holiness Methodist Church, Our Savior's Lutheran Church, Seneca Assemblies of God, First Methodist Church.

Local History—Grundy County

Local History—*Grundy County*—County Histories

Barge, William D. *The Genesis of Grundy County.* Chicago, 1920. 18 p. (Typewritten.)
ICHi

Bateman, Newton, ed. *Historical Encyclopedia of Illinois, Edited by Newton Bateman, LL.D., Paul Selby, A.M., and History of Grundy County (Historical and Biographical) by Special Authors and Contributors.* 2 v. Chicago: Munsell Publishing Company, 1914. front., plates, ports., maps.
ICN, ICU, IMoHi

Crawford, Jean. *Jugtown Pottery: History and Design.* Winston-Salem, Illinois: John F. Blair, Publisher, 1964.
IMo
Jugtown was in Section 9, Goose Lake Township, and was a famous terra cotta works.

History of Grundy County, Illinois: Containing a History from the Earliest Settlement to the Present Time, Embracing Its Topographical, Geological, Physical and Climatic Features; Its Agricultural, Railroad Interests, etc.; Giving an Account of Its Aboriginal Inhabitants, Early Settlement by the Whites, Pioneer Incidents, the County, the Judicial History, the Business and Industries, Churches, Schools, etc; Biographical Sketches; Portraits of Some of the Early Settlers, Prominent Men, etc. Chicago: O. L. Baskin & Company, 1882. 156 p.
ICN, IMoHi

Ullrich, Helen Stine. *This Is Grundy County: Its History from Beginning to 1968.* Dixon, Illinois: Rogers Printing Company, 1968. 338 p., illus., map.
ICN, IMo, IMoHi, ISe, IU—HS
Bibliography.

Local History—*Grundy County*—Morris

Armstrong, Perry. *Address 4th of July, 1876, at the Old Settlers Association at Morris, Illinois.* [Morris, Illinois, 1976].
IMo

"The Bell News Visits Your Home Town: Morris, Home of the Corn Festival." *Illinois Bell Telephone News* 41 (1951): 4–6. illus.
ICHi

The Morris Weekly Herald. Special Illustrated Souvenir Number Celebrating the 50th Anniversary of the Morris Weekly Herald; 25th Anniversary of the Morris Daily Herald. March 10, 1905. (Photocopy.)
IMo
City history, church histories, description of principal industrial and commercial firms, with photographs.

Local History—*Grundy County*—Minooka

Village of Minooka. Minooka, Illinois: Village Clerk's Office, 1984.
IMo
Contains a section on village history.

Local History—Will County

Local History—*Will County*—County Histories

Gleanings and Biographies. n.p., Will County Historical Society, 1969. 61 p.
ICHi
History of twenty-four Will County townships through 1918. Includes towns, churches, flora and fauna, industry, schools. Short biographies. 5 p.

Grinton, William. *Will County First Things: Manufacturing "Microbes" and "Germs" That Grow. . . .* Reprint ed. Lockport, Illinois: Will County Historical Society, 1973. 9 p.
ILo
A listing of first settlers and early businesses.

The History of Will County, Illinois, Containing a History of the County . . . A Directory of Its Real Estate Owners; Portraits of Early Settlers and Prominent Men; General and Local Statistics . . . History of Illinois . . . History of the Northwest. Chicago: W. LeBaron, Jr. Company, 1878. 995 p., illus., ports., tables, map.
ICN

Maue, August. *History of Will County, Illinois.* 2 v. Topeka, Kansas: Historical Publishing Company, 1928. 1,140 p., illus., ports.
ICN, ILo
Vol. 1: Contemporary photographs of schools, public buildings, and downtown business structures in Joliet, Lockport, Braidwood, Peotone, Plainfield, and Mokena. Reissued in 1944. Vol. 2: Biographies.

Schofield, William W. *Contemporary Local History, Volumes I and II.* 2 v. [Joliet, Illinois]: Will County Historical Society, 1972. 16 p.
ILo
Includes anecdotes of first settlers, first school in Joliet, the "winter of the deep snow' (1830–1831), Buffalo Bill in Joliet, "paper cities."

Souvenir of Settlement of Progress of Will County, Illinois . . . Complete History and Directory of Will County, Pioneers and Old Settlers, Early Settlement, Military History 1832–1865, Political History 1836–1884, Commercial History 1832–1884, Tax Roll of 1842, Tax Roll of 1884, Business Directory of Joliet, Societies, Schools, Churches, History of Townships, Cities, and Villages. . . . Chicago: Historical Directory Publishing Company, 1884. 458 p., front., map.
ICHi, ICU

Stevens, William Wallace. *Past and Present of Will County. . . .* 2 v. Chicago: S. J. Clarke Publishing Company, 1907.
IU

Where There's A Will. . . . Joliet, Illinois: Will County 125th Anniversary Committee, Inc., 1961. 75 p., illus.
IJo
Early history of Will County and Joliet, Crest Hill, Braidwood, and Lockport. Advertisements.

Where the Trails Cross. Vol. 1–. Homewood, Illinois. 1970–.
ICN
Official publication of the South Cook and North Will Counties Genealogical and Historical Society.

Will County Pioneer Association. *6th Annual Reunion.* Joliet, Illinois, 1886.
ICHi
Address by George H. Woodruff.

Woodruff, George H. *Fifteen Years Ago, or The Patriotism of Will County, Designed to Preserve the Names and Memory of Will County Soldiers, Both Officers and Privates—Both Living and Dead: To Tell Something of What They Did, and of What They Suffered in the Great Struggle to Preserve our Nationality. . . .* Joliet, Illinois: J. Goodspeed, 1876. 515 p., front.
ICHi, ICN
History of Illinois regiments 20th, 39th, 64th, 90th, and 100th Infantry; 1st Artillery.

Woodruff, George H. *Forty Years Ago! A Contribution to the Early History of Joliet and Will County: Two Lectures Delivered Before the Historical Society of Joliet, December 17th, 1873, and March 24th, 1874.* Joliet, Illinois: Jas. Goodspeed, 1874. 108 p.
ICHi, ICN, IGK
Indexed.

Woodruff, George. *History of Will County, Illinois.* Chicago: W. LeBaron, Jr. and Company, 1878.
DLC

Local History—*Will County*—Joliet

Cox, Charles E. "Sketch of Robert Mann Woods." *Journal of the Illinois State Historical Society* 12 (July 1919): 259–263.
DLC, I, IC, ICHi, ICN, ICU, IEN, IU

Woods was publisher of the *Joliet Daily Republican* from 1877 to 1893.

Ferris, Jas. H., ed. *Joliet News Historical Edition.* Joliet, Illinois, 1884. 57 p., illus., ports.
ICHi

Engravings of individuals, buildings, bridges, residences, churches, penitentiary, Fort Nonsense.

Grinton, William. *Cass Street Sketches (Joliet, Illinois). By the Old Man.* Joliet, Illinois: C. B. Hayward Company, 1897. 183 p., front.
ICHi, IJo

Literary sketches of Joliet personalities, locations, institutions.

Grinton, William. *Juliet and Joliet. . . .* Joliet, Illinois: News Printing Co., 1904. 55 p.
ICN

Includes poem about I&M Canal.

Hobbs, Clarissa Emily Gear. "Autobiography of Clarissa Emily Gear Hobbs." *Journal of the Illinois State Historical Society* 17 (January 1925): 612–714.
DLC, I, IC, ICHi, ICN, ICU, IEN, IU

Includes a section on life in Joliet in the 1850s and 1860s.

Joliet Daily News, Press Edition. Tuesday, November 28, 1911. 84 p., illus., ports.
ICHi

Contains historical and descriptive articles on Joliet. History of *Daily News.* Officers and histories of 1911 Joliet organizations: Merchants Association, judges, lawyers, officials, Illinois Steel Company, banks, laborers, doctors, lodges, library, parks, Illinois Brick Company, churches, W.C.T.U. History of I&M Canal. History of wars, 3rd Illinois Regiment.

Joliet, Illinois. Joliet Public Library. *Clippings: Joliet Herald News.* Special Edition, 1936. Compiled by Mary Loskill. Indexed by Terry Rettberg. Joliet, Illinois, 1936. 33 p.
IJo

Contains many photographs and drawings of residences, factories, and downtown stores and institutional structures, along with short historical sketches depicting various phases of the city's history.

Joliet Illustrated, Historical, Descriptive, and Biographical. Joliet: *Daily Republican,* 1897. 140 p.
ICHi, IJo

Engravings of E. Porter Brewing Co., Joliet Manufacturing Co., Fred Sehring Brewing Co., residences, individuals, churches, industrial sites.

"The Naming of Joliet." *Journal of the Illinois State Historical Society* 47 (September 1944): 266.
DLC, I, IC, ICHi, ICN, ICU, IEN, IU

Sorensen, Andrew A. "Lester Frank Ward, 'The American Aristotle' in Illinois." *Journal of the Illinois State Historical Society* 63 (Summer 1970): 158–166.
DLC, I, IC, ICHi, ICN, ICU, IEN, IU

Biography of Joliet native Ward, biologist, anthropologist, psychologist, and sociologist. Photographs.

Speech of Judge G. D. A. Parks, at a Meeting Held in Aid of Ireland at the Opera House, Joliet, Illinois, December 20th, 1879. Joliet, Illinois: Sun Steam Book and Job Print, 1880.
IJo

Also contains some of Parks's speeches, including 1882, Pioneer Association of Will County; 1889, Centennial Banquet of First Universalist Church; 1895, Pig Silver.

Local History—*Will County*—Lockport

Civic and Commerce Association. *Hail and Farewell, 1935–1980.* Lockport, Illinois, 1980. 56 p.
ICHi

Contains photographs of individuals and scenes from Lockport's history: I&M Canal lock, railroads, Evangelical Association Church, street scenes during World War I, homes, class pictures, Lockport Township High School.

Hamzik, Joseph. *Gleanings of Archer Road.* Chicago, 1961. 109 p., port. (Typewritten.)
ICHi

History of early Archer Road area. Section on I&M Canal, Lockport, Bridgeport, Brighton, Summit. Photograph of W. B. Archer.

"Illinois Sesquicentennial: Lockport-Homer Townships Celebration and Homecoming, October 18–19–20, 1968." Supplement to the *Lockport Herald,* October 17, 1968.
IBP

Articles on I&M Canal, Great Fire in Lockport (1895), high school, churches, history of Lewis University, Lemont refinery, Crest Hill Incorporates (1960), Texaco, Lockport Incorporates (1904), papers.

Lockport Has a Birthday: 1830–1930. [Lockport, Illinois]: Publicity Committee of the Centennial Celebration, 1930. 37 p., ports., illus.
ICHi, ICN, IU

Company record of 90th regiment volunteers. Photographs of mills along I&M Canal, school buildings, churches, street scenes.

"Old Canal Days Special." *Lockport Free Press.* June 15, 1978.
ILo

Contains map of historic sites in Lockport, description of structures, valley greatest influence on area, John Lane and the first steel plow, Lockport viewed by 1940s visitor, "Drunken, Dirty" Irish build Canal, culture came to Lockport in 1850, Homer, Lockport always close, I&M boatyard saw heavy use, Lockport as financial center. (All articles written by John Lamb.)

Lockport, Illinois: A Collective Heritage. Lockport, Illinois: American Printers and Lithographers for the Sesquicentennial Committee of the Bank of Lockport, 1980. 32 p., illus., maps.
ILe, ILeHi, ILo

Extensively illustrated historical guide published to commemorate Lockport's 150th anniversary.

Lockport, Illinois. Woman's Club. *Lockport.* Issued by Lockport Woman's Club, December 1905. Joliet, Illinois: Will County Historical Society, 1972. 9 p.
IHi

U.S. Department of the Interior. Heritage Conservation and Recreation Service. *Lockport, Illinois: A HCRS Project Report.* Washington: U.S. Government Printing Office, 1979. illus.
ILo

Report of team of eight student and professional historians, architects, and planners to develop historic preservation. Includes photographs of I&M locks, early history of Lockport, 9th Street Bridge over DesPlaines, buildings, street scenes. Plans for restoration of Norton building, canal front, Hyland building, Commerce Street.

Local History—*Will County*—
Romeoville

Bingle, James D., comp. *Bolingbrook Does Too Have a History.* Bolingbrook, Illinois: Bolingbrook Historical Society, [1975]. 19 p., illus., maps, ports.
IU—HS

Contains "Our Neighbor to the South: A Brief History of Romeoville, Courtesy of James Scyepaniak," pp. 18–19.

Romeo. Romeoville, Illinois: Romeoville Historical Society, n.d.
ILeHi

Historical sketch with seven pages of recollections of social life in the village during the early-twentieth century.

Local History—*Will County*—
Channahon

Dillon, Phyllis. *History of Channahon, Homecoming of 1972.* [Channahon, Illinois], 1972. illus.
IHi

Includes advertising.

Local History—*DuPage County*

Bateman, Newton, ed. *Historical Encyclopedia of Illinois and History of DuPage County.* 2 v. Chicago: Munsell Publishing Company, 1913. front., plates, ports., maps.
ICarbS, ICN, ICU, IU

Includes historical and biographical sketch of DuPage County by special authors and contributors.

Blanchard, Rufus. *History of DuPage County, Illinois.* Chicago: O. L. Baskin & Company, 1882. 247 p., ports.
DLC, ICN, MWA
Historical and biographical.

DuPage County, Illinois. Board of Supervisors. *History of DuPage County, Illinois.* Aurora, Illinois: Knickerbocker & Hodder, 1877. 250 p., front., port.
ICHi, ICN
Compiled under the direction and supervision of the board of supervisors, 1876. "Patrons' Directory," pp. [220]–244.

DuPage Historical Review. Vol. 1–3. Glen Ellyn, Illinois, 1950–1952. illus., ports.
ICHi, ICN
Bimonthly, 1950. Quarterly, 1951–1952.

Federal Writers' Project. Illinois. *DuPage County, a Descriptive and Historical Guide, 1831–1939.* Elmhurst, Illinois: I. A. Ruby, 1948. 253 p.
ICN, ICU, IU—HS
Marion Knoblavch reedited this publication in 1948.

Maas, David E. and Weber, Charles W., eds. *DuPage Discovery, 1776–1976: A Bicentennial View.* n.p., Columbian Lithographic, 1976. 208 p., illus.
ICN
DuPage history, addresses, essays, lectures. Index.

Richmond, Charles W. and Vallette, Henry F. *A History of the County of DuPage, Illinois: Containing an Account of Its Early Settlement and Present Advantages, a Separate History of the Several Towns, Including Notices of Religious Organizations, Education, Agriculture and Manufactures, with the Names and Some Account of the First Settlers in Each Township, and Much Valuable Statistical Information.* Chicago: Steam Presses of Scripps, Bross & Spears, 1857. 212 p.
DLC, ICHi, ICJ, ICN, IHi

Local History—Cook County

Local History—*Cook County*—County Histories

Andreas, Alfred T. *History of Cook County, Illinois, from the Earliest Period to the Present Time.* Chicago: A. T. Andreas, 1884. 888 p., front., illus., port., maps.
DLC, ICHi

Barge, William D. *The Genesis of Cook County.* Chicago, 1919. 23 p., maps. (Typewritten.)
ICHi

Bateman, Newton. *Historical Encyclopedia of Illinois; Cook County Edition.* 2 v. Chicago: Munsell Publishing Company, 1905. fronts., plates, ports., maps.
DLC, ICHi

Johnson, Charles B. *Growth of Cook County.* Chicago: Board of Commissioners of Cook County, 1960. illus.
DLC, ICHi

Our Suburbs: A Resume of the Origin, Progress and Present Status of Chicago's Environs. Chicago: Chicago Times, 1873.
ICN

Goodspeed, Weston A., *et al.*, eds. *History of Cook County, Illinois: Being a General Survey of Cook County History, Including a Condensed History of Chicago and Special Account of District Outside the City Limits; From the Earliest Settlement to the Present Time.* 2 v. Chicago: The Goodspeed Historical Assoc., [1911]. fronts., plates, ports., maps.
DLC, ICJ

Waterman, Arba Nelson, ed. *Historical Review of Chicago and Cook County.* 3 v. Chicago: The Lewis Publishing Company, 1908.
DLC, ICHi, ICJ
With selected biographies.

Local History—*Cook County*—Lemont

Buschman, Barbara, ed. *Lemont, Illinois: Its History in Commemoration of the Centennial of Its Incorporation.* [Des Plaines, Illinois: King/Man Yearbook Center, 1973.] 208 p., illus., map.

ICHi, ILeHi

Photographs of limestone quarries, early street scenes, school classes. Histories of church organizations, including St. Adolphus (German Catholic), Swedish Evangelical Bethany Lutheran, Ss. Cyril and Methodius, Polish Catholic, St. James (Sag), Catholic, St. Matthew's Lutheran (German), St. Patrick's (Irish Catholic), Lemont United Methodist. Institutions include St. Mary's Retreat House, Franciscan Brothers, Holy Family Villa (Lithuanian Catholic), Mother Theresa Home, Franciscan Sisters.

Lemont History and Anecdotes: Dedicated to the School Children of Our Town. Lemont, Illinois: Lemont Area Historical Society, 1975. (Typewritten.)
ILe, ILeHi

Includes history of Old Stone Church, Sioux and Ojibway pictography, transportation and Lemont trolley cars, Indians of the area, Jimmy Barry—American Bantam-weight champ, the First National Bank holdup, labor and the quarries, unlucky 252, the siege of Lemont, street names, clothing in 1873, Altgeld and Lemont, Ruby Kling—"The Pride of Lemont," legend of the Sag Church Ghosts, Lincoln's part in the I&M Canal, I&M Canal sparks Lemont's growth, Lemont's volunteer fire department.

Local History—*Cook County*—Chicago

Jewell, Frank. *Annotated Bibliography of Chicago History.* Chicago: Chicago Historical Society, 1979. 414 p.
ICHi, ICU

An extensive bibliography.

The Chicagoan. Vol. 1–15. Chicago: The Chicagoan Publishing Company, 1926–1935. illus., ports.
IC, NN

March 26, 1927, to July 1931, fortnightly; August 1931, monthly.

The Chicagoan. Vol. 1–. Chicago: City Publications Co., 1972–.
IC, ICU

Monthly.

Chicago History. Vol. 1–. Chicago: Chicago Historical Society, 1945–.
DLC, IC, ICF, ICHi, ICN, ICU, IU

Quarterly. Articles deal with city and surrounding area.

Adelman, William. *Touring Pullman: A Study in Company Paternalism. A Walking Guide to the Pullman Community in Chicago, Illinois.* Chicago: Illinois Labor History Society and the Ralph Helstein Fund, 1977. 46 p., facsim., views, map.
DLC

Andreas, Alfred Theodore. . . . *History of Chicago, From the Earliest Period to the Present Time.* . . . 3 v. Chicago: A. T. Andreas, 1884–1886. fronts., illus., plates, ports., maps.
DLC, ICU, IaU, MiU

Vol. I: 1670–1857; Vol. II: 1857–1871; Vol. III: 1871–1885. Business statistics, histories of voluntary organizations, arts, press, corporations, churches.

Bach, Ira J. "Pullman: A Town Reborn." *Chicago History* 4 (Spring 1975): 44–53.
DLC, IC, ICF, ICHi, ICN, ICU, IU

Pullman in nineteenth and twentieth centuries, with photographs and engravings of churches, residences, factories, and the arcade.

Chicago, Illinois. Chicago Historical Society. *Documents: History of . . . Communities, Chicago. Prepared for the Chicago Historical Society and Local Community Research Committee, University of Chicago. Research Under the Direction of Vivien M. Palmer.* 6 v. Chicago, 1925–1930. (Typewritten.)
ICHi

Vol. 6: Riverdale.

Chicago, Illinois. *Chicago in Periodical Literature, a Summary of Articles . . . Compiled by the Workers of the Writer's Program of the W.P.A. in the State of Illinois.* Chicago, 1940. (Typewritten.)
DLC

Doty, Mrs. Duane. *The Town of Pullman: Its Growth with Brief Descriptions of Its Industries.* Pullman, Illinois: T. P. Struhsacker, 1893. 208 p., illus.
DLC

Fanning, Charles F., Jr. "Mr. Dooley's Bridgeport Chronicle." *Chicago History* 2 (Spring 1972): 47–57.
DLC, IC, ICF, ICHi, ICN, ICU, IU

Politics and social life, with photographs of residences and saloons.

Gillette, John Morris. "... Culture Agencies of a Typical Manufacturing Group: South Chicago...." Ph.D. dissertation, University of Chicago, 1901. 66 p., maps, tables.
ICHi, ICU

Hauser, Philip M. and Ritagawa, Evelyn M. *Local Community Fact Book for Chicago, 1950.* Chicago: Chicago Community Inventory, University of Chicago, 1953.
DLC, ICU

Brief histories of each community area of Chicago, along with census statistics.

Holt, Glen E. and Pacyga, Dominic A. *Chicago: A Historical Guide to the Neighborhoods; The Loop and South Side.* Chicago: Chicago Historical Society, 1979. 174 p., illus.
ICHi, ICU

Contains history and photographs of sixteen Chicago neighborhoods including the Loop, Armour Square, and Bridgeport. Includes bibliography and index.

Pacyga, Dominic and Skerrett, Ellen. *Chicago: City of Neighborhoods.* Chicago: Loyola University Press, 1986. 582 p., illus.
ICL, ICU

Contains tours of all I&M Canal neighborhoods.

Janik, Phillip F. "Looking Backward from 'The Bush' to the Open Hearth." *Chicago History* 10 (Spring, 1981): 49–56.
DLC, IC, ICF, ICHi, ICN, ICU, IU

Concerns South Chicago.

The Kelly Community. Chicago: Thomas Kelly High School, 1938. 64 p., illus., maps.
ICHi

High school for Archer Heights and Brighton Park. History sections on I&M Canal, Drainage Canal in relation to typhoid, information on ethnic groups, transportation, churches.

Kijewski, Marcia, Borsch, David and Balanda, Robert. *The Historical Development of Three Chicago Millgates: South Chicago, East Side, South Deering.* 3 v. Chicago: Illinois Labor History Society, 1972. illus., ports., maps.
ICHi

Kogan, Herman. *Chicago: A Pictorial History....* New York: E. P. Dutton, 1958. 224 p., illus., plans, maps, photos.
DLC, ICU

Koopman, H. R. *Pullman, the City of Brick.* Roseland, Illinois: H. R. Koopman, 1893. 2 p.
DLC

Illustrated.

Mayer, Harold Melvin. *Chicago: Growth of a Metropolis.* Chicago: University of Chicago Press, 1969. 510 p., illus., maps, plans.
DLC, ICHi, ICU

Panorama of city views before and after fire, by Alexander Hesler. Plat of Blue Island. Chicago River scenes. Loop scenes. Plat of Pullman. J. W. Taylor 1913 panorama. 1937 panorama.

Petraitis, Paul W. "Henry Koopman II: The Life and Times of a Neighborhood Photographer." *Chicago History* 7 (Fall 1978): 161–177.
DLC, IC, ICF, ICHi, ICN, ICU, IU

Koopman lived in Roseland and worked in the Pullman-Kensington area. Article contains several photographs of area architecture.

Pierce, Bessie Louise. ... *A History of Chicago....* 3 v. New York, London: A. A. Knopf, 1937–1957. illus., plates, maps, diagrs.
DLC, ICHi, ICU

Bibliography. Vol. I: 1673–1848; Vol. II: 1848–1871; Vol. III: 1871–1893.

Motley, Archie. "Manuscript Sources on Frontier Chicago." *Chicago History* 9 (Summer 1980): 122–127.
DLC, IC, ICF, ICHi, ICN, ICU, IU

Local History—*Cook County*—Argo-Summit

Hill, Robert Milton. *A Little Known Story of the Land Called Clearing.* n.p., By the Author, 1983.
IBP

Six parts: French and Indians, ?–1762; Scalps and Civilization, 1763–1848; Railroads, 1848–1914; Village of Clearing, 1912–1915; Let the Good Times Roll, 1915–1929; Hungry but Happy, 1930–1940.

"History of Summit." Unpublished paper, Bedford Park Library, n.d. 21 p.
IBP

Sections on railroads, education, recreation, population by nationality, churches. *The Argo-Summit Survey* [Congregational Church].

Summit Heritage. Summit, Illinois: Summit Bicentennial Commission, 1977.
ISA

Local History—*Cook County*—Justice

Krbecek, Norene. "Unpublished History of Indian Springs School District #109." Unpublished paper, Bridgeview Public Library, n.d.
IBr, IJu
History of Justice and Bridgeview area, Indians, early explorers, I&M Canal, Chicago and Joliet Electric Railway, cemeteries (including Lithuanian), early settlers, pioneers of Justice, Justice Police Department, major area roads, photographs of Archer Road in 1930s, libraries, pioneers of Bridgeview, Bridgeview Fire Department, Bridgeview Police Department, Bridgeview Park District, Common School District #109 (1870–), Argo High School (1920), original boundaries of Bridgeview in 1947, copy of landowners maps of 1860, 1875, 1886, 1902, 1930.

Local History—*Cook County*—Bedford Park

Roots. Vol. 1–5. Bedford Park Historical Newsletter, 1974–1978.
IBP
Photographs and notices of elderly residents.

Local History—*Cook County*—Bridgeview

A History of Bridgeview, Illinois. n.p., Copyright Rich Peksa, 1972. 80 p., ports., photos., maps.
IBP, IBr
Twenty-fifth anniversary commemorative history. Includes information on the area prior to incorporation (1947).

Local History—*Cook County*—Sag Towns

Beaudette, E. P., comp. *Blue Island: An Illustrated Review of Its Leading Industries, Churches, Schools, Societies, Officials, Business Men and Citizens; Burr Oak, West Pullman, Posen, Oak Forest, Tinley Park, Worth, Mount Greenwood.* Chicago: Holland Press, 1915. 92 p., illus., ports.
ICHi, ICN
Picture collections of police and fire departments in Blue Island. Information on Liederkranz (German singing society). Street views, residences, churches, Opera House. Photographs of steam shovel used in building Sanitary and Ship Canal. One-page histories of West Pullman and Worth.

City of Palos Heights, 1959–1984: Silver Jubilee. n.p., 1984.
IPHei
Includes brief historical sketch, advertisements.

Dilg, Charles Augustus. *Blue Island History.* n.p., 1903.
ICHi, ICN
Clippings from the *Blue Island Standard,* August 8–October 3, 1903.

Despise Not the Day of Small Beginnings: Dolton, Illinois, by . . . Students of Thornridge High School. Dolton, Illinois: The First National Bank in Dolton, 1960. 35 p.
ICHi, ICN
Bibliography. Based on newspapers, directories, public documents, interviews.

Dolton–South Holland Woman's Club. *Dolton, Illinois, 1892–1976.* Dolton, Illinois, 1976. 68 p., illus., ports.
ICHi
Photographs of street scenes in 1910s, onion fields, railroad depots.

"Fünfzig Jahre deutschen Liedes in Blue Island." *Deutsch-Amerikanische Geschichtsblätter* 3 (October 1903): 21–23.
DLC, IC, ICJ, ICN, ICU, IU
In German. Singing organization in Blue Island.

Hewitt, Gwen. *The History of Palos Park.* n.p., 1971. 1 p.
IU—HS
A bibliography.

"How Blue Island Got Its Name." *Rock Island Magazine* 26 (June 1931): 11.
DLC, ICHi, IU

Huizenga, Pat. *Dolton, 1892–1976.* [Dolton, 1976], 68 p., illus., ports.
ICN
Bibliography.

Jebsen, Harry A. A. "Blue Island, Illinois: The History of a Working Class Suburb." Ph.D. dissertation, University of Cincinnati, 1971.
OCU

Jebsen, Harry A. "The Role of Blue Island in the Pullman Strike of 1894." *Journal of the Illinois State Historical Society* (1974): 275–293.
DLC, I, IC, ICHi, ICN, ICU, IEN, IU

The League of Women Voters of Riverdale, Illinois. *Spotlight on Riverdale.* [Chicago], 1958. 49 p.
ICHi
Contains short history of Riverdale, pp. 1–6.

McCoo, F. A. *"Say It with Pictures": Achievements of the Negro in Chicago, Illinois the Past Twenty-five Years.* Chicago: F. A. McCoo, Sr., 1937. 70 p., illus., ports.
ICHi
Contains a brief history of village of Robbins.

Pashley, Hattie Sinnard. *Pageant of Palos, Presented by the People of Palos Township, Saturday Afternoon, September 16, 1916, at Palos Park, Illinois, Under the Auspices of the Palos Improvement Club.* Chicago: The Hildmann Printing Company, 1916. 21 p., illus., music.
ICHi
History of Palos Township presented in a play. Includes references to I&M Canal and its effect on area population.

Potter, Earl. "History of Palos Hills." Unpublished paper, Green Hills Public Library. 22 p.
IPHil

Richards, Harold J. *The Blue Island Story: An Historical Sketch of the First One Hundred and Twenty-seven Years of Our City on the Hill Blue Island, Illinois. Written and Published as Part of the Fourth of July Celebration. Sponsored by the Lions Club of Blue Island.* Blue Island, Illinois, 1962. 185 p., illus., ports.
ICHi
Photographs of residences, buildings, street scenes, great fire of 1896.

Schapper, Ferdinand. *Southern Cook County and History of Blue Island Before the Civil War. . . .* 3 v. n.p., 1917. illus., maps, plans, photos. (Typewritten.)
ICHi
Vol. 1: Southern Cook County and history of Blue Island. Vol. 2: Early settlers and their families. Vol. 3: Views of Blue Island.

Spiegl, Marie. *A History of Palos [Township].* n.p., Palos Historical Society, 23 p., illus.
IPHil
Originally in *Bulletin of Illinois Geographical Society* 17 (December 1975).

Volp, John H. *The First Hundred Years, 1835–1935, Historical Review of Blue Island, Illinois.* n.p., n.d. 384 p.
ICHi

Local History—*Archive Sources*

Bedford Park, Illinois. Bedford Park Public Library. Local History Collection.
IBP
Historical reviews of Clearing, 3 p. (typewritten); Clearing History folder, copy of I&M Canal $5.00 note; Map of Clearing growth, 1900–1910; Bedford Park bus tour, 2 p.; "An Area's Story," grade eight graduating classes, Graves School, 1960 and 1965, 29 p., maps; Summit history. Sections on quarries, churches, schools, annexation of Argo to Summit, fire department, police, roads, bridges, early years of corn products, community in 1919, early residents and history of Bedford Park (1930).

Bedford Park, Illinois. Bedford Park Public Library. Local History Collection: Scrapbook on Plans for Bedford Park's Celebration of the 300th Anniversary of the Birth of Père Marquette.
IBP
The festival took place in 1937. The scrapbook contains correspondence, minutes of planning meetings, and clippings of newspaper articles.

Bridgeview, Illinois. Bridgeview Public Library. Vertical File. Bridgeview.
IBr
File includes twenty-fifth anniversary supplement to *The Times,* Wednesday, July 5, 1972. n.p.

Chicago, Illinois. Art Institute. National Register of Historic Places: Nomination Forms for Historic Places in Illinois, Outside Chicago. 1981–. Vol. [1–3], illus., maps.
ICA

Photocopies of nomination forms and supporting evidence. Information provided includes name, address, building type, owner, condition, building description, building's architectural significance, history of ownership and function, sources of further information on building, photographs of building.

Chicago, Illinois. Chicago Historical Society. Emma Lillian Baird Collection. 50 p.
ICHi

Personal and family recollections of Lockport resident before 1890.

Chicago, Illinois. Chicago Historical Society. Benjamin F. Barker Collection. Twenty-four items.
ICHi

Letters about conditions in Chicago and Joliet, 1832–1840.

Chicago, Illinois. Chicago Historical Society. Benton House Collection. Thirteen hundred items.
ICHi

Minutes, reports, correspondence of settlement house operated by Episcopalians in the Bridgeport area from 1892. Information on economic and social conditions.

Chicago, Illinois. Chicago Historical Society. Cyrus Bryant Collection. 3 p.
ICHi

Includes petition by people of Peru for a new county in 1841.

Chicago, Illinois. Chicago Historical Society. Andrew J. Galloway Collection. 3 p.
ICHi

Memories of Marseilles from 1841.

Chicago, Illinois. Chicago Historical Society. Daniel Healy Collection. Three pieces.
ICHi

Two descriptions of early days in Bridgeport. Naturalization certificate from 1857.

Chicago, Illinois. Chicago Historical Society. Cecil C. Moss Papers. 31 p.
ICHi

Concerning new settlements along the Illinois River.

Chicago, Illinois. Chicago Historical Society. Ottawa, Illinois. [Miscellaneous Pamphlets, Brochures, etc].
ICHi

High school theater programs from 1923, Ottawa Chautauqua pamphlet from 1909, Ottawa industrial folder from 1925, Christ Episcopal Church program from 1923, Ottawa Township High School Commencement program from 1898, Ottawa Theatre programs, Ottawa Opera House program from 1879.

Chicago, Illinois. Chicago Historical Society. Bessie Louise Pierce Papers.
ICHi

Files of notes used in preparation of her three-volume history of Chicago and an unpublished fourth volume covering the years 1893–1915. Grouped by volume years (to 1848, 1848–1871, and 1871–1893), subject (transportation, industry, and so on). Material on I&M Canal transcribed from newspapers, books, reports, and archives.

Chicago, Illinois. Chicago Historical Society. Charles P. Toot Collection. 4 p.
ICHi

Typed account of early history of South Chicago, first known as Ainsworth.

Chicago, Illinois. Chicago Historical Society. George Van Zandt Collection.
ICHi

Includes "Recollections of My Early Years in Chicago." 41 p. (photocopy.) This work contains remarks on a trip on the I&M Canal to Morris.

Chicago, Illinois. Federal Archives and Records Center. Records of the General Land Office. Chicago, Illinois, Land Office. Local Office Abstract of Cash Entries, Numbered 1–5874, 1835–1839, 1 v. Local Office Abstract of Cash Entries, Numbered 5875–14210, 1839–1843, 1 v. Local Office Abstract of Cash Entries, Numbered 25870–30160, 1847–1855, 1 v. Abstracts of Warrant Locations Numbered 1–277, Warrants Under the Act of 1847, 1 v.
IC—FARC

Information provided includes date of certificate, name of purchaser, county of residence, location of tract (including township and range), number of acres purchased, price per acre, total price of purchase, date when patent was received at land office.

Crest Hill, Illinois. Lockport Township Public Library. Vertical File. Crest Hill.
ICrH

Includes newspaper clippings from *Chicago Tribune,* December 4, 1978, on Lidice subdivision of Crest Hill, named such after Nazis leveled Czechoslovakian town of that name.

Crest Hill, Illinois. Lockport Township Public Library. Vertical File. Local Drawer. Joliet, Illinois. Two folders.
ICrH

Files include one-page brochure on Joliet Public Library (photographs), "Rialto Square Highlights" prerestoration fund raiser, Vol.1, No. 1, March 1980, with photographs, history of Rialto Square, "Places to Go, Things to See in Joliet."

Crest Hill, Illinois. Lockport Township Public Library. Vertical File. Lockport.
ICrH

Includes 1982 "Lockport Old Canal Days" supplement to *Joliet Herald-News.* Article on Irish labor and I&M Canal, historic churches. *Hail and Farewell, 1935–1980.* Published to commemorate Lockport Sesquicentennial. Lockport, Civic and Commerce Association, 1980. 59 p., illus. Old group photographs of school classes, school officials, homes, street scenes.

DeKalb, Illinois. Northern Illinois University. Illinois Regional Archives Depository. Vertical File. C. C. Tisler. Newspaper Columns. Ottawa, Illinois.
IDeKN—IRAD

Fifteen columns on Ottawa area history written for *Daily Republican-Times,* 1940s and 1950s. Indians, debate, Marseilles fort.

Joliet, Illinois. Joliet Public Library. Illinois Vertical File. Schofield, William W. "Contemporary Local History."
IJo

Typewritten. Historical anecdotes on social life of Joliet, 1830–1920.

Joliet, Illinois. Joliet Public Library. *Joliet Herald News.* Local History. One card file drawer.
IJo

Index of newspaper articles on historical subjects (articles published 1961–1963).

Justice, Illinois. Justice Public Library. Uncatalogued materials. Local History.
IJu

Materials include newspaper clippings, genealogical materials, village newsletters (1930s), real estate assessment for 1928, town of Lyons (Township 38, Range 12, Section 22), publication list, Cook County personal property assessment for 1935, town of Lyons (photocopy), 16 p., incorporation materials, 1911 (photocopy), 6 p., photocopy of documents disconnecting part of Justice, 1914.

Justice, Illinois. Justice Public Library. Vertical File. Justice.
IJu

Includes "Haunt These Eerie Places for a Supernatural Time, Resurrection Mary," *Economist,* October 29, 1980. "SW Ghost Legend Revived," *Economist,* January 22, 1984. "Resurrection Cemetery Opened in 1904," *Economist,* 1971. "Thirty-eight Votes Establish Justice Village Back in October, 1911," *DesPlaines Valley News.* "Justice Firemen Organized in 1938," *DesPlaines Valley News,* n.d. "Fifteen Lutheran Parishes Founded Bethamia Cemetery," *DesPlaines Valley News,* n.d. "Lutheran National Cemetery Started by German Lodges," *DesPlaines Valley News,* October 7, 1981. "Thirty-eight Voters Petition for Justice Incorporation," *DesPlaines Valley News,* October 7, 1971.

LaSalle, Illinois. LaSalle Public Library. Scrapbook.
ILa

Newspaper clippings on mid- to late-nineteenth-century LaSalle and early-twentieth century. Pictures and portraits of prominent figures.

Lemont, Illinois. Lemont Area Historical Society. Harry J. Swanson Memorial Library. Local History File. Two file drawers.
ILeHi

Files on parks, sports, canals, churches, buildings, censuses, Lemont centennial, leading citizens, roads, Cook County, Lemont folklore, Indian tribes, Joliet mound, mayors, population, library, Willow Springs, genealogy, schools, Lockport, folklore.

Lemont, Illinois. Lemont Area Historical Society. Harry J. Swanson Memorial Library. Local History File. Lockport.
ILeHi
Includes April 21, 1984, *Tribune* article on Gaylord Building.

Lemont, Illinois. Lemont Area Historical Society. Harry J. Swanson Memorial Library. Local History File. World War I: Correspondence.
ILeHi
Letters from and to Lemont residents. From France, New York City, and Kansas City, Missouri.

Lemont, Illinois. Lemont Public Library. Vertical File. Lemont History and I&M Canal.
ILe
Contains wide assortment of clippings, maps, brochures, and typewritten articles on Lemont's role in the I&M Canal history. Includes topics on engineers, Sanitary and Ship Canal, articles relating to I&M historical status as park, Walter Howe's "Documentary History . . . ," and other pieces on canal and river life.

Lemont, Illinois. Lemont Public Library. Vertical File. Lemont History.
ILe
"Lemont's Volunteer Fire Department," by Sonia Kallicke. (Typewritten). Map of sections and early settlers. "Walking Tour of Lemont." *Early Cook County Roads. Chicago Tribune,* "Meet the Folks on Archer—the Dead Ones," by Kenan Heise. Article on ghosts and cemeteries along Archer Avenue. Assorted clippings, brochures, maps, and walking "Keepataw Trail" tours.

Lockport, Illinois. Lockport Township Public Library. Vertical File. Will County History. Two folders.
ILo
Includes newsletter of Will County Historical Society. Publications of Will County Historical Society. "The Channahon Area," by Rose Bucciferro, 2 p. (Typewritten.) "Will County and the Barbed Wire Industry: A Challenge Met," by Hope Rajala, 1975, illus. (Typewritten.)

Lockport, Illinois. Lockport Township Public Library. Vertical File. Will County. Will County Historical Society. One folder.
ILo
File includes published excerpt of 1933 Harvard Ph.D. dissertation, "Will County Agriculture, 1830–1870," by Dr. Fayette Baldwin Shaw, 18 p. "Trails of the Past: The Road to Ottawa and the Southwest" (excerpted from M. M. Quaife), Will County Historical Society, 1979, 18 p. "A Final Tribute: Merchant's Row, 1837–1967," by Jack Schauer, published by the Will County Historical Society, 1978, 7 p. (Merchant's Row is in Joliet.) "The Reed Family: An Historic Narrative of the Early Midwest and of the First White Settler of Joliet, Illinois, Charles Reed," by Samuel Edward Reed, published by the Will County Historical Society, 1979, 18 p. *Joliet Herald-News, Supplement,* "1858–1970: Will County Historical Society," 16 p., photos., articles on the I&M Canal. Pamphlet on the Canal Commissioner's Office, published by the Will County Historical Society; photographs.

Lockport, Illinois. Will County Historical Society. Land Sales. Illinois and Michigan Canal Book of Register of Certificates. 1830–1843.
ILoHi

Marseilles, Illinois. Marseilles Public Library. "Quarter Century History of Marseilles." Compiled and published by Terry Simmons.
IMa
From *The Plaindealer.* Starts February 7, 1902. Clipped and pasted inside scrapbook. Scrapbook also includes other clippings of local interest.

Morris, Illinois. Morris Public Library. Local History File. Aux Sable Township. One folder.
IMo
Contains essays on sites, including Broadway School, Brown School, Aux Sable Methodist Episcopal Church, pioneers' homes, Meade School, Samuel Randall farm, Sand Ridge School, Ness Honey farm, Aux Sable Creek Bridge, Aux Sable Cemetery, Dresden Hills School, I&M Canal Lock 8, canal aqueduct, Chicago, Ottawa and Peoria Interurban Station. Also contains various newspaper clippings (*Joliet Herald-News*); genealogical essays; Aux Sable historical tour guide; Minooka historical eight-mile bike tour guide; photo of

wooden I&M Canal aqueduct over Aux Sable Creek, 1848–1931; a historical tour of Aux Sable Township; narration for history of Minooka and Aux Sable Township, 1979.

Morris, Illinois. Morris Public Library. Local History File. Channahon.
IMo

Includes "History of Channahon, Homecoming of 1972," photographs of homes, locktender's house, street scenes. Newspaper clippings.

Morris, Illinois. Morris Public Library. Local History File. Coal City.
IMo

Newspaper clippings from *Coal City Courant,* history of voluntary organizations, photograph of Coal City Turners, photographs of Coal City, school photographs, typewritten history of Italian immigrants, notes on Coal City elevator.

Morris, Illinois. Morris Public Library. Local History File. Dresden.
IMo

Includes typewritten two-page "How Dresden Got its Name," by Tom Smith, 1978. Newspaper clippings. Sketch of Dresden in 1842.

Morris, Illinois. Morris Public Library. Local History File. Erienna Township. One folder.
IMo

Contains newspaper clippings on Erienna Township history, Grundy County historic sites survey inventory, Castle Denger site, interurban site, Hoge or Stockdale School, Five Mile Bridge, Old Stage Road, Hill Croft farm, the Prairie Road, Horrom City (ghost, or paper town).

Morris, Illinois. Morris Public Library. Local History File. Felix Township. One folder.
IMo

Contains historical essay, newspaper clippings on Carbon Hill history, and essays on Carbon Hill, Suffern, Eileen, Harrisonville, Jugtown.

Morris, Illinois. Morris Public Library. Local History File. Goose Lake Township. One folder.
IMo

Contains newspaper clippings, map of township with Grundy County historic sites inventory, Goose Lake, Prairie State Park, Jugtown.

Morris, Illinois. Morris Public Library. Local History File. Grundy County.
IMo

Newspaper clippings from *Morris Herald* on local history.

Morris, Illinois. Morris Public Library. Local History File. Grundy County Historical Society.
IMo

Newspaper clippings and photographs of bridges, roads, school photographs, society events, constitution of society, 1923, Lock 8.

Morris, Illinois. Morris Public Library. Local History File. Minooka. One folder.
IMo

Contains various newspaper clippings, pencil sketches of Minooka street scenes, nineteenth century, genealogical newspaper clippings (mostly obituaries), photographs of Minooka Fire Department members, 1907 (newspaper), essay on Minooka in 1867, 1 p., essays (mostly genealogical), copy of expense book, 1880 (household budget), mimeo, 1 p., directory of Minooka, containing sketch of Minooka history, n.d., poem about Minooka by resident born in Channahon, 1920s (author, 1857–1940), map of original town plan (copy), essay on the geology of the Minooka Ridge, essays on St. Mary's Cemetery, Minooka, Chicago, Rock Island R.R. Depot, St. Mary's Catholic Church, Minooka United Methodist Church, Union Hotel, grain elevator, first edition of Minooka Directory, n.d.

Morris, Illinois. Morris Public Library. Local History File. Minooka. Churches. One folder.
IMo

Contains various newspaper articles on St. Mary's Catholic Church, Channahon Methodist Episcopal Church, Aux Sable Methodist Church, Minooka Methodist Episcopal Church. Pamphlets on Minooka and Aux Sable centennial, September 1956 (centennial of Methodist churches). Photographs of former pastors. Essays on Minooka United Methodist Church, history. Pamphlet on 125th anniversary celebration, 1856–1981, Minooka United Methodist

Church. Includes short history. List of subscribers to Debt Discharging Fund of St. Mary's Catholic church, 1911. Pamphlet, "St. Mary's Church, Minooka, Illinois: One Hundred Years of Grace, 1864–1964," includes history of parish, with photographs.

Morris, Illinois. Morris Public Library. Local History File. Minooka. Clubs. One folder.
IMo

Contains ribbon, Grundy County Democratic Club, 1884.

Files on banks, cemeteries, churches, clubs, community high schools, clothing, hospital, monuments, newspapers, police, schools, WPA projects.

Morris, Illinois. Morris Public Library. Local History File. Norman Township. One folder.
IMo

Contains registry return receipt from the Longham P.O., 1901.

Morris, Illinois. Morris Public Library. Local History File. Saratoga Township. One folder.
IMo

Contains short history of Saratoga Township. Grundy County historic sites inventory, Hiram Thayer–Philip Zink House (south side of Route 6, west of Bungalow Road, Section 23). Matteson Hill (Section 23). Michael Henry Cryder Centennial Farm (Route 6, one mile east of Morris, Section 27). Cryder School (Section 27), 1865. Waters Limestone Quarry (Section 24). Fox, Illinois and Union Electric R.R. (passed through Sections 4, 9, 16, 21, 28, 33).

Morris, Illinois. Morris Public Library. Local History File. Wauponsee Township. One folder.
IMo

Contains various newspaper clippings on churches and schools.

Morris, Illinois. Morris Public Library. The Winterbottom Letters. 4 v.
IMo

Covers 1844–1867. James Winterbottom and his five children. Forty letters. From Ashton-under-Lyne, Lancashire, England, Champaign, Illinois, Rockdale, and Morris. Index.

Ottawa, Illinois. Reddick Library. Vertical File. Lincoln-Douglas Debate. One folder.
IO

Includes text of debate in Ottawa, bibliography of debate, newspaper clipping on debate history.

Ottawa, Illinois. Reddick Library. Vertical File. Ottawa. Monuments. One folder.
IO

Contains photographs of Lincoln-Douglas debate monument and construction, 1903.

Palos Heights, Illinois. Palos Heights Public Library. List of Original Owners, Township 37N, 12E, Sections 24, 25, 36, 19, 29, 30, 31.
IPHe

Photocopies.

Palos Heights, Illinois. Palos Heights Public Library. Local History Pamphlet File. Early History. Three folders.
IPHe

Includes various newspaper clippings from *Palos Regional, Chicago Tribune, Where the Trails Cross,* essays.

Palos Heights, Illinois. Palos Heights Public Library. Local History Pamphlet File. Early History. Adjacent Areas.
IPHe

Includes information on Palos Township, Blue Island, Bridgeview, Palos Hills, Palos Park, Summit, Willow Springs, Worth.

Palos Heights, Illinois. Palos Heights Public Library. Local History Pamphlet File. Palos Historical Society. One folder.
IPHe

Includes various newspaper clippings, such as "Palos in the Past," from the *Palos Regional.*

Palos Hills, Illinois. Green Hills Public Library. Vertical File. "History of 'The Hills.'"
IPHil

Contains photocopies of lengthy articles on Palos's history from *Surburban Tribune,* June 4, 1980. Photocopy of the history of Palos from unknown source.

Palos Hills, Illinois. Green Hills Public Library. Vertical File. History of Palos Hills and Surrounding Area: Past to Present.
IPHil

Typewritten historical chronology with photocopies of maps.

Palos Hills, Illinois. Green Hills Public Library. Vertical File. Palos Hills.
IPHil

Map of Palos Township, 1862, showing land ownership. *History of the City of Palos Hills: Founded October 25, 1958.* William L. Potters, "The Forts of Palos," 1983. (Typewritten.) Photographs of archaeological sites.

Palos Hills, Illinois. Green Hills Public Library. Photo File. Summit-Argo.
IPHil

Includes "An Area's Story—Miscellaneous Information." On schools and churches.

Palos Hills, Illinois. Green Hills Public Library. Photo File. Worth.
IPHil

Contains *Reporter* article, March 20, 1975, "Historically Speaking." Samuel Huntington came to Worth Township in 1844, driving a flock of the area's first sheep. He and the sheep huddled in a shanty near what is now 99th Street to survive their first bitter winter. After settling down, he married and had three children, served as a constable and a deputy sheriff, and headed the township's draft board during the Civil War.

Palos Park, Illinois. Palos Park Public Library. Pamphlet File. Palos Park History. Early History.
IPP

Contains "Palos Historical Map Fact Sheet," and map. *A History of Palos.* Student papers including "The Population Growth of Palos" and "Early Settlers and Their Daily Habits."

Palos Park, Illinois. Palos Park Public Library. Pamphlet File. Palos Park History. General History.
IPP

Palos Park, Nature's Masterpiece, n.p., n.d. [1920s], photos. Contains short history and photographs of homes and nature areas. "Large Estates Dotted Area in 1920's." *Palos Regional,* April 9, 1981. *Pageant of Palos.*

Palos Park, Illinois. Palos Park Public Library. Pamphlet File. Palos Park History. Locations.
IPP

Various news clippings from *Palos Regional,* July 16, 1981; Palos ski jump; August 20, 1981; roads in 1929; July 23, 1981, Sag Channel. Photographs

Peru, Illinois. Peru Public Library. Peru, Illinois. Local History. Scrapbook. 5 v., and index.
IPe

Original photographs (many of houses, factories, and work crews), newspaper articles (mostly recent ones providing historical information), and assorted programs, bills, and miscellaneous items.

Peru, Illinois. Peru Public Library. Peru, Illinois. Local History. Scrapbooks and Index. 6 v.
IPe

Contains original photographs (residences, factories, work scenes).

Romeoville, Illinois. Fountaindale Public Library. Vertical File on the DesPlaines Valley.
IRo

Contains assorted clippings, photographs, maps, and brochures relating to the DesPlaines valley and the I&M Canal.

Romeoville, Illinois. Fountaindale Public Library. Vertical File. Romeoville. History. One folder.
IRo

Includes "History of Romeoville," a four-page typewritten paper written by Romeoville resident in 1969. Thirteen pages of information on Romeoville prepared for American Guide series. Various newspaper clippings. Township map of Will County. Original plan of Lockport.

Romeoville, Illinois. Fountaindale Public Library. Vertical File. Will County.
IRo

Includes Langford article, "Stratified Indian Mounds of Will County." Scholfield essay, "The Trail of the Potowatomi," *Incidents from Will County History Re-Told,* Will County Historical Society, 1977. *A Quartet of Will County Libraries,* Will County Historical Society, 1977 (Lockport Township, Crest Hill Branch, New Lenox, Mokena Community). *They Helped to Keep Our Country Free,* Will County Historical Society, 1977. List of some Will County veterans from Revolution to Vietnam.

Springfield, Illinois. Archives of the State of Illinois. Federal Records. U.S. General Land Office Records for Illinois. Kaskaskia Land District Office.
I—Ar

The Kaskaskia Land District Office was formed in 1804 and began to sell land in 1814. It was the District Land Office for the corridor until the creation of the Shawneetown Land District Office in 1812.

Records include Receiver and Register: correspondence (1804–1875), forms and instructions for keeping books (1805). Board of commissioners: transcripts of documents collected by the Board (1804–1814), claims confirmed by the governors (1804), orders of surveys (1805), donation lists for head grants and militia claims (1805), register of persons who received residue land from head and militia grants (n.d.), depositions regarding claims (1807–1809–1812), claims for which certificates of confirmation granted (1814–1817), tracts located by assignees (1802–1804), claims not submitted within time limit (comp. 1815), claims suspended for lack of record of assignment (1812), board of commissioners, ancient grants rejected by the board (1809), donations granted to heads of families by the governors (1804–1809), head grants affirmed by the board (1809), head grants rejected by the board (1804–1809), head grants for which certificates of confirmation issued (1814), improvement claims submitted to the governors (1804–1809), improvement claims confirmed by the governors (1804–1809), improvement claims affirmed by the governors (1809), improvement claims rejected by the board (1804–1809), confirmed unlocated improvement claims for which certificates of confirmation issued (1814–1815), militia claims confirmed by the governors (1804–1809), militia claims affirmed by the board (1809), militia claims rejected by the board (1804–1809), militia claims submitted to the board (1809–1813), militia claims for which certificates of confirmation issued (1814).

Receiver: journal (credit system) (1814–1831), general and individual ledger (credit system) (1814–1831), monthly accounts of payments received from land purchasers (1814–1819), register of receipts (credit system) (1814–1829), copies of receipts issued to land purchasers (credit system) (1814–1831).

Register: general and individual ledger (credit system) (1814–1841), certificates issued to land purchasers (credit system) (1814–1820), abstract of applications to purchase land and land forfeited for nonpayment (1814–1820), monthly accounts of payments made by individuals for land purchases (1814–1817), patents received and delivered (1814–1847), register of applications and permissions to remain on tracts as tenants of will (1814–1815, 1816–1822), papers relating to land in Kaskaskia District (1783–1956).

Springfield, Illinois. Archives of the State of Illinois. Federal Records. U.S. General Land Office Records for Illinois. Shawneetown Land District Office.
I—Ar

The Shawneetown Land District Office was formed in 1812 and began to sell land in 1814. It was the district land office for the corridor until the creation of the Vandalia and Palestine districts in 1820.

Records include Receiver and Register: correspondence (1812–1876).

Receiver: journal (credit system) (1814–1831), general ledger (credit system) (1814–1831), individual ledger (credit system) (1814–1820), individual ledger for Shawneetown lots (credit system) (1814–1829), register of receipts (credit system) (1814–1831), journal (credit system) (1814–1819, 1821–1831), general ledger (credit system) (1814–1831), individual ledger (credit system) (1814–1831), individual ledger for Shawneetown lots (credit system) (1814–1829), certificates issued to land purchasers (credit system) (1814–1820), record of applications to purchase land and payments of subsequent installments (1814–1819), record of applications to purchase Shawneetown lots and payments of subsequent installments (1814–1831), applications to purchase land (1814–1819), applications to purchase Shawneetown lots (1814–1819), applications to remain on tracts of lands as tenants at will (1816), receipts for patents on land or Shawneetown lots (1815–1819), powers of attorney (1818–1830), enumeration of land contained in Shawneetown District (1814), classification of land

(1820), survey bearing marks and land discriptions (1814), abstract from surveyor's field notes of land contained in Shawneetown District (transcribed 1850), tract books of land sold within Shawneetown District (1820–1866), papers relating to land in Shawneetown District (1812–1956).

Springfield, Illinois. Archives of the State of Illinois. Federal Records. U.S. General Land Office Records for Illinois. Palestine Land District Office.
I—Ar

The Palestine Land District Office was created in 1820. It was the district land office for the western portion of the corridor until the creation of the Danville district in 1831.

Records include Receiver and Register: incoming correspondence (1821–1876).

Receiver: outgoing correspondence (1822, 1831–1855), journal (1821–1834), ledger (1821–1834), register of receipts (1821–1855), register of forfeited land stock and military land scrip received (1831–1851), outgoing correspondence (1822–1855), journal (1821–1851), outgoing correspondence (1822–1855), journal (1821–1834), ledger (1821–1834), sales book (1821–1830), stubs for land purchasers (1821–1850), abstract of land sold (1831–1845), tract books of land sold within Palestine District (1820–1873), papers relating to land in Palestine District (1821–1956).

Springfield, Illinois. Archives of the State of Illinois. Federal Records. U.S. General Land Office Records for Illinois. Vandalia Land District Office.
I—Ar

The Vandalia Land District Office was created in 1820. It was the district land office for the eastern portion of the corridor until the creation of the Danville district in 1831.

Records include Receiver and Register: correspondence and circulars, received from the General Land Office (1821–1876).

Receiver: journal (1823–1834), ledger (1823–1834), register of receipts (1823–1855), register of forfeited land stock and military land scrip received (1831–1837), outgoing correspondence (1820–1849, 1851–1856), journal (1821–1834), ledger (1820–1834), sales book (1821–1834), stubs for certificates issued to land purchases (1821–1848), list of patents received from General Land Office (1822–1823), land within the Vandalia Land District sold at other district offices (1815–1833), abstract of land sold (1831–1841), tract book of land sold within Vandalia District (1821–1873), survey bearing marks and land descriptions (n.d.), papers relating to land in Vandalia District (1820–1856).

Springfield, Illinois. Archives of the State of Illinois. Federal Records. U.S. General Land Office. Records for Illinois. Danville Land District Office.
I—Ar

The Danville Land District Office was created in 1831. It was the district land office for the corridor until the creation of the Northwestern and Northeastern Land district offices in 1834.

Records include Receiver and Register: incoming correspondence (1831–1876).

Receiver: outgoing correspondence (1831–1856); journal (1831–1834); ledger (1831–1834); quarterly accounts (1834–1856); register of receipts (1831–1842); outgoing correspondence (1831–1855); affidavits filed by preemption claimants (1832–1857); register of preemption claims filed under Act of June 19, 1834; posers of attorney (1834–1853); abstract of land sold (1831–1841); tract books of land sold within Danville District (1822–1864); papers relating to land in Danville District (1831–1857).

Springfield, Illinois. Archives of the State of Illinois. Federal Records. U.S. General Land Office. Records for Illinois. Northeastern Land District Office.
I—Ar

The Northeastern Land District Office was formed in 1834. It was the district land office for all but the western two-thirds of LaSalle County until district land offices were consolidated in Springfield in 1855.

Records include Receiver and Register: circulars of instruction (1830–1855).

Receiver: correspondence (1835–1875); quarterly accounts (1835–1855); monthly accounts (1839–1843, 1849–1855); weekly accounts (1839–1846); quarterly accounts acting as disbursing agent under Act of March 3, 1846 (1849–1855); weekly accounts acting as depositary for U.S. Treasury (1846–1853); register of receipts (1835–1855); register of U.S. Treasury notes received in payment for land (1839–1853); register of receipts (1835–1855); register of U.S. Treasury notes received in payment for land (1839–1843); correspondence (1835–1855); record of applications made to purchase land (1843–1846); register of military land warrants received in payment for land (1843–1850); register of preemption declaration statements (1841–1845); protests of preemption claims (1841–1842); docket of preemption claim protests (1842–1849); record of land sold to aid Illinois Central Railroad construction (1852); land offered at public auction (1835–1851); abstracts of land sold (1839–1847); abstract of land in Northeastern District sold at Danville and Palestine Land District Offices (1831–1835); tract books of land sold within Northeastern District (1834–1859); abstracts from surveyor's field notes of land contained in Northeastern District (transcribed 1850); papers relating to land in Northeastern District (1834–1856).

Springfield, Illinois. Archives of the State of Illinois. Federal Records. U.S. General Land Office. Records for Illinois. Northwestern Land District Office.
I—Ar

The Northwestern Land District Office was formed in 1834. It was the district land office for the western two-thirds of LaSalle County until district land offices were consolidated in Springfield in 1855.

Records include Receiver and Register: incoming correspondence (1834–1875).

Receiver: outgoing correspondence (1835–1852), quarterly accounts (1835–1855), monthly accounts (1841–1843), weekly accounts (1845–1849), register of receipts (1835–1837, 1839, 1841–1855), register of canceled U.S. Treasury notes (1838–1841, 1842–1843, 1844, 1847), register of military land scrip or U.S. Treasurer's receipts received (1840–1844), sales blotter (1841–1842).

Register: outgoing correspondence (1835–1855); sales book (1841–1846); applications to purchase land (1836–1855); register of preemption declaration statements (1841–1847, 1848–1855); preemption declaration statements (1841–1855); record of preemption proofs to land situated in mineral district on which a tender of purchase money has been made (1841–1850); monthly abstract of land located on military land warrant certificates (1849–1855); register of military land warrants received (1848); abstract of expired or conditional military land warrant locations (1847–1849); canal, mineral, and seminary lands selected under Act of September 4, 1841 (1842); list of townships compiled in preparation for sale of land under Graduation Act of 1854 (1854); land offered at public auction (1839–1847); abstracts of land sold (1835–1847, 1852, 1854–1855); abstracts from surveyor's field notes of land contained in Northwestern District (transcribed 1850); tract books of land sold within Northwestern District (1835–1870); papers relating to land in Northwestern District (1828–1862).

Springfield, Illinois. Archives of the State of Illinois. Federal Records. U.S. General Land Office. Records for Illinois. Springfield Land District Office.
I—Ar

The Springfield Land District Office was created in 1822. After 1855–1856, all land district offices were consolidated, and the Springfield office assumed responsibility for the remaining land.

Records include Receiver and Register: correspondence (1823–1877).

Receiver: quarterly accounts (1834–1875); register of receipts (1823–1874); lists of patents delivered to patentees (1859–1876); register of preemption declaration statements filed under Act of September 4, 1841 (1841–1858); preemption declaration statements (1845–1876); register of individuals purchasing land under Graduation Act of 1854 (1856); records of notices given to graduators (1856); tract books of land sold within Springfield District (1825–1861); papers relating to land in Springfield District (1823–1856).

Springfield, Illinois. Archives of the State of Illinois. Federal Land Surveyors' Field Notes, 1804–1856. 495 v.

I—Ar

Notes of individual surveyors. Includes descriptions of methods, topographical features, directions. Used in preparation of Federal Township Plats. Indexed.

Springfield, Illinois. Archives of the State of Illinois. Meanders of Various Bodies of Water and Islands, 1830–1855. 4 v.
I—Ar

Survey notes of the causes and banks of bodies of water. Notes include directions and distances. Rivers surveyed include Calumet, Chicago, DesPlaines, Illinois, Kankakee. Lakes include Calumet and Michigan. No index.

Springfield, Illinois. Archives of the State of Illinois. Register of Field Notes of Boundary Lines and Subdivisions of Townships, 1804–1839. 2 v.
I—Ar

Serves as an index to federal surveys. Includes legal descriptions of townships, dates surveyed, names of surveyors, numbers of field books in which notes contained.

Springfield, Illinois. Archives of the State of Illinois. Federal Township Plats. 1807–1822, 1830–1862, 1868–1891, 1962, 1970. 53 v.
I—Ar

Using surveyors' notes, plats were prepared for each township. Each plat includes legal description of township, sections within township, measurement, various topographical features and vegetation, bodies of water. Index.

Springfield, Illinois. Archives of the State of Illinois. Land Sales Receipts, 1830–1842. One-half cubic foot.
I—Ar

Copies of receipts issued to individuals for purchases of I&M Canal lands. Entries include date, name of purchaser, description of tract, price per acre, total purchase price. No index.

Springfield, Illinois. Archives of the State of Illinois. Tract Book of Canal Land Sales, 1830–1927. 17 v.
I—Ar

Lists of town lots and other land sold by commissioners. Entries contain name of purchaser, description of tract, number of acres, price per acre, total purchase price. No index.

Springfield, Illinois. Archives of the State of Illinois. List of Town Lots Sold by the Board of Canal Commissioners, 1830–1843. 1 v.
I—Ar

An 1878 compilation of town lots sold by commissioners. Entries include name of purchaser, name of town and number of block, number of lot, date. No index.

Springfield, Illinois. Archives of the State of Illinois. Certificates for Land and Lots, 1848–1870. Four cubic feet.
I—Ar

Contains records of first payments to I&M Canal commissioners for the purchase of canal land. Entries include name of purchaser, lot number, number of acres, price per acre, date. No index.

Springfield, Illinois. Archives of the State of Illinois. Land Patents Issued by the I&M Canal, 1842–1878. One-half cubic foot.
I—Ar

Copies of patents issued to individuals who bought canal lands. Entries include date, name of purchaser, description of tract. No index.

Springfield, Illinois. Archives of the State of Illinois. List of Land Patents issued by the State of Illinois, 1831–1885. 2 v.
I—Ar

Includes some patents issued to persons who bought canal lands. Entrees contain description of tract, name of purchaser, and date. Index.

Springfield, Illinois. Archives of the State of Illinois. Illinois and Michigan Canal Pre-emption Applications, 1845–1854. Three-quarters cubic foot.
I—Ar

Claims by individuals who had settled on canal lands prior to public sales. Claimant had to show that he had occupied and improved tract in question. Applications include name, description of tract, date, description of improvements, and signature of justice of the peace. No index.

Springfield, Illinois. Archives of the State of Illinois. Records of the Illinois Territory.
I—Ar

Records are grouped in the following manner:

Territorial Governor: Correspondence. March 10, 1809–August 19, 1813; August 8, 9, 1814; January 5, 17, 1816. 2 v. Partial index. Correspondence with private citizens and government officials. Contains information on civil and military affairs including forts and Indians.

Secretary of the Territory: Executive Records. May 17, 1809–December 3, 1818. One cubic foot. No index. Executive Register. April 25, 1809–September 9, 1818. 2 v., 1 partial v., index. Extradition Papers. July 1809–August 1809. One folder. No index. Enrolled Acts of the Territorial Council of Revision. June 13, 1809–June 26, 1811. One-quarter cubic foot. Calendar. Enrolled Acts of the Territorial General Assembly. December 13, 1812–January 26, 1818. Three-quarters cubic foot. No index. Record of Bills and Acts. November 26, 1812–December 3, 1818. 1 v. Index. Territorial Census. [May 1818–July 1818]. 1 v. Index. Minutes of Council Meetings. June 13, 1809–November 25, 1812. 1 v. Index.

Territorial General Assembly: Journals of the Legislative Council. November 25, 1812–December 26, 1812; November 8, 1813; November 14, 1814–December 24, 1814; December 4, 1815–January 11, 1816; December 2, 1816–January 14, 1817; December 1, 1817–January 12, 1818. Journals of the House of Representatives. November 25, 1812–December 26, 1812; November 14, 1814–December 24, 1814; December 4, 1815–January 11, 1816. Legislative Records. November 14, 1813–January 14, 1817.

Territorial Adjutant General: Militia Muster Roll. February 27, 1813–March 17, 1813.

Springfield, Illinois. Illinois State Historical Library. Wallace Dickey Family Papers, 1816–1934.
IHi

Letters and diaries of Ottawa family.

Springfield, Illinois. Illinois State Historical Library. Reminiscences of Pioneer Days in LaSalle County, Illinois. 9 p.
IHi

Written March 27, 1918, by "a Woman Aged 92 Years." Name indecipherable.

Summit, Illinois. Summit-Argo Public Library. Local History File. Village of Summit. History. One folder.
ISA

Contains street scenes photographs, c. 1930; various newspaper clippings; street car routes; telephone history; historical essays; Harry Sklenar, "Village of Summit/ 1890–1965: Seventy-five Years of Progress: A Historical Profile of the Summit Community Area"; DesPlaines Valley News Publishing Company, 1965. 67 p., illus., photos., facsims., ports., maps.

Urbana, Illinois. Illinois Historical Survey Library. Vertical Files. Palos, Illinois.
IU—HS

Includes "Home Tour," Palos Historical Society, 1976.

Utica, Illinois. LaSalle County Historical Society Museum. Clippings Book.
IUtHi

Contains clippings about LaSalle County and canal life in and around LaSalle.

Utica, Illinois. LaSalle County Historical Society Museum. Letters to Joseph Mason, Ottawa, Illinois, 1887–1896.
IUtHi

Letters from Iowa to Mason, from family.

Utica, Illinois. LaSalle County Historical Society Museum. Records of the Organization of the Town of Utica, 1850–1900.
IUtHi

Town meeting minutes.

Utica, Illinois. LaSalle County Historical Society Museum. Scrapbook of Newspaper Articles (1908) on Ottawa History.
IUtHi

Articles commemorate Lincoln-Douglas debate. One includes list of people who attended the debate, along with city of residence.

Worth, Illinois. Worth Public Library. Vertical File. Village of Worth.
IWo

Village incorporated 1914. Twenty-one-page typewritten, photocopied history of Worth, with photographs in 1910s including Methodist Church, Volunteer Fire Department. *Golden Anniversary Souvenir Edition of the*

Worth Palos Reporter Presents the Story of Worth, Fifty Years as a Village, 1914–1964. 32 p. August 27, 1964. Articles on Indians, history of Worth, genealogy, Sag Channel, schools, city services, churches. photos., ports. *The Worth Palos Reporter,* Section 3, September 9, 1982. Pioneer Day Edition. Historical notes section includes articles on early settlement, Civil War, incorporation. Map of Worth Township, 1977. Highway Department. Palos *Regional News,* Section 3, September 8, 1983, "Worth Day" section. Includes articles on medicine in early Worth, reminiscences, photographs of Cal Sag Channel, 1912. Aerial photograph, c. 1930. Various newspaper clippings.

PART 14 Genealogy and Biography

The recent interest in historical subjects in the United States has often taken the form of biographical or genealogical research. Individuals who wish to trace the wanderings of and the relationships among their ancestors might begin with the sources in this part of the Bibliography.

The listings are generally of four sorts: genealogical publications, censuses, vital records, and biographical collections. The information contained in the first three types of sources is explained in detail in the annotations. However, the last type, biographical collections, warrants a word of caution. These "mug books" or "potted biographies" were written during the late-nineteenth and early-twentieth centuries and were usually sold on a subscription basis. That is, the information was usually written or dictated by the subject, who tended to aggrandize his "rags to riches" life story. The information about dates and places is usually factual, but the moral tinge to the biographies should probably be taken with a grain of salt and viewed in the light of late-nineteenth-century values and aspirations.

Genealogy and Biography—*General*

"Family Histories." *Journal of the Illinois State Historical Society* 57 (Winter 1964): 406–410.
DLC, I, IC, ICHi, ICN, ICU, IEN, IU

Alphabetical list of family and town histories held by the Illinois State Historical Library.

"Family Histories." *Journal of the Illinois State Historical Society* (Winter 1965): 424–430.
DLC, I, IC, ICHi, ICN, ICU, IEN, IU

Alphabetical list of family histories received by Illinois State Historical Library between July 1, 1964, and June 30, 1965. Also county histories.

"Family Histories." *Journal of the Illinois State Historical Society* (Winter 1966): 407–416.
DLC, I, IC, ICHi, ICN, ICU, IEN, IU

Alphabetical list of family histories received by the Illinois State Historical Library between July 1, 1965, and June 30, 1966.

Illinois State Genealogical Society. *Quarterly.* Vol. 1–. Springfield, Illinois, 1969–.
DLC, ICU

Quarterly. Indexes: Vol. 1–5: 1969–1973.

Osborne, Georgia L., comp. "A List of the Genealogical Works in the Illinois State Historical Library." *Publications of the Illinois State Historical Library* 18 (1914): 1–163.
DLC, IC, ICN, ICU, IO, IU

Listings by state and county and city. County histories, biographies, directories.

Pastfinders. Journal of the Genealogy Guild of the LaSalle County Historical Society. Vol. 1., No. 1. n.p., n.d. 27 p.
IUtHi

Excerpts from diaries.

Collins, Raymond, comp. *Genealogy Resources at Bur Oak Library System Headquarters.* Shorewood, Illinois: Bur Oak Library System, 1981.
ILo

Explains systematic methods for the beginning genealogist. Includes county histories, directories, maps, passenger lists, newspapers, oral history.

Schulz, Mildred. "Family Histories." *Journal of the Illinois State Historical Society* 62 (Winter 1969): 407–417.
DLC, I, IC, ICHi, ICN, ICU, IEN, IU

Alphabetical list of ninety-four books and pamphlets on Illinois families received by Illinois State Historical Library between July 1, 1968, and June 30, 1969.

Schulz, Mildred. "Family Histories." *Journal of the Illinois State Historical Society* 63 (Autumn 1970): 303–314.
DLC, I, IC, ICHi, ICN, ICU, IEN, IU

Alphabetical list of family histories received by the Illinois State Historical Library between July 1, 1969, and April 30, 1970.

Shull, Tressie Nash. "County Atlases for Genealogical Use." *National Genealogical Society Quarterly* 37 (March 1949): 4–11.
DLC, ICN

Wolf, Joseph C. *A Reference Guide for Genealogical and Historical Research in Illinois.* Detroit, Michigan: The Detroit Society for Genealogical Research, 1963. 140 p.
ICU, NNC

Details availability of public and private records for genealogical research. Censuses, churches, military rosters, newspapers, historical and genealogical societies.

Genealogy and Biography—Biographical and Genealogical Collections

Genealogy and Biography—*Biographical and Genealogical Collections*—LaSalle County

Biographical and Genealogical Record of LaSalle County, Illinois. 2 v. Chicago: Lewis Publishing Company, 1900. index, illus., ports.
ICHi, ICN

Approximately 600 sketches of turn-of-the-century county residents.

Biographical and Genealogical Record of LaSalle and Grundy Counties. 2 v. Chicago: Lewis Publishing Company, 1900.
ICHi, ICN, IMoHi

Dunn, Sheldon H. *An Index to the Biographical Sketches in the Past and Present of LaSalle County, Illinois.* Fort Wayne, Indiana: Fort Wayne and Allen County Public Library, 1963. 51 p.
ICN

History of LaSalle County, Illinois . . . and Biographies of Representative Citizens . . . Also a Condensed History of Illinois. . . . 2 v. Chicago: Inter-State Publishing Company, 1886. illus., plates, port.
ICHi, ICU

LaSalle County Centennial. *Directory of Former Ottawa Residents, 1831–1931.* Ottawa, Illinois: *Daily Republican Times,* 1931. 45 p., illus., ports.
ICN

LaSalle County Old Settler's Association. *Twenty-Ninth Annual Reunion-Picnic . . . Old Settler's Association of LaSalle County, Illinois. Ottawa, Illinois, 19 Aug. 1897.* n.p. [1897].
IO

Also *30th Annual Reunion and Picnic, 25 Aug. 1898,* and *33rd Annual Picnic, 5 Sept. 1901.*

The Past and Present of LaSalle County, Illinois, Containing a History of the County—Its Cities, Towns, etc., a Biographical Directory of its Citizens, War Record of Its Volunteers in the Late Rebellion, Portraits of Early Settlers and Prominent Men, General and Local Statistics, Map of LaSalle County, History of Illinois, Constitution of the United States, Miscellaneous Matters, etc., etc. Chicago: H. F. Klett & Company, 1877. 653 p., ports., map.
ICHi, ICU

Genealogy and Biography—*Biographical and Genealogical Collections*—Grundy County

An Index to the Names of Persons Appearing in History of Grundy County, Illinois. Chicago: O. L. Baskin & Company, 1882. 53 p.
ICN

Prepared by the Winnetka Genealogy Projects Committee, Winnetka Public Library, Winnetka, Illinois, 1979.

Genealogy and Biography—*Biographical and Genealogical Collections*—Will County

Genealogical and Biographical Record of Kendall and Will Counties, Illinois, Containing Biographies of Well Known Citizens of the Past and Present. Chicago: Biographical Publishing Company, 1901. 670 p.
ICN

An Index to the Names of Persons Appearing in the History of Will County, Illinois. Chicago: Wm. LeBaron, Jr. & Company, 1978. Winnetka, Illinois: The Winnetka Public Library, 1973. 101 p.
ILo

Portrait and Biographical Album of Will County, Illinois, Containing Full Page Portraits and Biographical Sketches of Prominent and Representative Citizens of the County Together with Portraits and Biographies of All the Presidents of the United States and Governors of the State. Chicago, 1890.
ICN

Genealogy and Biography—*Biographical and Genealogical Collections*—DuPage County

Lombard Suburban Genealogical Society. *Genealogical Holdings of DuPage Public Libraries: A Subject Guide.* Lombard, Illinois: The Society, 1979. 60 p.
ILomGe

Portrait and Biographical Record of DuPage and Cook Counties, Illinois, Containing Biographical Sketches of Prominent and Representative Citizens of the County, Together with Biographies and Portraits of All the Presidents of the United States. Chicago: Lake City Publishing Company, 1894. 490 p., ports.
DLC, ICHi, ICN

Winnetka, Illinois. Winnetka Public Library. Genealogy Projects Committee. *An Index to the Names of Persons Appearing in History of DuPage County, Illinois. [By Rufus Blanchard].* Thomson, Illinois: Heritage House, 1973. 105 p.
IU—HS

Genealogy and Biography—*Biographical and Genealogical Collections*—Cook County

Album of Genealogy and Biography, Cook County, Illinois. 3rd ed. Chicago: Calumet Book & Engraving Company, 1895. 658 p., ports.
DLC, ICJ, ICU

Also 8th edition, 1897, and 13th edition, 1900.

Genealogical and Biographical Record of Cook County, Illinois, Containing Biographical Sketches of Prominent and Representative Citizens of the County. Chicago: Lake City Publishing Company, 1894. 501 p., ports.
CtY, DLC, WHi, IU

Waterman, Arba Nelson. *Historical Review of Chicago and Cook County and Selected Biography. . . .* 3 v. Chicago, New York: The Lewis Publishing Company, 1908. front., illus., plates, ports.
DLC, ICU

Wilkie, Franc Bangs. *Sketches and Notices of the Chicago Bar: Including the More Prominent Lawyers and Judges of the City and Suburban Towns.* 4th ed. Chicago: The Western News Company, 1872. 128 p.
DLC, ICN, ICHi, ICU, IHi

Genealogy and Biography—Censuses

Genealogy and Biography—*Censuses*—General

Kirkham, E. Kay. *A Survey of American Census Schedules: An Explanation and Description of our Federal Census Enumerations 1790–1950.* Salt Lake City, Utah: Deseret Book Company, [1959]. 102 p.
ICN

Explanation of schedules 1790 to 1950.

Norton, Margaret C. "Census Records in the Archives Department of the Illinois State Library." *Illinois Libraries* 26 (May 1944): 178–184.
DLC, I, IC, ICJ, ICN, ICU, IU

Manuscripts in Illinois archives, detailing dates, data, and extant counties. Territorial, state, and federal censuses to 1880.

Norton, Margaret Cross, ed. *Illinois Census Returns, 1810, 1818.* Collections of the Illinois State Historical Library, No. 24. Springfield, 1935. 329 p.
DLC, ICF, ICN, ICU, IEN

Indexed.

Norton, Margaret Cross. *Illinois Census Returns, 1820.* Collections of the Illinois State Historical Library, No. 26. Springfield, 1934. 466 p.
DLC, ICF, ICN, ICU, IEN

Indexed. Bond, Crawford, Franklin, Gallatin, Jackson, Johnson, Madison, Monroe, Pope, Randolph, St. Clair, Union, Washington, White counties.

Genealogy and Biography—*Censuses*—Published

Lemont Township Census, 1860: The Town of Lemont in the County of Cook, Illinois. South Holland, Illinois: South Suburban Genealogical and Historical Society, n.d. 19 p.
ILo

Index of heads of households and transcription of census.

U.S. Department of State. *Fourth Federal Census: Population Schedules for Illinois, 1820.* (Microfilm.)
I—Ar, IC—FARC, ICRL

Nineteen Illinois counties. 3 v. Index. Information entered for each household: name of head of household; numbers of free white males and females in six age groups; numbers of persons engaged in agriculture, commerce, and manufacturing; number of aliens; numbers of male and female slaves and free negroes in each age group; number of all other nontaxable persons, excluding Indians. Returns for the following counties: Alexander, Bond, Clark, Crawford, Edwards, Franklin, Gallatin, Jackson, Jefferson, Johnson, Madison, Monroe, Pope, Randolph, St. Clair, Union, Washington, Wayne, White.

U.S. Department of State. *Fifth Federal Census: Population Schedules for Illinois, 1830.* (Microfilm.)
I—Ar, IC—FARC, ICRL

Fifty-one Illinois counties. Four reels of microfilm. Index. Information entered for each household: name of head of household; numbers of free white males and females in thirteen age groups; numbers of male and female slaves and free colored persons in five age groups; total number of inhabitants in household; numbers of deaf and dumb white persons and slaves and colored persons in three age groups; number of blind white aliens. Counties included are Adams, Alexander, Bond, Calhoun, Clark, Clay, Clinton, Crawford, Edgar, Edwards, Fayette, Franklin, Fulton, Gallatin, Greene, Hamilton, Hancock, Henry, Jackson, Jefferson, JoDaviess, Johnson, Knox, Lawrence, McDonough, Macon, Macoupin, Madison, Marion, Mercer, Monroe, Montgomery, Morgan, Peoria, Perry, Pike, Pope, Putnam, Randolph, St. Clair, Sangamon, Schuyler, Shelby, Tazewell, Union, Vermillion, Wabash, Warren, Washington, Wayne, White.

U.S. Department of State. *Sixth Federal Census: Population Schedules for Illinois, 1840.* (Microfilm.)
I—Ar, IC—FARC, ICRL

Eighty-eight Illinois counties. Twenty reels of microfilm. Index. Information entered for household: name of head of household; numbers of free white males and females in thirteen age groups; numbers of male and female free negroes and slaves in six age groups; total number of inhabitants in household; number employed in mining, agriculture, commerce, manufactures and trades, navigation, learned professions; names and ages of military pensioners; number deaf and dumb; number blind; number insane. Counties include LaSalle, Grundy, Will, DuPage, and Cook.

U.S. Department of Interior. *Seventh Federal Census: Population Schedules for Illinois, 1850.* (Microfilm.)
I—Ar, IC—FARC, ICRL

Ninety-nine Illinois counties. Thirty-eight reels of microfilm. Index. Information entered for household: numbers assigned to dwelling and family in order of visitation and name of each individual. Information entered for individual: name, age, sex, color, occupation of males over fifteen, value of real estate owned, birthplace, marital status, whether attended school in last year, ability to read and write, whether deaf and dumb, blind, insane, idiotic, pauper, or convict. Counties include LaSalle, Grundy, Will, DuPage, and Cook.

U.S. Department of Interior. *Eighth Federal Census: Population Schedules for Illinois, 1860.* (Microfilm.)
I—Ar, IC—FARC, ICRL

One-hundred-two Illinois counties. Eighty-eight reels of microfilm. Partial index. Information entered for household: numbers assigned to dwelling and family in order of visitation and name of each individual. Information entered for individual: name, age, sex, color, occupation of males over 15, value of real and personal property owned, birthplace, marital status, whether attended school in last year, ability to read and write, whether deaf and dumb, blind, insane, idiotic, pauper, or convict. Counties include LaSalle, Grundy, Will, DuPage, and Cook.

U.S. Department of Interior. *Ninth Federal Census: Population Schedules for Illinois, 1870.* (Microfilm.)
I—Ar, IC—FARC, ICRL

One-hundred-two Illinois counties. 109 reels of microfilm. No index. Information entered for household: numbers assigned to dwelling and family in order of visitation and name of each individual. Information entered for individual: name, age, sex, color, occupation of males over fifteen, value of real and personal property owned, birthplace, marital status, whether attended school in last year, ability to read and write, whether deaf and dumb, blind, insane, idiotic, pauper, or convict. Counties include LaSalle, Grundy, Will, DuPage, and Cook.

U.S. Department of Interior. *Tenth Federal Census: Population Schedules for Illinois, 1880.* (Microfilm.)
I—Ar, IC—FARC, ICRL

One-hundred-two Illinois counties. 59 v. Soundex for families having children under eleven (143 reels of microfilm). Information entered for household: numbers assigned to dwelling and family in order of visitation, name of street and house number, and name of each individual. Information entered for individual: name, occupation, age, sex, color, months employed during year, permanent illness or disability, temporary disability, whether attended school in last year, ability to read and write, birthplace, birthplace of parents. Counties include LaSalle, Grundy, Will, DuPage and Cook.

U.S. Department of Interior. *Eleventh Federal Census: Population Schedules for Illinois, 1900.* (Microfilm.)
I—Ar, IC—FARC, ICRL

One-hundred-two Illinois counties. 121 reels of microfilm. Soundex for families having children under eleven (479 reels of microfilm). Information entered for individual: name; address; relationship to head of household; color; sex; month and year of birth; age; marital status; number of years married; number of children; number of living children; birthplace; birthplace of parents; citizenship, if foreign born; year of immigration and years in United States; citizenship status; ability to read and write and speak English; home owned or rented; whether home is a farm; whether home is mortgaged. Counties include LaSalle, Grundy, Will, DuPage, and Cook.

U.S. Department of Labor and Commerce. *Twelth Federal Census: Population Schedules for Illinois, 1910.* (Microfilm.)
IC—FARC

One-hundred-two Illinois counties. 108 reels of microfilm. Miracode index (491 reels of microfilm). Information entered for individual: name; relationship to head of household; sex; color; age; marital status; length of present marriage; number of children; number of living children; birthplace; birthplace of parents; if foreign born, year of immigration and citizenship status; language spoken; occupation; type of industry; whether employer, employee, or self-employed; if unemployed, number of weeks unemployed in 1909; ability to read and write; whether attended daytime school since September 1, 1909; home owned or rented; whether home is a farm; whether survivor of Union or Confederate army or navy; whether blind; whether deaf and dumb. Counties include LaSalle, Grundy, Will, DuPage, and Cook.

Utica, Illinois. LaSalle County Historical Society. *Census of the City of Ottawa, 1867, for the Board of Education.* One package.
IUtHi

Genealogy and Biography—*Censuses*—Indexes

Frederick, Nancy Gubb. *The 1880 Illinois Census Index: Soundex Code 0200-0240, the Code That Was Not Filmed.* Evanston, Illinois: N. G. Frederick, 1981. 287 p.
DLC

Includes registers of birth, and so on, based on 1880 census of United States.

Jackson, Ronald Vern, Polson, Altha, and Zachrison, Shirley P. *Early Illinois.* Vol. 1: [*1787–1819*]. Bountiful, Utah: Accelerated Indexing Systems, 1980.
DLC

An early Illinois census index; includes genealogy, register of births, and so forth.

Jackson, Ronald Vern, and Teeples, Gary Ronald, eds. *Illinois 1820 Census Index.* Bountiful, Utah: Accelerated Indexing Systems, c. 1977. 155 p.
DLC

Bibliography, p. 9.

Jackson, Ronald Vern, and Teeples, Gary Ronald, eds. *Illinois 1830 Census Index.* Bountiful, Utah: Accelerated Indexing Systems, c. 1976. 63 p., map.
DLC

Jackson, Ronald Vern, and Teeples, Gary Ronald, eds. *Illinois 1840 Census Index.* Bountiful, Utah: Accelerated Indexing Systems, c. 1976. 192 p., map.
DLC
Includes bibliographies.

Jackson, Ronald Vern, and Teeples, Gary Ronald, eds. *Illinois 1850 Census Index.* Bountiful, Utah: Accelerated Indexing Systems, c. 1976. 192 p., map.
DLC
Includes bibliographies.

Jackson, Ronald Vern, Winmill, Wylma, and Zachrison, Shirley P., eds. *Illinois 1850 Mortality Schedule.* Bountiful, Utah: Accelerated Indexing Systems, 1980. 150 p.
DLC
Based on 1850 U.S. Census. Includes register of births, and so on.

Lundberg, G. W. *North-East Illinois Genealogical Source Materials: Will County 1850 Census, Township 4, Lockport. Homewood, Illinois.* Homewood, Illinois: Root & Tree Publications, n.d., 39 p. (Mimeographed).
ILo
Transcript of the census.

Richard, Bernice C. *1850 Federal Census of Grundy County, Illinois.* n.p., [1978]. 379 p.
ICN, IU—HS
Includes index.

Robb, Ruth Flesher. *1840 DuPage County, Illinois Federal Census.* Lombard, Illinois: By the Author, 1978. 14 p.
ICN, IU—HS

Robb, Ruth Flesher. *1850 DuPage County, Illinois Federal Census.* Lombard, Illinois: By the Author, 1976. 14 p.
ICN, IU—HS
Indexed.

Robb, Ruth Flesher. *1860 DuPage County, Illinois Federal Census/Transcribed, Indexed, Typed, and Published. . . .* Lombard, Illinois: By the Author, 1983. 18 p.
IU—HS
Includes index.

Volkel, Lowell. *1850 Illinois Mortality Schedule, Volume III, Counties Peoria through Woodford.* n.p., By the Author, 1973.
IJo

Wormer, Maxine E. *Illinois 1840 Census Index.* 5 v. Thomson, Illinois: Heritage House, c. 1973–1979. map.
DLC
Based on Sixth U.S. Census, 1840.

U.S. Census Office. *Seventh Census, 1850: Will County 1850 Census.* 22 v. Compiled by G. W. Lundberg. Homewood, Illinois: Root & Tree Publications, [1972–1973].
ICN, IU—HS

Genealogy and Biography—*Cemetery Inventories*

Bethany Lutheran Cemetery, A Reading. Read by Lemont Area Historical Society. Lemont, Illinois, 1984. 33 p., diagrs.
ILeHi
Location of burials in alphabetical order.

Carr, Martin and Carr, Diana. *Hadly Cemetery, Homer Township, Will County.* Listed by South Suburban Genealogical and Historical Society, n.p., n.d. 14 p., appendices, map.
ILo
Latter Day Saints Records were incorporated into this volume. Appendices include list of names found by Latter Day Saints but not by current researchers, list of Civil War veterans, transcripts of some early minutes of Hadly Cemetery Association meetings, record of plot owners, chart, map. Index in front.

Cemetery Records, DuPage County. Elmhurst, Illinois: Daughters of the American Revolution, 1952. 269 p.
ICN

Cemetery Records, LaSalle and Livingston Counties. Streator, Illinois: Daughters of the American Revolution, 1954. 175 p.
ICN

Daughters of the American Revolution. Illinois. *List of the Cemeteries in DuPage County, Illinois.* n.p., 1938. 14 p. (Typewritten.)
ICN

Daughters of the American Revolution. Illinois. Martha Ibbetson Chapter, Elmhurst, Illinois. *Cemetery Records, DuPage and Cook Counties.* Elmhurst, Illinois, 1953. 162 p. (Typewritten.)
ICN

Daughters of the American Revolution. Illinois. Illini Chapter, Ottawa. *Roll of the Cemeteries of LaSalle County, Illinois: Listing Names and Locations of Pioneer, Private, Family, Abandoned or Otherwise, and Those Cemeteries Now in Use.* Ottawa, Illinois, 1971. map.
IO
Indexed by name.

Daughters of the American Revolution. Illinois. Illini Chapter, Ottawa. *Seventeen Cemeteries, LaSalle County.* Ottawa, Illinois, 1955. 195 p. (Typewritten.)
ICN

Illinois Adjutant General's Office. *Roll of Honor Record of Burial Places of Soldiers, Sailors, Marines, and Army Nurses of All Wars of the United States Buried in the State of Illinois.* 2 v. Springfield, Illinois: Adjutant General, 1929.
DLC, ICJ, ICN

Irgang, George L. *LaSalle County Cemeteries/ Inventoried and Contributed....* Normal, Illinois: Bloomington-Normal Genealogical Society, [1971].
ICN, IU—HS

Morris, Illinois. Morris Public Library. *Evergreen Cemetery Records.* Two reels. (Microfilm).
IMo
Covers 1853–1982.

St. Alphonsus Cemetery, A Reading. Read by the Lemont Area Historical Society, Assisted by Members of the Southwest Suburban Genealogical Society. Lemont, Illinois, 1983. 67 p., diagrs.
ILeHi
Location of burials in alphabetical order.

St. Cyril's Cemetery, A Reading. Read by the Lemont Area Historical Society. Lemont, Illinois, 1983. 63 p., diagrs.
ILeHi
Location of burials in alphabetical order.

Sharp, Lea. *Grundy County Cemeteries: A List of Unrecorded Burials in Township Cemeteries.* n.p., 1979. 57 p., maps.
IMo
Cemeteries in ten townships.

"They Helped to Keep Our Country Free." *Will County Historical Society Quarterly,* November 1977.
IJo
U.S. Veterans buried in Will County.

Genealogy and Biography—*Vital Records*

Allison, Linda S. and Taylor, Harlin B. *Records of LaSalle County, Illinois.* Decatur, Illinois: Vio-Lin Enterprises, 1972.
ICN
Indexed. Names of Old Settlers' Association and 1929 Patron's Reference Directory.

County of LaSalle, Illinois. *LaSalle County Marriages on Record in Court House.* Ottawa, Illinois, 1931. (Typewritten.)
ICN
From June 22, 1831, the beginning of record, to July 19, 1851, the end of the first book.

Daughters of the American Revolution. Illinois. *Boone County, DuPage County, Kane County, Knox County, Genealogical Records....* Compiled by Gertrude S. Wheeler. Evanston, Illinois, 1945. 117 p.
ICN

Daughters of the American Revolution. Illinois. *DuPage County Genealogical Records....* Compiled from Records Copied by Laura Kendall Thomas. Elmhurst, Illinois, 1945. (Typewritten.)
ICN
Marriage records. Covers 1839–1905.

Daughters of the American Revolution. Illinois. *LaSalle County Genealogical Records.* 4 v. Indexed by Mrs. Burt T. Wheeler. Evanston, Illinois, 1943. (Typewritten.)
ICN
Covers 1831–1962.

Daughters of the American Revolution. Illinois. *White County, Will County, Genealogical Records. . . .* Compiled by Gertrude S. Wheeler. Evanston, Illinois, 1943–1945. 154 p. (Typewritten.)
ICN

Historical Records Survey, Illinois. *Guide to Public Vital Statistics Records in Illinois.* Chicago: Illinois Historical Records Survey, 1941. 138 p. (Mimeographed.)
ICU

Lists all available records alphabetically by county.

Index to Register of Deaths, 1878–1930: An Index to Death Records Held at the Grundy County Courthouse. n.p., n.d. 177 p.
IMo

LaSalle County Marriage Records, 1859–1862. 4 v. Ottawa, Illinois: Daughters of the American Revolution, 1959.
ICN

Lombard Suburban Genealogical Society. *Genealogical Sources: DuPage County, Illinois.* Lombard, Illinois: Lombard Suburban Genealogical Society, 1978. 97 p.
IDeKN—IRAD, ILomGe

Includes locations and description of vital statistics and wills, church records, census records, cemeteries, land records, military records, school records, newspapers, maps.

Peters, Marjorie Herlache, ed. *DuPage County, Illinois: Churches and Their Records: 1833–1920.* Lombard, Illinois: Lombard Suburban Genealogical Society, 1981. 62 p., illus., maps.
ICHi

Indexed.

Vital Records from Chicago Newspapers, 1833–1839, 1840–1842, 1843–1844, 1845, 1846. 4 v. Prepared by Newspaper Research Committee, Chicago Genealogical Society. Chicago, 1972–1976.
DLC, ILo

Lists marriages, deaths in Chicago newspapers. Indexed. Areawide coverage.

Genealogy and Biography—*Archive Sources*

Chicago, Illinois. Federal Archives and Records Center. Records of the Immigration and Naturalization Service.
IC—FARC

A Soundex index of all naturalizations in corridor cities (1840–1950) is available at FARC, as are dexagraph copies of naturalization petitions filed in local courts in Cook County for 1871–1906. Records for all other counties are kept in county courthouses. Genealogists would therefore want to use the Soundex index first in order to obtain the location of the records for a particular individual.

Joliet, Illinois. Joliet Public Library. *Joliet Herald News.* Biography. One card file drawer.
IJo

Index to newspaper articles published 1963–1970.

Joliet, Illinois. Joliet Public Library. *Joliet Herald News.* Obituary Index. Eight card file drawers.
IJo

Entries begin 1981.

Joliet, Illinois. Joliet Public Library. Obituaries. Three card file drawers.
IJo

Entries copied from *Joliet Herald News,* 1915–1916, 1918.

Lemont, Illinois. Lemont Area Historical Society. Harry J. Swanson Memorial Library. Cemetery Reading Index. Five catalogue drawers.
ILeHi

Names of burials in Bethany Lutheran, St. Matthew's, Franciscan, Sisters of Chicago (Our Lady's of Victory), St. Mary's, Ss. Cyril and Methodius, St. Alphonsus, St. Patrick's, Danish, Union Oil Refinery.

Lemont, Illinois. Lemont Area Historical Society. Harry J. Swanson Memorial Library. Newspaper Genealogy Index. Two catalogue drawers.
ILeHi

Vital statistics: births, deaths, marriages, christenings reported in *Lemont Observer,* 1896–1897; *Optimist News,* 1916–1927, 1928–1930; *Lemonter,* 1927, 1931–1969.

Lockport, Illinois. Will County Historical Society. Cemetery Inventory and Obituary Files. Sixty-six drawers.
ILoHi

Inventories for the following cemeteries: St. John's in Joliet, McCane in Channahon, St. Michael's, Gooding Farm and Brooks in Homer Township, Rudd in Joliet, Lockport City, Calvary, Barnet, Hadley, Runyon, Sisson-Bronson and South Lockport in Lockport, Bourdman and Resurrection in Romeoville.

Lockport, Illinois. Will County Historical Society. Genealogical File. Twenty-five boxes.
ILoHi
Thirty thousand names of Will County from church records, family Bibles, and county histories.

Lockport, Illinois. Will County Historical Society. Surname and Subject File.
ILoHi
Sixty-four thousand references to records, letters, news clippings, diaries, tax lists, deeds, and so on, on documents in Will County Historical Society.

Morris, Illinois. Morris Public Library. Local History File. Biography, 1900–1940. Two folders.
IMo
Newspaper clippings and obituaries of Grundy County residents.

Morris, Illinois. Morris Public Library. Local History File. Goose Lake Township Cemeteries. One folder.
IMo
Contains historical essay of the White-Holderman Cemetery, essay on Short Cemetery with inventory, White-Holderman Cemetery inventory.

Morris, Illinois. Morris Public Library. Local History File. Minooka. Marriages. One folder.
IMo
Contains newspaper clippings of marriage notices, c. 1902–.

Morris, Illinois. Morris Public Library. Local History File. Minooka Obituaries. One folder.
IMo
Contains newspaper clippings of Minooka deaths, c. 1902–.

Morris, Illinois. Morris Public Library. Local History Room. Registers of Interment Permits, 1902–1917. 3 v.
IMo

Morris, Illinois. Morris Public Library. *Morris Herald* Obituaries, 1967–1984. Index. Nine card catalogue drawers.
IMo

Palos Hills, Illinois. Green Hills Public Library. Sacred Heart Cemetery Plots. 1 v.
IPHil
Notebook locating plots and the interred.

Palos Park, Illinois. Palos Park Public Library. Local History Pamphlet File. Cemeteries. One folder.
IPHe
List of Chicagoland cemeteries. Also inventory of St. Patrick's in Lemont, by South Suburban Genealogical and Historical Society.

Peru, Illinois. Peru Public Library. Peru Cemetery Plots.
IPe
Laid out in 1847. By block and lot. Lists names of people buried (not life dates).

Springfield, Illinois. Archives of the State of Illinois. Illinois. Secretary of State. State Census, 1820.
I—Ar
Eighteen Illinois counties. 2 v. Index. Information entered for household: name of head of household, numbers of free white males over twenty, other white inhabitants, slaves and servants, free negroes, and mulattoes. Counties included are Alexander, Bond, Clark, Crawford, Franklin, Gallatin, Jackson, Jefferson, Johnson, Madison, Monroe, Pope, Randolph, St. Clair, Union, Washington, Wayne, and White.

Springfield, Illinois. Archives of the State of Illinois. Illinois. Secretary of State. State Census, 1825.
I—Ar
Three Illinois counties. Two folders and one reel of microfilm. Index. Information entered for household: name of head of household, number of free white males over twenty, number of free white males under twelve, number of free white females, number of male and female servants and slaves, free persons of color, type and number of manufacturing establishments. Counties included are Edwards, Fulton, and Randolph.

Springfield, Illinois. Archives of the State of Illinois. Illinois. Secretary of State. State Census, 1830.
I—Ar

Morgan County. 1 v. Index. Information entered for household: name of head of household, numbers of males and females in each decennial age group, numbers of male and female negroes and mulattoes, indentured or registered servants, French negroes and mulattoes held in bondage, total number of inhabitants in household, number of males subject to duty in state militia, type and numbers of manufacturing establishments.

Springfield, Illinois. Archives of the State of Illinois. Illinois. Secretary of State. State Census, 1835.
I—Ar

Four Illinois counties (and summary account of Cook). 3 v. Index. Information entered for household: name of head of household, numbers of free white males and females in each decennial age group, numbers of male and female negroes and mulattoes, indentured or registered servants and their children, French negroes and mulattoes held in bondage, total number of inhabitants in each household, number of males subject to duty in state militia, type and number of manufacturing establishments. Counties included are Fayette, Fulton, Jaspar, and Morgan. Summary account of Cook County but no individual names.

Springfield, Illinois. Archives of the State of Illinois. Illinois. Secretary of State. State Census, 1840.
I—Ar

Thirty-five Illinois counties. 7 v. One folder. Partial index (includes Cook and LaSalle, summary account for Will). Information entered for household: name of head of household, numbers of free white males and females in each decennial age group, numbers of male and female negroes and mulattoes, indentured and registered servants and their children, French negroes and mulattoes held in bondage, number of males subject to duty in state militia, total number of inhabitants in household, type and number of manufacturing establishments. Counties included are Adams, Bond, Brown, Calhoun, Champaign, Clark, Clay, Clinton, Coles, Cook, Crawford, Edgar, Effingham, Franklin, Fulton, Hamilton, Hardin, Jackson, Jasper, Jo Daviess, Johnson, Knox, LaSalle, Lawrence, Livingston, Monroe, Randolph, Rock Island, Schuyler, Stark, Tazewell, Union, Vermillion, White, Whiteside. Summary account with no individual names for Will.

Springfield, Illinois. Archives of the State of Illinois. Illinois. Secretary of State. State Census, 1845.
I—Ar

Three Illinois counties. 2 v. One folder. Index. Information entered for household: name of head of household, numbers of free white males and females in each decennial age group, numbers of male and female negroes and mulattoes, indentured or registered servants, French negroes and mulattoes held in bondage, total number of inhabitants in household, number of males subject to duty in state militia, type and number of manufacturing establishments. Counties included are Cass, Putnam, and Tazewell.

Springfield, Illinois. Archives of the State of Illinois. Illinois. Secretary of State. State Census, 1855.
I—Ar

Ninety Illinois counties. 59 v. Two folders. Partial index. Information entered for household: name of head of household, numbers of free white males and females in each decennial age group, numbers of male and female negroes and mulattoes, total number of inhabitants in household, number of males eligible for duty in state militia, type and value of products from manufacturing establishments, value of livestock and products of coal mines, quantity of wool produced, occupation of head of household. Returns also include numbers of colleges and common schools and pupils enrolled in each. Counties include LaSalle, Grundy, DuPage, and Cook.

Springfield, Illinois. Archives of the State of Illinois. Illinois. Secretary of State. Census of Deaf and Dumb, Blind, and Insane, 1855.
I—Ar

Sixty Illinois counties. 1 v. No index. Information entered for each individual: name, age, address, ailment, name of head of family. Counties include Grundy, Will, and DuPage.

Springfield, Illinois. Archives of the State of Illinois. Illinois. Secretary of State. State Census, 1865.
I—Ar

Information entered for household: name of head of household, numbers of free white males and females in each decennial age group, numbers of male and female negroes, total number of inhabitants in household, number of males eligible for duty in state militia, type and value of products of manufacturing establishments, value of livestock, grain products, quantity of coal produced, quantity of wool products, number of flour and gristmills, sawmills, and distilleries. Returns also include numbers of schools and attendance. Counties include LaSalle, Grundy, Will, DuPage, and Cook.

Springfield, Illinois. Archives of the State of Illinois. Illinois Territory. Governor. Territorial Census, 1818.
I—Ar

Fourteen Illinois counties. 1 v. Index. Information entered for household: name of head of household, numbers of free white males over twenty, other white inhabitants, free negroes and mulattoes, and servants and slaves. Counties included are Bond, Crawford, Franklin, Gallatin, Jackson, Johnson, Madison, Monroe, Pope, Randolph, St. Clair, Union, Washington, White.

Springfield, Illinois. Archives of the State of Illinois. U.S. Department of Interior. Seventh Federal Census. Mortality Schedules for Illinois, 1850.
I—Ar

Ninety-nine Illinois counties. 1 v. No index. Information entered for each deceased individual in year ending June 1, 1850: name, occupation, age, sex, race, free or slave, marital status, birthplace, length of illness, month of death, cause of death. Counties include LaSalle, Grundy, Will, DuPage, and Cook.

Springfield, Illinois. Archives of the State of Illinois. U.S. Department of Interior. Eighth Federal Census. Mortality Schedules for Illinois, 1860.
I—Ar

One-hundred-two Illinois counties. 1 v. No index. Information entered for each deceased individual in year ending June 1, 1860: name, occupation, age, sex, race, free or slave, marital status, birthplace, length of illness, month of death, cause of death. Counties include LaSalle, Grundy, Will, DuPage, and Cook.

Springfield, Illinois. Archives of the State of Illinois. U.S. Department of Interior. Ninth Federal Census. Mortality Schedules for Illinois, 1870.
I—Ar

One-hundred-two Illinois counties. 1 v. No index. Information entered for each deceased individual in year ending June 1, 1870: name, occupation, age, race, marital status, birthplace, birthplace of parents, month of death, cause of death. Counties include LaSalle, Grundy, Will, DuPage, and Cook.

Springfield, Illinois. Archives of the State of Illinois. U.S. Department of Interior. Tenth Federal Census. Mortality Schedules for Illinois, 1880.
I—Ar

One-hundred-two Illinois counties. 3 v. No index. Information entered for each deceased individual in year ending May 31, 1880: name, occupation, age, sex, race, marital status, birthplace, birthplace of parents, month of death, cause of death, length of residence in county, place where disease was contracted, name of attending physician. Counties include LaSalle, Grundy, Will, DuPage, and Cook.

Springfield, Illinois. Archives of the State of Illinois. U.S. Department of Interior. Tenth Federal Census. Schedules of Handicapped, Dependent and Delinquent Inhabitants of Illinois, 1880.
I—Ar

One-hundred-two Illinois counties. 3 v. No index. Information entered for the insane: name, residence, whether institutionalized, disease, history, restraint. Idiotic: name, residence, dependency, cause of idiocy, school record. Deaf-mutes: name, residence, dependency, cause of deafness, condition, record. Blind: name, residence, dependency, form of blindness, cause, degree, record. Homeless children: name, residence, status, previous condition. Prisoners: name, residence, place of imprisonment, type of prison, reason for imprisonment, date of incarceration, crime, sentence. Paupers: name, residence, means of support, condition, nature of disability, date of admission, relatives in institution. Counties include LaSalle, Grundy, DuPage, and Cook.

Utica, Illinois. LaSalle County Historical Society Museum. Bible Collection. 20 v.
IUtHi

Various family Bibles, nineteenth century, some in German.

PART 15 Maps and Atlases

The graphic history of the I&M corridor landscape reflects the history of the settlement and transportation interest in the area. The earliest maps—drawn by French, English, and American explorers—show the connections between the midwestern river systems and reflect a continuing fascination with the strategic importance of the Chicago portage. As the Illinois territory was brought into the United States public land disposal system in the early-nineteenth century, drawings of the corridor were included in numerous maps designed to attract settlers to the farms and to the towns of northeastern Illinois. Therefore, as time went by and as the canal and the population grew, maps were drawn in greater numbers and included more details on a smaller scale. Therefore, only pre-1860 maps of the entire state are included in this section. More localized representations were drawn in larger quantities afterward.

Since individual maps are shaped differently from most books, libraries usually store and catalogue them separately from other collections. Researchers who wish to take advantage of the often unique information contained in maps should be prepared to make a special effort to learn the existence and location of map collections in libraries and archives. The best bibliography for maps and atlases that covers the corridor is the checklist by Robert Karrow, listed in the following.

Unlike most of the other parts of the Bibliography, which are arranged alphabetically, the following subsections that list actual maps and atlases are arranged chronologically.

Maps and Atlases—*General*

Conzen, Michael P., ed. *The Chicago Mapmakers: Essays on the Rise of the City's Map Trade.* Chicago: Chicago Historical Society for the Chicago Map Society, 1984. 76 p.
ICHi, ICN, ICU, IU

Essays about maps made in Chicago during the nineteenth century and their makers. Includes maps of Chicago, northern Illinois, and the corridor.

Karrow, Robert W., Jr., gen. ed. *Checklist of Printed Maps of the Middle West to 1900.* 13 v. Boston: G. K. Hall & Co., 1981.
ICHi, ICN, ICU, IU

The most comprehensive finding aid for maps of the region. Vol. 4: Covers Illinois and is arranged alphabetically by geographical location or place and chronologically within these categories.

Karrow, Robert W., Jr., comp. *Index to Checklist of Printed Maps of the Middle West Before 1900.* Chicago: The Newberry Library, 1984.
ICHi, ICN, ICU, IU

Author, title, and subject indexes make this an excellent adjunct to the *Checklist.*

Maps and Atlases—*Prestatehood Manuscripts and Reconstructions*

Beckwith, Hiram W. "A Map of Illinois in 1680." *American Antiquarian* 17 (July 1895): 231–236.
ICU

Description of mounds overlooked by early Illinois explorers. Includes commentary on Starved Rock and Mount Joliet.

[Blanchard, Rufus]. *Map Showing the Indian Tribes in Illinois in 1684 and 1765 and 1812.* In his *History of Illinois.* Chicago, 1883.
IU

Franquelin, Jean B. L. "Carte de la Louisiane on des Voyages du Sr. de la Salle . . . (Map.)" Manuscript in the Library of Congress, Washington, 1684.
DLC

Reproduced in Charles A. Hanna, *The Wilderness Trail: Or the Ventures and Adventures of the Pennsylvania Traders on the Allegheny Path, with Some New Annals of the Old West, and the Records of Some Strong Men and Some*

Bad Ones. 2 v. New York and London: G. P. Putnam's Sons, 1911.

Kellogg, Louise P. "Marquette's Authentic Map Possibly Identified." *Proceedings of the State Historical Society of Wisconsin for 1906*. Madison, Wisconsin, 1907. pp. 183–193.
WU

Marcel, Gabriel. *Reproductions de Cartes et de Globes Relatifs à la Découverte de l'Amérique du XVIe au XVIIe Siècle*. Atlas and Test. Paris, 1892.
DLC

Marquette, Father Pierre. *Map of the Mississippi River*. n.p., 1673–1674.
ICHi
Copy of original.

Musham, Harry Albert. *Chicago in 1808: Prepared from the Official Report of Captain John Whistler . . . Early U.S. Government Surveys and Other Authentic Sources*. Chicago, 1936. (Blueprint.)
ICN
Detailed layout of buildings, routes, and sites in 1808 Chicago. Blueprint.

Musham, Harry Albert. *The Chicago Portage in 1812: Prepared from Early Maps, United States Government Surveys and Other Authentic Sources*. Chicago, 1936.
ICN
Insets include copy of map of the country from Lake Michigan to the Illinois River, Lake Michigan to the Mississippi River. Also includes distances. Musham used the papers of Gen. William Hull, governor of Michigan from 1805 to 1812.

Musham, Harry Albert. *General Situation Map, May 1812: Prepared from Report by Governor N. Edwards of Illinois Territory to Secretary of War Eustis*. Chicago, 1934.
ICN
With a key giving the location of the Indian tribes and the number of men in each, in Illinois Territory, 1812. Indicates at least four Indian villages in the corridor region.

Steward, John Fletcher. *Chicago Portage*. Chicago, 1904. (Blueprint.)
ICN
Insets include details from an unidentified map of 1681, details from Hutchins's map of 1778; Andrews's map, 1782; Hull's map, 1812.

Steward, John F. "De Lery's Error Again." *Illinois State Historical Society Transactions* 19 (1913): 91.
ICU
Brief commentary on the Illinois River as found in Franquelin's 1684 map. (Illinois River is labeled as the Macoupin.) Map faces p. 91.

Storm, Colton. "Lieutenant John Armstrong's Map of the Illinois River, 1790." *Journal of the Illinois State Historical Society* 37 (March 1944): 48–55. illus.
DLC, I, IC, ICHi, ICN, ICU, IEN, IU
Good early map with landmarks indicated. Original copy in Harmar Papers, Vol. 12, p. 122b, held at the Clements Library, University of Michigan.

Tucker, Sara Jones. *Indian Villages of the Illinois Country, 1670–1830*. Illinois State Museum. Scientific Papers Series, Vol. 2, Pt. 1. Springfield: Printed by Authority of the State of Illinois, 1942. 18 p., 54 plates. (Copies of originals.)
ISM
Supplement by Wayne C. Temple, 1975. Contains maps 55–93. Annotated.

U.S. Northwest Territory Celebration Commission. *Historical Map of the Old Northwest Territory*. Marietta, Ohio: Northwest Territory Celebration Commission, 1937.
ICN

Maps and Atlases—*General Illinois (to 1860)*

Carey, [Matthew]. *Carey's American Pocket Atlas . . . With a Concise Description of Each State*. Philadelphia: Carey. c. 1815. 118 p., 19 maps.
DLC
Four editions. Illinois is covered under the Northwest of Indiana Territory. Fourth edition contains a two-page account of Illinois Territory.

Melish, John. *Map of Illinois Constructed from the Surveys of Its General Land Office*. Phila-

delphia: John Melish and Samuel Harrison, 1818.
DLC, IHi
Reprinted in 1819.

Illinois. Philadelphia: A. Finley, 1821.
IHi

Beck, Lewis Caleb. "Map of the States of Illinois and Missouri." In *A Gazetteer of the State of Illinois and Missouri.* By Lewis C. Beck. Albany, New York, 1823.
ICN

Jocelyn [N. and S. S.]. "Illinois and Missouri." In *An Atlas of the United States.* By Sidney Edwards Morse. New Haven: S. E. Morse, 1823.
DLC, IHi

Lucas, Fielding, Jr. *Illinois.* Baltimore: J. Lucas, Print., 1823.
IHi

Browne, E. *Map of the States of Missouri and Illinois and Territory of Arkansas Taken from Recent Surveys in the Office of the Surveyor General at St. Louis. . . .* [St. Louis]: B. Rogers, 1827.
DLC

Tanner, Henry Schenck. *Illinois and Missouri.* Philadelphia: H. S. Tanner, 1825.
IU, IHi
Reprinted in 1827, 1831, 1833, 1836, 1841.

[Melish, John]. *Illinois and Missouri.* Philadelphia: H. C. Carey and I. Lea, 1826.
IU

Finley, Anthony. *Illinois.* Philadelphia: A. Finley [1829].
IU
Reprinted in 1831, 1834.

Tanner, Henry Schenk. *The Travellers Pocket Map of Illinois with Its Proposed Canals, Roads and Distances from Place to Place. . . .* Philadelphia: H. S. Tanner, c. 1830.
IU

Carpenter, Justin. *Indiana, Illinois and Part of Missouri.* [New York]: Justin Carpenter, c. 1831.
InHi

Tanner, Henry Schenk. *A New Map of Illinois with Its Proposed Canals, Roads and Distances from Place to Place. . . .* Philadelphia: H. S. Tanner, c. 1833.
IHi
Reprinted in 1836, 1841.

Young, James Hamilton. *Illinois.* Drawn by J. H. Young. Engraved by J. H. Young and E. Yeager. Philadelphia: Anthony Finley, 1833.
DLC, ICHi
Reprinted in 1834.

Burr, David H. *Illinois.* New York: Engraved and Printed by Illinois & Pilbrow, c. 1834.
IHi
Reprinted in 1835.

Bromme, Traugott. *Karte der Staaten Illinois und Missouri.* Baltimore: Verlag von C. Scheld & Co., 1835.
DLC

Young, James Hamilton. *The Tourist's Pocket Map of the State of Illinois Exhibiting Its Internal Improvements, Roads, Distances, etc.* Philadelphia: S. Augustus Mitchell, 1835.
IU
Reprinted in 1836, 1837, 1839, 1849.

Peck, J. M. and Messenger, J. *A New Map of Illinois and Part of the Wisconsin Territory.* Cincinnati, Ohio: Doolittle and Munson, 1835.
ICN

Peck, J. M. and Messenger, John. *New Sectional Map of the State of Illinois. . . .* New York: J. H. Colton and Co., 1836.
ICHi, IU
Reprinted in 1838, 1839.

Squire, Bela S. *Map of Illinois with a Plan of Chicago.* Engraved by J. R. Hammond. New York: B. S. Squire, Print., 1836.
IHi

Bufford, John H. *A Map of Illinois, Exhibiting the Railroads, and Other Improvements Projected.* New York: J. H. Bufford's Lithogy, [1836].
IDeKN—IRAD, IHi

Hammond, John T. *Map of Illinois with a Plan of Chicago.* Engraved by J. J. Hammond. New York: B. S. Squire, Jr., 1836.
IU

Young, James Hamilton. *Mitchell's Map of Illinois Exhibiting its Improvements, Counties,*

Towns, Roads, etc. Engraved by J. H. Young. Philadelphia: S. A. Mitchell, 1837.
ICN, IDeKN—IRAD, IHi
Reprinted in 1838, 1848.

Boynton, George W. *Illinois.* Engraved by G. W. Boynton. [Boston]: T. G. Bradford, c. 1838.
ICN

Eddy, James. *Illinois: Exhibiting the Latest Surveys and Improvements.* Boston: Weeks, Jordan & Co., 1838.
IU

Burr, David H. *Map of Illinois and Missouri Exhibiting the Post Offices, Post Roads, Canals, Railroads, etc.* [Washington], 1839.
DLC

Peck, John Mason. *Map of the State of Illinois Compiled from the United States Surveys, Exhibiting the Sections, with Internal Improvements. . . .* By J. G. Peck and John Messinger. Engraved by Stiles, Sherman & Smith. New York: J. H. Colton, 1840.
IU
In Colton, J. H., *The Traveler's Directory for Illinois.* New York, 1839.

Peck, J. M. and Messenger, John. *New Sectional Map of the State of Illinois.* New York: J. H. Colton and Co., 1843.
ICHi

Peck, J. M., Messenger, John, and Mathewson, A. J. *New Sectional Map of the State of Illinois Compiled from the United States Surveys, Also Exhibiting the Internal Improvements, Distances Between Towns, Villages, and Post Offices, the Outlines of Prairies, Woodlands, Marshes . . . Includes a Profile of the Illinois and Michigan Canal.* New York: J. H. Colton and Co., 1844.
DLC, IU

Tanner, Henry Schenk. *Sectional Map of Illinois and Missouri.* Engraved by H. S. Tanner & Assistants. New York: H. S. Tanner, 1844.
DLC, IHi
Reprinted in 1846.

[Drown, Simeon DeWitt]. *A Map of the State of Illinois, and a Table of Distances from Peoria City to Different Points Throughout the State, Which is Four Hundred Miles in Length and Two-Hundred and Twenty in Breadth.* [Peoria, 1845].
IHi

Mitchell, Samuel Augustus. *A New Map of Illinois with Proposed Canals, Roads, and Distances from Place to Place. . . .* Philadelphia: Published by S. Augustus Mitchell, 1847.
IU
Reprinted 1849.

Peck, J. M., Messenger, John, and Mathewson, A. J. *New Sectional Map of the State of Illinois Compiled from U.S. Surveys. . . .* New York: J. H. Colton and Co., 1848.
DLC, ICHi, ICN, IHi, IU
Reprinted in 1850, 1851, 1852, 1853, 1854, 1855, 1856, 1857.

Cowperthwait, Thomas, & Co. *Map of the State of Illinois.* Philadelphia: Thomas Cowperthwait & Co., c. 1850.
IHi, IU
Reprinted in 1851, 1852, 1854.

Colton's Sectional Map of Illinois. New York: J. H. Colton and Co., 1852.
IHi, IU
Reprinted in 1853, 1854.

Morse, Charles Walker. *Morse's Map of Illinois.* Chicago: Rufus Blanchard, 1854.
ICN, IHi

Colton, Joseph Hutchins. *Colton's Illinois.* New York: J. H. Colton & Co., c. 1855.
DLC, ICHi, IDeKN—IRAD, IHi, IU
Reprinted in 1856, 1859.

Ensign, Bridgman & Fanning, pub. *Map of Illinois.* New York: Ensign, Bridgman & Fanning, 1855.
ICHi, IHi
Reprinted in 1856, 1857.

Chapman, Silas. *Chapman's Sectional Map of Illinois.* Milwaukee, Wisconsin: Silas Chapman, c. 1856.
IU
Reprinted in 1857.

DeSilver, Charles. *A New Map of the State of Illinois.* Philadelphia: Charles DeSilver, c. 1856.
ICHi, IU
Reprinted 1859.

Mendenhall, Edward. *A New Map of Illinois Exhibiting the Counties, Townships, Cities, Villages & Post Offices, the Railroads, Canals, Common Roads....* Cincinnati, Ohio: E. Mendenhall, 1856.
DLC

[Gerhard, Ferd.]. *Map of Illinois Showing Its Prairies, Woods, Swamps, Bluffs.* Chicago, 1857.
IHi
In Gerhard, Ferd., *Illinois As It Is.* Chicago, 1857. Opposite p. 216.

Larrance, Isaac. *Larrance's Post Office Chart.* [Cincinnati, Ohio]: Isaac Larrance, c. 1858.
DLC

Maps and Atlases—*Canal and Waterway*

Thompson, James. *Map of That Part of the State of Illinois Which Is Contemplated to Construct a Canal.* n.p., 1829.
DLC, ICHi

Thompson, James. *Map of the State of Illinois Through Which It Is Contemplated to Construct a Canal.* n.p., 1829.
DLC

Quion, Walter Burling. *Map and Profile of the Proposed Route for the Michigan and Illinois Canal.* S. 23rd Congress, First Session, Washington: Claussen and Friis, 1830.
ICN

Belin, H. *Map of Canal Route.* U.S. House Report. Washington, 1834.
ICHi

Map of Lands in the State of Illinois Embracing the Canal Route from Lake Michigan to the Head of Steam Boat Navigation on the Illinois River Compiled from Surveys Authenticated by the Surveyor General of the United States. New York: C. B. and J. R. Graham's Lithography, 1835.
DLC

Stone, William J. *Map Exhibiting Routes by Which the Navigation of the Mississippi River May Be Connected with the Navigation of the Lakes.* U.S. 26th Congress, First Session, Senate Document 318, Section 259. Washington, 1839–1840.
IU

Mathewson, A. J. *Sectional Map of Lands Donated by Congress to the State of Illinois to Aid in Constructing the Illinois and Michigan Canal.* Lockport, Illinois: [Illinois and Michigan Canal Commission], 1844.
ICHi

Brown, W. S. *Map of the Illinois and Michigan Canal and the Illinois and Mississippi Rivers Showing the Navigable Route from Chicago to St. Louis.* New York: Mayer and Korff Lithography, 1851.
ICHi

Calumet and Chicago Canal and Dock Co. *Subdivision of the Calumet and Chicago Canal and Dock Co., ... at South Chicago, Cook County, Illinois....* Chicago c. 1870.
ICN
Engraved by R. W. Dobson.

Denyuard, Wm. Henry Harrison. *Sketch of the Illinois and Michigan Canal and the Proposed Hennepin Canal Showing Their Relations to the Illinois River, Mississippi River, and Lake Michigan.* Washington: Government Printing Office, 1884.
IU

Map of the Illinois and Michigan Canal and Proposed Hennepin Canal. Washington: Corps of Engineers, United States Army, 1886.
DLC

Cooley, Lyman Edgar. *Watersheds of the Des-Plaines River....* Chicago: Chicago Sanitary District Committee on Boundaries, 1890.
DLC

Marshall, William Louis. *Tracing Map of DesPlaines and Illinois Rivers from Joliet to LaSalle, Survey of 1883, Showing Location of Locks and Dams for Proposed Waterway....* Chicago: [U.S. Engineer Dept.], 1890.
DLC

Outline Map of Waterway Between Lake Michigan and LaSalle, Illinois Showing Location of Proposed Locks and Dams. House Executive Document, 51st Congress, First Session, Washington, 1890.
ICHi

Map and Profile of Proposed Waterway Routes Between Lake Michigan and Mississippi River. 51st Congress, First Session, House Executive Document, Washington, 1890.
ICHi
Series of six maps showing vegetation along canal routes.

Map and Profile of the Main Drainage Channel from Chicago to Joliet. Chicago: Chicago Sanitary District, 1893.
DLC

U.S. Corps of Engineers. *Atlas Containing Maps of Chicago River, Illinois and Its Branches Showing Result of Improvement by the U.S. Government,* n.p., Drawn by A. T. Grohmann. 1896–1899. Twenty-nine maps.
ICHi

Property of the Calumet and Chicago Canal & Dock Company on the Calumet River, Cook County, Illinois. [Chicago], 1897.
ICHi
Includes South Deering, Hegewisch.

Maps and Atlases—*Railroads*

U.S. Surveyor General for Illinois and Missouri. *Diagram of the State of Illinois Showing the Six and Fifteen Mile Limits on Each Side of Its Railroad and Townships Originally Withdrawn from Market.* St. Louis: Surveyor's Office, 1848.
ICHi

A New Map of the Great West. New York: Miller, Orton and Mauli, c. 1850.
IDeKN—IRAD
Shows Rock Island and Chicago Railroad, Morris.

Cooke, D. B. & Co. *Cooke's Railway Guide for Illinois Showing All the Stations with Their Respective Distances Connecting with Chicago.* Chicago: D. B. Cooke and Co., 1854.
DLC, IU
Reprinted in 1855.

Ensign, Bridgman & Fanning, pubs. *Railroad and County Map of Illinois Showing Its Internal Improvements.* Printed by D. McLellan. New York: Ensign, Bridgman & Fanning, 1854.
DLC, ICHi
Reprinted in 1857.

Cooke's Great Western Railway Guide. Chicago: D. B. Cooke and Co., 1855.
IHi

Greenbaum, Henry. *Map of the State of Illinois N. America Showing All Its Rail-Roads Completed or in Progress. . . .* Chicago: Ed. Mendel's Lith., 1855.
ICHi
From *The Illinois Gazetteer and Immigrant's Western Guide.* Chicago, 1855.

Blanchard, Rufus. *Township Map of Illinois Showing Railroads, Stations, and Towns.* Chicago: Rufus Blanchard, 1863.
ICHi

Illinois. Railroad and Warehouse Commission. *Railroad Map of Illinois.* Chicago: Rand, McNally & Co., c. 1885.
ICN, IDeKN—IRAD
Prepared for the 1885 report of the Railroad and Warehouse Commissioners.

Illinois. Railroad and Warehouse Commission. *Railroad Map of Illinois.* Chicago: Rand, McNally & Co., 1890.
ICN, IDeKN—IRAD

Rand, McNally & Co. *Rand, McNally & Co.'s New Sectional Railroad Map of Cook and DuPage Counties with Parts of Adjoining Counties Including the Manufacturing District in Lake County, Indiana.* Chicago: Rand, McNally & Co., c. 1893.
DLC, IHi

Blanchard, Rufus. *Map of Six Counties Around Chicago, Showing Railroads, Junction Points, Stations, Post Offices and Villages. . . .* [Chicago: Rufus Blanchard, 1899].
ICHi

Illinois. Railroad and Warehouse Commission. *Railroad Commissioner's Official Map of Illinois.* Chicago, 1908.
DLC

Maps and Atlases—Counties and Cities

Maps and Atlases—*Counties and Cities*—LaSalle County

Mesier, Peter A. *Ottawa.* New York: P. A. Mesier's Lith., c. 1850.
DLC

Price, I. *Ottawa.* Engraved on Stone by I. Price. New York: P. A. Mesier's Lith., [1850].
IHi

[Walling, Henry Francis]. *City of LaSalle, LaSalle County.* Inset on his *Map of the State of Illinois.* New York, 1863.
DLC

[Walling, Henry Francis]. *City of Ottawa.* Inset on his *Map of the State of Illinois.* New York, 1863.
DLC

[Walling, Henry Francis]. *City of Peru, LaSalle County.* Inset on his *Map of the State of Illinois.* New York, 1863.
DLC

Thompson and Everts. *Thompson's Maps of LaSalle County, Illinois.* Geneva, Illinois: C. L. F. Thompson, 1870. Thirty-two maps.
ICU
Thirty-two township maps.

Warner and Beers. *Atlas of LaSalle County and the State of Illinois, to Which Is Added an Atlas of the United States, Maps of the Hemispheres, etc.* Chicago: Warner and Beers, 1876. 93 p. Eighty-two maps, illus.
IU
Thirty-five township maps showing owners. Plats of towns.

[Baldwin, Elmer]. "Survey of Old Fort on Bluff South of Starved Rock." In *History of LaSalle County, Illinois.* By Elmer Baldwin. Chicago: Rand, McNally & Co., 1877. p. 338.
IU

[Wilson, Charles F.]. *Map of the City of Ottawa.* [Ottawa, Illinois]: Maierhofer, Fourlaugh & Goudolf, 1888.
IHi

Alden, Ogle and Company. *Plat Book of LaSalle County, Illinois.* Chicago: Alden, Ogle and Company, 1892. 110 p. Sixty-two maps.
ICJ, ICU, IG

Dunaway, W. A. *Map of LaSalle County, Illinois. . . .* Ottawa, Illinois: Maierhofer and Briel, 1895.
DLC

W. W. Hixson and Company. *Plat Book of LaSalle County, Illinois.* Rockford, Illinois: W. W. Hixson and Company [1900]. Thirty-three maps.
IDeKN—IRAD

Hixson Maps and Lith. Company. *Map of LaSalle County, Illinois.* Ottawa, Illinois: The Fair Dealer, 1902.
IDeKN—IRAD

George A. Ogle and Company. *Standard Atlas of LaSalle County, Illinois, Including a Plat Book of the Villages, Cities and Townships of the County, Map of the State, United States and World. . . .* Chicago: G. A. Ogle and Company, 1906. 123 p. Seventy-eight maps, illus.
I, IU

Ottawa Printing Company. *Plat Book of LaSalle County and Roster of LaSalle County Soldiers, Sailors and Nurses of the World War.* Ottawa, Illinois: Ottawa Printing Company, Inc., 1921. 93 p.
IMa, IO, IUtHi
Advertisements. Thirty-two maps showing owners.

Brock and Company. *Standard Atlas of LaSalle County, Illinois, Including a Plat Book of the Villages, Cities and Townships of the County, Map of the State, United States and World. . . .* Chicago: Brock and Company, 1929. 139 p. Seventy-eight maps, illus.
I, IU
Thirty-two township maps showing owners. Plats of LaSalle, Marseilles, Utica, Ottawa, Peru, Science, Seneca.

Plat Book of LaSalle County, Illinois. Rockford, Illinois: The Globe Map & Atlas Publishers, Comp. & Pub., 1937.
IO

Maps and Atlases—*Counties and Cities*—Grundy County

[Burhans, S. H.]. *Plat of Channahon.* Inset on his *Map of Will County, Illinois.* [Chicago], 1862.
DLC

Doran, Thomas. *Map of Grundy County, Illinois.* Chicago: Thomas Doran, 1863.
IMoHi

Ten views. Copy in possession of Virginia Sparr Brown, Morris, Illinois.

[Walling, Henry Francis]. *City of Morris, Grundy County.* Inset on his *Map of the State of Illinois.* New York, 1863.
DLC

Sanford, E. *Map of Grundy County, Illinois.* Morris, Illinois: E. Sanford, Attorney & Real Estate Agt., c. 1868.
DLC

Warner and Beers. *Atlas of Grundy County and the State of Illinois, to Which Is Added an Atlas of the United States, Maps of the Hemisphere, etc.* Chicago: Warner and Beers, 1874. 93 p. Fifty-four maps, illus.
ICHi, IU

Ten township maps. Plat and business directory of Morris.

Ogle, George A. and Company. *Plat Book of Grundy County, Illinois.* Chicago: George A. Ogle and Company, 1892. 75 p. Twenty-four maps.
IHi

Hixson, W. W. and Company. *Map of Grundy County, Illinois.* Morris: Daily and Weekly Sentinel, 1901.
IDeKN—IRAD

Ogle, George A. and Company. *Standard Atlas of Grundy County, Illinois, Including A Plat Book of the Villages, Cities, and Townships of the County: Map of the State, United States and World. . . .* Chicago: George A. Ogle and Company, 1909. 107 p. Twenty-four maps, illus.
I, ICHi

Seventeen township maps showing owners. Plats of Coal City and Morris.

W. W. Hixson and Company. *Plat Book of Grundy County.* Rockford, Illinois: W. W. Hixson and Company, c. 1930. Thirteen maps.
IDeKN—IRAD

Maps and Atlases—*Counties and Cities*—Will County

Mesier, Peter A. *Map of Juliet [sic] and Additions.* New York: P. A. Mesier's Lith., [1840].
IHi

Veith, A. *Map of Joliet, Will County, Illinois.* Joliet, Illinois: Drawn and Published by A. Veith, Surveyor, 1859.
DLC

Burhans, S. H. *Map of Will County, Illinois: Compiled and Drawn from Records and Actual Surveys. . . .* Chicago: Engraved, Printed, Colored and Mounted by Edward Mendel, 1862.
DLC

Insets of Lockport, Joliet.

[Burhans, S. H.] *Map of Joliet.* Inset on his *Map of Will County, Illinois.* [Chicago], 1862.
DLC

[Burhans, S. H.] *Map of Lockport.* Inset on his *Map of Will County, Illinois.* [Chicago], 1862.
DLC

Walling, Henry Francis. *City of Joliet.* Inset on his *Map of the State of Illinois.* New York, 1863.
DLC

Radford, P. M. *Sectional Map of the Counties of Will, Kankakee and Part of Cook.* Joliet, Illinois: P. M. Radford [1872].
ICHi

Thompson Brothers and Burr. *Combination Atlas of Will County, Illinois.* Elgin, Illinois: Thompson Brothers and Burr, 1873. 135 p. Thirty-one maps, illus.
I, ICHi, ICN, IU

Lithographs of Joliet, penitentiary, quarries, breweries. Township maps with owners. Plats of Lockport and Channahon.

Whitley, Noah. *City of Joliet, Illinois. Compiled from Original and Recent Surveys.* Engraved by Wm. Wangersheim. Chicago, 1887.
DLC

Ogle, George A. and Company. *Plat Book of Will County, Illinois.* Chicago: George A. Ogle and Company, 1893. 81 p. Fifty-seven maps.
IHi

Whitley, Noah. *Will County [Illinois] Atlas.* [Joliet, Illinois, 1900]. 23 p. Twenty-four maps.
IG

Hixson, W. W. and Company. *Map of Will County, Illinois.* Joliet, Illinois: Joliet News, 1902.
IDeKN—IRAD

Whitley, N[oah]. *Map of the City of Joliet, Illinois.* Compiled and Drawn by N. Whitley and W. H. Zarley. . . . Joliet, Illinois: Finley, 1903. 17 p.
ICN

Ogle, George A. and Company. *Standard Atlas of Will County, Illinois, Including a Plat Book of the Villages, Cities and Townships of the County, Map of the State, United States and World. . . .* Chicago: George A. Ogle and Company, 1909–1910. 163 p. Fifty-nine maps, illus.
I, ICU, IU

Hixson, W. W. and Company. *Plat Book of Will County, Illinois.* Rockford, Illinois: W. W. Hixson and Company, c. 1924. Twenty-four maps.
IDeKN—IRAD

Maps and Atlases—*Counties and Cities*—DuPage County

Bennett, Lyman G., Lyon, E. A., and Brooks, Horace, comps. *Map of DuPage County, Illinois.* Chicago: Lyman G. Bennett and Horace Brooks, 1862.
ICN

With sixteen views.

Thompson Brothers and Burr. *Combination Atlas Map of DuPage County, Illinois.* Elgin, Illinois: Thompson Brothers and Burr, 1874, 71 p. Nineteen maps, illus.
ICN, ICU, IU

Middle-West Publishing Company. *Twentieth Century Atlas of DuPage County, Illinois, Containing Maps of Villages, Cities and Townships of the County, of the State, United States and World.* Chicago: Middle-West Publishing Company, 1904. 89 p. Thirty maps, illus.
IU

Thrift Press. *Atlas, Plat Book of DuPage County, Illinois, Containing Outline Map of County and Plats of All the Townships with Owners' Names.* Rockford, Illinois: Thrift Press, 1927. Nine maps.
ICN

Steinbrecher, Harold F. *Atlas of DuPage County, Illinois, Showing Ownership, Acreage, Roads, Railroads, City Limits, Subdivided Areas, Sections and Quarter Sections. . . .* Wheaton, Illinois: Harold F. Steinbrecher, 1930. Eleven maps.
DLC

Hixson, W. W. and Company. *Plat Book of DuPage County, Illinois.* Rockford, Illinois: W. W. Hixson and Company, c. 1930. Eleven maps.
IDeKN—IRAD

Sidwell Studio. *DuPage County, Illinois. . . .* Lombard, Illinois: Sidwell Studio, 1936. 25 p. Twelve maps.
DLC

Sidwell Studio. *Aer-o-Plat of DuPage County, Illinois.* Lombard, Illinois: Sidwell Studio, 1940. Fifty maps.
IU—HS

This aer-o-plat of DuPage is the first of its kind to be published. Compiled by tracing aerial survey maps and supplementing the legal descriptive matter.

Maps and Atlases—*Counties and Cities*—Cook County

Cook, DuPage, Will and Kankakee Counties. U.S. Government Survey. n.p., 1832.
ICHi

Atlas.

Rees, James H. *Map of the Counties of Cook and DuPage, the East Part of Kane and Kendall, the North Part of Will, State of Illinois.* Chicago: Ferdinand Mayer's Lithography, 1851.
DLC, ICHi

Flower, W. L. *Map of Cook County.* [Chicago]: S. H. Burnhans and J. Van Vechten, 1861.
DLC, ICHi, ICN

[Flower, Walter L.]. *Map of Blue Island.* Inset on his *Map of Cook County, Illinois.* [Chicago], 1861.
ICHi

[Flower, Walter L.]. *Plat of Lemont.* Inset on his *Map of Cook County, Illinois.* [Chicago], 1861.
ICHi

[Flower, Walter L.]. *Plat of Long John.* Inset on his *Map of Cook County, Illinois.* [Chicago], 1861.
ICHi

Long John was Willow Springs.

Flower, W. L. *Map of Cook County.* [Chicago]: S. H. Burnhans and J. Van Vechten, 1862.
DLC, ICHi, ICN, IU

Hewitt, John H. *Sectional Map of Cook County, Illinois.* Chicago: John H. Hewitt, 1868.
DLC

Blanchard, Rufus. *Blanchard's Map of Cook and DuPage Counties.* Chicago: Rufus Blanchard, 1868.
ICHi

Blanchard, Rufus. *Blanchard's Map of Cook and DuPage Counties.* Chicago: Rufus Blanchard, 1869.
ICHi

Stewart, Charles W. *Map Showing Hill's Addition to South Chicago.* Compiled from Actual Surveys by C. W. Stewart, Surveyor. Robert Lyons Conroy, Draughtsman. Chicago, [1869].
ICHi

Van Vechten, J. *Map of Cook and DuPage Counties.* Chicago: J. Van Vechten, 1870.
DLC

Blanchard, Rufus. *Blanchard's Map of Cook and DuPage Counties Showing the Streets, Blocks, Parks, Boulevards, and Subdivisions of Chicago and Its Environs. . . .* Chicago: Rufus Blanchard, 1871.
ICHi, IU

Blanchard, Rufus. *Map of Cook and DuPage Counties.* On his *Map of Chicago.* Chicago: Rufus Blanchard, 1872.
DLC

Van Vechten, James. *Van Vechten's Map of Cook and DuPage Counties, Also the Northern Portion of Lake County, Indiana.* Chicago: J. Van Vechten, 1872.
DLC

Iron Workers' Addition to South Chicago. [Chicago, 1973].
ICHi

Shows New York silicon steel rail mill grounds.

Roy, Peter. *Map of Cook and DuPage Counties, Showing the Suburban Towns of Chicago.* [Chicago]: Peter Roy, 1873.
ICHi

Blanchard, Rufus. *Map of Cook and DuPage Counties.* Engraved by Rufus Blanchard. Chicago, 1874.
ICHi, IHi

Dobson, Robert W. *Map of Riverdale and Surroundings, Cook County, Illinois.* Chicago: R. W. Dobson, Surveyor and Lithographer, 1874.
ICHi

Van Vechten, J. and Snyder, L. M. *Van Vechten and Snyder's Real Estate Map of Cook and DuPage Counties. . . .* Chicago: J. Van Vechten and L. M. Snyder, 1875.
DLC

Henbach, Emil. *Map of Chicago and Adjacent Towns, in the Counties of Cook, Lake, McHenry, Kendall, Grundy, Kane, DuPage, Will, Kankakee, etc.* n.p., 1876.
ICHi

Blanchard, Rufus. *Map of Cook and DuPage Counties.* Chicago: Rufus Blanchard, 1877.
ICHi

Van Vechten and Snyder. *Guide Map of Cook, DuPage and Parts of Will and Kane Counties, Illinois. . . .* Chicago: Van Vechten & Snyder, 1881.
DLC

Rand, McNally & Co. *Map of Cook and DuPage Counties, Illinois, With Part of Lake County, Indiana.* Chicago: Rand, McNally & Co., c. 1882.
ICN

Index to location and population of townships, villages, post offices, and railway stations.

Snyder, L. M. and Company. *Snyder's Real Estate Map of Cook County, Illinois.* Chicago: Engraved and Published by L. M. Snyder & Co., 1886.
ICHi

Insets of Blue Island, Lemont, Worth, Dolton.

[Snyder, L. M. & Co.]. *Blue Island.* Inset on *Snyder's Real Estate Map of Cook County, Illinois.* Chicago, 1886.
ICHi

[Snyder, L. M. & Co.]. *Dolton.* Inset on *Snyder's Real Estate Map of Cook County, Illinois.* Chicago, 1886.
ICHi

[Snyder, L. M.]. *Long John.* Inset on his *Snyder's Real Estate Map of Cook County, Illinois.* Chicago, 1886.
ICHi

Long John was Willow Springs.

Snyder, Frank Miles. *Snyder's Real Estate Map of Cook and DuPage Counties, Illinois.* Chicago: F. M. Snyder, 1890.
DLC

Inset of Blue Island.

[Snyder, Frank Miles]. *Blue Island.* Inset on *Snyder's Real Estate Map of Cook and DuPage Counties, Illinois.* Chicago, 1890.
DLC

Lemont, Illinois. Lemont Area Historical Society. *Land Ownership Map of Lemont Area.* n.p., c. 1890.
ILeHi

Blanchard, Rufus. *Map of the Counties of Cook, DuPage and Lake with Parts of Adjacent Counties. . . .* Chicago: Rufus Blanchard, 1891.
ICHi

Reprinted in 1892.

Inman, G. S. *The Authentic Real Estate Investors Map of Cook, DuPage and Part of Will Counties, Illinois. . . .* n.p., G. S. Inman, F. F. Short, c. 1891.
DLC

Rossiter, F. C. *Map of Cook County, Illinois Showing Chicago, Its Suburbs and Railroad Connections.* Compiled and Published by F. C. Rossiter, Chicago, 1891.
ICHi

Map of the Calumet District, Cook County, Illinois. n.p., 1897.
ICHi

Includes Hegewisch, South Deering, Calumet City.

Mitchell, Wm. L. *Snyder's Real Estate Map of Cook, DuPage and Part of Will Counties, Illinois.* Chicago: William L. Mitchell, 1898.
DLC

Mitchell, Wm. C. *Real Estate Map of Cook, DuPage, and Part of Will Counties, Illinois.* Chicago: Wm. C. Mitchell, 1902.
DLC, ICHi

Mitchell, Wm. L. *Mitchell's Real Estate Map of Cook and DuPage Counties and Part of Will County. . . .* Chicago: Wm. L. Mitchell, 1904.
DLC

Cook County, Illinois. Board of Commissioners. *Map of Cook County, Illinois.* Chicago: Board of Commissioners, 1928.
ICN

Showing highways and forest preserves.

Thrift Press. *Atlas and Plat Book of Cook County, Illinois, Containing Outline Map of the County and Plats of All the Townships with Owners' Names.* Rockford, Illinois: Thrift Press, 1926. Thirty maps.
ICHi

Hixson, W. W. and Company. *Plat Book of Cook County, Illinois.* Rockford, Illinois: W. W. Hixson and Company, c. 1930. Twenty-four maps.
IDeKN—IRAD

Cook County, Illinois. Board of Commissioners. *Map of Cook County, Illinois.* Chicago: Board of Commissioners, 1935.
ICN

Showing highways and forest preserves.

Maps and Atlases—Fire Insurance

Maps and Atlases—*Fire Insurance*—LaSalle County

Sanborn Fire Insurance Company. *Peru, LaSalle County.* New York: Sanborn Map and Publishing Co., 1888, 1892, 1897, 1902, 1909, 1916, 1926, 1926–1941.
DLC, IU

Sanborn Fire Insurance Company. *LaSalle, LaSalle County.* New York: Sanborn Map and Publishing Co., 1888, 1892, 1898, 1906, 1911, 1926, 1926–1941.
DLC, IU

Sanborn Fire Insurance Company. *Oglesby, LaSalle County.* New York: Sanborn Map and Publishing Co., 1911, 1930, 1930–1943.
DLC, IU

Sanborn Fire Insurance Company. *Utica, LaSalle County.* New York: Sanborn Map and Publishing Co., 1888, 1891, 1896, 1901, 1909, 1929.
DLC, IU

Sanborn Fire Insurance Company. *Ottawa, LaSalle County.* New York: Sanborn Map and Publishing Co., 1888, 1891, 1898, 1913, 1925, 1925–1943.
DLC, IU

Sanborn Fire Insurance Company. *Marseilles, LaSalle County.* New York: Sanborn Map and Publishing Co., 1889, 1892, 1898, 1907, 1913, 1929, 1929–1935.
DLC, IU

Sanborn Fire Insurance Company. *Seneca, LaSalle County.* New York: Sanborn Map and Publishing Co., 1892, 1898, 1907, 1913, 1924, 1924–1939.
DLC, IU

Maps and Atlases—*Fire Insurance*—Grundy County

Sanborn Fire Insurance Company. *Morris, Grundy County.* New York: Sanborn Map and Publishing Co., 1889, 1894, 1900, 1909, 1916, 1927–1937.
DLC, IU

Sanborn Fire Insurance Company. *Minooka, Grundy County.* New York: Sanborn Map and Publishing Co., 1893, 1898, 1907, 1926.
DLC, IU

Sanborn Fire Insurance Company. *Coal City, Grundy County.* New York: Sanborn Map and Publishing Co., 1892, 1898, 1907, 1933, 1933–1943.
DLC, IU

Maps and Atlases—*Fire Insurance*—Will County

Sanborn Fire Insurance Company. *Joliet, Will County.* New York: Sanborn Map and Publishing Co., 1886, 1891, 1898, 1898–1914, 1924, 1924–1943.
DLC, IU
Includes Rockdale.

Sanborn Fire Insurance Company. *Lockport, Will County.* New York: Sanborn Map and Publishing Co., 1886, 1891, 1897, 1902, 1909, 1926, 1926–1941.
DLC, IU

Maps and Atlases—*Fire Insurance*—Cook County

Sanborn Fire Insurance Company. *Lemont, Cook County.* New York: Sanborn Map and Publishing Co., 1886, 1894.
DLC, IU

Sanborn Fire Insurance Company. *Chicago, Cook County.* New York: Sanborn Map and Publishing Co. Vol. E: 1897, 1910, 1920, 1925, 1925–1943.
DLC, IU
Includes Argo, Bedford Park, Clearing, and Summit.

Sanborn Fire Insurance Company. *Chicago, Cook County.* New York: Sanborn Map and Publishing Co. Vol. H: 1911, 1917, 1919, 1921, 1911–1943.
DLC, IU
Includes Blue Island, Justice, Lemont, Riverdale, Willow Springs, Worth.

Sanborn Fire Insurance Company. *Chicago, Cook County.* New York: Sanborn Map and Publishing Co. Vol. I: 1911, 1922, 1911–1943.
DLC, IU
Includes Calumet City and Dolton.

Sanborn Fire Insurance Company. *Chicago, Cook County.* New York: Sanborn Map and Publishing Co., Vol. 34: 1930, 1930–1944.
DLC, IU
Includes Hodgkins.

Western Insurance Survey Co. *Insurance Map of Blue Island, Cook County, Illinois.* Chicago: Western Insurance Survey Co., c. 1894.
DLC

Sanborn Fire Insurance Company. *Blue Island, Cook County.* New York: Sanborn Map and Publishing Co., 1886, 1899.
DLC, IU

Maps and Atlases—*Government Surveys*

Weller, Stuart. *The Geological Map of Illinois.* Urbana, Illinois: State Geological Survey, 1906. 20 p.
IU

Urbana, Illinois. University of Illinois. Agricultural Experiment Station. "Illinois Land Use Maps, April, 1934." Urbana, Illinois: University of Illinois, 1934. 22 p., mounted maps.
IU

Urbana, Illinois. University of Illinois. Agricultural Experiment Station. *Soil Survey Maps.* 3 v. Urbana, Illinois: University of Illinois, n.d.
ICJ

Vol. 1: Alexander to Jasper counties. Vol. 2: Livingston to Pulaski counties. Vol. 3: St. Clair to White counties.

Important Farmlands. n.p., U.S. Department of Agriculture. Soil Conservation Service, 1975. Two maps.
IMa

Accompanied by three-page discussion. Farmlands map of LaSalle County, Illinois.

U.S. Department of the Interior. Geological Survey. *Quadrangle Maps.* Scale 1:62,500. Reston, Virginia: The Geological Survey.
ICU, IU

Maps of various quadrangles in the corridor include Joliet (1890, 1923), LaSalle (1891, 1913), Marseilles (1890, 1916), Morris (1890, 1918, 1954), Ottawa (1890, 1915, 1946), Wilmington (1890, 1918, 1954), Chicago (1889, 1899).

U.S. Department of the Interior. Geological Survey. *Quadrangle Maps.* Scale 1:24,000. Reston, Virginia: The Geological Survey.
ICU, IU

Maps of various quadrangles in the corridor include Blue Island (1927, 1953), Berwyn (1925, 1953), Calumet Lake (1953, 1973), Calumet City (1926, 1953), Channahon (1954), Chicago Loop (1953, 1972), Coal City (1953), Elwood (1953), Englewood (1926, 1963), Hinsdale (1925, 1953), Joliet (1954), Ladd (1966), LaSalle (1966), Lisbon (1953), Marseilles (1970), Minooka (1954), Morris (1953), Ottawa (1970), Palos Park (1953), Plainfield (1954), Prairie Center (1970), Romeoville (1954, 1962), Sag Bridge (1925, 1953), Starved Rock (1970), Stavanger (1970), Troy Grove (1966), Wedrow (1970), Wilmington (1954.)

Maps and Atlases—*Archive Sources*

Chicago, Illinois. Chicago Historical Society. Manuscript Map Collection.
ICHi

"Maps of the Illinois River." 1674–1755. Five maps.

"Hull Map of the Upper Illinois." 1805–1812.

Thompson, James. "Map of That Part of the State of Illinois Through Which It Is Contemplated to Construct a Canal." 1829.

W. B. Quion and H. Belin. "Proposed Route of the Michigan and Illinois Canal." 1830.

"Sectional Map of the Lands Donated by Congress to the State of Illinois to Aid in Constructing the Illinois and Michigan Canal." 1844.

Corps of Engineers. "Map of the Illinois and Michigan Canal and Proposed Hennepin Canal." 1886.

"Sketch Showing the Illinois and Michigan Canal and the Different Routes of the Proposed Hennepin Canal." 1887.

"DesPlaines and Illinois Rivers from Joliet to LaSalle." 1883.

"Diagram of Termination of the Illinois and Michigan Canal at the South Branch of the Chicago River on Section 19." c. 1880.

Board of Engineers. "Map of the Illinois and DesPlaines Rivers from Chicago, Illinois to the Mouth of the Illinois River, in Fourteen Sheets Including an Index Map." 1902–1905.

"Consolidation of Exhibits in Case of People Versus Economy Light and Power Co." n.d. Colored map of I&M Canal and Calumet Feeder.

"Illinois." 1918. Shows I&M and Chicago Drainage Canals.

"Pictorial Profile of the Illinois Waterway." 1960, 1967. Shows locations of dams and locks.

Housby, James. "Illinois-Michigan Canal: Points of Historical Significance Dating Back to 1848." [1980]. LaSalle–Peru to Utica.

Chicago South Branch Canal Co. "Map of

Canal and Canal Lots Along South Branch of the River." 1864.

U.S. Army Corps of Engineers. "Charts of the Illinois Waterway from Mississippi River at Grafton, Illinois to Lake Michigan at Chicago and Calumet Harbors." 1951.

Chicago, Illinois. Chicago Historical Society. U.S. Government Survey Maps, 1827–1832. Thirty-two maps.
ICHi

Bound collection. Cook County townships.

DeKalb, Illinois. Northern Illinois University. Illinois Regional Archives Depository. Map Collection.
IDeKN—IRAD

"IL Paese de Selvaggi Out Agamiani, Mascoutense, Illine Si e Parte delle VI Nazioni." 1748.

"Carte des Cinq Grand Lacs du Canada." 1764. Shows R. Checagon.

"A New Map of Upper and Lower Canada." John Cary, Engraver, 1819. Shows Illinois River area as territory of Potawatomis.

"Chicago in Connection with the North West to the Principal Lines of Rail Roads, Canals, Navigable Streams and Lakes, Together with the Most Important Towns, and Their Distances from Chicago." 1860.

"Illinois." [1838]. Shows county divisions, I&M Canal.

Campbell, R. A. "Climatological Map of the State of Illinois." 1869. Shows isothermal lines.

"Coal Mines and Coal Fields of Illinois." State Geological Survey, 1916. Shows coal field boundary through Will, Grundy, and LaSalle counties. Also shipping points in LaSalle, Oglesby, and Seneca.

Blum, Max L. *Blum's Commercial Traveler's Map of Illinois*. 1921. Shows Interurban trolleys.

Map of Illinois. Des Moines, Iowa: The Kenyon Company, 1921. Shows automobile highways. No. 44, Starved Rock Trail.

State Bond Issue Road System. n.p., State of Illinois, Dept. of Public Works and Buildings, 1923. Shows existing and proposed routes.

Illinois Official Auto Trails Map. n.p., Secretary of State, 1924.

"Mileage Map of the Best Roads of Illinois." 1925.

Morris, Illinois. Morris Public Library. Manuscript Map Collection. Three drawers.
IMo

Cemetery maps include Ward Cemetery, St. Mary's Cemetery (Minooka), Gardner Prairie Cemetery, Mazon Brookside Cemetery, Wheeler Cemetery (Mazon), and Saratoga Cemetery.

Lockport, Illinois. Lewis University. Canal Archives and Local History Collection. Seven map drawers.
ILoL

Drawer 1: Seventy-four sheets of I&M Canal Survey. Surveyed 1950, by State of Illinois.

Drawer 2: One hundred twenty-six sheets of I&M Canal Survey. Surveyed 1958, by State of Illinois.

Drawer 3: U.S. Geological Survey Maps. Approximately twenty-five maps of the I&M and Chicago area.

Drawer 4: Reproduction of various older canal maps and of foreign canals. Also an original sheet of various canal contractors from 1830s.

Drawer 5: Town and canal maps. Approximately fifteen maps of the area, reproduced.

Drawer 6: Maps of presettlement Illinois.

Drawer 7: Miscellaneous maps and other papers, including blueprints for canal boats, aerial photographs of the canal (1970) by Army Corps of Engineers, various drainage maps, and maps constructed from aerial photographs by Army Corps of Engineers.

Palos Heights, Illinois. Palos Heights Public Library. Manuscript Map Collection. Fifteen items.
IPHei

"Aerial Views of Palos Heights." 1930, 1938, 1940, 1930–1940.

"Aerial View of Worth." 1930.

Palos Park, Illinois. Palos Park Public Library. Pamphlet File. Palos Park. Maps. One folder.
IPP

Includes State Geological Survey Map, "Surficial Geology of the Palos Park Quadrangle," by J. Harlen Bretz, 1925. "A Tour of Palos' Past Brings History Alive," *The Palos Regional*, May 17, 1979.

Springfield, Illinois. Illinois State Historical Library. "Map of the Country Between Chicago, Galena, Rock Island, etc." [July 1832].
IHi

Probably drawn by Lt. M. L. Clark, aide-de-camp to Gen. H. Atkinson. $7\frac{7}{8}$ by $10\frac{1}{4}$ inches. Manuscript map shows but does not highlight the Upper Illinois River valley.

Springfield. Illinois State Museum. Department of Anthropology. Map Drawers. Starved Rock Area. One drawer.
ISM

Copied and manuscript. Maps.

Urbana, Illinois. Illinois Historical Survey Library. Manuscript Map Collection.
IU—HS

"Illinois State Water Survey, Watershed of Illinois." n.d.

"Illinois General Assembly District Maps." 1854–1856, 1856–1858.

Burr, David H. "Map of Illinois and Missouri, Exhibiting the Post Offices, Post Roads, Canals, Railroads, etc." c. 1834. Facsimile of original at Library of Congress.

Tanner, H. F. "A New Map of Illinois with Its Proposed Canals, Roads and Distances from Places Along the Stage and Steamboat Routes." 1842.

"Base Map of Illinois." State Geological Survey. 1911, 1941, 1945.

"Map of Illinois Showing Major Archaeological Sites in Illinois." c. 1915.

"Map of Illinois Showing Indian Cessions to the Kickapoo Tribe." c. 1915.

"Map of Illinois Showing Indian Cessions to the Ottawa and Chippewa Tribes." c. 1915.

"Map of Illinois Showing Indian Cessions to the Kaskaskia and League of the Illinois Tribes." c. 1915.

"Map of Illinois Showing Indian Cessions to the Potawatomi Tribes." c. 1915.

"Map of Illinois Showing Indian Cessions to the Sac and Fox Tribes." c. 1915.

"Map of Illinois Showing Indian Cessions to the Winnebago Tribes." c. 1915.

"Illinois Base Map with Highways." U.S. Dept. of the Interior Geological Survey, 1927.

PART 16 Newspapers

A town's newspapers are often the only primary sources for continuous local history. And the history of the towns within the corridor is particularly well documented because the surviving newspaper files are from the earliest white settlement and are nearly complete.

Any researcher who uses newspapers as sources for family or local history should be aware that nineteenth-century journals were founded and operated for different purposes than those of today. Local newspapers were often founded as mouthpieces for various political parties, voluntary organizations, and ethnic groups. Since many were not conceived as profit-making businesses, they were often short-lived or were bought by more successful concerns. Therefore, the newspaper histories of many of the corridor cities in the nineteenth and early-twentieth centuries are stories of constant competition and merger until one or two journals came to dominate towns or regions.

As one might expect, copies of the earliest and shortest-running newspapers are the least likely to have survived. Therefore, journals that are known to have existed but for which there are no known extant copies have been included in this part of the guide in the hope that readers will recognize the historical value of any copies they may own and make them available to researchers.

This section is organized on a town-by-town basis beginning with Peru in LaSalle County and progressing north and east along the I&M Canal. Then, the newspaper issues are arranged in chronological order. Users will notice that they can find copies of individual newspapers at varied locations but that the most complete collection is on microfilm at the Illinois State Historical Library in Springfield. Newspaper indexes and guides are also included and are a useful means of placing corridor newspapers within the context of national and state collections.

Newspapers—*General*

Center for Research Libraries. *Catalogue of Newspapers.* 2nd ed. Chicago: The Center for Research Libraries, 1978. 233 p.
ICRL, ICU

Newspapers held by Center for Research Libraries listed alphabetically by name of publication.

Gill, James V. "Rural Northern Illinois Newspapers and Newspapermen Before 1851." M.A. thesis, Northern Illinois University, 1982.
IDeKN—IRAD

Includes information on *Joliet Courier,* Joliet *Democratic Cudgel,* Joliet *Signal,* Joliet *True Democrat, Will County Telegraph,* Ottawa *Republican, Ottawa Democrat and Internal Improvement Advocate, Illinois Free Trader, Ottawa Constitutionalist,* Ottawa *United Irishman,* Peru *Ninewah Gazette,* Peru *Beacon Light, Peru Telegraph,* and *LaSalle County Democrat.*

Gregory, Winifred, ed. *American Newspapers: 1821–1936. A Union List of Files Available in the United States and Canada.* Under the Auspices of the Bibliographical Society of America. New York: The H. W. Wilson Company, 1937. 791 p.
ICU

Illinois. Secretary of State. *Laws of Illinois Relating to Publications Required to Be Made in Newspapers or Otherwise.* Springfield, Illinois: Schnepp & Barnes, Printers, 1930. 96 p.
DLC, ICJ

James, Edmund J. "A Bibliography of Newspapers Published in Illinois Prior to 1860." *Publications of the Illinois Historical Library* 1 (1899): 1–94.
ICN, ICU

Lists newspapers according to place of publication. Appendices list 1808–1897 Missouri and Illinois papers in the St. Louis Mercantile Library and county histories of Illinois.

Mabbott, Thomas O. and Jorsan, Philip D. "A Catalogue of Illinois Newspapers in the New York Historical Society." *Journal of the Illinois State Historical Society* 24 (July 1931): 187–242.
DLC, I, IC, ICHi, ICN, ICU, IEN, IU
Lists mostly single issues, Joliet, LaSalle, Marseilles, Morris, Ottawa, Peru, Seneca, South Chicago.

Newspapers in Libraries of Chicago, A Joint Check List. Chicago: The University of Chicago Libraries, 1936. 256 p.
ICU
Lists newspapers held by University of Chicago, Newberry Library, Chicago Public Library, Chicago Historical Society, John Crerar Library, Northwestern University.

Newspapers in the University of Illinois Library. Urbana, Illinois, 1942. 43 p. (Typewritten.)
ICU
Lists bound newspapers.

North, S. N. D. "The Newspaper and Periodical Press." U.S. Census Office. *Tenth Census of the United States, 1880.* Vol. 8: *Special Reports.* Washington: Government Printing Office, 1884. 446 p.
ICU
Chronological listing and contemporary directory of newspapers and periodicals in each county and municipality.

Scott, Franklin William. *Newspapers and Periodicals of Illinois, 1814–1879.* Collections of the Illinois State Historical Library. Vol. 6: *Bibliographical Series.* Springfield, Illinois: Trustees of the Illinois State Historical Library, 1910. 610 p., illus.
ICN, ICU
Newspapers listed according to place of publication. Includes life span of papers along with editors and political affiliation.

Stark, Sandra M. "Newspapers in the Illinois State Historical Library." *Illinois Libraries* 64 (March 1982): 203–334.
DLC, I, IC, ICJ, ICN, ICU, IU
All Illinois papers held by Illinois State Historical Library on microfilm. Special section lists missing issues.

U.S. Library of Congress. Catalog Publication Division. Processing Department. *Newspapers in Microfilm: United States, 1848–1972.* Washington: Library of Congress, 1973. 1,056 p.
ICU
Comprehensive list of papers in public and private libraries. Yearly updates.

Newspapers—Issues

Newspapers—*Issues*—LaSalle County

Newspapers—*Issues*—LaSalle County—*Peru*

Ninawah Gazette. 1840–1841.
ICU, IHi
Weekly. Successor of Lacon *Herald.* Continued as *Illinois Gazette.* Supported Harrison in 1840. Peru.

Illinois Gazette. 1841.
ICU, IHi
Weekly. Continues *Ninawah Gazette.* Moved to Lacon. Peru.

Beacon Light. 1846–1848.
***
Weekly. Peru.

Telegraph: 1848–1853.
***
Weekly. Freesoil in politics. Continued as *Chronicle* after merger with *Gazette and Chronicle.* Peru.

LaSalle County Democrat. 1850?–1851.
IHi
Weekly. Continued as *Democrat.* Peru.

Democrat. 1851–1853.
IHi
Weekly. Continues *LaSalle County Democrat.* Continued as *Gazette and Chronicle.* Peru.

Chronicle. 1853–1854.
IO
Daily. Continues weekly *Chronicle.* Peru.

Gazette and Chronicle. 1853.
IHi
Weekly. Continues *Democrat.* Continued as *Chronicle* following merger with *Telegraph.* Peru.

Chronicle. 1854–1856.
IHi, IO

Weekly. Formed by merger of *Telegraph* and *Gazette and Chronicle*. Continues daily *Chronicle*. Peru.

LaSalle County Sentinel. 1855–1858.
***
Weekly. Continues *Rattlesnake*. Democratic in politics. Peru.

Rattlesnake. 1855.
IHi
Weekly. Continued as *LaSalle County Sentinel*. Peru.

Commercial and Volksfreund. 1858–?
***
Weekly. In German. Peru.

Herald. 1858–1884.
ICHi
Weekly. Merged with *News* and continued as *Twin City News-Herald*. Peru.

Peruvian. 1863?
IHi
Monthly. Peru.

News. 1879–1884.
***
Semiweekly. Merged with *Herald* and continued as *Twin City News-Herald*. Peru.

Twin City News-Herald. 1884–1886.
***
Semiweekly. Formed by merger of *News* and *Herald*. Continued as weekly *Twin City News-Herald*. Peru.

News-Herald. 1886–1947.
ICHi, IHi, IU
Daily. Daily version of weekly *Twin City News-Herald*. Merged with *Post-Tribune* (LaSalle) and continued as *News-Tribune* (LaSalle). Peru.

Twin City News-Herald. 1886–.
***
Weekly. Continues semiweekly *Twin City News-Herald*. Peru.

Newspapers—*Issues*—LaSalle County—*LaSalle*

Standard. 1851–1852.
MWA
Weekly. LaSalle.

Herald. 1852–1854.
***
Weekly. Democratic in politics. Continued as *Journal*. LaSalle.

Watchman. 1852–1855.
MWA
Weekly. Whig in politics. Continued as *LaSalle County Press*. LaSalle.

Independent [*I*]. 1853.
***
Weekly. LaSalle.

Journal. 1854–1858.
IHi
Weekly. Continues *Herald*. Moved to Peru. LaSalle.

LaSalle County Press. 1856–1883.
MWA
Weekly. Republican in 1856. Sold to A. J. Reddick in 1883 (owner of *Democrat*) and continued as *Democrat-Press*. LaSalle.

Democrat Standard. 1858–1860.
***
Weekly. LaSalle.

Central Illinois Wochenblatt. 1868.
IHi
Weekly. In German. Moved to Ottawa. LaSalle.

Reporter. 1871–1876.
***
Weekly. LaSalle.

Independent [*II*]. 1875–1876.
***
Weekly. Purchased by A. J. Reddick in 1876 and continued as *Democrat*. LaSalle.

Democrat. 1876–1883.
***
Weekly. Continues *Independent* [*II*]. Edited and published by A. J. Reddick. Reddick purchased *LaSalle County Press* in 1883 and continued as *Democrat-Press*. LaSalle.

Volksblatt. 1877.
***
Weekly. In German. LaSalle.

Twin City Journal. 1880–1894?
IHi, IO
Daily. LaSalle and Peru.

Democrat-Press. 1883–?
***

Weekly. Continues *Democrat* and *LaSalle County Press*. Published by A. J. Reddick. LaSalle.

Tribune. 1890–1906?
IHi, ILa

Daily. LaSalle. Continued as *Tribune and Peru News* (LaSalle and Peru).

Tribune. 1890–1906?
***

Weekly. LaSalle. Continued as *Tribune and Peru News* (LaSalle and Peru).

Daily Post. 1894–1926.
***

Daily. Merged with daily *Tribune and Peru News* and continued as *Post-Tribune*. LaSalle.

Tribune and Peru News. 1906?–1926.
IHi, ILa

Daily. LaSalle and Peru. Continues *Tribune* (LaSalle). Merged with *Daily Post* and continued as *Post-Tribune*.

Tribune and Peru News. 1906?–1926.
IHi

Weekly. LaSalle and Peru. Continues *Tribune* (LaSalle). Merged with *Daily Post* and continued as *Post-Tribune*.

Post-Tribune. 1926–1947.
IHi, ILa

Daily. Formed by merger of *Daily Post* and *Tribune*. Merged with *News-Herald* (Peru) and continued as *News-Tribune*. LaSalle.

Newspapers—*Issues*—LaSalle County—*Ottawa*

Republican [*I*]. 1836.
IO

Weekly. Democratic in politics. Ottawa.

Democrat and Internal Improvement Advocate. 1838.
ICHi

Weekly. One issue. Ottawa.

Illinois Free Trader. 1840–1841.
DLC, ICU, IHi, IO

Weekly. Democratic in politics. Merged with *LaSalle County Commercial Advertiser* and continued as *Illinois Free Trader and LaSalle County Commercial Advertiser*. Ottawa.

Illinois Free Trader and LaSalle County Commercial Advertiser. 1841–1843.
IHi, IO

Weekly. Formed by merger of *Illinois Free Trader* and *LaSalle County Commercial Advertiser*. Continued as *Free Trader* [*I*]. Ottawa.

Free Trader [*I*]. 1843–1882.
IHi, IU, ICHi, IO, MWA

Weekly. Continues *Illinois Free Trader and LaSalle County Commercial Advertiser*. Continued as semiweekly. Democratic in politics. Ottawa.

Constitutionalist. 1844–1852.
IHi, IO

Weekly. Whig in politics. Continued as *Republican* [*II*]. Ottawa.

United Irishman. 1848–?
***

Weekly. Devoted to the repeal of Legislative Union of England and Ireland. Ottawa.

Republican [*II*]. 1852–1882.
ICHi, IHi, IO, IU, MWA, WHi

Weekly. Continuation of *Constitutionalist*. Continued as semiweekly. Whig until 1854, then Republican in politics. Ottawa.

Little Giant. 1858.
IHi

Daily. Ottawa.

Central Illinois Wochenblatt. 1868–1926?
ICHi, ICRL, IHi, IU

German. Independent-Republican in politics. Moved from LaSalle. Ottawa.

Statesman. 1868–1869.
ICHi, WHi

Weekly. Democratic in politics. Ottawa.

Commercial Miller. 1873–1874.
***

Monthly. Published by American Miller Publishing Company. Moved to Chicago. Ottawa.

Times [*I*]. 1877–1890.
IHi

Daily. Republican in politics. Merged with *Republican* and continued as *Republican-Times*. Ottawa.

Times. 1879–1890?
IHi, IU

Weekly. Republican in politics. Merged with *Republican* [*III*] and continued as *Republican-Times*. Ottawa.

Journal. 1880–1916.
IHi, IO, IU
Daily version of weekly *Journal* and *LaSalle County Journal*. Merged with daily *Free Trader* and continued as *Free Trader-Journal*. Ottawa.

Republican [*III*]. 1883–1890.
IHi, IO
Weekly. Continuation of semiweekly *Republican*. Merged with *Times* and continued as *Republican-Times*. Ottawa.

Free Trader. 1882.
IHi, IO
Semiweekly. Continuation of weekly *Free Trader* [*I*]. Continued as weekly *Free Trader* [*II*]. Ottawa.

Free Trader [*II*]. 1882–1916.
IHi, IO, IU, WHi
Weekly. Continuation of semiweekly *Free Trader*. Merged with *LaSalle County Journal* and continued as *Free Trader-Journal*. Ottawa.

Republican. 1882–1883.
IHi, IO, IU
Semiweekly. Continuation of weekly *Republican* [*II*]. Continued as weekly *Republican* [*III*]. Ottawa.

Journal. 1883–1892.
IHi
Weekly. Ottawa. Continued as *LaSalle County Journal* (Ottawa and LaSalle).

Free Trader. 1887–1916.
IHi, IO
Daily. Merged with Journal and continued as *Free Trader-Journal*. Ottawa.

Republican. 1887–1890.
IHi, IU
Daily. Daily version of weekly *Republican* [*III*]. Merged with *Times* and continued as *Republican-Times*. Ottawa.

Republican-Times. 1890–1967.
ICHi, IHi, IU
Daily. Formed by merger of *Republican* and *Times* [*I*]. Bought *Free Trader-Journal* in 1927. Continued as *Times* [*II*] in 1967. Ottawa.

Republican-Times. 1890–1918.
IHi, IO, IU
Weekly. Formed by merger of *Republican* [*III*] and *Times*. Weekly discontinued in 1918. Ottawa.

Fair Dealer. 1892–1920.
IHi, IO, IU
Weekly. Merged with daily *Free Trader-Journal* and weekly version discontinued. Daily continued as *Free Trader-Journal and Fair Dealer*. Ottawa.

LaSalle County Journal. 1892–1916.
IHi, IU
Weekly. Published in Ottawa and LaSalle. Continuation of *Journal* (Ottawa). Merged with weekly *Free Trader* [*II*] and continued as *Free Trader-Journal*.

Afholds-vennen. 1894–1901.
WHi
Weekly. Norwegian. Also dated in Chicago. Continued as *Illinois-Posten*. Ottawa.

Illinois-Posten. 1902–1910.
WHI
Weekly. Norwegian and Danish. Continues *Afhold-vennen*. Ottawa.

Tidende. 1907–1913.
IHi
Weekly. Norwegian. Continued as *LaSalle County Times*. Ottawa.

LaSalle County Record. 1913–1916.
IHi
Weekly. Continues LaSalle County Times. Ottawa.

LaSalle County Times. 1913.
IHi
Weekly. Continuation of *Tidende*. Continued as *LaSalle County Record*. Ottawa.

Free Trader-Journal. 1916–1920.
IHi, IO, IU
Daily. Formed by merger of *Free Trader* and *Journal*. Merged with weekly *Fair Dealer* and continued as daily *Free Trader-Journal and Fair Dealer*. Ottawa.

Free Trader-Journal. 1916–1918.
IHi
Weekly. Formed by merger of weekly *Free Trader* [*II*] and *LaSalle County Journal*. Ottawa.

Free Trader-Journal and Fair Dealer. 1920–1927.
IHi, IO
Daily. Formed by merger of weekly *Fair Dealer* and daily *Free Trader-Journal*. Bought by and continued as *Republican-Times*. Ottawa.

Newspapers—*Issues*—LaSalle County—*Utica*

Enterprise. 1876–1877.
***
Monthly. Utica.

Gazette. 1886–1921.
IHi, IU
Weekly. Utica.

Newspapers—*Issues*—LaSalle County—*Marseilles*

Gazette. 1867–1868?
***
Weekly. Marseilles.

Advertiser. 1869–1874.
***
Weekly. Independent in politics. Continued as *Herald*. Marseilles.

Citizen. 1869–1870.
***
Weekly. Marseilles.

Herald. 1874–1879.
ICHi
Weekly. Continues *Advertiser*. Continued as *Register*. Marseilles.

Plaindealer. 1876–1879.
IHi, IU
Monthly. Continued as semimonthly. Marseilles.

Plaindealer. 1879–1883.
IHi, IU
Semimonthly. Continues monthly *Plaindealer*. Continued as biweekly. Marseilles.

Register. 1879–1905?
IHi, IU
Weekly. Continues *Herald*. Continued as *Register-Chronicle* after merger with daily *Chronicle*. Marseilles.

Plaindealer. 1883–1885.
IHi
Biweekly. Continues semimonthly *Plaindealer*. Continued as weekly. Marseilles.

Plaindealer. 1885–?
IHi, IU
Weekly. Continues biweekly *Plaindealer*. Marseilles.

News. 1887–1890.
IU
Daily. Marseilles.

Plaindealer. 1887–?
IU
Daily version of weekly *Plaindealer*. Marseilles.

Eclipse. 1891–?
IU
Daily. Marseilles.

Chronicle. 1903–1905.
***
Daily. Merged with weekly *Register* to form weekly *Register-Chronicle*. Marseilles.

Register-Chronicle. 1905–1917.
***
Weekly. Continues *Register* and daily *Chronicle*. Marseilles.

Illinois Valley Tradesman. 1914?
IHi
Weekly. Marseilles.

Press. 1921–?
***
Daily. Marseilles.

Newspapers—*Issues*—LaSalle County—*Seneca*

Record. 1878–1901.
IU
Weekly. Merges with *News* and continues as *Record and News*. Seneca.

Messenger. 1887–?
IU
Daily. Seneca.

Messenger. 1887–1888?
IU
Weekly. Seneca.

News. 1892–1901.
IHi
Weekly. Merges with *Record* and continues as *Record and News*. Seneca.

Record and News. 1892–1918.
IU
Weekly. Independent in politics. Seneca.

Bumble Bee. 1893–1895.
IU
Weekly. Seneca.

Newspapers—*Issues*—Grundy County

Newspapers—*Issues*—Grundy County—*Morris*

Grundy Yeoman. 1852–1853?
IHi
Weekly. Continues as *Yeoman*. Morris.

Yeoman. 1852–1853.
IHi, MWA
Weekly. Continuation of *Grundy Yeoman*. Merges with *Gazette* and continues as *Grundy County Herald*. Morris.

Gazette. 1853–1855.
IHi
Weekly. Democratic in politics. Continued as *Grundy County Herald* after merger with *Yeoman*. Morris.

Grundy County Herald. 1855–1866.
ICHi, IHi
Weekly. Continuation of *Gazette* and *Yeoman*. Merged with *Advertiser* and continued as *Herald and Advertiser*. Morris.

Advertiser. 1865–1866.
ICHi, IHi
Weekly. Merged with *Grundy County Herald* and continued as *Herald and Advertiser*. Morris.

Herald and Advertiser. 1866–1874.
ICHi, IHi
Weekly. Formed by merger of *Grundy County Herald* and *Advertiser*. Continues as *Herald*. Morris.

Liberal Reformer. 1872–1876.
IHi
Weekly. Anti-Republican in politics. Continues as *Reformer*. Morris.

Herald. 1874–1926.
ICHi, IHi, IU
Weekly. Continuation of *Herald and Advertiser*. Morris.

Reformer. 1876–1879.
ICHi, IHi
Weekly. Greenback in politics. Continuation of *Liberal Reformer*. Morris.

Herald. 1878–.
IHi, IU
Daily. Daily version of weekly *Herald*. Continuation of *Herald and Advertiser*. Morris.

Independent. 1878–1893.
IHi
Weekly. Continues as *Grundy County Sentinel*. Morris.

Grundy County Sentinel. 1893–1908?
IHi
Weekly. Continuation of *Independent*. Morris.

Sentinel. 1895?–1908?
IHi
Daily. Daily version of *Grundy County Sentinel*. Continuation of *Independent*. Morris.

Newspapers—*Issues*—Grundy County—*Minooka*

Phoenix-Advertiser. 1903?–1906?
IHi
Weekly? Minooka.

Newspapers—*Issues*—Grundy County—*Coal City*

Courant. 1900–.
IHi, IU
Weekly. Coal City.

Newspapers—*Issues*—Will County

Newspapers—*Issues*—Will County—*Joliet*

Courier. 1839–1843.
ICU, IHi, IJo
Weekly. Democratic in politics. Continued as *Signal*. Joliet.

Democratic Cudgel. 1842?
***
Weekly. Democratic in politics. Joliet.

Signal. 1843–1893.
ICHi, IHi, IJo, ILoHi, MWA
Weekly. Continuation of *Courier*. Democratic in politics. Joliet.

True Democrat. 1847–1864.
ICHi, IHi, ILoHi
Weekly. Whig then Republican. Continues as *Republican* [*I*]. Joliet.

Republican [*I*]. 1864–1869.
DLC, IHi
Weekly. Continuation of *True Democrat*. Continues as *Republic*. Joliet.

People's Advocate. 1869–?
IHi
Weekly. Joliet.

Republic. 1869–1883.
ICHi, IHi
Daily. Merged with *Sun* and continued as *Republic and Sun*. Joliet.

Republic. 1869–1883.
ICHi, IHi
Weekly. Continuation of *Republican* [*I*]. Merged with *Sun* and continued as *Republic and Sun*. Joliet.

Record. 1870–1883.
ICHi, IHi
Weekly. Democratic in politics. Merged with *News*. Joliet.

St. Mary's Messenger. 1871.
IHi
Weekly. Joliet.

Mustard Plaster. 1872–?
IHi
Daily. Joliet.

Sun. 1872–1883.
ICHi, IHi, IJo, IU
Weekly. Continued as *Republic and Sun* after merger with *Republic*. Joliet.

Sun. 1874–1883.
ICHi, IHi, IJo, IU
Daily. Merged with *Republic* and continued as *Republic and Sun*. Joliet.

Will County Courier. 1874?–1884.
ICHi, IHi
Weekly. Granger organ. Moved from Lockport about 1874. Joliet.

Herald. 1875–1876.
ICHi
Weekly. In German. Joliet.

Morning News. 1877–1880.
IHi, ILoHi
Daily. Continued as *News* [*I*]. Greenback in 1877. Joliet.

News. 1877–1915.
IHi, IJo, ILoHi
Weekly. Greenback in 1877. Joliet.

Phoenix. 1877–?
***
Weekly. Joliet. Home office of circuit of *Phoenix* newspapers in Joliet, Lockport, Wilmington, Lemont, Braidwood, Peotone, and Plainfield.

Wochenblatt. 1877–1880?
***
Weekly. In German. Moved from Beecher. Joliet.

Greenback News. 1878?
IHi
Weekly. Joliet.

News [*I*]. 1880–1884.
IHi, IJo
Daily. Continues *Morning News*. Continued as *Joliet's Daily Newspaper*. Joliet.

Record. 1880–1883.
IHi
Daily. Democratic in politics. Merged with *News* [*II*]. Joliet.

Press. 1883–1885.
IHi
Weekly. Continued as *Will County Press*. Joliet.

Republic and Sun. 1883–1890?
IHi
Daily. Formed by merger of *Republic* and *Sun*. Continued as *Republican*. Joliet.

Republic and Sun. 1883–1890.
IHi, ICHi
Weekly. Formed by merger of *Republic* and *Sun*. Continued as *Republican* [*II*]. Joliet.

Will County Press. 1883–?
IHi
Daily. Joliet.

Joliet's Daily Newspaper. 1884.
IHi
Daily. Continuation of *News* [*I*]. Continued as *News* [*II*]. Joliet.

News [*II*]. 1884–1915.
IHi
Daily. Continuation of *Joliet's Daily Newspaper.* Merged with daily *Herald* and continued as *Herald-News*. Joliet.

Will County Press. 1885–?
IHi
Weekly. Continuation of *Press*. Joliet.

Republican. 1890–1911.
IHi, IJo, ILoHi
Daily. Continuation of *Republic and Sun*. Joliet.

Republican [*II*]. 1890–1906?
IHi, IJo
Weekly. Weekly version of daily *Republican*. Continuation of *Republic and Sun*. Joliet.

Times. 1893?–1922?
IHi
Daily. Joliet.

General-Anzeiger. 1896–?
ICRL, IU
Weekly. In German. Joliet.

Sentinel. 1896?
IHi
Monthly. Joliet.

Herald. 1904–1915.
IHi, IJo, ILoHi
Daily. Merged with daily *News* [*II*] and continued as *Herald-News*. Evening. Joliet.

Amerikanski Slovenec. 1913?
IHi
Weekly. Slovenian. Joliet.

Free Press. 1913?–1914?
IHi
Daily. Joliet.

Herald-News. 1915–?
IHi, IJo, ILoHi, IU
Daily. Formed by merger of *Herald* and *News* [*II*]. Joliet.

Glasilo K.S.K. Jednote. 1921–1926.
MnU
Weekly. Slovenian. Joliet. Published in Chicago 1915–1921, Cleveland 1926–1948.

Spectator. 1929?–1960?
IHi
Weekly. Joliet.

Labor Record. 1934–1965
WHi
Weekly. Continued as *Will County Labor Record*. Joliet.

Newspapers—*Issues*—Will County—*Lockport*

Will County Telegraph. 1848–1850?
ICHi, ICN
Weekly. Independent in politics. Continues as *Telegraph*. Lockport.

Telegraph. 1850–?
ICHi, ICN, IHi, ILo, ILoHi
Weekly. Continues *Will County Telegraph*. Lockport.

Mirror. 1870–?
IHi
Weekly. Lockport.

Courier. 1873–1874.
ILo
Weekly. Independent in politics. Lockport.

American Educator. 1875–1882?
***
Weekly. Lockport.

Phoenix. 1875–1901.
IHi
Weekly. Merges with *Will County Commercial Advertiser* and continues as *Phoenix-Advertiser* [*I*]. Lockport.

Standard. 1876–1878.
***
Weekly. Continues as *Will County Commercial Advertiser*. Lockport.

Will County Commercial Advertiser. 1878–1901.
IHi
Weekly. Republican. Merges with *Phoenix* and continues as *Phoenix-Advertiser* [*I*]. Lockport.

Phoenix-Advertiser [*I*]. 1901–1902.
IHi
Weekly. Formed by merger of *Phoenix* and *Will County Commercial Advertiser*. Merged with *Journal* and continued as *Phoenix-Advertiser and Journal*. Lockport.

Journal. 1899?–1902?
IHi

Weekly. Merges with *Phoenix-Advertiser* [*I*] and continues as *Phoenix-Advertiser and Journal.* Lockport.

Phoenix-Advertiser and Journal. 1902–1903.
IHi
Weekly. Continued as *Phoenix-Advertiser* [*II*]. Lockport.

Phoenix-Advertiser [*II*]. 1903–1918.
IHi, ILoHi, IU
Weekly. Continues *Phoenix-Advertiser and Journal.* Lockport.

Leader. 1929–?
IHi, ILo
Weekly. Lockport.

Herald. 1933–?
ILo
Weekly. Lockport.

Newspapers—*Issues*—Cook County

Newspapers—*Issues*—Cook County—*Lemont*

Gazette. 1870.
***
Weekly. Lemont.

Phoenix. 1877–1879.
***
Weekly. Printed at office of Joliet *Phoenix.* Served Lemont.

Press. 1887–1888?
IHi
Weekly. Lemont.

Observer [*I*]. 1894?
IHi
Weekly. Continues as *Observer and Ledger.* Lemont.

Advertiser. 1899?
IHi
Weekly. Lemont.

Observer and Ledger. 1899?
IHi
Weekly. Continues as *Observer* [*II*]. Lemont.

Observer [*II*]. 1899?–1901?
IHi
Weekly. Merges with *Phoenix-Advertiser* and continues as *Phoenix-Advertiser and Observer.* Lemont.

Phoenix-Advertiser. 1901?–1902?
IHi
Weekly. Merges with *Observer* [*II*] and continues *Phoenix-Advertiser and Observer.* Lemont.

Phoenix-Advertiser and Observer. 1902–?
IHi
Weekly. Formed by merger of *Phoenix-Advertiser* and *Observer* [*II*]. Lemont.

Newspapers—*Issues*—Cook County—*Chicago*

Hegewisch Journal.
IHi
Weekly. Chicago.

Pullman Review. 1891–1898?
IHi
Weekly. Chicago.

South Chicago Star.
IHi
Weekly. Chicago.

South Chicago Eagle. 1871.
ICHi
Weekly. Printed at office of *Chicago Sun.* Chicago.

Newspapers—*Issues*—Cook County—*Argo-Summit*

DesPlaines Valley News. 1913–?
ISA
Weekly. Argo-Summit.

Newspapers—*Issues*—Cook County—*Palos Park*

Palos Journal. 1928?
IPP
Published in Palos Park.

Newspapers—*Issues*—Cook County—*Calumet Sag Towns*

Crucible. 1887?–1892.
IHi
Weekly. Blue Island.

Herald. 1873–1876.
ICHi

Weekly. Blue Island.

Press. 1876.
ICHi
Daily. Continues as weekly *Standard*. Blue Island.

Standard. 1876–1917.
IHi
Weekly. Continues daily *Press*. Merged with *Sun* and continued as *Sun-Standard*. Independent in politics. Blue Island.

Sun. 1894–1917.
IHi
Weekly. Merged with *Standard* and continued as *Sun-Standard*. Blue Island.

Sun-Standard. 1918–1968.
IHi, ICE
Weekly. Formed by merger of *Sun* and *Standard*. Blue Island.

Review. 1921–1923.
IHi, IU
Weekly. Continuation of Chicago publication of 1905–1921. Continued in Chicago. Blue Island.

Suburban Star. 1923–1935.
IHi
Weekly. Also datelined in Chicago. Blue Island.

Daily Calumet. 1884–.
IHi, IU
Daily. Continuation of *Hyde Park Tribune*. Calumet.

Record. 1898–?
IHi
Monthly. Calumet.

World. 1924?–1928?
InG
Weekly. Calumet City.

Pointer. 1924?–1925?
ICE
Weekly. Calumet City.

Index. 1906–1946.
***
Weekly. Calumet City. Absorbed *South End Telegram*, 1907.

Dolton-Riverdale Review. 1875–.
***
Weekly. Dolton. Issued from office of Blue Island *Herald*.

Pointer. 1936–1957.
ICE, IHi
Weekly. Dolton. Moved from Riverdale.

Review. 1892?–1893?
IHi
Weekly. Riverdale.

Pointer. 1907–1936.
ICE, IHi, IU
Weekly. Riverdale. Moved to Dolton.

Newspapers—*Indexes*

The Chicago Record Herald Index, 1904–1912. 9 v. [Chicago, 1957].
ICHi

Federal Works Agency. Works Progress Administration. "The Chicago Daily Democratic Press Index." The Library Omnibus Project. Chicago, 1940. (Typewritten.)
ICHi
For the years 1855 and 1856. Articles on corridor towns catalogued under "Illinois. Local Divisions." Also contains articles on I&M Canal, railroads, and other subjects.

Index to the Springfield Journal. 2 v. Compiled from the Files of Illinois State Historical Library by James N. Adams. Springfield, 1944–1953. Vol. 1, Pts. 1–3: *1831–1850*. Vol. 2: *1851–1860*. (Typewritten.)
IJo
Contains many entries for the I&M Canal and for the cities and towns in the corridor. Also available in microfilmed edition.

Lockport, Illinois. Will County Historical Society. *Joliet Republican* Newspaper Ledger, 1869–1872.
ILoHi

Morris, Illinois. Morris Public Library. *Morris Herald* Newspaper Index. Seven file drawers.
IMo
Index consists of three- by five-inch cards arranged alphabetically by subject of article.

[Wentworth, John]. *Manuscript Indeces of Chicago Newspapers, 1835–1861.* 21 v.
ICHi

Titles indexed: *Chicago American,* 1835–1842; *Chicago Democrat,* 1837–1861; *Chicago Journal,* 1844–1852.

PART 17 Photographs

The history of the Illinois and Michigan Canal National Heritage Corridor is usually found in verbal sources. But the researcher who is interested in the complete development of the area might also gain valuable information from the use of the many photographs of the corridor. This section of the Bibliography outlines the places one might go to find photographic collections, both published and archival. One should be aware, however, that many of the entries in the other parts of the Bibliography also contain individual photographs that may be of some use.

Photographs—*Published Sources*

James, James Alton. *Chicago; A History in Block-Print . . . Block-Prints Executed by the Advanced Class in Design Under the Direction of Clara MacGowan . . . Northwestern University.* Chicago, 1934. 106 p., illus.
DLC, ICU

Jensen, James. *W. E. Bowman, General Photographer.* By the Author, 1979. 103 p., illus., port.
IUtHi

Published to accompany an exhibition at the LaSalle County Historical Society, Utica, Illinois, 1979.

Newberry, Lane K. "Portraits of Historic Spots in Illinois." *Journal of the Illinois State Historical Society* 28 (April 1935–January 1936): n.p.
DLC, I, IC, ICHi, ICN, ICU, IEN, IU

Includes Portage Trail.

U.S. Army Corps of Engineers. *Illinois Waterway.* n.p., U.S. Army Corps of Engineers, 1950. Forty-two minutes, color. (Motion Picture.)
IC—ACE

Photographs—*Archive Sources*

Chicago, Illinois. Art Institute. Photo Collection.
ICA

Four photographs of Locktender's House (1845) and Lock No. 6, I&M Canal, Channahon. Two photographs of the John Hossack House (1854–1855), Ottawa.

Chicago, Illinois. Chicago Historical Society. Chicago Waterways Survey.
ICHi

Photographs of Chicago harbor, junction of north-south branches; downtown Chicago; shipbuilding; drainage canal; I&M Canal at Summit, Chicago, Channahon, Joliet, Willow Springs, Romeo, Lockport, Calumet Sag, Mud Lake, Chicago Portage, Calumet Harbor, and River; Chicago River Tunnel; lumber yards. Drawings of St. Denis in Lockport, Lockport locks, drainage canal, Bridgeport lock. State Bank of Illinois I&M Canal note. Articles from Chicago newspapers about canal. Toll list.

Chicago, Illinois. Chicago Historical Society. Prints and Photographs Department. Photographs: [C-9], Chicago Portage in 1920. [C-11], Portage Creek east of Ogden Dam in 1920. [C-12], Chicago portage "after 1871."
ICHi

Chicago, Illinois. Chicago Historical Society. Prints and Photographs Department. Album of Photographs, 1887–1888.
ICHi

Includes photographs of residential houses of Lyons, limestone quarry, lime kiln, and the dam on the DesPlaines River. Also contains several views of the Chicago River.

Chicago, Illinois. Chicago Historical Society. Prints and Photographs Department. Illinois. Justice.
ICHi

Eight-by-ten-inch photograph of Resurrection Cemetery Gate.

Chicago, Illinois. Chicago Historical Society. Prints and Photographs Department. Illinois. Morris.
ICHi

Birds-eye photograph of city (1924). Grundy County Court House and Square (1915). Eight-by-ten-inch photographs (1950s and 1960s) of Court House, Shaft House, Number 4 mine, jail house. Interior view of telephone exchange (1903).

Chicago, Illinois. Chicago Historical Society. Prints and Photographs Department. Illinois. Peru.
ICHi

Large photograph of St. Bede's Academy (taken 1946).

Chicago, Illinois. Chicago Historical Society. Prints and Photographs Department. Illinois Waterways. Three vertical folders.
ICHi
File 1: Photographs of I&M Canal, (approximately twenty-five) of canal, locks, spillways, and buildings; DesPlaines River, I&M Canal near Joliet and Channahon, twelve photographs taken 1945–1960, lock gates, city of Pekin, Lockport locks, Calumet sag and oil barge.
File 2: Envelope containing about twenty-five snapshots of Chicago Portage, Mud Lake, Chicago Drainage Canal, Calumet River, Fox River taken in 1912. Photographs of Illinois Waterway, 1925–1933; construction of locks and dams below Joliet and at Marseilles; opening of Waterway. Four aerial photographs of Blue Island. Five photographs of construction of Calumet-Sag Channel. Six photographs of locks and power station at Lockport (one from 1907) and one of construction of dam at Dresden Heights.
File 3: Photographs of I&M Canal, grain elevators, locks, Lasker Iron Works, and other factories (1911). Photographs of Cal-Sag Channel (1922). Photographs of Drainage Canal (1896). Photographs of Illinois Waterway construction 1929 and 1933.

Chicago, Illinois. International Harvester Company Archives. Photograph and Graphics Collection.
IC—IHC
An extensive collection of photographs of factory buildings (with interior and exterior views) of International Harvester and its predecessor companies, dating back to 1847. The collection is partially catalogued. Catalogue available at library.

Lemont, Illinois. Lemont Area Historical Society. Harry J. Swanson Memorial Library. Photograph File. Local History File. Aerial view of Lemont Township.
ILeHi

Lemont, Illinois. Lemont Area Historical Society. Harry J. Swanson Memorial Library. Local History File. Old Photographs of Chicago Drainage Canal Construction.
ILeHi

Lemont, Illinois. Lemont Area Historical Society. Harry J. Swanson Memorial Library. Local History File. Photograph File. Photocopies of photographs on Sanitary and Ship Canal. 50 p.
ILeHi
Photographs of canal construction.

Lemont, Illinois. Lemont Area Historical Society. Museum. Photograph of Knights of Pythias, Charter Members, 1894.
ILeHi

Summit, Illinois. Summit-Argo Public Library. Local History File. Independence Day Parade, Argo, Monday, July 5, 1926. (sixteen-millimeter film).
ISA
Contains one reel of sixteen-millimeter film.

Urbana, Illinois. Illinois Historical Survey Library. Mounted Newspaper Cuttings Relating to the Board of Supervisors and the New Court House of LaSalle County, Illinois. 1880–1883. 383 p.
IU—HS

Utica, Illinois. LaSalle County Historical Society Museum. Scenic LaSalle County, Book I. Picture Book and Illustrations.
IUtHi
Contains bridges, early state park postcards, Starved Rock postcards (c. 1906), Illinois River at Starved Rock, pictures of area in winter, and Deer Park.

Utica, Illinois. LaSalle County Historical Society Museum. LaSalle County, Book II. Picture Book and Printed Illustrations.
IUtHi
Contains photographs of Deer Park, Starved Rock Park, Illinois River, and some bridges.

Utica, Illinois. LaSalle County Historical Society Museum. Utica.
IUtHi
A picture book. Contains photographs of grade school classes, high school classes, various associations, groups of men, baby pictures.

PART 18 Artifact Collections

Artifact collections of various sizes and emphases are available in each county in the corridor. A few of these are briefly described in this section. The largest, held by the Will County Historical Society, lays particular emphasis upon the different aspects of the canal itself. Strong local collections are also housed in the Lemont Area Historical Society, Grundy County Historical Society, and LaSalle County Historical Society Museum. Although not local in focus, the Illinois State Museum in Springfield and the Field Museum of Natural History in Chicago also hold artifacts of significance for the region, particularly collections relating to the American Indian.

Bedford Park, Illinois. Bedford Park Public Library. Artifacts.
IBP

Collected by Ray Douglas, leader of Boy Scout Troup Tribe of Delevan. Miscellaneous Indian artifacts include moccasins, tobacco pouches (beaded), pipe bud, pipestone pipes, war clubs, and arrowheads. Also includes the donator's own beadwork.

Chicago, Illinois. Chicago Historical Society. Museum Collection.
ICHi

Includes surveying compass, drafting instruments, shovel, and ruler used in building the I&M and Sanitary and Ship canals.

Lemont, Illinois. Lemont Area Historical Society. Museum.
ILeHi

Extensive collection of tools, clothing, machinery, furniture, Indian artifacts, military memorabilia, cooking utensils, and miscellaneous relics.

Lockport, Illinois. Will County Historical Society Museum. Artifacts. 1,284 items.
ILoHi

Household items, including kitchen and dining room utensils and furnishings, office, parlor, and bedroom furnishings, personal effects, sewing and quilting items, toys, surgeon and dental instruments, blacksmith and carpentry tools, farming implements, Indian artifacts, I&M Canal items, and some printed materials.

Morris, Illinois. Grundy County Historical Society. Artifacts.
IMoHi

Holdings include photographs, a wide range of military objects and memorabilia, tools, household goods and utensils, crafts, and Indian artifacts. Partial inventory available.

Utica, Illinois. LaSalle County Historical Society Museum. Artifacts.
IUtHi

Holdings include clothing, crafts, household and farm tools, and furniture.

Summit, Illinois. Summit Area Historical Society.
ISHi

Holdings include an extensive collection of prehistoric and historic artifacts uncovered in the Summit area.

PART 19 Oral History

Researchers often make the mistake of assuming that history can only be composed from written materials. But over at least the last decade, some individuals have recognized that there are living and breathing sources of corridor history that can tell us about almost one-half of the American period of occupation. This section, then, contains a sample of oral history sources held in the I&M Canal area. Some of the collections include only tapes of interviews with elderly residents, others also include transcripts of the tapes.

Joliet, Illinois. Joliet Junior College. Learning Resource Center. Oral History Collection. Social Science Interview. Sixty-five tapes.
IJoJ

Interviews conducted by social science students under the direction of Robert Sterling. Emphasis on the social history of Will County. Transcripts available.

Lockport, Illinois. Lewis University. Canal Archives. Oral History Collection. Will County Interviews. Seven tapes.
ILoL

Contains 1950s interview of the captain of a canal boat by members of his family; 1970s interview of Helen Poole, daughter of a boat captain, by John Lamb; 1973 interview of Bruce Cheadle of Lockport; 1978 recollection of Slovenian ethnic life in Joliet; 1978 interview of woman who spent time on a farm just west of Lewis University; and 1979 interview of Maurice Flavin of Lockport. Transcripts available.

Lockport, Illinois. Lockport Township Public Library. Oral History Collection. Retired Teachers. Fifteen tapes.
ILo

Contains fifteen packets, each of which includes taped interview, transcript, and photograph of the subject. Also six untranscribed tapes. Subjects were retired teachers from the Lockport area in 1976. Interviews by Helen Meurer. Focus on families, churches, world wars, natural disasters.

Lockport, Illinois. Lockport Township Public Library. Oral History Collection. Senior Citizens. Six tapes.
ILo

Untranscribed interviews with members of early Lockport families: Bruce Cheadle, Nelson Reed, Clarence Woock, Frank Milne, Esther McDonald, and Maurice Flavin.

Morris, Illinois. Morris Public Library. Oral History Collection. Bicentennial Interviews. Twenty-five tapes.
IMo

Sixty- to ninety-minute interviews conducted by Deborah Trotter between 1976 and 1981. Interviewees were professionals, industrial workers, a boat captain, and a farmer.

Ottawa, Illinois. Starved Rock Library System. Valley Oral History Association. Forty-five tapes.
IOS

Contains eight tapes of 1975 interviews with corridor residents: Burton Confrey, James Housby, John Mitchell, Alta Pierson, Hart Fisher, Jessie Dunlap, Myrtle Johnson, and Juliette Ricci.

PART 20 Directories

In the days before the invention of the telephone, inhabitants of cities, counties, and states kept track of each other with social and business directories and gazetteers. The directories were usually published annually by private concerns that specialized in canvassing neighborhoods for new residents or for changes in addresses. The directory companies then sold advertising space, published the volume, and sold copies to individual subscribers. But in order to be economically successful, directories had to include a large enough number of inhabitants and businesses to attract the necessary subscriptions. Therefore, the earliest examples of corridor directories cover the entire state of Illinois. But as the years went by and as the corridor area became more populated, directories were compiled for individual counties and, finally, for some of the larger towns. (References to the very earliest gazetteers can be found in the Description and Travel section of the Bibliography.)

Directories are potentially useful to many types of historical researchers. For those interested in learning about their family histories, the volumes can be used to track an individual's whereabouts from year to year. Social and economic historians can use directories for compiling and tracing trends in residence and employment patterns.

The amount of information in a particular directory varied according to date and company of publication. Most include the name and home address of heads of households. Others add employment information and business addresses. (The researcher should also keep in mind that *all* residents were not *always* listed.) Some directories also included community information that was printed in a separate part of the volume from the alphabetical roster of residents. For example, they might list officers of city governments, ministers of churches, and heads of voluntary organizations. And most also included an advertising section.

Directories—*General*

City Directories of the United States, 1860–1901. Guide to Microfilm Collection. Woodbridge, Connecticut: Research Publications, 1983.
ICRL

Spear, Dorothea N. *Bibliography of American Directories Through 1860.* Worcester, Massachusetts: American Antiquarian Society, 1961.
ICN, ICU, IEN, IU

Directories—*Early Illinois Directories*

Hall, E[dward] H. *The Northern Counties Gazetteer and Directory, for 1855/56: A Complete and Perfect Guide to Northern Illinois, Containing a Concise Description of the Cities, Towns and Principal Villages, with the Names of the Public Officers, Professional and Business Men, in the Counties of Boone, Cook, DeKalb, DuPage, JoDaviess, Kane, Lake, McHenry, Stephenson, Winnebago; and a Variety of Other Useful and Interesting Information. Brought Down to November, 1855.* Chicago: Fergus Printing, 1855. 152 p.
ICRL

Usually bound with the Chicago City Directory for 1855.

Hawes, George W., comp. *Illinois State Gazetteer and Business Directory for 1858 and 1859.* Chicago: [Scripps, Printers, 1858]. 444 p.
ICHi, ICRL, ICU, IHi

Illinois Annual Register and Western Business Directory. Norris and Gardiner, Editors and Proprietors. Nov. 1, 1847. Chicago: Geer & Wilson, Printers, Journal Office Print., 1847. 120 p.
DLC, ICHi

Illinois State Business Directory, 1860: In Which the Mercantile, Professional, Manufacturing and Mechanical Departments are Accurately Compiled and Alphabetically

Arranged. . . . Chicago: J. C. W. Bailey & Co., [1860]. 941 p., illus.
DLC, ICRL

Illinois State Gazetteer and Business Directory, for the Year 1864–5. . . . Chicago: J. C. W. Bailey, 1864. 820 p., illus., plates, map.
DLC, ICHi, ICN, ICU

Illinois State Gazetteer and Business Directory. 7 v. Chicago: R. L. Polk, 1878, 1882–1893. illus.
DLC

Montague's Illinois and Missouri State Directory for 1854/55: Containing the Names, Occupation and Post-Office Address of All the Principal Men of Business in the States of Illinois, Missouri, Classified and Alphabetically Arranged for Easy Reference. Also a Register of the Various Officers of the State and County Governments. . . . St. Louis, Missouri: Wm. L. Montague, 1854. 504 p.
ICRL, ICU

Directories—LaSalle County

Directories—*LaSalle County*—General

Bailey, John C. W. *LaSalle County Directory for 1858 and 1859: Containing the Name, Occupation, and Address of Every Resident Within the Cities of Ottawa, LaSalle, Peru, the Town of Mendota, and Other Villages, Together with the Resident Farmers and Others in the Several Townships of the County.* Chicago: William H. Rand, [1858]. 193 p.
ICHi, IO

Keyes, Robert F., comp. *LaSalle County General Directory for 1872–3.* Joliet, Illinois: Joliet Republican Steam Printing House, 1872. 288 p.
ICHi, IO

LaSalle County Directory, 1885–6. . . . Also a Classified Business Directory and an Editorial Review of Some of the Leading Merchants, Manufacturers, etc. Chicago: R. R. Donnelley & Sons, Printers, 1885. 320 p.
ICHi, IO

LaSalle County Gazetteer and Farmers' and Land Owners' Directory. Springfield, Illinois: J. E. Fitzpatrick, & Co., 1888.
IO, IUtHi

Contains business directory.

Directories—*LaSalle County*—Peru

R. L. Polk and Company's Peru and LaSalle Directory . . . 1898/99. Indianapolis, Indiana: R. L. Polk, 1899.
DLC

Directories—*LaSalle County*—LaSalle

Hennessey, A. L. *A Complete City Directory of LaSalle and Peru.* LaSalle, Illinois: Printed by A. L. Hennessey, 1876. 150 p.
ICN, IPe

Polk's LaSalle–Peru and Oglesby City Directory. . . . Peoria, Illinois: Leshnick Directory Co., n.d.
DLC

From the early-twentieth century.

Directories—*LaSalle County*—Ottawa

Ottawa, Illinois City Directories, 1858–1940. Imprint varies. Ottawa, Illinois: Ottawa Free Trader, 1858; Ottawa, Illinois: D. E. Hawley and Co., 1874/1875; Ottawa, Illinois: Osman and Hapeman, Book and Job Printers, 1868–1879; n.p., 1884; Columbus, Ohio: R. L. Polk and Co., 1894/1895; Blue Island, Illinois: Boehl and Dale Directory Publishers, 1898; Columbus, Ohio: R. L. Polk and Co., 1901/1902; Keokuk, Iowa: W. H. McCoy, 1902/1903, 1904/1905, 1906/1906; Rockford, Illinois: The McCoy Directory Co., 1907/1908, 1909/1910, 1911/1912, 1913; Peoria, Illinois: Leshnick Directory Co., 1916/1917, 1918, 1920, 1921, 1922/1923, 1924/1925, 1926/1927, 1928; Chicago: R. L. Polk and Co., 1930, 1935, 1937, 1939; St. Louis: R. L. Polk and Co., 1940.
IO

Woltz, J. N. *Ottawa City Directory and Business Advertiser, for 1866–67.* Ottawa, Illinois: Republican Job Printing Office, 1866. 168 p.
ICHi, IO

Holland Brothers. *Holland's Ottawa City Directory for 1869–70: Containing a Complete List of All Residents in the City. Also a Classified Business Directory, with the Names and Addresses of the Merchants, Manufacturers, Professional Men, etc., in the City.* Chicago: Western Publishing Company [1869]. 196 p.

ICN, IO
Advertisements.

The Ottawa City Directory . . . Including . . . Ottawa and South Ottawa Townships Outside the City Limits. . . . Ottawa, Illinois: W. Osman & Sons, Printers, 1888. 188 p. map.
DLC, IO

Maierhofer, Albert, and Son. *The Ottawa City Directory . . . Including . . . Ottawa and South Ottawa Townships Outside the City Limits.* Ottawa, Illinois: Globe Steam Printing House, 1891. 290 p., front., illus.
ICHi, IO

Polk's Ottawa City Directory. . . . Peoria, Illinois: Leshnick Directory Co., [1914–1915].
DLC, IO

United Telephone Company. *United Telephone Company Directory of Ottawa, Utica, and Harding, Grand Ridge and Marseilles.* Ottawa, Illinois: Record Press, 1916.
ICHi

Telephone Directory of Ottawa and Harding. Chicago: Illinois Bell, 1937, 1938.
IUtHi

Directories—Grundy County

Directories—*Grundy County*—General

Lawrence and Thompson's Grundy County Directory, 1877–1878: A Classified Business Directory: A Complete List of All the Residents. Morris, Illinois: *Reformer* Office. 300 p.
ICHi, IMoHi
Historical sketch, biographies.

Directories—*Grundy County*—Morris

Illinois Bell Telephone Company. *Morris, Illinois Directory.* December 1912 through March 1958. (Microfilm.)
IMo

Morris City Directory. . . . 4 v. [Morris, Illinois]: Johnson Publishing Co., 1917, 1929/1930, 1938/1939, 1940.
IMo

Directories—Will County

Directories—*Will County*—General

Bailey, John C. W. *Will County Directory, 1859–1860.* Chicago: John C. W. Bailey, 1859. 179 p.
ICHi, ICRL, MWA
Contains information for Joliet, Lockport, Wilmington, Plainfield, Mokena, Channahon, Crete, Monee, Elwood.

Goodspeed, James. *Will County General Directory for 1872–3, Containing the Name, Occupation and Post Office, of Every Resident Within the County.* Joliet, Illinois: Republican Book and Job Printing House, 1872. 203 p.
ICHi

Directories—*Will County*—Joliet

Joliet, Illinois City Directories, 1875–1940. Imprint varies. n.p., 1875; Chicago: Western Publishing Co., 1877; Joliet, Illinois: Joliet Sun Printing Company, 1881; n.p., W. R. Curtis and Co., 1884, 1887, 1888; Joliet, Illinois: Joliet Directory Co., 1892, 1893, 1895, 1896; n.p., W. F. Curtis, 1897; n.p., R. L. Polk and Co., 1899, 1900, 1901; n.p., 1902–1906, 1908–1909, 1912, 1914, 1916, 1918, 1920, 1921, 1923, 1925, 1927, 1930, 1933–1935, 1937–1938, 1940.
ICRL, IJo

Joliet City Directory [*1885/1886, 1889/90*]. 2 v. Joliet, Illinois: W. F. Curtis, 1885–1889. plan.
DLC, ICRL, IJo

Joliet City Directory. Joliet, Illinois: The Joliet News Bindery Co., 1890.
DLC
City Directory for Joliet, 1891.

R. L. Polk and Company's Joliet City Directory, 1904/1905–1908. 4 v. Chicago, 1904–1908.
DLC, ICRL, IJo

Directories—*DuPage County*

Bumstead's Directory of Wheaton City and DuPage County, 1915/1916. Chicago: Bumstead & Company, 1915.
ICHi

DuPage County, Illinois Directory . . . 1924/1925–. Chicago: McDonough & Company, 1924–. map.
DLC, ICJ, ICN

Directories—Cook County

Directories—*Cook County*—General

Cook County Suburban and Rural Directory. Chicago: Smith Directory Co., 1929. 536 p. (Photocopied.)
ICN

Directories—*Cook County*—Lemont

Lemont, Lockport and Plainfield City Directories, 1927–1928. Chicago: The Union Directory Company of Illinois, 1927.
ICJ, ILo

Includes village and township officers.

Directories—*Cook County*—Argo-Summit

Directory of Summit, Argo and Clearing, 1922/23. Chicago: McDonough & Co., 1922.
DLC

Directories—*Cook County*—Calumet Sag Towns

The Hammond Historical Society Presents the First City Directory for the Following Cities: Hammond, Indiana; East Chicago, Indiana; Hegewisch, Illinois; Burnham, Illinois; West Hammond, Illinois (now Calumet City), 1889–1890. Hammond, Indiana: The Society, 1976. 95 p., maps, ports.
ICN

Reprint of the 1889 edition of *Tri-Urban Directory of Hammond, East Chicago, and Hegewisch. . . .* by F. E. Gero.

Boehl, Henry. *Boehl's Blue Island City Directory; Including Also a Business Directory . . . Together with an Annex of Useful Information on the Churches, Schools, Societies, Banks. . . .* Blue Island, Illinois: Henry Boehl, 1897. 100 p., illus., map.
ICHi

Bumstead's Blue Island City Directory, 1904–05. . . . Chicago: Bumstead & Co., 1904.
DLC

Blue Island City Directory. . . . Chicago: McDonough Directory System, 1914.
ICHi

Blue Island Directory, 1921/22. Chicago: McDonough & Co., 1921.
DLC

Directory of Riverdale, Dolton and South Holland, 1922/23. Chicago: McDonough & Co., 1922.
DLC

Six

LIBRARIES, COLLECTIONS, AND MUSEUMS HOLDING MATERIALS RELEVANT TO CORRIDOR HISTORY

Each of the institutions listed in this chapter meets either or both of the following criteria: it is located within the Illinois and Michigan Canal National Heritage Corridor and/or it is noted in the Guide to Historical Sources as containing materials relevant to the corridor's history. Any of the libraries, museums, historical societies, or archives listed here but that are clearly outside of the northeastern Illinois–northwestern Indiana–southern Wisconsin area covered by the Bibliography are included because they hold materials that are unavailable at a closer location.

Public Libraries

Alsip-Merrionette Park Public Library
11960 South Pulaski
Alsip, Illinois 60658

Argonne National Laboratory
Technical Information Services Department
9700 South Cass Avenue
Argonne, Illinois 60439

Bedford Park Public Library
7816 West 65th Place
Bedford Park, Illinois 60501

Blue Island Public Library
2433 York Street
Blue Island, Illinois 60406

Boston Public Library
Copley Square
Box 286
Boston, Massachusetts 02117

Bridgeview Public Library
7840 West 79th Street
Bridgeview, Illinois 60455

Calumet City Public Library
760 Wentworth Avenue
Calumet City, Illinois 60409

Chicago Public Library
425 North Michigan Avenue
Chicago, Illinois 60611

Chicago Public Library
Pullman Branch
11001 South Indiana Avenue
Chicago, Illinois 60628

Coal City Public Library
515 South Broadway Street
Coal City, Illinois 60416

Dolton Public Library
14037 Lincoln Avenue
Dolton, Illinois 60419

Florida State University Library
Robert Manning Strozier Library
Tallahassee, Florida 32306

Fountaindale Public Library
201 Normantown Road
Romeoville, Illinois 60441

Galesburg Public Library
40 East Simmons Street
Galesburg, Illinois 61401

Gary Public Library
220 West Fifth Avenue
Gary, Indiana 46402

Green Hills Public Library
8611 West 103rd Street
Palos Hills, Illinois 60465

Hayner Public Library
401 State Street
Alton, Illinois 62002

Hodgkins Public Library
6500 Wenz Avenue
Hodgkins, Illinois 60525

Illinois Department of Conservation
405 East Washington
Springfield, Illinois 62706

Illinois Department of Transportation
126 East Ash
Springfield, Illinois 62704

Illinois Historical Survey Library
1A University of Illinois Library
Urbana, Illinois 61801

Illinois State Historical Library
Old State Capitol Building
Springfield, Illinois 62706

Illinois State Library
Centennial Building
Springfield, Illinois 62756

Illinois State University
Gilner Library
Normal, Illinois 61761

Illinois Valley Community College
Jacobs Library
Oglesby, Illinois 61348

Indiana University at Bloomington
University Libraries
Tenth Street and Jordan Avenue
Bloomington, Indiana 47405

Joliet Junior College
Learning Resource Center
1216 Houbolt Avenue
Joliet, Illinois 60436

Joliet Public Library
150 North Ottawa Street
Joliet, Illinois 60431

The John Crerar Library
The University of Chicago
5730 Ellis Avenue
Chicago, Illinois 60616

Justice Public Library
7641 Oak Grove Avenue
Justice, Illinois 60458

LaSalle Public Library
305 Marquette Street
LaSalle, Illinois 61301

Lemont Public Library
800 Porter Street
Lemont, Illinois 60439

Lockport Township Public Library
Theodore Street and Willowbridge Road
Crest Hill, Illinois 60435

Lockport Township Public Library
121 East 8th Street
Lockport, Illinois 60441

Marseilles Public Library
155 East Bluff Street
Marseilles, Illinois 61341

Metropolitan Sanitary District Library
100 East Erie Street
Chicago, Illinois 60611

Michigan State University
Library
East Lansing, Michigan 48824

Moraine Valley Community College Library
10900 South 88th Avenue
Palos Hills, Illinois 60465

Morris Public Library
604 Liberty Street
Morris, Illinois 60450

Municipal Reference Library
Room 104, City Hall
Chicago, Illinois 60602

Museum of Science and Industry Library
57th Street and Lake Shore Drive
Chicago, Illinois 60637

New York Public Library
Fifth Avenue and 42nd Street
New York, New York 10018

New York State Library
State Education Building
Albany, New York 12234

Northern Illinois University
Swen Parson Library
DeKalb, Illinois 60115

Oglesby Public Library
128 West Walnut Street
Oglesby, Illinois 61348

Palos Heights Public Library
12501 South 71st Avenue
Palos Heights, Illinois 60463

Palos Park Public Library
12330 Forest Glen Boulevard
Palos Park, Illinois 60464

Peru Public Library
627 Putnam Street
Peru, Illinois 61354

Reddick Library
1010 Canal Street
Ottawa, Illinois 61350

Riverdale Public Library
208 West 144th Street
Riverdale, Illinois 60627

Robbins Public Library District
13822 Central Park
Robbins, Illinois 60472

Seneca Public Library
210 North Main Street
Seneca, Illinois 61360

Smithsonian Institution Libraries
Constitution Avenue at Tenth Street, N.W.
Washington, D.C. 20560

Southern Illinois University
Morris Library
Carbondale, Illinois 62901

Starved Rock Library System
900 Hitt Street
Ottawa, Illinois 61350

State University of Iowa
Library
Ames, Iowa 50011

State University of New York
College at Buffalo Library
Buffalo, New York 14222

Summit-Argo Public Library
6209 South Archer Road
Summit, Illinois 60501

Three Rivers Public Library
210 Channon Drive
Channahon, Illinois 60410

U.S. Army Corps of Engineers
North Central Division Library
536 South Clark Street
Chicago, Illinois 60605

U.S. Army Corps of Engineers
Technical Library, Rock Island District
Clock Tower Building
Rock Island, Illinois 61204

U.S. Department of Health and Human Services Library
330 Independence Avenue, S.W.
Washington, D.C. 20201

U.S. Library of Congress
Washington, D.C. 20540

U.S. National Archives Library
8th Street and Pennsylvania Avenue, N.W.
Washington, D.C. 20408

U.S. National Library of Medicine
Bethesda, Maryland 20209

The University of California at Berkeley
The Bancroft Library
Berkeley, California 94720

The University of Illinois
Library
Urbana, Illinois 61801

The University of Illinois at Chicago Library
80 South Morgan Street
Chicago, Illinois 60680

The University of Iowa
Library
Iowa City, Iowa 52242

The University of Michigan
Library
Ann Arbor, Michigan 48109

The University of Minnesota
Library
Minneapolis, Minnesota 55455

The University of Missouri at Columbia
Library
Columbia, Missouri 65201

The University of Nebraska at Lincoln
Library
Lincoln, Nebraska 68588

The University of Oklahoma Libraries
401 West Brooks
Norman, Oklahoma 73019

The University of Wisconsin at Madison
Library
Madison, Wisconsin 53706

Utica Public Library
Mill and Grove Streets
Utica, Illinois 61373

Worth Public Library
6917 West 111th Street
Worth, Illinois 60482

Private Libraries

American Antiquarian Society
185 Salisbury Street
Worcester, Massachusetts 01609

American Slovenian Catholic Union
351–53 North Chicago Street
Joliet, Illinois 60431

Art Institute of Chicago
Ryerson and Burnham Libraries
Michigan Avenue at Adams Street
Chicago, Illinois 60603

Bowdoin College
Library
Brunswick, Maine 04011

Catholic University of America
Library
Washington, D.C. 20064

Center for Research Libraries
6046 S. Kenwood
Chicago, Illinois 60637

Chicago Theological Seminary
Hammond Library
5757 South University Avenue
Chicago, Illinois 60637

College of St. Francis Library
600 Taylor Street
Joliet, Illinois 60435

Columbia College Library
600 South Michigan Avenue
Chicago, Illinois 60605

Columbia University
Library
New York, New York 10027

Cornell University
Library
Ithaca, New York 14853

DeAndreis Seminary Library
511 East 127th Street
Lemont, Illinois 60439

DePaul University Library
2323 North Seminary Avenue
Chicago, Illinois 60614

Garrett Theological Seminary Library
2121 Sheridan Road
Evanston, Illinois 60201

Harvard University
Graduate School of Business
Baker Library
Cambridge, Massachusetts 02138

Henry E. Huntington Library
1151 Oxford Road
San Marino, California 91108

Illinois Agricultural Association Library
1701 Towanda Avenue
Bloomington, Illinois 61701

Illinois Baptist Historical Library
Springfield, Illinois 62706

Iowa Masonic Library
813 First Avenue, S.E.
Cedar Rapids, Iowa 52406

Knox College
Seymour Library
Galesburg, Illinois 61401

LeHigh University
Library
Bethlehem, Pennsylvania 18015

Lewis University
Learning Resource Center
Route 53
Lockport, Illinois 60441

Loyola University of Chicago
E. M. Cudahy Memorial Library
6525 North Sheridan Road
Chicago, Illinois 60626

McCormick Theological Seminary
McGaw Library
800 West Belden Avenue
Chicago, Illinois 60614

Marquette University Library
1415 West Wisconsin Avenue
Milwaukee, Wisconsin 53233

Meadville Theological School of Lombard College Library
5701 South Woodlawn Avenue
Chicago, Illinois 60637

The Newberry Library
60 West Walton Street
Chicago, Illinois 60610

Northwestern University Library
1935 Sheridan Road
Evanston, Illinois 60201

Occidental College Library
1600 Campus Road
Los Angeles, California 90041

Princeton University
Library
Princeton, New Jersey 08540

St. Louis University
Pius XII Memorial Library
St. Louis, Missouri 63108

St. Mary of the Lake Seminary
Feehan Memorial Library
Mundelein, Illinois 60060

St. Vincent College and Archabbey
Library
Latrobe, Pennsylvania 15650

Syracuse University
Library
Syracuse, New York 13210

Tulane University
Howard-Tilton Memorial Library
New Orleans, Louisiana 10118

The University of Chicago
The Joseph Regenstein Library
1100 East 57th Street
Chicago, Illinois 60637

The University of Cincinnati Libraries
Central Library
University and Woodside
Cincinnati, Ohio 45221

The University of Notre Dame
Library
Notre Dame, Indiana 46556

Yale University
Sterling Memorial Library
New Haven, Connecticut 06520

Museums

American Lithuanian Art Association
112 Charlton Avenue
Willow Springs, Illinois 60480

Balzekas Museum of Lithuanian Culture
4012 Archer Avenue
Chicago, Illinois 60632

DuPage County Historical Museum
102 East Wesley
Wheaton, Illinois 60187

Field Museum of Natural History
Library
Roosevelt Road and Lake Shore Drive
Chicago, Illinois 60605

Illinois and Michigan Canal Museum
803 South State Street
Lockport, Illinois 60441

Illinois State Museum
State Museum Building
Springfield, Illinois 62706

Illinois Valley Museum
835 East Southmor Road
Route 1
Morris, Illinois 60450

Isle a la Cache Museum
501 East Romeo Road
Romeoville, Illinois 60441

LaSalle County Historical Society Museum
P.O. Box 278
Utica, Illinois 61373

Will County Museum
803 South State Street
Lockport, Illinois 60441

Historical Societies

Blue Island Library Historical Society
2433 York Street
Blue Island, Illinois 60406

Calumet Historical Society
1400 Torrence
Calumet City, Illinois 60409

Chicago Historical Society
Clark Street and North Avenue
Chicago, Illinois 60614

Czechoslovak Society of America
2701 S. Harlem Avenue
Berwyn, Illinois 60402

Grundy County Historical Society
P.O. Box 224
Morris, Illinois 60450

Historic Pullman Foundation, Inc.
1111 South Forrestville Avenue
Chicago, Illinois 60628

Illinois Canal Society
1109 Garfield Street
Lockport, Illinois 60441

Illinois State Historical Society
Old State Capitol Building
Springfield, Illinois 62706

Illinois Valley Historical Society
835 East Southmor Road, Route 1
Morris, Illinois 60450

Indiana Historical Society
140 North Senate Avenue
Indianapolis, Indiana 46204

Joliet Area Historical Society
P.O. Box 477
Joliet, Illinois 60435

LaSalle County Historical Society
Box 577
Ottawa, Illinois 61350

Lemont Area Historical Society
306 Lemont Street
Lemont, Illinois 60439

DuPage County Genealogical Society
Box 133
Lombard, Illinois 60148

Oglesby Historical Society
128 West Walnut
Oglesby, Illinois 61348

Palos Historical Society
12021 South 93rd Avenue
Palos Park, Illinois 60464

Presbyterian Historical Society
425 Lombard Street
Philadelphia, Pennsylvania 19147

Robbins Historical Society
3329 West 137th Street
Robbins, Illinois 60472

Romeoville Historical Society
707 Echo Avenue
Romeoville, Illinois 60441

Summit Area Historical Society
5410 South Third
Summit, Illinois 60501

Swedish Pioneer Historical Society
5125 North Spaulding Avenue
Chicago, Illinois 60625

Will County Historical Society
803 South State Street
Lockport, Illinois 60441

Wisconsin State Historical Society
816 State Street
Madison, Wisconsin 53706

Archives and Depositories

Archives of the State of Illinois
State Archives Building
Springfield, Illinois 62706

Commonwealth Edison Company Library
One First National Plaza
P.O. Box 676
Chicago, Illinois 60690

Economist Newspapers
5959 South Harlem Avenue
Chicago, Illinois 60637

Episcopal Diocese of Chicago
Archives and Historical Collections
65 East Huron Street
Chicago, Illinois 60611

Evangelical Covenant Church of America
Archives and Historical Library
5125 North Spaulding Avenue
Chicago, Illinois 60625

Illinois and Michigan Canal State Trail Archives
Gebhard Woods State Park
Morris, Illinois 60450

Illinois Bell Telephone
Company Library
Chicago, Illinois 60606

Illinois Regional Archives Depository
Illinois State University
Normal, Illinois 61761

Illinois Regional Archives Depository
Northern Illinois University
DeKalb, Illinois 60115

Illinois State Geological Survey Library
469 Natural Resources Building
Urbana, Illinois 61801

Illinois State Water Survey Library
605 East Springfield Avenue
Champaign, Illinois 61820

Immigration History Research Center
University of Minnesota
826 Berry Street
St. Paul, Minnesota 55114

International Harvester Company
Corporate Archives
401 North Michigan Avenue
Chicago, Illinois 60611

Lutheran Church in America
Archives
Lutheran School of Theology
1100 East 55th Street
Chicago, Illinois 60615

Methodist Archives
Illinois Wesleyan University
Bloomington, Illinois 61701

National Archives and Records Service
Federal Archives and Records Center
Archives Branch
1557 St. Joseph Avenue
East Point, Georgia 30344

National Archives and Records Service
Federal Archives and Records Center
Archives Branch
7358 South Pulaski Road
Chicago, Illinois 60629

National Climatic Center
Federal Building
Asheville, North Carolina 28801

Norwegian American Historical Association
Archives
St. Olaf College
Northfield, Minnesota 55057

Polish Museum of America Library and Archives
984 Milwaukee Avenue
Chicago, Illinois 60622

The University of Illinois Archives
19 Library
Urbana, Illinois 61801

Contributors

Gerald W. Adelmann is executive director of the Upper Illinois Valley Association. A sixth-generation native of Lockport, in the corridor, he earned a Bachelor's degree in art and architectural history from Georgetown University. Graduate studies in Paris, Boston, and Washington in historic preservation, urban planning, and American history led to a predoctoral fellowship at the Smithsonian Institution. Long active in open space and historic preservation in Chicago, he was uniquely instrumental in gaining passage of the congressional act creating the Illinois and Michigan Canal National Heritage Corridor, in recognition of which Lewis University in 1986 conferred on him an honorary Doctorate of Humanities. He is on the Board of Advisers of the National Trust for Historic Preservation, and a director of The Nature Conservancy and the Chicago Maritime Society.

Kay J. Carr is assistant professor of history at Mercer University in Macon, Georgia. She earned a Bachelor's degree in history and German at Knox College in 1979, where she was elected Phi Beta Kappa, and recently completed a doctorate at the University of Chicago, where she was a Bessie Louise Pierce Fellow in American history. The subject of her dissertation is a comparative study of frontier decision making and political culture in early Belleville and Galesburg, Illinois.

Michael P. Conzen is professor of geography at the University of Chicago. Educated at the Universities of Cambridge, Giessen, and Wisconsin (Madison), he taught previously at Boston University before coming to Chicago in 1976. He has served on the Illinois Historic Sites Advisory Council and the Governor's Task Force to establish an Illinois Historic Preservation Agency. He has been a National Endowment for the Humanities Fellow at the Newberry Library and a director of the Chicago Map Society and currently serves on the Social Science Research Council's Committee on New York City. Author of *Frontier Farming in an Urban Shadow* and *Boston: A Geographical Portrait,* and editor of *World Patterns of Modern Urban Change* and *Chicago Mapmakers,* his scholarly interests include the urban and historical geography of North America and the study of American landscapes.

Chris E. Copenhaver is an analyst with the U.S. Defense Intelligence Agency in Washington, D.C. He earned a Bachelor's degree in political science from Valparaiso University in 1979 and completed a Master of Arts degree in geography at the University of Chicago in 1983 with a study on the geography of Soviet foreign aid and its policy implications.

G. Gray Fitzsimons is a historian of technology at the Historic Engineering Record, National Park Service, U. S. Department of the Interior, in Washington, D.C. He earned an undergraduate degree in civil engineering from the University of Maryland and is currently in the graduate program in history at the University of Washington. For the past two years he has directed the Historic American Buildings Survey/Historic American Engineering Record's survey and documentation work in the Illinois and Michigan Canal National Heritage Corridor.

Stephen Freedman is a research associate at the Manpower Demonstration Research Corporation in New York City. He earned a Bachelor's degree from Oberlin College in 1976 and is a doctoral candidate in American history at the University of Chicago. The subject of his dissertation research is a study of the evolution of class relations in Rockford, Peoria, and Joliet, Illinois, between 1870 and 1920, a portion of which, devoted to the union movement in Joliet, he recently published in the *Illinois Historical Journal.* He served as leader of the bibliography team for this project.

Jean M. O'Brien is a doctoral candidate in American history at the University of Chicago. She earned a Bachelor's degree from Bemidji State University, Bemidji, Minnesota, in 1980, and a Master's degree from the University of Chicago in 1982. The topic of the doctoral dissertation she is currently working on is a study of community dynamics in the Anglo-Indian town of Natick, Massachusetts, between 1650 and 1790.

Edmund B. Thornton is Chairman of the Illinois and Michigan Canal National Heritage Corridor Commission. He attended Phillips Academy and earned a Bachelor's degree in geography from Yale University in 1954 before serving in the U.S. Marine Corps. He has been associated with the Ottawa Silica Company since 1959, serving as Chairman from 1975 until recently, and is President of the Ottawa Silica Foundation. He has contributed for many years to the advancement of natural conservation and historic preservation, serving at various times as Chairman of the Illinois Nature Preserves Commission, the National Parks Centennial Commission, and the Illinois Historic Sites Advisory Council. He is a Past Vice President of the Illinois State Historical Society and, in 1974, received the Conservation Service Award, the highest civilian honor granted by the United States Department of the Interior.

Index